BEGINNING
MICROSOFT® VISUAL BASIC 2010

BEGINNING

Microsoft® Visual Basic 2010

BEGINNING

Microsoft® Visual Basic 2010

Thearon Willis
Bryan Newsome

WILEY

Wiley Publishing, Inc.

Beginning Microsoft® Visual Basic 2010

Published by
Wiley Publishing, Inc.
10475 Crosspoint Boulevard
Indianapolis, IN 46256
www.wiley.com

Copyright © 2010 by Wiley Publishing, Inc., Indianapolis, Indiana

Published simultaneously in Canada

ISBN: 978-0-470-50222-8

Manufactured in the United States of America

10 9 8 7 6 5 4 3 2 1

For general information on our other products and services please contact our Customer Care Department within the United States at (877) 762-2974, outside the United States at (317) 572-3993 or fax (317) 572-4002.

Wiley also publishes its books in a variety of electronic formats. Some content that appears in print may not be available in electronic books.

Library of Congress Control Number: 2009943647

For my daughter, Stephanie, my most precious gift from God.
For Wendy, my wife and friend in Christ

— THEARON

For my wife Jennifer and daughter Katelyn.

— BRYAN

ABOUT THE AUTHORS

 THEARON WILLIS currently works as a senior developer and develops Windows applications and add-ins for Microsoft Office products using Microsoft Visual Basic .NET. Over the years, Thearon has worked on a variety of systems from mainframe to client-server development.

 BRYAN NEWSOME leads a team of lead developers specializing in Microsoft solutions. Since starting his career building Visual Basic 5 solutions, he has embraced each new version Visual Basic and now creates all new solutions leveraging the .NET platform and VB.NET. He provides clients with solutions and mentoring on leading edge Microsoft technologies. For VB.NET, Bryan is a Microsoft Certified Application Developer.

ABOUT THE TECHNICAL EDITOR

DAMIEN FOGGON is a developer, writer, and technical reviewer in cutting-edge technologies and has contributed to more than 50 books on .NET, C#, Visual Basic, and ASP.NET. He is a multiple MCPD in .NET 2.0 and .NET 3.5 and can be found online at `http://blog.littlepond.co.uk`.

CREDITS

ACQUISITIONS EDITOR
Paul Reese

PROJECT EDITOR
Maureen Spears

TECHNICAL EDITOR
Damien Foggon

PRODUCTION EDITOR
Eric Charbonneau

COPY EDITOR
Luann Rouff

EDITORIAL DIRECTOR
Robyn B. Siesky

EDITORIAL MANAGER
Mary Beth Wakefield

MARKETING MANAGER
David Mayhew

PRODUCTION MANAGER
Tim Tate

**VICE PRESIDENT AND EXECUTIVE GROUP
PUBLISHER**
Richard Swadley

**VICE PRESIDENT AND EXECUTIVE
PUBLISHER**
Barry Pruett

ASSOCIATE PUBLISHER
Jim Minatel

PROJECT COORDINATOR, COVER
Lynsey Stanford

PROOFREADER
Jen Larsen, Word One

INDEXER
Johnna VanHoose Dinse

COVER IMAGE
© biffspandex/istockphoto

ACKNOWLEDGMENTS

FIRST AND FOREMOST I WANT to thank God for giving me the wisdom and knowledge to share with others and for the many talents that he has blessed me with. I would also like to thank all the people at Wiley who work so hard to bring this book to market. I'd be remiss if I didn't thank my good friend and co-author Bryan Newsome; thanks for your hard work and dedication.

— THEARON

THANKS TO EVERYONE AT WILEY who worked so hard to get this book on the shelves. Special thanks to Maureen Spears who went above and beyond to help me finish my review on schedule. Of course, thanks goes out to Thearon Willis for completing one more edition.

— BRYAN

CONTENTS

INTRODUCTION

Visual Basic 2010 is Microsoft's latest version of the highly popular Visual Basic .NET programming language, one of the many languages supported in Visual Studio 2010. Visual Basic 2010's strength lies in its ease of use and the speed at which you can create Windows Forms applications, WPF Windows applications, Web applications, WPF Browser applications, mobile device applications, and Web Services.

In this book, we introduce you to programming with Visual Basic 2010 and show you how to create these types of applications and services. Along the way you'll also learn about object-oriented techniques and learn how to create your own business objects and Windows controls.

Microsoft's .NET Framework provides Visual Basic 2010 programmers with the capability to create full object-oriented programs, just like the ones created using C# or C++. The .NET Framework provides a set of base classes that are common to all programming languages in Visual Studio 2010, which provides you with the same capability to create object-oriented programs as a programmer using C# or C++.

This book will give you a thorough grounding in the basics of programming using Visual Basic 2010; from there the world is your oyster.

WHOM THIS BOOK IS FOR

This book is designed to teach you how to write useful programs in Visual Basic 2010 as quickly and easily as possible.

There are two kinds of beginners for whom this book is ideal:

➤ You're a beginner to programming and you've chosen Visual Basic 2010 as the place to start. That's a great choice! Visual Basic 2010 is not only easy to learn, it's also fun to use and very powerful.

➤ You can program in another language but you're a beginner to .NET programming. Again, you've made a great choice! Whether you've come from Fortran or Visual Basic 6, you'll find that this book quickly gets you up to speed on what you need to know to get the most from Visual Basic 2010.

WHAT THIS BOOK COVERS

Visual Basic 2010 offers a great deal of functionality in both tools and language. No one book could ever cover Visual Basic 2010 in its entirety — you would need a library of books. What this book aims to do is to get you started as quickly and easily as possible. It shows you the roadmap, so to speak, of what there is and where to go. Once we've taught you the basics of creating working applications (creating the windows and controls, how your code should handle unexpected events, what object-oriented programming is, how to use it in your applications, and so on) we'll show you some of the areas you might want to try your hand at next:

- ➤ Chapters 1 through 9 provide an introduction to Visual Studio 2010 and Windows programming.

- ➤ Chapter 6 provides an introduction to XAML and Windows Presentation Foundation (WPF) programming.

- ➤ Chapter 10 provides an introduction to application debugging and error handling.

- ➤ Chapters 11 through 13 provide an introduction to object-oriented programming and building objects.

- ➤ Chapter 14 provides an introduction to creating Windows Forms user controls.

- ➤ Chapters 15 and 16 provide an introduction to programming with databases and covers Access, SQL Server, and ADO.NET.

- ➤ Chapters 17 and 18 provide an introduction to Dynamic Data Web Sites and ASP.NET and show you how to write applications for the Web.

- ➤ Chapter 19 provides a brief introduction to XML, a powerful tool for integrating your applications with others — regardless of the language they were written in.

- ➤ Chapter 20 introduces you to deploying applications using ClickOnce technology.

WHAT YOU NEED TO USE THIS BOOK

Apart from a willingness to learn, all you'll need for the first 15 chapters are a PC running Windows 7 (preferred), or Windows Vista, Windows XP (Home or Professional Edition), Windows Server 2008, Windows Server 2003; Internet Explorer; and of course:

- ➤ Microsoft Visual Basic 2010 Professional Edition

    or

- ➤ Microsoft Visual Basic 2010 Premium Edition

    or

- ➤ Microsoft Visual Basic 2010 Ultimate Edition

    or

- ➤ Microsoft Visual Basic 2010 Team Edition

CONVENTIONS

To help you get the most from the text and keep track of what's happening, we've used a number of conventions throughout the book.

TRY IT OUT

The *Try It Out* is an exercise you should work through, following the text in the book.

1. They usually consist of a set of steps.

2. Each step has a number.

3. Follow the steps through with your copy of the database.

How It Works

After each *Try It Out*, the code you've typed will be explained in detail.

WARNING *Boxes like this one hold important, not-to-be forgotten information that is directly relevant to the surrounding text.*

NOTE *Tips, hints, tricks, and asides to the current discussion look like this.*

As for other conventions in the text:

➤ New terms and important words are *highlighted* in italics when first introduced.

➤ Keyboard combinations are treated like this: Ctrl+R.

➤ Filenames, URLs, and code within the text are treated like so: `persistence.properties`.

```
This book uses monofont type with no highlighting for most code examples.
This book uses bolding to emphasize code that is of particular importance in the
present context.
```

SOURCE CODE

As you work through the examples in this book, you may choose either to type in all the code manually or to use the source-code files that accompany the book. All of the source code used in this book is available for download at `www.wrox.com`. Once at the site, simply locate the book's title (either by using the Search box or by using one of the title lists) and click the Download Code link on the book's detail page to obtain all the source code for the book.

NOTE *Because many books have similar titles, you may find it easiest to search by ISBN; this book's ISBN is 978-0-470-50222-8.*

Once you download the code, just decompress it with your favorite compression tool. Alternately, you can go to the main Wrox code download page at www.wrox.com/dynamic/books/download.aspx to see the code available for this book and all other Wrox books.

ERRATA

We make every effort to ensure that there are no errors in the text or in the code. However, no one is perfect, and mistakes do occur. If you find an error in one of our books, like a spelling mistake or faulty piece of code, we would be very grateful for your feedback. By sending in errata, you may save another reader hours of frustration, and at the same time you will be helping us provide even higher-quality information.

To find the errata page for this book, go to www.wrox.com and locate the title using the Search box or one of the title lists. Then, on the book details page, click the Book Errata link. On this page you can view all errata that have been submitted for this book and posted by Wrox editors. A complete book list, including links to each book's errata, is also available at www.wrox.com/misc-pages/booklist.shtml.

If you don't spot "your" error on the Book Errata page, go to www.wrox.com/contact/techsupport. shtml and complete the form there to send us the error you have found. We'll check the information and, if appropriate, post a message to the book's errata page and fix the problem in subsequent editions of the book.

P2P.WROX.COM

For author and peer discussion, join the P2P forums at p2p.wrox.com. The forums are a web-based system on which you can post messages relating to Wrox books and related technologies and interact with other readers and technology users. The forums offer a subscription feature to e-mail you topics of interest of your choosing when new posts are made to the forums. Wrox authors, editors, other industry experts, and your fellow readers are present on these forums.

At http://p2p.wrox.com you will find a number of different forums that will help you not only as you read this book, but also as you develop your own applications. To join the forums, just follow these steps:

1. Go to p2p.wrox.com and click the Register link.

2. Read the terms of use and click Agree.

3. Complete the required information to join as well as any optional information you wish to provide, and click Submit.

4. You will receive an e-mail with information describing how to verify your account and complete the joining process.

> **NOTE** *You can read messages in the forums without joining P2P, but in order to post your own messages, you must join.*

Once you join, you can post new messages and respond to messages other users post. You can read messages at any time on the Web. If you would like to have new messages from a particular forum e-mailed to you, click the Subscribe to this Forum icon by the forum name in the forum listing.

For more information about how to use the Wrox P2P, be sure to read the P2P FAQs for answers to questions about how the forum software works, as well as many common questions specific to P2P and Wrox books. To read the FAQs, click the FAQ link on any P2P page.

1

Welcome to Visual Basic 2010

WHAT YOU WILL LEARN IN THIS CHAPTER:

➤ Using event-driven programming

➤ Installing Visual Basic 2010

➤ A tour of the Visual Basic 2010 integrated development environment (IDE)

➤ Creating a simple Windows program

➤ Using the integrated Help system

This is an exciting time to enter the world of programming with Visual Basic 2010 and Windows 7. Windows 7 represents the latest Windows operating system from Microsoft and is packed with a lot of new features to make Windows programming fun. Much has changed in the Windows user interface, and Visual Basic 2010 makes it easy to write professional-looking Windows applications as well as web applications and web services. Haven't upgraded to Windows 7 yet? No worries, Visual Basic 2010 also enables you to write professional-looking applications for previous versions of Windows as well.

The goal of this book is to help you use the Visual Basic 2010 programming language, even if you have never programmed before. You will start slowly and build on what you have learned in subsequent chapters. So take a deep breath, let it out slowly, and tell yourself you can do this. No sweat! No kidding!

Programming a computer is a lot like teaching a child to tie his shoes. Until you find the correct way of giving the instructions, not much is accomplished. Visual Basic 2010 is a language you can use to tell your computer how to do things; but, like a child, the computer will understand only if you explain things very clearly. If you have never programmed before, this sounds like an arduous task, and sometimes it can be. However, Visual Basic 2010 offers an easy-to-use language to explain some complex tasks. Although it never hurts to have an understanding of what is happening at the lowest levels, Visual Basic 2010 frees the programmer from having to deal with the mundane complexities of writing Windows applications. You are free to concentrate on solving real problems.

Visual Basic 2010 helps you create solutions that run on the Microsoft Windows operating systems, such as Windows 7, Windows Server 2008, and Windows Mobile 6.1. If you are looking at this book, you might have already felt the need or desire to create such programs. Even if you have never written a computer program before, as you progress through the Try It Out exercises in this book, you will become familiar with the various aspects of the Visual Basic 2010 language, as well as its foundations in the Microsoft .NET Framework. You will find that it is not nearly as difficult as you imagined. Before you know it, you will feel quite comfortable creating a variety of different types of programs with Visual Basic 2010.

Visual Basic 2010 can also be used to create web applications and web services, as well as mobile applications that can run on Pocket PCs or smartphones. However, you will begin by focusing on Windows applications before extending your boundaries to other platforms.

EVENT-DRIVEN PROGRAMMING

A Windows program is quite different from yesteryear's MS-DOS program. A DOS program follows a relatively strict path from beginning to end. Although this does not necessarily limit the functionality of the program, it does limit the road the user has to take to get to it. A DOS program is like walking down a hallway; to get to the end you have to walk down the entire hallway, passing any obstacles that you may encounter. A DOS program would only let you open certain doors along your stroll.

Windows, on the other hand, opened up the world of *event-driven programming*. *Events* in this context include clicking a button, resizing a window, or changing an entry in a text box. The code that you write responds to these events. In terms of the hallway analogy: In a Windows program, to get to the end of the hall you just click the end of the hall. The hallway itself can be ignored. If you get to the end and realize that is not where you wanted to be, you can just set off for the new destination without returning to your starting point. The program reacts to your movements and takes the necessary actions to complete your desired tasks.

Another big advantage in a Windows program is the *abstraction of the hardware,* which means that Windows takes care of communicating with the hardware for you. You do not need to know the inner workings of every laser printer on the market just to create output. You do not need to study the schematics for graphics cards to write your own game. Windows wraps up this functionality by providing generic routines that communicate with the drivers written by hardware manufacturers. This is probably the main reason why Windows has been so successful. The generic routines are referred to as the Windows *application programming interface (API)*, and most of the classes in the .NET Framework take care of communicating with those APIs.

Before Visual Basic 1.0 was introduced to the world in 1991, developers had to be well versed in C and C++ programming, as well as the building blocks of the Windows system itself, the Windows API. This complexity meant that only dedicated and properly trained individuals were capable of turning out software that could run on Windows. Visual Basic changed all of that, and it has been estimated that there are now as many lines of production code written in Visual Basic as in any other language.

Visual Basic changed the face of Windows programming by removing the complex burden of writing code for the user interface (UI). By allowing programmers to *draw* their own UI, it freed them to concentrate on the business problems they were trying to solve. When the UI is drawn, the programmer can then add the code to react to events.

Visual Basic has also been *extensible* from the very beginning. Third-party vendors quickly saw the market for reusable modules to aid developers. These modules, or *controls*, were originally referred to as VBXs (named after their file extension). Prior to Visual Basic 5.0, if you did not like the way a button behaved, you could either buy or create your own, but those controls had to be written in C or C++. Database access utilities were some of the first controls available. Version 5 of Visual Basic introduced the concept of *ActiveX*, which enabled developers to create their own *ActiveX controls*.

When Microsoft introduced Visual Basic 3.0, the programming world changed significantly. Now you could build database applications directly accessible to users (so-called *front-end applications*) completely with Visual Basic. There was no need to rely on third-party controls. Microsoft accomplished this task with the introduction of *Data Access Objects (DAOs)*, which enabled programmers to manipulate data with the same ease as manipulating the user interface.

Versions 4.0 and 5.0 extended the capabilities of Version 3.0 to enable developers to target the new Windows 95 platform. They also made it easier for developers to write code, which could then be manipulated to make it usable to other language developers. Version 6.0 provided a new way to access databases with the integration of *ActiveX Data Objects (ADOs)*. The ADO feature was developed by Microsoft to aid web developers using *Active Server Pages (ASP)* to access databases. All of the improvements to Visual Basic over the years have ensured its dominant place in the programming world — it helps developers write robust and maintainable applications in record time.

With the release of Visual Basic .NET in February 2002, most of the restrictions that used to exist were obliterated. In the past, Visual Basic was criticized and maligned as a "toy" language, because it did not provide all of the features of more sophisticated languages such as C++ and Java. Microsoft removed these restrictions with Visual Basic .NET, which was rapidly adopted as a very powerful development tool. This trend has continued with the release of Visual Basic 2003, Visual Basic 2005, Visual Basic 2008, and the latest release, Visual Basic 2010. Each new release of the Visual Basic .NET programming language offers many new features, improvements, and trends, making it a great choice for programmers of all levels.

INSTALLING VISUAL BASIC 2010

You may own Visual Basic 2010 in one of the following forms:

> As part of Visual Studio 2010, a suite of tools and languages that also includes C# (pronounced "C-sharp") and Visual C++. The Visual Studio 2010 product line includes Visual Studio Professional Edition or Visual Studio Tools Team Editions. The Team Edition versions come with progressively more tools for building and managing the development of larger, enterprise-wide applications.

> As Visual Basic 2010 Express Edition (a free edition for students and beginners), which includes the Visual Basic 2010 language, and a smaller set of the tools and features available with Visual Studio 2010.

Both of these products enable you to create your own applications for the Windows platform. The installation procedure is straightforward. In fact, the Visual Studio Installer is smart enough to figure out exactly what your computer requires to make it work.

The descriptions in the following Try It Out exercise are based on installing Visual Studio 2010 Professional Edition Beta 1. Most of the installation processes are straightforward, and you can accept the default installation options for most environments. Therefore, regardless of which edition you are installing, the installation process should be smooth when accepting the default installation options.

TRY IT OUT Installing Visual Basic 2010

The Visual Studio 2010 DVD has an auto-run feature, but if the Setup screen does not appear after inserting the DVD, you need to run `Setup.exe` from the root directory of the DVD. To do this, follow these steps:

1. Click the Windows Start menu at the bottom left of your screen and then select Run or browse to the Setup program on the DVD. In the Run dialog, you can click the Browse button to locate the `Setup.exe` program on your DVD. Then click the OK button to start the setup program. After the setup program initializes, you will see the initial screen, as shown in Figure 1-1.

2. The dialog shown in Figure 1-1 shows the order in which the installation will occur. To function properly, Visual Studio 2010 requires various updates to be installed depending on the operating system that you have (e.g., Service Pack 3 on Windows XP). The setup program will automatically inform you of these updates if they are not installed. You should install those updates first and then return to the Visual Studio 2010 setup program. The individual updates required are different from the service releases listed as the third option in Figure 1-1. Step 1 of the setup program will install Visual Studio 2010, so click the Install Visual Studio 2010 link shown in Figure 1-1.

FIGURE 1-1

3. The next step in the installation process asks whether you want to send the setup information from the installation of Visual Studio 2010 to Microsoft. This is a good idea to help streamline the installation process of future editions of Visual Studio, and no personal information is sent. After you have selected or cleared the check box, indicating whether or not you want this information sent, click the Next button.

4. The third step in the installation process is the license agreement. Read the license agreement and then select the option button indicating your acceptance of the licensing terms. Then click the Next button to continue.

5. As with most setup programs, you are then presented with a list of installation options, as shown in Figure 1-2. You can install the .NET Development Environment, which is the option you need to choose for this book, and you can also install the C++ Development Environment. After checking the .NET Development Environment installation option, click the Install button to have this feature installed.

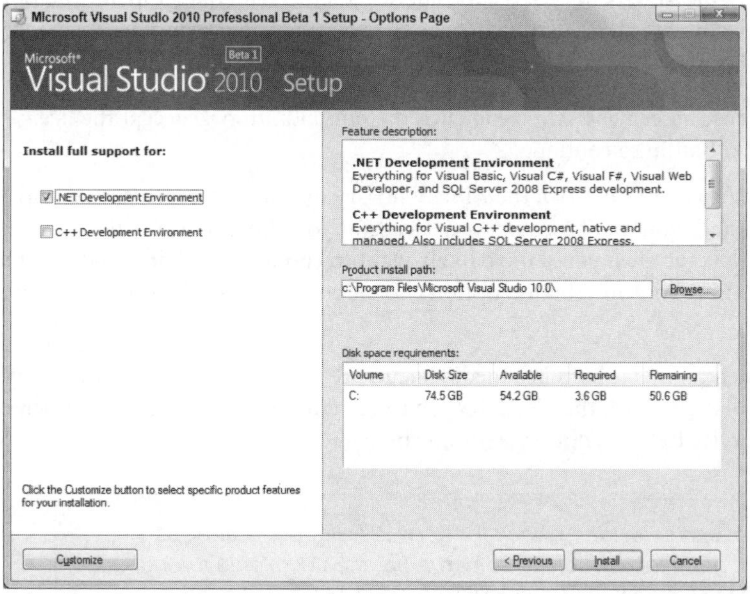

FIGURE 1-2

6. The first components to be installed are the runtime components for C++ followed by the Microsoft .NET Framework version 4.0. During installation of this component you will be required to restart your computer. After your computer has restarted and you log back in, the setup program will continue.

> **NOTE** *Note to Windows Vista and Windows 7 users: You may be prompted that the setup program needs to run, in which case you will need to grant permission to let the setup program continue. After the setup program continues, you can sit back and relax while all of the features are being installed. The setup program can take 20 minutes or more depending on the installation features chosen and the speed of your computer.*

7. Once the installation has been completed, you are presented with a dialog informing you of the status of the installation. Here you can see any problems that the setup program encountered. At this point you are encouraged to update your computer with the latest security patches, and a link is provided in the notes to Windows Update. When you have finished reviewing the setup status, click the Finish button to move on to the next step.

8. If you chose to have your setup information sent to Microsoft, the next step is a dialog sending the setup information. This dialog requires no action on your part and will automatically close when finished. The next dialog is the one shown earlier in Figure 1-1 with the option to install the production documentation enabled. Click the Install Product Documentation link to install the MSDN library.

9. The first step in installing the MSDN library is choosing whether to send the setup information to Microsoft. Make the appropriate choice and then click the Next button to continue. Again, it is recommended to send this information to help streamline future MSDN library installations.

10. Read and accept the license agreement. After you click the option button to accept the license agreement, click the Next button to continue.

11. Like the installation of Visual Studio 2010, the MSDN library installation provides you with options to choose the installation that best suits your needs. If you chose to install the complete Visual Studio 2010 product set, then you'll most likely want to choose the full installation of the MSDN library. After making your installation option choice, click the Install button to begin the installation.

12. After the MSDN documentation has been installed, you are presented with a dialog informing you of the status of the installation. Click the Finish button to be returned to the initial Setup screen again. The Check for Service Releases option is now available.

> **NOTE** *It is a good idea to select the Check for Service Releases option, as Microsoft has done a good job of making software updates available through the Internet. These updates can include anything from additional documentation to bug fixes. You will be given the choice to install any updates through a Service Pack CD or the Internet. Obviously, the Internet option requires an active connection. Since updates can be quite large, a fast connection is highly recommended.*

After you have performed the update process, Visual Studio 2010 is ready to use. Now the real fun can begin — so get comfortable, relax, and enter the world of Visual Basic 2010.

THE VISUAL STUDIO 2010 IDE

You don't need Visual Basic 2010 to write applications in the Visual Basic .NET language. The capability to run Visual Basic .NET code is included with the .NET Framework. You could write all of your Visual Basic .NET code using a text editor such as Notepad. You could also hammer nails using your shoe as a hammer, but that slick pneumatic nailer sitting there is a lot more efficient. In the same way, by far the easiest way to write in Visual Basic .NET code is by using the Visual Studio 2010 IDE. This is what you see when working with Visual Basic 2010 — the windows, boxes, and so on. The IDE provides a wealth of features unavailable in ordinary text editors — such as code checking, visual representations of the finished application, and an explorer that displays all of the files that make up your project.

The Profile Setup Page

An IDE is a way of bringing together a suite of tools that makes developing software a lot easier. Fire up Visual Studio 2010 and see what you've got. If you used the default installation, go to your Windows Start menu and then select All Programs ⇨ Microsoft Visual Studio 2010 ⇨ Microsoft Visual Studio 2010. A splash screen will briefly appear, and then you see the Choose Default Environment Settings dialog. Select the Visual Basic Development Settings option and click Start Visual Studio. After Visual Studio configures the environment based on the chosen settings, the Microsoft Development Environment will appear, as shown in Figure 1-3.

The Menu

By now, you may be eager to start writing some code; but hold off and begin your exploration of the IDE by looking at the menu and toolbar, which are not really all that different from the toolbars and menus available in other Windows applications (although they differ from the Ribbon in Microsoft Office 2007 and some of the newer Windows applications).

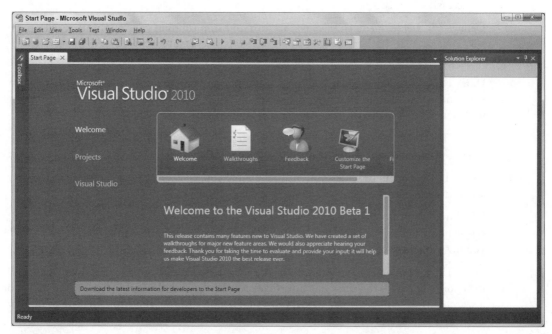

FIGURE 1-3

The Visual Studio 2010 menu is dynamic, which means items are added or removed depending on what you are trying to do. When looking at the blank IDE, the menu bar consists only of the File, Edit, View, Tools, Test, Window, and Help menus. When you start working on a project, however, the full Visual Studio 2010 menu appears, as shown in Figure 1-4.

FIGURE 1-4

At this point, there is no need to cover each menu topic in detail. You will become familiar with each of them as you progress through the book. Here is a quick rundown of what activities each menu item pertains to:

➤ **File:** Most software programs have a File menu. It has become the standard where you should find, if nothing else, a way to exit the application. In this case, you can also find ways of opening and closing single files and whole projects.

➤ **Edit:** The Edit menu provides access to the common items you would expect: Undo, Redo, Cut, Copy, Paste, and Delete.

➤ **View:** The View menu provides quick access to the windows that exist in the IDE, such as the Solution Explorer, Properties window, Output window, Toolbox, and so on.

➤ **Project:** The Project menu enables you to add various files to your application, such as forms and classes.

➤ **Build:** The Build menu becomes important when you have completed your application and want to run it without the use of the Visual Basic 2010 environment (perhaps running it directly from your Windows Start menu, as you would any other application such as Word or Access).

➤ **Debug:** The Debug menu enables you to start and stop running your application within the Visual Basic 2010 IDE. It also gives you access to the Visual Studio 2010 debugger. The debugger enables you to step through your code while it is running to see how it is behaving.

➤ **Data:** The Data menu enables you to use information that comes from a database. You can view and add data sources, and preview data. Chapters 15 and 16 introduce you to working with databases.

➤ **Tools:** The Tools menu has commands to configure the Visual Studio 2010 IDE, as well as links to other external tools that may have been installed.

➤ **Test:** The Test menu provides options that enable you to create and view unit tests for your application to exercise the source code in various scenarios.

➤ **Window:** The Window menu has become standard for any application that allows more than one window to be open at a time, such as Word or Excel. The commands on this menu enable you to switch between the windows in the IDE.

➤ **Help:** The Help menu provides access to the Visual Studio 2010 documentation. There are many different ways to access this information (e.g., through the Help contents, an index, or a search). The Help menu also has options that connect to the Microsoft website to obtain updates or report problems.

The Toolbars

Many toolbars are available within the IDE, including Formatting, Image Editor, and Text Editor, which you can add to and remove from the IDE through the View ➪ Toolbars menu option. Each one provides quick access to frequently used commands, preventing you from having to navigate through a series of menu options. For example, the leftmost icon (New Project) on the default toolbar (called the Standard toolbar), shown in Figure 1-5, is available from the menu by navigating to File ➪ New Project.

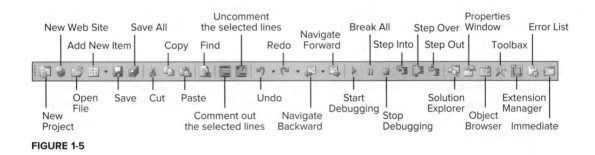

FIGURE 1-5

The toolbar is segmented into groups of related options, which are separated by vertical bars:

➤   The first six icons provide access to the commonly used project and file manipulation options available through the File and Project menus, such as opening and saving files.

➤   The next group of icons is for editing (Cut, Copy, and Paste). The next icon is for finding and replacing items in your code.

➤   The third group of icons is used for commenting out and un-commenting sections of code. This can be useful in debugging when you want to comment out a section of code to determine what results the program might produce by not executing those lines of code.

➤   The fourth group of icons is for undoing and redoing edits and for navigating through your code.

➤   The fifth group of icons provides the ability to start (via the green triangle), pause, and stop your application. You can also use the last three icons in this group to step into your code line by line, step over entire sections of code, and step out of a procedure. These icons will be covered in depth in Chapter 10.

➤   The final group of icons provides quick links to the Solution Explorer, Properties window, Object Browser, Toolbox, Error List, Extension Manager, and the Immediate window. If any of these windows is closed, clicking the appropriate icon will bring it back into view.

If you forget what a particular icon does, you can hover your mouse pointer over it so that a tooltip appears displaying the name of the toolbar option.

You could continue to look at each of the windows in the IDE by clicking the View menu and choosing the appropriate window, but as you can see, they are all empty at this stage and therefore not very revealing. The best way to look at the capabilities of the IDE is to use it while writing some code.

CREATING A SIMPLE APPLICATION

To finish your exploration of the IDE, you need to create a project so that the windows shown earlier in Figure 1-3 have some interesting content for you to look at.

TRY IT OUT   Creating a Hello User Project

Code file Chapter 1\Hello User.zip available for download at Wrox.com.

In this Try It Out exercise, you are going to create a very simple application called Hello User that will allow you to enter a person's name and display a greeting to that person in a message box.

1. Click the New Project button on the toolbar.

2. In the New Project dialog, select Visual Basic in the Installed Templates tree-view box to the left and then select Windows beneath it. The Templates pane on the right will display all of the available templates for the project type chosen. Select the Windows Forms Application template. Finally, type Hello User in the Name text box and click OK. Your New Project dialog should look like Figure 1-6.

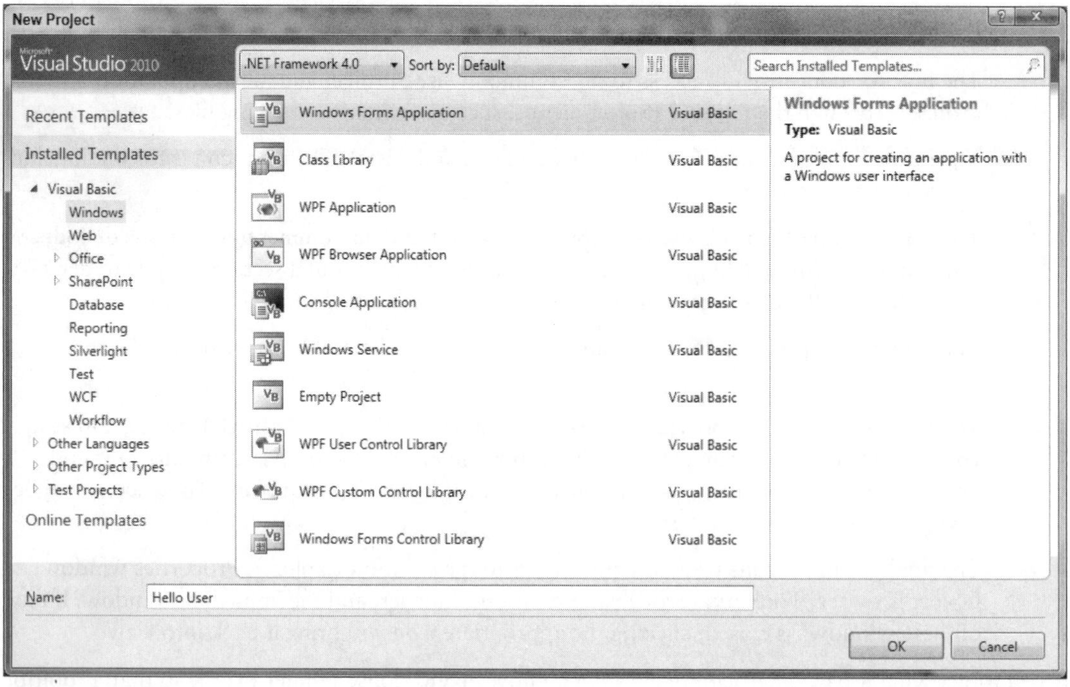

FIGURE 1-6

Visual Studio 2010 allows you to target your application to a specific version of the Microsoft .NET Framework. The combo box at the top of the Templates pane in the New Project dialog has version

4.0 selected, but you can target your application to version 3.5, version 3.0, or even version 2.0 of the .NET Framework.

The IDE will then create an empty Windows application for you. So far, your Hello User program consists of one blank window, called a Windows Form (or sometimes just a form), with the default name of Form1.vb, as shown in Figure 1-7.

Whenever Visual Studio 2010 creates a new file, either as part of the project creation process or when you create a new file, it will use a name that describes what it is (in this case, a form) followed by a number.

Windows in the Visual Studio 2010 IDE

At this point, you can see that the various windows in the IDE are beginning to show their purposes, and you should take a brief look at them now before you come back to the Try It Out exercise.

> **NOTE** *Note that if any of these windows are not visible on your screen, you can use the View menu to show them. Also, if you do not like the location of any particular window, you can move it by clicking its title bar (the blue bar at the top) and dragging it to a new location. The windows in the IDE can float (stand out on their own) or be docked (as they appear in Figure 1-7).*

FIGURE 1-7

The following list introduces the most common windows:

➤ **Toolbox:** The Toolbox contains reusable controls and components that can be added to your application. These range from buttons to data connectors to customized controls that you have either purchased or developed.

➤ **Design window:** The Design window is where a lot of the action takes place. This is where you will draw your user interface on your forms. This window is sometimes referred to as *the Designer*.

➤ **Solution Explorer:** The Solution Explorer window contains a hierarchical view of your solution. A *solution* can contain many projects, whereas a *project* contains forms, classes, modules, and components that solve a particular problem.

➤ **Properties:** The Properties window shows what *properties* the selected object makes available. Although you can set these properties in your code, sometimes it is much easier to set them while you are designing your application (for example, drawing the controls on your form). You will notice that the `File Name` property has the value `Form1.vb`. This is the physical filename for the form's code and layout information.

TRY IT OUT   **Creating a Hello User Project** *(continued)*

Code file Chapter 1\Hello User.zip available for download at Wrox.com.

Next, you'll give your form a name and set a few properties for it:

1. Change the name of your form to something more indicative of your application. Click `Form1.vb` in the Solution Explorer window. Then, in the Properties window, change the `File Name` property from `Form1.vb` to **HelloUser.vb** and press Enter, as shown in Figure 1-8. When changing properties you must either press Enter or click another property for it to take effect.

2. Note that the form's filename has also been updated in the Solution Explorer to read `HelloUser.vb`.

3. Click the form displayed in the Design window. The Properties window will change to display the form's `Form` properties (instead of the `File` properties, which you have just been looking at).

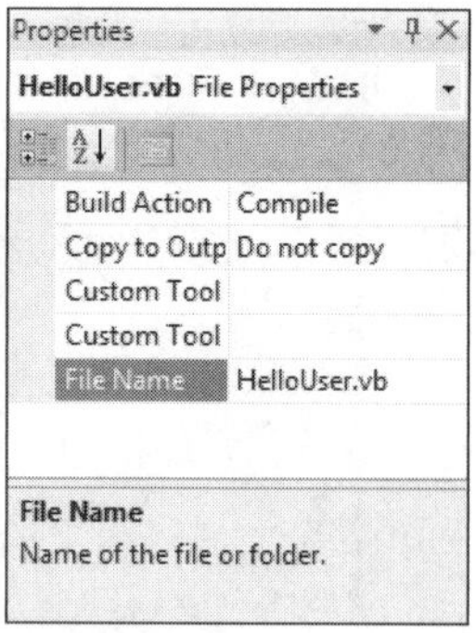

FIGURE 1-8

> **NOTE** *Note that the Properties window is dramatically different. This difference is the result of two different views of the same file. When the form name is highlighted in the Solution Explorer window, the physical file properties of the form are displayed. When the form in the Design window is highlighted, the visual properties and logical properties of the form are displayed.*

The Properties window allows you to set a control's properties easily. Properties are a particular object's set of internal data; they usually describe appearance or behavior. In Figure 1-9 you can see that properties are displayed alphabetically. The properties can also be grouped together in categories — Accessibility, Appearance, Behavior, Data, Design, Focus, Layout, Misc, and Window Style.

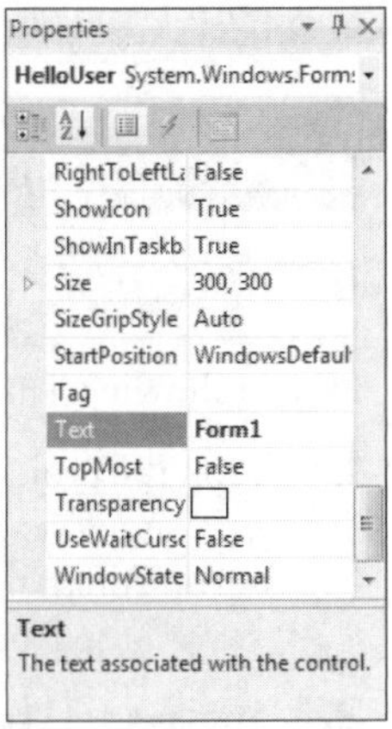

4. Right now, the title (`Text` property) of your form (displayed in the bar at the top of the form) is `Form1`. This is not very descriptive, so change it to reflect the purpose of this application. Locate the `Text` property in the Properties window. Change the `Text` property's value to `Hello from Visual Basic 2010` and press Enter. Note that the form's title has been updated to reflect the change.

FIGURE 1-9

> **NOTE** *If you have trouble finding properties, click the little AZ icon on the toolbar toward the top of the Properties window. This changes the property listing from being ordered by category to being ordered by name.*

5. You are now finished with this procedure. Click the Start button on the Visual Studio 2010 toolbar (the green triangle) to run the application. As you work through the book, whenever we say "run the project" or "start the project," just click the Start button. An empty window with the title Hello from Visual Basic 2010 is displayed.

That was simple, but your little application isn't doing much at the moment. Let's make it a little more interactive. To do this, you are going to add some controls — a label, a text box, and two buttons — to the form. This will enable you to see how the Toolbox makes adding functionality quite simple. You may be wondering at this point when you will actually look at some code. Soon! The great thing about Visual Basic 2010 is that you can develop a fair amount of your application without writing any code. Sure, the code is still there, behind the scenes, but, as you will see, Visual Basic 2010 writes a lot of it for you.

The Toolbox

The Toolbox is accessed through the View ➪ Toolbox menu option, by clicking the Toolbox icon on the Standard menu bar, or by pressing Ctrl+Alt+X. Alternatively, the Toolbox tab is displayed on the left of the IDE; hovering your mouse over this tab will cause the Toolbox window to fly out, partially covering your form.

The Toolbox contains a Node-type view of the various controls and components that can be placed onto your form. Controls such as text boxes, buttons, radio buttons, and combo boxes can be selected and then *drawn* onto your form. For the HelloUser application, you will be using only the controls in the Common Controls node. Figure 1-10 shows a listing of common controls for Windows Forms.

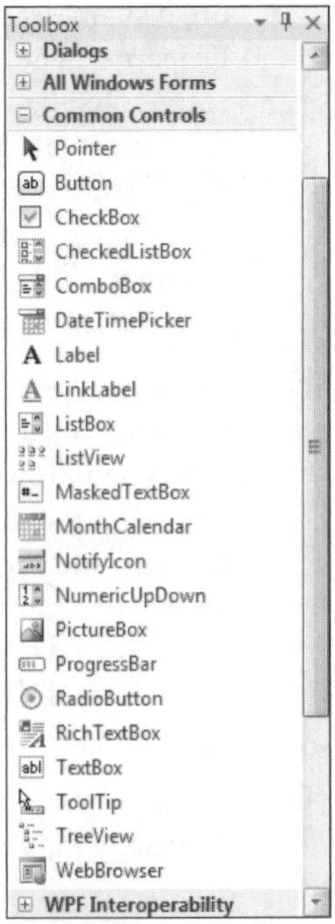

FIGURE 1-10

Controls can be added to your forms in any order, so it doesn't matter if you add the label control after the text box or the buttons before the label.

TRY IT OUT   Adding Controls to the Hello User Application

Code file Chapter 1\Hello User.zip available for download at Wrox.com.

In the following Try It Out exercise, you start adding controls.

1. Stop the project if it is still running, because you now want to add some controls to your form. The simplest way to stop your project is to click the close (X) button in the top-right corner of the form. Alternatively, you can click the blue square on the toolbar (which displays a ToolTip that says "Stop Debugging" if you hover over it with your mouse pointer).

2. Add a Label control to the form. Click Label in the Toolbox, drag it over to the form's Designer and drop it in the desired location. (You can also place controls on your form by double-clicking the required control in the Toolbox or clicking the control in the Toolbox and then drawing it on the form.)

4. If the Label control you have just drawn is not in the desired location, no problem. When the control is on the form, you can resize it or move it around. Figure 1-11 shows what the control looks like after you place it on the form. To move it, click the control and drag it to the desired location. The label will automatically resize itself to fit the text that you enter in the `Text` property.

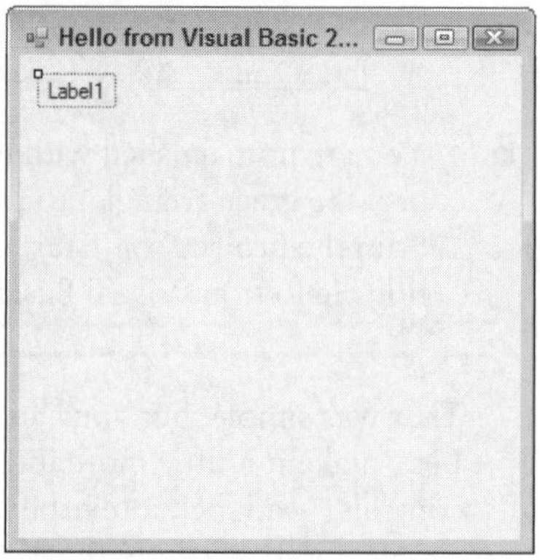

FIGURE 1-11

5. After drawing a control on the form, you should at least configure its name and the text that it will display. You will see that the Properties window to the right of the Designer has changed to `Label1`, telling you that you are currently examining the properties for the label. In the Properties window, set your new label's `Text` property to **Enter Your Name**. Note that after you press Enter or click on another property, the label on the form has automatically resized itself to fit the text in the `Text` property. Now set the `Name` property to **lblName**.

5. Directly beneath the label, you want to add a text box so that you can enter a name. You are going to repeat the procedure you followed for adding the label, but this time make sure you select the TextBox control from the toolbar. After you have dragged and dropped (or double-clicked) the control into the appropriate position as shown in Figure 1-12, use the Properties window to set its `Name` property to **txtName**. Notice the sizing handles on the left and right side of the control. You can use these handles to resize the text box horizontally.

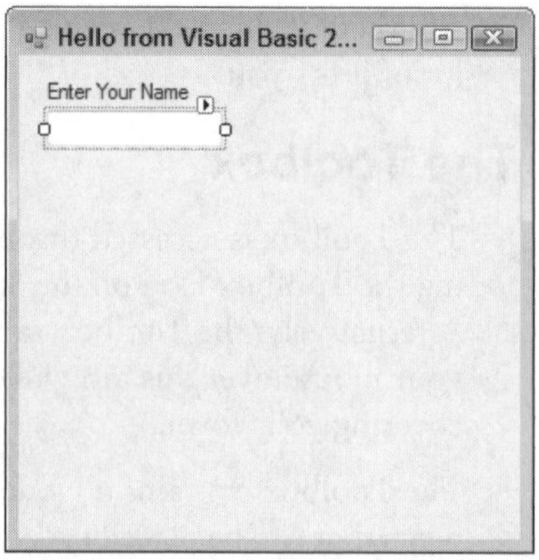

6. In the bottom left corner of the form, add a Button control in exactly the same manner as you added the label and text

FIGURE 1-12

box. Set its `Name` property to **btnOK** and its `Text` property to **&OK**. Your form should now look similar to the one shown in Figure 1-13.

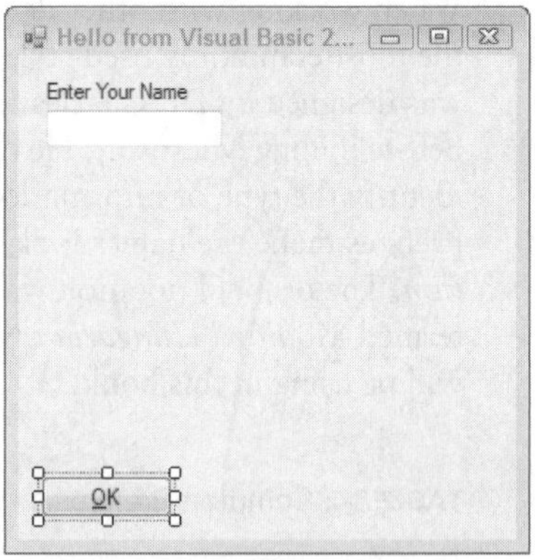

The ampersand (&) is used in the `Text` property of buttons to create a keyboard shortcut (known as a *hot key*). The letter with the & sign placed in front of it will become underlined (as shown in Figure 1-13) to signal users that they can select that button by pressing the Alt+letter key combination, instead of using the mouse (on some configurations the underline doesn't appear until the user presses Alt). In this particular instance, pressing Alt+O would be the same as clicking the OK button. There is no need to write code to accomplish this.

FIGURE 1-13

7. Now add a second Button control to the bottom right corner of the form by dragging the Button control from the Toolbox onto your form. Notice that as you get close to the bottom right of the form, a blue snap line appears, as shown in Figure 1-14. This snap line enables you to align this new Button control with the existing Button control on the form. The snap lines assist you in aligning controls to the left, right, top, or bottom of each other, depending on where you are trying to position the new control. The light blue line provides you with a consistent margin between the edge of your control and the edge of the form. Set the `Name` property to **btnExit** and the `Text` property to **E&xit**. Your form should look similar to Figure 1-15.

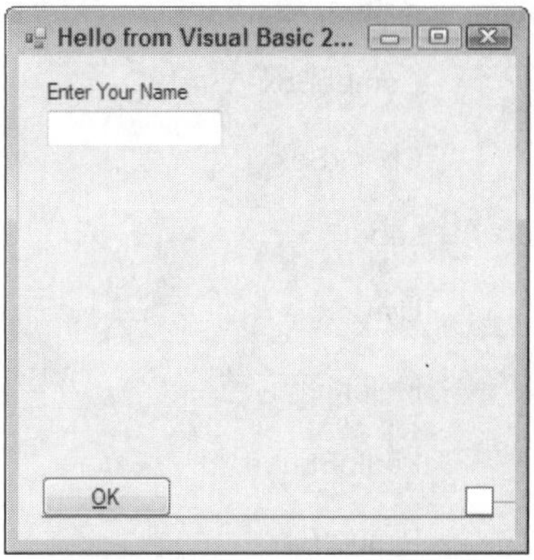

FIGURE 1-14

Now, before you finish your sample application, the following section briefly discusses some coding practices that you should be using.

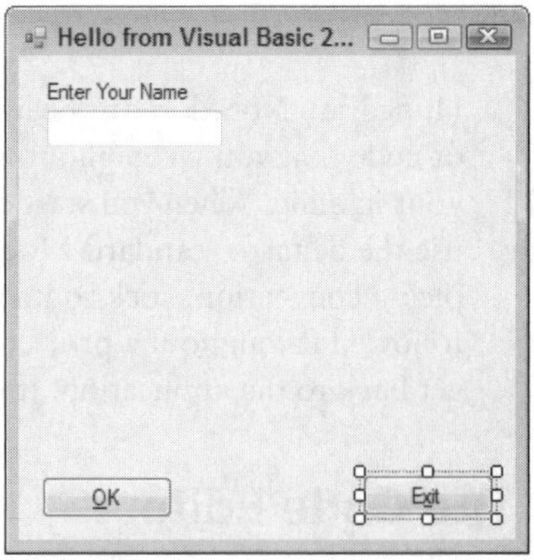

Modified Hungarian Notation

You may have noticed that the names given to the controls look a little funny. Each name is prefixed with a shorthand identifier describing the type of control it is. This makes it much easier to understand what type of control you are working with as you look through the code. For example, say you had a control called simply Name, without a prefix of lbl or txt. You would not know whether you were working with a text box that accepted a name or with a label that displayed a name. Imagine if, in the previous

FIGURE 1-15

Try It Out exercise, you had named your label Name1 and your text box Name2 — you would very quickly become confused. What if you left your application for a month or two and then came back to it to make some changes?

When working with other developers, it is very important to keep the coding style consistent. One of the most commonly used styles for control names within application development in many languages was designed by Dr. Charles Simonyi, who worked for the Xerox Palo Alto Research Center (XPARC) before joining Microsoft. He came up with short prefix mnemonics that allowed programmers to easily identify the type of information a variable might contain. Because Simonyi is from Hungary, and the prefixes make the names look a little foreign, this naming system became known as *Hungarian Notation*. The original notation was used in C/C++ development, so the notation for Visual Basic 2010 is termed *Modified Hungarian Notation*. Table 1-1 shows some of the commonly used prefixes that you will be using in this book.

TABLE 1-1: Common Prefixes in Visual Basic 2010

CONTROL	PREFIX
Button	btn
ComboBox	cbo
CheckBox	chk
Label	lbl
ListBox	lst
MainMenu	mnu
RadioButton	rdb
PictureBox	pic
TextBox	txt

Hungarian Notation can be a real time-saver when you are looking at either code someone else wrote or code that you wrote months earlier. However, by far the most important thing is to be consistent in your naming. When you start coding, choose a convention for your naming. It is recommended that you use the de facto standard Modified-Hungarian for Visual Basic 2010, but it is not required. After you pick a convention, stick to it. When modifying others' code, use theirs. A standard naming convention followed throughout a project will save countless hours when the application is maintained. Now let's get back to the application. It's time to write some code.

The Code Editor

Now that you have the HelloUser form defined, you have to add some code to make it actually do something interesting. You have already seen how easy it is to add controls to a form. Providing the functionality behind those on-screen elements is no more difficult. To add the code for a control, you just double-click the control in question. This opens the Code Editor in the main window, shown in Figure 1-16.

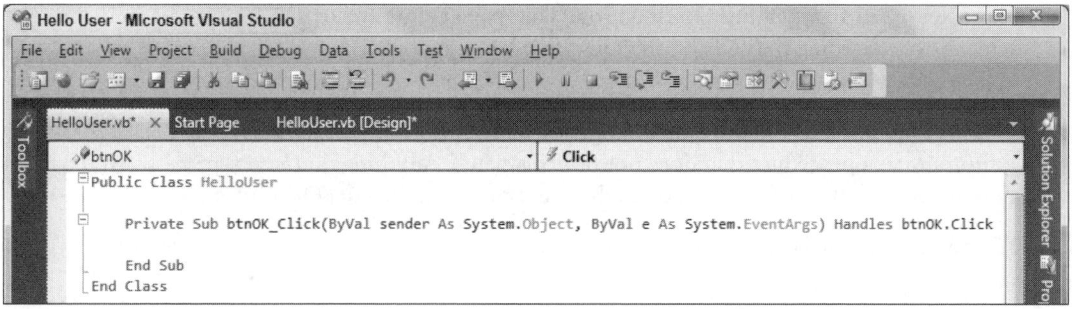

FIGURE 1-16

Note that an additional tab has been created in the main window. Now you have the Design tab and the Code tab, each containing the name of the form you are working on. You draw the controls on your form in the Design tab, and you write code for your form in the Code tab. One thing to note here is that Visual Studio 2010 has created a separate file for the code. The visual definition and the code behind it exist in separate files: HelloUser.Designer.vb and HelloUser.vb. This is actually the reason why building applications with Visual Basic 2010 is so slick and easy. Using the design mode you can visually lay out your application; then, using Code view, you add just the bits of code to implement your desired functionality.

Note also the two combo boxes at the top of the window. These provide shortcuts to the various parts of your code. The combo box on the left is the Class Name combo box. If you expand this combo box, you will see a list of all the objects within your form. The combo box on the right is the Method Name combo box. If you expand this combo box, you will see a list of all defined functions and events for the object selected in the Class Name combo box. If this particular form had a lot of code behind it, these combo boxes would make navigating to the desired code area very quick — jumping to the selected area in your code. However, all of the code for this project so far fits in the window, so there aren't a lot of places to get lost.

TRY IT OUT Adding Code to the Hello User Project

Code file Chapter 1\Hello User.zip available for download at Wrox.com.

1. To begin adding the necessary code, click the Design tab to show the form again. Then double-click the OK button. The code window will open with the following code. This is the shell of the button's Click event and the place where you enter the code that you want to run when you click the button. This code is known as an *event handler*, sometimes also referred to as an *event procedure*:

```
Private Sub btnOK_Click(ByVal sender As System.Object, _
    ByVal e As System.EventArgs) Handles btnOK.Click

End Sub
```

As a result of the typographic constraints in publishing, it is not possible to put the Sub declaration on one line. Visual Basic 2010 allows you to break up lines of code by using the underscore character (_) to signify a line continuation. The space before the underscore is required. Any whitespace preceding the code on the following line is ignored.

Sub is an example of a *keyword*. In programming terms, a keyword is a special word that is used to tell Visual Basic 2010 to do something special. In this case, it tells Visual Basic 2010 that this is a *subroutine,* a procedure that does not return a value. Anything that you type between the lines Private Sub and End Sub will make up the event procedure for the OK button.

2. Now add the bolded code to the procedure:

```
Private Sub btnOK_Click(ByVal sender As System.Object, _
    ByVal e As System.EventArgs) Handles btnOK.Click
    'Display a message box greeting to the user
    MessageBox.Show("Hello, " & txtName.Text & _
        "! Welcome to Visual Basic 2010.", _
        "Hello User Message")
End Sub
```

Throughout this book, you will be presented with code that you should enter into your program if you are following along. Usually, we will make it pretty obvious where you put the code, but as we go, we will explain anything that looks out of the ordinary. The code with the gray background is code that you should enter.

3. After you have added the preceding code, go back to the Design tab and double-click the Exit button. Add the following bolded code to the btnExit_Click event procedure:

```
Private Sub btnExit_Click(ByVal sender As System.Object, _
    ByVal e As System.EventArgs) Handles btnExit.Click
    'End the program and close the form
    Me.Close()
End Sub
```

4. Now that the code is finished, the moment of truth has arrived and you can see your creation. First, however, save your work by using File ➪ Save All from the menu or by clicking the Save All button on the toolbar. The Save Project dialog is displayed, as shown in Figure 1-17, prompting you for a name and location for saving the project.

Save Project			? X
Name:	Hello User		
Location:	C:\Users\thearon\documents\visual studio 10\Projects	▾	Browse...
Solution Name:	Hello User	☐ Create directory for solution	
		Save	Cancel

FIGURE 1-17

By default, a project is saved in a folder with the project name; in this case Hello User. Since this is the only project in the solution, there is no need to create a separate folder for the solution, which contains the same name as the project, thus the "Create directory for solution" check box is unselected.

5. Now click the Start button on the toolbar. At this point Visual Studio 2010 will *compile* the code. Compiling is the activity of taking the Visual Basic 2010 source code that you have written and translating it into a form that the computer understands. After the compilation is complete, Visual Studio 2010 *runs* (also known as *executes*) the program, and you'll be able to see the results.

Any errors that Visual Basic 2010 encounters will be displayed as tasks in the Error List window. Double-clicking a task transports you to the offending line of code. You will learn more about how to debug the errors in your code in Chapter 3.

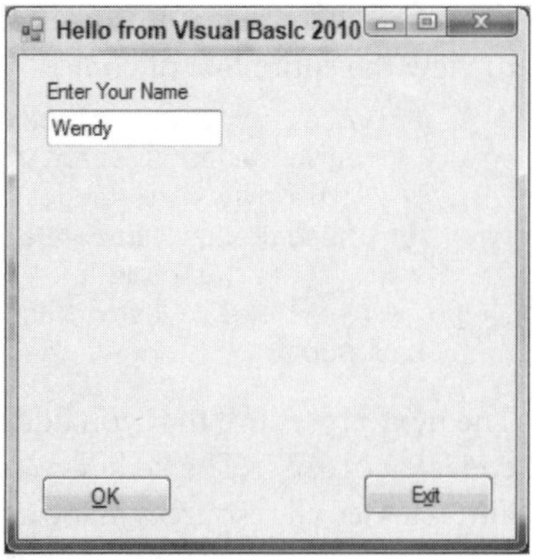

6. When the application loads, you see the main form. Enter a name and click OK or press the Alt+O key combination (see Figure 1-18).

A window known as a message box appears as shown in Figure 1-19, welcoming the person whose name was entered in the text box on the form — in this case, Wendy.

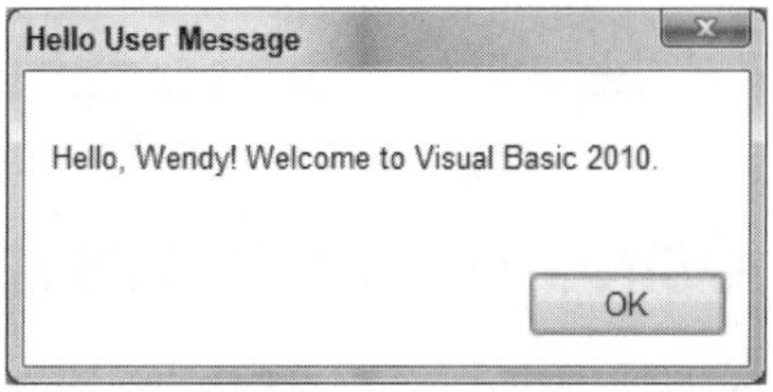

7. After you close the message box by clicking the OK button, click the Exit button on your form. The application closes and you will be returned to the Visual Studio 2010 IDE.

FIGURE 1-18

FIGURE 1-19

How It Works

The code that you added to the Click event for the OK button will take the name that was entered in the text box and use it as part of the message that was displayed in Figure 1-19.

The first line of text you entered in this procedure ('Display a message box greeting to the user) is actually a *comment*, text that is meant to be read by the human programmer who is writing or maintaining the code, not by the computer. Comments in Visual Basic 2010 begin with a single quote ('), and everything following on that line is considered a comment and ignored by the compiler. Comments are discussed in detail in Chapter 3.

The MessageBox.Show method displays a message box that accepts various parameters. As used in your code, you have passed the string text to be displayed in the message box. This is accomplished through the *concatenation* of string constants defined by text enclosed in quotes. Concatenation of strings into one long string is performed through the use of the ampersand (&) character.

The code that follows concatenates a string constant of "Hello," followed by the value contained in the Text property of the txtName text box control, followed by a string constant of "! Welcome to Visual Basic 2010." The second parameter passed to the MessageBox.Show method is the caption to be used in the title bar of the Message Box dialog.

Finally, the underscore (_) character used at the end of the lines in the following code enables you to split your code onto separate lines. This tells the compiler that the rest of the code for the parameter is continued on the next line. This is very useful when building long strings because it enables you to view the entire code fragment in the Code Editor without having to scroll the Code Editor window to the right to view the entire line of code.

```
Private Sub btnOK_Click(ByVal sender As System.Object, _
    ByVal e As System.EventArgs) Handles btnOK.Click
    'Display a message box greeting to the user
    MessageBox.Show("Hello, " & txtName.Text & _
        "! Welcome to Visual Basic 2010.", _
        "Hello User Message")
End Sub
```

The next procedure that you added code for was the Exit button's `Click` event. Here you simply enter the code: `Me.Close()`.The `Me` keyword refers to the form itself. The `Close` method of the form closes the form and releases all resources associated with it, thus ending the program:

```
Private Sub btnExit_Click(ByVal sender As System.Object, _
    ByVal e As System.EventArgs) Handles btnExit.Click
    'End the program and close the form
    Me.Close()
End Sub
```

USING THE HELP SYSTEM

The Help system included in Visual Basic 2010 is an improvement over the Help systems in earliest versions of Visual Basic. As you begin to learn Visual Basic 2010, you will probably become very familiar with the Help system. However, a brief overview would be useful, just to help speed your searches for information.

The Help menu contains the items shown in Figure 1-20.

As you can see, this menu contains a few more items than the typical Windows application. The main reason for this is the vastness of the documentation. Few people could keep it all in their heads — but luckily that is not a problem, because you can always quickly and easily refer to the Help system or search the forums for people who are experiencing or have experienced a similar programming task. Think of it as a safety net for your brain.

You can also quickly access the Help documentation for a particular subject by simply clicking on a keyword in the Code Editor and pressing the F1 key.

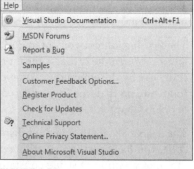

FIGURE 1-20

SUMMARY

Hopefully, you are beginning to see that developing basic applications with Visual Basic 2010 is not very difficult. You have taken a look at the IDE and have seen how it can help you put together software very quickly. The Toolbox enables you to add controls to your form and design a user interface very quickly and easily. The Properties window makes configuring those controls a snap, while the Solution Explorer gives you a bird's-eye view of the files that make up your project. You even wrote a little code.

In the coming chapters, you will go into even more detail and get comfortable writing code. Before you get too far into Visual Basic 2010 itself, however, the next chapter provides an introduction to the Microsoft .NET Framework, which is what gives all of the .NET languages their ease of use, ease of interoperability, and simplicity in learning.

EXERCISE

The answers for this exercise and those at the end of each chapter in this book can be found in Appendix A.

Code file Chapter 1\Exercise 1.zip available for download at Wrox.com.

1. Create a Windows application with a Textbox control and a Button control that will display whatever is typed in the text box when the user clicks the button.

▶ **WHAT YOU LEARNED IN THIS CHAPTER**

TOPIC	CONCEPTS
The integrated development environment (IDE)	How to create projects in the IDE, how to navigate between Design View and Code View, and how to run and debug projects.
Adding controls to your form in the Designer	How to use the toolbox to drag and drop controls onto your form and how to move and resize controls on your form.
Setting the properties of your controls	How to display text in the control and to name the controls to something meaningful.
Adding code to your form in the code window	How to add code to control what your program does.

2

The Microsoft .NET Framework

WHAT YOU WILL LEARN IN THIS CHAPTER:

➤ What the .NET Framework is

➤ Using the .NET vision

➤ Why Microsoft dared to spend billions on a single development project

The .NET Framework provides an unprecedented platform for building Windows, web, and mobile applications with one or more languages. It is a definitive guide, encompassing and encapsulating where we have come from as a development community and, of course, where we are going.

.NET has been a success in many respects. Within the .NET Framework, new languages (C# and F#) have been born, and the well-established Visual Basic language has been reborn. The .NET Framework even supports legacy languages such as C++.

The .NET Framework provides the base for all development using Visual Studio 2010. It provides base classes, available to all Visual Studio 2010 languages for such functions as accessing databases, parsing XML, displaying and processing Windows and web forms, and providing security for your applications. All languages in Visual Studio 2010 share and use the same base classes, making your choice of a programming language in Visual Studio 2010 a matter of personal preference and syntax style.

MICROSOFT'S RELIANCE ON WINDOWS

In terms of the great corporations of the world, Microsoft is still a new kid on the block. It is a fabulously rich and successful business. Nonetheless, the company has grown from nothing to a corporate superpower in a very short time.

What is perhaps more interesting is that although the origins of Microsoft can be traced to the mid-1970s, it is really the Windows family of operating systems that has brought the company great success. Based on Presentation Manager for OS/2, Windows has seen many incarnations from Windows/286 to Windows 7, but the essential way that you use Windows and Windows applications has not changed in all that time. (Granted, there have been advances in the user interface and the hardware, but you still use the version of Excel included with Office 2007 in roughly the same way that you used the first version.)

The scary thing to Microsoft and its investors is that the pace of technological change means that they cannot be sure that Windows is going to be as relevant in 2020 as it is today. All it takes is one change in the way that people want to use computers, and the Windows platform's current incarnation may become obsolete.

It would be unfair to say that Microsoft has been extremely lucky over the past several years in the way that it has reacted to the opportunities offered by the Internet. Do not underestimate the number of smart people working for that company. When they discovered that companies such as Netscape were making money with the Internet and identified the risk, they turned a large corporation on a dime and went after an unexplored market with teeth bared. Their gambles paid off, and with the invention of the .NET Framework, corporations and users are leveraging the power of the Internet in new ways.

Luckily for Microsoft, the applications that drove the adoption of the Internet worked well on a desktop operating system. Microsoft managed to adapt the Windows platform to provide the two killer Internet applications, e-mail and the web browser, to end users with a minimum of hassle, securing the Windows platform for another few years. It also delivered several powerful tools for developers, such as Active Server Pages Extended (ASPX), web services, and Internet Information Server (IIS), and improved existing tools such as Visual Basic and SQL Server, all of which made it easier for developers to build advanced Internet applications.

MSN 1.0

When the Internet started to become popular in the early 1990s, Microsoft was trying to push the original incarnation of Microsoft Network (MSN). Rather than the successful portal that it is today, MSN was originally a proprietary dial-up service much like CompuServe. In the beginning, MSN did not provide access to the rich world of the Internet as we know it today; it was a closed system. Let us call the original MSN "MSN 1.0."

MSN 1.0 provided an opportunity for innovative companies to steal a march on Microsoft, which was already seen as an unshakable behemoth thanks to the combination of Windows and Office. As it turned out, it was a missed opportunity.

Imagine an alternative 1995 in which Microsoft stuck to its guns with MSN 1.0, rather than plotted the course that brought it where it is today. Imagine that a large computer manufacturer, such as Dell, identified this burgeoning community of forward-thinking business leaders and geeks called the Internet. Also suppose Dell predicted that Microsoft's strategy was to usurp this community with MSN 1.0 — in other words, rather than cooperate with this community, Microsoft would decide to crush it at all costs.

Now Dell needs to find a way to build this community. It predicts that home users and small businesses will love the Internet and so puts together a very low-cost PC. They need software to run on it and, luckily, they predict that the Web and e-mail will be the killer applications of this new community.

They find Linus Torvalds, who has been working on this thing called Linux since 1991, and they find Sun, which is keen to start pushing Java as a programming language to anyone who will listen. Another business partner builds a competent, usable suite of productivity applications for the platform using Java. Another business partner builds easy-to-use connectivity solutions that enable the computers to connect to the Internet and other computers in the LAN, easily and cheaply.

Dell, Sun, and their selected business partners start pushing this new computer to anyone and everyone. The concept is a success and, for the first time since 1981, the dominance of the IBM-compatible PC is over, and sales of Microsoft products plummet — all because Microsoft did not move on a critical opportunity.

We all know that this did not happen, but there is nothing outlandish or crazy about this scenario. It could have happened, and that is what scared Microsoft. It came very close to losing everything, and .NET is its insurance against this happening again.

The .NET Vision

To understand .NET, you have to ignore the marketing hype from Microsoft and really think about what it is doing. With the first version of the .NET Framework and indeed even now, Microsoft appears to be pushing .NET as a platform for building web services and large-scale enterprise systems. Web services is a tiny, tiny part of what .NET is all about. In simple terms, .NET splits an operating system's platform (be it Windows, Linux, Mac OS, or any other OS) into two layers: a programming layer and an execution layer.

All computer platforms are trying to achieve roughly the same effect: to provide applications to the user. If you wanted to write a book, you would have the choice of using the word processor in StarOffice under Linux, or Word under Windows. However, you would use the computer in the same way; in other words, the application remains the same, irrespective of the platform.

It is a common understanding that software support is a large part of any platform's success. Typically, the more high-quality the available software is for a given platform, the larger the consumer adoption of that platform will be. The PC is the dominant platform because, back in the early 1980s, it was the predominant target for software writers. That trend has continued to this day, and people are writing applications that run on Windows, which targets the 32-bit and 64-bit Intel processors. The Intel processor harks back to the introduction of the Intel 8086 processor in 1979 and today includes the Intel Core family of processors. It also includes competitors such as AMD's Athlon and Turion.

Without .NET, developers are still reliant on Windows, and Windows is still reliant on Intel. Although the relationship between Microsoft and Intel is thought to be fairly symbiotic, it is reasonable to assume that the strategists at Microsoft, who are feeling (rightly) paranoid about the future, might want to lessen the dependence on a single family of chips, too.

The Windows/Intel combination (sometimes known as *Wintel*) is also known as the *execution layer*. This layer takes the code and runs it — simple as that.

Although .NET originally targeted and still targets only the Windows platform, you are seeing development communities using open-source projects to convert .NET to run on other platforms such as Linux and Unix. This means that a program written by a .NET developer on Windows could run unchanged on Linux. In fact, the Mono project (www.mono-project.com) has already released several versions of its product. This project has developed an open-source version of a C# and VB.NET compiler, a runtime for the Common Language Infrastructure (CLI, also known as the Common Intermediate Language, or CIL), a subset of the .NET classes, and other .NET goodies independent of Microsoft's involvement.

.NET is a *programming layer*. It is totally owned and controlled by Microsoft. By turning all developers into .NET programmers, rather than Windows programmers, software is written as .NET software, not Windows software.

To understand the significance of this, imagine that a new platform is launched and starts eating up market share like crazy. Imagine that, like the Internet, this new platform offers a revolutionary way of working and living that offers real advantages. With the .NET vision in place, all Microsoft has to do to gain a foothold on this platform is develop a version of .NET that works on it. All of the .NET software now runs on the new platform, lessening the chance that the new platform will usurp Microsoft's market share.

This Sounds Like Java

Some of this does sound a lot like Java. In fact, Java's mantra of "write once, run anywhere" fits nicely into the .NET doctrine. However, .NET is not a Java clone. Microsoft has a different approach.

To write in Java, developers were expected to learn a new language. This language was based on C++, and although C++ is a popular language, it is not the most popular language. In fact, the most popular language in terms of number of developers is Visual Basic, and, obviously, Microsoft owns it. Some estimates put the number of Visual Basic developers at approximately three million worldwide, but bear in mind that this number includes both Visual Basic professionals and people who tinker with macros in the various Office products.

Whereas Java is "one language, many platforms," .NET is "many languages, one platform — for now." Microsoft wants to remove the barrier to entry for .NET by making it accessible to anyone who has used pretty much any language. The two primary languages for .NET are Visual Basic 2010 and C#. Visual Studio 2010 comes supplied with both of these. Although C# is not C++, developers of C++ applications should be able to migrate to C# with about the same amount of relearning that a Visual Basic 6 developer will have to do in order to move to Visual Basic 2010. Of course, the .NET Framework supports developers using C++ and allows them to write C++ applications using the .NET Framework.

With Java, Sun attempted to build from the ground up something so abstracted from the operating system that when you compare an application written natively in something like Visual C++ with a Java equivalent, it becomes fairly obvious that the Java version will run slower and not look as good in terms of user interface. Sun tried to take too big a bite out of the problem by attempting to support everything, so in the end it did not support one single thing completely. That's probably why Java developers have so many third-party and open-source tools, such as Eclipse and Ruby.

Microsoft's .NET strategy is more like a military campaign. First, it will use its understanding of the Windows platform to build .NET into something that will stand against a native C++ application. After it wins over the voters on Windows, it may invade another platform, most likely Linux. This second stage will prove the concept that .NET applications can be ported from one platform to the next. After invading and conquering Linux, it may move to another platform. Microsoft has been attempting to shake Solaris from the top spot in the server market for a long time, so it's likely that it'll go there next.

Where Now?

Microsoft has bet its future on .NET and rightly so, with its ever-increasing adoption by developers and businesses alike. With developers writing software for the programming layer, rather than an execution layer, it really does not matter whether Windows or Linux or some other software is the dominant platform in 2020. The remainder of this chapter drills into the mechanics of .NET and takes a detailed look at how the whole thing works.

WRITING SOFTWARE FOR WINDOWS

To understand how .NET works, you need to look at how developers used to write software for Windows. The general principle was the same as with .NET, only they had to do things in different ways to work with different technologies — the Component Object Model (COM), ActiveX Data Objects (ADO), and so forth.

Any software that you write has to interact with various parts of the operating system to do its job. If the software needs a block of memory to store data in, it interacts with the memory manager subsystem. To read a file from disk, you use the disk subsystem. To request a file from the network, you use the network subsystem. To draw a window on the screen, you use the graphics subsystem, and so on.

This *subsystems* approach breaks down as far as .NET is concerned, because there is no commonality between the ways you use the subsystems on different platforms, despite the fact that platforms tend to have things in common. For example, if you are writing an application for Linux, you may still need to use the network, disk, and screen subsystems. However, because different organizations developed these platforms, the way you open a file using the Linux platform is different from the way you do it on Windows. If you want to move code that depends on one platform to another, you will probably have to rewrite portions of the code. You will also have to test the code to ensure it still works as intended.

Windows software communicates with the operating system and various subsystems using something called the *Windows 32-bit Application Programming Interface (Win32 API)*. Although object-orientation in programming was around at the time, this API was designed to be an evolution of the original Windows API, which predates the massive adoption of object-oriented techniques, which are discussed in Chapter 11.

It is not easy to port the Win32 API to other platforms, which is why there is no version of the Win32 API for Linux, even though Linux has been around for over a decade. There is a cut-down version of the Win32 API for the Mac, but this has never received much of an industry following.

The Win32 API provides all basic functionality, but now and again, Microsoft extends the capabilities of Windows with a new API. A classic example is the Windows Internet API, also known as the *WinInet API*. This API enables an application to download resources from a web server, upload files to an FTP server, discover proxy settings, and so on. Again, it is not object oriented, but it does work. Another example of this is the Win32 API that is part of the Windows 7 operating system. Because so many of the core components of the operating system have changed, a new version of the Win32 API had to be developed for this operating system.

A large factor in the success of early versions of Visual Basic is that it took the tricky-to-understand Win32 API calls and packaged them in a way that could be easily understood. Using the native Win32 API, it takes about 100 lines of code to draw a window on the screen. The same effect can be achieved in Visual Basic with a few gestures of the mouse. Visual Basic represents an abstraction layer on top of the Win32 API that makes it easier for developers to use.

A long-time frustration for C++ developers was that a lot of the things that were very easy to do in Visual Basic remained not so much hard as laborious in C++. Developers like C++ because it gives them an amazing amount of control over how a program works, but their programs take longer to write. Microsoft introduced the Microsoft Foundation Classes (MFC) because of this overhead, which, along with the IDE of Visual Studio, brought the ease of Visual C++ development closer to that of Visual Basic.

The .NET Framework Classes

Unlike the Win32 API, .NET is totally object-oriented. Anything you want to do in .NET, you are going to be doing with an object. If you want to open a file, you create an object that knows how to do this. If you want to draw a window on the screen, you create an object that knows how to do this. When you get to Chapter 11, you will discover that this is called *encapsulation*; the functionality is encapsulated in an object, and you don't really care how it's done behind the scenes.

Although the concept of subsystems still exists in .NET, these subsystems are never accessed directly — instead, they are abstracted away by the Framework classes. Either way, your .NET application never has to talk directly to the subsystem (although you can do so if you really need or want to). Rather, you talk to objects, which then talk to the subsystem. In Figure 2-1, the box marked System.IO.File is a class defined in the .NET Framework.

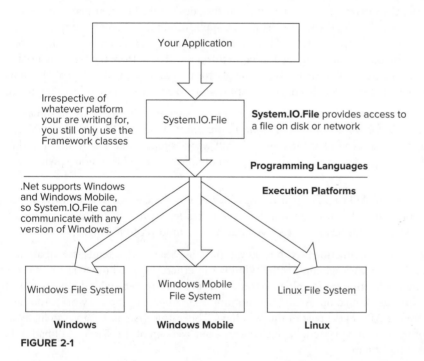

FIGURE 2-1

If you are talking to objects that talk to subsystems, do you really care what the subsystem looks like? Thankfully, the answer is no, and this is how Microsoft removes your reliance on Windows. If you know the name of a file, you use the same objects to open it whether you are running on a Windows 7 machine, a Pocket PC, or even the Mono Project version of the .NET Framework, Linux. Likewise, if you need to display a window on the screen, you don't care whether it is on a Windows operating system or a Mac.

The .NET Framework is actually a set of classes called *base classes*. The base classes in the .NET Framework are rather extensive and provide the functionality for just about anything that you need to do in a Windows or web environment, from working with files to working with data to working with forms and controls.

The class library itself is vast, containing several thousand objects available to developers, although in your daily development you only need to understand a handful of these to create powerful applications.

Another really nice thing about the base classes in the .NET Framework is that they are the same irrespective of the language used, so if you are writing a Visual Basic 2010 application, you use the same object you would use from within a C# application. That object will have the same methods, properties, and events, meaning there is very little difference in capabilities between the languages, as they all rely on the Framework.

Executing Code

The base class library is only half the equation. After you have written the code that interacts with the classes, you still need to run it. This poses a tricky problem; to remove the reliance on the platform is to remove the reliance on the processor.

Whenever you write software for Windows, you are guaranteed that this code will run on an Intel chip. With .NET, Microsoft does not want to make this guarantee. It might be that the dominant chip in 2020 is a Transmeta chip, or something never yet seen or heard of. What needs to be done is to abstract .NET from the processor, in a similar fashion to the way .NET is abstracted from the underlying subsystem implementations.

Programming languages are somewhere in between the languages that people speak every day and the language that the computer itself understands. The language that a computer uses is the *machine code* (sometimes called *machine instructions* or *machine language*) and consists entirely of zeros and ones, each corresponding to electrical current flowing or not flowing through this or that part of the chip. When you are using a PC with an Intel or compatible processor, this language is more specifically known as *x86 machine instructions*.

If you wrote an application with Visual Basic 6, you had to *compile* it into a set of x86 machine instructions before you could deploy it. This machine code would then be installed and executed on any machine that supported x86 instructions and was also running Windows.

If you write an application with Visual Basic 2010, you still have to compile the code. However, you do not compile the Visual Basic 2010 code directly into x86 machine instructions, because that would mean that the resulting program would run only on processors that support this language — in other words, the program would run only on Intel chips and their compatible competitors. Instead, compilation creates something called *Microsoft Intermediate Language (MSIL)*. This language is not dependent on any processor. It is a layer above the traditional machine code.

MSIL code will not just run on any processor, because processors do not understand MSIL. To run the code, it has to be further compiled, as shown in Figure 2-2, from MSIL code into the native code that the processor understands.

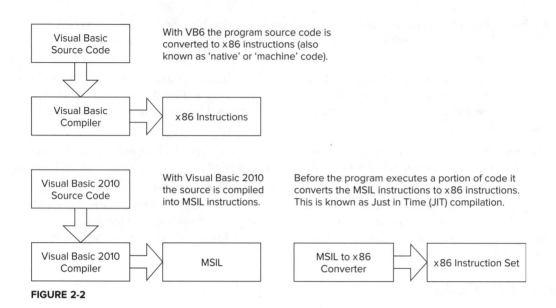

FIGURE 2-2

However, this approach also provides the industry with a subtle problem. In a world where .NET is extremely popular (some might say dominant), who is responsible for developing an MSIL-to-native compiler when a new processor is released? Is the new processor at the mercy of Microsoft's willingness to port .NET to the chip? Time will tell.

The next section describes what makes .NET work: the Common Language Runtime.

COMMON LANGUAGE RUNTIME

The Common Language Runtime (CLR) is the heart of .NET. CLR takes your .NET application, compiles it into native processor code, and runs it. It provides an extensive range of functionalities to help applications run properly:

➤ Code loading and execution

➤ Application isolation

➤ Memory management

➤ Security

➤ Exception handling

➤ Interoperability

Don't worry if you don't understand what all these are — the following sections discuss all of them except for memory management. Memory management is quite a complex subject and is discussed in Chapter 12.

Code Loading and Execution

The code loading and execution part of the CLR deals with reading the MSIL code from the disk and running it. It compiles the code from MSIL into the native code (machine code) that the processor understands.

Java also has a concept similar to MSIL, known as *byte code,* which the Java runtime loads and executes.

Application Isolation

One important premise of modern operating systems such as Windows and Linux is that applications are isolated from one another. This is critically important from the standpoint of both security and stability.

Imagine that you have a badly written program and it crashes the PC. This shouldn't happen; only the badly behaved program should crash. You don't want other applications or the operating system itself to be affected by a program running on it. For example, if your e-mail program crashes, you do not want to lose any unsaved changes in your word processor. With proper application isolation, one application crashing should not cause others to crash.

In some instances, even under Windows XP, a badly behaved program can do something so horrendous that the entire machine crashes. This is commonly known as the *Blue Screen of Death (BSOD),* so called because your attractive Windows desktop is replaced with a stark blue screen with a smattering of white text explaining the problem. This problem should be alleviated in .NET, but it is unlikely to be completely solved.

The other aspect to application isolation is one of security. Imagine that you are writing a personal and sensitive e-mail. You do not want other applications running on your computer to be able to grab, or even stumble across, the contents of the e-mail and pass it on to someone else. Applications running in an isolated model cannot just take what they want. Instead, they have to ask whether they can have something, and they are given it only if the operating system permits it.

This level of application isolation is already available in Windows. .NET extends and enhances this functionality by further improving it.

Security

.NET has powerful support for the concept of code security. The Framework was designed to give system administrators, users, and software developers a fine level of control over what a program can and cannot do.

Imagine you have a program that scans your computer's hard disk looking for Word documents. You might think this is a useful program if it is the one that you run to find documents that are missing. Now imagine that this program is delivered through e-mail and it automatically runs and e-mails copies of any "interesting" documents to someone else. You are less likely to find that useful.

This is the situation you find yourself in today with old-school Windows development. To all intents and purposes, Windows applications have unrestricted access to your computer and can do pretty much anything they want. That is why the Melissa and I Love You–type viruses are possible — Windows does not understand the difference between a benign script file you write that, say, looks through your address book and sends e-mails to everyone, and those written by others and delivered as viruses.

Windows 7 solves this problem by locking down the security aspects of Windows applications. If an application is not properly signed, Windows 7 will prompt you for permission to let the program run. Likewise, Windows 7 will prompt you for any program needing administrative permission to do operating system tasks. You then have the option to let these programs run or to cancel them, thus protecting your computer from rogue viruses.

With .NET this situation changes because of the security features built into the CLR. Under the CLR, code requires *evidence* to run. This evidence can consist of policies set by you and your system administrator, as well as the origin of the code (for example, whether it came off your local machine, off a machine on your office network, or over the Internet).

> **NOTE** *Security is a very involved topic and beyond the scope of this book. However, you can find many books that cover only the topic of .NET security and it is worthwhile to find the book that best meets your needs.*

Interoperability

Interoperability in the .NET Framework is achieved on various levels not covered here. However, we must point out some of the types of interoperation that it provides. One kind of interoperation is at the core of the framework, where data types are shared by all managed languages. This is known as the *Common Type System (CTS)*. This is a great improvement for language interoperability (see the section "The Common Type System and Common Language Specification" later in this chapter).

The other type of interoperation is that of communicating with existing Component Object Model (COM) interfaces. Because a large application-software base is written in COM, it was inevitable that .NET should be able to communicate with existing COM libraries. This is also known as *COM interop*.

Exception Handling

Exception handling is the concept of dealing with exceptional happenings when you are running the code. Imagine that you have written a program that opens a file on disk. What if that file is not there? Well, the fact that the file is not there is exceptional, and you need to handle it in some way. It could be that you crash, or you could display a window asking the user to supply a new filename. Either way, you have a fine level of control over what happens when an error does occur.

.NET provides a powerful exception handler that can catch exceptions when they occur and give your programs the opportunity to react and deal with the problem in some way. Chapter 10 talks about exception handling in more detail, but for now, think of exception handling as something provided by the CLR to all applications.

THE COMMON TYPE SYSTEM AND COMMON LANGUAGE SPECIFICATION

One of the most important aspects of .NET that Microsoft had to get right is inter-language operation. Remember, Microsoft's motivation was to get any developer using any language to use .NET; and for this to happen, all languages had to be treated equally. Likewise, applications created in one language have to be understood by other languages. For example, if you create a class in Visual Basic 2010, a C# developer should be able to use and extend that class. Alternatively, you may need to define a string in C#, pass that string to an object built in Visual Basic 2010, and make that object understand and manipulate the string successfully.

The Common Type System (CTS) enables software written in different languages to work together. Before .NET, Visual Basic and C++ handled strings completely differently, and you had to go through a conversion process each time you went from one to the other. With the CTS in place, all .NET languages use strings, integers, and so on in the same way, so no conversion needs to take place.

In addition, the Common Language Specification (CLS) was introduced by Microsoft to make it easier for language developers to adapt their languages to be compatible with .NET.

The Common Type System and Common Language Specification are the foundation for this interoperation, but detailed discussion is, unfortunately, beyond the scope of this book.

When talking to other .NET developers, you will likely hear the term *managed code*. This simply describes code that runs inside the CLR. In other words, you get all of the advantages of the CLR, such as the memory management and all of the language interoperability features previously mentioned.

Code written in Visual Basic 2010 and C# is automatically created as managed code. C++ code is not automatically created as managed code, because C++ does not fit well into the memory management scheme implemented by the CLR. You can, if you are interested, turn on an option to create managed code from within C++, in which case you use the term *managed C++*.

Hand-in-hand with managed code is *managed data*. As you can probably guess, this is data managed by the CLR, although in nearly all cases this data actually consists of objects. Objects managed by the CLR can easily be passed between languages.

SUMMARY

This chapter introduced the Microsoft .NET Framework and explained why Microsoft chose to radically change the way programs were written for Windows. You also learned that part of Microsoft's motivation for this was to move the dependence of developers from the execution platform (Windows, Linux, or whatever) over to a new programming platform that it would always own.

After learning about why Microsoft developed .NET, you saw how writing for it is not much different from writing for Windows. You still have a layer that you program against; it is just that now, rather than being flat like the Win32 API, it is a rich set of classes that enables you to write true object-oriented programs no matter what .NET language you choose to develop in. This chapter also discussed how these classes could be ported to other platforms and how your applications could transfer across.

Finally, you looked at some of the more technical aspects of the .NET Framework, specifically the Common Language Runtime.

To summarize, you should now understand:

- ➤ Microsoft's new business venture
- ➤ Goals of the .NET Framework
- ➤ Abstractions provided by the .NET Framework
- ➤ The core of the .NET Framework

▶ **WHAT YOU LEARNED IN THIS CHAPTER**

TOPIC	CONCEPTS
The .NET Vision	A set of .NET Framework classes that isolate the operating system details from the developer and provides a set of classes that can be used by any .NET programming language.
Object-Oriented Programming	The .NET Framework base classes provide objects that every other class in the framework derives from. Thus developers write object-oriented code consuming the .NET Framework objects.
Common Language Runtime	The CLR takes .NET code written in any .NET language (e.g., Visual Basic or C#) and compiles that code into a native processor code targeted for the processor your computer is using.

3

Writing Software

WHAT YOU WILL LEARN IN THIS CHAPTER:

➤   Understanding algorithms

➤   Using variables

➤   Exploring different data types, including integers, floating-point numbers, strings, and dates

➤   Studying code scope

➤   Understanding debugging applications basics

➤   Understanding how computers store data in memory

Now that you have Visual Basic 2010 up and running and have even written a simple program, you're going to look at the fundamentals behind the process of writing software and start putting together some exciting programs of your own.

INFORMATION AND DATA

Information describes facts and can be presented or found in any format, whether that format is optimized for humans or computers. For example, if you send four people to different intersections to manually survey traffic, at the end of the process you will end up with four handwritten tallies of the number of cars that went past (say, a tally for each hour).

The term *data* is used to describe information that has been collated, ordered, and formatted in such a way that it can be used by a piece of computer software. The information you have (several notebooks full of handwritten tallies) cannot be directly used by a piece of software. Rather, someone has to work with it to convert it into usable data the computer can understand. For example, the tallies can be transferred to an Excel spreadsheet that can be directly used by a piece of software designed to read that Excel spreadsheet and analyze the results.

Algorithms

The computer industry changes at an incredible speed. Most professionals retrain and reeducate themselves on an ongoing basis to keep their skills sharp and up-to-date. However, some aspects of computing haven't really changed since they were first invented and perhaps won't change within our lifetimes. The process and discipline of software development is a good example of an aspect of computer technology whose essential nature hasn't changed since its inception.

For software to work, you need to have some data to work with. The software then takes that data and manipulates it into another form. For example, software may take your customer database, stored as ones and zeroes on your computer's hard drive, and make it available for you to read on your computer's monitor. The on-board computer in your car constantly examines the environmental and performance information, adjusting the fuel mix to make your car run at maximum efficiency. For every call you make or receive, your cell phone provider records the phone number and the length of the call in order to generate a bill based on this information.

The base underpinning of all software is the *algorithm*. Before you can write software to solve a problem, you have to break it down into a step-by-step description of how the problem is going to be solved. An algorithm is independent of the programming language, so, if you like, you can describe it to yourself either as a spoken language, with diagrams, or with whatever helps you visualize the problem. Imagine that you work for a wireless telephone company and need to produce bills based on calls that your customers make. Here's an algorithm that describes a possible solution:

1. On the first day of the month, you need to produce a bill for each customer.

2. For each customer, you have a list of calls that the customer has made in the previous month.

3. You know the duration of each call, and the time of day when the call was made. Based on this information, you can determine the cost of each call.

4. For each bill, you total the cost of each call.

5. If a customer exceeds a preset time limit, you charge the customer a certain rate for each minute that exceeds the allotted time.

6. You apply sales tax to each bill.

7. After you have the final bill, you need to print and mail it.

Those seven steps describe, fairly completely, an algorithm for a piece of software that generates bills for a wireless telephone company for outgoing calls made by a customer. At the end of the day, it doesn't matter whether you build this solution in C++, Visual Basic 2010, C#, Java, or whatever — the basic algorithms of the software never change. However, it's important to realize that each of those seven parts of the algorithm may well be made up of smaller, more detailed algorithms.

The good news for a newcomer to programming is that algorithms are usually easy to construct. There shouldn't be anything in the preceding algorithm that you don't understand. Algorithms always follow commonsense reasoning, although you may have to code algorithms that contain complex mathematical or scientific reasoning. It may not seem like common sense to you, but it will to someone else! The bad news is that the process of turning the algorithm into code can be arduous. As a programmer, learning how to construct algorithms is the most important skill you will ever obtain.

All good programmers respect the fact that the preferred language of the programmer is largely irrelevant. Different languages are good at doing different things. C++ gives developers a lot of control over the way a program works; however, it's harder to write software in C++ than it is in Visual Basic 2010. Likewise, building the user interface for desktop applications is far easier to do in Visual Basic 2010 than it is in C++. (Some of these issues are eliminated when you use managed C++ with .NET, so this statement is less true today than it was years ago.) What you need to learn to do as a programmer is adapt different languages to achieve solutions to a problem in the best possible way. Although when you begin programming you'll be hooked on one language, remember that different languages are focused on developing different kinds of solutions. At some point, you may have to take your basic skills as an algorithm designer and coder to a new language.

What Is a Programming Language?

A programming language is anything capable of making a decision. Computers are very good at making decisions, but the problems or questions they need to answer have to be fairly basic, such as "Is this number greater than three?" or "Is this car blue?"

If you have a complicated decision to make, the process of making that decision has to be broken down into simple parts that the computer can understand. You use algorithms to determine how to break down a complicated decision into simpler ones.

A good example of a problem that's hard for a computer to solve is recognizing peoples' faces. You can't just say to a computer, "Is this a picture of Dave?" Instead, you have to break the question down into a series of simpler questions that the computer can understand.

The decisions that you ask computers to make must have one of two possible answers: yes or no. These possibilities are also referred to as true and false, or 1 and 0. In software terms, you cannot make a decision based on the question "How much bigger is 10 compared to 4?" Instead, you have to make a decision based on the question "Is 10 bigger than 4?" The difference is subtle, yet important — the first question does not yield an answer of yes or no, whereas the second question does. Of course, a computer is more than capable of answering the first question, but this is actually done through an operation; in other words, you have to actually subtract 4 from 10 to use the result in some other part of your algorithm.

You might be looking at the requirement for yes/no answers as a limitation, but it isn't really. Even in our everyday lives the decisions we make are of the same kind. Whenever you decide something, you accept (yes, true, 1) something and reject (no, false, 0) something else.

You are using Visual Basic 2010 for a language, but the important aspects of programming are largely independent of the language. The key is understanding that any software, no matter how flashy it is, or which language it is written in, is made up of *methods* (functions and subroutines, the lines of code that actually implement the algorithm) and *variables* (placeholders for the data the methods manipulate).

WORKING WITH VARIABLES

A variable is something that you store a value in as you work through your algorithm. You can then make a decision based on that value (for example, "Is it equal to 7?" or "Is it more than 4?"), or you can perform operations on that value to change it into something else (for example, "Add 2 to the value," "Multiply it by 6", and so on).

Before you get bogged down in code, take a moment to look at another algorithm:

1. Create a variable called `intNumber` and store in it the value 27.

2. Add 1 to the value of the variable called `intNumber` and store the new value in the same variable.

3. Display the value of the variable called `intNumber` to the user.

This algorithm creates a variable called `intNumber` and stores in it the value 27. This means that a part of the computer's memory is being used by the program to store the value 27. That piece of memory keeps storing that value until you change it or tell the program that you don't need it anymore.

In the second step, an add operation is performed. You're taking the value contained in `intNumber` and adding 1 to its value. After you've performed this operation, the piece of memory given over to storing `intNumber` contains the value 28.

In the final step, you want to tell the user the value of `intNumber`, so you read the current value from memory and write it out to the screen.

Again, there's nothing about the algorithm there that you can't understand. It's just common sense! However, the Visual Basic 2010 code looks a little more cryptic.

TRY IT OUT **Working with Variables**

Code file Chapter 3\Variables.zip available for download at Wrox.com

In the following Try It Out, you learn more about working with variables firsthand.

1. Create a new project in Visual Studio 2010 by selecting File ➪ New Project from the menu bar. In the New Project dialog, select Windows Forms Application from the right-hand pane, enter the project name as **Variables,** and click OK (see Figure 3-1).

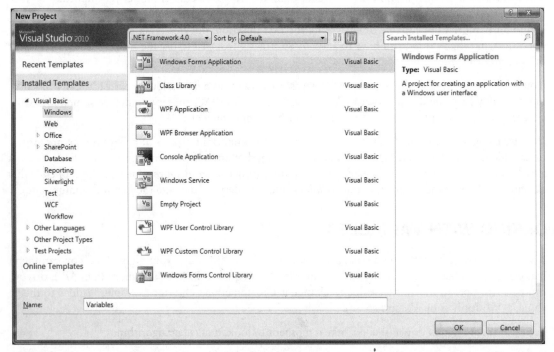

FIGURE 3-1

2. Make Form1 a little smaller and add a Button control from the Toolbox to it. Set the button's Text property to Add 1 to intNumber and its Name property to btnAdd. Your form should look similar to Figure 3-2.

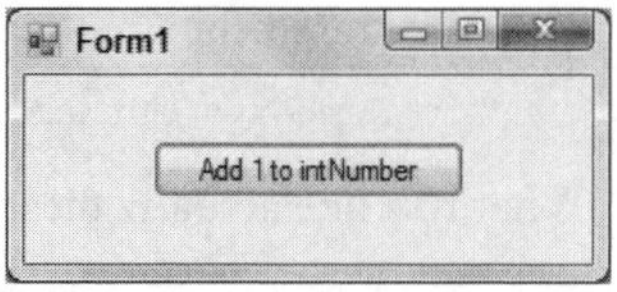

3. Double-click the button to open the btnAdd_Click event handler. Add the following bolded code to it:

FIGURE 3-2

```
Private Sub btnAdd_Click(ByVal sender As System.Object, _
    ByVal e As System.EventArgs) Handles btnAdd.Click
    Dim intNumber As Integer
    intNumber = 27
    intNumber = intNumber + 1
    MessageBox.Show("Value of intNumber + 1 = " & intNumber.ToString, _
        "Variables")
End Sub
```

4. Click the Save All button on the toolbar, verify the information in the Save Project dialog, and then click the Save button to save your project.

5. Run the project, click the Add 1 to intNumber button, and you'll see a message box like the one shown in Figure 3-3.

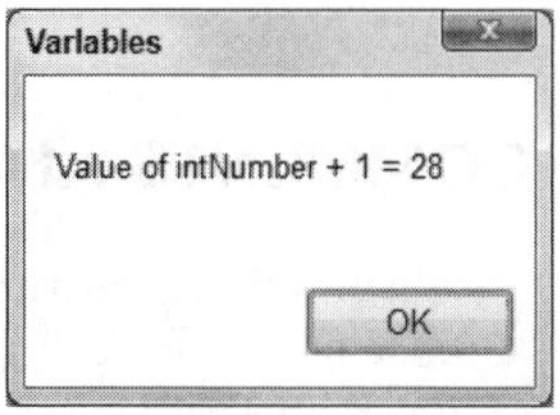

FIGURE 3-3

How It Works

After clicking the button, the program calls the btnAdd_Click event handler and program execution starts at the top and works its way down, one line at a time, to the bottom. The first line defines a new variable, called intNumber:

```
Dim intNumber As Integer
```

Dim is a keyword. As stated in Chapter 1, a keyword has a special meaning in Visual Basic 2010 and is used for things such as commands. Dim tells Visual Basic 2010 that what follows is a variable definition.

> *Its curious name harks back to the original versions of the BASIC language. BASIC has always needed to know how much space to reserve for an array (arrays are discussed in Chapter 5), so it had a command to indicate the dimensions of the array — Dim for short. Visual Basic extends that command to all other kinds of variables as well to mean "make some space for" in general.*

The variable name, intNumber, comes next. Note that the variable name uses the Modified Hungarian Notation discussed in Chapter 1. In this case the prefix int is short for integer, which represents the data type for this variable, as described in the following paragraph. Then a name was chosen for this variable; in this case the name is Number. Whenever you see this variable throughout your code, you know that this variable will represent a number that is of the Integer data type.

An Integer tells Visual Basic 2010 what kind of value you want to store in the variable. This is known as the *data type*. For now, all you need to know is that this is used to tell Visual Basic 2010 that you expect to store an integer (whole number) value in the variable.

The next line sets the value of intNumber:

```
intNumber = 27
```

In other words, it stores the value 27 in the variable intNumber.

The next statement simply adds 1 to the variable intNumber:

```
intNumber = intNumber + 1
```

What this line actually means is: Keep the current value of intNumber and add 1 to it.

The final line displays a message box with the text Value of intNumber + 1 = and the current value of intNumber. You've also set the title of the message box to Variables to match the project name. When using numeric variables in text, it is a good idea to use the ToString method to cast the numeric value to a string. This makes the code easier to read and understand because you know that you are working with strings at this:

```
MessageBox.Show("Value of intNumber + 1 = " & intNumber.ToString, _
    "Variables")
```

COMMENTS AND WHITESPACE

When writing software code, you must be aware that you or someone else may have to change that code in the future. Therefore, you should try to make it as easy to understand as possible. Comments and whitespace and the two primary means of making your code as legible as possible.

Comments

Comments are parts of a program that are ignored by the Visual Basic 2010 compiler, which means you can write whatever you like in them, be it English, C#, Perl, FORTRAN, Chinese, whatever. What they're supposed to do is help the human developer reading the code understand what each part of the code is supposed to be doing.

All languages support comments, not just Visual Basic 2010. If you're looking at C# code, for example, you'll find that comments start with a double forward slash (//).

How do you know when you need a comment? Well, it varies from one case to another, but a good rule of thumb is to think about the algorithm involved. The program in the previous Try It Out exercise had the following algorithm:

1. Define a valusssse for inNumber.

2. Add 1 to the value of intNumber.

3. Display the new value of intNumber to the user.

You can add comments to the code from that example to match the steps in the algorithm:

```
'Define a variable for intNumber
Dim intNumber As Integer

'Set the initial value
intNumber = 27

'Add 1 to the value of intNumber
intNumber = intNumber + 1
```

```
'Display the new value of intNumber
MessageBox.Show("Value of intNumber + 1 = " & intNumber.ToString, _
    "Variables")
```

In Visual Basic 2010, you begin your comments with an apostrophe ('). Anything on the same line following that apostrophe is your comment. You can also add comments onto a line that already has code, like this:

```
intNumber = intNumber + 1 'Add 1 to the value of intNumber
```

This works just as well, because only comments (not code) follow the apostrophe. Note that the comments in the preceding code, more or less, match the algorithm. A good technique for adding comments is to write a few words explaining the stage of the algorithm that's being expressed as software code.

You can also use the built-in XML Documentation Comment feature of Visual Studio 2010 to create comment blocks for your methods. To use this feature, place your cursor on the blank line preceding your method definition and type three consecutive apostrophes. The comment block is automatically inserted as shown in the code here:

```
''' <summary>
'''
''' </summary>
''' <param name="sender"></param>
''' <param name="e"></param>
''' <remarks></remarks>
    Private Sub btnAdd_Click(ByVal sender As System.Object, _
        ByVal e As System.EventArgs) Handles btnAdd.Click
```

What's really cool about this feature is that Visual Studio 2010 automatically fills in the name values of the parameters in the comment block based on the parameters defined in your method. If your method does not have any parameters, the <param> tag will not be inserted into the comment block.

Once a comment block has been inserted, you can provide a summary of what the method does and any special remarks that may need to be noted before this method is called or any other special requirements of the method. If the method returns a value, then a <returns> tag will also be inserted, and you can insert the return value and description.

Comments are primarily used to make the code easier to understand, either to a new developer who's never seen your code before or to you when you haven't reviewed your code for a while. The purpose of a comment is to point out something that might not be immediately obvious or to summarize code to enable the developer to understand what's going on without having to ponder each and every line.

You'll find that programmers have their own guidelines about how to write comments. If you work for a larger software company, or your manager/mentor is hot on coding standards, they'll dictate which formats your comments should take and where you should and should not add comments to the code.

Whitespace

Another important aspect of writing readable code is to leave a lot of whitespace. *Whitespace* (space on the screen or page not occupied by characters) makes code easier to read, just as spaces do in English.

In the previous example, there is a blank line before each comment. This implies to anyone reading the code that each block is a unit of work, which it is.

You'll be coming back to the idea of whitespace in the next chapter, which discusses controlling the flow through your programs using special code blocks, but you'll find that the use of whitespace varies between developers. For now, remember not to be afraid to space out your code — it will greatly improve the readability of your programs, especially as you write long chunks of code.

The compiler ignores whitespace and comments, so there are no performance differences between code with a lot of whitespace and comments, and code with none.

DATA TYPES

When you use variables, it's a good idea to know ahead of time the things that you want to store in them. So far in this chapter, you've seen a variable that holds an integer number.

When you define a variable, you must tell Visual Basic 2010 the type of data that should be stored in it. As you might have guessed, this is known as the *data type*, and all meaningful programming languages have a vast array of different data types from which to choose. The data type of a variable has a great impact on how the computer will run your code. In this section, you'll take a deeper look at how variables work and how their types affect the performance of your program.

Working with Numbers

When you work with numbers in Visual Basic 2010, you'll be working with two kinds of numbers: integers and floating-point numbers. Both have very specific uses. *Integers* are usually not very useful for calculations of quantities — for example, calculating how much money you have left on your mortgage or calculating how long it would take to fill a swimming pool with water. For these kinds of calculations you're more likely to use *floating-point* variables, which can be used to represent numbers with fractional parts, whereas integer variables can hold only whole numbers.

On the other hand, oddly, you'll find that in your day-to-day activities you're far more likely to use integer variables than floating-point variables. Most of the software that you write will use numbers to keep track of what is going on by counting, rather than calculating quantities.

For example, suppose you are writing a program that displays customer details on the screen. Furthermore, suppose you have 100 customers in your database. When the program starts, you'll display the first customer on the screen. You also need to keep track of which customer is being displayed, so that when the user says, "Next, please," you'll actually know which one is next.

Because a computer is more comfortable working with numbers than with anything else, you'll usually find that each customer has been given a unique number. In most cases, this unique number will be an integer. What this means is that each of your customers will be assigned a unique integer number between 1 and 100. In your program, you'll also have a variable that stores the ID of the customer you're currently looking at. When the user asks to see the next customer, you add one to that ID (also called *incrementing by one*) and display the new customer.

You'll see how this works as you move on to more advanced topics, but for now, rest assured that you're more likely to use integers than floating-point numbers. Take a look now at some common operations.

Common Integer Math Operations

In this section, you create a new project for your math operations. In the Try It Out exercise that follows, you'll see how to add, subtract, multiple, and divide integer numbers.

TRY IT OUT   Common Integer Math

Code file Chapter 3\ Integer Math.zip available for download at Wrox.com

1. Create a new project in Visual Studio 2010 by selecting File ➪ New Project from the menu. In the New Project dialog, select Windows Forms Application from the right pane (refer to Figure 3-1), enter the project name as **Integer Math**, and click OK.

2. Using the Toolbox, add a new Button control to Form1 as before. Set its Name property to btnIntMath and its Text property to Math Test. Double-click it and add the following bolded code to the new Click event handler that will be created:

```
Private Sub btnIntMath_Click(ByVal sender As System.Object, _
    ByVal e As System.EventArgs) Handles btnIntMath.Click
    'Declare variable
    Dim intNumber As Integer

    'Set number, add numbers, and display results
    intNumber = 16
    intNumber = intNumber + 8
    MessageBox.Show("Addition test. " & intNumber.ToString, _
        "Integer Math")

    'Set number, subtract numbers, and display results
    intNumber = 24
    intNumber = intNumber - 2
    MessageBox.Show("Subtraction test. " & intNumber.ToString, _
        "Integer Math")

    'Set number, multiply numbers, and display results
    intNumber = 6
    intNumber = intNumber * 10
    MessageBox.Show("Multiplication test. " & intNumber.ToString, _
        "Integer Math")

    'Set number, divide numbers, and display results
    intNumber = 12
    intNumber = CType(intNumber / 6, Integer)
    MessageBox.Show("Division test. " & intNumber.ToString, _
        "Integer Math")
End Sub
```

3. Save your project by clicking the Save All button on the toolbar.

4. Run the project and click the Math Test button. You'll be able to click through four message box dialogs, as shown in Figure 3-4.

How It Works

None of the code should be too baffling. You've already seen the addition operator. Here it is again:

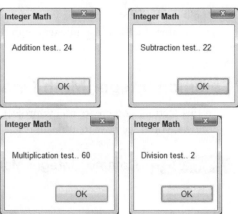

FIGURE 3-4

```
'Set number, add numbers, and display
results
intNumber = 16
intNumber = intNumber + 8
MessageBox.Show("Addition test. " & intNumber.ToString, _
    "Integer Math")
```

Let intNumber be equal to the value of 16.

Then, let intNumber be equal to the current value of intNumber (which is 16) plus 8.

As shown in the first message dialog in Figure 3-4, you get a result of 24, which is correct.

The subtraction operator is a minus (-) sign. Here it is in action:

```
'Set number, subtract numbers, and display results
intNumber = 24
intNumber = intNumber-2
MessageBox.Show("Subtraction test. " & intNumber.ToString, _
    "Integer Math")
```

Again, the same deal as before:

Let intNumber be equal to the value 24.

Let intNumber be equal to the current value of intNumber (which is 24) minus 2.

The multiplication operator is an asterisk (*). Here it is in action:

```
'Set number, multiply numbers, and display results
intNumber = 6
intNumber = intNumber * 10
MessageBox.Show("Multiplication test. " & intNumber.ToString, _
    "Integer Math")
```

Here your algorithm states the following:

Let intNumber be equal to the value 6.

Let intNumber be equal to the current value of intNumber (which is 6) times 10.

Finally, the division operator is a forward slash (/). Here it is in action:

```
'Set number, divide numbers, and display results
intNumber = 12
intNumber = CType(intNumber / 6, Integer)
```

```
MessageBox.Show("Division test. " & intNumber.ToString, _
    "Integer Math")
```

Again, all you're saying is this:

Let `intNumber` be equal to the value of `12`.

Let `intNumber` be equal to the current value of `intNumber` (which is `12`) divided by `6`.

The division of `intNumber` by the value of `6` has been enclosed in the `CType` function. The `CType` function returns the result of explicitly converting an expression to a specified data type, which in this case is an integer number as indicated by the `Integer` type name. Because the division of two numbers can result in a floating-point number, you should use the `CType` function to force the results to an integer number.

This explicit conversion is not necessary when the Option Strict setting is set to Off but is required when this setting is set to On. The Option Strict setting ensures compile-time notification of narrowing conversion of numeric operations so they can be avoided and prevent run-time errors.

To access the settings for Option Strict, click the Tools ⇨ Options menu item in Visual Studio 2010. In the Options dialog, expand the Projects and Solutions node and then click VB Defaults. From here you can turn the Option Strict setting on and off.

Integer Math Shorthand

In the next Try It Out, you'll see how you can perform the same operations without having to write as much code by using *shorthand operators* (assignment operators). Although they look a little less logical than their more verbose counterparts, you'll soon learn to love them.

TRY IT OUT   **Using Shorthand Operators**

In this Try It Out exercise, you'll modify the code from the last Try It Out exercise and use Integer shorthand operators to add, subtract, and multiply Integer numbers.

1. Go back to Visual Studio 2010 and open the code for `Form1.vb` again. Change the following bolded lines:

```
Private Sub btnIntMath_Click(ByVal sender As System.Object, _
    ByVal e As System.EventArgs) Handles btnIntMath.Click
    'Declare variable
    Dim intNumber As Integer
    'Set number, add numbers, and display results
    intNumber = 16
    intNumber += 8
    MessageBox.Show("Addition test. " & intNumber.ToString, _
        "Integer Math")
    'Set number, subtract numbers, and display results
    intNumber = 24
    intNumber -= 2
    MessageBox.Show("Subtraction test. " & intNumber.ToString, _
        "Integer Math")
    'Set number, multiply numbers, and display results
    intNumber = 6
```

```
intNumber *= 10
MessageBox.Show("Multiplication test. " & intNumber.ToString, _
    "Integer Math")
'Set number, divide numbers, and display results
intNumber = 12
intNumber = CType(intNumber / 6, Integer)
MessageBox.Show("Division test. " & intNumber.ToString, _
    "Integer Math")
```
```
End Sub
```

2. Run the project and click the Math Test button. You'll get the same results as in the previous Try It Out exercise.

How It Works

To use the shorthand version, you just drop the last intNumber variable and move the operator to the left of the equals sign. Here is the old version:

```
intNumber = intNumber + 8
```

Here's the new version:

```
intNumber += 8
```

Integer shorthand math works well for adding, subtracting, and multiplying Integer numbers. However, it cannot be used when dividing numbers, as the results could return a number that contains a remainder.

The Problem with Integer Math

The main problem with integer math is that you can't do anything that involves a number with a fractional part. For example, you can't do this:

```
'Try multiplying numbers.
intNumber = 6
intNumber = intNumber * 10.23
```

Or, rather, you can actually run that code, but you won't get the result you were expecting. Because intNumber has been defined as a variable designed to accept an integer only, the result is rounded up or down to the nearest integer. In this case, although the actual answer is 61.38, intNumber will be set to the value 61. If the answer were 61.73, intNumber would be set to 62.

> **NOTE** With the Option Strict setting set to On, the preceding code would produce an error in the IDE and the program would not compile. With the Option Strict setting set to Off, this code is allowed.

A similar problem occurs with division. Here's another piece of code:

```
'Try dividing numbers.
intNumber = 12
intNumber = intNumber / 7
```

This time the answer is 1.71. However, because the result has to be rounded up in order for it to be stored in intNumber, you end up with intNumber being set equal to 2. As you can imagine, if you were trying to write programs that actually calculated some form of value, you'd be in big trouble, as every step in the calculation would be subject to rounding errors.

In the next section, you'll look at how you can do these kinds of operations with floating-point numbers.

Floating-Point Math

You know that integers are not good for most mathematical calculations because most calculations of these types involve a fractional component of some quantity. Later in this chapter, you'll see how to use floating-point numbers to calculate the area of a circle. The following Try It Out introduces the concepts.

TRY IT OUT Floating-Point Math

Code file Chapter 3\Floating Point Math.zip available for download at Wrox.com

In this Try it Out exercise, you will create a project that multiplies and divides floating point numbers.

1. Create a new Windows Forms Application project in Visual Studio 2010 called Floating Point Math. As before, place a button on the form, setting its **Name** property to **btnFloatMath** and its **Text** property to **Double Test**.

2. Double-click btnFloatMath and add the following bolded code:

```
Private Sub btnFloatMath_Click(ByVal sender As System.Object, _
    ByVal e As System.EventArgs) Handles btnFloatMath.Click

    'Declare variable
    Dim dblNumber As Double

    'Set number, multiply numbers, and display results
    dblNumber = 45.34
    dblNumber *= 4.333
    MessageBox.Show("Multiplication test. " & dblNumber.ToString, _
        "Floating Points")

    'Set number, divide numbers, and display results
    dblNumber = 12
    dblNumber /= 7
    MessageBox.Show("Division test. " & dblNumber.ToString, _
        "Floating Points")
End Sub
```

3. Save your project by clicking the Save All button on the toolbar.

4. Run the project. You should see the results shown in Figure 3-5.

How It Works

Perhaps the most important change in this code is the way you're defining your variable:

```
'Declare variable
Dim dblNumber As Double
```

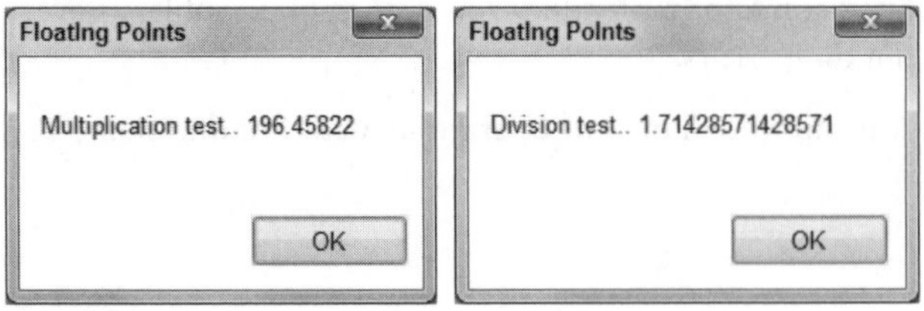

FIGURE 3-5

Rather than saying "As Integer" at the end, you're saying "As Double." This tells Visual Basic 2010 that you want to create a variable that holds a double-precision floating-point number, rather than an integer number. This means that any operation performed on dblNumber will be a floating-point operation, rather than an integer operation. Also note that you have used a different Modified Hungarian Notation prefix to signify that this variable contains a number that is of the Double data type.

However, there's no difference in the way either of these operations is performed. Here, you set dblNumber to be a decimal number and then multiply it by another decimal number:

```
'Set number, multiply numbers, and display results
dblNumber = 45.34
dblNumber *= 4.333
MessageBox.Show("Multiplication test. " & dblNumber.ToString, _
    "Floating Points")
```

When you run this, you get a result of 196.45822, which, as you can see, has a decimal component, and therefore you can use this in calculations.

Of course, floating-point numbers don't have to have an explicit decimal component:

```
'Set number, divide numbers, and display results
dblNumber = 12
dblNumber /= 7
MessageBox.Show("Division test. " & dblNumber.ToString, _
    "Floating Points")
```

This result still yields a floating-point result because dblNumber has been set up to hold such a result. You can see this by your result of 1.71428571428571, which is the same result you were looking for when you were examining integer math.

This time, the code allows you to use the math shorthand to divide two numbers, as the variable that holds the results will accept a floating-point number. Thus, you do not have to use the CType function to convert the results to an integer value.

A floating-point number gets its name because it is stored like a number written in scientific notation on paper. In scientific notation, the number is given as a power of 10 and a number between 1 and 10 that is multiplied by that power of 10 to get the original number. For example, 10,001 is written 1.0001×10^4, and 0.0010001 is written 1.0001×10^{-3}. The decimal point *floats* to the position after the first digit in both cases. The advantage is that large numbers and small numbers are represented with the same degree of precision (in this example, one part in 10,000). A floating-point variable is stored in the same way inside the computer, but in base-2 instead of base-10 (see the section "Storing Variables," later in this section).

Other States

Floating-point variables can hold a few other values besides decimal numbers. Specifically, these are:

➤ NaN, which means *not a number*

➤ Positive infinity, positive numbers without end

➤ Negative infinity, negative numbers without end

We won't show how to get all of the results here, but the mathematicians among you will recognize that .NET caters to your advanced math needs.

Single-Precision Floating-Point Numbers

We've been saying *double-precision floating-point*. In .NET, there are two main ways to represent floating-point numbers, depending on your needs. In certain cases the decimal fractional component of numbers can zoom off to infinity (pi being a particularly obvious example), but the computer does not have an infinite amount of space to hold digits, so there has to be some limit at which the computer stops keeping track of the digits to the right of the decimal point. This limit is related to the size of the variable, which is a subject discussed in much more detail toward the end of this chapter. There are also limits on how large the component to the left of the decimal point can be.

A double-precision floating-point number can hold any value between -1.7×10^{308} and $+1.7 \times 10^{308}$ to a great level of accuracy (one penny in 45 trillion dollars). A single-precision floating-point number can only hold between -3.4×10^{38} and $+3.4 \times 10^{38}$. Again, this is still a pretty huge number, but it holds decimal components to a lesser degree of accuracy (one penny in only $330,000) — the benefits being that single-precision floating-point numbers require less memory, and calculations involving them are faster on some computers.

You should avoid using double-precision numbers unless you actually require more accuracy than the single-precision type allows. This is especially important in very large applications, where using double-precision numbers for variables that only require single-precision numbers could slow your program significantly.

The calculations you're trying to perform will dictate which type of floating-point number you should use. If you want to use a single-precision number, use As Single, rather than As Double, like this:

```
Dim sngNumber As Single
```

Working with Strings

A *string* is a sequence of characters, and you use double quotes to mark its beginning and end. You've seen how to use strings to display the results of simple programs on the screen. Strings are commonly used for exactly this function — telling the user what happened and what needs to happen next. Another common use is storing a piece of text for later use in an algorithm. You'll see a lot of strings throughout the rest of the book. So far, you've used strings like this:

```
MessageBox.Show("Multiplication test. " & dblNumber.ToString, _
    "Floating Points")
```

"Multiplication test." and "Floating Points" are strings; you can tell because of the double quotes
("). However, what about dblNumber? The value contained within dblNumber is being converted to a
string value that can be displayed on the screen by use of the ToString method of the Double structure,
which defines the variable type. For example, if dblNumber represents the value 27, to display it on the
screen it has to be converted into a quoted string two characters in length, and this is what the ToString
method does.

TRY IT OUT   **Using Strings**

Code file Chapter 3\Strings.zip available for download at Wrox.com

This Try It Out demonstrates some of the things you can do with strings.

1. Create a new Windows Forms Application using the File ➪ New Project menu option. Call it
Strings.

2. Using the Toolbox, draw a button with the Name property **btnStrings** on the form and set its Text
property to **Using Strings.** Double-click it and then add the following bolded code:

```
Private Sub btnStrings_Click(ByVal sender As System.Object, _
    ByVal e As System.EventArgs) Handles btnStrings.Click
    'Declare variable
    Dim strResults As String

    'Set the string value
    strResults = "Hello World!"

    'Display the results
    MessageBox.Show(strResults, "Strings")
End Sub
```

3. Save your project by clicking the Save All button on the toolbar.

4. Run the project and click the Using Strings button. You'll see a message like the
one shown in Figure 3-6.

How It Works

You can define a variable that holds a string using a notation similar to that used with
the number variables, but this time using As String:

FIGURE 3-6

```
'Declare variable
Dim strResults As String
```

You can also set that string to have a value, again as before:

```
'Set the string value
strResults = "Hello World!"
```

You need to use double quotes around the string value to *delimit* the string, which means marking where
the string begins and ends. This is an important point, because these double quotes tell the Visual Basic
2010 compiler not to try to compile the text contained within the string. If you don't include the quotes,

Visual Basic 2010 treats the value stored in the variable as part of the program's code, tries to compile it and can't, causing the whole program to fail to compile.

With the value `Hello World!` stored in a string variable called `strResults`, you can pass that variable to the message box whose job it is to extract the value from the variable and display it. Therefore, you can see that strings can be defined and used in the same way as the numeric values shown earlier. The next section looks at how to perform operations on strings.

Concatenation

> *Concatenation* means linking things together in a chain or series, to join them. If you have two strings that you join together, one after the other, you say they are concatenated.

TRY IT OUT   Concatenation

You can think of concatenation as addition for strings. In the next Try It Out, you work with concatenation.

1. Using the same Strings project, view the Designer for Form1 and add a new button. Set its `Name` property to **btnConcatenation** and its `Text` property to **Concatenation**. Double-click the button and add the following bolded code:

```
Private Sub btnConcatenation_Click(ByVal sender As System.Object, _
    ByVal e As System.EventArgs) Handles btnConcatenation.Click
        'Declare variables
        Dim strResults As String
        Dim strOne As String
        Dim strTwo As String

        'Set the string values
        strOne = "Hello"
        strTwo = " World!"

        'Concatenate the strings
        strResults = strOne & strTwo

        'Display the results
        MessageBox.Show(strResults, "Strings")
End Sub
```

2. Run the project and click the Concatenation button. You'll see the same results that were shown in Figure 3-6.

How It Works

In this Try It Out, you started by declaring three variables that are `String` data types:

```
'Declare variables
Dim strOne As String
Dim strTwo As String
Dim strResults As String
```

Then you set the values of the first two strings:

```
'Set the string values
strOne = "Hello"
strTwo = " World!"
```

After you set the values of the first two strings, you use the & operator to concatenate the two previous strings, setting the results of the concatenation in a new string variable called strResults:

```
'Concatenate the strings
strResults = strOne & strTwo
```

Using the Concatenation Operator Inline

You don't have to define variables to use the concatenation operator. You can use it on the fly, as shown in the Floating-Point Math, Integer Math, and Variables projects. You've already seen the concatenation operator being used like this in previous examples. What this is actually doing is converting the value stored in dblNumber to a string so that it can be displayed on the screen. Consider the following code:

```
MessageBox.Show("Division test. " & dblNumber.ToString, _
    "Floating Points")
```

The portion that reads, "Division test." is actually a string, but you don't have to define it as a string variable. In Visual Basic 2010 parlance, this is called a *string literal*, meaning that it's exactly as shown in the code and doesn't change. When you use the concatenation operator on this string together with dblNumber.ToString, the value contained in the dblNumber variable is converted into a string and tacked onto the end of "Division test.". Remember that the ToString method converts the value contained in a variable to a string value. The result is one string that is passed to MessageBox.Show and that contains both the base text and the current value of dblNumber.

More String Operations

You can do plenty more with strings! Take a look at some examples in the next Try It Out.

TRY IT OUT Returning the Length of a String

1. The first thing you'll do is look at a property of the string that can be used to return its length.

2. Using the Strings project, return to the designer for Form1. Add a TextBox control to the form and set its Name property to **txtString**. Add another Button control and set its Name property to **btnLength** and its Text property to **Length**. Rearrange the controls so that they look like Figure 3-7.

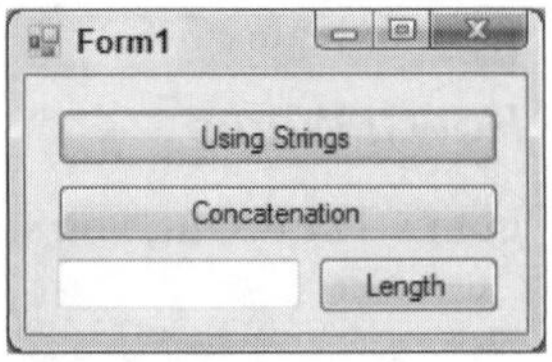

3. Double-click the Length button to open its Click event handler. Add the following bolded code:

```
Private Sub btnLength_Click(ByVal sender As System.Object, _
    ByVal e As System.EventArgs) Handles btnLength.Click
    'Declare variable
    Dim strResults As String
```

FIGURE 3-7

```
'Get the text from the TextBox
strResults = txtString.Text

'Display the length of the string
MessageBox.Show(strResults.Length.ToString & " characters(s)", _
    "Strings")
End Sub
```

4.   Run the project and enter some text into the text box.

5.   Click the Length button. You'll see results similar to those shown in Figure 3-8.

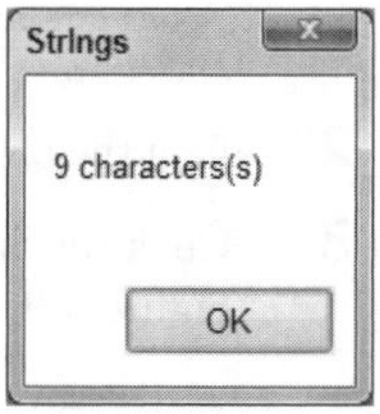

How It Works

The first thing you do is declare a variable to contain string data. Then you extract the text from the text box and store it in your string variable called strResults:

FIGURE 3-8

```
'Declare variable
Dim strResults As String

'Get the text from the TextBox
strResults = txtString.Text
```

When you have the string, you can use the Length property to get an integer value that represents the number of characters in it. Remember that as far as a computer is concerned, characters include things like spaces and other punctuation marks. Since the Length property returns the number of characters as an Integer data type, you want to convert that number to a string using the ToString method:

```
'Display the length of the string
MessageBox.Show(strResults.Length.ToString & " characters(s)", _
    "Strings")
```

Substrings

Common ways to manipulate strings in a program include using a set of characters that appears at the start, a set that appears at the end, or a set that appears somewhere in between. These are known as *substrings*.

TRY IT OUT   **Working with Substrings**

In the following Try It Out, you build on your previous application in order to have it display the first three, middle three, and last three characters.

1.   Using the Strings project, return to the designer for Form1. Add another Button control to Form1 and set its Name property to **btnSubStrings** and its Text property to **SubStrings**. Double-click the button and add the bolded code that follows:

```
Private Sub btnSubStrings_Click(ByVal sender As System.Object, _
    ByVal e As System.EventArgs) Handles btnSubStrings.Click
  'Declare variable
  Dim strResults As String

  'Get the text from the TextBox
  strResults = txtString.Text
```

```
        'Display the first three characters
        MessageBox.Show(strResults.Substring(0, 3), "Strings")

        'Display the middle three characters
        MessageBox.Show(strResults.Substring(3, 3), "Strings")

        'Display the last three characters
        MessageBox.Show(strResults.Substring(strResults.Length–3), "Strings")
    End Sub
```

2. Run the project. Enter the word **Cranberry** in the text box.

3. Click the SubStrings button and you'll see three message boxes, one after another, as shown in Figure 3-9.

FIGURE 3-9

How It Works

The Substring method lets you grab a set of characters from any position in the string. The method can be used in one of two ways. The first way is to give it a starting point and a number of characters to grab. In the first instance, you're telling it to start at character position 0 — the beginning of the string — and grab three characters:

```
        'Display the first three characters
        MessageBox.Show(strResults.Substring(0, 3), "Strings")
```

In the next instance, you start three characters in from the start and grab three characters:

```
        'Display the middle three characters
        MessageBox.Show(strResults.Substring(3, 3), "Strings")
```

In the final instance, you're providing only one parameter. This tells the Substring method to start at the given position and grab everything right up to the end. In this case, you're using the Substring method in combination with the Length method, so you're saying, "Grab everything from three characters in from the right of the string to the end":

```
        'Display the last three characters
        MessageBox.Show(strResults.Substring(strResults.Length – 3), "Strings")
```

Formatting Strings

Often when working with numbers, you'll need to alter the way they are displayed as a string. Figure 3-5 shows how a division operator works. In this case, you don't really need to see 14 decimal places — two or three would be fine! What you need is to format the string so that you see everything to the left of the decimal point, but only three digits to the right, which is what you do in the next Try It Out.

TRY IT OUT Formatting Strings

In this Try It Out exercise, you'll modify the Floating Point Math project you created earlier to display numbers in various string formats.

1. Open the Floating Point Math project that you created earlier in this chapter.

2. Open the Code Editor for Form1 and make the following bolded changes to the **btnFloatMath _Click** procedure:

```
'Set number, divide numbers, and display results
dblNumber = 12
dblNumber /= 7

'Display the results without formatting
MessageBox.Show("Division test without formatting. " & _
    dblNumber.ToString, "Floating Points")

'Display the results with formatting
MessageBox.Show("Division test with formatting. " & _
    String.Format("{0:n3}", dblNumber), "Floating Points")
End Sub
```

3. Run the project. After the message box dialog for the multiplication test is displayed, you'll see two more message boxes, as shown in Figure 3-10.

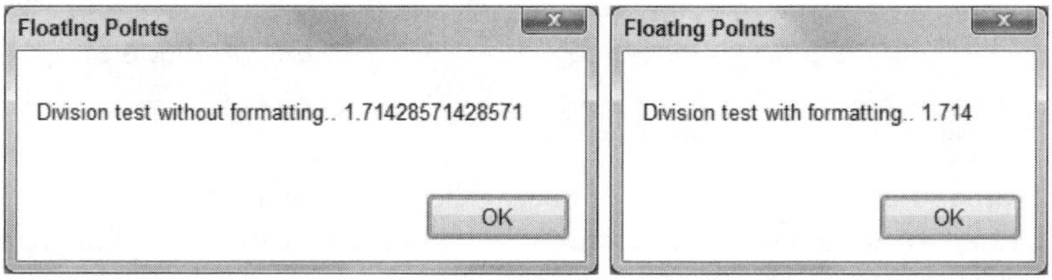

FIGURE 3-10

How It Works

The magic here is in the call to `String.Format`. This powerful method allows the formatting of numbers. The key is all in the first parameter, as this defines the format the final string will take:

```
MessageBox.Show("Division test with formatting. " & _
    String.Format("{0:n3}", dblNumber), "Floating Points")
```

You passed `String.Format` two parameters. The first parameter, `"{0:n3}"`, is the format that you want. The second parameter, `dblNumber`, is the value that you want to format. Note that because you are formatting a number to a string representation, you do not need to provide the `ToString` method after `dblNumber` as in the previous call to the `Show` method of the `MessageBox` class. This is because the `String.Format` method is looking for a number, not a string.

The `0` in the format tells `String.Format` to work with the zero[th] data parameter, which is just a cute way of saying "the second parameter," or `dblNumber`. What follows the colon is how you want `dblNumber` to be formatted. In this case it is n3, which means "floating-point number, three decimal places." You could have said n2 for "floating-point number, two decimal places."

Localized Formatting

When building .NET applications, it's important to realize that the user may be familiar with cultural conventions that are uncommon to you. For example, if you live in the United States, you're used to seeing the decimal separator as a period (.). However, if you live in France, the decimal separator is actually a comma (,).

Windows can deal with such problems for you based on the locale settings of the computer. If you use the .NET Framework in the correct way, by and large you'll never need to worry about this problem.

Here's an example: If you use a formatting string of n3 again, you are telling .NET that you want to format the number with thousands separators and that you want the number displayed to three decimal places (1,714.286).

> **NOTE** *The equation changed from 12 / 7 to 12000 / 7 to allow the display of the thousands separator (,).*

Now, if you tell your computer that you want to use the French locale settings, and you run the *same code* (making no changes whatsoever to the application itself), you'll see 1 714,286.

> **NOTE** *You can change your language options by going to the Control Panel and clicking the Regional and Language Options icon and changing the language to French.*

In France, the thousands separator is a space, not a comma, while the decimal separator is a comma, not a period. By using String.Format appropriately, you can write one application that works properly regardless of how the user has configured the locale settings on the computer.

Replacing Substrings

Another common string manipulation replaces occurrences of one string with another.

TRY IT OUT   Replacing Substrings

To demonstrate replacing a substring, in this Try It Out you'll modify your Strings application to replace the string "Hello" with the string "Goodbye".

1.   Open the Strings project that you were working with earlier.

2.   Return to the Forms Designer for Form1, add another Button control and set its Name property to **btnReplace** and set its Text property to **Replace**. Double-click the button and add the following bolded code to its Click event handler:

```
Private Sub btnReplace_Click(ByVal sender As System.Object, _
    ByVal e As System.EventArgs) Handles btnReplace.Click
    'Declare variables
    Dim strData As String
    Dim strResults As String
```

```
'Get the text from the TextBox
strData = txtString.Text

'Replace the string occurence
strResults = strData.Replace("Hello", "Goodbye")

'Display the new string
MessageBox.Show(strResults, "Strings")
End Sub
```

3.   Run the project and enter **Hello World!** into the text box (using this exact capitalization).

4.   Click the Replace button. You should see a message box that says Goodbye World!

How It Works

The Replace method works by taking the substring to look for as the first parameter and the new substring to replace it with as the second parameter. After the replacement is made, a new string is returned that you can display in the usual way:

```
'Replace the string occurence
strResults = strData.Replace("Hello", "Goodbye")
```

You're not limited to a single search and replace within this code. If you enter **Hello** twice into the text box and click the button, you'll notice two Goodbye returns. However, case is important — if you enter **hello**, it will not be replaced. You'll take a look at case-insensitive string comparisons in the next chapter.

Using Dates

Another data type that you'll often use is Date. This data type holds, not surprisingly, a date value.

TRY IT OUT   **Displaying the Current Date**

Code file Chapter 3\Date Demo.zip available for download at Wrox.com

You learn to display the current date in the next Try It Out.

1.   Create a new Windows Forms Application project called Date Demo.

2.   In the usual way, use the Toolbox to draw a new Button control on the form. Call it **btnShowDate** and set its Text property to **Show Date.**

3.   Double-click the button to bring up its Click event handler and add the following bolded code:

```
Private Sub btnShowDate_Click(ByVal sender As System.Object, _
    ByVal e As System.EventArgs) Handles btnShowDate.Click

    'Declare variable
    Dim dteResults As Date

    'Get the current date and time
    dteResults = Now

    'Display the results
    MessageBox.Show(dteResults.ToString, "Date Demo")
End Sub
```

4. Save your project by clicking the Save All button on the toolbar.

5. Run the project and click the button. You should see something like what is shown in Figure 3-11, depending on the locale settings on your machine.

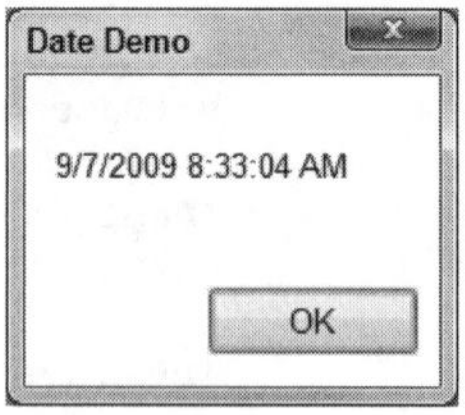

How It Works

The Date data type can be used to hold a value that represents any date and time. After creating the variable, you initialized it to the current date and time using the Now property. Then you display the date in a message box dialog. Note that because you want to display a Date data type as a string, you once again use the ToString method to convert the results to a string format:

```
'Declare variable
Dim dteResults As Date

'Get the current date and time
dteResults = Now

'Display the results
MessageBox.Show(dteResults.ToString, "Date Demo")
```

FIGURE 3-11

Date data types aren't any different from other data types, although you can do more with them. The next couple of sections demonstrate ways to manipulate dates and control how they are displayed on the screen.

Formatting Date Strings

You've already seen one way in which dates can be formatted. By default, if you pass a Date variable to MessageBox.Show, the date and time are displayed as shown in Figure 3-11.

Because this machine is in the United States, the date is shown in m/d/yyyy format and the time is shown using the 12-hour clock. This is another example of how the computer's locale setting affects the formatting of different data types. For example, if you set your computer to the United Kingdom locale, the date is in dd/mm/yyyy format and the time is displayed using the 24-hour clock — for example, 07/08/2004 07:02:47.

Although you can control the date format to the nth degree, it's best to rely on .NET to ascertain how the user wants strings to look and then automatically display them in their preferred format.

TRY IT OUT Formatting Dates

In this Try It Out, you'll look at four useful methods that enable you to format dates.

1. Return to the Code Editor for Form1, find the Click event handler for the button, and add the following bolded code:

```
'Display the results
MessageBox.Show(dteResults.ToString, "Date Demo")

'Display dates
MessageBox.Show(dteResults.ToLongDateString, "Date Demo")
MessageBox.Show(dteResults.ToShortDateString, "Date Demo")
```

```
'Display times
MessageBox.Show(dteResults.ToLongTimeString, "Date Demo")
MessageBox.Show(dteResults.ToShortTimeString, "Date Demo")
```

2. Run the project. You'll be able to click through five message boxes. You have already seen the first message box dialog; it displays the date and time according to your computer's locale settings. The next message box dialog displays the long date, and the next one displays the short date. The fourth message box displays the long time, and the last one displays the short time.

How It Works

This demonstrates the four basic ways that you can display dates and times in Windows applications — namely, long date, short date, long time, and short time. The names of the formats are self-explanatory:

```
'Display dates
MessageBox.Show(dteResults.ToLongDateString, "Date Demo")
MessageBox.Show(dteResults.ToShortDateString, "Date Demo")

'Display times
MessageBox.Show(dteResults.ToLongTimeString, "Date Demo")
MessageBox.Show(dteResults.ToShortTimeString, "Date Demo")
```

Extracting Date Properties

When you have a variable of type Date, there are several properties that you can call to learn more about the date; let's look at them.

TRY IT OUT   **Extracting Date Properties**

In this Try It Out exercise, you'll see how to extract portions of the date and portions of the time contained in a DateTime variable.

1. Return to the Forms Designer for the Date Demo project and add another Button control to Form1. Set its Name property to **btnDateProperties** and its Text property to **Date Properties**. Double-click the button and add the following bolded code to the Click event:

```
Private Sub btnDateProperties_Click(ByVal sender As System.Object, _
    ByVal e As System.EventArgs) Handles btnDateProperties.Click
    'Declare variable
    Dim dteResults As Date

    'Get the current date and time
    dteResults = Now

    'Display the various date properties
    MessageBox.Show("Month: " & dteResults.Month, "Date Demo")
    MessageBox.Show("Day: " & dteResults.Day, "Date Demo")
    MessageBox.Show("Year: " & dteResults.Year, "Date Demo")
    MessageBox.Show("Hour: " & dteResults.Hour, "Date Demo")
    MessageBox.Show("Minute: " & dteResults.Minute, "Date Demo")
    MessageBox.Show("Second: " & dteResults.Second, "Date Demo")
```

```
      MessageBox.Show("Day of week: " & dteResults.DayOfWeek, "Date Demo")
      MessageBox.Show("Day of year: " & dteResults.DayOfYear, "Date Demo")
   End Sub
```

2.   Run the project. If you click the button, you'll see a set of fairly self-explanatory message boxes.

How It Works

Again, there's nothing here that's rocket science. If you want to know the hour, use the `Hour` property. To get the year, use `Year`, and so on.

Date Constants

In the preceding Try It Out, when you called the `DayOfWeek` property, you were actually given an integer value, as shown in Figure 3-12.

The date that we're working with, September 7, 2009, is a Monday, and, although it may not be immediately obvious, Monday is represented as 1. Because the first day of the week is Sunday in the United States, you start counting from Sunday, with Sunday being 0. However, there is a possibility that you're working on a computer whose locale setting starts the calendar on a Monday, in which case `DayOfWeek` would return 0. Complicated? Perhaps, but just remember that you can't guarantee that what you think is `"Day 1"` is always going to be Monday. Likewise, what's Wednesday in English is Mittwoch in German.

FIGURE 3-12

TRY IT OUT   Getting the Names of the Weekday and the Month

If you need to know the name of the day or the month in your application, a better approach is to have .NET get the name for you, again from the particular locale settings of the computer, as demonstrated in the next Try It Out.

1.   Return to the Forms Designer in the Date Demo project and add a new Button control. Set its `Name` property to **btnDateNames** and its `Text` property to **Date Names**. Double-click the button and add the following bolded code to the `Click` event handler:

```
Private Sub btnDateNames_Click(ByVal sender As System.Object, _
    ByVal e As System.EventArgs) Handles btnDateNames.Click
    'Declare variable
    Dim dteResults As Date

    'Get the current date and time
    dteResults = Now

    MessageBox.Show("Weekday name: " & dteResults.ToString("dddd"), _
        "Date Demo")
    MessageBox.Show("Month name: " & dteResults.ToString("MMMM"), _
        "Date Demo")
End Sub
```

2.   Run the project and click the button. You will see a message box indicating the weekday name (e.g., Monday), and a second one indicating the month (e.g., September).

How It Works

When you used your `ToLongDateString` method and its siblings, you were basically allowing .NET to look in the locale settings for the computer for the date format the user preferred. In this example, you're using the `ToString` method but supplying your own format string:

```
MessageBox.Show("Weekday name: " & dteResults.ToString("dddd"), _
    "Date Demo")
MessageBox.Show("Month name: " & dteResults.ToString("MMMM"), _
    "Date Demo")
```

Usually, it's best practice not to use the `ToString` method to format dates to different string values, because you should rely on the built-in formats in .NET, but here you're using the `"dddd"` string to get the weekday name, and `"MMMM"` to get the month name. (Note that case is important here — `"mmmm"` won't work.)

To show how this works, if the computer is set to use Italian locale settings, you get one message box telling you the weekday name is `Lunedi` and another telling you the month name is `Settembre`.

Defining Date Literals

You know that if you want to use a string literal in your code, you can do this:

```
Dim strResults As String
strResults = "Woobie"
```

Date literals work in more or less the same way. However, you use the pound sign (#) to delimit the start and end of the date.

TRY IT OUT **Defining Date Literals**

You learn to define date literals in this Try It Out.

1. Return to the Forms Designer for the Date Demo project and add another Button control to the form. Set its `Name` property to **btnDateLiterals** and its `Text` property to **Date Literals**. Double-click the button and add the following bolded code to the `Click` event handler:

```
Private Sub btnDateLiterals_Click(ByVal sender As
  System.Object, _
    ByVal e As System.EventArgs) Handles btnDateLiterals.Click
    'Declare variable
    Dim dteResults As Date

    'Set a date and time
    dteResults = #1/1/2010 8:01:00 AM#

    'Display the date and time
    MessageBox.Show(dteResults.ToLongDateString
      & " " & _
        dteResults.ToLongTimeString, "Date Demo")
End Sub
```

2. Run the project and click the button. You should see the message box shown in Figure 3-13.

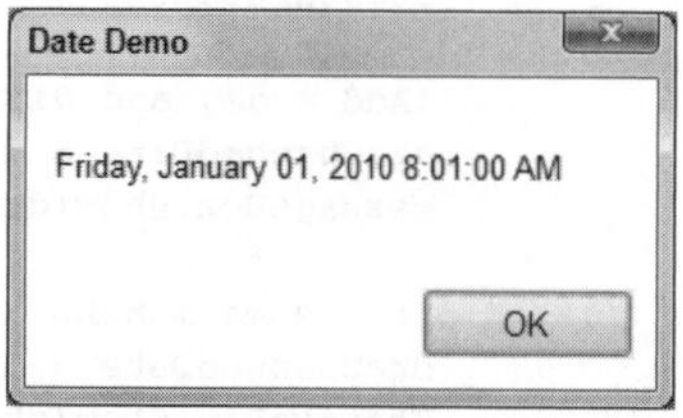

FIGURE 3-13

How It Works

When defining a date literal, it must be defined in the mm/dd/yyyy format, regardless of the actual locale settings of the computer. You may or may not see an error if you try to define the date in the format dd/mm/yyyy. This is because you could enter a date in the format dd/mm/yyyy (for example, 06/07/2010) that is also a valid date in the required mm/dd/yyyy format. This requirement reduces ambiguity: Does 6/7/2010 mean July 6 or June 7?

> **NOTE** *In fact, this is a general truth of programming as a whole: There are no such things as dialects when writing software. It's usually best to conform to North American standards. As you'll see throughout the rest of this book, this includes variables and method names — for example,* `GetColor` *rather than* `GetColour`.

It's also worth noting that you don't have to supply both a date and a time. You can supply one, the other, or both.

Manipulating Dates

One thing that's always been pretty tricky for programmers to do is manipulate dates. Most of you will remember New Year's Eve 1999, waiting to see whether computers could deal with tipping into a new century. Also, dealing with leap years has always been a bit of a problem.

The next turn of the century that also features a leap year will be 2399 to 2400. In the next Try It Out, you'll take a look at how you can use some of the methods available on the Date data type to adjust the date around that particular leap year.

TRY IT OUT   Manipulating Dates

1. Return to the Forms Designer for the Date Demo project and add another Button control to the form. Set its Name property to **btnDateManipulation** and its Text property to **Date Manipulation**. Double-click the button and add the following bolded code to the Click event handler:

```
Private Sub btnDateManipulation_Click(ByVal sender As System.Object, _
    ByVal e As System.EventArgs) Handles btnDateManipulation.Click
    'Declare variables
    Dim dteStartDate As Date
    Dim dteChangedDate As Date

    'Start in the year 2400
    dteStartDate = #2/28/2400#

    'Add a day and display the results
    dteChangedDate = dteStartDate.AddDays(1)
    MessageBox.Show(dteChangedDate.ToLongDateString, "Date Demo")

    'Add some months and display the results
    dteChangedDate = dteStartDate.AddMonths(6)
    MessageBox.Show(dteChangedDate.ToLongDateString, "Date Demo")
```

```
    'Subtract a year and display the results
    dteChangedDate = dteStartDate.AddYears(-1)
    MessageBox.Show(dteChangedDate.ToLongDateString, "Date Demo")
End Sub
```

2. Run the project and click the button. You'll see three message boxes, one after another. The first message box displays the long date for 2/29/2400, whereas the second message box displays the long date for 8/28/2400. The final message box displays the long date for 2/28/2399.

How it Works

The Date data type supports several methods for manipulating dates. Here are three of them:

```
'Add a day and display the results
dteChangedDate = dteStartDate.AddDays(1)
MessageBox.Show(dteChangedDate.ToLongDateString, "Date Demo")

'Add some months and display the results
dteChangedDate = dteStartDate.AddMonths(6)
MessageBox.Show(dteChangedDate.ToLongDateString, "Date Demo")

'Subtract a year and display the results
dteChangedDate = dteStartDate.AddYears(-1)
MessageBox.Show(dteChangedDate.ToLongDateString, "Date Demo")
```

It's worth noting that when you supply a negative number to any of the Add methods when working with Date variables, the effect is subtraction (demonstrated by going from 2400 back to 2399). The other important Add methods are AddHours, AddMinutes, AddSeconds, and AddMilliseconds.

Boolean

So far, you've seen the Integer, Double, Single, String, and Date data types. The other one you need to look at is Boolean. After you've done that, you've seen all of the simple data types that you're most likely to use in your programs.

A Boolean variable can be either True or False. It can never be anything else. Boolean values are extremely important when it's time for your programs to start making decisions, which is something you look at in more detail in Chapter 4.

STORING VARIABLES

The most limited resource on your computer is typically its memory. It is important that you try to get the most out of the available memory. Whenever you create a variable you are using a piece of memory, so you must strive to use as few variables as possible and use the variables that you do have in the most efficient manner.

Today, absolute optimization of variables is not something you need to go into a deep level of detail about, for two reasons. First, computers have far more memory these days, so the days when programmers tried to cram payroll systems into 32 KB of memory are long gone. Second, the compilers themselves have a great deal of intelligence built into them these days, to help generate the most optimized code possible.

Binary

Computers use binary to represent everything. That means that whatever you store in a computer must be expressed as a binary pattern of ones and zeros. Take a simple integer, 27. In binary code, this number is actually 11011, each digit referring to a power of two. The diagram in Figure 3-14 shows how you represent 27 in the more familiar base-10 format, and then in binary (base-2).

10^7	10^6	10^5	10^4	10^3	10^2	10^1	10^0
10,000,000	1,000,000	100,000	10,000	1,000	100	10	1
0	0	0	0	0	0	2	7

In base-10, each digit represents a power of ten. To find what number the "pattern of base-10 digits" represents, you multiply the relevant number by the power of ten that the digit represents and add the results.

$$2 \times 10 + 7 \times 1 = 27$$

2^7	2^6	2^5	2^4	2^3	2^2	2^1	2^0
128	64	32	16	8	4	2	1
0	0	0	1	1	0	1	1

In base-2, or binary, each digit represents a power of two. To find what number the "pattern of binary" represents, you multiply the relevant number by the power of two that the digit represents and add the results.

$$1 \times 16 + 1 \times 8 + 1 \times 2 + 1 \times 1 = 27$$

FIGURE 3-14

Although this may appear to be a bit obscure, note what is happening. In base-10, the decimal system that you're familiar with, each digit fits into a *slot*. This slot represents a power of 10 — the first representing 10 to the power zero, the second 10 to the power one, and so on. If you want to know what number the pattern represents, you take each slot in turn, multiply it by the value it represents, and add the results.

The same applies to binary — it's just that you're not familiar with dealing with base-2. To convert the number back to base-10, you take the digit in each slot in turn and multiply that power of *two* by the number that the slot represents (zero or one). Add all of the results together and you get the number.

Bits and Bytes

In computer terms, a binary slot is called a *bit*. It is the smallest possible unit of information, the answer to a single yes/no question, represented by a part of the computer's circuitry that either has electricity flowing in it or not. The reason why there are eight slots/bits on the diagram in Figure 3-14 is that there are eight bits in a *byte*. A byte is the unit of measurement that you use when talking about computer memory.

A *kilobyte,* or *KB,* is 1,024 bytes. You use 1,024 rather than 1,000 because 1,024 is the 10th power of 2, so as far as the computer is concerned it's a round number. Computers don't tend to think of things in terms of 10s like you do, so 1,024 is more natural to a computer than 1,000 is.

Likewise, a *megabyte* is 1,024 kilobytes, or 1,048,576 bytes. Again, that is another round number because this is the 20th power of 2. A *gigabyte* is 1,024 megabytes, or 1,073,741,824 bytes. (Again, think 2 to the power of 30 and you're on the right track.) Finally, a *terabyte* is 2 to the 40th power, and a *petabyte* is 2 to the 50th power.

So what's the point of all this? Well, having an understanding of how computers store variables helps you design your programs better. Suppose your computer has 256MB of memory. That's 262,144 KB or 268,435,456 bytes or (multiply by 8) 2,147,483,648 bits. As you write your software, you have to make the best possible use of this available memory.

Representing Values

Most desktop computers in use today are 32-bit, which means that they're optimized for dealing with integer values that are 32 bits in length. The number shown in the last example was an 8-bit number. With an 8-bit number, the largest value you can store is as follows:

```
1x128 + 1x64 + 1x32 + 1x16 + 1x8 + 1x4 + 1x2 + 1x1 = 255
```

A 32-bit number can represent any value between –2,147,483,648 and 2,147,483,647. Now, if you define a variable like

```
Dim intNumber As Integer
```

you want to store an integer. In response to this, .NET will allocate a 32-bit block of memory in which you can store any number between 0 and 2,147,483,647. Also, remember you have only a finite amount of memory; and on your 256MB computer, you can store only a maximum of 67,108,864 long numbers. It sounds like a lot, but remember that memory is for sharing. You shouldn't write software that deliberately tries to use as much memory as possible. Be frugal!

You also defined variables that were double-precision floating-point numbers, like this:

```
Dim dblNumber As Double
```

To represent a double-precision floating-point number, you need 64 bits of memory. That means you can store only a maximum of 33,554,432 double-precision floating-point numbers.

> **NOTE** Single-precision floating-point numbers take up 32 bits of memory — in other words, half as much as a double-precision number and the same as an integer value.

If you do define an integer, whether you store 1, 3, 249, or 2,147,483,647, you're always using exactly the same amount of memory, 32 bits. The size of the number has no bearing on the amount of memory required to store it. This might seem incredibly wasteful, but the computer relies on numbers of the same type taking the same amount of storage. Without this, it would be unable to work at a decent speed.

Now look at how you define a string:

```
Dim strResults As String
strResults = "Hello World!"
```

Unlike integers and doubles, strings do not have a fixed length. Each character in the string takes up two bytes, or 16 bits. Therefore, to represent this 12-character string, you need 24 bytes, or 192 bits. That means your computer is able to store only a little over two million strings of that length. Obviously, if the string is twice as long, you can hold half as many, and so on.

A common mistake that new programmers make is not taking into consideration what impact the data type has on storage. Suppose you have a variable that's supposed to hold a string, and you try to hold a numeric value in it, like this:

```
Dim strData As String
strData = "65536"
```

You're using 10 bytes (or 80 bits) to store it. That's less efficient than storing the value in an `Integer` data type. To store this numerical value in a string, each character in the string has to be converted into a numerical representation. This is done according to something called *Unicode*, which is a standard way of defining the way computers store characters. Each character has a unique number between 0 and 65,535, and it's this value that is stored in each byte allocated to the string.

Here are the Unicode codes for each character in the string:

➤ **6:** Unicode 54, binary 0000000000110110

➤ **5:** Unicode 53, binary 0000000000110101

➤ **5:** Unicode 53, binary 0000000000110101

➤ **3:** Unicode 51, binary 0000000000110011

➤ **6:** Unicode 54, binary 0000000000110110

Each character requires 16 bits, so storing a five-digit number in a string requires 80 bits — five 16-bit numbers. What you should do is this:

```
Dim intNumber As Integer
intNumber = 65536
```

This stores the value as a single number binary pattern. An `Integer` uses 32 bits, so the binary representation will be 00000000000000010000000000000000, far smaller than the space needed to store it as a string.

Converting Values

Although strings seem natural to us, they're unnatural to a computer. A computer wants to take two numbers and perform some simple mathematical operation on them. However, a computer can perform such a vast number of these simple operations each second that you, as a human, get the results you want.

Let's imagine that a computer wants to add 1 to the value 27. You already know that you can represent 27 in binary as 11011. Figure 3-15 shows what happens when you want to add 1 to the value 27.

As you can see, binary math is no different from decimal (base-10) math. If you try to add one to the first bit, it won't fit, so you revert it to zero and carry the one to the next bit. The same happens, and you carry the one to the third bit. At this point, you've finished, and if you add up the value you get 28, as intended.

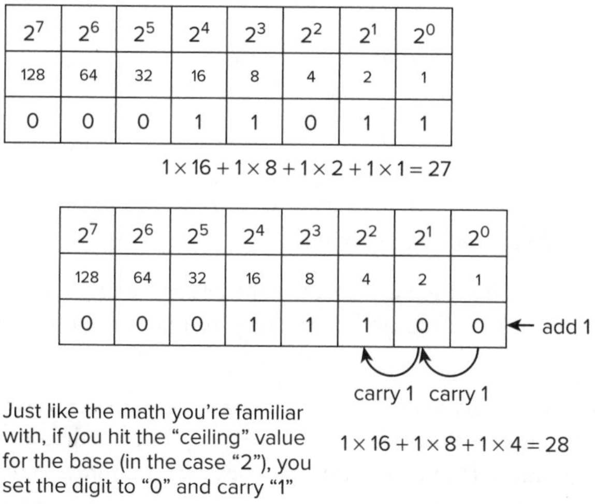

2^7	2^6	2^5	2^4	2^3	2^2	2^1	2^0
128	64	32	16	8	4	2	1
0	0	0	1	1	0	1	1

$$1 \times 16 + 1 \times 8 + 1 \times 2 + 1 \times 1 = 27$$

2^7	2^6	2^5	2^4	2^3	2^2	2^1	2^0
128	64	32	16	8	4	2	1
0	0	0	1	1	1	0	0

← add 1

carry 1   carry 1

Just like the math you're familiar with, if you hit the "ceiling" value for the base (in the case "2"), you set the digit to "0" and carry "1"

$$1 \times 16 + 1 \times 8 + 1 \times 4 = 28$$

FIGURE 3-15

Any value that you have in your program ultimately has to be converted to simple numbers in order for the computer to do anything with them. To make the program run more efficiently, you have to keep the number of conversions to a minimum. Here's an example:

```
Dim strResults As String
strResults = "27"
strResults = strResults + 1
MessageBox.Show(strResults)
```

Let's look at what's happening:

1. You create a string variable called `strResults`.

2. You assign the value 27 to that string. This uses 4 bytes of memory.

3. To add 1 to the value, the computer has to convert 27 to an internal, hidden `Integer` variable that contains the value 27. This uses an additional 4 bytes of memory, taking the total to 8. However, more important, this conversion takes time!

4. When the string is converted to an integer, 1 is added to it.

5. The new value then has to be converted into a string.

6. The string containing the new value is displayed on the screen.

To write an efficient program, you don't want to be constantly converting variables between different types. You want to perform the conversion only when it's absolutely necessary.

Here's some more code that has the same effect:

```
Dim intNumber As Integer
intNumber = 27
```

```
intNumber += 1
MessageBox.Show(intNumber.ToString)
```

1. You create an integer variable called `intNumber`.

2. You assign the value `27` to the variable.

3. You add `1` to the variable.

4. You convert the variable to a string and display it on the screen.

In this case, you have to do only one conversion, and it's a logical one; use the `ToString` method on the `Integer` data type. `MessageBox.Show` works in terms of strings and characters, so that's what it is most comfortable with.

What you have done is reduce the number of conversions from two (string to integer, integer to string) to one. This makes your program run more efficiently and use less memory. Again, it's a small improvement, but imagine this improvement occurring hundreds of thousands of times each minute — you'll get an improvement in the performance of the system as a whole.

> **NOTE** It is absolutely vital that you work with the correct data type for your needs. In simple applications like the ones you've created in this chapter, a performance penalty is not really noticeable. However, when you write more complex, sophisticated applications, you want to optimize your code by using the right data type.

METHODS

A *method* is a self-contained block of code that does something. Methods, also called *procedures,* are essential for two reasons. First, they break a program up and make it more understandable. Second, they promote code *reuse* — a topic you'll be spending most of your time on throughout the rest of this book.

As you know, when you write code you start with a high-level algorithm and keep refining the detail of that algorithm until you have the software code that expresses all of the algorithms up to and including the high-level one. A method describes a line in one of those algorithms — for example, "open a file," "display text on screen," "print a document," and so on.

Knowing how to break up a program into methods is something that comes with experience. To add to the frustration, it's far easier to understand why you need to use methods when you're working on far more complex programs than the ones you've seen so far. In the rest of this section, we'll endeavor to show you why and how you use methods.

Why Use Methods?

In day-to-day use, you need to pass information to a method for it to produce the expected results. This might be a single integer value, a set of string values, or a combination of both. These are known as *input values.* However, some methods don't take input values, so having input values is not a requirement of a method. The method uses these input values and a combination of environmental information (for instance, facts about the current state of the program that the method knows about) to do something useful.

When you give information to a method, you are said to *pass* it data. You can also refer to that data as *parameters*. Finally, when you want to use a method, you *call* it.

> **NOTE** To summarize, you call a method, passing data in through parameters.

The reason for using methods is to promote this idea of code reuse. The principle behind using a method makes sense if you consider the program from a fairly high level. If you have an understanding of all the algorithms involved in a program, you can find commonality. If you need to do the same thing more than once, you should wrap it up into a method that you can reuse.

Imagine you have a program that comprises many algorithms, and some of those algorithms call for the area of a circle to be calculated. Because *some* of those algorithms need to know how to calculate the area of a circle, it's a good candidate for a method. You write code that knows how to find the area of a circle given its radius, and *encapsulate* it (wrap it up) into a method, which you can reuse when you're coding the other algorithms. This means you don't have to keep writing code that does the same thing — you do it once and reuse it as often as needed.

It might be the case that one algorithm needs to work out the area of a circle with 100 for its radius, and another needs to work out one with a radius of 200. By building the method in such a way that it takes the radius as a parameter, you can use the method from wherever you want.

> **NOTE** With Visual Basic 2010, you can define a method using the `Sub` keyword or the `Function` keyword. `Sub`, short for subroutine, is used when the method doesn't return a value, as mentioned in Chapter 1. `Function` is used when the method returns a value.

Methods You've Already Seen

The good news is that you've been using methods already. Consider the following bolded code that you wrote at the beginning of this chapter:

```
Private Sub btnAdd_Click(ByVal sender As System.Object, _
    ByVal e As System.EventArgs) Handles btnAdd.Click
    'Define a variable for intNumber
    Dim intNumber As Integer

    'Set the initial value
    intNumber = 27

    'Add 1 to the value of intNumber
    intNumber = intNumber + 1
```

```
        'Display the new value of intNumber
        MessageBox.Show("Value of intNumber + 1 = " & intNumber.ToString, _
            "Variables")
    End Sub
```

That code is a method — it's a self-contained block of code that does something. In this case, it adds 1 to the value of intNumber and displays the result in a message box.

This method does not return a value (that is, it's a subroutine, so it starts with the Sub keyword and ends with the End Sub statement). Anything between these two statements is the code assigned to the method. Let's take a look at how the method is defined (this code was automatically created by Visual Basic 2010):

```
    Private Sub btnAdd_Click(ByVal sender As System.Object, _
        ByVal e As System.EventArgs) Handles btnAdd.Click
```

1. First, you have the word Private. The meaning of this keyword is discussed in later chapters. For now, think of it as ensuring that this method cannot be called by any code outside of this class.

2. Second, you have the keyword Sub to tell Visual Basic 2010 that you want to define a subroutine.

3. Third, you have btnAdd_Click. This is the name of the subroutine.

4. Fourth, you have ByVal sender As System.Object, ByVal e As System.EventArgs. This tells Visual Basic 2010 that the method takes two parameters: sender and e. We'll talk about this more later.

5. Finally, you have Handles btnAdd.Click. This tells Visual Basic 2010 that this method should be called whenever the Click event on the control btnAdd is fired.

TRY IT OUT **Using Methods**

Code file Chapter 3\Three Buttons.zip available for download at Wrox.com

This Try It Out takes a look at how you can build a method that displays a message box and calls the same method from three separate buttons.

1. Create a new Windows Forms Application project called Three Buttons.

2. Use the Toolbox to draw three buttons on the form.

3. Double-click the first button (Button1) to create a new Click event handler. Add the following bolded code:

```
    Private Sub Button1_Click(ByVal sender As System.Object, _
        ByVal e As System.EventArgs) Handles Button1.Click
        'Call your method
        SayHello()
    End Sub

    Private Sub SayHello()
        'Display a message box
        MessageBox.Show("Hello World!", "Three Buttons")
    End Sub
```

4. Save your project by clicking the Save All button on the toolbar.

5. Run the project. You'll see the form with three buttons appear. Click the topmost button to see "Hello World!" displayed in a message box.

How It Works

As you know now, when you double-click a Button control in the Designer, a new method is automatically created:

```
Private Sub Button1_Click(ByVal sender As System.Object, _
    ByVal e As System.EventArgs) Handles Button1.Click

End Sub
```

The `Handles Button1.Click` statement at the end tells Visual Basic 2010 that this method should automatically be called when the `Click` event on the button is fired. As part of this, Visual Basic 2010 provides two parameters, which you don't have to worry about for now. Outside of this method, you've defined a new method:

```
Private Sub SayHello()
    'Display a message box
    MessageBox.Show("Hello World!", "Three Buttons")
End Sub
```

The new method is called `SayHello`. Anything that appears between the `Sub` and `End Sub` keywords is part of the method and when that method is called, the code is executed. In this case, you've asked it to display a message box.

So you know that when the button is clicked, Visual Basic 2010 will call the `Button1_Click` method. You then call the `SayHello` method. The upshot of all this is that when the button is clicked, the message box is displayed:

```
Private Sub Button1_Click(ByVal sender As System.Object, _
    ByVal e As System.EventArgs) Handles Button1.Click

    'Call your method
    SayHello()
End Sub
```

That should make the general premise behind methods a little clearer, but why did you need to break the code into a separate method to display the message box? You learn more about that in the next Try It Out.

TRY IT OUT   Reusing the Method

In this exercise, you'll see how you can reuse a method by calling it from other areas of your code.

1. If your project is still running, stop it.

2. Return to the Forms Designer, double-click the second button, and add the following bold code to the new event handler:

```
Private Sub Button2_Click(ByVal sender As System.Object, _
    BCyVal e As System.EventArgs) Handles Button2.Click
```

```
          'Call your method
          SayHello()
     End Sub
```

3.   Switch back to the Forms Designer, double-click the third button, and add the bold code:

```
     Private Sub Button3_Click(ByVal sender As System.Object, _
          ByVal e As System.EventArgs) Handles Button3.Click
          'Call your method
          SayHello()
     End Sub
```

4.   Now run the project. You'll notice that when you click each of the buttons, they all bring up the same message box.

5.   Stop the project and find the SayHello method definition. Change the text to be displayed, like this:

```
     Private Sub SayHello()
          'Display a message box
          MessageBox.Show("I have changed!", "Three Buttons")
     End Sub
```

6.   Run the project again and click each of the three buttons. You'll notice that the text displayed on the message boxes has changed.

How It Works

Each of the event handlers calls the same SayHello() method:

```
     Private Sub Button1_Click(ByVal sender As System.Object, _
          ByVal e As System.EventArgs) Handles Button1.Click
          'Call your method
          SayHello()
     End Sub

     Private Sub Button2_Click(ByVal sender As System.Object, _
          ByVal e As System.EventArgs) Handles Button2.Click
          'Call your method
          SayHello()
     End Sub

     Private Sub Button3_Click(ByVal sender As System.Object, _
          ByVal e As System.EventArgs) Handles Button3.Click
          'Call your method
          SayHello()
     End Sub
```

You'll also notice that the Handles keyword on each of the methods ties the method to a different control — Button1, Button2, or Button3.

What's really important (and clever) here is that when you change the way that SayHello works, the effect you see on each button is the same. This is a really important programming concept. You can central-ize code in your application so that when you change it in once place, the effect is felt throughout the application, enabling you to avoid entering the same or very similar code repeatedly.

Building a Method

In the last Try It Out exercise, you built a method that simply displayed static text. Methods are most useful when they accept data and then actually do something useful with that data. Sometimes you'll want a method to return a value, as you'll see in the next Try It Out exercise.

TRY IT OUT **Building a Method**

In the next Try It Out, you'll build a method that's capable of returning a value. Specifically, you'll build a method that can return the area of a circle if its radius is provided. You can do this with the following algorithm:

➤   Square the radius.

➤   Multiply it by pi.

To try out this exercise, reuse the Three Buttons project and return to the Code Editor.

1.   Add the following code to define a new method (which will be a function, because it returns a value):

```
'CalculateAreaFromRadius-find the area of a circle
Private Function CalculateAreaFromRadius(ByVal radius As Double) As Double
    'Declare variables
    Dim dblRadiusSquared As Double
    Dim dblResult As Double

    'Square the radius
    dblRadiusSquared = radius * radius

    'Multiply it by pi
    dblResult = dblRadiusSquared * Math.PI

    'Return the result
    Return dblResult
End Function
```

2.   Now delete the existing code from the Button1_Click event handler, and add the following bolded code:

```
Private Sub Button1_Click(ByVal sender As System.Object, _
    ByVal e As System.EventArgs) Handles Button1.Click
    'Declare variable
    Dim dblArea As Double

    'Calculate the area of a circle with a radius of 100
    dblArea = CalculateAreaFromRadius(100)

    'Display the results
    MessageBox.Show(dblArea.ToString, "Area of 100")
End Sub
```

3.   Run the project and click Button1. You'll see results like the one shown in Figure 3-16.

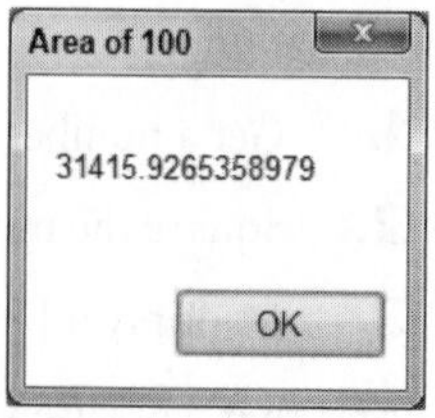

FIGURE 3-16

How It Works

In this exercise, you first build a separate method called `CalculateAreaFromRadius`. You do this by using the `Private Function . . . End Function` block:

```
Private Function CalculateAreaFromRadius(ByVal radius As Double) As Double
.
End Function
```

Anything between `Function` and `End Function` is the *body* of the method and will be executed only when the method is called.

The `ByVal radius As Double` portion defines a parameter for the method. When a parameter is passed by value, as indicated here by the keyword `ByVal`, .NET in effect creates a new variable and stores the passed parameter information in it. Even if the method is called with a variable given for the parameter, the contents of that original variable are not modified by the method. In this case, you're telling .NET that you want to pass a parameter into the method called `radius`. In effect, this statement creates a variable called `radius`, just as if you had done this:

```
Dim radius As Double
```

In fact, there's a little more. The variable is automatically set to the value passed through as a parameter, so if you pass 200 through as the value of the parameter, what you're effectively doing is this:

```
Dim radius As Double = 200
```

If you passed 999 as the value of the parameter, you'd have this:

```
Dim radius As Double = 999
```

> **NOTE** *Another way of passing a parameter is by reference, using the keyword* `ByRef` *instead of* `ByVal`. *When a parameter is passed by reference, the parameter name used within the method body effectively becomes another name for the variable specified when the method is called, so anything the method does that modifies the parameter value modifies the original variable value as well.*

The `As Double` sitting at the end of the method declaration tells Visual Basic 2010 that this method will return a double-precision floating-point number back to whomever called it:

```
Private Function CalculateAreaFromRadius(ByVal radius
As Double) As Double
```

Now you can look at the method properly. First, you know that to find the area of a circle you have this algorithm:

1. Get a number that represents the radius of a circle.

2. Square the number.

3. Multiply it by pi (p).

And that's precisely what you've done:

```
'Declare variables
Dim dblRadiusSquared As Double
```

```
Dim dblResult As Double

'Square the radius
dblRadiusSquared = radius * radius

'Multiply it by pi
dblResult = dblRadiusSquared * Math.PI
```

The `Math.PI` in the previous code is a constant defined in .NET that defines the value of pi (p) for us. After the last line, you need to return the result to whatever code called the method. That's done with the following statement:

```
'Return the result
Return dblResult
```

The code you added in `Button1_Click` calls the method and tells the user the results:

```
'Declare variable
Dim dblArea As Double

'Calculate the area of a circle with a radius of 100
dblArea = CalculateAreaFromRadius(100)

'Display the results
MessageBox.Show(dblArea.ToString, "Area of 100")
```

The first thing to do is define a variable called `dblArea` that will contain the area of the circle. You set this variable to whatever value `CalculateAreaFromRadius` returns. Using parentheses at the end of a method name is how you send the parameters. In this case, you're passing just one parameter, and you're passing the value 100.

After you call the method, you wait for the method to finish calculating the area. This area is returned from the method (the `Return` result line defined within `CalculateAreaFromRadius`) and stored in the variable `dblArea`. You can then display this on the screen in the usual way.

Choosing Method Names

The .NET Framework has a few standards for how things should be named. These conventions help developers move between languages — a topic discussed in Chapter 2. We recommend that whenever you create a method, you use *Pascal casing*. This is a practice in which the first letter in each word in the method is uppercase but nothing else is. This is merely a suggestion for best coding practices and is not a requirement of Visual Basic 2010. An example of this is as follows:

➤   `CalculateAreaFromRadius`

➤   `OpenXmlFile`

➤   `GetEnvironmentValue`

Note that even when an abbreviation is used (in this case, XML), it *isn't* written in uppercase. This alleviates confusion for developers, who may or may not know how something should be capitalized.

We recommend that you always write parameter names in *camel casing*. (If you've ever seen Java code, you'll be familiar with this.) To get camel casing, you do the same as Pascal casing, but you don't capitalize the very first letter:

➤ `myAccount`

➤ `customerDetails`

➤ `updatedDnsRecord`

Again, abbreviations (such as DNS) are not treated as a special case, so they appear as a mix of uppercase and lowercase letters, just like in Pascal casing.

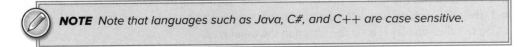

> **NOTE** *The name camel casing comes from the fact that the identifier has a hump in the middle — for example,* `camelCasing`*. Pascal casing is so called because the convention was invented for use with the programming language Pascal.*

In Chapter 2, you saw that .NET isn't tied to a particular language. Because some languages are *case sensitive* and others are not, it's important that you define standards to make life easier for programmers who may be coming from different programming language backgrounds.

The term *case sensitive* means that the positions of uppercase and lowercase letters are important. In a case-sensitive language, `MYACCOUNT` is not the same as `myAccount`. However, Visual Basic 2010 is *not* a case-sensitive language, meaning that for all intents and purposes you can do whatever you like with respect to capitalization; in other words, `MYACCOUNT` would be the same as `mYacCounT`.

> **NOTE** *Note that languages such as Java, C#, and C++ are case sensitive.*

Scope

When introducing the concept of methods, we described them as *self-contained*. This has an important effect on the way that variables are used and defined in methods. Imagine you have the following two methods, both of which define a variable called `strName`:

```
Private Sub DisplaySebastiansName()
    'Declare variable and set value
    Dim strName As String
    strName = "Sebastian Blackwood"

    'Display results
    MessageBox.Show(strName, "Scope Demo")
End Sub

Private Sub DisplayBalthazarsName()
    'Declare variable and set value
```

```
        Dim strName As String
        strName = "Balthazar Keech"

        'Display results
        MessageBox.Show(strName, "Scope Demo")
    End Sub
```

Even though both of these methods use a variable with the same name (strName), the self-contained feature of methods means that this is perfectly practicable and the variable names won't affect each other. Try it out next.

TRY IT OUT   Scope

Code file Chapter 3\Scope Demo.zip available for download at Wrox.com

In this exercise, you'll start exploring the scope of variables by using the same variable name in two different methods.

1. Create a new Windows Forms Application project called Scope Demo.

2. Add a Button control to the form, setting its Name property to **btnScope** and its Text property to **Scope**. Double-click the button and add the following bolded code to the Click event handler, and add the other two methods:

```
Private Sub btnScope_Click(ByVal sender As System.Object, _
    ByVal e As System.EventArgs) Handles btnScope.Click
    'Call a method
    DisplayBalthazarsName()
End Sub

Private Sub DisplaySebastiansName()
    'Declare variable and set value
    Dim strName As String
    strName = "Sebastian Blackwood"

    'Display results
    MessageBox.Show(strName, "Scope Demo")
End Sub

Private Sub DisplayBalthazarsName()
    'Declare variable and set value
    Dim strName As String
    strName = "Balthazar Keech"

    'Display results
    MessageBox.Show(strName, "Scope Demo")
End Sub
```

3. Save your project by clicking the Save All button on the toolbar.

4. Run the project. You'll see the message box displaying the name Balthazar Keech when you click the button.

How It Works

This exercise illustrates that even though you've used the same variable name in two separate places, the program still works as intended:

```
Private Sub DisplaySebastiansName()
    'Declare variable and set value
    Dim strName As String
    strName = "Sebastian Blackwood"

    'Display results
    MessageBox.Show(strName, "Scope Demo")
End Sub

Private Sub DisplayBalthazarsName()
    'Declare variable and set value
    Dim strName As String
    strName = "Balthazar Keech"

    'Display results
    MessageBox.Show(strName, "Scope Demo")
End Sub
```

When a method starts running, the variables defined within that method (in other words, between `Sub` and `End Sub`, or between `Function` and `End Function`) are given *local scope*. The *scope* defines which parts of the program can see the variable, and *local* specifically means *within the current method*.

The `strName` variable technically doesn't exist until the method starts running. At this point, .NET and Windows allocate memory to the variable so that it can be used in the code. First you set the value and then you display the message box. Therefore, in this case, as you're calling the method `DisplayBalthazarsName`, the variable is created the moment the method is called, you run the code in the method that alters the newly created version of `strName`, and when the method has finished, the variable is deleted.

> **NOTE** *You will see in Chapter 4 that scope can even be limited to loops within your subroutines and functions.*

SUMMARY

This chapter introduced the concept of writing software not just for Visual Basic 2010 but also for all programming languages. We started by introducing the concept of an algorithm — the underpinnings of all computer software. We then introduced the concept of variables, and looked closely at the most commonly used data types: `Integer`, `Double`, `String`, `Date`, and `Boolean`. You saw how you could use these data types to perform operations such as mathematical operations, concatenating strings, returning the length of a string, splitting text into substrings, retrieving the current date, and extracting date properties. You then looked at how variables are stored in the computer.

After this, you looked at methods — what they are, why you need them, how to create them, and how the variables you declare within your methods have local scope within that method and do not apply outside of it. We also described the difference between a function and a subroutine.

EXERCISES

1. Create a Windows application with two button controls. In the `Click` event for the first button, declare two `Integer` variables and set their values to any number that you like. Perform any math operation on these variables and display the results in a message box.

In the Click event for the second button, declare two String variables and set their values to anything that you like. Perform a string concatenation on these variables and display the results in a message box.

2. Create a Windows application with a text box and a button control. In the button's `Click` event, display three message boxes. The first message box should display the length of the string that was entered into the text box. The second message box should display the first half of the string, and the third message box should display the last half of the string.

▶ WHAT YOU LEARNED IN THIS CHAPTER

TOPIC	CONCEPTS
Algorithms	What an algorithm is and how it applies to software development.
Variables	How to declare and use the most common types of variables.
String functions	How to use the most common string functions when working with the `String` data type.
Date data type	How to use the `Date` data type and display dates and times so that they are automatically localized to the user's computer settings.
Methods	How to create and use simple methods that either accept parameters or not and either return a value or not.

4

Controlling the Flow

WHAT YOU WILL LEARN IN THIS CHAPTER:

➤ How to use the `If` statement

➤ How to use `Select Case`

➤ How to use `For` loops and `Do` loops

In Chapter 3, you learned about algorithms and their role in programming. In this chapter, you're going to look at how you can control the flow through your algorithms so that you can make decisions like "If X is the case, go and do A; otherwise do B." This ability to make decisions is known as *branching*. You'll also see how you can repeat a section of code (a process known as *looping*) a specified number of times, or while a certain condition applies.

MAKING DECISIONS

Algorithms often include decisions. It's this decision-making ability that makes computers do what they do so well. When you're writing code, you make two kinds of decisions. The first kind is used to find out what part of an algorithm you're currently working on or to cope with problems. For example, imagine you have a list of 10 people and need to write a piece of code to send an e-mail to each of them. To do this, after sending each e-mail, you ask, "Have I finished?" If so, you quit the algorithm; otherwise, you get the next person in the list. As another example, you might need to open a file, so you ask, "Does the file exist?" You have to deal with both possible answers to that question.

The second kind of decision is used to perform a different part of the algorithm depending on one or more facts. Imagine you're going through your list of 10 people so that you can send an e-mail to those who own a computer, but telephone those who don't. As you look at each person, you use the fact that the person does or doesn't own a computer to choose what you should do.

These decisions are all made in the same way, and it doesn't matter whether you have more of the first kind, more of the second kind, or whatever. Now, let's take a look at how to make a decision using the If statement.

THE IF STATEMENT

The simplest way to make a decision in a Visual Basic 2010 program is to use the If ... Then statement. You learn to use an If ... Then statement in the following Try It Out exercise.

TRY IT OUT   **A Simple If ... Then Statement**

Code file Simple If.zip available for download at Wrox.com

Let's look at the If ... Then statement.

1. Create a Windows Forms Application project called **Simple If**. Add a Button control, setting its Name property to **btnIf**, and its Text property to **If**. Double-click the button and add the following bolded code:

```
Private Sub btnIf_Click(ByVal sender As System.Object, _
    ByVal e As System.EventArgs) Handles btnIf.Click
    'Declare and set a variable
    Dim intNumber As Integer = 27

    'Here's where you make a decision,
    'and tell the user what happened
    If intNumber = 27 Then
        MessageBox.Show("'intNumber' is, indeed, 27!", "Simple If")
    End If
End Sub
```

2. Save your project and then run it. Click the If button and you'll see the message box shown in Figure 4-1.

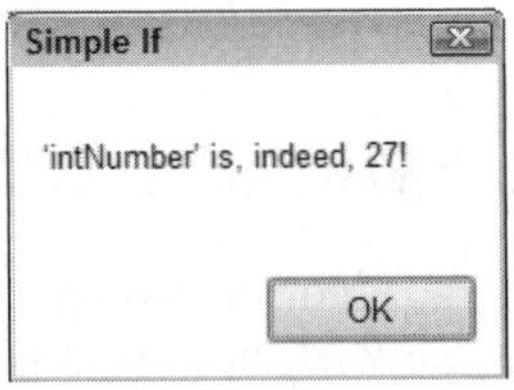

How It Works

In this example, first you declare an Integer variable called **intNumber** and set its value to **27**, all in the same line of code, as shown here:

```
'Declare and set a variable
Dim intNumber As Integer = 27
```

FIGURE 4-1

Then you use an If ... Then statement to determine what you should do next. In this case, you say, "If intNumber is equal to 27 ... ":

```
'Here's where you make a decision,
'and tell the user what happened
If intNumber = 27 Then
    MessageBox.Show("'intNumber' is, indeed, 27!", "Simple If")
End If
```

The code block that follows this will be executed only if intNumber equals 27. You end the code block with End If. Anything between If and End If is called only if the expression you're testing for is true.

So, as you walk through the code, you get to the `If` statement, and it's true. You drop into the code block that runs if the expression is true, and the text is displayed in a message box.

> **NOTE** Notice that the code within the `If ... End If` block is automatically indented for you. This is to increase readability so that you can tell what code will run in the event that the condition is true. It's also good to add some whitespace before the `If ... Then` statement and after the `End If` statement to enhance readability further.
>
> A simple `If` block like the previous one may also be written on one line, without an `End If` statement:
>
> ```
> If intNumber = 27 Then MessageBox.Show("'intNumber' is, indeed, 27!",
>     "Simple If")
> ```

This works equally well — although you are limited to only one line of code within the `If` statement. Now you know what happens if your condition is true; but what happens if you fail the test and the result is false? You find out in the next Try It Out.

TRY IT OUT Failing the Test

Code file Simple If.zip available for download at Wrox.com

In this example, you will see how to code for when the If statement is not true.

1. Return to the Forms Designer for the Simple If program. Add another Button control to the form and set its `Name` property to **btnAnotherIf** and its `Text` property to **Another If**. Double-click the button and add the following bolded code:

```
Private Sub btnAnotherIf_Click(ByVal sender As System.Object, _
    ByVal e As System.EventArgs) Handles btnAnotherIf.Click

        'Declare and set a variable
        Dim intNumber As Integer = 27

        'Here's where you make a decision,
        'and tell the user what happened
        If intNumber = 1000 Then
            MessageBox.Show("'intNumber' is, indeed, 1000!", "Simple If")
        End If
End Sub
```

2. Run your project and click the Another If button; nothing will happen.

How It Works

In this case, the question "Is `intNumber` equal to 1000?" comes out false. The code block executes only if the statement is true, so it's skipped. If the statement were true, the line between the `If` and `End If` lines would have executed. However, in this instance the statement was false, so the next line to be executed was the first line directly following the End If line (which is End Sub). In effect, the true code block is skipped.

The Else Statement

If you want to run one piece of code if the condition is true and another piece if the condition is false, then you use the Else statement. This expands on the previous Try It Out.

The Else Statement

Code file Simple If.zip available for download at Wrox.com

This Try It Out builds on the previous Try It Out to show how the Else statement works.

1.   Return to the Code Editor in the Simple If project and modify the code in the btnAnotherIf_Click procedure so that it looks like this:

```
Private Sub btnAnotherIf_Click(ByVal sender As System.Object, _
    ByVal e As System.EventArgs) Handles btnAnotherIf.Click

    'Declare and set a variable
    Dim intNumber As Integer = 27

    'Here's where you make a decision,
    'and tell the user what happened
    If intNumber = 1000 Then
        MessageBox.Show("'intNumber' is, indeed, 1000!", "Simple If")
    Else
        MessageBox.Show("'intNumber' is not 1000!", "Simple If")
    End If
End Sub
```

2.   Run the project and you'll see the message box shown in Figure 4-2.

How It Works

Here, the code following the Else statement runs if the condition in the If statement is not met. In this case, the value of intNumber is 27, but the condition being tested for is intNumber = 1000, so the code after the Else statement is run:

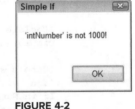

FIGURE 4-2

```
    MessageBox.Show("'intNumber' is not 1000!", "Simple If")
```

Allowing Multiple Alternatives with ElseIf

If you want to test for more than one condition, you need to make use of the ElseIf statement.

TRY IT OUT   The ElseIf Statement

Code file Simple If.zip available for download at Wrox.com

In this Try It Out, you'll use your Simple If program to see how you can test for the value of intNumber being 27 and 1000.

1. Return to the Code Editor and change the code in the btnAnotherIf_Click procedure so that it looks like this:

```
Private Sub btnAnotherIf_Click(ByVal sender As System.Object, _
    ByVal e As System.EventArgs) Handles btnAnotherIf.Click

    'Declare and set a variable
    Dim intNumber As Integer = 27

    'Here's where you make a decision,
    'and tell the user what happened
    If intNumber = 1000 Then
        MessageBox.Show("'intNumber' is, indeed, 1000!", "Simple If")
    ElseIf intNumber = 27 Then
        MessageBox.Show("'intNumber' is 27!", "Simple If")
    Else
        MessageBox.Show("'intNumber' is neither 1000 nor 27!", "Simple If")
    End If
End Sub
```

2. Run the project and click the Another If button. You'll see the message box shown in Figure 4-3.

How It Works

This time the code in the ElseIf statement ran because intNumber met the condition intNumber = 27. Note that you can still include the Else statement at the end to catch instances where intNumber is neither 27 nor 1000, but something else entirely:

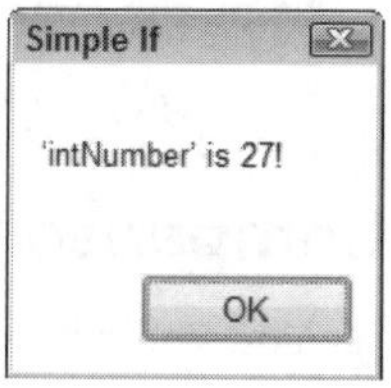

```
ElseIf intNumber = 27 Then
    MessageBox.Show("'intNumber' is 27!", "Simple If")
Else
    MessageBox.Show("'intNumber' is neither 1000 nor 27!", "Simple If")

End If
```

FIGURE 4-3

> **NOTE** *You can add as many ElseIf statements as you need to test for conditions. However, bear in mind that each ElseIf statement is executed as Visual Basic 2010 attempts to discover whether the condition is true. This slows your program if you have a lot of conditions to be tested. If this is the case, you should try to put the statements in the order they are most likely to be executed, with the most common one at the top. Alternatively, you should use a Select Case block, which you will be looking at later in the chapter.*

Nested If Statements

It's possible to nest an `If` statement inside another:

```
If intX = 3 Then
    MessageBox.Show("intX = 3")

    If intY = 6 Then
        MessageBox.Show("intY = 6")
    End If

End If
```

There's no real limit to how far you can nest your `If` statements. However, the more levels of nesting you have, the harder it is to follow what's happening in your code, so try to keep the nesting of `If` statements to a minimum.

Single-Line If Statement

The single-line form of the `If` statement is typically used for short, simple tests, and it saves space in the code editor. However, it doesn't provide the structure and flexibility of the multiline form and is usually harder to read:

```
If intX = 3 Then MessageBox.Show("intX = 3") Else MessageBox.Show("intX is not 3")
```

You don't need an `End If` at the end of a single-line `If ... Then` statement.

Multiple statements can also be executed within a single-line `If ... Then` statement. All statements must be on the same line and must be separated by colons, as in the following example:

```
If intX = 3 Then MessageBox.Show("intX = 3"): intX = intX + 1: Total += intX
```

Comparison Operators

You know how to check whether a particular variable is equal to some value and execute code if this is the case. In fact, `If` is far more flexible than this. You can ask questions such as these, all of which have yes/no answers.

➤ Is `intNumber` greater than 49?

➤ Is `intNumber` less than 49?

➤ Is `intNumber` greater than or equal to 49?

➤ Is `intNumber` less than or equal to 49?

➤ Is `strName` not equal to `Ben`?

When working with string values, most of the time you'll use the Equal To or Not Equal To operator. When working with numeric values (both integer and floating-point), you can use all of these arithmetic operators discussed in the previous chapter.

Using Not Equal To

You have not used Not Equal To yet, so test the Not Equal To operator with strings.

TRY IT OUT   Using Not Equal To

Code file If Demo.zip available for download at Wrox.com

The Not Equal To operator will be false when Equal To is true and it will be true when Equal To is false. Let's try this out.

1. Create a Windows Forms Application project called **If Demo**. Add a TextBox control and a Button control. Set the Name property for TextBox1 to **txtName** and the Text property to **Stephanie**. Set the Name property for Button1 to **btnCheck** and the Text property to **Check**.

2. Double-click the Button control to create its Click event handler. Add the bolded code:

```
Private Sub btnCheck_Click(ByVal sender As System.Object, _
    ByVal e As System.EventArgs) Handles btnCheck.Click

    'Declare a variable and get the name from the text box
    Dim strName As String
    strName = txtName.Text

    'Is the name Wendy?
    If strName <> "Wendy" Then
        MessageBox.Show("The name is *not* Wendy.", "If Demo")
    End If
End Sub
```

3. Save your project and then run it. When the form is displayed, click the Check button and you will see a message box indicating that the name is not Wendy.

How It Works

The Not Equal To operator looks like this: <>. When the button is clicked, the first thing you do is retrieve the name from the text box by looking at its Text property:

```
'Declare a variable and get the name from the text box
Dim strName As String
strName = txtName.Text
```

After you have the name, you use an If statement. This time, however, you use the Not Equal To operator, rather than the Equal To operator. Also note that you are comparing two string values:

```
'Is the name Wendy?
If strName <> "Wendy" Then
    MessageBox.Show("The name is *not* Wendy.", "If Demo")
End If
```

The code between Then and End If executes only if the answer to the question asked in the If statement is True. You may find this to be a bit of a heady principle, because the question you're asking is, "Is strName not equal to Wendy?" to which the answer is "Yes, the strName is *not* equal to Wendy." Because the answer to this question is yes, or True, the code runs and the message box displays. However, if you enter Wendy into the text box and click Check, nothing happens, because the answer to the question is "No, the strName *is* equal to Wendy"; therefore, you have a no, or False, answer.

> **NOTE** If you try this, be sure to enter Wendy with an uppercase W and the rest of the letters in lowercase; otherwise, the application won't work properly. You'll see why later.

An alternative way of checking that something does not equal something else is to use the Not keyword. The condition in the If statement could have been written as follows:

```
If Not strName = "Wendy" Then
```

Using the Numeric Operators

In this section, you take a look at the four other comparison operators you can use. These are all fairly basic, so you'll go through this quite fast.

TRY IT OUT Using Less Than

Code file If Demo.zip available for download at Wrox.com

In this try it out, you will work with greater than, less than, greater than or equal to, and less than or equal to.

1. Return to the Forms Designer for the If Demo project. Add another TextBox control and set its Name property to **txtValue**. Add another Button control and set its Name property to **btnCheck-Numbers** and its Text property to **Check Numbers**.

2. Double-click the Check Numbers button and add the following bolded code to its Click event handler:

```
Private Sub btnCheckNumbers_Click(ByVal sender As System.Object, _
    ByVal e As System.EventArgs) Handles btnCheckNumbers.Click

    'Declare variable
    Dim intNumber As Integer

    Try
        'Get the number from the text box
        intNumber = CType(txtValue.Text, Integer)
    Catch
        Exit Sub
    End Try

    'Is intNumber less than 27?
    If intNumber < 27 Then
        MessageBox.Show("Is 'intNumber' less than 27? Yes!", "If Demo")
    Else
        MessageBox.Show("Is 'intNumber' less than 27? No!", "If Demo")
    End If
End Sub
```

3. Run the project. Enter **14** into the text box and click the Check Numbers button. You'll be told whether the number entered is less than or greater than 27, as shown in Figure 4-4.

How It Works

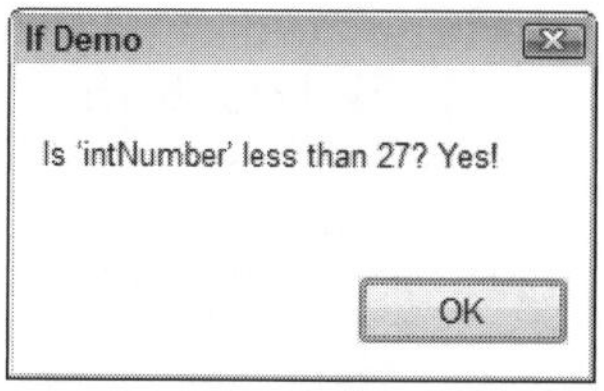

First, you get the value back from the text box. However, there is a slight wrinkle. Because this is a text box, end users are free to enter anything they like into it, and if a series of characters that cannot be converted into an integer is entered, the program will crash. Therefore, you add an *exception handler* to ensure that you always get a value back. Also, with the Option Strict option turned on, you'll need to convert the string value in the text box to an Integer data type using the CType function as you did in the last chapter. If the user enters something invalid, intNumber remains 0 (the default value); otherwise, it will be whatever is entered:

FIGURE 4-4

```
'Declare variable
Dim intNumber As Integer

Try
    'Get the number from the text box
    intNumber = CType(txtValue.Text, Integer)
Catch
End Try
```

> **NOTE** *You'll be introduced to exception handling properly in Chapter 10. For now, you can safely ignore it!*

The Less Than operator looks like this: <. Here, you test to determine whether the number entered was less than 27, and if it is, you say so in a message box; otherwise, you say No:

```
'Is intNumber less than 27?
If intNumber < 27 Then
    MessageBox.Show("Is 'intNumber' less than 27? Yes!", "If Demo")
Else
    MessageBox.Show("Is 'intNumber' less than 27? No!", "If Demo")
End If
```

Here's something interesting, though. If you actually enter **27** into the text box and click the button, you'll see a message box that tells you intNumber is not less than 27. The If statement said No, and it's right; intNumber is actually equal to 27, and the cutoff point for this operator is anything up to *but not including* the value itself. You can get around this problem with a different operator, as you'll see in the next Try It Out.

TRY IT OUT   Using the Less Than Or Equal To Operator

Code file If Demo.zip available for download at Wrox.com

The Less Than Or Equal To operator will be true when the tested value is less than the comparison value and also when the two values are equal. You will see this next.

1. Return to the Code Editor and change the `If` statement in the `btnCheckNumbers_Click` event handler as shown here:

```
Try
    'Get the number from the text box
    intNumber = CType(txtValue.Text, Integer)
Catch
    Exit Sub
End Try

 'Is intNumber less than or equal to 27?
If intNumber <= 27 Then
    MessageBox.Show("Is 'intNumber' less than or equal to 27? Yes!", _
        "If Demo")
Else
    MessageBox.Show("Is 'intNumber' less than or equal to 27? No!", _
        "If Demo")
End If
```

2. Now run the project and enter 27 into the text box. Click the Check Numbers button and you should see the results shown in Figure 4-5.

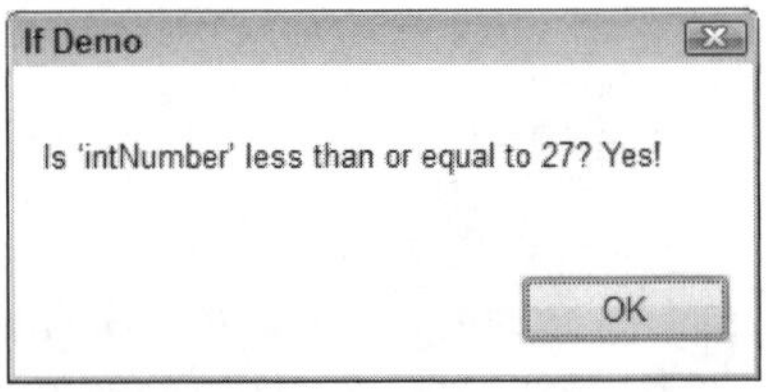

FIGURE 4-5

How It Works

In this example, the Less Than Or Equal To operator looks like this: `<=`. In this situation, you're extending the possible range of values up to and including the value you're checking. Therefore, in this case when you enter **27**, you get the answer `Yes`, n is `less than or equal` to `27`. This type of operator is known as an *inclusive operator*.

The final two operators look very similar to this, so let's look at them now.

TRY IT OUT   **Using Greater Than and Greater Than Or Equal To**

Code file If Demo.zip available for download at Wrox.com

In this example, you see how to use the Greater Than and Greater Than Or Equal To Operators.

1. Return to the Code Editor and add two additional `If` statements in the `btnCheckNumbers_Click` event handler, as shown here:

```
'Is intNumber less than or equal to 27?
If intNumber <= 27 Then
    MessageBox.Show("Is 'intNumber' less than or equal to 27? Yes!", _
        "If Demo")
Else
    MessageBox.Show("Is 'intNumber' less than or equal to 27? No!", _
        "If Demo")
End If

 'Is intNumber greater than 27?
If intNumber > 27 Then
```

```
        MessageBox.Show("Is 'intNumber' greater than 27? Yes!", _
            "If Demo")
    Else
        MessageBox.Show("Is 'intNumber' greater than 27? No!", _
            "If Demo")
    End If

    'Is intNumber greater than or equal to 27?
    If intNumber >= 27 Then
        MessageBox.Show("Is 'intNumber' greater than or equal to 27? Yes!", _
            "If Demo")
    Else
        MessageBox.Show("Is 'intNumber' greater than or equal to 27? No!", _
            "If Demo")
    End If
End Sub
```

2. Run the program. This time enter a value of **99** and click the Check Numbers button. You'll see three message boxes, one after the other. The first message box will indicate that `intNumber` is not less than or equal to 27, while the second message box will indicate that `intNumber` is greater than 27. The final message box will indicate that `intNumber` is greater than or equal to 27.

How It Works

The Greater Than and Greater Than Or Equal To operators are basically the opposite of their Less Than counterparts. This time, you're asking, "Is `intNumber` greater than 27?" and, "Is `intNumber` greater than or equal to 27?" The results speak for themselves.

The And and Or Operators

What happens when you need your `If` statement to test more than one condition? For example, suppose you want to ensure that `intNumber` is less than 27 *and* greater than 10. Or, how about checking that `strName` is "Wendy" or "Stephanie"? You can combine operators used with an `If` statement with the `And` and `Or` operators, as you do in the next Try It Out.

TRY IT OUT Using the Or Operator

Code file And Or Demo.zip available for download at Wrox.com

1. Create a new Windows Forms Application called **And Or Demo**.

2. In the Forms Designer for Form1, add two TextBox controls and a Button control. Set the `Name` properties of the text boxes to **txtName1** and **txtName2** and the `Name` property of the button to **btnOrCheck**.

3. Set the `Text` property for txtName1 to **Wendy** and the `Text` property for txtName2 to **Stephanie**. Finally, set the `Text` property for btnOrCheck to **Or Check**. Your completed form should look similar to the one shown in Figure 4-6.

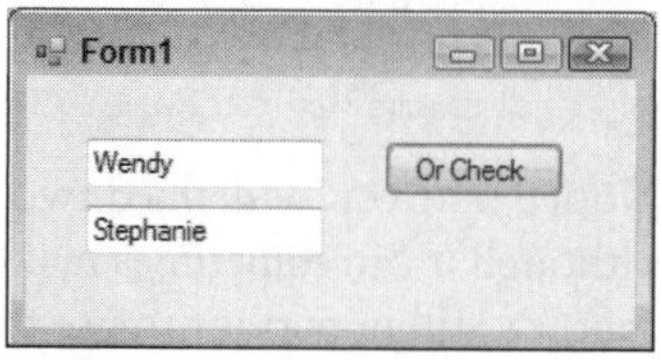

FIGURE 4-6

4. Double-click the Or Check button and add the following code to its `Click` event handler:

```
Private Sub btnOrCheck_Click(ByVal sender As System.Object, _
    ByVal e As System.EventArgs) Handles btnOrCheck.Click

    'Declare variables
    Dim strName1 As String, strName2 As String

    'Get the names
    strName1 = txtName1.Text
    strName2 = txtName2.Text

    'Is one of the names Wendy?
    If strName1 = "Wendy" Or strName2 = "Wendy" Then
        MessageBox.Show("One of the names is Wendy.", _
            "And Or Demo")
    Else
        MessageBox.Show("Neither of the names is Wendy.", _
            "And Or Demo")
    End If
End Sub
```

5. Run the project and click the button. You should see the results shown in Figure 4-7.

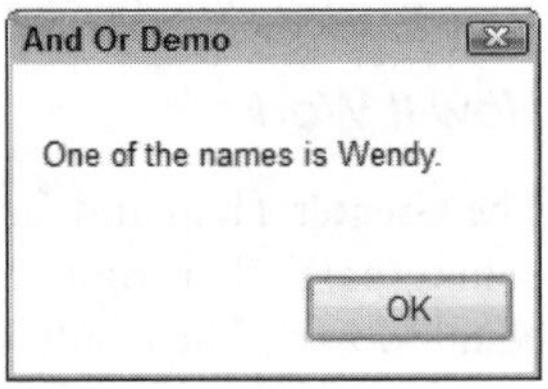

6. Click OK to dismiss the message box dialog and flip the names around so that the top one (txtName1) is **Stephanie** and the bottom one (txtName2) is **Wendy**. Click the button again. You'll see a message box indicating that one of the names is Wendy.

FIGURE 4-7

7. Click OK to dismiss the message box again and this time change the names so that neither of them is Wendy. Click the button and you should see a message box indicating that neither of the names is Wendy.

How It Works

This example shows that the `Or` operator is a great way of building `If` statements that compare two different values in a single hit. In your `Click` event handler, you first declare your variables and then retrieve both names and store them in variables `strName1` and `strName2`:

```
'Declare variables
Dim strName1 As String, strName2 As String

'Get the names
strName1 = txtName1.Text
strName2 = txtName2.Text
```

Notice that you've defined two variables on the same line. This is a perfectly legitimate coding practice, although it can sometimes make the code look congested. The variables are separated with commas; note that it's still important to use the `As` keyword to tell Visual Basic 2010 the data type of each variable.

Once you have both names, you use the `Or` operator to combine two separate `If` statements. The question you're asking here is, "Is `strName1` equal to `Wendy` or is `strName2` equal to `Wendy`?" The answer to this question (provided that one of the text boxes contains the name Wendy) is, "Yes, either `strName1` is equal to `Wendy` or `strName2` is equal to `Wendy`." Again, it's a yes/no or true/false answer, even though the question is seemingly more complex:

```
'Is one of the names Wendy?
If strName1 = "Wendy" Or strName2 = "Wendy" Then
    MessageBox.Show("One of the names is Wendy.", _
        "And Or Demo")
Else
    MessageBox.Show("Neither of the names is Wendy.", _
        "And Or Demo")
End If
```

Using the And Operator

The `And` operator is conceptually similar to `Or`, except that both parts of the condition need to be satisfied, as you will see in the next Try It Out.

TRY IT OUT   Using the And Operator

Code file And Or Demo.zip available for download at Wrox.com

Let's see how to use the And operator.

1.   Return to the Forms Designer in the And Or Demo project. Add another Button control to the form. Set its `Name` property to **btnAndCheck** and its `Text` property to **And Check**. Double-click the button and add the following bolded code to its `Click` event handler:

```
Private Sub btnAndCheck_Click(ByVal sender As System.Object, _
    ByVal e As System.EventArgs) Handles btnAndCheck.Click

    'Declare variables
    Dim strName1 As String, strName2 As String

    'Get the names
    strName1 = txtName1.Text
    strName2 = txtName2.Text

    'Are both names Wendy?
    If strName1 = "Wendy" And strName2 = "Wendy" Then
        MessageBox.Show("Both names are Wendy.", _
            "And Or Demo")
    Else
        MessageBox.Show("One of the names is not Wendy.", _
            "And Or Demo")
    End If
End Sub
```

2.   Run the program and click the And Check button. A message box will tell you that one of the names is not Wendy.

3.   Change both names so that they are both Wendy and click the button. You'll see the results shown in Figure 4-8.

How It Works

Let's review why this works. After you retrieve both names from the text boxes, you compare them. In this case, you're asking the question, "Is strName1 equal to Wendy *and* is strName2 equal to Wendy?" In this case, both parts of the If statement must be satisfied in order for the "Both names are Wendy" message box to be displayed:

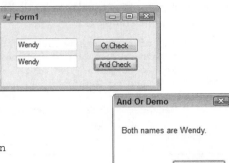

```
'Are both names Wendy?
If strName1 = "Wendy" And strName2 = "Wendy" Then
    MessageBox.Show("Both names are Wendy.", _
        "And Or Demo")
Else
    MessageBox.Show("One of the names is not
        Wendy.", _
        "And Or Demo")
End If
```

FIGURE 4-8

More on And and Or

You've seen And and Or used with strings. They can also be used with numeric values, like this:

```
If intX = 2 And intY = 3 Then
    MessageBox.Show("Hello, both of the conditions have been satisfied!")
End If
```

or

```
If intX = 2 Or intY = 3 Then
    MessageBox.Show("Hello, one of the conditions has been satisfied!")
End If
```

In Visual Basic 2010, there's no realistic limit to the number of And operators or Or operators that you can include in a statement. It's perfectly possible to do the following, although it's unlikely you'd want to do so:

```
If intA = 1 And intB = 2 And intC = 3 And intD = 4 And intE = 5 And _
    intF = 6 And intG = 7 And intH = 1 And intI = 2 And intJ = 3 And _
    intK = 4 And intL = 5 And intM = 6 And intN = 7 And intO = 1 And _
    intP = 2 And intQ = 3 And intR = 4 And intS = 5 And intT = 6 And _
    intU = 7 And intV = 1 And intW = 2 And intX = 3 And intY = 4 And _
    intZ = 5 Then
    MessageBox.Show("That's quite an If statement!")
End If
```

Finally, it's possible to use parentheses to group operators and look for a value within a range. For example, say you want to determine whether the value of intX is between 12 and 20 exclusive or between 22 and 25 exclusive. You can use the following If ... Then statement:

```
If (intX > 12 And intX < 20) Or (intX > 22 And intX < 25) Then
```

There are many other combinations of operators, far more than we have room to go into here. Rest assured that if you want to check for a condition, there is a combination to suit your needs.

String Comparison

When working with strings and If statements, you often run into the problem of uppercase and lowercase letters. A computer treats the characters A and a as separate entities, even though people consider them to be similar. This is known as *case sensitivity* — meaning that the case of the letters does matter when comparing strings. For example, if you run the following code, the message box would *not* be displayed:

```
Dim strName As String
strName = "Winston"
If strName = "WINSTON" Then
    MessageBox.Show("Aha! You are Winston.")
End If
```

Because WINSTON is not, strictly speaking, the same as Winston, this If statement will not return a message. However, in many cases you don't actually care about case, so you have to find a way of comparing strings and ignoring the case of the characters.

TRY IT OUT Using Case-Insensitive String Comparisons

Code file And Or Demo.zip available for download at Wrox.com

In this Try It Out, you work with case-insensitive strings.

1. Return to the Forms Designer in the And Or Demo project and add another TextBox and Button control to the form.

2. Set the Name property of the TextBox to **txtName3** and the Text property to **Bryan**. Set the Name property of the Button to **btnStringCompare** and the Text property to **String Compare**.

3. Double-click the String Compare button to open its Click event handler and add the following bolded code:

```
Private Sub btnStringCompare_Click(ByVal sender As System.Object, _
    ByVal e As System.EventArgs) Handles btnStringCompare.Click

    'Declare variable
    Dim strName As String

    'Get the name
    strName = txtName3.Text

    'Compare the name
    If String.Compare(strName, "BRYAN", True) = 0 Then
        MessageBox.Show("Hello, Bryan!", "And Or Demo")
    End If
End Sub
```

4. Run the project and click the button. You should see results like the ones shown in Figure 4-9.

5. Dismiss the message box and enter the name in the last text box as **BrYaN**, or some other combination of uppercase and lowercase letters, and click the button. You should still see a message box that says "Hello, Bryan!"

6. However, if you enter a name that isn't Bryan, the message box will not be displayed when you click the button.

How It Works

After you get the name back from the text box, you have to use a function to compare the two values, rather than use the basic Equal To operator. In this instance, you're using the Compare method on System.String, passing it the two strings you want to compare. The first string is the value stored in strName (which is the value entered into the text box), with the second string being "BRYAN". The last parameter that you supply is True, which tells Compare to perform a case-insensitive match; in other words, it should ignore the differences in case. If you supplied False for this parameter, the comparison would be case sensitive, in which case you would be no better off than using the vanilla Equal To operator:

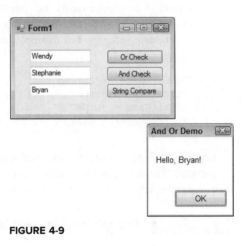

FIGURE 4-9

```
'Compare the name
If String.Compare(strName, "BRYAN", True) = 0 Then
    MessageBox.Show("Hello, Bryan!", "And Or Demo")
End If
```

String.Compare returns a fairly curious result. It actually returns an integer, rather than a True or False value. This is because String.Compare can be used to determine *how* two strings differ, rather than just a straightforward, "Yes, they are," or "No, they're not." If the method returns 0, the strings match. If the method returns a value that is not 0, the strings do not match.

> **NOTE** *String.Compare returns an indication of how different two strings are in order to help you build sorting algorithms.*

SELECT CASE

On occasion, you need to make a set of similar decisions such as this:

➤ Is the customer called Bryan? If so, do this.

➤ Is the customer called Stephanie? If so, do this.

➤ Is the customer called Cathy? If so, do this.

➤ Is the customer called Betty? If so, do this.

➤ Is the customer called Edward? If so, do this.

You can obviously do this with a set of If . . . Then statements. In fact, it would look a little like this:

```
If Customer.Name = "Bryan" Then
    (do something)
```

```
ElseIf Customer.Name = "Stephanie" Then
        (do something)
ElseIf Customer.Name = "Cathy" Then
        (do something)
ElseIf Customer.Name = "Betty" Then
        (do something)
ElseIf Customer.Name = "Edward" Then
        (do something)
End If
```

What happens if you decide you want to check `Customer.FirstName` instead of `Customer.Name`? You'd have to change every `If` statement, which is a pain. In addition, if `Customer.Name` turns out to be `"Edward"`, you still have to go through the other four `If` statements, which is very inefficient. In the next Try It Out, you learn a better way.

TRY IT OUT   Using Select Case

Code file Select Demo.zip available for download at Wrox.com

1. Create a new Windows Forms Application project. Call it **Select Demo**. Set the `Text` property of the form to **Select Case**.

2. From the Toolbox, add a ListBox control to the form and set its `Name` property to **lstData**, its `Dock` property to **Fill**, and its `IntegralHeight` property to **False**.

3. With lstData selected in the Forms Designer, look at the Properties window and select the Items property. Click the ellipses button to the right of the property, and in the String Collection Editor that appears, add the five names on separate lines as shown in Figure 4-10.

4. Click OK to save the changes. The names will be added to your list box.

5. Now double-click lstData to create a new `SelectedIndexChanged` event handler and add the following bolded code:

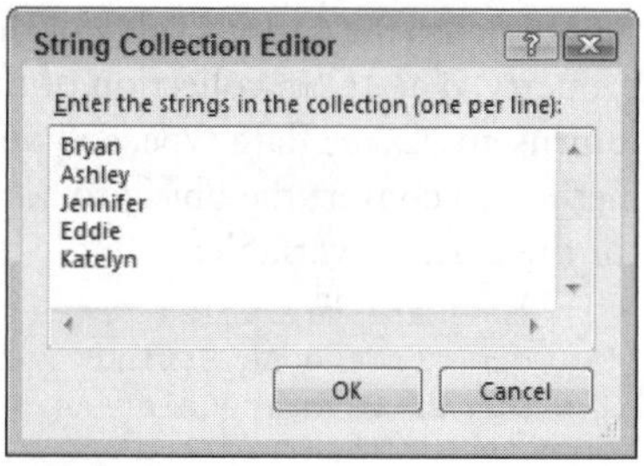

FIGURE 4-10

```
Private Sub lstData_SelectedIndexChanged(ByVal sender As System.Object, _
    ByVal e As System.EventArgs) Handles lstData.SelectedIndexChanged

    'Declare variables
    Dim strName As String
    Dim strFavoriteColor As String

    'Get the selected name
    strName = lstData.Items(lstData.SelectedIndex).ToString

    'Use a Select Case statement to get the favorite color
    'of the selected name
    Select Case strName
        Case "Bryan"
            strFavoriteColor = "Madras Yellow"
```

```
        Case "Ashley"
            strFavoriteColor = "Sea Blue"

        Case "Jennifer"
            strFavoriteColor = "Morning Mist"

        Case "Eddie"
            strFavoriteColor = "Passionate Purple"

        Case "Katelyn"
            strFavoriteColor = "Red"
    End Select

    'Display the favorite color of the selected name
    MessageBox.Show(strName & "'s favorite color is " & _
        strFavoriteColor, "Select Demo")
End Sub
```

6. Save your project and then run it. Whenever you click one of the names, a message box like the one shown in Figure 4-11 will appear.

How It Works

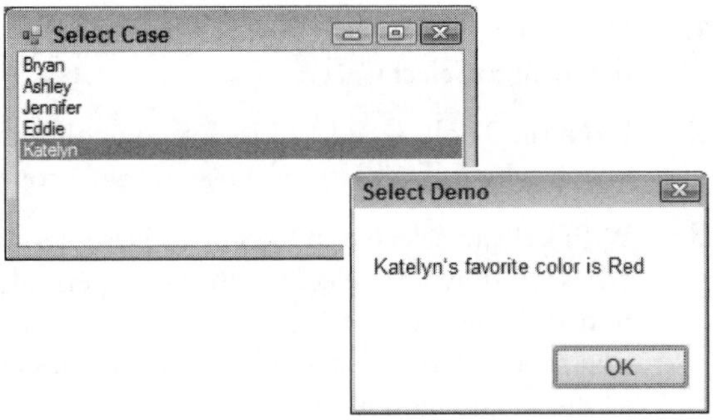

In this Try It Out, the first thing you need to do in the `SelectedIndexChanged` event handler is declare your variables and determine which name was selected. You do this by finding the item in the list that matches the current value of the `SelectedIndex` property. The `Items` collection of the `ListBox` class returns an `Object` data type, so you use the `ToString` method to convert the object to a `String` data type for the `strName` variable:

FIGURE 4-11

```
'Declare variables
Dim strName As String
Dim strFavoriteColor As String

'Get the selected name
strName = lstData.Items(lstData.SelectedIndex).ToString
```

When you have that, you start a `Select Case ... End Select` block. To do this, you need to supply the variable that you're matching against; in this case, you're using the name that was selected in the list.

Inside the `Select Case ... End Select` block, you define separate `Case` statements for each condition to be checked against. In this example, you have five, and each is set to respond to a different name. If a match can be found, Visual Basic 2010 executes the code immediately following the relevant `Case` statement.

For example, if you clicked Katelyn, the message box would display Red as her favorite color, because Visual Basic 2010 would execute the line, `strFavoriteColor = "Red"`. If you clicked Ashley, the message box would display Sea Blue as her favorite color, because Visual Basic 2010 would execute `strFavoriteColor = "Sea Blue"`.

```
    'Use a Select Case statement to get the favorite color
    'of the selected name
```

```
Select Case strName
    Case "Bryan"
        strFavoriteColor = "Madras Yellow"

    Case "Ashley"
        strFavoriteColor = "Sea Blue"

    Case "Jennifer"
        strFavoriteColor = "Morning Mist"

    Case "Eddie"
        strFavoriteColor = "Passionate Purple"

    Case "Katelyn"
        strFavoriteColor = "Red"
End Select
```

After the `Select Case ... End Select` block, you display a message box:

```
'Display the favorite color of the selected name
MessageBox.Show(strName & "'s favorite color is " & _
    strFavoriteColor, "Select Demo")
```

How do you get out of a `Select Case ... End Select` block? As you're processing code that's beneath a `Case` statement, if you meet another `Case` statement, Visual Basic 2010 jumps out of the block and down to the line immediately following the block. Here's an illustration:

1. The user clicks Katelyn. The `SelectedIndexChanged` event is activated, and you store "`Katelyn`" in `strName`.

2. You reach the `Select Case` statement. This is set to compare the value in `strName` with one of the five supplied names.

3. Visual Basic 2010 finds a `Case` statement that satisfies the request and immediately moves to `strFavoriteColor = "Red"`.

4. Visual Basic 2010 moves to the next line. This is another `Case` statement, and, seeing that you're already in one, you move to the first line after the `Select Case ... End Select` block and display the message box.

`Select Case` is a powerful and easy-to-use technique for making a choice from several options. However, you must leave the block as soon as another `Case` statement is reached.

Case-Insensitive Select Case

Just like `If`, `Select Case` is case sensitive; prove it in the next Try It Out.

TRY IT OUT   Using Case-Sensitive Select Case

Code file Select Demo.zip available for download at Wrox.com

In this Try It Out, you will prove that case matters when using `Select Case` to compare strings.

1. Return to the Select Demo project and open the Forms Designer. Locate the `Items` property for the list box and open the String Collection Editor again.

2. Change all the names so that they appear in all uppercase letters, as shown in Figure 4-12.

3. Click OK to save your changes and then run the project. You'll notice that when you click a name, the message box doesn't specify a favorite color, as shown in Figure 4-13.

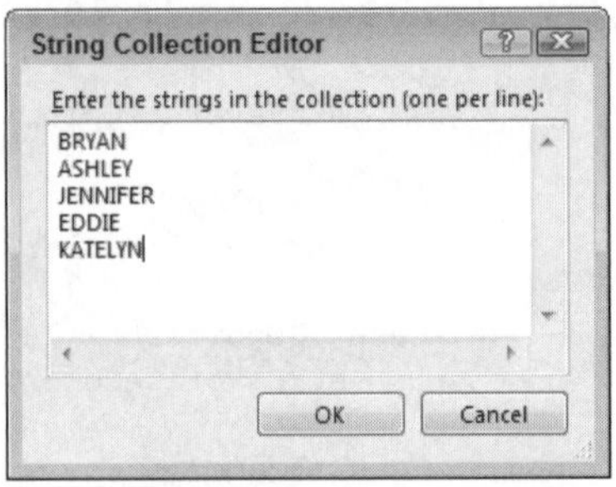

String Collection Editor

Enter the strings in the collection (one per line):

```
BRYAN
ASHLEY
JENNIFER
EDDIE
KATELYN
```

OK   Cancel

FIGURE 4-12

How It Works

`Select Case` performs a case-sensitive match, just like `If`. This means that if you provide the name `BRYAN` or `EDDIE` to the statement, there won't be a corresponding `Case` statement because you're trying to say:

```
If "EDDIE" = "Eddie"
```

or

```
If "BRYAN" = "Bryan"
```

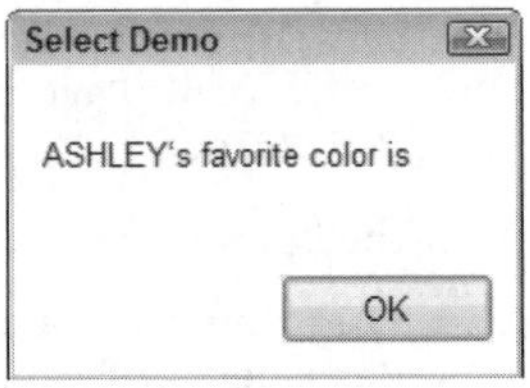

Select Demo

ASHLEY's favorite color is

OK

FIGURE 4-13

Earlier in this chapter, you learned how to use the `String.Compare` method to perform case-insensitive comparisons with `If` statements. With `Select Case`, you can't use this method, so if you want to be insensitive towards case, you need to employ a different technique — the one you learn in the next Try It Out.

TRY IT OUT   Case-Insensitive Select Case

Code file Select Demo.zip available for download at Wrox.com

In this example, you will learn another way to compare strings using `Select Case`.

1. Return to the Select Demo project, open the Code Editor for Form1, and make the following changes to the event handler for `SelectedIndexChanged`. Pay special attention to the `Case` statements — the name that you're trying to match *must* be supplied in all lowercase letters:

```
Private Sub lstData_SelectedIndexChanged(ByVal sender As System.Object, _
    ByVal e As System.EventArgs) Handles lstData.SelectedIndexChanged

        'Declare variables
        Dim strName As String
        Dim strFavoriteColor As String

        'Get the selected name
        strName = lstData.Items(lstData.SelectedIndex).ToString

        'Use a Select Case statement to get the favorite color
        'of the selected name
        Select Case strName.ToLower
            Case "bryan"
                strFavoriteColor = "Madras Yellow"
```

```
        Case "ashley"
            strFavoriteColor = "Sea Blue"

        Case "jennifer"
            strFavoriteColor = "Morning Mist"

        Case "eddie"
            strFavoriteColor = "Passionate Purple"

        Case "katelyn"
            strFavoriteColor = "Red"
    End Select

    'Display the favorite color of the selected name
    MessageBox.Show(strName & "'s favorite color is " & strFavoriteColor, _
        "Select Demo")
End Sub
```

2. Run the project and try selecting a name again. This time you will see that the message box includes the favorite color of the person you clicked, as shown in Figure 4-14.

How It Works

To make the selection case insensitive in this example, you have to convert the strName variable into all lowercase letters. This is done using the ToLower method:

```
Select Case strName.ToLower
```

This means that whatever string you're given (whether it's "BRYAN" or "Bryan"), you always convert it to all lowercase ("bryan"). However, when you do this, you have to ensure that you're comparing apples to apples (and not to Apples), which is why you had to convert the values you're checking against in the Case statements to all lowercase too. Therefore, when given "BRYAN", you convert this to "bryan", and then try to find the Case that matches "bryan":

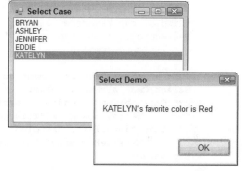

FIGURE 4-14

```
        Case "bryan"
            strFavoriteColor = "Madras Yellow"

        Case "ashley"
            strFavoriteColor = "Sea Blue"

        Case "jennifer"
            strFavoriteColor = "Morning Mist"

        Case "eddie"
            strFavoriteColor = "Passionate Purple"

        Case "katelyn"
            strFavoriteColor = "Red"
    End Select
```

Finally, once you have the favorite color, you display a message box as usual.

> **NOTE** *You could have done the opposite of this and converted all the names to uppercase and used `strName.ToUpper` instead of `strName.ToLower`.*

Multiple Selections

You're not limited to matching one value inside a `Select Case ... End Select` block. You can also match multiple items.

TRY IT OUT   Multiple Selections

Code file Select Demo.zip available for download at Wrox.com

In this Try It Out, you'll modify the application so that you also report the sex of whoever you click on.

1. Return to the Select Demo project, open the Code Editor for Form1, and add the bolded code in the `SelectedIndexChanged` handler:

```
'Display the favorite color of the selected name
MessageBox.Show(strName & "'s favorite color is " & strFavoriteColor, _
    "Select Demo")

'Use a Select Case statement to display a person's gender
Select Case strName.ToLower
    Case "bryan", "eddie", "ashley"
        MessageBox.Show("This person's gender is male.", "Select Demo")
    Case "jennifer", "katelyn"
        MessageBox.Show("This person's gender is female.", "Select Demo")
End Select
End Sub
```

2. Run the project and click one of the female names. You will see results as shown in Figure 4-15, following the message box indicating the person's favorite color.

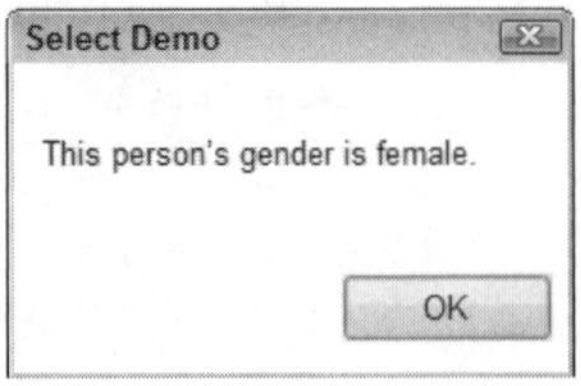

How It Works

OK, now let's look at how multiple selections work. The code you use to get back the name and initialize the `Select Case` block remains the same. However, in each `Case` statement you can provide a list of possible values, separated with commas. In the first one, you look for bryan *or* edward *or* ashley. If any of these matches, you run the code under the `Case` statement:

FIGURE 4-15

```
Case "bryan", "eddie", "ashley"
    MessageBox.Show("This person's gender is male.", "Select Demo")
```

In the second statement, you look for jennifer *or* katelyn. If any of these two matches, you again run the code under the `Case` statement:

```
Case "jennifer", "katelyn"
    MessageBox.Show("This person's gender is female.", "Select Demo")
```

It's important to realize that these are all *or* matches. You're saying "one *or* the other," not "one *and* the other."

The Case Else Statement

What happens if none of the Case statements that you've included is matched? You saw this before in the demonstration of the case-sensitive nature of Select Case. In the next Try It Out, you see it with the Case Else statement.

TRY IT OUT   Using Case Else

Code file Select Demo.zip available for download at Wrox.com

1. Return to the Forms Designer, locate the Items property for the list box, and open the String Collection Editor again. Add another name in all uppercase letters to the collection and then click the OK button.

2. In the lstData_SelectedIndexChanged event handler, add the following bolded code:

```
'Use a Select Case statement to display a person's gender
Select Case strName.ToLower
    Case "bryan", "edward"
        MessageBox.Show("This person's gender is male.", "Select Demo")
    Case "stephanie", "cathy", "betty"
        MessageBox.Show("This person's gender is female.", "Select Demo")
    Case Else
        MessageBox.Show("I don't know this person's gender.", _
            "Select Demo")
End Select
End Sub
```

3. Run the project and click the last name that you just added. You will see results similar to those shown in Figure 4-16.

How It Works

The Case Else statement is used if none of the other supplied Case statements match what you're looking for. There isn't a Case "tony" defined within the block, so you default to using whatever is underneath the Case Else statement. In this instance, you display a message box indicating that you do not know the gender of the person who's been selected.

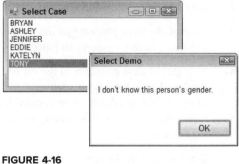

FIGURE 4-16

Different Data Types with Select Case

In this chapter, you used Select Case with variables of type String. However, you can use Select Case with all basic data types in Visual Basic 2010, such as Integer, Double, and Boolean.

In day-to-day work, the most common types of `Select Case` are based on `String` and `Integer` data types. However, as a general rule, if a data type can be used in an `If` statement with the Equals (=) operator, it will work with `Select Case`.

LOOPS

When writing computer software, you often need to perform the same task several times to get the effect you want. For example, you might need to create a telephone bill for *all* customers, or read in 10 files from your computer's disk.

To accomplish this, you use a *loop,* and in this section you'll take a look at the two main types of loops available in Visual Basic 2010:

➤   `For` loops: These loops occur a certain number of times (for example, exactly 10 times).

➤   `Do` loops: These loops keep running until a certain condition is reached (for example, until all of the data is processed).

The For . . . Next Loop

The simplest loop to understand is the `For . . . Next` loop.

TRY IT OUT   Building a For . . . Next Loop

Code file Loops.zip available for download at Wrox.com

You will learn to build a `For . . . Next` Loop in this Try It Out.

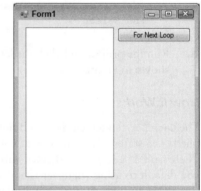

FIGURE 4-17

1.   Create a new Windows Forms Application project called **Loops**.

2.   Add a ListBox and a Button control to the form.

3.   Change the `Name` property of the list box to **lstData** and its `IntegralHeight` property to **False**.

4.   Change the `Name` property of the button to **btn-ForNextLoop**. Set its `Text` property to **For Next Loop**. You'll be adding more buttons later so make this button a little wider, as shown in Figure 4-17.

5.   Double-click the button to create its `Click` event handler and add the following bolded code:

```
Private Sub btnForNextLoop_Click(ByVal sender As System.Object, _
    ByVal e As System.EventArgs) Handles btnForNextLoop.Click

        'Declare variable
        Dim intCount As Integer

        'Clear the list
        ClearList()
```

```
'Perform a loop
For intCount = 1 To 5
    'Add the item to the list
    lstData.Items.Add("I'm item " & intCount.ToString & _
        " in the list!")
Next
End Sub
```

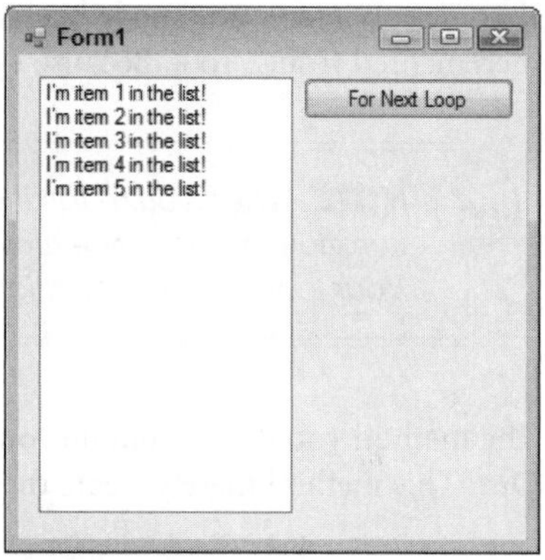

6. Now create the following method:

```
Private Sub ClearList()
    'Clear the list
    lstData.Items.Clear()
End Sub
```

7. Save and run the project and then click the For Next Loop button. You should see results like those in Figure 4-18.

```
I'm item 1 in the list!
I'm item 2 in the list!
I'm item 3 in the list!
I'm item 4 in the list!
I'm item 5 in the list!
```

For Next Loop

FIGURE 4-18

How It Works

First, inside the Click event handler, you define a variable:

```
'Declare variable
Dim intCount As Integer
```

Next, you clear the list box by calling the ClearList method. Although the list is empty at this point, you'll be adding more buttons to this project in the following Try It Out exercises, and may want to compare the results of the each of the buttons.

```
'Clear the list
ClearList()
```

Then you start the loop by using the For keyword. This tells Visual Basic 2010 that you want to create a loop. Everything that follows the For keyword is used to define how the loop should act. In this case, you're giving it the variable you just created and then telling it to count *from* 1 *to* 5:

```
'Perform a loop
For intCount = 1 To 5
```

The variable that you give the loop (in this case, intCount) is known as the *control variable*. When you first enter the loop, Visual Basic 2010 sets the control variable to the initial count value — in this case, 1. After the loop starts, Visual Basic 2010 moves to the first line within the For loop — in this case, the line that adds a string to the list box:

```
'Add the item to the list
lstData.Items.Add("I'm item " & intCount.ToString & _
    " in the list!")
```

This time, this line of code adds I'm item 1 in the list! to the list box. Visual Basic 2010 then hits the Next statement, and that's where things start to get interesting:

```
Next
```

When the Next statement is executed, Visual Basic 2010 increments the control variable by one. The first time Next is executed, the value in intCount changes from 1 to 2. Providing that the value of the control variable is less than or equal to the "stop" value (in this case, 5), Visual Basic 2010 moves back to the first line after the For statement, in this case:

```
'Add the item to the list
```

```
lstData.Items.Add("I'm item " & intCount.ToString & _
    " in the list!")
```

This time, this line of code adds I'm item 2 in the list! to the list box. Again, after this line is executed, you run the Next statement. The value of intCount is now incremented from 2 to 3, and because 3 is less than or equal to 5, you move back to the line that adds the item to the list. This happens until intCount is incremented from 5 to 6. Because 6 is greater than the stop value for the loop, the loop stops.

> **NOTE** *When you're talking about loops, you tend to use the term iteration. One iteration includes one movement from the* For *statement to the* Next *statement. Your loop has five iterations.*

The method you define contains only one line of code but its reuse becomes apparent in the next Try It Out. This method merely clears the Items collection of the list box:

```
Private Sub ClearList()
    'Clear the list
    lstData.Items.Clear()
End Sub
```

Using the Step Keyword

You don't have to start your loop at 1 — you can pick any value you like. Nor do you have to increment the control value by 1 on each iteration — again, you can increment by any value you like.

TRY IT OUT **Using Step**

Code file Loops.zip available for download at Wrox.com

In this Try It Out, you learn about the flexibility of the step keyword.

1. Return to the Forms Designer for the Loops project. Add a Button control to your form. Set its Name property to **btnForNextLoopWithStep** and its Text property to **For Next Loop w/Step**.

2. Double-click the button and add the following bolded code in the Click event handler:

```
Private Sub btnForNextLoopWithStep_Click(ByVal sender As System.Object, _
    ByVal e As System.EventArgs) Handles btnForNextLoopWithStep.Click

    'Clear the list
    ClearList()

    'Perform a loop
    For intCount As Integer = 4 To 62 Step 7
        'Add the item to the list
        lstData.Items.Add(intCount.ToString)
    Next
End Sub
```

3. Run the project and click the For Next Loop w/Step button. You will see results like those in Figure 4-19.

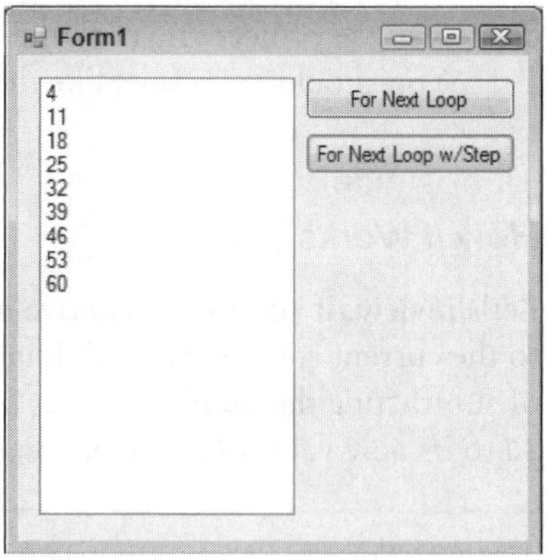

How It Works

The magic in this example all happens with this statement:

```
'Perform a loop
For intCount As Integer = 4 To 62 Step 7
```

First, note that you didn't declare the intCount variable using a Dim statement. This has been done as part of the For statement and makes this variable local to this loop. Using the As keyword and the data type for the variable (in this case, Integer), you have effectively declared an inline variable.

FIGURE 4-19

Next, instead of using 1 as the start value, you're using 4. This means that on the first iteration of the loop, intCount is set to 4, which you can see because the first item added to the list is indeed 4. You've used the Step keyword to tell the loop to increment the control value by 7 on each iteration, rather than by the default of 1. This is why, by the time you start running the second iteration of the loop, intCount is set to 11, not 5.

Although you gave For a stop value of 62, the loop has actually stopped at 60 because the stop value is a *maximum*. After the ninth iteration, intCount is actually 67, which is more than 62, so the loop stops.

Looping Backwards

By using a Step value that's less than 0 (or a negative number), you can make the loop go backward, rather than forward, as demonstrated in the next Try It Out.

TRY IT OUT   Looping Backward

Code file Loops.zip available for download at Wrox.com

In this example, you will make a loop go backwards.

1. Return to the Forms Designer and add another Button control to your form, setting its Name property to **btnBackwardsForNextLoop** and its Text property to **Backwards For Next Loop**.

2. Double-click the button and add the following bolded code in the Click event handler:

```
Private Sub btnBackwardsForNextLoop_Click(ByVal sender As System.Object, _
    ByVal e As System.EventArgs) Handles btnBackwardsForNextLoop.Click

    'Clear the list
    ClearList()

    'Perform a loop
    For intCount As Integer = 10 To 1 Step -1
        'Add the item to the list
```

```
            lstData.Items.Add(intCount.ToString)
        Next
    End Sub
```

3. Run the project and click the Backwards for Next Loop button. You should see results like those shown in Figure 4-20.

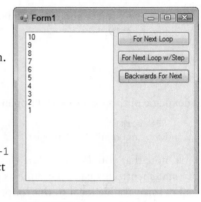

How It Works

Let's review. If you use a negative number, like -1, For tries to add -1 to the current control value. Adding a negative number has the effect of subtracting the number, so intCount goes from its start value of 10 to its new value of 9, and so on until the stop value is reached.

FIGURE 4-20

The For Each . . . Next Loop

In practical, day-to-day work, it's unlikely that you'll use For . . . Next loops as illustrated here. Because of way the .NET Framework typically works, you'll usually use a derivative of the For . . . Next loop called the For Each . . . Next loop.

In the algorithms you design, whenever a loop is necessary, you'll have a collection of things to work through, and usually this set is expressed as an *array*. For example, you might want to look through all of the files in a folder, looking for those that are larger than a particular size. When you ask the .NET Framework for a list of files, you are returned an array of strings, with each string in that array describing a single file.

TRY IT OUT   For Each Loop

In this Try It Out, you'll modify your Loops application so that it returns a list of folders contained at the root of your C drive.

1. Return to the Forms Designer, add another Button control to your form, and set its Name property to **btnForEachLoop** and its Text property to **For Each Loop**.

2. Double-click the button and add the following bolded code to the Click event handler:

```
Private Sub btnForEachLoop_Click(ByVal sender As System.Object, _
    ByVal e As System.EventArgs) Handles btnForEachLoop.Click

        'Clear the list
        ClearList()

        'List each folder at the root of your C drive
        For Each strFolder As String In _
            My.Computer.FileSystem.GetDirectories("C:\")

            'Add the item to the list
            lstData.Items.Add(strFolder)
        Next
    End Sub
```

3. Run the project and click the For Each Loop button. You should see a list of folders that are at the root of your C drive.

How It Works

In the For Each Loop example, the My namespace in the .NET Framework exposes several classes that make it easy to find the information that you'll use on a daily basis. In particular, the Computer class provides several other classes related to the computer on which your program is running. Since you want to find out about files and folders, you use the FileSystem class, which provides methods and properties for working with files and folders.

The GetDirectories method returns a *collection* of strings representing names of directories (or folders) on your computer. In this case, you use it to return a collection of folder names in the root of the computer's C drive.

The concept with a For Each ... Next loop is that for each iteration, you'll be given the "thing" that you're supposed to be working with. You need to provide a source of things (in this case, a collection of strings representing folder names) and a control variable into which the current thing can be put. The GetDirectories method provides the collection, and the inline variable strFolder provides the control variable:

```
'List each folder at the root of your C drive
For Each strFolder As String In _
    My.Computer.FileSystem.GetDirectories("C:\")
Next
```

This means that on the first iteration, strFolder is equal to the first item in the string collection (in this case, "C:\$Recycle.Bin"). You then add that item to the list box:

```
'Add the item to the list
lstData.Items.Add(strFolder)
```

As with normal For ... Next loops, for every iteration of the loop, you're given a string containing a folder name, and you add that string to the list. When there are no more folders to be returned, execution automatically drops out of the loop.

The Do ... Loop Loops

The other kind of loop you can use is one that keeps happening until a certain condition is met. This is known as a Do ... Loop, and there are a number of variations.

The first one you'll learn about is the Do Until ... Loop. This kind of loop keeps going until something happens.

TRY IT OUT   **Using the Do Until ... Loop**

For this Try It Out, you're going to use the random number generator that's built into the .NET Framework and create a loop that will keep generating random numbers *until* it produces the number 10. When you get the number 10, you'll stop the loop.

1. Return to the Forms Designer in the Loops project, add another Button control to your form, and set its Name property to **btnDoUntilLoop** and its Text property to **Do Until Loop**.

2. Double-click the button and add the following bolded code to its Click event handler:

```
Private Sub btnDoUntilLoop_Click(ByVal sender As System.Object, _
    ByVal e As System.EventArgs) Handles btnDoUntilLoop.Click

        'Declare variables
        Dim objRandom As New Random
        Dim intRandomNumber As Integer = 0

        'Clear the list
        ClearList()

        'Process the loop until intRandomNumber = 10
        Do Until intRandomNumber = 10
            'Get a random number between 0 and 24
            intRandomNumber = objRandom.Next(25)
            'Add the number to the list
            lstData.Items.Add(intRandomNumber.ToString)
        Loop
End Sub
```

3. Run the project and click the Do Until Loop button. You'll see results similar to the results shown in Figure 4-21. Keep clicking the button. The number of elements in the list is different each time.

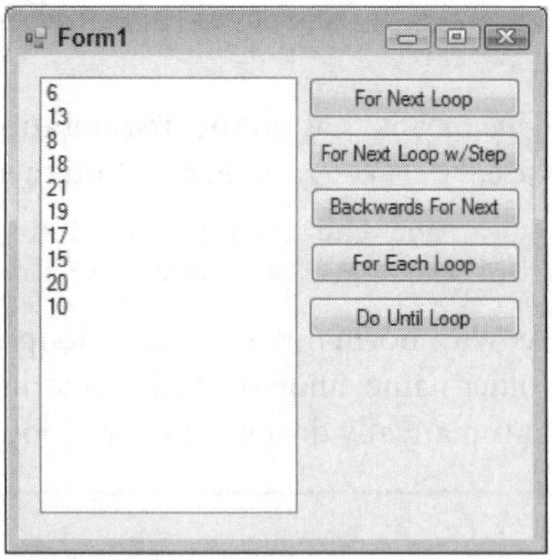

How It Works

A Do Until ... Loop keeps running the loop until the given condition is met. When you use this type of loop, there isn't a control variable per se; rather, you have to keep track of the current position of the loop yourself. You begin by declaring a variable (also known as an object) for the Random class, which provides methods for generating random numbers. This object has been prefixed with obj to specify that this is an object derived from a class. The next variable that you declare is the intRandomNumber, which is used to receive the random number generated by your objRandom object:

FIGURE 4-21

```
'Declare variables
Dim objRandom As New Random()
Dim intRandomNumber As Integer = 0
```

Then you clear the list of any previous items that may have been added:

```
'Clear the list
ClearList()
```

Next, you set up the loop, indicating that you want to keep running the loop until intRandomNumber is equal to 10:

```
'Process the loop until intRandomNumber = 10
Do Until intRandomNumber = 10
```

With each iteration of the loop, you ask the random number generator for a new random number and store it in intRandomNumber. This is done by calling the Next method of objRandom to get a random number.

In this case, you've passed 25 as a parameter to Next, meaning that any number returned should be between 0 and 24 inclusive — that is, the number you supply must be one larger than the biggest number you ever want to get. In other words, the bounds that you ask for are non-inclusive. You then add the number that you got to the list:

```
'Get a random number between 0 and 24
intRandomNumber = objRandom.Next(25)
'Add the number to the list
lstData.Items.Add(intRandomNumber.ToString)
Loop
```

The magic happens when you get to the Loop statement. At this point, Visual Basic 2010 returns not to the first line within the loop, but instead to the Do Until line. When execution returns to Do Until, the expression is evaluated. Provided it returns False, the execution pointer moves to the first line within the loop. However, if intRandomNumber is 10, the expression returns True, and instead of moving to the first line within the loop, you continue at the first line immediately after Loop. In effect, the loop is stopped.

Do While . . . Loop

The conceptual opposite of a Do Until . . . Loop is a Do While . . . Loop. This kind of loop keeps iterating while a particular condition is true. Let's see it in action.

TRY IT OUT   Using the Do While . . . Loop

Code file Loops.zip available for download at Wrox.com

In this Try It Out, you will use a Do While . . . Loop to continue while a random number is less than 15.

1. Return to the Forms Designer again and add another Button control to your form. Set its Name property to **btnDoWhileLoop** and its Text property to **Do While Loop**.

2. Double-click the button and add the following bolded code to the Click event handler:

```
Private Sub btnDoWhileLoop_Click(ByVal sender As System.Object, _
    ByVal e As System.EventArgs) Handles btnDoWhileLoop.Click

    'Declare variables
    Dim objRandom As New Random
    Dim intRandomNumber As Integer = 0

    'Clear the list
    ClearList()

    'Process the loop while intRandomNumber < 15
    Do While intRandomNumber < 15
        'Get a random number between 0 and 24
        intRandomNumber = objRandom.Next(25)
        'Add the number to the list
        lstData.Items.Add(intRandomNumber.ToString)
    Loop
End Sub
```

3.   Run the project and click the Do While Loop button. You'll see something similar to the results shown in Figure 4-22.

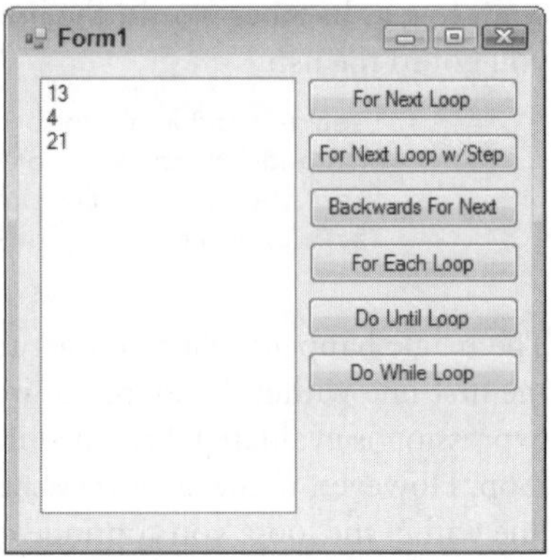

How It Works

Every time you press the button, the loop executes as long as the random number generator produces a number less than 15.

A Do While ... Loop keeps running as long as the given expression remains True. As soon as the expression becomes False, the loop quits. When you start the loop, you check to ensure that intRandomNumber is less than 15. If it is, the expression returns True, and you can run the code within the loop:

FIGURE 4-22

```
'Process the loop while intRandomNumber < 15
Do While intRandomNumber < 15
    'Get a random number between 0 and 24
    intRandomNumber = objRandom.Next(25)
    'Add the number to the list
    lstData.Items.Add(intRandomNumber.ToString)
Loop
```

Again, when you get to the Loop statement, Visual Basic 2010 moves back up to the Do While statement. When it gets there, it evaluates the expression again. If it's True, you run the code inside the loop once more. If it's False (because intRandomNumber is greater than or equal to 15), you continue with the first line after Loop, effectively quitting the loop.

Acceptable Expressions for a Do ... Loop

You might be wondering what kind of expressions you can use with the two variations of Do ... Loop. If you can use it with an If statement, then you can use it with a Do ... Loop. For example, you can write this:

```
Do While intX > 10 And intX < 100
```

or

```
Do Until (intX > 10 And intX < 100) Or intY = True
```

or

```
Do While String.Compare(strA, strB) > 0
```

In short, it's a pretty powerful loop!

Other Versions of the Do ... Loop

It's possible to put the Until or While statements after Loop, rather than after Do. Consider these two loops:

```
Do While intX < 3
    intX += 1
Loop
```

and

```
Do
```

```
        intX += 1
    Loop While intX < 3
```

At first glance, it looks like the `While intX < 3` has just been moved around. You might think that these two loops are equivalent — but there's a subtle difference. Suppose the value of `intX` is greater than 3 (such as 4) when these two `Do` loops start. The first loop will not run at all. However, the second loop will run *once*. When the `Loop While intX < 3` line is executed, the loop will be exited. This happens despite the condition saying that `intX` must be less than 3.

Now consider these two `Do Until` loops:

```
    Do Until intX = 3
        intX += 1
    Loop
```

and

```
    Do
        intX += 1
    Loop Until intX = 3
```

Again, although at first glance it looks like these two loops are equivalent, they're not; and they behave slightly differently. Let's say that `intX` is 3 this time. The first loop isn't going to run, as `intX` already meets the exit condition for this loop. However, the second loop will run *once*. Then, when you execute `Loop Until intX = 3` the first time, `intX` is now 4, so you go back to the start of the loop and increment `intX` to 5, and so on. In fact, this is a classic example of an *infinite loop* (discussed later in this chapter) and will not stop.

> **NOTE** When you use `Loop While` or `Loop Until`, you are saying that, no matter what, you want the loop to execute at least once. In general, it's best to stick with `Do While` and `Do Until`, rather than use `Loop While` and `Loop Until`.

You may also come across a variation of `Do While ... Loop` called `While ... End While`. This convention is a throwback to previous versions of Visual Basic, but old-school developers may still use it with .NET code, so it's important that you can recognize it. These two are equivalent, but you should use the first one:

```
    Do While intX < 3
        intX += 1
    Loop
```

and

```
    While intX < 3
        intX += 1
    End While
```

Nested Loops

You might need to start a loop even though you're already working through another loop. This is known as *nesting,* and it's similar in theory to the nesting demonstrated when you looked at `If` statements.

TRY IT OUT Using Nested Loops

Code file Loops.zip available for download at Wrox.com

In this Try It Out, you'll see how you can create and run through a loop, even though you're already working through another one.

1. In the Forms Designer, add another Button control to your form and set its Name property to **btnNestedLoops** and its Text property to **Nested Loops**.

2. Double-click the button and add the following bolded code to its Click event handler:

```
Private Sub btnNestedLoops_Click(ByVal sender As System.Object, _
    ByVal e As System.EventArgs) Handles btnNestedLoops.Click

    'Clear the list
    ClearList()

    'Process an outer loop
    For intOuterLoop As Integer = 1 To 2
        'Process a nested (inner) loop
        For intInnerLoop As Integer = 1 To 3
            lstData.Items.Add(intOuterLoop.ToString & _
                ", " & intInnerLoop.ToString)
        Next
    Next
End Sub
```

3. Run the program and click the Nested Loops button. You should see results that look like those shown in Figure 4-23.

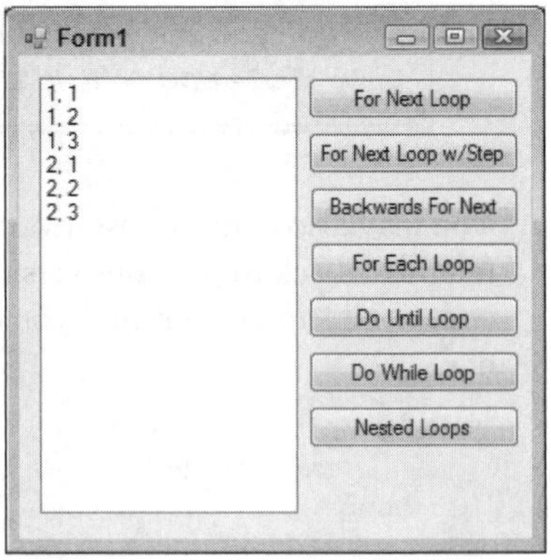

How It Works

This code is really quite simple. Your first loop (outer loop) iterates intOuterLoop from 1 to 2, and the nested loop (inner loop) iterates intInnerLoop from 1 to 3. Within the nested loop, you have a line of code to display the current values of intOuterLoop and intInnerLoop:

```
'Process an outer loop
For intOuterLoop As Integer = 1 To 2
    'Process a nested (inner) loop
    For intInnerLoop As Integer = 1 To 3
        lstData.Items.Add(intOuterLoop.ToString & _
            ", " & intInnerLoop.ToString)
    Next
Next
```

FIGURE 4-23

Each For statement must be paired with a Next statement, and each Next statement that you reach always "belongs" to the last created For statement. In this case, the first Next statement you reach is for the 1 To 3 loop, which results in intInnerLoop being incremented. When the value of intInnerLoop gets to be 4, you exit the inner loop.

After you've quit the inner loop, you hit another Next statement. This statement belongs to the first For statement, so intOuterLoop is set to 2 and you move back to the first line within the first, outer loop — in this case, the other For statement. Once there, the inner loop starts once more. Although in this Try It Out you've seen two For ... Next loops nested together, you can nest Do ... While loops and even mix them, so you can have two Do ... Loop statements nested inside a For loop and vice versa.

Quitting Early

Sometimes you don't want to see a loop through to its natural conclusion. For example, you might be looking through a list for something specific, and when you find it, there's no need to go through the remainder of the list.

TRY IT OUT Quitting a Loop Early

Code file Loops.zip available for download at Wrox.com

In this Try It Out, you'll look through folders on your local drive, but this time, when you get to c:\Program Files, you'll display a message and quit.

1. Return to the Forms Designer, add another Button control to your form, and set its Name property to **btnQuittingAForLoop** and its Text property to **Quitting A For Loop**.

2. Double-click the button and add the following bolded code to the Click event handler:

```
Private Sub btnQuittingAForLoop_Click(ByVal sender As System.Object, _
    ByVal e As System.EventArgs) Handles btnQuittingAForLoop.Click

        'Clear the list
        ClearList()

        'List each folder at the root of your C drive
        For Each strFolder As String In _
            My.Computer.FileSystem.GetDirectories("C:\")

            'Add the item to the list
            lstData.Items.Add(strFolder)

            'Do you have the folder C:\Program Files?
            If String.Compare(strFolder, "c:\program files", True) = 0 Then

                'Tell the user MessageBox.Show("Found it, exiting the loop now.", "Loops")

                'Quit the loop early
                Exit For

            End If
        Next
End Sub
```

3. Run the program and click the Quitting a For Loop button. You'll see something similar to the results shown in Figure 4-24.

How It Works

This time, with each iteration, you use the `String.Compare` method that was discussed earlier to check the name of the folder to see whether it matches `C:\Program Files`:

```
'Do you have the folder C:\Program Files?
If String.Compare(strFolder, "c:\program files", True) = 0 Then
```

If it does, then the first thing you do is display a message box:

```
'Tell the user
MessageBox.Show("Found it, exiting the loop now.", "Loops")
```

After the user has clicked OK to dismiss the message box, you use the `Exit For` statement to quit the loop. In this instance, the loop is short-circuited, and Visual Basic 2010 moves to the first line after the `Next` statement:

```
'Quit the loop early
Exit For
```

Of course, if the name of the folder doesn't match the one you're looking for, you keep looping. Using loops to find an item in a list is one of their most common uses. Once you've found the item you're looking for, using the `Exit For` statement to short-circuit the loop is a very easy way to improve the performance of your application. The `Exit For` statement will only exit one loop at a time so if you are nesting loops be sure to exit the correct one.

Imagine you have a list of a thousand items to look through. You find the item you're looking for on the

FIGURE 4-24

tenth iteration. If you don't quit the loop after you've found the item, you're effectively asking the computer to look through another 990 useless items. If, however, you do quit the loop early, you can move on and start running another part of the algorithm.

Quitting Do . . . Loops

As you might have guessed, you can quit a `Do . . . Loop` in more or less the same way, as you see in the next Try It Out.

TRY IT OUT   Quitting a Do . . . Loop

Code file Loops.zip available for download at Wrox.com

In this example, you will use `Exit Do` to quit a `Do . . . Loop`.

1. Return to the Forms Designer one last time and add another Button control to your form. Set its Name property to **btnQuittingADoLoop** and its Text property to **Quitting a Do Loop**.

2. Double-click the button and add the following bolded code to the Click event handler:

```
Private Sub btnQuittingADoLoop_Click(ByVal sender As System.Object, _
    ByVal e As System.EventArgs) Handles btnQuittingADoLoop.Click

        'Declare variable
        Dim intCount As Integer = 0

        'Clear the list
        ClearList()

        'Process the loop
        Do While intCount < 10

            'Add the item to the list
            lstData.Items.Add(intCount.ToString)

            'Increment the count by 1
            intCount += 1

            'Should you quit the loop
            If intCount = 3 Then

                Exit Do
            End If

        Loop
End Sub
```

3. Run the project and click the Quitting a Do Loop button. You'll see a list containing the values 0, 1, and 2.

How It Works

In this case, because you're in a Do ... Loop, you have to use Exit Do, rather than Exit For. However, the principle is exactly the same. Exit Do will work with both the Do While ... Loop and Do Until ... Loop loops.

Infinite Loops

When building loops, you can create something called an *infinite loop*. This is a loop that, once started, will never finish. Consider this code:

```
Dim intX As Integer = 0
Do
    intX += 1
Loop Until intX = 0
```

This loop will start and run through the first iteration. Then, when you execute Loop Until intX = 0 the first time, intX is 1. Therefore, you return to the start of the loop again and increment intX to 2, and so on. What's important here is that it will never get to 0. The loop becomes infinite, and the program won't crash (at least not instantly), but it may well become unresponsive.

When you suspect a program has dropped into an infinite loop, you need to force the program to stop. If you are running your program in Visual Studio 2010, flip over to it, and select Debug ⇨ Stop Debugging from the menu. This will immediately stop the program. If you are running your compiled program, you'll need to use the Windows Task Manager. Press Ctrl+Alt+Del and select Task Manager. Your program should appear as Not Responding. Select your program in the Task Manager and click End Task. Eventually this opens a dialog indicating that the program is not responding (which you knew already) and asking whether you want to kill the program stone dead, so click End Task again.

In some extreme cases, the loop can take up so much processing power or other system resources that you won't be able to open Task Manager or flip over to Visual Studio. In these cases, you can persevere and try to use either of these methods; or you can reset your computer and chalk it up to experience.

Visual Studio 2010 does not automatically save your project before running the application the first time, so you're likely to lose all of your program code if you have to reset. Therefore, it would be wise to save your project before you start running your code.

SUMMARY

This chapter took a detailed look at the various ways that programs can make decisions and loop through code. You first saw the alternative operators that can be used with If statements and examined how multiple operators can be combined by using the And and Or keywords. Additionally, you examined how case-insensitive string comparisons could be performed.

You then looked at Select Case, an efficient technique for choosing one outcome out of a group of possibilities. Next you examined the concept of looping within a program and were introduced to the two main types of loops: For loops and Do loops. For loops iterate a given number of times, and the derivative For Each loop can be used to loop automatically through a list of items in a collection. Do While loops iterate while a given condition remains True, whereas Do Until loops iterate until a given condition becomes True.

In summary, you should know how to use:

➤   If, ElseIf, and Else statements to test for multiple conditions

➤   Nested If statements

➤   Comparison operators and the String.Compare method

➤   The Select Case statement to perform multiple comparisons

➤   For ... Next and For ... Each loops

➤   Do ... Loop and Do While ... Loop statements

EXERCISES

1. When using a `Select Case` statement, how do you allow for multiple items in the `Case` statement?

2. What is the difference between a `Do Until` and a `Loop Until Do` loop?

3. Is "Bryan" and "BRYAN" the same string as Visual Basic sees it?

4. When you use the `string.compare` method, what is the last parameter (a Boolean parameter) used for?

5. In a `Select Case` statement, how do you put in a catch all case for items that do not have a match?

6. When writing a `For Each` Loop, how do you have the loop iterate backwards?

7. What keyword do you use to exit a loop early?

▶ **WHAT YOU HAVE LEARNED IN THIS CHAPTER**

TOPIC	CONCEPTS
Comparison Operators	To compare items, you can use the following operators: >, >=, <, <=, =, <>, And, Or.
Using `If`	Use `If` statements to make decisions. For multiple decisions, you can also use `If ... Else` or `ElseIf`. You can nest `If ... Else` statements for more complex decisions. For simple decisions, you can even use a single-line If statement.
Using `Select Case`	Use `Select Case` to test an item for one of many possible values. To make sure you find a match, use the `Case Else` statement.
Using `For Loops`	Use `For Loops` to execute tasks for a certain number of times. The statement `Exit For` is used to quit a `For Loop`.
Using `Do Loops`	Use `Do Loops` to execute tasks while or until a condition is reached. The statement `Exit Do` is used to quit a `Do Loop`.

5

Working with Data Structures

WHAT YOU WILL LEARN IN THIS CHAPTER:

➤   Using Arrays

➤   Working with Enumerations

➤   Using Constants

➤   Working with Structures

In the previous chapters, you worked with simple data types — namely, `Integer` and `String` variables. Although these data types are useful in their own right, more complex programs call for working with *data structures* — that is, groups of data elements that are organized in a single unit. In this chapter, you learn about the various data structures available in Visual Basic 2010. You also will see some ways in which you can work with complex sets of data. Finally, you learn how you can build powerful collection classes for working with, maintaining, and manipulating lists of complex data.

UNDERSTANDING ARRAYS

A fairly common requirement in writing software is the need to hold lists of similar or related data. You can provide this functionality by using an *array*. Arrays are just lists of data that have a single data type. For example, you might want to store a list of your friends' ages in an integer array or their names in a string array.

This section explains how to define, populate, and use arrays in your applications.

Defining and Using Arrays

When you define an array, you're actually creating a variable that has more than one dimension. For example, if you define a variable as a string, you can only hold a single string value in it:

```
Dim strName As String
```

However, with an array you create a kind of multiplier effect with a variable, so you can hold more than one value in a single variable. An array is defined by entering the size of the array after the variable name. For example, if you wanted to define a string array with 10 elements, you'd do this:

```
Dim strName(9) As String
```

> **NOTE** *The reason why you use* `(9)` *instead of* `(10)` *to get an array with 10 elements is explained in detail later. The basic explanation is simply that because numbering in an array starts at zero, the first element in an array is zero, the second element is one, and so on.*

When you have an array, you can access individual elements in it by providing an index value between 0 and a maximum possible value — this maximum possible value happens to be one less than the total size of the array.

For example, to set the element with index 2 in the array, you'd do this:

```
strName(2) = "Katie"
```

To get that same element back again, you'd do this:

```
MessageBox.Show(strName(2))
```

What's important is that other elements in the array are unaffected when you set their siblings, so if you do this:

```
strName(3) = "Betty"
```

`strName(2)` remains set to `"Katie"`.

TRY IT OUT   **Defining and Using a Simple Array**

Code file Array Demo.zip is available for download at Wrox.com

Perhaps the easiest way to understand what an array looks like and how it works is to write some code.

1. In Visual Studio 2010, click File ⇨ New Project. In the New Project dialog, create a new Windows Forms Application called **Array Demo**.

2. When the Designer for Form1 appears, add a ListBox control to the form. Using the Properties window set its `Name` property to **lstFriends** and its `IntegralHeight` property to `False`.

3. Add a Button control to the form. Set its `Name` property to **btnArrayElement** and set its `Text` property to **Array Element**. Arrange your controls so that your form looks similar to Figure 5-1, as you'll be adding more Button controls to this project later.

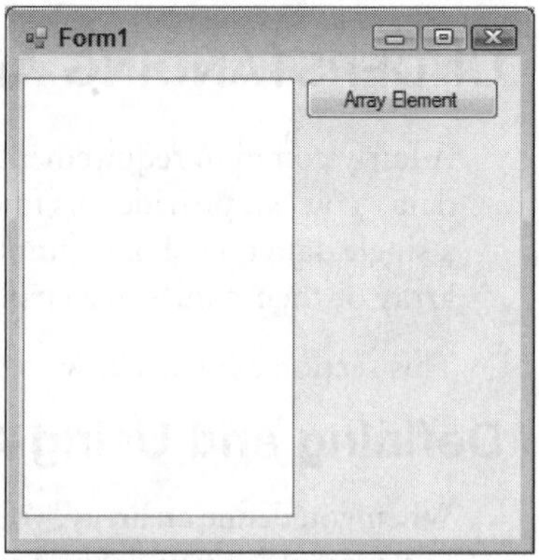

FIGURE 5-1

4. Double-click the button and add the following bolded code to its `Click` event handler. You'll receive an error message that the `ClearList` procedure is not defined. You can ignore this error because you'll be adding that procedure in the next step:

```
Private Sub btnArrayElement_Click(ByVal sender As System.Object, _
            ByVal e As System.EventArgs) Handles btnArrayElement.Click

        'Clear the list
        ClearList()

        'Declare an array
        Dim strFriends(4) As String

        'Populate the array
        strFriends(0) = "Wendy"
        strFriends(1) = "Harriet"
        strFriends(2) = "Jay"
        strFriends(3) = "Michelle"
        strFriends(4) = "Richard"

        'Add the first array item to the list
        lstFriends.Items.Add(strFriends(0))
    End Sub
```

5. Now create the following procedure:

```
Private Sub ClearList()
    'Clear the list
    lstFriends.Items.Clear()
End Sub
```

6. Save your project by clicking the Save All button on the toolbar and then run it. When the form displays, click the Array Element button. The list box on your form will be *populated* with the name `Wendy`.

How It Works

In this example, you clear the list box by calling the `ClearList` method. Although the list is empty at this point, you'll be adding more buttons to this project in the following Try It Out exercises, and may want to compare the results of the each of the buttons:

```
'Clear the list
ClearList()
```

When you define an array, you have to specify a data type and a size. In this case, you're specifying an array of type `String` and defining an array size of 5. Recall that the way the size is defined is a little quirky. You have to specify a number one less than the final size you want (more on that shortly). Therefore, here you have used the following line:

```
'Declare an array
Dim strFriends(4) As String
```

This way, you end up with an array of size 5. Another way of expressing this is to say that you have an array consisting of 5 *elements*.

When you are done, you have your array, and you can access each item in the array by using an *index*. The index is given as a number in parentheses after the name of the array. Indexes begin at zero and go up to one less than the number of items in the array. The following example sets all five possible items in the array to the names:

```
'Populate the array
strFriends(0) = "Wendy"
strFriends(1) = "Harriet"
strFriends(2) = "Jay"
strFriends(3) = "Michelle"
strFriends(4) = "Richard"
```

Just as you can use an index to set the items in an array, you can use an index to get items back out. In this case, you're asking for the item at position 0, which returns the first item in the array — namely, Wendy:

```
'Add the first array item to the list
lstFriends.Items.Add(strFriends(0))
```

The reason why the indexes and sizes seem skewed is that the indexes are zero-based, whereas humans tend to number things beginning at 1. When putting items into or retrieving items from an array, you have to adjust the position you want down by one to get the actual index; for example, the fifth item is actually at position 4, the first item is at position 0, and so on. When you define an array, you do not actually specify the size of the array but rather the upper *index bound* — that is, the highest possible value of the index that the array will support.

> **NOTE** *Why should the indexes be zero-based? Remember that to the computer, a variable represents the address of a location in the computer's memory. Given an array index, Visual Basic 2010 just multiplies the index by the size of one element and adds the product to the address of the array as a whole to get the address of the specified element. The starting address of the array is also the starting address of the first element in it. That is, the first element is zero times the size of an element away from the start of the whole array; the second element is 1 times the size of an element away from the start of the whole array; and so on.*

The method you define contains only one line of code but its reuse becomes apparent in the next Try It Out. This method merely clears the `Items` collection of the list box.

```
Private Sub ClearList()
    'Clear the list
    lstFriends.Items.Clear()
End Sub
```

Using For Each . . . Next

One common way to work with arrays is by using a `For Each..Next` loop. This loop was introduced in Chapter 4, when you used it with a string collection returned from the `My.Computer.FileSystem.GetDirectories` method.

TRY IT OUT   **Using For Each . . . Next with an Array**

Code file Array Demo.zip is available for download at Wrox.com

This Try It Out demonstrates how you use For Each..Next with an array.

1. Close your program if it is still running and open the Code Editor for Form1. Add the following bolded variable declaration at the top of your form class:

```
Public Class Form1
    'Declare a form level array
    Private strFriends(4) As String
```

2. In the Class Name combo box at the top left of your Code Editor, select (Form1 Events). In the Method Name combo box at the top right of your Code Editor, select the Load event. This causes the Form1_Load event handler to be inserted into your code. Add the following bolded code to this procedure:

```
Private Sub Form1_Load(ByVal sender As Object, _
    ByVal e As System.EventArgs) Handles Me.Load

    'Populate the array
    strFriends(0) = "Wendy"
    strFriends(1) = "Harriet"
    strFriends(2) = "Jay"
    strFriends(3) = "Michelle"
    strFriends(4) = "Richard"
End Sub
```

3. Switch to the Forms Designer and add another Button control. Set its Name property to **btn EnumerateArray** and its Text property to **Enumerate Array**.

4. Double-click this new button and add the following bolded code to its Click event handler:

```
Private Sub btnEnumerateArray_Click(ByVal sender As System.Object, _
    ByVal e As System.EventArgs) Handles btnEnumerateArray.Click

    'Clear the list
    ClearList()

    'Enumerate the array
    For Each strName As String In strFriends
        'Add the array item to the list
        lstFriends.Items.Add(strName)
    Next
End Sub
```

5. Run the project and click the button. You'll see results like those in Figure 5-2.

FIGURE 5-2

How It Works

You start this exercise by declaring an array variable that is local to the form, meaning the variable is available to all procedures in the form class. Whenever variables are declared outside a method in the form class, they are available to all methods in the form:

```
'Declare a form level array
Private strFriends(4) As String
```

Next you added the `Load` event handler for the form and then added code to populate the array. This procedure will be called whenever the form loads, ensuring that your array always gets populated:

```
Private Sub Form1_Load(ByVal sender As Object, _
    ByVal e As System.EventArgs) Handles Me.Load

    'Populate the array
    strFriends(0) = "Wendy"
    strFriends(1) = "Harriet"
    strFriends(2) = "Jay"
    strFriends(3) = "Michelle"
    strFriends(4) = "Richard"
End Sub
```

Chapter 4 shows the `For Each..Next` loop iterate through a string collection; in this example, it is used in an array. The principle is similar; you create a control variable that is of the same type as an element in the array and give this to the loop when it starts. This has all been done in one line of code. The control variable, `strName`, is declared and used in the `For Each` statement by using the `As String` keyword.

The internals behind the loop move through the array starting at element 0 until reaching the last element. For each iteration, you can examine the value of the control variable and do something with it; in this case, you add the name to the list:

```
'Enumerate the array
For Each strName As String In strFriends
    'Add the array item to the list
    lstFriends.Items.Add(strName)
Next
```

Note that the items are added to the list in the same order that they appear in the array. That's because `For Each..Next` proceeds from the first item to the last item as each item is defined.

Passing Arrays As Parameters

It's extremely useful to be able to pass an array (which could be a list of values) to a function as a parameter.

TRY IT OUT   Passing Arrays As Parameters

Code file Array Demo.zip is available for download at Wrox.com

In this Try It Out, you'll look at how to pass an array to a function as a parameter.

1. Return to the Forms Designer in the Array Demo project and add another Button control. Set its `Name` property to **btnArraysAsParameters** and its `Text` property to **Arrays as Parameters**.

2. Double-click the button and add the following bolded code to its `Click` event handler. You'll receive an error message that the `AddItemsToList` procedure is not defined. You can ignore this error because you'll be adding that procedure in the next step:

```
Private Sub btnArraysAsParameters_Click(ByVal sender As System.Object, _
    ByVal e As System.EventArgs) Handles btnArraysAsParameters.Click
```

```
      'Clear the list
      ClearList()

      'List your friends
      AddItemsToList(strFriends)
   End Sub
```

3. Add the `AddItemsToList` procedure as follows:

```
Private Sub AddItemsToList(ByVal arrayList() As String)
    'Enumerate the array
    For Each strName As String In arrayList
        'Add the array item to the list
        lstFriends.Items.Add(strName)
    Next
End Sub
```

4. Run the project and click the button. You'll see the same results that were shown in Figure 5-2.

How It Works

The trick here is to tell the `AddItemsToList` method that the parameter it's expecting is an array of type `String`. You do this by using empty parentheses, like this:

```
Sub AddItemsToList(ByVal arrayList() As String)
```

If you specify an array but don't define a size (or upper-bound value), you're telling Visual Basic 2010 that you don't know or care how big the array is. That means you can pass an array of any size through to `AddItemsToList`. In the `btnArraysAsParameters_Click` procedure, you're sending your original array:

```
'List your friends AddItemsToList(strFriends)
```

TRY IT OUT   Adding More Friends

Code file Array Demo.zip is available for download at Wrox.com

What happens if you define another array of a different size? In this Try It Out, you'll see.

1. Return to the Forms Designer of the Array Demo project. Add another Button control and set its `Name` property to **btnMoreArrayParameters** and its `Text` property to **More Array Parameters**.

2. Double-click the button and add the following bolded code to its `Click` event handler:

```
Private Sub btnMoreArrayParameters_Click(ByVal sender As System.Object, _
    ByVal e As System.EventArgs) Handles btnMoreArrayParameters.Click

    'Clear the list
    ClearList()

    'Declare an array
    Dim strMoreFriends(1) As String

    'Populate the array
    strMoreFriends(0) = "Elaine"
    strMoreFriends(1) = "Debra"
```

```
          'List your friends
          AddItemsToList(strFriends)
          AddItemsToList(strMoreFriends)
      End Sub
```

3. Run the project and click the button. You will see the form shown in Figure 5-3.

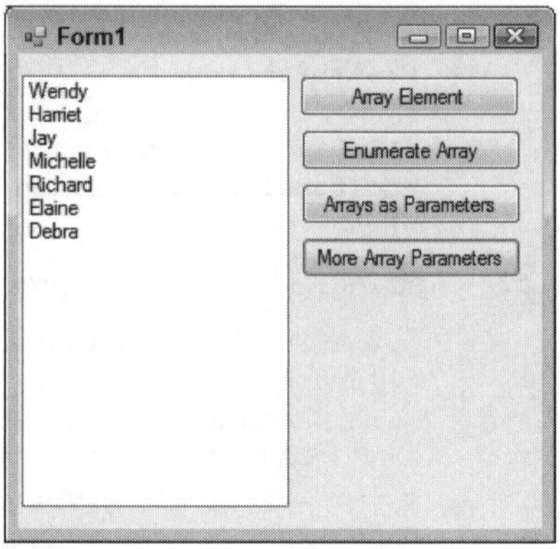

How It Works

What you have done here is prove that the array you pass as a parameter does not have to be of a fixed size. You created a new array of size 2 and passed it through to the same `AddItemsToList` function.

As you're writing code, you can tell whether a parameter is an array type by looking for empty parentheses in the IntelliSense pop-up box, as illustrated in Figure 5-4.

FIGURE 5-3

```
'List your frie...
AddItemsToList( Common  All
AddItemsToList(
 AddItemsToList(arrayList() As String)
```

FIGURE 5-4

> **NOTE** *Not only are you informed that `arrayList` is an array type, but you also see that the data type of the array is `String`.*

Sorting Arrays

It is sometimes useful to be able to sort an array. You may find this useful when you display data to the user in a manner they can easily search or when you need to evaluate data logically.

TRY IT OUT   Sorting Arrays

Code file Array Demo.zip is available for download at Wrox.com

This Try It Out demonstrates how you can sort an array alphabetically.

1. Return to the Forms Designer in the Array Demo project and add another Button control. Set its `Name` property to **btnSortingArrays** and its `Text` property to **Sorting Arrays.**

2. Double-click the button and add the following bolded code to its `Click` event handler:

```
Private Sub btnSortingArrays_Click(ByVal sender As System.Object, _
    ByVal e As System.EventArgs) Handles btnSortingArrays.Click

    'Clear the list
    ClearList()

    'Sort the array
    Array.Sort(strFriends)
```

```
        'List your friends
        AddItemsToList(strFriends)
    End Sub
```

3. Run the project and click the button. You'll see the list box on your form populated with the names from your array sorted alphabetically.

How It Works

All arrays are internally implemented in a class called `System.Array`. In this case, you use a method called `Sort` on that class. The `Sort` method takes a single parameter — namely, the array you want to sort. The method then does what its name suggests, sorting it for you into an order appropriate to the data type of the array elements. In this case you are using a string array, so you get an alphanumeric sort. If you were to attempt to use this technique on an array containing integer or floating-point values, the array would be sorted in numeric order.

```
    'Sort the array
    Array.Sort(strFriends)
```

The capability to pass different parameter types in different calls to the same method name and to get behavior that is appropriate to the parameter types actually passed is called *method overloading.* `Sort` is referred to as an overloaded method.

Going Backwards

`For Each ... Next` will go through an array in only one direction. It starts at position 0 and loops through to the end of the array. If you want to go through an array backwards (from the length −1 position to 0), you have two options.

One, you can step through the loop backwards by using a standard `For ... Next` loop to start at the upper index bound of the first dimension in the array and work your way to 0 using the `Step -1` keyword, as shown in the following example:

```
    For intIndex As Integer = strFriends.GetUpperBound(0) To 0 Step -1
        'Add the array item to the list
        lstFriends.Items.Add(strFriends(intIndex))
    Next
```

Alternately, you can call the `Reverse` method on the `Array` class to reverse the order of the array and then use your `For Each ... Next` loop

TRY IT OUT **Reversing an Array**

Code file Array Demo.zip is available for download at Wrox.com

This Try It Out shows you how to call the `Reverse` method on the `Array` class to reverse the order of an array.

1. Return to the Forms Designer and add another Button control. Set its `Name` property to **btn ReversingAnArray** and its `Text` property to **Reversing an Array**.

2. Double-click the button and add the following bolded code to its `Click` event handler:

```
Private Sub btnReversingAnArray_Click(ByVal sender As System.Object, _

    ByVal e As System.EventArgs) Handles btnReversingAnArray.Click


    'Clear the list
    ClearList()

    'Reverse the order — elements will be in
        descending order
    Array.Reverse(strFriends)

    'List your friends
    AddItemsToList(strFriends)
End Sub
```

3. Run the project and click the button. You'll see the friends listed in reverse order, as shown in Figure 5-5.

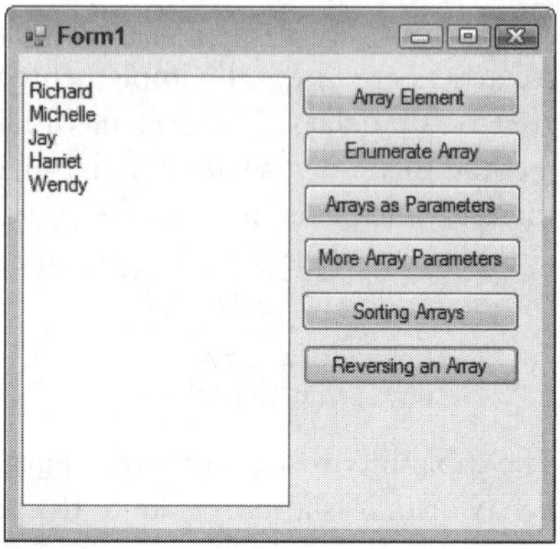

How It Works

FIGURE 5-5

The `Reverse` method reverses the order of elements in a one-dimensional array, which is what you are working with here. By passing the `strFriends` array to the `Reverse` method, you are asking the `Reverse` method to re-sequence the array from bottom to top:

```
'Reverse the order — elements will be in descending order
Array.Reverse(strFriends)
```

After the items in your array have been reversed, you simply call the `AddItemsToList` procedure to have the items listed:

```
'List your friends
AddItemsToList(strFriends)
```

> **NOTE** *If you want to list your array in descending sorted order, you would call the* `Sort` *method on the* `Array` *class to have the items sorted in ascending order and then call the* `Reverse` *method to have the sorted array reversed, putting it into descending order.*

Initializing Arrays with Values

It is possible to create an array in Visual Basic 2010 and populate it in one line of code, rather than having to write multiple lines of code to declare and populate the array, as shown here:

```
'Declare an array
Dim strFriends(4) As String

'Populate the array
strFriends(0) = "Wendy"
```

```
strFriends(1) = "Harriet"
strFriends(2) = "Jay"
strFriends(3) = "Michelle"
strFriends(4) = "Richard"
```

TRY IT OUT   Initializing Arrays with Values

Code file Array Demo.zip is available for download at Wrox.com

---

You learn more about initializing arrays with values in this Try It Out.

1.   Return to the Forms Designer in the Array Demo project and add one last Button control. Set its
Name property to **btnInitializingArraysWithValues** and its Text property to **Initializing Arrays with
Values.**

2.   Double-click the button and add the following bolded code to its Click event handler:

```
Private Sub btnInitializingArraysWithValues_Click( _
    ByVal sender As System.Object, ByVal e As System.EventArgs) _
    Handles btnInitializingArraysWithValues.Click

    'Clear the list
    ClearList()

    'Declare and populate an array
    Dim strMyFriends() As String = {"Elaine", "Richard", "Debra", _
        "Wendy", "Harriet"}
    'List your friends
    AddItemsToList(strMyFriends)
End Sub
```

3.   Run the project and click the button. Your list box will be populated with the friends listed in this
array.

How It Works

The pair of braces ({}) allows you to set the values that should be held in an array directly. In this instance,
you have five values to enter into the array, separated with commas. Note that when you do this, you
don't specify an upper bound for the array; instead, you use empty parentheses. Visual Basic 2010 prefers
to calculate the upper bound for you based on the values you supply:

```
'Declare and populate an array
Dim strMyFriends() As String = {"Elaine", "Richard", "Debra", _
    "Wendy", "Harriet"}
```

This technique can be quite awkward to use when populating large arrays. If your program relies on
populating large arrays, you might want to use the method illustrated earlier: specifying the positions and
the values. This is especially true when populating an array with values that change at runtime.

UNDERSTANDING ENUMERATIONS

So far, the variables you've seen had virtually no limitations on the kinds of data you can store in
them. Technical limits notwithstanding, if you have a variable defined As Integer, you can put any
number you like in it. The same holds true for String and Double. You have seen another variable

type, however, that has only two possible values: Boolean variables can be either True or False and nothing else.

Often, when writing code, you want to limit the possible values that can be stored in a variable. For example, if you have a variable that stores the number of doors that a car has, do you really want to be able to store the value 163,234?

Using Enumerations

Enumerations enable you to build a new type of variable, based on one of these data types: Integer, Long, Short, or Byte. This variable can be set to one value of a set of possible values that you define, ideally preventing someone from supplying invalid values. It is used to provide clarity in the code, as it can describe a particular value.

TRY IT OUT   **Using Enumerations**

Code file Enum Demo.zip is available for download at Wrox.com

In this Try It Out, you'll look at how to build an application that checks the time of day and, based on that, can record a DayAction of one of the following possible values:

➤ Asleep

➤ Getting ready for work

➤ Traveling to work

➤ At work

➤ At lunch

➤ Traveling from work

➤ Relaxing with friends

➤ Getting ready for bed

1.   Create a new Windows Forms application in Visual Studio 2010 called **Enum Demo**.

2.   Set the Text property of Form1 to **What's Richard Doing?**

3.   Now add a DateTimePicker control and set the following properties:

➤ Set Name to **dtpHour**.

➤ Set Format to **Time**.

➤ Set ShowUpDown to **True**.

➤ Set Value to **01:00 am**. VS will add the current date in the property to the time.

➤ Set Size to **90, 20**.

4.   Add a Label control to the form, setting its Name property to **lblState** and its Text property to **State Not Initialized**. Resize your form so it looks similar to Figure 5-6.

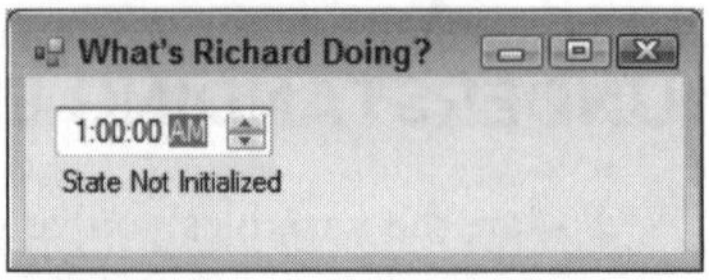

FIGURE 5-6

5. View the Code Editor for the form by right-clicking the form and choosing View Code from the context menu. At the top of the class add the following bolded enumeration:

```
Public Class Form1

    'DayAction Enumeration
    Private Enum DayAction As Integer
        Asleep = 0
        GettingReadyForWork = 1
        TravelingToWork = 2
        AtWork = 3
        AtLunch = 4
        TravelingFromWork = 5
        RelaxingWithFriends = 6
        GettingReadyForBed = 7
    End Enum
```

6. With an enumeration defined, you can create new member variables that use the enumeration as their data type. Add this member:

```
'Declare variable
Private CurrentState As DayAction
```

7. Add the following code below the variable you just added:

```
'Hour property
Private Property Hour() As Integer
    Get
        'Return the current hour displayed
        Return dtpHour.Value.Hour
    End Get
    Set(ByVal value As Integer)
        'Set the date using the hour passed to this property
        dtpHour.Value = _
            New Date(Now.Year, Now.Month, Now.Day, value, 0, 0)
        'Set the display text
        lblState.Text = "At " & value & ":00, Richard is "
    End Set
End Property
```

8. In the Class Name combo box at the top of the Code Editor, select (Form1 Events), and in the Method Name combo box, select the Load event. Add the following bolded code to the event handler:

```
Private Sub Form1_Load(ByVal sender As System.Object, _
    ByVal e As System.EventArgs) Handles MyBase.Load

    'Set the Hour property to the current hour
    Me.Hour = Now.Hour
End Sub
```

9. In the Class Name combo box at the top of the Code Editor, select **dtpHour**, and in the Method Name combo box, select the ValueChanged event. Add the following bolded code to the event handler:

```
Private Sub dtpHour_ValueChanged(ByVal sender As Object, _
    ByVal e As System.EventArgs) Handles dtpHour.ValueChanged
```

```
        'Update the Hour property
        Me.Hour = dtpHour.Value.Hour
    End Sub
```

10. Save your project and then run it. You will be able to click the up and down arrows in the DateTimePicker control and see the text updated to reflect the hour selected, as shown in Figure 5-7.

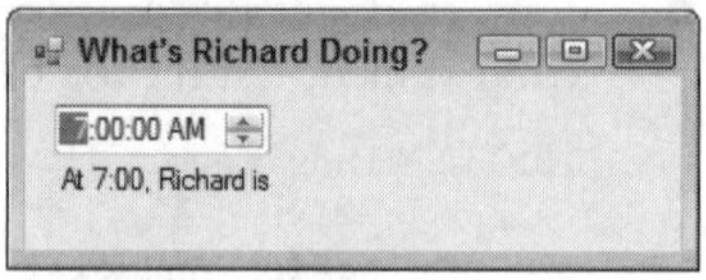

FIGURE 5-7

How It Works

In this application, the user will be able to use the DateTimePicker to choose the hour. The program then looks at the hour and determines which one of the eight states Richard is in at the given time. To achieve this, you have to keep the hour around somehow. To store the hour, you have created a property for the form in addition to the properties it already has, such as `Name` and `Text`. The new property is called `Hour`, and it is used to set the current hour in the DateTimePicker control and the Label control. The property is defined with a `Property.End Property` statement:

```
Private Property Hour() As Integer
    Get
        'Return the current hour displayed
        Return dtpHour.Value.Hour
    End Get
    Set(ByVal value As Integer)
        'Set the date using the hour passed to this property
        dtpHour.Value = _
            New Date(Now.Year, Now.Month, Now.Day, value, 0, 0)
        'Set the display text
        lblState.Text = "At " & value & ":00, Richard is "
    End Set
End Property
```

Note the `Get.End Get` and `Set.End Set` blocks inside the `Property.End Property` statement. The `Get` block contains a `Return` statement and is called automatically to return the property value when the property name appears in an expression. The data type to be returned is not specified in the `Get` statement because it was already declared `As Integer` in the `Property` statement. The `Set` block is called automatically when the value is set, such as by putting the property name to the left of an equals sign.

When the application starts, you set the `Hour` property to the current hour on your computer. You get this information from `Now`, a `Date` variable containing the current date and time:

```
Private Sub Form1_Load(ByVal sender As System.Object, _
    ByVal e As System.EventArgs) Handles MyBase.Load

    'Set the Hour property to the current hour
    Me.Hour = Now.Hour
End Sub
```

You also set the `Hour` property when the `Value` property changes in the DateTimePicker control:

```
Private Sub dtpHour_ValueChanged(ByVal sender As Object, _
    ByVal e As System.EventArgs) Handles dtpHour.ValueChanged

    'Update the Hour property
    Me.Hour = dtpHour.Value.Hour
End Sub
```

When the `Hour` property is set, you have to update the value of the DateTimePicker control to show the new hour value, and you have to update the label on the form as well. The code to perform these actions is put inside the `Set` block for the `Hour` property.

The first update that you perform is to update the `Value` property of the DateTimePicker control. The `Value` property of the date-time picker is a `Date` data type; thus, you cannot simply set the hour in this control, although you can retrieve just the hour from this property. To update this property, you must pass it a `Date` data type.

You do this by calling `New` (see Chapter 11) for the `Date` class, passing it the different date and time parts as shown in the code: year, month, day, hour, minute, second. You get the year, month, and day by extracting them from the `Now` variable. The hour is passed using the `value` parameter that was passed to this `Hour` property, and the minutes and seconds are passed as `0`, since you do not want to update the specific minutes or seconds:

```
'Set the date using the hour passed to this property
dtpHour.Value = _
    New Date(Now.Year, Now.Month, Now.Day, value, 0, 0)
```

The second update performed by this `Hour` property is to update the label on the form using some static text and the hour that is being set in this property:

```
'Set the display text
lblState.Text = "At " & value & ":00, Richard is "
```

You have not evaluated the `Hour` property to determine the state using the `DayAction` enumeration, but you do that next.

Determining the State

In the next Try It Out, you look at determining the state when the `Hour` property is set. You can take the hour returned by the DateTimePicker control and use it to determine which value in your enumeration it matches.

TRY IT OUT   Determining State

Code file Enum Demo.zip is available for download at Wrox.com

This exercise demonstrates this and displays the value on your form.

1.   Open the Code Editor for Form1 and modify the `Hour` property as follows:

```
Set(ByVal value As Integer)
    'Set the date using the hour passed to this property
    dtpHour.Value = _
        New Date(Now.Year, Now.Month, Now.Day, value, 0, 0)

    'Determine the state
    If value >= 6 And value < 7 Then
        CurrentState = DayAction.GettingReadyForWork
    ElseIf value >= 7 And value < 8 Then
        CurrentState = DayAction.TravelingToWork
```

```
        ElseIf value >= 8 And value < 13 Then
            CurrentState = DayAction.AtWork
        ElseIf value >= 13 And value < 14 Then
            CurrentState = DayAction.AtLunch
        ElseIf value >= 14 And value < 17 Then
            CurrentState = DayAction.AtWork
        ElseIf value >= 17 And value < 18 Then
            CurrentState = DayAction.TravelingFromWork
        ElseIf value >= 18 And value < 22 Then
            CurrentState = DayAction.RelaxingWithFriends
        ElseIf value >= 22 And value < 23 Then
            CurrentState = DayAction.GettingReadyForBed
        Else
            CurrentState = DayAction.Asleep
        End If


        'Set the display text
        lblState.Text = "At " & value & ":00, Richard is " & _
            CurrentState
    End Set
```

2. Run the project. You'll see something like Figure 5-8.

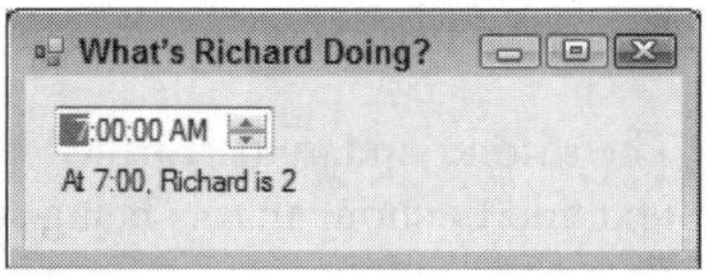

3. Here's the problem: The user doesn't know what 2 means. Close the project and find the following section of code at the end of the `Hour` property:

FIGURE 5-8

```
        'Set the display text
        lblState.Text = "At " & value & ":00, Richard is " & _
            CurrentState
    End Set
```

4. Change the last line to read as follows:

```
        'Set the display text
        lblState.Text = "At " & value & ":00, Richard is " & _
            CurrentState.ToString()
    End Set
```

5. Now run the project and you'll see something like Figure 5-9.

How It Works

FIGURE 5-9

As you typed the code in this example, you might have noticed that whenever you tried to set a value against `CurrentState`, you were presented with an enumerated list of possibilities, as shown in Figure 5-10.

Visual Studio 2010 knows that `CurrentState` is of type `DayAction`. It also knows that `DayAction` is an enumeration and that it defines eight possible values, each of which is displayed in the IntelliSense pop-up box. Clicking an item in the enumerated list causes a ToolTip to be displayed with the actual value of the item; for example, clicking `DayAction.RelaxingWithFriends` will display a ToolTip with a value of 6.

Fundamentally, however, because `DayAction` is based on an integer, `CurrentState` is an integer value. That's why, the first time you ran the project with the state determination code in place, you saw an integer at the end of the status string. At 7:00 A.M., you know that Richard is traveling to work, or rather `CurrentState` equals `DayAction.TravelingToWork`. You defined this as 2, which is why 2 is displayed at the end of the string.

```
'Determine the state
If value >= 6 And value < 7 Then
    CurrentState = DayAction.GettingReadyForWork
ElseIf value >= 7 A | DayAction.Asleep
    CurrentState =   | DayAction.AtLunch
ElseIf value >= 8 A | DayAction.AtWork
    CurrentState =   | DayAction.GettingReadyForBed
ElseIf value >= 13  | DayAction.GettingReadyForWork
    CurrentState =   | DayAction.RelaxingWithFriends
ElseIf value >= 14  | DayAction.TravelingFromWork
    CurrentState =   | DayAction.TravelingToWork
ElseIf value >= 17  |
```

FIGURE 5-10

What you've done in this Try It Out is to tack a call to the ToString method onto the end of the CurrentState variable. This results in a string representation of DayAction being used, rather than the integer representation.

Enumerations are incredibly useful when you want to store one of a possible set of values in a variable. As you start to drill into more complex objects in the Framework, you'll find that they are used all over the place!

Setting Invalid Values

One of the limitations of enumerations is that it is possible to store a value that technically isn't one of the possible defined values of the enumeration. For example, you can change the Hour property so that rather than setting CurrentState to Asleep, you can set it to 999:

```
ElseIf value >= 22 And value < 23 Then
    CurrentState = DayAction.GettingReadyForBed
Else
    CurrentState = 999
End If
```

If you build the project, you'll notice that Visual Basic 2010 doesn't flag this as an error if you have the Option Strict option turned off. When you run the project, you'll see that the value for CurrentState is shown on the form as 999.

So, you can set a variable that references an enumeration to a value that is not defined in that enumeration and the application will still "work" (as long as the value is of the same type as the enumeration). If you build classes that use enumerations, you have to rely on the consumer of that class being well behaved. One technique to solve this problem would be to disallow invalid values in any properties that used the enumeration as their data type.

UNDERSTANDING CONSTANTS

Another good programming practice to be aware of is the *constant*. Imagine you have the following two methods, each of which does something with a given file on the computer's disk (obviously, we're omitting the code here that actually manipulates the file):

```
Public Sub DoSomething()
    'What's the filename?
```

```
          Dim strFileName As String = "c:\Temp\Demo.txt"
          'Open the file
          ..
      End Sub
      Public Sub DoSomethingElse()
          'What's the filename?
          Dim strFileName As String = "c:\Temp\Demo.txt"
          'Do something with the file
          ..
      End Sub
```

Using Constants

The code defining a string literal gives the name of a file twice. This is poor programming practice, because if both methods are supposed to access the same file, and if that filename changes, this change has to be made in two separate places.

In this instance, both methods are next to each other and the program itself is small. However, imagine you have a massive program in which a separate string literal pointing to the file is defined in 10, 50, or even 1,000 places. If you needed to change the filename, you'd have to change it many times. This is exactly the kind of thing that leads to serious problems for maintaining software code.

What you need to do instead is define the filename globally and then use that global symbol for the filename in the code, rather than use a string literal. This is what a constant is. It is, in effect, a special kind of variable that cannot be varied when the program is running.

TRY IT OUT   Using Constants

Code file Constants Demo.zip is available for download at Wrox.com

In this Try It Out, you learn to use constants.

1. Create a new Windows Forms application in Visual Studio 2010 called **Constants Demo**.

2. When the Forms Designer appears, add three Button controls. Set the Name property of the first button to **btnOne**, the second to **btnTwo**, and the third to **btnThree**. Change the Text property of each to **One**, **Two**, and **Three**, respectively. Arrange the controls on your form so it looks similar to Figure 5-11.

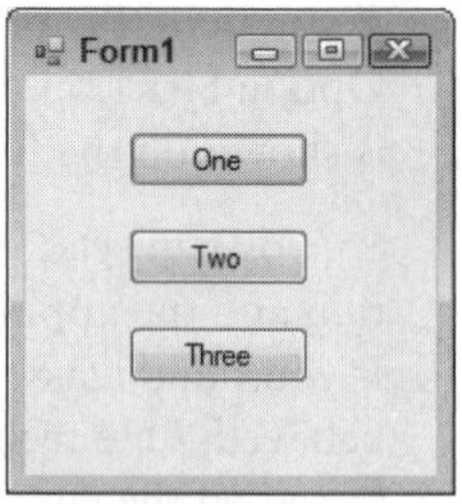

FIGURE 5-11

3. View the Code Editor for the form by right-clicking the form and choosing View Code from the context menu. At the top of the class definition, add the following bolded code:

```
Public Class Form1
```

```
    'File name constant
    Private Const strFileName As String = "C:\Temp\Hello.txt"
```

4. In the Class Name combo box at the top of the editor, select **btnOne**, and in the Method Name combo box select the Click event. Add the following bolded code to the Click event handler:

```
Private Sub btnOne_Click(ByVal sender As Object, _
    ByVal e As System.EventArgs) Handles btnOne.Click
```

```
    'Using a constant
    MessageBox.Show("1: " & strFileName, "Constants Demo")
End Sub
```

5. Select **btnTwo** in the Class Name combo box and select its Click event in the Method Name combo box. Add the bolded code here:

```
Private Sub btnTwo_Click(ByVal sender As Object, _
    ByVal e As System.EventArgs) Handles btnTwo.Click

    'Using the constant again
    MessageBox.Show("2: " & strFileName, "Constants Demo")
End Sub
```

6. Select **btnThree** in the Class Name combo box and the Click event in the Method Name combo box. Add this code to the Click event handler:

```
Private Sub btnThree_Click(ByVal sender As Object, _
    ByVal e As System.EventArgs) Handles btnThree.Click

    'Reusing the constant one more time
    MessageBox.Show("3: " & strFileName, "Constants Demo")
End Sub
```

7. Save and run your project and then click button One. You'll see the message box shown in Figure 5-12.

FIGURE 5-12

Likewise, you'll see the same filename when you click buttons Two and Three.

How It Works

This example demonstrates that a constant is actually a type of value that cannot be changed when the program is running. It is defined as a variable, but you add Const to the definition, indicating that this variable is constant and cannot change:

```
'File name constant
Private Const strFileName As String = "C:\Temp\Hello.txt"
```

You'll notice that it has a data type, just like a variable, and you have to give it a value when it's defined — which makes sense, because you can't change it later.

When you want to use the constant, you refer to it just as you would refer to any variable:

```
Private Sub btnOne_Click(ByVal sender As Object, _
    ByVal e As System.EventArgs) Handles btnOne.Click

    'Using a constant
    MessageBox.Show("1: " & strFileName, "Constants Demo")
End Sub
```

As mentioned before, the appeal of a constant is that it enables you to change a value that's used multiple times by altering a single piece of code. However, note that you can change constants only at design time; you cannot change their values at runtime. Look at how this works.

Different Constant Types

You've seen how to use a string constant, but in this section, you can use other types of variables as constants. Basically, a constant must not be able to change, so you should not store an object data type (which we will discuss in Chapter 11) in a constant.

Integers are very common types of constants. They can be defined like this:

```
Public Const intHoursAsleepPerDay As Integer = 8
```

Also, it's fairly common to see constants used with enumerations, like this:

```
Public Const intRichardsTypicalState As DayAction = DayAction.AtWork
```

STRUCTURES

Applications commonly need to store several pieces of information of different data types that all relate to one thing and must be kept together in a group, such as a customer's name and address (strings) and balance (a number). Usually, an object of a class is used to hold such a group of variables, as you'll discover in Chapter 11, but you can also use a *structure*.

Building Structures

Structures are similar to class objects but are somewhat simpler, so they're discussed here.

Later, as you design applications, you need to be able to decide whether a structure or a class is appropriate. As a rule of thumb, we suggest that if you end up putting a lot of methods on a structure, it should probably be a class. It's also relatively tricky to convert from a structure to a class later, because structures and objects are created using different syntax rules, and sometimes the same syntax produces different results between structures and objects. Therefore, choose once and choose wisely!

TRY IT OUT | **Building a Structure**

Code file Structure Demo.zip is available for download at Wrox.com

Take a look at how you can build a structure.

1. Create a new Windows Forms application in Visual Studio 2010 called **Structure Demo**.

2. When the Forms Designer appears, add four Label controls, four TextBox controls, and a Button control. Arrange your controls so that they look similar to Figure 5-13.

3. Set the Name properties as follows:

> ➤ Set Label1 to **lblName**.

> ➤ Set TextBox1 to **txtName**.

> ➤ Set Label2 to **lblFirstName**.

> ➤ Set TextBox2 to **txtFirstName**.

> ➤ Set Label3 to **lblLastName**.

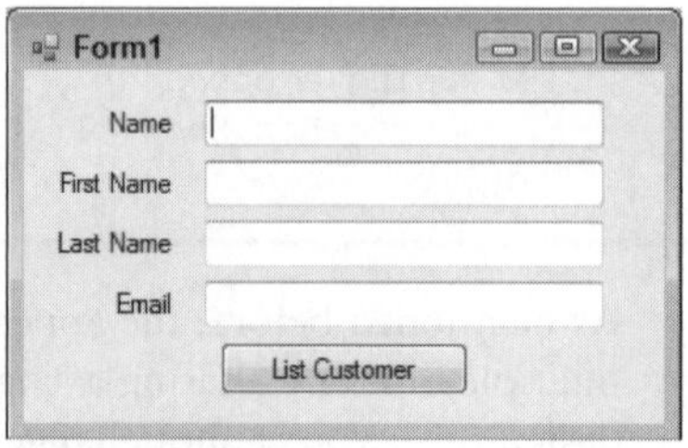

FIGURE 5-13

➤ Set TextBox3 to **txtLastName**.

➤ Set Label4 to **lblEmail**.

➤ Set TextBox4 to **txtEmail**.

➤ Set Button1 to **btnListCustomer**.

4. Set the Text properties of the following controls:

➤ Set lblName to **Name**.

➤ Set lblFirstName to **First Name**.

➤ Set lblLastName to **Last Name**.

➤ Set lblEmail to **E-mail**.

➤ Set btnListCustomer to **List Customer**.

5. Right-click the project name in the Solution Explorer, choose the Add menu item from the context menu, and then choose the Class submenu item. In the Add New Item – Structure Demo dialog, enter **Customer** in the Name field and then click the Add button to have this item added to your project.

6. When the Code Editor appears, replace all existing code with the following code:

```
Public Structure Customer
    'Public members
    Public FirstName As String
    Public LastName As String
    Public Email As String
End Structure
```

> **NOTE** Be sure to replace the Class definition with the Structure definition!

7. View the Code Editor for the form and add this procedure:

```
Public Class Form1

    Public Sub DisplayCustomer(ByVal customer As Customer)
        'Display the customer details on the form
        txtFirstName.Text = customer.FirstName
        txtLastName.Text = customer.LastName
        txtEmail.Text = customer.Email
    End Sub
```

8. In the Class Name combo box at the top of the editor, select btnListCustomer, and in the Method Name combo box select the Click event. Add the following bolded code to the Click event handler:

```
Private Sub btnListCustomer_Click(ByVal sender As System.Object, _
    ByVal e As System.EventArgs) Handles btnListCustomer.Click

    'Create a new customer
    Dim objCustomer As Customer
    objCustomer.FirstName = "Michael"
```

```
      objCustomer.LastName = "Dell"
      objCustomer.Email = "mdell@somecompany.com"

      'Display the customer
      DisplayCustomer(objCustomer)
End Sub
```

9.   Save and run your project. When the form appears, click the
List Customer button and you should see results similar to
those shown in Figure 5-14.

FIGURE 5-14

How It Works

In this example, you define a structure using a `Structure.End Structure` statement. Inside this block, the
variables that make up the structure are declared by name and type: These variables are called *members* of
the structure:

```
Public Structure Customer
        'Public members
        Public FirstName As String
        Public LastName As String
        Public Email As String
End Structure
```

Notice the keyword `Public` in front of each variable declaration, as well as in front of the `Structure`
statement. You have frequently seen `Private` used in similar positions. The `Public` keyword means that
you can refer to the member (such as `FirstName`) outside of the definition of the `Customer` structure
itself.

In the `btnListCustomer_Click` procedure, you define a variable of type `Customer` using the `Dim` statement.
(If `Customer` were a class, you would also have to initialize the variable by setting `objCustomer` equal to
`New Customer`, as discussed in Chapter 11.)

```
Private Sub btnListCustomer_Click(ByVal sender As System.Object, _
      ByVal e As System.EventArgs) Handles btnListCustomer_Click.Click

      'Create a new customer
      Dim objCustomer As Customer
```

Then you can access each of the member variables inside the `Customer` structure `objCustomer` by giving the
name of the structure variable, followed by a dot, followed by the name of the member:

```
      objCustomer.FirstName = "Michael"
      objCustomer.LastName = "Dell"
      objCustomer.Email = "mdell@somecompany.com"

      'Display the customer
      DisplayCustomer(objCustomer)
End Sub
```

The `DisplayCustomer` procedure simply accepts a `Customer` structure as its input parameter and then
accesses the members of the structure to set the `Text` properties of the text boxes on the form:

```
Public Sub DisplayCustomer(ByVal customer As Customer)
      'Display the customer details on the form
```

```
        txtFirstName.Text = customer.FirstName
        txtLastName.Text = customer.LastName
        txtEmail.Text = customer.Email
    End Sub
```

Adding Properties to Structures

When you need to store basic information, you can add properties to a structure just as you did to the form in the Enum Demo project earlier in the chapter. You learn how in the next Try It Out.

TRY IT OUT Adding a Name Property

Code file Structure Demo.zip is available for download at Wrox.com

In this Try It Out, you add a ReadOnly name property.

1. Open the Code Editor for Customer and add this bolded code to create a read-only property Name:

```
'Public members
Public FirstName As String
Public LastName As String
Public Email As String

'Name property
Public ReadOnly Property Name() As String
    Get
        Return FirstName & " " & LastName
    End Get
End Property
```

2. Open the Code Editor for Form1. Modify the DisplayCustomer method with the bolded code:

```
Public Sub DisplayCustomer(ByVal customer As Customer)
    'Display the customer details on the form
    txtName.Text = customer.Name
    txtFirstName.Text = customer.FirstName
    txtLastName.Text = customer.LastName
    txtEmail.Text = customer.Email
End Sub
```

3. Run the project and click the List Customer button. You'll see that the Name text box, which was empty in Figure 5-14, is now populated with the customer's first name and last name.

How It Works

First, you create the property and mark it as **ReadOnly** so it cannot be changed.

```
'Name property
Public ReadOnly Property Name() As String
    Get
```

```
            Return FirstName & " " & LastName
        End Get
    End Property
```

Next, you use the new name property to populate the textbox for Name.

```
    txtName.Text = customer.Name
```

WORKING WITH ARRAYLISTS

Suppose you need to store a set of `Customer` structures. You could use an array, but in some cases the array might not be so easy to use:

> ➤ If you need to add a new `Customer` to the array, then you need to change the size of the array and insert the new item in the new last position in the array. (You'll learn how to change the size of an array later in this chapter.)

> ➤ If you need to remove a `Customer` from the array, you need to look at each item in the array in turn. When you find the one you want, you have to create another version of the array one element smaller than the original array and copy every item except the one you want to delete into the new array.

> ➤ If you need to replace a `Customer` in the array with another customer, you need to look at each item in turn until you find the one you want and then replace it manually.

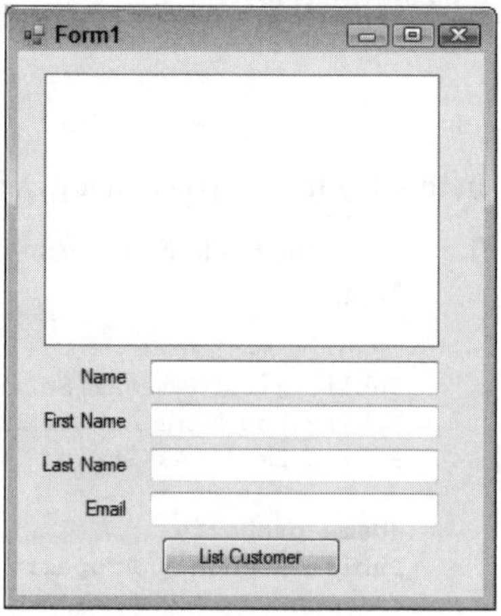

FIGURE 5-15

The `ArrayList` provides a way to create an array that can be easily manipulated as you run your program.

Using an ArrayList

`ArrayLists` allow for a collection of objects that is dynamically sized. You can add and remove items at any point. When you are not sure how many items your collection will contain, the `ArrayList` is a good option. Look at using an `ArrayList` in this next Try It Out.

TRY IT OUT Using an ArrayList

Code file Structure Demo.zip is available for download at Wrox.com

In this Try It Out, you see how to use an `ArrayList`.

1. Return to the Structure Demo project in Visual Studio 2010. Make the form larger, move the existing controls down, and then add a new ListBox control as shown in Figure 5-15. Set the `Name` property of the list box to **lstCustomers** and its `IntegralHeight` property to `False`.

> **NOTE** *You can click the form and press Ctrl+A to select all of the controls and then drag them to their new location. Once highlighted, you can also move them with the keyboard arrows in tiny increments or by pressing Ctrl and the arrows for larger movements.*

2. Open the Code Editor for Form1 and add the member bolded here to the top of the class definition:

```
Public Class Form1

    'Form level members
    Private objCustomers As New ArrayList
```

3. Add this method to Form1 to create a new customer:

```
Public Sub CreateCustomer(ByVal firstName As String, _
    ByVal lastName As String, ByVal email As String)

    'Declare a Customer object
    Dim objNewCustomer As Customer

    'Create the new customer
    objNewCustomer.FirstName = firstName
    objNewCustomer.LastName = lastName
    objNewCustomer.Email = email

    'Add the new customer to the list
    objCustomers.Add(objNewCustomer)

    'Add the new customer to the ListBox control
    lstCustomers.Items.Add(objNewCustomer)
End Sub
```

4. Modify the `btnListCustomer_Click` method next, making these code changes:

```
Private Sub btnListCustomer_Click(ByVal sender As
System.Object, _
    ByVal e As System.EventArgs) Handles
  btnListCustomer.Click

    'Create some customers
    CreateCustomer("Darrel", "Hilton",
  "dhilton@somecompany.com")
    CreateCustomer("Frank", "Peoples",
  "fpeoples@somecompany.com")
    CreateCustomer("Bill", "Scott",
  "bscott@somecompany.com")
End Sub
```

5. Run the project and click the List Customer button. You'll see results like those shown in Figure 5-16.

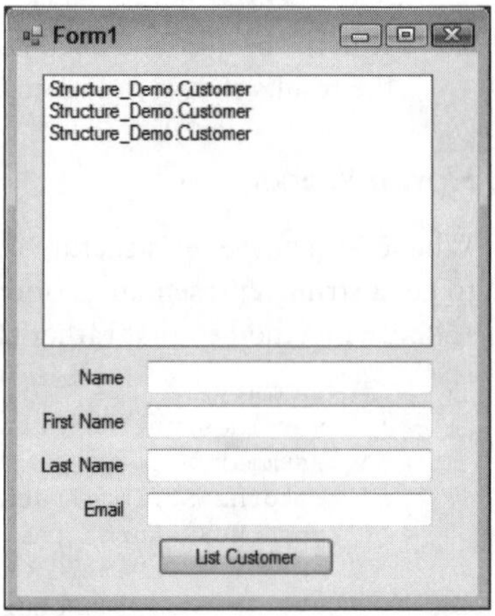

FIGURE 5-16

How It Works

You are adding `Customer` structures to the list, but they are being displayed by the list as `Structure_Demo.Customer`; this is the full name of the structure. The ListBox control accepts string values, so by specifying that you wanted to add the `Customer` structure to the list box, Visual Basic 2010 called the `ToString` method of the `Customer` structure. By default, the `ToString` method for a structure returns the structure name, which is not the contents that you wanted to see. Therefore, you need to tweak the `Customer` structure so that it can display something more meaningful.

TRY IT OUT   Overriding ToString

> *Code file Structure Demo.zip is available for download at Wrox.com*

In this Try It Out, when you tweak the `Customer` structure, you'll see how the `ArrayList` works.

1. Return to the Structure Demo project and open the Code Editor for `Customer` and add the following method to the structure, ensuring that it is below the member declarations. Remember from Chapter 3 that to insert an XML Document Comment block, you type three apostrophes above the method name:

```
'" <summary>
'" Overrides the default ToString method
'" </summary>
'" <returns>String</returns>
'" <remarks>Returns the customer name and email
'"     address</remarks>
Public Overrides Function ToString() As String
    Return Name & " (" & Email & ")"
End Function
End Structure
```

2. Run the project and click the List Customer button. You'll see the results shown in Figure 5-17.

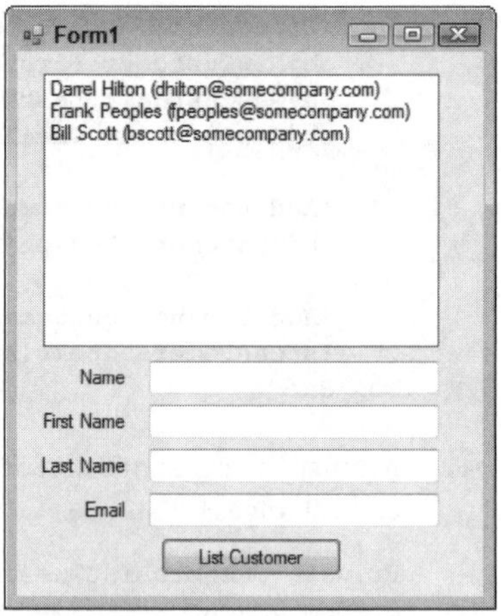

How It Works

FIGURE 5-17

Whenever a `Customer` structure is added to the list, the list box calls the `ToString` method on the structure to get a string representation of that structure. With this code, you *override* the default functionality of the `ToString` method so that rather than returning just the name of the structure, you get some useful text:

```
'" <summary>
'" Overrides the default ToString method
'" </summary>
'" <returns>String</returns>
'" <remarks>Returns the customer name and email address</remarks>
        Public Overrides Function ToString() As String
            Return Name & " (" & Email & ")"
        End Function
```

An `ArrayList` can be used to store a list of objects/structures of any type (in contrast to a regular array). In fact, you can mix the types within an `ArrayList` — a topic we'll be talking about in a little while. In this example, you created a method called CreateCustomer that initializes a new Customer structure based on parameters that were passed to the method:

```
Public Sub CreateCustomer(ByVal firstName As String, _
    ByVal lastName As String, ByVal email As String)

    'Declare a Customer object
    Dim objNewCustomer As Customer

    'Create the new customer
    objNewCustomer.FirstName = firstName
    objNewCustomer.LastName = lastName
    objNewCustomer.Email = email
```

After the structure has been initialized, you add it to the ArrayList stored in objCustomers:

```
    'Add the new customer to the list
    objCustomers.Add(objNewCustomer)
```

You also add it to the list box itself, like this:

```
    'Add the new customer to the ListBox control
    lstCustomers.Items.Add(objNewCustomer)
```

With CreateCustomer defined, you can call it to add new members to the ArrayList and to the ListBox control when the user clicks the List Customer button:

```
    Private Sub btnListCustomer_Click(ByVal sender As System.Object, _
        ByVal e As System.EventArgs) Handles btnListCustomer.Click

        'Create some customers
        CreateCustomer("Darrel", "Hilton", "dhilton@somecompany.com")
        CreateCustomer("Frank", "Peoples", "fpeoples@somecompany.com")
        CreateCustomer("Bill", "Scott", "bscott@somecompany.com")
    End Sub
```

Deleting from an ArrayList

OK, so now you know the principle behind an ArrayList. You use it to do something that's traditionally hard to do with arrays but is pretty easy to do with an ArrayList, such as dynamically add new values.

TRY IT OUT   Deleting from an ArrayList

Code file Structure Demo.zip is available for download at Wrox.com

This Try It Out shows you how easy it is to delete items from an ArrayList.

1.   Return to the Code Editor in the Structure Demo project and add the SelectedCustomer property to the form as follows:

```
Public ReadOnly Property SelectedCustomer() As Customer
    Get
        If lstCustomers.SelectedIndex <> -1 Then
            'Return the selected customer
            Return CType(objCustomers(lstCustomers.SelectedIndex), Customer)
```

```
        End If
    End Get
End Property
```

2. Now switch to the Forms Designer and add a new Button control to the bottom of the form and set its Name property to **btnDeleteCustomer** and its Text property to **Delete Customer.**

3. Double-click the button and add the bolded code:

```
Private Sub btnDeleteCustomer_Click(ByVal sender As System.Object, _
    ByVal e As System.EventArgs) Handles btnDeleteCustomer.Click

        'If no customer is selected in the ListBox then.
        If lstCustomers.SelectedIndex = -1 Then

            'Display a message
            MessageBox.Show("You must select a customer to delete.", _
                "Structure Demo")

            'Exit this method
            Exit Sub
        End If

        'Prompt the user to delete the selected customer
        If MessageBox.Show("Are you sure you want to delete " & _
            SelectedCustomer.Name & "?", "Structure Demo", _
            MessageBoxButtons.YesNo, MessageBoxIcon.Question) = _
            DialogResult.Yes Then

            'Get the customer to be deleted
            Dim objCustomerToDelete As Customer = SelectedCustomer

            'Remove the customer from the ArrayList
            objCustomers.Remove(objCustomerToDelete)

            'Remove the customer from the ListBox
            lstCustomers.Items.Remove(objCustomerToDelete)
        End If
End Sub
```

4. Run the project and click the List Customer button. *Do not* select a customer in the list box and then click the Delete Customer button. You'll see a message box indicating that you must select a customer.

5. Now select a customer and click Delete Customer. You'll see a confirmation dialog similar to the one shown in Figure 5-18.

6. Click Yes, and the customer you selected will be removed from the list.

How It Works

The trick here is to build a read-only property that returns the Customer structure selected in the list box back to the caller on demand. The SelectedIndex property of the list box returns a value of -1 if no selection has been made. Otherwise, it returns the zero-based index of the selected customer. Because the

Items collection of the list box contains a collection of Object data types, you must convert the object returned to a Customer object, which you do by using the CType function:

```
Public ReadOnly Property SelectedCustomer() As Customer
    Get
        If lstCustomers.SelectedIndex <> -1 Then
            'Return the selected customer
            Return CType(objCustomers(lstCustomers.SelectedIndex), Customer)
        End If
    End Get
End Property
```

FIGURE 5-18

Because there is no else statement for the If, you will see a warning about a non-returning code path. Be aware of these when you are writing your code. To correct this, you could add an else statement for the situation.

Like the Name property that you added to the Customer structure, this property is identified as read-only by the keyword ReadOnly. It contains a Get block but no Set block. The reason for making it read-only is that it constructs the value it returns from other information (the contents of the Customer structures in the list) that can be set and changed by other means.

Inside the Click event handler for the Delete Customer button, you first test to see whether a customer has been selected in the list box. If no customer has been selected, then you display a message box indicating that a customer must be selected. Then you exit the method, allowing the user to select a customer and try again:

```
'If no customer is selected in the ListBox then.
If lstCustomers.SelectedIndex = -1 Then

    'Display a message
    MessageBox.Show("You must select a customer to delete.", _
        "Structure Demo")
```

```
        'Exit this method
        Exit Sub
    End If
```

If a customer has been selected, you prompt the user to confirm the deletion:

```
    'Prompt the user to delete the selected customer
    If MessageBox.Show("Are you sure you want to delete " & _
        SelectedCustomer.Name & "?", "Structure Demo", _
        MessageBoxButtons.YesNo, MessageBoxIcon.Question) = _
        DialogResult.Yes Then
```

If the user does want to delete the customer, you get a return value from `MessageBox.Show` equal to `DialogResult.Yes`. Then you declare a `customer` structure to save the customer to be deleted and populate that structure with the selected customer:

```
    'Get the customer to be deleted
    Dim objCustomerToDelete As Customer = SelectedCustomer
```

The `Remove` method of the `ArrayList` can then be used to remove the selected customer:

```
    'Remove the customer from the ArrayList
    objCustomers.Remove(objCustomerToDelete)
```

You also use a similar technique to remove the customer from the list box:

```
    'Remove the customer from the ListBox
    lstCustomers.Items.Remove(objCustomerToDelete
```

Showing Items in the ArrayList

For completeness, you'll want to add one more piece of functionality to enhance the user interface of your application.

TRY IT OUT   Showing Details of the Selected Item

Code file Structure Demo.zip is available for download at Wrox.com

In this Try It Out, you add code in the `SelectedIndexChanged` event for the Customers list box. Every time a new customer is selected, the customer's details will be displayed in the text boxes on the form.

1.   Return to the Forms Designer in the Structure Demo project and double-click the list box. This creates a new `SelectedIndexChanged` event handler. Add the bolded code:

```
Private Sub lstCustomers_SelectedIndexChanged( _
    ByVal sender As System.Object, ByVal e As System.EventArgs) _
    Handles lstCustomers.SelectedIndexChanged

    'Display the customer details
    DisplayCustomer(SelectedCustomer)
End Sub
```

2. Run the project and click the List Customer button to populate the list box. Now when you select a customer in the list box, that customer's information will appear in the fields at the bottom of the form, as shown in Figure 5-19.

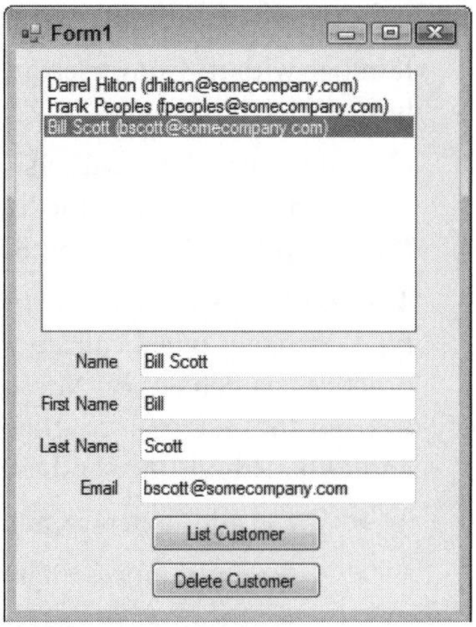

How It Works

In this example, you hook up the `SelectedIndexChanged` event so the new selected customer is displayed when the event fires.

```
DisplayCustomer(SelectedCustomer)
```

FIGURE 5-19

WORKING WITH COLLECTIONS

The `ArrayList` is a kind of *collection*, which the .NET Framework uses extensively. A collection is a way of easily creating ad hoc groups of similar or related items. If you refer back to your Structure Demo code and peek into the `CreateCustomer` method, you'll notice that when adding items to the `ArrayList` and to the list box, you use a method called `Add`:

```
'Add the new customer to the list
objCustomers.Add(objNewCustomer)

'Add the new customer to the ListBox control
lstCustomers.Items.Add(objNewCustomer)
```

The code that deletes a customer uses a method called `Remove` on both objects:

```
'Remove the customer from the ArrayList
objCustomers.Remove(objCustomerToDelete)

'Remove the customer from the ListBox
lstCustomers.Items.Remove(objCustomerToDelete)
```

Microsoft is very keen to see developers use the collection paradigm whenever they need to work with a list of items. They are also keen to see collections work in the same way, irrespective of what they actually hold, which is why you use `Add` to add an item and `Remove` to remove an item, even though you're using a `System.Collections.ArrayList` object in one case and a `System.Windows.Forms.ListBox.ObjectCollection` object in another. Microsoft has taken a great deal of care with this feature when building the .NET Framework.

Consistency is good — it enables developers to map an understanding of one thing and use that same understanding with a similar thing. When designing data structures for use in your application, you should take steps to follow the conventions that Microsoft has laid down. For example, if you have a collection class and want to create a method that removes an item, call it `Remove`, not `Delete`.

Developers using your class will have an intuitive understanding of what `Remove` does because they're familiar with it. Conversely, developers would do a double-take on seeing `Delete`, because that term has a different connotation.

One of the problems with using an `ArrayList` is that the developer who has an array list cannot guarantee that every item in the list is of the same type. For this reason, each time an item is extracted from the `ArrayList`, the type should be checked to avoid causing an error.

The solution is to create a *strongly typed* collection, which contains only elements of a particular type. Strongly typed collections are very easy to create. According to .NET best-programming practices as defined by Microsoft, the best way to create one is to derive a new class from `System.Collections.CollectionBase` (discussed in the explanation for the next two Try It Outs) and add two methods (`Add` and `Remove`) and one property (`Item`):

➤   `Add` adds a new item to the collection.

➤   `Remove` removes an item from the collection.

➤   `Item` returns the item at the given index in the collection.

Creating CustomerCollection

Sometimes, you will need to store many of your structures together. You can do that using a collection.

TRY IT OUT   **Creating CustomerCollection**

> *Code file Structure Demo.zip is available for download at Wrox.com*

In this Try It Out, you create a `CustomerCollection` designed to hold a collection of `Customer` structures.

1.   Return to the Structure Demo project in Visual Studio 2010 and in the Solution Explorer, right-click the project and choose Add from the context menu and then choose the Class submenu item. In the Add New Item – Structure Demo dialog, enter **CustomerCollection** in the Name field and then click the Add button to have the class added to your project.

2.   Add the following bolded line in the Code Editor:

```
Public Class CustomerCollection
    Inherits CollectionBase

End Class
```

3.   You need to add an `Add` method to add a customer to the collection. Add the following code:

```
'Add a customer to the collection
Public Sub Add(ByVal newCustomer As Customer)
    Me.List.Add(newCustomer)
End Sub
```

4.   You also need to add a `Remove` method to remove a customer from the collection, so add this method:

```
'Remove a customer from the collection
Public Sub Remove(ByVal oldCustomer As Customer)
    Me.List.Remove(oldCustomer)
End Sub
```

5. Open the Code Editor for the form and find the definition for the `objCustomers` member. Change its type from `ArrayList` to `CustomerCollection` as bolded here:

```
Public Class Form1

     'Form level members
     Private objCustomers As New CustomerCollection
```

6. Finally, run the project. You'll notice that the application works as before.

How It Works

Now, your `CustomerCollection` class is the first occasion for you to create a *class* explicitly (although you have been using them implicitly from the beginning). Classes and objects are discussed in Chapter 11 and subsequent chapters. For now, note that, like a structure, a class represents a data type that groups one or more members that can be of different data types, and it can have properties and methods associated with it. Unlike a structure, a class can be *derived* from another class, in which case it *inherits* the members, properties, and methods of that other class (which is known as the *base class*), and it can have further members, properties, and methods of its own.

Your `CustomerCollection` class inherits from the `System.Collections.CollectionBase` class, which contains a basic implementation of a collection that can hold any object. In that respect it's very similar to an `ArrayList`. The advantage comes when you add your own methods to this class.

Since you provided a version of the `Add` method that has a parameter type of `Customer`, it can accept and add only a `Customer` structure. Therefore, it's impossible to put anything into the collection that isn't a `Customer`. You can see there that IntelliSense is telling you that the only thing you can pass through to `Add` is a `Structure_Demo.Customer` structure. See Chapter 10 for more on IntelliSense.

Internally, `CollectionBase` provides you with a property called `List`, which in turn has `Add` and `Remove` methods that you can use to store items. That's precisely what you use when you need to add or remove items from the list:

```
'Add a customer to the collection
Public Sub Add(ByVal newCustomer As Customer)
     Me.List.Add(newCustomer)
End Sub

'Remove a customer from the collection
Public Sub Remove(ByVal oldCustomer As Customer)
     Me.List.Remove(oldCustomer)
End Sub
```

Building collections this way is a .NET best practice. As a newcomer to .NET programming, you may not appreciate just how useful this is, but trust us — it is. Whenever you need to use a collection of classes, this technique is the right way to go and one that you'll be familiar with.

Adding an Item Property

At the beginning of this section, you read that you were supposed to add two methods and one property. You've seen the methods but not the property, so take a look at it in the next Try It Out.

TRY IT OUT Adding an Item Property

In this Try It Out, you will add an `Item` property and make it the default property of the class.

1. Return to Visual Studio 2010, open the Code Editor for the `CustomerCollection` class, and add this code:

```
'Item property to read or update a customer at a given position
'in the list
Default Public Property Item(ByVal index As Integer) As Customer
    Get
        Return CType(Me.List.Item(index), Customer)
    End Get
    Set(ByVal value As Customer)
        Me.List.Item(index) = value
    End Set
End Property
```

2. To verify that this works, open the Code Editor for Form1. Modify the `SelectedCustomer` property with this code:

```
Public ReadOnly Property SelectedCustomer() As Customer
    Get
        If lstCustomers.SelectedIndex <> -1 Then
            'Return the selected customer
            Return objCustomers(lstCustomers.SelectedIndex)
        End If
    End Get
End Property
```

3. Run the project. Click the List Customer button and note that when you select items in the list, the details are shown in the fields as they were before.

How It Works

The `Item` property is actually very important; it gives the developer direct access to the data stored in the list but maintains the strongly typed nature of the collection.

If you look at the code again for `SelectedCustomer`, you'll notice that when you wanted to return the given item from within `objCustomers`, you didn't have to provide the property name of `Item`. Instead, `objCustomers` behaved as if it were an array:

```
If lstCustomers.SelectedIndex <> -1 Then
    'Return the selected customer
    Return objCustomers(lstCustomers.SelectedIndex)
End If
```

IntelliSense tells you to enter the index of the item that you require and that you should expect to get a `Customer` structure in return.

You don't have to specify the property name of `Item` because you marked the property as the default by using the `Default` keyword:

```
'Item property to read or update a customer at a given position
'in the list
Default Public Property Item(ByVal index As Integer) As Customer
    Get
```

```
            Return CType(Me.List.Item(index), Customer)
        End Get
        Set(ByVal value As Customer)
            Me.List.Item(index) = value
        End Set
    End Property
```

A given class can have only a single default property, and that property must take a parameter of some kind. This parameter must be an index or search term of some description. The one used here provides an index to an element in a collection list. You can have multiple overloaded versions of the same property so that, for example, you could provide an e-mail address rather than an index. This provides a great deal of flexibility, further enhancing your class.

What you have at this point is the following:

➤ A way to store a list of `Customer` structures, and just `Customer` structures

➤ A way to add new items to the collection on demand

➤ A way to remove existing items from the collection on demand

➤ A way to access members in the collection as if it were an `ArrayList`

BUILDING LOOKUP TABLES WITH HASHTABLE

So far, whenever you want to find something in an array or in a collection, you have to provide an integer index representing the position of the item. It's common to end up needing a way to look up an item in a collection when you have something other than an index. For example, you might want to find a customer when you provide an e-mail address.

In this section you'll take a look at the `Hashtable`. This is a special kind of collection that works on a *key-value* principle.

Using Hashtables

A `Hashtable` is a collection in which each item is given a *key*. This key can be used at a later time to unlock the value. For example, if you add Darrel's `Customer` structure to the `Hashtable`, you would give it a key that matches his e-mail address of `dhilton@somecompany.com`. If later you come along with that key, you'll be able to find his record quickly.

Whenever you add an object to the `Hashtable`, it calls a method `System.Object.GetHashCode`, which provides a unique integer value for that object that is the same every time it is called, and internally uses this integer ID as the key. Likewise, whenever you want to retrieve an object from the `Hashtable`, it calls `GetHashCode` on the object to get a lookup key and matches that key against the ones it has in the list. When it finds it, it returns the related value to you.

Lookups from a `Hashtable` are very, very fast. Irrespective of the object you pass in, you're only matching on a relatively small integer ID. An integer ID takes up 4 bytes of memory, so if you pass in a 100-character string (which is 200 bytes long), the lookup code only needs to compare 4 bytes, which makes everything run very quickly.

TRY IT OUT Using a Hashtable

Code file Structure Demo.zip is available for download at Wrox.com

You learn to use a `Hashtable` in this Try It Out.

1. Return to Visual Studio 2010 and open the Code Editor for the `CustomerCollection` class. Add the bolded member to the top of the class definition:

```
Public Class CustomerCollection
    Inherits CollectionBase

    'Private member
    Private objEmailHashtable As New Hashtable
```

2. Add the following read-only property to the class:

```
'EmailHashtable property to return the Email Hashtable
Public ReadOnly Property EmailHashtable() As Hashtable
    Get
        Return objEmailHashtable
    End Get
End Property
```

3. Now make this change to the `Add` method:

```
'Add a customer to the collection
Public Sub Add(ByVal newCustomer As Customer)
    Me.List.Add(newCustomer)

    'Add the email address to the Hashtable
    EmailHashtable.Add(newCustomer.Email, newCustomer)
End Sub
```

4. Next, add this overloaded version of the `Item` property that allows you to find a customer by e-mail address:

```
'Overload Item property to find a customer by email address
Default Public ReadOnly Property Item(ByVal email As
    String) As Customer
    Get
        Return CType(EmailHashtable.Item(email),
    Customer)
    End Get
End Property
```

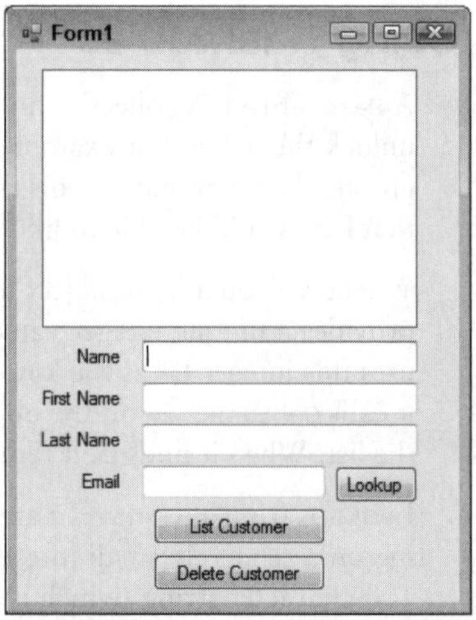

5. Open the Forms Designer for Form1, resize the controls on your form, and add a new Button control next to the E-mail text box as shown in Figure 5-20. Set the `Name` property of the button to **btnLookup** and the `Text` property to **Lookup**.

6. Double-click the Lookup button and add the following bolded code to its `Click` event handler:

```
Private Sub btnLookup_Click(ByVal sender As System.
    Object, _
    ByVal e As System.EventArgs) Handles btnLookup.
    Click
```

FIGURE 5-20

```
'Declare a customer object and set it to the customer
'with the email address to be found
Dim objFoundCustomer As Customer = objCustomers(txtEmail.Text)

If Not IsNothing(objFoundCustomer.Email) Then
    'Display the customers name
    MessageBox.Show("The customers name is: " & _
        objFoundCustomer.Name, "Structure Demo")
Else
    'Display an error
    MessageBox.Show("There is no customer with the e-mail" & _
        " address " & txtEmail.Text & ".", "Structure Demo")
End If
End Sub
```

7. Run the project and click the List Customer button to populate the list of customers. If you enter an e-mail address that does not exist into the E-mail text box and then click the Lookup button, you'll see a message box similar to the one shown in Figure 5-21.

FIGURE 5-21

If you enter an e-mail address that does exist — for example, dhilton@somecompany.com — the name of the customer is shown in the message box.

How It Works

In this example, you added a new member to the `CustomerCollection` class that can be used to hold a `Hashtable`:

```
'Private member
Private objEmailHashtable As New Hashtable
```

Whenever you add a new `Customer` to the collection, you also add it to the `Hashtable`:

```
'Add a customer to the collection
Public Sub Add(ByVal newCustomer As Customer)
    Me.List.Add(newCustomer)
```

```
      'Add the email address to the Hashtable
      EmailHashtable.Add(newCustomer.Email, newCustomer)
   End Sub
```

However, unlike the kinds of `Add` methods shown earlier, the `EmailHashtable.Add` method takes two parameters. The first is the key, and you're using the e-mail address as the key. The key can be any object you like, but it must be unique. You cannot supply the same key twice. (If you do, an exception will be thrown.) The second parameter is the value that you want to link the key to, so whenever you give that key to the `Hashtable`, you get that object back.

The next trick is to create an overloaded version of the default `Item` property. This one, however, takes a string as its only parameter. IntelliSense displays the overloaded method as items 1 and 2 when you access it from your code.

This time you can provide either an index or an e-mail address. If you use an e-mail address, you end up using the overloaded version of the `Item` property, and this defers to the `Item` property of the `Hashtable` object. This takes a key and returns the related item, provided that the key can be found:

```
   'Overload Item property to find a customer by email address
   Default Public ReadOnly Property Item(ByVal email As String) As Customer
      Get
         Return EmailHashtable.Item(email)
      End Get
   End Property
```

At this point, you have a collection class that not only enables you to look up items by index, but also allows you to look up customers by e-mail address.

Cleaning Up: Remove, RemoveAt, and Clear

Because it isn't possible to use the same key twice in a `Hashtable`, you have to take steps to ensure that what's in the `Hashtable` matches whatever is in the list itself.

Although you implemented the `Remove` method in your `CustomerCollection` class, the `CollectionBase` class also provides the `RemoveAt` and `Clear` methods. Whereas `Remove` takes an object, `RemoveAt` takes an index.

TRY IT OUT Cleaning Up the List

Code file Structure Demo.zip is available for download at Wrox.com

In this Try It Out, you need to provide new implementations of these methods to adjust the `Hashtable`.

1. Return to Visual Studio 2010 and open the Code Editor for Form1. Locate the `btnListCustomer_Click` method and add the bolded code to clear the two lists:

```
   Private Sub btnListCustomer_Click(ByVal sender As System.Object, _
      ByVal e As System.EventArgs) Handles btnListCustomer.Click

      'Clear the lists
      objCustomers.Clear()
      lstCustomers.Items.Clear()
```

```
        'Create some customers
        CreateCustomer("Darrel", "Hilton", "dhilton@somecompany.com")
        CreateCustomer("Frank", "Peoples", "fpeoples@somecompany.com")
        CreateCustomer("Bill", "Scott", "bscott@somecompany.com")
    End Sub
```

2. To demonstrate how a `Hashtable` cannot use the same key twice, run your project and click the List Customer button to have the customer list loaded. Now click the List Customer button again and you'll see the error message shown in Figure 5-22.

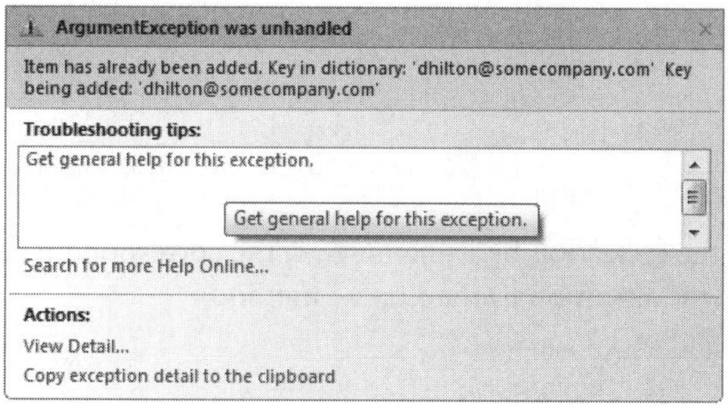

FIGURE 5-22

3. Click the Stop Debugging button on the toolbar in Visual Studio 2010 to stop the program.

4. Add the following method to the `CustomerCollection` class:

```
    'Provide a new implementation of the Clear method
    Public Shadows Sub Clear()
        'Clear the CollectionBase
        MyBase.Clear()
        'Clear your hashtable
        EmailHashtable.Clear()
    End Sub
```

5. Modify the `Remove` method as follows:

```
    'Remove a customer from the collection
    Public Sub Remove(ByVal oldCustomer As Customer)
        Me.List.Remove(oldCustomer)

        'Remove customer from the Hashtable
        EmailHashtable.Remove(oldCustomer.Email.ToLower)
    End Sub
```

6. Add the `RemoveAt` method to override the default method defined in the `CollectionBase` class:

```
    'Provide a new implementation of the RemoveAt method
    Public Shadows Sub RemoveAt(ByVal index As Integer)
        Remove(Item(index))
    End Sub
```

7. Run the project and click the List Customer button to load the customers. Click the List Customer button again to have the existing list of customers cleared before the customers are added again. Note that this time no exception is thrown.

How It Works

With these changes, the exception isn't thrown the second time around because you have ensured that the `Hashtable` and the internal list maintained by `CollectionBase` are properly synchronized. Specifically, whenever your `CustomerCollection` list is cleared using the `Clear` method, you ensure that the `Hashtable` is also cleared.

To clear the internal list maintained by `CollectionBase`, you ask the base class to use its own `Clear` implementation, rather than try to provide your own implementation. You do this by calling `MyBase.Clear`. Right after that, you call `Clear` on the `Hashtable`:

```
'Provide a new implementation of the Clear method
Public Shadows Sub Clear()
    'Clear the CollectionBase
    MyBase.Clear()
    'Clear your hashtable
    EmailHashtable.Clear()
End Sub
```

You'll also find that when you delete items from the collection by using `Remove`, the corresponding entry is also removed from the `Hashtable`, because of the modification to the `Remove` method:

```
'Provide a new implementation of the RemoveAt method
Public Shadows Sub RemoveAt(ByVal index As Integer)
    Remove(Item(index))
End Sub
```

EmailHashtable.Remove(oldCustomer.Email.ToLower)

The `Shadows` keyword indicates that this `Clear` procedure and `RemoveAt` procedure should be used instead of the `Clear` procedure and `RemoveAt` procedure in the base class. The arguments and the return type do not have to match those in the base class procedure, even though they do here.

> **NOTE** You don't need to worry too much about the details of *Shadows* and *Overrides* at this point, as they are discussed in detail in Chapter 11.

Case Sensitivity

It's about this time that case sensitivity rears its ugly head again. If you run your project and click the List Customer button and then enter a valid e-mail address in all uppercase letters, you'll see a message box indicating that there is no customer with that e-mail address.

TRY IT OUT Case Sensitivity

Code file Structure Demo.zip is available for download at Wrox.com

You need to get the collection to ignore case sensitivity on the key. In this Try It Out, you do this by ensuring that whenever you save a key, you transform the e-mail address into all lowercase characters. Whenever you perform a lookup based on a key, you transform whatever you search for into lowercase characters too.

1. Return to Visual Studio 2010, open the Code Editor for the `CustomerCollection` class, and make the bolded change to the `Add` method:

```
'Add a customer to the collection
Public Sub Add(ByVal newCustomer As Customer)
    Me.List.Add(newCustomer)

    'Add the email address to the Hashtable
    EmailHashtable.Add(newCustomer.Email.ToLower, newCustomer)
End Sub
```

2. Find the overloaded `Item` property that takes an e-mail address and modify the code as shown here:

```
'Overload Item property to find a customer by email address
Default Public ReadOnly Property Item(ByVal email As String) As Customer
    Get
        Return CType(EmailHashtable.Item(email.ToLower), Customer)
    End Get
End Property
```

3. Find the `Remove` method and modify the code as shown here:

```
'Remove a customer from the collection
Public Sub Remove(ByVal oldCustomer As Customer)
    Me.List.Remove(oldCustomer)

    'Remove customer from the Hashtable
    EmailHashtable.Remove(oldCustomer.Email.ToLower)
End Sub
```

4. Run the project and click the List Customer button. Now if you enter a valid e-mail address in all uppercase characters, the lookup will still work.

How It Works

In Chapter 4 you saw how you could perform case-insensitive string comparisons using the `String.Compare` method. You can't use this technique here because the `Hashtable` is handling the comparison and, ideally, you don't want to produce your own version of the comparison code that the `Hashtable` uses just to do a case-insensitive match.

You can use the `ToLower` method available on strings. This creates a new string in which all of the characters are transformed into their lowercase equivalents, so whether you pass DHILTON@SOMECOMPANY.COM or DHilton@SomeCompany.com in, you always get dhilton@somecompany.com out.

When you add an item to the collection, you can get `ToLower` to convert the e-mail address stored in the `Customer` structure so that it is always in lowercase:

```
'Add the email address to the Hashtable
EmailHashtable.Add(newCustomer.Email.ToLower, newCustomer)
```

Likewise, when you actually do the lookup, you also turn whatever value is passed in as a parameter into all lowercase characters:

```
Return CType(EmailHashtable.Item(email.ToLower), Customer)
```

When you're consistent with it, this action makes uppercase characters "go away" — in other words, you'll never end up with uppercase characters being stored in the key or being checked against the key.

> **NOTE** *This technique for removing the problem of uppercase characters can be used for normal string comparisons, but* `String.Compare` *is more efficient.*

ADVANCED ARRAY MANIPULATION

Being able to manipulate the size of an array from code and store complex sets of data in an array is important, but with .NET it's far easier to achieve both of these using the collection functionality that the majority of this chapter has discussed. The following two sections are included for completeness and to enable you to compare the two for yourself.

Dynamic Arrays

When using an array, if you want to change its size in order to add items, or clean up space when you remove items, you need to use the `ReDim` keyword to make it a dynamic array. This is a short form of, not surprisingly, *redimension*.

TRY IT OUT Using the ReDim Keyword

Code file Array Demo.zip is available for download at Wrox.com

In this Try It Out, you'll reuse the Array Demo project you created at the beginning of the chapter and tweak it so that you can add new friends to the array after the initial array has been created.

1. Find and open the Array Demo project in Visual Studio 2010. Open the Code Editor for Form1 and modify the code in the `AddItemsToList` method so that it looks like this:

```
Private Sub AddItemsToList(ByVal arrayList() As String)
    'Enumerate the array
    For Each strName As String In arrayList
        'Add the array item to the list
        lstFriends.Items.Add("[" & strName & "]")
    Next
End Sub
```

2. Run the project and click the Initializing Arrays with Values button. Your form should look like Figure 5-23; note the square brackets around each name.

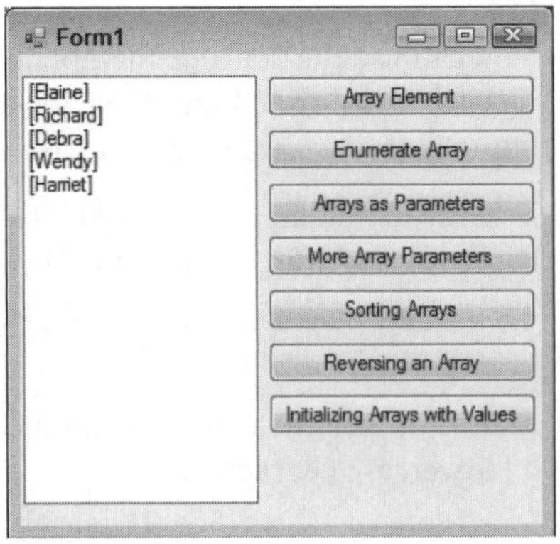

3. Stop the project and make the bolded change to the `btnInitializingArraysWithValues_Click` method:

```
    Private Sub btnInitializingArraysWithValues_Click( _
        ByVal sender As System.Object, ByVal e As System.
        EventArgs) _
        Handles btnInitializingArraysWithValues.Click
```

FIGURE 5-23

```
    'Clear the list
    ClearList()

    'Declare and populate an array
    Dim strMyFriends() As String =
{"Elaine", "Richard", "Debra", _
        "Wendy", "Harriet"}

    'Make the strMyFriends array larger
    ReDim strMyFriends(6)
    strMyFriends(5) = "Lane"
    strMyFriends(6) = "Joel"

    'List your friends
    AddItemsToList(strMyFriends)
End Sub
```

FIGURE 5-24

4. Run the project again and click the Initializing Arrays with Values button. Your form should look like the one shown in Figure 5-24.

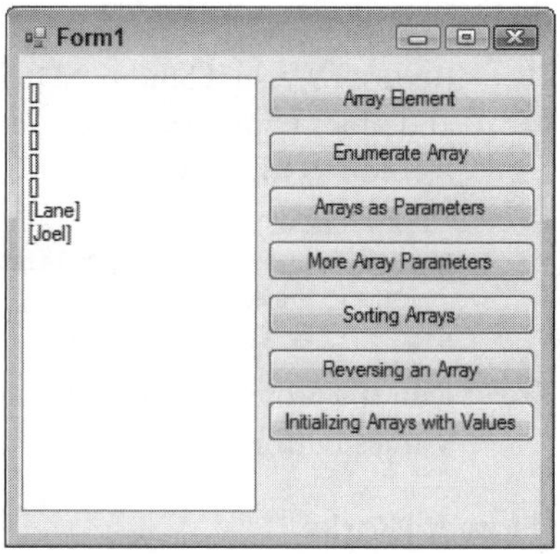

How It Works

After defining an array of five items, you use the ReDim keyword to redimension the array to have an upper boundary of 6, which, as you know, gives it a size of 7. After you do that, you have two new items in the array to play with — items 5 and 6:

```
'Make the strMyFriends array larger
ReDim strMyFriends(6)
strMyFriends(5) = "Lane"
strMyFriends(6) = "Joel"
```

Then, you can pass the resized array through to AddItemsToList:

```
'List your friends
AddItemsToList(strMyFriends)
```

However, as shown in the results, the values for the first five items have been lost. (This is why you wrapped brackets around the results — if the name stored in the array is blank, you still see something appear in the list.) ReDim does indeed resize the array, but when an array is redimensioned, by default all of the values in the array are cleared, losing the values you defined when you initialized the array in the first place.

You can solve this problem by using the Preserve keyword.

Using Preserve

By including the Preserve keyword with the ReDim keyword, you can instruct Visual Basic 2010 to not clear the existing items. One thing to remember is that if you make an array smaller than it originally was, data will be lost from the eliminated elements even if you use Preserve.

TRY IT OUT Using the Preserve Keyword

Code file Array Demo.zip is available for download at Wrox.com

In this Try It Out, you use the `Preserve` keyword.

1. Return to Visual Studio 2010, open the Code Editor for Form1, and modify the `btnInitializingArraysWithValues_Click` method as follows:

```
'Make the strMyFriends array larger
ReDim Preserve strMyFriends(6)
strMyFriends(5) = "Lane"
strMyFriends(6) = "Joel"
```

2. Run the project again and click the Initializing Arrays with Values button.

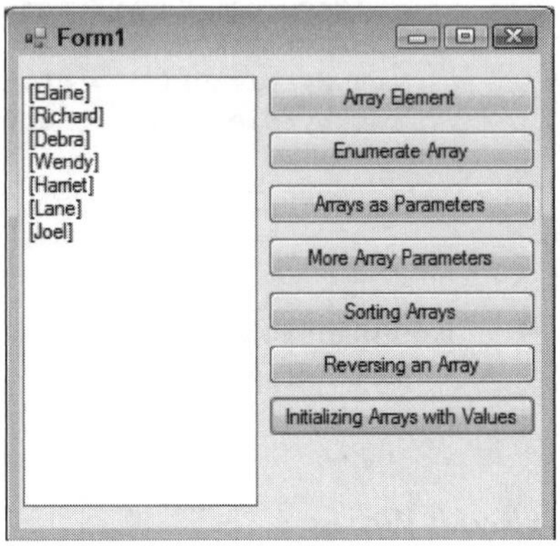

How It Works

You should now find that the existing items in the array are preserved, as shown in Figure 5-25.

FIGURE 5-25

SUMMARY

In this chapter, you saw some ways in which you can manage complex groups of data. You started by looking at the concept of an array, or rather, defining a special type of variable that's configured to hold a one-dimensional list of similar items rather than a single item.

You then looked at the concepts behind enumerations and constants. Both of these can be used to great effect in making more readable and manageable code. An enumeration enables you to define human-readable, commonsense titles for basic variable types. For example, rather than say `"CurrentState = 2"`, you can say `"CurrentState = DayAction.TravelingToWork"`. Constants enable you to define literal values globally and use them elsewhere in your code.

You then looked at structures. These are similar to classes and are well suited for storing groups of items of information that all pertain to a particular thing or person. After looking at these, you learned about various types of collections, including the basic `ArrayList`, and then you saw how you can build your own powerful collection classes inherited from `CollectionBase`. Finally, you looked at the `Hashtable` class and some of the less commonly used array functionality.

To summarize, you should know how to:

➤ Define and redimension fixed and dynamic string arrays

➤ Enumerate through arrays and find their upper dimension

➤ Define an enumeration of values using the `Enum` class

➤ Create and use structures to manipulate sets of related data

➤ Use an `ArrayList` to hold any type of object

➤ Use collections to manage sets of related data

EXERCISES

1. What keyword do you use to keep the values in an array that you `ReDim`? Where do you insert it?

2. How do you order an array?

3. Are arrays zero-based or one-based?

4. Why would you use an enumeration in code?

5. When initializing an array with values, what characters do you use to enclose the values?

6. How does a constant differ from a normal variable?

7. Structures are simpler and similar to what object?

8. `Hashtables` provide a fast mechanism for what?

▶ **WHAT YOU HAVE LEARNED IN THIS CHAPTER**

TOPIC	CONCEPTS
Arrays	List of a single data type. Sorting can be done using `Array.Sort`. `Array.Reverse` can reverse the order of the array.
Enumerations	Use enumerations to prevent invalid values from being used and to add clarity to your code.
Constants	Constants are variables that cannot be changed. They are typically global in scope.
Structures	Allow you to store different types of data together. Similar to a class but typically simpler in design.

6

Extensible Application Markup Language (XAML)

WHAT YOU WILL LEARN IN THIS CHAPTER:

➤   What XAML is and how it applies to the .NET Framework

➤   How XAML relates to the Windows Presentation Foundation (WPF)

➤   How to create WPF applications in Visual Studio 2010

In the past, user interface (UI) designers have often relied on tools like Adobe Dreamweaver and Photoshop to develop screen mockups of Windows applications and HTML for web applications. Although these tools do provide designers with cutting-edge tools to create graphics, they are limited to creating graphics and have limited ability to create actual Windows forms and web forms. Up to this point, these limited tools have hindered UI designers from creating rich user interfaces, forcing them to rely on developers who have access to tools like Visual Studio.

Microsoft has recognized the separation of duties between UI designers and developers and has created a new language and a new set of tools to assist UI designers, enabling them to create the Windows forms and web forms that will be used by developers to create world-class applications.

This new language comes in the form of the Extensible Application Markup Language (XAML), pronounced *Zammel*. Because XAML is an extensible application markup language, the language defines the elements of the user interface. This enables not only Microsoft to create tools for designing user interfaces, such as Expression Blend and Expression Design, but other companies as well. One such example of this is the Aurora XAML Designer from Mobiform Software, which enables UI designers to create user interfaces for Windows and web applications.

WHAT IS XAML?

As previously mentioned, XAML is an *Extensible Application Markup Language*. But what exactly does this mean? Wikipedia (www.wikipedia.org) defines XAML as a declarative XML-based language used to initialize structured values and objects. Others define XAML as a declarative XML-based language that defines objects and their properties.

Given these definitions you can begin to understand how the acronym for this new language was formed. You can see that this new language is based on XML, which has become the industry standard for sharing structured data between applications. The A in XAML is the application part of the acronym, and the declarative part of the definition refers to the language's ability to declare objects that represent controls on a form.

So you can start to visualize that this new language defines an application's UI in an XML-type language by defining the controls on a form. The controls that XAML defines map to classes in the .NET Framework. Keep in mind that XAML is an application markup language used to define a user interface, and should not be confused with a programming language such as Visual Basic 2010.

To illustrate this point, Figure 6-1 shows a basic Windows application defined in XAML, and the output that it produces. You can see that XAML looks a lot like XML because it is an XML-based language and adheres to the XML standard. You can also see that the controls are defined in the sample map to classes in the .NET Framework and that the output looks like a standard Windows application that you've already created in previous chapters.

```
<Window x:Class="Window1"
    xmlns="http://schemas.microsoft.com/winfx/2006/xaml/presentation"
    xmlns:x="http://schemas.microsoft.com/winfx/2006/xaml"
    Title="Window1" Height="164" Width="207">
    <Grid>
        <Label Name="Label1" Height="23" Width="106"
            VerticalAlignment="Top" HorizontalAlignment="Left"
            Margin="11,15,0,0">Enter your name:</Label>
        <TextBox Name="txtFirstName" Height="21" Width="121"
            VerticalAlignment="Top" HorizontalAlignment="Left"
            Margin="16,42,0,0"  />
        <Button Name="btnSubmit" Height="23" Width="74"
            VerticalAlignment="Top" HorizontalAlignment="Left"
            Margin="16,72,0,0">Submit</Button>
    </Grid>
</Window>
```

FIGURE 6-1

Given the nature of XAML and the output that it produces, you can start to visualize how XAML can more completely separate the duties of the UI designer from the developer. The UI designer would typically create the XAML code shown in the figure, using a tool such as Expression Blend, Expression Design, or Aurora XAML Designer, by visually creating the Windows form and having the tool create the XAML.

The next step would be for the UI designer to give the developer the XAML, which is stored in a file with a .xaml extension. The developer would import that XAML file into Visual Studio 2010 and then write the code to make the form have functional meaning so that when the user clicks the button something useful happens.

This should give you the bigger picture and illustrate the concept behind XAML and what role you might play in this picture in the future. In larger organizations that have a person or team dedicated to creating user interfaces, this scenario may soon become a reality. Your job in that organization might then be to write the code to make these user interfaces functional.

XAML SYNTAX

The best way to learn about XAML syntax and how it all works is to take an in-depth look at an actual example. Using the XAML code shown previously in Figure 6-1, this section breaks down the pieces so you have an understanding of how it all fits together and how it relates to the .NET Framework, and explains the syntax along the way.

Every element in a XAML file maps to a .NET Framework class, thus creating a corresponding object at runtime. XAML files can be parsed at runtime although they are typically part of an application and are compiled into an executable file.

The following code defines the basic Windows form that you have dealt with in the previous chapters. Here, notice that the element name is `Window`, which corresponds to the `Window` class in the .NET Framework instead of the typical `Form` class that you've been dealing with. The `Window` element is the root element in this XAML document, and like every well-formed XML document it must contain only one root element.

The attributes of the `Window` element define the namespaces used in this XAML document and map to properties of the `Window` class. The XML standard `xmlns` attribute, typical of most XML documents, defines the schema used with this XAML document. The `xmlns:x` attribute defines a custom namespace within the document with the name of `x`, and custom namespaces can also be found in other complex XML documents.

The `x:Class` attribute provides a name for the `Window` class, and in this example the class name is `MainWindow`. The `Title` attribute maps to the `Title` property of the `Window` class and sets the title that is displayed in the window, as shown in the form in Figure 6-1.

The `Height` and `Width` attributes map to the `Height` and `Width` properties of the `Window` class. These attributes are used to define the height and width of the window, as shown in Figure 6-1:

```
<Window x:Class="MainWindow"
    xmlns="http://schemas.microsoft.com/winfx/2006/xaml/presentation"
    xmlns:x="http://schemas.microsoft.com/winfx/2006/xaml"
    Title="Window1" Height="164" Width="207">
</Window>
```

Unlike the Windows forms that you've been using in the previous chapters, the `Window` class does not have a design surface that allows you to just start drawing controls on; it needs to have a container control that will in turn host other controls. Several different container controls are available for use in XAML, each with its own purpose. The `Grid` class, however, is the default container that gets added to XAML when using Visual Studio 2010 to design a XAML window. This is represented in the following code by the `Grid` element.

The Grid element enables you to precisely position controls in the window using columns and rows. Basically, it behaves in the same manner as the forms that you've been using up to this point. You can add rows and columns to the Grid control and place your controls into the grid in a table-like layout. In this chapter, you will not add row and columns to the grid control.

```
<Window x:Class="MainWindow"
    xmlns="http://schemas.microsoft.com/winfx/2006/xaml/presentation"
    xmlns:x="http://schemas.microsoft.com/winfx/2006/xaml"
    Title="MainWindow" Height="164" Width="207">
    <Grid>
    </Grid>
</Window>
```

Regarding the code:

➤ The first control shown in the window in Figure 6-1 is a label that contains the text "Enter your name:" This is represented in XAML by the Label element, which maps to the Label class in the .NET Framework.

➤ The Name attribute on the Label element maps back to the Name property of the Label class and is the name that you would reference in the code should you choose to the change the text displayed in the label. The Height and Width attributes map to the Height and Width attributes of the Label class and specify the height and width of the label in the window.

➤ The VerticalAlignment attribute maps to its corresponding property in the Label class and sets the label's vertical alignment within the Grid. This attribute has a value of Top, indicating that this control should align to the top of the Grid. Other possible values are Center, Bottom, and Stretch.

➤ The HorizontalAlignment attribute specifies the horizontal alignment of the Label within the Grid and maps to the same named property in the Label class. Possible values for this attribute are Left, Right, Center, and Stretch.

➤ The Margin attribute maps to the Margin property of the Label class and specifies the outer margin of the element. The Margin property defines a Thickness structure that contains Double values for the Left, Top, Right, and Bottom sides of the rectangle.

To put this into perspective, the Enter your name: label has a Left margin of 11 and a Top margin of 15. If you set both of these margins to a value of 0, it would cause the label to be aligned to the very left and very top of the Grid.

➤ The inner text of the Label element is the text that is displayed on the form. In a label on a Windows form that you've been using up to this point, the text in the label would be set using the Text property. The inner text of the Label element in XAML instead maps back to the Content property in the Label class in the .NET Framework. This is a little confusing and is worth keeping in the back of your mind in case you ever want to change the text of a label in code.

At this point you can start to see how a complete window is starting to take shape with the various XAML elements and their attributes:

```
<Window x:Class="MainWindow"
    xmlns="http://schemas.microsoft.com/winfx/2006/xaml/presentation"
```

```
    xmlns:x="http://schemas.microsoft.com/winfx/2006/xaml"
    Title="Window1" Height="164" Width="207">
    <Grid>
        <Label Name="Label1" Height="23" Width="106"
            VerticalAlignment="Top" HorizontalAlignment="Left"
            Margin="11,15,0,0">Enter your name:</Label>
    </Grid>
</Window>
```

Let's continue building out the code for this simple form to see how the next element, a text box control, aligns using the `Margin` attribute. In the following code you can see that the text box control is represented by the `TextBox` element, which maps to the `TextBox` class in the .NET Framework. The `Name` attribute also maps to the `Name` property of the class — and, again, this is the property that you will use to access the text contained in this control in your code.

Continuing the code discussion:

➤ The `Height` and `Width` attributes also map to their named counterparts in the `TextBox` class in the .NET Framework and specify the height and width of the text box. The `Vertical Alignment` and `HorizontalAlignment` attributes set the vertical and horizontal alignment in the grid, specifying that this control should be aligned to the left and top of the `Grid`.

➤ The `Margin` attribute is what is really interesting here. This attribute maps to the `Margin` property in the `TextBox` class and behaves in the same manner as it does for the `Label` element. Remember that the `Margin` property defines a `Thickness` structure that contains `Double` values for the `Left`, `Top`, `Right`, and `Bottom` sides of the rectangle.

➤ The `Left` attribute, as you would guess, specifies the distance from the left side of the `Grid`.

➤ Similarly, the `Top` margin specifies the top of this control from the top of the `Grid`, not from the bottom of the previous control as you might expect.

➤ If you wanted to specify some initial text for the `TextBox` element, you would create an ending tag of `</TextBox>` and place the text between the beginning tag and ending tag just as it was specified in the `Label` element. You can also access the text entered by the user in your code by querying the `Text` property of the `TextBox` class:

```
<Window x:Class="MainWindow"
    xmlns="http://schemas.microsoft.com/winfx/2006/xaml/presentation"
    xmlns:x="http://schemas.microsoft.com/winfx/2006/xaml"
    Title="Window1" Height="164" Width="207">
    <Grid>
        <Label Name="Label1" Height="23" Width="106"
            VerticalAlignment="Top" HorizontalAlignment="Left"
            Margin="11,15,0,0">Enter your name:</Label>
        <TextBox Name="txtFirstName" Height="21" Width="121"
            VerticalAlignment="Top" HorizontalAlignment="Left"
            Margin="16,42,0,0" />
    </Grid>
</Window>
```

➤ The final control in this sample XAML code is a Button control. The `Button` element in the following code maps to the `Button` class in the .NET Framework, and all of the attributes specified map to their counterparts in the `Button` class and behave as already discussed.

The text that is displayed on the button lies between the beginning and ending tags of the `Button` element. Like the `Label` element, this text is accessed through code via the `Content` property:

```
<Window x:Class="MainWindow"
    xmlns="http://schemas.microsoft.com/winfx/2006/xaml/presentation"
    xmlns:x="http://schemas.microsoft.com/winfx/2006/xaml"
    Title=" Window1" Height="164" Width="207">
    <Grid>
        <Label Name="Label1" Height="23" Width="106"
            VerticalAlignment="Top" HorizontalAlignment="Left"
            Margin="11,15,0,0">Enter your name:</Label>
        <TextBox Name="txtFirstName" Height="21" Width="121"
            VerticalAlignment="Top" HorizontalAlignment="Left"
            Margin="16,42,0,0" />
        <Button Name="btnSubmit" Height="23" Width="74"
            VerticalAlignment="Top" HorizontalAlignment="Left"
            Margin="16,72,0,0">Submit</Button>
    </Grid>
</Window>
```

At this point, you've seen what XAML looks like and the results that it can produce. You should have a basic understanding of XAML and how it relates to XML and the .NET Framework. The one piece that is missing is how XAML relates to Windows Presentation Foundation, which is the next topic of conversation.

WINDOWS PRESENTATION FOUNDATION

Windows Presentation Foundation, better known as WPF, is a presentation technology built into the .NET Framework and used to build rich user interfaces in WPF Windows and WPF Browser applications. WPF Windows applications differ from the Windows Forms applications that you've built thus far, as they separate the user interface code from the application's business logic code in much the same way that web forms in a web application do. The user interface code, as you might have guessed, is XAML. You'll learn more about web forms and code separation in Chapter 18.

WPF is represented in the .NET Framework in the `PresentationFramework.dll` and contains its own set of classes for building controls in WPF. For instance, if you display the Button Class topic in the MSDN Library that is installed with Visual Studio 2010, you'll get an index result prompting you to select the appropriate class: Web, WPF, or Windows.

You'll find most of the common controls (such as Label, TextBox, ComboBox, and Button) that exist for Windows Forms also exist in WPF. Although most of the properties, events, and methods are the same, there are some subtle differences, as you will soon discover.

At this point you may be wondering what you can do in WPF applications that you can't do in a Windows Forms application. Most everything that can be done in a WPF application can be done in a Windows Forms application. However, WPF applications make it easier to do more complex tasks such as working with video and manipulating images.

Figure 6-2 demonstrates some of the power of Windows Presentation Foundation in a WPF application. Notice that the image displayed on the form is skewed at an angle and contains a partial shadow of the image that fades out. The presentation code for this entire form is represented in XAML, and you will walk through the steps to create this form in the first Try It Out.

FIGURE 6-2

Creating a Rich WPF User Interface

One of the strong points of WPF Windows applications is the ease with which you can create rich three-dimensional images in a user interface such as the one shown in Figure 6-2. You can take a two-dimensional image, skew it at an angle, and add a drop shadow of the image that fades out.

TRY IT OUT Creating a Rich WPF User Interface

Code file Credit Card.zip available for download at Wrox.com

You will start to create the user interface shown in Figure 6-2 in this Try It Out. If you want to use the same credit card image shown in Figure 6-2, you can download the code for this chapter at the Wrox website at www.wrox.com. The download includes this image as well as the code for this application.

1. Open Visual Studio 2010 and select File ➪ New Project. In the New Project dialog, select Visual Basic in the Project Types list and WPF Application in the Templates list. Enter **Credit Card** in the Name field and click OK.

2. Note that the Forms Designer is divided into two sections. The top section contains the visual representation of the form, while the bottom section contains the XAML code used to create the visual representation. You can modify the form contents by clicking on the form or form controls and setting their properties in the Properties window or you can modify the properties directly in the XAML code.

Modify the properties for the Window element in the XAML editor by setting the `Height` property to **600** and the `Width` property to 800. You will see the window resize as you make the changes. Now, set the `Title` to Window1.

3. Before adding any controls to the form, you want to add the credit card image to your project. Right-click the Credit Card project in the Solution Explorer and select Add ⇨ Existing Item. Browse to the downloaded credit card image or an image of your choice and then click Add in the Add Existing Item dialog.

4. Click in the middle of the window in the Forms Designer, which is the Grid control. Now drag a Label control from the Toolbox and align it at the top of the window and center it from left to right. In the Properties window, set the `Content` property to **Apply for Your Card Today**.

5. Scroll down in the Properties window until you find the `FontFamily` property and then set it to **Segoe UI**. Set the `FontSize` property to **18** and the `FontWeight` property to **Bold**.

6. Resize the Label control in the window until all of the text appears and then reposition it so it is centered in the form.

7. A Border control will be used to apply the various effects to the image. Drag a Border from the Toolbox and drop it on your window. In the XAML Code Editor, set the `Margin` property to **0,60,0,0**. Set the following properties in the Properties window:

➤ Set `Width` to **380**.

➤ Set `Height` to **200**.

8. Drag an Image control from the Toolbox and drop it in the Border control in the window. Set the following properties in the Properties window:

➤ Set `Source` to **CreditCard.jpg** (or whatever name you gave it).

➤ Set `Height` to **185**.

➤ Set `Width` to **300**.

9. In the XAML Code Editor, click the `Border` element. In the XAML window, add the `BitmapEffect` element below.

```
<Border.BitmapEffect></Border.BitmapEffect>
```

10. Inside the `BitmapEffect` property in the XAML Code Editor are the subproperties. Add the following subproperties to BitmapEffect:

```
<Border.BitmapEffect>
    <DropShadowBitmapEffect Opacity="0.5" ShadowDepth="8" Softness="1" />
</Border.BitmapEffect>
```

11. At this point your image has a shadow around the bottom and right edges. In order to skew the image, you need to modify the XAML code in the XAML Code Editor. After adding the following code, your image should look similar to the one shown in Figure 6-3:

```
</Border.BitmapEffect>
<Border.RenderTransform>
<SkewTransform CenterX="0" CenterY="0" AngleX="0" AngleY="-3" />
    </Border.RenderTransform>
```

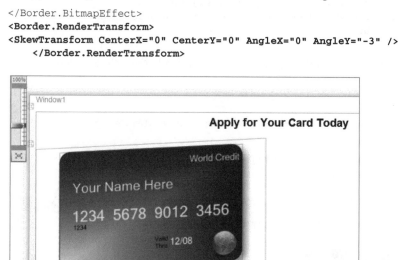

FIGURE 6-3

12. Now you need to create a second border to contain the upside-down faded reflection of the credit card. Drag a Border control from the Toolbox and place it beneath the first Border control. Set the following properties in the Properties window:

> ➤ Set `Margin` to **41,251,0,110**.

> ➤ Set `Width` to **300**.

13. In the XAML Code Editor, modify the second `Border` element by adding an ending `Border` element and removing the forward slash from the end of the `Border` element. Then add the following code:

```
<Border Margin="41,259,0,102" Name="Border2" HorizontalAlignment="Left"
    Width="300">
    <Border.Background>
        <VisualBrush Visual="{Binding ElementName=Image1}">
            <VisualBrush.Transform>
                <ScaleTransform CenterX="300" CenterY="100" ScaleX="1"
                    ScaleY="-1" />
            </VisualBrush.Transform>
        </VisualBrush>
    </Border.Background>
</Border>
```

14. To make the image fade out from top to bottom, add the following code:

```
</VisualBrush>
```

```
    </Border.Background>
    <Border.OpacityMask>
        <LinearGradientBrush StartPoint="0,0" EndPoint="0,1">
            <GradientStop Offset="0" Color="Black"></GradientStop>
            <GradientStop Offset="0.7" Color="Transparent"></GradientStop>
        </LinearGradientBrush>
    </Border.OpacityMask>
```

15. Finally, to skew the image shown in the second Border control, add the following code:

```
        </LinearGradientBrush>
    </Border.OpacityMask>
    <Border.RenderTransform>
        ,<SkewTransform CenterX="0" CenterY="0" AngleX="30" AngleY="-3.3" />
    </Border.RenderTransform>
```

16. Save your project by clicking the Save All button on the toolbar. After your project has been saved, go ahead and run it. Your window should look similar to the one shown in Figure 6-4.

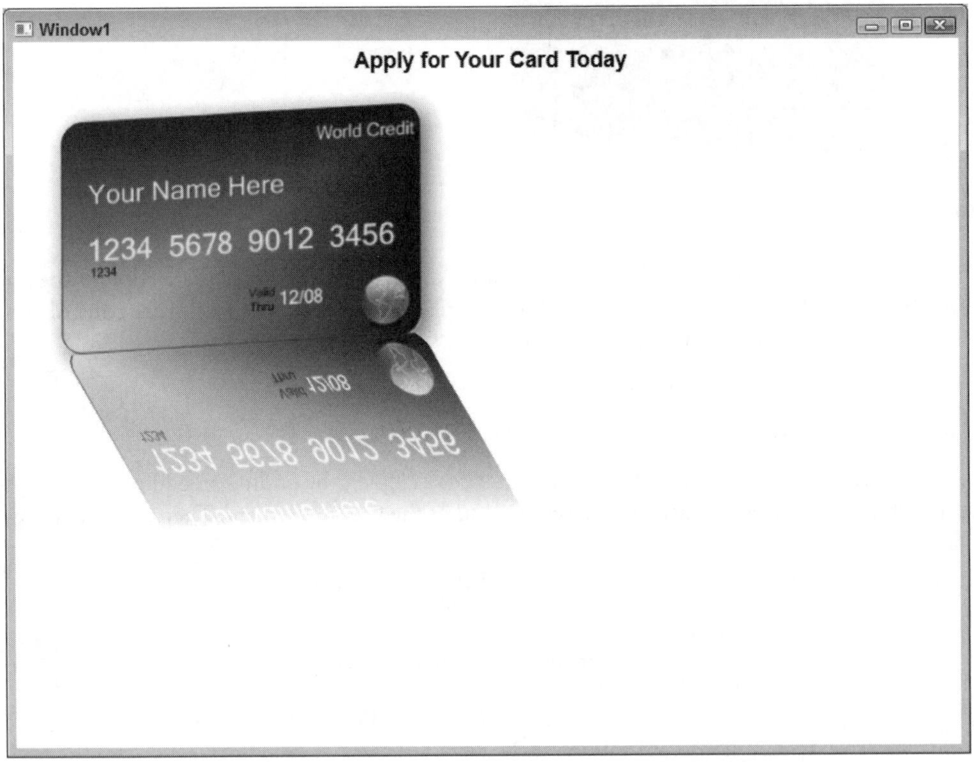

FIGURE 6-4

How It Works

You start by modifying the size of the form, and you have a choice of setting the `Height` and `Width` properties in the Properties window or using the XAML editor. You selected to modify the `Height` and `Width` properties in the XAML editor, and as you changed the `Height` property you saw the form resized immediately.

Next, you add an existing image to the project to be used in the Image control. You then add the Label control for the title and modify the properties for that control to have it centered in the window and to display the Segoe UI font.

The Border control has numerous built-in properties that enable you to render various effects on the objects contained in it. You add an Image control inside the Border control in order to apply the effects available in the Border control to the image.

The `BitmapEffect` property enables you to create a shadow effect around the bottom and right edges of the image by setting this property to `DropShadowBitmapEffect`. You fine-tune the shadow created by the `BitmapEffect` property by setting the subproperty `Opacity` to control the darkness of the shadow, the `ShadowDepth` subproperty to control the width of the shadow, and the `Softness` subproperty to control the shadow's softness from one edge to the other. After you apply the `BitmapEffect` property, your image has a shadow around the bottom and right edges at runtime.

In order to skew the image at an angle, you add the following code. The `RenderTransform` property sets the transformation that affects the rendering of the contents contained in the Border control. The `SkewTransform` element is used to transform a two-dimensional object into a three-dimensional object — in this case, the image of the credit card.

The `CenterX` and `CenterY` attributes specify the center coordinates of the transform and have been set to a value of `0` to specify the center of the image. The `AngleX` attribute specifies the X coordinate of the skew angle, which in this case is the starting point. The `AngleY` attribute specifies the Y coordinate of the skew, which in this case has been set to a value of `-3`:

```
<Border.RenderTransform>
    <SkewTransform CenterX="0" CenterY="0" AngleX="0" AngleY="-3" />
</Border.RenderTransform>
```

The second Border control that you added to the window provides the upside-down faded reflection of the credit card. When you add the following code, you immediately see an upside-down image of the credit card contained in the `Image` element.

The `Background` property of the border sets the brush that will fill the inside area of the border. However, instead of using a solid color to fill the area inside the border you use a `VisualBrush`. A `VisualBrush` paints an area with a visual image — in this case, the image of the credit card. The `Visual` attribute shown in the following code is used to set the visual content of the `VisualBrush` and is bound to the `Image` element whose `Name` property is set to `Image1`. You specify the `Binding ElementName` keywords to bind the Image to the `Visual` attribute. This is known as data binding. Data binding will be used in many other places in VS 2010.

The `Transform` property is used to apply a transformation to the image contained in the `VisualBrush`. The `ScaleTransform` element is used to rotate the image upside-down. The `CenterX` and `CenterY` attributes are used to specify the center point of the transform, and the `ScaleX` and `ScaleY` attributes are used to specify the X and Y axis for scaling.

The `CenterX` attribute has been set to the width of the image, and the `CenterY` attribute has been set to a value of `100` to show only a portion of the credit card contained in the `Image` element. `ScaleX` has been set to a value of 1 to indicate that the image should be scaled to a one-to-one ratio — in other words, its normal size. The ScaleY value has been set to a value of -1 in order to rotate the image upside-down:

```
<Border.Background>
    <VisualBrush Visual="{Binding ElementName=Image1}">
        <VisualBrush.Transform>
            <ScaleTransform CenterX="300" CenterY="100" ScaleX="1"
                ScaleY="-1" />
        </VisualBrush.Transform>
    </VisualBrush>
</Border.Background>
```

The OpacityMask element uses a Brush element to set the opacity of a UI element — in this case, the image of the credit card contained in the second Border control. The LinearGradientBrush element specifies a brush that paints an area with a linear gradient (for example, horizontal). The StartPoint attribute specifies the two-dimensional starting point to begin the gradient and the EndPoint attribute specifies the two-dimensional ending point to end the gradient. The StartPoint and EndPoint attributes can be set to a double between 0 and 1.

The GradientStop elements are used to specify the location and color of a transition point in a gradient. The first GradientStop element is used to specify the color Black with an offset of 0, indicating the gradient vector should stop at offset 0. The second GradientStop element uses the color Transparent and specifies an offset of 0.7. This provides the faded look starting at the top of the image where it is darker, to the bottom of the image where it is barely visible:

```
<Border.OpacityMask>
    <LinearGradientBrush StartPoint="0,0" EndPoint="0,1">
        <GradientStop Offset="0" Color="Black"></GradientStop>
        <GradientStop Offset="0.7" Color="Transparent"></GradientStop>
    </LinearGradientBrush>
</Border.OpacityMask>
```

The RenderTransform property and the SkewTransform element have already been covered during the creation of the first Border control. Here you set the AngleX attribute to a value of 30, indicating the angle of the transform starting at the upper-left corner. The AngleY attribute controls the angle of the upper-right corner and has been set to a value of -3.3:

```
<Border.RenderTransform>
    <SkewTransform CenterX="0" CenterY="0" AngleX="30" AngleY="-3.3" />
</Border.RenderTransform>
```

Using WPF Common Controls

You worked with the Label, TextBox, and Button controls in the Windows Forms applications that you built in the previous chapters. At this point you should be quite familiar with the more common properties of these controls — namely, the Name and Text properties.

In the following Try It Out, you will complete the user interface in the WPF Credit Card application that you have started building by adding Label, TextBox, Button, and ComboBox controls.

TRY IT OUT   Using WPF Common Controls

Code file Credit Card.zip available for download at Wrox.com

In this Try It Out, as you add the Label, TextBox, Button, and ComboBox controls to your window and set their properties, you will begin to see how they differ from their Windows Forms counterparts.

1. If your project is still running, stop it and return to the Forms Designer. Drag a Label control from the Toolbox and drop it on your window towards the upper-right corner. Set the following properties for this control in the Properties window:

➤ Set Content to **Personal Information.**

➤ Set Margin to **0,38,100,0.**

➤ Set FontFamily to **Segoe UI.**

➤ Set FontSize to **11.**

➤ Set FontWeight to **Bold.**

➤ Set HorizontalAlignment to Right.

2. Drag another Label control from the Toolbox and position it slightly beneath and to the left of the previous Label control. Set the following properties for this label:

➤ Set Content to **First Name.**

➤ Set Width to **95.**

➤ Set Margin to **0,69,225,0.**

➤ Set FontFamily to **Segoe UI.**

➤ Set FontSize to **11.**

➤ Set HorizontalAlignment **to Right.**

3. Drag a TextBox control from the Toolbox and position it to the right of the second label. The Name property is in the top border area of the Properties window. Set the following properties:

➤ Set Name to **txtFirstName.**

➤ Set Width to **185.**

➤ Set Margin to **0,71,35,0.**

➤ Set FontFamily to **Segoe UI.**

➤ Set FontSize to **11.**

➤ Set HorizontalAlignment **to Right.**

4. Drag a Label control from the Toolbox and align it beneath the second Label control. Set the following properties:

➤ Set Content to **Last Name.**

- ➤ Set `Width` to **95**.
- ➤ Set `Margin` to **0,99,225,0**.
- ➤ Set `FontFamily` to **Segoe UI**.
- ➤ Set `FontSize` to **11**.
- ➤ Set `HorizontalAlignment` **to Right**.

5. Drag a TextBox control from the Toolbox and position it beneath the previous TextBox control. Set the following properties:

- ➤ Set `Name` to **txtLastName**.
- ➤ Set `Width` to **185**.
- ➤ Set `Margin` to **0,101,35,0**.
- ➤ Set `FontFamily` to **Segoe UI**.
- ➤ Set `FontSize` to **11**.
- ➤ Set `HorizontalAlignment` **to Right**.

6. Drag a Label control from the Toolbox and align it beneath the previous Label control. Set the following properties:

- ➤ Set `Content` to **Address**.
- ➤ Set `Width` to **95**.
- ➤ Set `Margin` to **0,129,225,0**.
- ➤ Set `FontFamily` to **Segoe UI**.
- ➤ Set `FontSize` to **11**.
- ➤ Set `HorizontalAlignment` **to Right**.

7. Drag a TextBox control from the Toolbox and position it beneath the previous TextBox control. Set the following properties:

- ➤ Set `Name` to **txtAddress**.
- ➤ Set `Width` to **185**.
- ➤ Set `Margin` to **0,131,35,0**.
- ➤ Set `FontFamily` to **Segoe UI**.
- ➤ Set `FontSize` to **11**.
- ➤ Set `HorizontalAlignment` **to Right**.

8. Drag a Label control from the Toolbox, align it beneath the previous Label control, and set the following properties:

- ➤ Set `Content` to **City**.
- ➤ Set `Width` to **95**.

➤ Set `Margin` to **0,159,225,0**.

➤ Set `FontFamily` to **Segoe UI**.

➤ Set `FontSize` to **11**.

➤ Set `HorizontalAlignment` to **Right**.

9. Drag a TextBox control from the Toolbox, position it beneath the previous TextBox control, and set the following properties:

➤ Set `Name` to **txtCity**.

➤ Set `Width` to **185**.

➤ Set `Margin` to **0,161,35,0**.

➤ Set `FontFamily` to **Segoe UI**.

➤ Set `FontSize` to **11**.

➤ Set `HorizontalAlignment` to **Right**.

10. Drag a Label control from the Toolbox, align it beneath the previous Label control, and set the following properties:

➤ Set `Content` to **State**.

➤ Set `Width` to **95**.

➤ Set `Margin` to **0,189,225,0**.

➤ Set `FontFamily` to **Segoe UI**.

➤ Set `FontSize` to **11**.

➤ Set `HorizontalAlignment` to **Right**.

11. Drag a ComboBox control from the Toolbox, position it beneath the previous TextBox control, and set the following properties:

➤ Set `Name` to **cboState**.

➤ Set `Width` to **95**.

➤ Set `Margin` to **0,191,125,0**.

➤ Set `FontFamily` to **Segoe UI**.

➤ Set `FontSize` to **11**.

➤ Set `HorizontalAlignment` to **Right**.

12. Drag a Label control from the Toolbox, align it beneath the previous Label control, and set the following properties:

➤ Set `Content` to **Postal Code**.

➤ Set `Width` to **95**.

➤ Set `Margin` to **0,219,225,0**.

➤ Set `FontFamily` to **Segoe UI.**

➤ Set `FontSize` to **11.**

➤ Set `HorizontalAlignment` **to Right.**

13. Drag a TextBox control from the Toolbox, position it beneath the previous ComboBox control, and set the following properties:

➤ Set `Name` to **txtPostalCode.**

➤ Set `Width` to **95.**

➤ Set `Margin` to **0,221,125,0.**

➤ Set `FontFamily` to **Segoe UI.**

➤ Set `FontSize` to **11.**

➤ Set `HorizontalAlignment` **to Right.**

14. Drag a Button control from the Toolbox, position it in the bottom-right corner of the window, and set the following properties:

➤ Set `Name` to **btnApplyNow.**

➤ Set `Content` to **Apply Now.**

➤ Set `Margin` to **0,0,35,16.**

➤ Set `FontFamily` to **Segoe UI.**

➤ Set `FontSize` to **11.**

➤ Set `VerticalAlignment` **to Bottom. (The default is Top, which is how the other controls are vertically aligned.)**

15. Save your project and then run it. Your completed form should look similar to Figure 6-5.

How It Works

Adding controls to a WPF window is no different from adding controls to a Windows form, as you discovered. You simply drag the control from the Toolbox and drop it on the window. The difference is when you try to position a control and align it to other controls.

In a Windows Forms application, you can drag a control from the Toolbox and align it to other controls with snap lines before releasing the left mouse button. In a WPF application, you drag the control and place it on the form first and then reposition the control before you see any snap lines when aligning it with other controls.

A TextBox control in a WPF application has a `Text` property to specify the text displayed in the control, just as it does in a Windows Form application. However, the Label and Button control do not use the `Text` property to specify the text displayed in the control as they do in a Windows Forms application; instead, they use the `Content` property.

FIGURE 6-5

You'll undoubtedly have noticed that you must use the Margin property to reposition controls from within the Properties window, unlike using the Location property in a Windows Forms application. The differences in the properties do not stop at being named differently. The Location property uses a set of X,Y coordinates that position a control relative to the upper-left corner of the form.

The Margin property of a WPF control specifies the outer margins of the control as Left, Top, Right, and Bottom.

You may also have noticed that the Properties window does not provide as rich an interface as the Properties windows in a Windows Forms application. Case in point is the FontFamily property. In a Windows Forms application, the Font property provides the Font dialog that enables you to choose the font, style, and size desired.

Aside from these differences and limitations, WPF applications do enable you to create some stunning graphics in your applications. Although WPF may not be the norm for most applications, it does have a growing presence in desktop and browser applications.

Wiring Up Events

When you write code using Visual Basic, you will be required to handle events. An event happens when something, like clicking a button, happens. You will learn more about handling events in Chapter 7.

TRY IT OUT Wiring Up Events

Code file Credit Card.zip available for download at Wrox.com

In this Try It Out you will wire up some event handlers in the code to load the combo boxes on the form and handle the button being clicked. This will enable you to see firsthand how similar events in WPF applications are compared to Window Forms applications and how to add code to make your WPF application functional.

1. If your project is still running, stop it. Right-click `MainWindow.xaml` in the Solution Explorer and choose View Code in the context menu. Add the following `Imports` statement at the top of the class:

```
Imports System.Text

Class MainWindow
```

2. Declare a string array to hold the abbreviations of the states that will be loaded in the combo boxes. To keep the code short, we've only included the first six state abbreviations in alphabetical order. Add the following bolded code to your class:

```
Class MainWindow
'Private variables
Private strStates() As String = {"AL", "AK", "AZ", "AR", "CA", "CO"}
```

3. You want to load the combo boxes with the data from the `strStates` array. The best time to do this is when the window is loaded and after all the controls have been initialized. Select `(Windows1 Events)` in the Class Name combo box at the top of the Code Editor and then select the `Loaded` event in the Method Name combo box. Add the following bolded code to the event handler:

```
Private Sub MainWindow_Loaded(ByVal sender As Object, _
    ByVal e As System.Windows.RoutedEventArgs) Handles Me.Loaded

    'Bind the combo box to the strStates array
    cboState.ItemsSource = strStates
End Sub
```

4. When the user clicks the button on the window, you want the application to perform some action. To keep the code simple, display a message box with some information from the window. Select `btnApplyNow` in the Class Name combo box and the `Click` event in the Method Name combo box. Add the following bolded code to the event handler:

```
Private Sub btnApplyNow_Click(ByVal sender As Object, _
    ByVal e As System.Windows.RoutedEventArgs) Handles btnApplyNow.Click

    'Declare and instantiate a StringBuilder object
    Dim objStringBuilder As New StringBuilder

    'Add the question
    objStringBuilder.AppendLine("Is your personal " & _
```

```
            "information listed here correct?")
        objStringBuilder.AppendLine(String.Empty)

        'Add the personal information
        objStringBuilder.AppendLine(txtFirstName.Text & " " & _
            txtLastName.Text)
        objStringBuilder.AppendLine(txtAddress.Text)
        objStringBuilder.AppendLine(txtCity.Text & ", " & _
            cboState.SelectedItem.ToString() & " " & txtPostalCode.Text)

        'Display a message box to verify the information
        If MessageBox.Show(objStringBuilder.ToString, _
            My.Application.Info.Title, MessageBoxButton.YesNo, _
            MessageBoxImage.Question) = MessageBoxResult.Yes Then
            'Do some processing here
        Else
            'Return to the window and let the user correct
            'their information
        End If
    End Sub
```

5. Save your project and then run it. Enter some data in the Personal Information section of the window and click the Apply Now button. You should see results similar to those shown in Figure 6-6.

FIGURE 6-6

How It Works

In this example, you start the code by adding the following `Imports` statement, which is needed for the `StringBuilder` class:

```
Imports System.Text
```

The `strStates` variable is declared as a `String` array because of the parentheses after the variable name. Next you set the array values in the string, enclosing each string value in double quotes and separating each value with a comma. The entire list of values is enclosed in curly brackets:

```
'Private variables
Private strStates() As String = {"AL", "AK", "AZ", "AR", "CA", "CO"}
```

The code in the `MainWindow_Loaded` event handles loading the combo boxes with the items contained in the `strStates` string array. The `ItemsSource` property of the `ComboBox` class is used to set the `Items` collection to a list of items. You use the `ItemsSource` property when you want to bind a list of items to a combo box, such as items in a `String` array, a `DataSet`, or a `DataView`. You'll learn about the `DataSet` and `DataView` in Chapter 16.

```
Private Sub MainWindow_Loaded(ByVal sender As Object, _
    ByVal e As System.Windows.RoutedEventArgs) Handles Me.Loaded

    'Bind the combo box to the strStates array
    cboState.ItemsSource = strStates
End Sub
```

When a user clicks the Apply Now button, the `Click` event handler for this control is fired. The first thing you do here is declare and instantiate a `StringBuilder` object. The `StringBuilder` object is an efficient way to build large strings using fewer system resources than simply appending text to a `String` variable.

The `AppendLine` method of the `StringBuilder` class appends the text to the string and then automatically appends a line terminator after the data. The first line of text that you specify is a question for the user, and then you append a blank line by supplying an empty string. This provides a separation between the question in the message box and the data that is displayed:

```
Private Sub btnApplyNow_Click(ByVal sender As Object, _
    ByVal e As System.Windows.RoutedEventArgs) Handles btnApplyNow.Click

    'Declare and instantiate a StringBuilder object
    Dim objStringBuilder As New StringBuilder

    'Add the question
    objStringBuilder.AppendLine("Is your personal " & _
        "information listed here correct?")
    objStringBuilder.AppendLine(String.Empty)
```

Next, you start appending the information entered in the window to the string. First, you append the first name and last name on a single line, and then append the address information on the next line. The city, state, and postal code are added to the next line:

```
'Add the personal information
objStringBuilder.AppendLine(txtFirstName.Text & " " & _
    txtLastName.Text)
objStringBuilder.AppendLine(txtAddress.Text)
objStringBuilder.AppendLine(txtCity.Text & ", " & _
    cboState.SelectedItem.ToString() & " " & txtPostalCode.Text)
```

Next, you want to display the results of the string in a message box. Just as you've done before, you use the `MessageBox` class and call the `Show` method. The first parameter to the `Show` method uses the `ToString` method of the `StringBuilder` class to output the string that has been built. The caption for the message box is set in the next parameter to the `Show` method. Here you use the `Title` property from the `My.Application.Info` object. This object contains useful information about your application. You'll learn more about the `My` namespace in Chapters 10 and 11.

The next parameter to the `Show` method specifies the buttons that should be displayed on the message box. Here you specify the `YesNo` constant from the `MessageBoxButton` enumeration. The last parameter to the `Show` method is the icon that should be displayed in the message box. In this parameter you specify the Question icon, as you are asking the user a question.

The `Show` method will return a dialog result based on the buttons that you specify. Because you specify that the Yes and No buttons be displayed, the `Show` method will return a dialog result of either `Yes` or `No`. You handle this in an `If. . .Then` statement, checking for a dialog result of `Yes`.

The appropriate comments have been added in the following code to indicate where you provide your own code to perform some processing. You'll learn more about the `MessageBox` and how to use its buttons and icons in the `If. . .Then` statement blocks in Chapter 8.

```
    'Display a message box to verify the information
    If MessageBox.Show(objStringBuilder.ToString, _
        My.Application.Info.Title, MessageBoxButton.YesNo, _
        MessageBoxImage.Question) = MessageBoxResult.Yes Then
        'Do some processing here
    Else
        'Return to the window and let the user correct
        'their information
    End If
End Sub
```

SUMMARY

In this chapter you learned what XAML is and how it can be used to build WPF applications in Visual Studio 2010. You have also seen firsthand the power of XAML and WPF in building applications with interfaces that provide rich graphic manipulation that is not easily achieved with Windows Forms applications.

In building the Credit Card application, you not only learned how to create a WPF application that provides rich graphic manipulation, but you also learned how to wire events to the controls in a window. At this point you should realize the potential of WPF applications and understand how they differ from Windows Forms applications. You'll learn more about Windows Forms applications in the next chapter, which will help to tie all this information together.

To summarize, you should now know:

➤ What XAML is

➤ What WPF is and how XAML relates to it

➤ How to build a WPF application using Visual Studio 2010

➤ How to work with graphics in a WPF application

➤ How to work with control event handlers in a WPF application

EXERCISES

1. WPF makes it easy for organizations to separate which parts of software development?

2. XAML is based on another type of language. What is it?

3. What property do you set to position a WPF control in a Grid control?

4. In WPF design, you cannot place controls onto a window class, as the window does not have a design surface. To place controls onto a form, Visual Studio adds what container by default?

▶ **WHAT YOU HAVE LEARNED IN THIS CHAPTER**

TOPIC	CONCEPTS
XAML	XML based language to define objects and values in a WPF application.
Basic WPF controls	Grid, Label, TextBox, ComboBox, Image and Button controls are some of the common controls you will use when building WPF applications
Creating a gradient	To create a gradient, use the `LinearGradientBrush` and set the `GradientStops` to define how the gradient is shown.
Image Manipulation	You can skew images, display a reflection and add borders to images with ease in WPF using `SkewTransform`, `Border`, `ScaleTransform` and other WPF elements.
`My.Application`	To get information about the application at runtime, you can use the `My.Application` class.

7

Building Windows Applications

WHAT YOU WILL LEARN IN THIS CHAPTER:

➤ How to add more features using buttons, text boxes, and radio buttons

➤ How to create a simple toolbar and toolbar buttons to respond to events

➤ How to create additional forms and windows in your applications

When Microsoft first released Visual Basic 1.0, developers fell in love with it because it made building the user interface components of an application very simple. Instead of having to write thousands of lines of code to display windows — the very staple of a Windows application — developers could simply draw the window on the screen.

In Visual Basic (any version), a window is known as a *form*. With the .NET Framework, this form design capability has been brought to all of the managed languages — as *Windows Forms* in Windows Forms applications and as *Windows* in WPF applications. You've been using Windows Forms over the course of the previous chapters, and in the last chapter you learned about Windows in WPF applications. However, you haven't really given that much thought to them — focusing instead on the code that you've written inside them.

In this chapter, you'll look in detail at Windows Forms and WPF applications and learn how you can use Visual Basic 2010 to put together fully featured Windows applications using Windows Forms Application projects and WPF Application projects.

RESPONDING TO EVENTS

Building a user interface using Windows Forms or Windows is all about responding to *events* (such as the Click event), so programming for Windows is commonly known as *event-driven programming.* To build a form, you paint controls onto a blank window called the Designer using the mouse. Each of these controls is able to tell you when an event happens. For example, if you run your program and click a button that's been painted onto a form, that button will say, "Hey, I've been clicked!" and give you an opportunity to execute some code that you provide to respond to that event. You have already been using this feature.

Event-driven programming has two basic objects, a sender and a handler. In the next example, you will use a Button as a sender and a procedure (button_click) as a handler. When you click the button, it will raise or broadcast the event of clicking the Button and that event will be handled by the click event procedure you create. Once the handler receives the event notification, the code you write inside of the procedure will be executed. Your click event has sender and EvenTargs (RoutedEventArgs in WPF) parameters. The sender will be the object that raised the event, which in this case, is a Button object. The EventArgs may be nothing or a class derived from EventArgs like MouseEventArgs. The EventArgs will contain information on what caused the event, and in the case of MouseEventArgs it will have information like which button was clicked.

Setting Up a Button Event

A good way to illustrate the event philosophy is to wire up a button to an event. An example would be the Click event, which is *fired or raised* whenever the button is clicked. You have more events than just the Click event, although in day-to-day practice it's unlikely you'll use more than a handful of these. Even though you've already seen the Click event in action, this next Try It Out goes into some of the details of the Code Editor and new Button events that you have not seen up until this point.

In the real world, you'll more than likely be tasked to work on multiple projects at the same time. When you have down time in one project, you switch to the other project and work on it.

TRY IT OUT   **Using Button Events**

Code file Button Events.zip is available for download at Wrox.com

In this Try It Out, you'll work on multiple projects at one time: one Windows Forms Application project and one WPF Application project. This will enable you to see firsthand how button events are handled in both types of Windows application.

1.   Start Visual Studio 2010. Select File ⇨ New Project from the menu. In the New Project dialog, select Visual Basic as the Project type and Windows Forms Application as the Templates type. Enter a project name, **Windows Forms Button Events**, in the Name field and then click the OK button.

2.   Click the form in the Forms Designer. In the Properties window, change the Text property from Form1 to **Windows Button Events**.

3. From the Toolbox, drag a Button control onto the form. Change its Text property to **Hello World!** and its Name property to **btnSayHello**. Resize your button and form so that it looks similar to the one shown in Figure 7-1.

FIGURE 7-1

4. Save your project by clicking the Save All button on the toolbar.

5. Open a second instance of Visual Studio 2010, select File ➪ New Project from the menu. In the New Project dialog, select Visual Basic as the Project type and WPF Application as the Templates type. Enter the project name **WPF Button Events** in the Name field and then click the OK button.

6. In the WPF Button Events project, click the top of the window in the Forms Designer. In the Properties window, change the Title property to **WPF Button Events**.

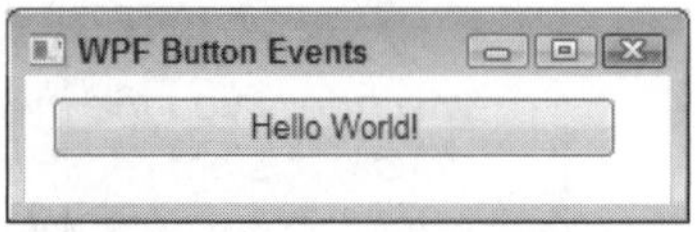

FIGURE 7-2

7. From the Toolbox, drag a Button control onto the form. Change its Content property to **Hello World!** and its Name property to **btnSayHello**. Resize your button and window so that it looks similar to the one shown in Figure 7-2.

8. Save your project by clicking the Save All button on the toolbar.

9. At this point, run both projects to get an idea of how both application types look very similar, as shown in Figure 7-3.

10. Stop both projects and return to the Forms Designer in the Windows Forms Button Events project.

FIGURE 7-3

11. Double-click the button and add the following bolded code to the Click event handler:

```
Private Sub btnSayHello_Click(ByVal sender As System.Object, _
    ByVal e As System.EventArgs) Handles btnSayHello.Click

    MessageBox.Show("Hello World!", Me.Text)
End Sub
```

> **NOTE** *Visual Basic 2010 added the ability to continue a line without the underscore (_) in many cases. Because this is not handled in every case and if you use any version before 2010 which is most likely going to be true, we chose to not add this into the examples. For the code above, you could have entered it without the underscore (_) and it would not have an error. Be aware that this is new to VB 2010 and take advantage of it when you can.*

12. Drop down the list in the Class Name combo box at the top of the code window. You'll see the options shown in the top portion of Figure 7-4. The bottom portion of Figure 7-4 shows the class members from the WPF Button Events project.

> **NOTE** *Visual Basic 2010 adds a small icon to the left of everything it displays in these lists. These can tell you what the item in the list actually is. A small purple box represents a method, a small blue box represents a member, four books stacked together represent a library, three squares joined together with lines represent a class, and a yellow lightning bolt represents an event.*
>
> *Visual Studio may also decorate these icons with other icons to indicate the way they are defined. For example, next to Finalize in Figure 7-5 you'll see a small key, which tells you the method is protected. The padlock icon tells you the item is private. It's not really important to memorize all these now, but Visual Basic 2010 is fairly consistent with its representations, so if you do learn them over time they will help you understand what's going on.*

Notice that the last two items in the list are slightly indented. This tells you that (Form1 Events) and btnSayHello are all related to Form1. That is, the btnSayHello class is a member of Form1. As you add more members to the form, they will appear in this list.

In the WPF Button Events project, this indentation tells you that (MainWindow Events) and btnSayHello are all related to MainWindow. Again, as you add more members to the window, they will appear in this list.

Now select Form1 in this list.

FIGURE 7-4

FIGURE 7-5

13. Open the drop-down list from the Method Name combo box to the right of the Class Name combo box and you'll see the options shown in Figure 7-5; the top portion of the figure lists the events in the Windows Form Button Events project and the bottom portion of the figure lists the events in the WPF Button Events project. These options are described in the list that follows the figure.

➤ The contents of the Method Name combo box vary according to the item selected in the Class Name combo box. This list lets you navigate through the methods related to the selected class. In this case, its main job is to show you the methods and properties related to the class. This applies to both Windows Forms Applications and WPF Applications.

➤ The (Declarations) entry takes you to the top of the class, where you can change the definition of the class and add member variables.

➤ The New method will create a new constructor for the class that you are working with. The constructor should contain any initialization code that needs to be executed for the class.

➤ The Finalize method creates a new method called Finalize and adds it to the class. It will be called when your program ends, to release any unmanaged resources.

➤ The Dispose method (not available in WPF Applications) takes you to the Dispose method for the class that you are working with and allows you to add any additional clean-up code for your class.

➤ The InitializeComponent method takes you to the code that initializes the controls for the class you are working with. You should not modify this method directly. Instead, use the Forms Designer to modify the properties of your form's controls.

14. Select btnSayHello in the Class Name combo box. Now, drop down the Method Name combo box, as shown in Figure 7-6. The list on the left is from the Windows Forms Button Events project and the list on the right is from the WPF Button Events project.

Because you selected btnSayHello in the Class Name combo box, the Method Name combo box now contains items that are exclusively related to that control. In this case, you have a huge list of events. One of those events, Click, is shown in bold because you provided a definition for that event. If you select Click, you'll be taken to the method in the form that provides an event handler for this method.

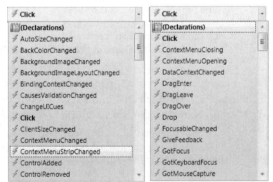

FIGURE 7-6

15. Now add another event handler to the Button control. With btnSayHello still selected in the Class Name combo box, select the MouseEnter event in the Method Name combo box. A new event handler method will be created, to which you need to add the following bolded code:

```
Private Sub btnSayHello_MouseEnter(ByVal sender As Object, _
    ByVal e As System.EventArgs) Handles btnSayHello.MouseEnter
```

```
        'Change the Button text
        btnSayHello.Text = "The mouse is here!"
End Sub
```

The `MouseEnter` event will be fired whenever the mouse pointer enters the control — in other words, crosses its boundary.

16. To complete this exercise, you need to add another event handler. With `btnSayHello` still selected in the Class Name combo box, select the `MouseLeave` event in the Method Name combo box. Again, a new event will be created, so add the bolded code here:

```
Private Sub btnSayHello_MouseLeave(ByVal sender As Object, _
    ByVal e As System.EventArgs) Handles btnSayHello.MouseLeave

        'Change the Button text
        btnSayHello.Text = "The mouse has gone!"
End Sub
```

The `MouseLeave` event will be fired whenever the mouse pointer moves back outside of the control.

17. Switch over to the Forms Designer in the WPF Button Events project. Double-click the button and add the following bolded code to the `Click` event handler:

```
Private Sub btnSayHello_Click(ByVal sender As System.Object, _
    ByVal e As System.Windows.RoutedEventArgs) Handles btnSayHello.Click

        MessageBox.Show("Hello World!", Me.Title)
End Sub
```

18. Now add another event handler to the Button control. With `btnSayHello` still selected in the Class Name combo box, select the `MouseEnter` event in the Method Name combo box. A new event handler method will be created, to which you need to add the following bolded code:

```
Private Sub btnSayHello_MouseEnter(ByVal sender As Object, _
    ByVal e As System.Windows.Input.MouseEventArgs) _
    Handles btnSayHello.MouseEnter

        'Change the Button text
        btnSayHello.Content = "The mouse is here!"
End Sub
```

19. To complete this project, you need to add an event handler for the `MouseLeave` event. With `btnSayHello` still selected in the Class Name combo box, select the `MouseLeave` event in the Method Name combo box. Add the bolded code to the event handler as shown:

```
Private Sub btnSayHello_MouseLeave(ByVal sender As Object, _
    ByVal e As System.Windows.Input.MouseEventArgs) _
    Handles btnSayHello.MouseLeave

        'Change the Button text
        btnSayHello.Content = "The mouse has gone!"
End Sub
```

20. Run both projects to compare how they look and perform. Note that both forms look very similar and that both forms behave exactly the same way.

The two forms in Figure 7-7 show the Windows Buttons Events form and the WPF Button Events form. The WPF Buttons Events form has focus and the mouse has been hovered over the button.

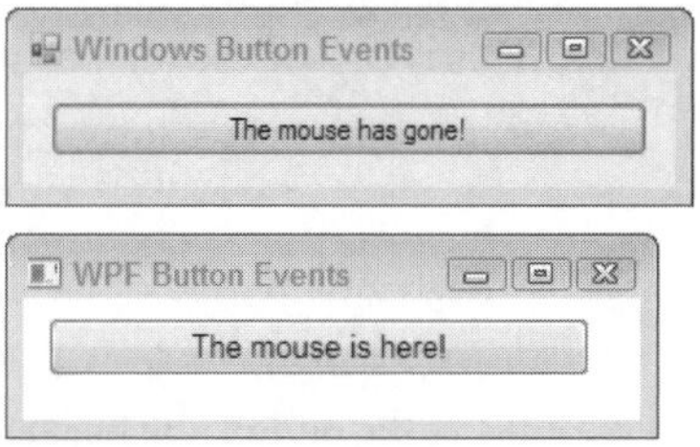

The two forms in Figure 7-7 show that the mouse has left the region of the button in the Windows Buttons Events form and has entered the button region in the WPF Button Events form. As you compare the minor differences in how the forms look, you should realize that both forms behave exactly the same way.

FIGURE 7-7

How It Works

Most of the controls that you use will have a dazzling array of events, although in day-to-day programming only a few of them will be consistently useful. For the Button control, the most useful event is usually the `Click` event.

Visual Basic 2010 knows enough about the control to create the event handlers for you automatically when you select them. This makes your life a lot easier and saves on typing!

You've seen the `Click` event handler for buttons in Windows forms in Chapters 1, 3, 4, and 5. The one parameter that I want to point out in the `btnSayHello_Click` method is the parameter defined as a `System.EventArgs`. The `EventArgs` class is defined in the `System` namespace and is used for most common controls in Windows Forms applications.

The `EventArgs` class will contain various data depending on the event being raised. For example, when the button is clicked and the `Click` event is raised, `EventArgs` will contain `MouseEventArgs`, enabling you to determine which mouse button was clicked and the X and Y coordinates of the mouse within the button:

```
Private Sub btnSayHello_Click(ByVal sender As System.Object, _
    ByVal e As System.EventArgs) Handles btnSayHello.Click

    MessageBox.Show("Hello World!", Me.Text)
End Sub
```

Did you notice the class that was specified in the `Click` event handler in your WPF application that corresponds to the `EventArgs` class is defined in a Windows Forms application? The parameter defined in the `Click` event handler for the button in your WPF application is defined as `System.Windows.RoutedEventArgs`. The `RoutedEventArgs` class is part of the `System.Windows` namespace, and is derived from EventArgs.

In a WPF application, this class does not provide any useful information about the mouse button that was clicked. This is one of the major differences between Windows Forms applications and WPF applications.

```
Private Sub btnSayHello_Click(ByVal sender As System.Object, _
    ByVal e As System.Windows.RoutedEventArgs) Handles btnSayHello.Click

    MessageBox.Show("Hello World!", Me.Title)
End Sub
```

If you look at the end of the btnSayHello_MouseEnter method definition for both application types, you'll notice the Handles keyword. This ties the method definition into the btnSayHello.MouseEnter event. When the button fires this event, your code will be executed.

```
Private Sub btnSayHello_MouseEnter(ByVal sender As Object, _
    ByVal e As System.EventArgs) Handles btnSayHello.MouseEnter

    'Change the Button text
    btnSayHello.Text = "The mouse is here!"
End Sub

Private Sub btnSayHello_MouseEnter(ByVal sender As Object, _
    ByVal e As System.Windows.Input.MouseEventArgs) _
    Handles btnSayHello.MouseEnter

    'Change the Button text
    btnSayHello.Content = "The mouse is here!"
End Sub
```

Although you set the button's Text property (for the Windows Forms Button Event project) and the button's Content property (for the WPF Button Events project) at design time using the Properties window, here you can see that you can change those properties at runtime too.

> **NOTE** As a quick reminder here, design time is the term used to define the period of time when you are actually writing the program — in other words, working with the Designer or adding code. Runtime is the term used to define the period of time when the program is running.

Likewise, the MouseLeave event works in a similar way for both applications:

```
Private Sub btnSayHello_MouseLeave(ByVal sender As Object, _
    ByVal e As System.EventArgs) Handles btnSayHello.MouseLeave

    'Change the Button text
    btnSayHello.Text = "The mouse has gone!"
End Sub

Private Sub btnSayHello_MouseLeave(ByVal sender As Object, _
    ByVal e As System.Windows.Input.MouseEventArgs) _
    Handles btnSayHello.MouseLeave

    'Change the Button text
    btnSayHello.Content = "The mouse has gone!"
End Sub
```

BUILDING A SIMPLE APPLICATION

Visual Studio 2010 comes with a comprehensive set of controls that you can use in your projects. For the most part, you'll be able to build all your applications using just these controls, but in Chapter 14 you look at how you can create your own controls.

In this section, you use some of the provided controls to put together a basic application.

Building the Form

The first job in creating your application is to start a new project and build a form. This form will contain a multiline text box in which text can be entered. It will also contain two radio buttons that give you the option of counting either the words or the number of characters in the text box.

TRY IT OUT Building the Form

Code file Word Counter.zip is available for download at Wrox.com

In this Try It Out, you build a basic Windows Forms application that enables users to enter text into a form. The application will count the number of words and letters in the block of text that is entered.

1. Select File ⇨ New Project from the Visual Studio 2010 menu and create a new Windows Forms Application project. Enter the project name **Windows Forms Word Counter** and click OK.

2. Click Form1 in the Forms Designer and in the Properties window, set the `Size` property to **442, 300**, the `StartPosition` property to **CenterScreen**, and the `Text` property to **Word Counter**.

FIGURE 7-8

3. To instruct users what to do with the form, add a label. Select the Label control from the Toolbox and drag it to the top-left corner of the form. Use the snap lines to align this control in the upper-left corner of the form as shown in Figure 7-8 before releasing the mouse button to add the control. Change the `Text` property to **Enter some text for counting:**

Strictly speaking, unless you have to talk to the control from your code, you don't need to change its `Name` property. With a text box, you need to use its properties and methods in code to make the application work. However, a label is just there for aesthetics, so you don't need to change the name for Label1.

> **NOTE** *When you are referring to a control from code, it's a good coding practice to give the control a name. Other developers should be able to determine what the control represents based on its name, even if they've never seen your code before. Refer to the section "Modified Hungarian Notation" in Chapter 1 for prefixes to use with your control names.*

4. Drag a TextBox control from the Toolbox and use the snap lines as shown in Figure 7-9 to align it beneath the Label control that you just added. Once the snap lines show the position of the control (refer to Figure 7-9), release the mouse button to have the control created and positioned.

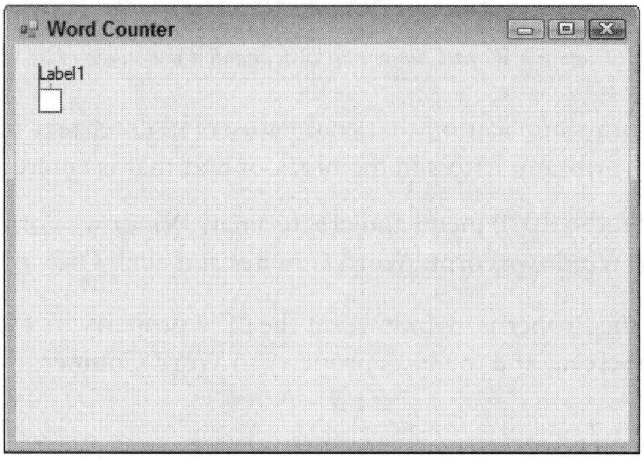

FIGURE 7-9

Now change the properties of the text box as follows:

➤   Set Name to **txtWords.**

➤   Set Multiline to **True.**

➤   Set ScrollBars to **Vertical.**

➤   Set Size to **390, 190.**

5. Your application will be capable of counting either the characters the user entered or the number of words. To allow users to select the preferred count method, you use two *radio buttons*. Draw two RadioButton controls onto the form next to each other below the text box. You need to refer to the radio buttons from your code, so change the properties as follows:

For the first radio button:

➤   Set Name to **radCountChars.**

➤   Set Checked to **True.**

➤   Set Text to **Chars.**

For the second radio button:

➤ Set `Name` to **radCountWords**.

➤ Set `Text` to **Words**.

6. As the user types, the characters or words that the user enters will be counted as appropriate. You want to pass your results to the user, so add two new Label controls next to the RadioButton controls that you just added.

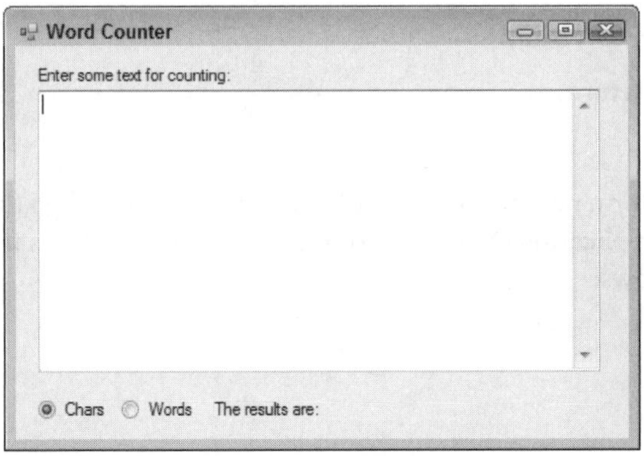

Word Counter

Enter some text for counting:

◉ Chars ○ Words The results are:

FIGURE 7-10

7. The first Label control is just for aesthetics, so leave the `Name` property as is and change its `Text` property to **The results are:**. The second Label control will report the results, so you need to give it a name. Set the `Name` property as **lblResults** and clear the `Text` property. Your completed form should look similar to the one shown in Figure 7-10.

8. Now that you have the controls laid out on your form the way you want, you can ensure that they stay that way. Select one of the controls and not the actual form, and then select Format ➪ Lock Controls from the menu. This sets the `Locked` property of each of the controls to `True` and prevents them from accidentally being moved, resized, or deleted.

9. Save your project by clicking the Save All button on the toolbar.

10. Start another instance of Visual Studio 2010. Select File ➪ New Project from the Visual Studio 2010 menu and create a new WPF Application project. Enter the project name **WPF Word Counter** and click OK.

11. Click MainWindow in the Designer. In the Properties window, set the `Width` property to **442**, the `WindowStartupLocation` property to **CenterScreen**, and the `Title` property to **Word Counter**.

12. Drag a Label control from the Toolbox and drop it onto the window.

Now change the properties of the label as follows:

➤ Set `Content` to **Enter some text for counting:**

➤ Set `Width` to **180**.

➤ Set `Margin` to **8,8,0,0**.

13. Drag a TextBox control from the Toolbox and drop it on the form. Using the following list, set the properties of the text box:

➤   Set `Name` to **txtWords.**

➤   Set `Width` to **390.**

➤   Set `Height` to **190.**

➤   Set `Margin` to **13,34,13,0.**

➤   Set `VerticalScrollBarVisibility` to **Visible.**

➤   Enable the check box for **AcceptsReturn.**

➤   Set `TextWrapping` to **Wrap.**

14. Draw two RadioButton controls onto the form next to each other below the text box. Align them the same as they appear in the Windows Application. You need to refer to the radio buttons from your code, so change the properties as follows:

For the first radio button:

➤   Set `Name` to **radCountChars.**

➤   Set `Content` to **Chars.**

➤   Set `IsChecked` to **True.**

For the second radio button:

➤   Set `Name` to **radCountWords.**

➤   Set `Content` to **Words.**

15. Draw a Label control on the form. Align it the same as in the Windows Application and set its properties as follows:

➤   Set `Content` to **The results are:.**

➤   Set `Width` to **100.**

16. Draw another Label control. Align it on the form the same way it appears in the Windows Application and set its properties as follows:

➤   Set `Name` to **lblResults.**

➤   Clear Content.

➤   Set `Width` to **175.**

17. There are no lock control features for a WPF window so just save your project by clicking the Save All button on the toolbar.

COUNTING CHARACTERS

With your forms designed, you'll want to build some event handlers to count the number of characters in a block of text that the user types. Because your application will be able to count words and characters, you build separate functions for each.

Code file Word Counter.zip is available for download at Wrox.com

In this Try It Out, you write the code to count characters.

1. Return to the Windows Forms Word Counter project and view the code for Form1. Add the following code to count characters. Remember that in order to insert an XML Document Comment block, you need to type three apostrophes above the function after you have written the code:

```
''' <summary>
''' Count the characters in a block of text
''' </summary>
''' <param name="text">The string containing the text to count
''' characters in</param>
''' <returns>The number of characters in the string</returns>
''' <remarks></remarks>
Private Function CountCharacters(ByVal text As String) As Integer
    Return text.Length
End Function
```

2. Now you need to build an event handler for the text box. Select txtWords in the Class Name combo box and, in the Method Name combo box, select the TextChanged event. Add the following bolded code to the event handler:

```
Private Sub txtWords_TextChanged(ByVal sender As Object, _
    ByVal e As System.Windows.Controls.TextChangedEventArgs) _
    Handles txtWords.TextChanged

    'Count the number of characters
    Dim intChars As Integer = CountCharacters(txtWords.Text)

    'Display the results
    lblResults.Text = intChars &
" characters"
    End Sub
```

3. Run the project. Enter some text into the text box and you'll see a screen like the one in Figure 7-11.

FIGURE 7-11

4. Now return to the WPF Word Counter project and view the code for Window1. Add the following code to count characters:

```
''' <summary>
''' Count the characters in a block of text
''' </summary>
''' <param name="text">The string containing the text to count</param>
''' <returns>The number of characters in the string</returns>
''' <remarks></remarks>
Private Function CountCharacters(ByVal text As String) As Integer
    Return text.Length
End Function
```

5. To build the TextChanged event handler, select txtWords in the Class Name combo box and, in the Method Name combo box, select the TextChanged event. Add this bolded code:

```
Private Sub txtWords_TextChanged(ByVal sender As Object, _
    ByVal e As System.Windows.Controls.TextChangedEventArgs) _
    Handles txtWords.TextChanged

    'Count the number of characters
    Dim intChars As Integer = CountCharacters(txtWords.Text)

    'Display the results
    lblResults.Content = intChars & " characters"
End Sub
```

6. Now run the WPF Word Counter project and enter some text. You'll see a screen similar to the one shown in Figure 7-12.

How It Works

Whenever a character is typed into the text box, the label at the bottom of the form reports the current number of characters. That's because the TextChanged event is fired whenever the user changes the text in the box. This happens when new text is entered, when changes are made to existing text, and when old text is deleted. The application is listening for this event, and whenever you hear it (or rather receive it), you call CountCharacters and pass in the block of text from the text box. As the user types text into the txtWords text box, the Text property is updated to reflect the text that has been entered. You can get the value for this property (in other words, the block of text) and pass it to CountCharacters:

```
'Count the number of characters
Dim intChars As Integer = CountCharacters(txtWords.Text)
```

The CountCharacters function in return counts the characters and passes back an integer representing the number of characters that it has counted:

```
Return text.Length
```

After the number of characters is known, the lblResults control for your Windows form can be updated using . . .

```
'Display the results
lblResults.Text = intChars & " characters"
```

. . . and for the WPF window using

```
'Display the results
lblResults.Content = intChars & " characters"
```

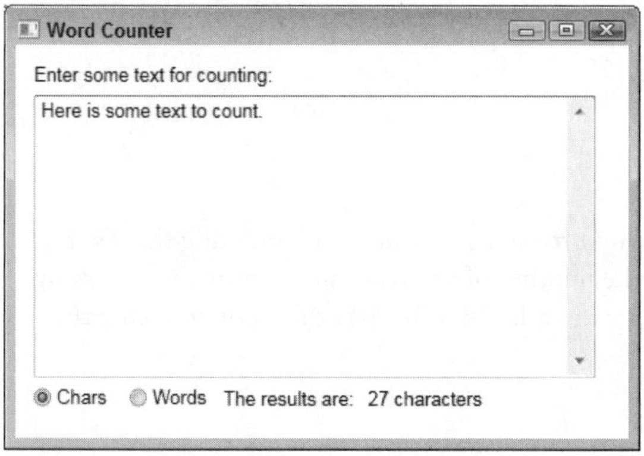

FIGURE 7-12

COUNTING WORDS

Although building a Visual Basic 2010 application is actually very easy, building an elegant solution to a problem requires a combination of thought and experience.

Take your application, for example. When the Words radio button is checked, you want to count the number of words, whereas when Chars is checked, you want to count the number of characters. This has two implications.

First, when you respond to the TextChanged event, you need to call a different method that counts the words, rather than your existing method for counting characters. This isn't too difficult. Second, whenever a different radio button is selected, you need to change the text in the results from "characters" to "words" or back again. Again, this isn't that difficult.

TRY IT OUT Counting Words

Code file Word Counter.zip is available for download at Wrox.com

In this Try It Out, you'll add some more event handlers to your code, and when you finish, you'll examine the logic behind the techniques you used.

1. Return to the Windows Forms Word Counter project and stop it if is still running. The first thing you want to do is add another function that will count the number of words in a block of text. Add this code to create the `CountWords` function:

```vb
''' <summary>
''' Count the number of words in a block of text
''' </summary>
''' <param name="text">The string containing the text to count</param>
''' <returns>The number of words in the string</returns>
''' <remarks></remarks>
Private Function CountWords(ByVal text As String) As Integer
    'Is the text empty?
    If text.Trim.Length = 0 Then Return 0

    'Split the words
    Dim strWords() As String = text.Split(" "c)

    'Return the number of words
    Return strWords.Length
End Function
```

2. The `UpdateDisplay` procedure handles getting the text from the text box and updating the display. It also understands whether it's supposed to find the number of words or number of characters by looking at the `Checked` property on the `radCountWords` radio button. Add this code to create the procedure:

```vb
Private Sub UpdateDisplay()
    'Do we want to count words?
    If radCountWords.Checked Then
        'Update the results with words
        lblResults.Text = CountWords(txtWords.Text) & " words"
    Else
        'Update the results with characters
        lblResults.Text = CountCharacters(txtWords.Text) & " characters"
    End If
End Sub
```

3. Now, instead of calling `CountCharacters` from within your `TextChanged` handler, you want to call `UpdateDisplay`. Make the following change:

```vb
Private Sub txtWords_TextChanged(ByVal sender As Object, _
    ByVal e As System.EventArgs) Handles txtWords.TextChanged

    'Something changed so display the results
    UpdateDisplay()
End Sub
```

4. You want the display to change when you change the radio button from Chars to Words and vice versa. To add the `CheckedChanged` event, select `radCountWords` in the Class Name combo box at the top of the code window and the `CheckedChanged` event in the Method Name combo box. Add the following bolded code to the event handler procedure:

```
Private Sub radCountWords_CheckedChanged(ByVal sender As Object, _
    ByVal e As System.EventArgs) Handles radCountWords.CheckedChanged

    'Something changed so display the results
    UpdateDisplay()
End Sub
```

5. Repeat the previous step for the `radCountChars` radio button:

```
Private Sub radCountChars_CheckedChanged(ByVal sender As Object, _
    ByVal e As System.EventArgs) Handles radCountChars.CheckedChanged

    'Something changed so display the results
    UpdateDisplay()
End Sub
```

6. Run the project, enter some text, and then check the Words radio button. Notice that the display changes to show the number of words, as shown in Figure 7-13.

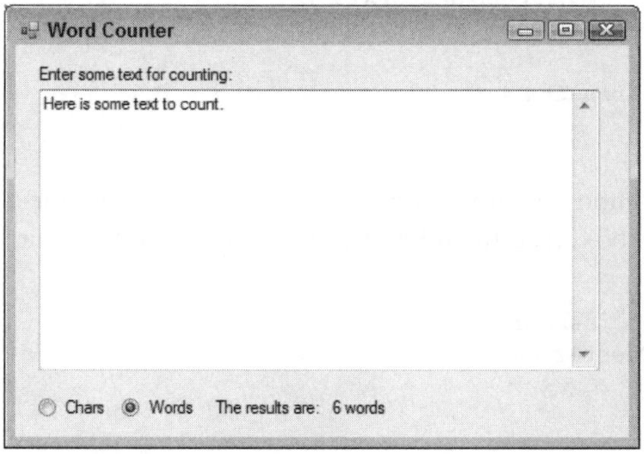

FIGURE 7-13

7. Return to the WPF Word Counter project and stop it if it is still running. Add this code to create the `CountWords` function:

```
''' <summary>
''' Count the number of words in a block of text
''' </summary>
''' <param name="text">The string containing the text to count</param>
''' <returns>The number of words in the string</returns>
''' <remarks></remarks>
Private Function CountWords(ByVal text As String) As Integer
    'Is the text empty?
    If text.Trim.Length = 0 Then Return 0

    'Split the words
    Dim strWords() As String = text.Split(" "c)

    'Return the number of words
    Return strWords.Length
End Function
```

8. Add the following code to create the `UpdateDisplay` procedure:

```
Private Sub UpdateDisplay()
    'If the window has not completed initialization then exit
    'this procedure as the radCountWords radio button has not
    'been created yet
    If Not Me.IsInitialized Then Exit Sub

    'Do we want to count words?
    If radCountWords.IsChecked Then
        'Update the results with words
        lblResults.Content = CountWords(txtWords.Text) & " words"
    Else
        'Update the results with characters
        lblResults.Content = CountCharacters(txtWords.Text) & " characters"
    End If
End Sub
```

9. Modify the `txtWords_TextChanged` event handler as follows:

```
Private Sub txtWords_TextChanged(ByVal sender As Object, _
    ByVal e As System.Windows.Controls.TextChangedEventArgs) _
    Handles txtWords.TextChanged

    'Something changed to display the results
    UpdateDisplay()
End Sub
```

10. Select `radCountWords` in the Class Name combo box at the top of the code window and the `Checked` event in the Method Name combo box. Add the following bolded code to the event handler procedure:

```
Private Sub radCountWords_Checked(ByVal sender As Object, _
    ByVal e As System.Windows.RoutedEventArgs) _
    Handles radCountWords.Checked

    'Update the display
    UpdateDisplay()
End Sub
```

11. Repeat the previous step for the radCountChars radio button:

```
Private Sub radCountChars_Checked(ByVal sender As Object, _
    ByVal e As System.Windows.RoutedEventArgs) _
    Handles radCountChars.Checked

    'Update the display
    UpdateDisplay()
End Sub
```

12. Run the project and enter some text. Then select the Words radio button and notice that the display changes to show the number of words, as shown in Figure 7-14.

How It Works

Before you look at the technique that you used to put the form together, take a quick look at the `CountWords` function:

```
''' <summary>
''' Count the number of words in a block of text
''' </summary>
```

```
''' <param name="text">The string containing the text to count</param>
''' <returns>The number of words in the string</returns>
''' <remarks></remarks>
Private Function CountWords(ByVal text As String) As Integer
    'Is the text empty?
    If text.Trim.Length = 0 Then Return 0

    'Split the words
    Dim strWords() As String = text.Split(" "c)

    'Return the number of words
    Return strWords.Length
End Function
```

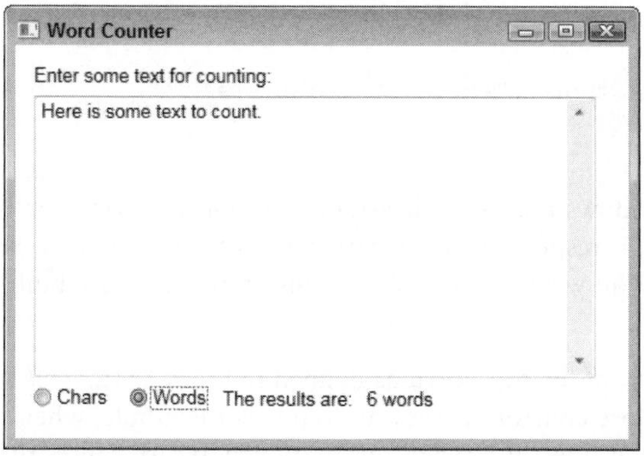

FIGURE 7-14

You start by checking to see whether the string passed to this function is empty by first trimming the blank spaces from the end of the string using the Trim method of the String class and then comparing the Length property of the String class to a value of 0. If no text has been passed to this procedure, then you immediately return from the function with a value of 0, indicating zero words were counted.

The Split method of the String class is used to take a string and turn it into an array of string objects. There are several overloaded methods of the Split method and the parameter you passed here is a Char data type. You want to split the string using the space character, so you specify a space in double quotes and add a lowercase "c" following the quotes to let the compiler know that this is a Char data type, enabling the compiler to convert the space. This means that Split returns an array containing each of the words in the string. You then return the length of this array — in other words, the number of words — back to the caller.

> **NOTE** *Because this code uses a single space character to split the text into words, you'll get unexpected behavior if you separate your words with more than one space character or use the Return key to start a new line.*

One of the golden rules of programming is to never write more code than you absolutely have to. In particular, when you find yourself in a position where you are going to write the same piece of code twice, try to find a workaround that requires that you write it only once. In this example, you have to change the value displayed in `lblResults` from different places. The most sensible way to do this is to split the code that updates the label into a separate method: `UpdateDisplay`. You can then easily set up the `TextChanged` and `CheckedChanged` event handlers to call this method in your Windows Forms Word Counter project or the `TextChanged` and `Checked` event handlers in your WPF Word Counter project.

The upshot of this is that you only have to write the tricky routine to get the text, find the results, and update them once. This technique also creates code that is easier to change in the future and easier to debug when a problem is found. Here is the code for the `UpdateDisplay` method:

```
Private Sub UpdateDisplay()
    'Do we want to count words?
    If radCountWords.Checked Then
        'Update the results with words
        lblResults.Text = CountWords(txtWords.Text) & " words"
    Else
        'Update the results with characters
        lblResults.Text = CountCharacters(txtWords.Text) & " characters"
    End If
End Sub
```

A WPF application starts a little differently from a Windows Forms application. A Windows Forms application calls an `InitializeComponent` procedure, which is responsible for creating all of the controls on the form. This procedure is executed before the code that you write so that all controls on the form are built and initialized before your code accesses those controls.

A WPF application builds and initializes the controls from the top down as defined in the XAML. This causes a problem because events start to be fired on those controls as they are built. For example, when the `radCountChars` radio button is built and initialized, it fires the `Checked` event, which in turn causes the `UpdateDisplay` method to be called when the `IsChecked` property is set to `True` on this control.

At this point, the `radCountWords` radio button has not been built by the application and a `NullReferenceException` is thrown when your code tries to access the `radCountWords` control. To handle this behavior, you'll want to check the `IsInitialized` property of the window. This property returns a `Boolean` value indicating if the window has been completely initialized, and by using this property you can exit this method if the controls in the window are still being built and initialized:

```
Private Sub UpdateDisplay()
    'If the window has not completed initialization then exit
    'this procedure as the radCountWords radio button has not
    'been created yet
    If Not Me.IsInitialized Then Exit Sub

    'Do we want to count words?
    If radCountWords.IsChecked Then
        'Update the results with words
        lblResults.Content = CountWords(txtWords.Text) & " words"
    Else
        'Update the results with characters
        lblResults.Content = CountCharacters(txtWords.Text) & " characters"
    End If
End Sub
```

You'll find as you build applications that this technique of breaking out the code for an event handler is something you'll do quite often.

CREATING MORE COMPLEX APPLICATIONS

Normal applications generally have a number of common elements. Among these are toolbars and status bars. Putting together an application that has these features is a fairly trivial task in Visual Basic 2010.

In the next Try It Out, you build an application that enables you to make changes to the text entered into a text box, such as changing its color and making it all uppercase or lowercase. You'll be using a ToolBar control to change both the color of the text in your text box and the case of the text to either all uppercase letters or all lowercase letters.

The StatusBar control will also be used in your project to display the status of your actions as a result of clicking a button on the toolbar.

The Text Editor Project

Your first step on the road to building your application is to create a new project.

TRY IT OUT   Creating the Text Editor Project

Code file Text Editor.zip is available for download at Wrox.com

You will be building the Text Editor project using both Windows Forms and WPF.

1.   Create a new Windows Forms Application project and name it **Windows Forms Text Editor**.

2.   Most of the time, Form1 isn't a very appropriate name for a form, as it's not very descriptive. Right-click the form in the Solution Explorer, select Rename, and change its name to **TextEditor.vb** as shown in Figure 7-15. Then press Enter to save the changes.

3.   Click the form in the Forms Designer, and in the Properties window change the Text property to **Text Editor**.

4.   The screenshots show the design window as quite small, to save paper. Using the Properties window of the form, you should explicitly set the size of the form by setting the Size property to **600, 460**.

FIGURE 7-15

5.   Save your project by clicking the Save All button on the toolbar.

6.   Start a new instance of Visual Studio 2010. Create a new WPF Application project and name it **WPF Text Editor**.

7.   In the Solution Explorer, rename MainWindow.xaml to **TextEditor.xaml** as shown in Figure 7-16 and press Enter to save the changes.

8.   Click the form in the Designer, and in the Properties window change the Title property to **Text Editor**.

9.   Set the Width property to **600** and the Height property to **460**.

10.   Save your project by clicking the Save All button on the toolbar.

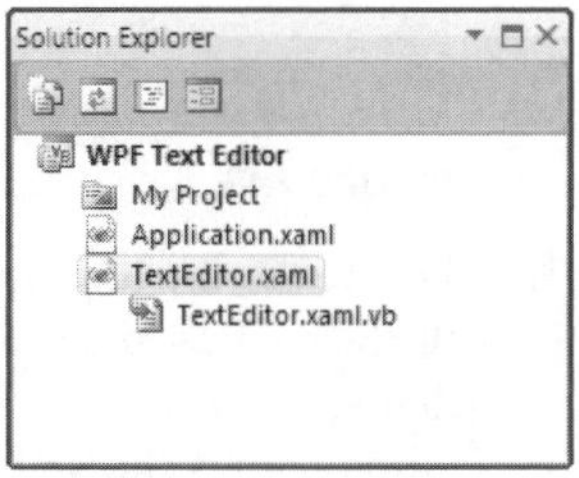

FIGURE 7-16

In the next section, you start building the user interface part of the application.

CREATING THE TOOLBAR

The toolbar you are building will contain a collection of buttons, like the toolbar in Visual Studio 2010.

TRY IT OUT Adding the Toolbar

Code file Text Editor.zip is available for download at Wrox.com

In this Try It Out, you will create the toolbar and add the buttons to it.

1. Return to the Forms Designer in the Windows Forms Text Editor project. Select the ToolStrip control from the Toolbox and drag and drop it on the form. It will automatically dock at the top of the form. Set the `Stretch` property to `True` to cause the toolbar to stretch across the entire form at runtime.

2. To add buttons to the toolbar you use a built-in editor. Find the `Items` property in the Properties window, select it, and left-click the collection button to the right of (Collection)(look for ...).

3. You're going to add six buttons to the toolbar: Clear, Red, Blue, Uppercase, Lowercase, and About. To add the first button, click the Add button in the Items Collection Editor. The Items Collection Editor displays a properties palette much like the one that you're used to using. For each button you need to change its name, change its display style, give it an icon, clear its text, and provide some explanatory ToolTip text. Change the `Name` property to **tbrClear** as shown in Figure 7-17.

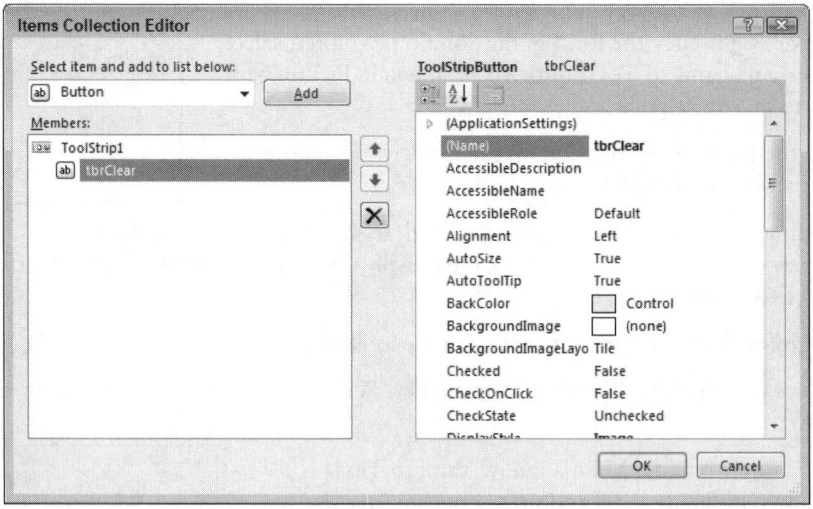

FIGURE 7-17

4. Locate the `Image` property and select it. Then click the ellipses button for this property to invoke the Select Resource editor. In the Select Resource editor, click the Import button. In the Open dialog, browse to the installation folder where Visual Studio 2010 was installed (the default installation path is shown here) and locate the following folder:

```
C:\Program Files\Microsoft Visual Studio 10.0\Common7\VS2010ImageLibrary\1033
```

If you have not previously extracted the contents of the `VS2010ImageLibrary.zip` file you will need to do so now.

From the installation folder, browse to the `VS2010ImageLibary\Actions\32bitcolor bitmaps\16x16` folder. Select the `New_DocumentHS.bmp` file and then click Open to import the resource. Next, click OK in the Select Resource editor and you'll be returned to the Items Collection Editor.

5. The background color of the bitmap is black so you need to adjust the image transparency color so the image displays correctly in the toolbar. Locate the `ImageTransparentColor` property and click the drop-down arrow next to the text "Magenta." Then locate the color black near the top of the list and select it.

6. Set the `ToolTipText` property to **New**. This completes the steps necessary to create the first button.

7. You want to create a Separator between the Clear button and the Red button. Add this control using the Add ToolStripButton tool. Select the ToolStrip at the top of the form. You will see the drop-down to add a new item. Open the drop-down and select Separator. A Separator will be added to the ToolStrip. You can accept all the default properties for this button.

8. Repeat steps 3 through 6 to create the Red button and use the following properties for this button. Use the image library you used for Clear (`VS2010ImageLibary\Actions\32bitcolor bitmaps\16x16\`) for all of the images you import unless instructed to use another folder.

- ➤ Set `Name` to **tbrRed** and clear the `Text` property.
- ➤ Use **Color_fontHS.bmp** for the `Image` property.
- ➤ Set `ImageTransparentColor` to **Black**.
- ➤ Set the `ToolTipText` property to **Red**.

9. Next is the Blue button. For this button and the others, you will copy and paste the Red button. In the ToolStrip, select the Red button. Press Ctrl+C, select the ToolStrip (if the button is selected when you paste a new button it will be before the button you copied, not after it) and then press Ctrl+V. A copy of the Red button is added with a new name. This will copy the properties of the Red button; you only need to update properties that are different. Use the following properties for this button; if you cannot make the copy paste work, you can just add the other buttons as before.

- ➤ Set `Name` to **tbrBlue**.
- ➤ Use `Color_lineHS.bmp` for the `Image` property.
- ➤ Set the `ToolTipText` property to **Blue**.

10. You want to create a separator between the Blue button and the Uppercase button. Create the Uppercase button and use the following properties for this button:

- ➤ Set `Name` to **tbrUpperCase**.
- ➤ Use `FillUpHS.bmp` for the `Image` property.
- ➤ Set the `ToolTipText` property to **Upper Case**.

11. Create the Lowercase button and use the following properties for it:

➤ Set `Name` to **tbrLowerCase.**

➤ Use `FillDownHS.bmp` for the `Image` property.

➤ Set the `ToolTipText` property to **Lower Case.**

12. You want to create a separator between the Lowercase button and the Help button.

13. Create the Help button and use the following properties for it. Note the different image path for the help image.

➤ Set `Name` to **tbrHelpAbout.**

➤ Use `VS2010ImageLibary\Annotation&Buttons\bmp_format\ Help.bmp` for the `Image` property.

➤ Set the `ToolTipText` property to **About.**

➤ Set the `ImageTransparentColor` to **Fuchsia**

14. Click the OK button in the Items Collection Editor to close it.

15. Save your project by clicking the Save All button on the toolbar.

16. Switch to the WPF Text Editor project and click the window in the Designer. Next, select the ToolBarTray control from the Toolbox and drag it and drop it on the Grid. Reposition the Tool-BarTray control to the upper-left corner of the Grid. Drag the right edge of the ToolBarTray control to the right side of the Grid until it snaps into place. The ToolBarTray is now set to expand with the width of the window at runtime.

17. Drag a ToolBar control from the Toolbox and drop it on the ToolBarTray control. Expand its width until it completely fills the ToolBarTray control.

18. Click in the XAML editor on the definition for the ToolBar control and modify the code for this control as follows:

```
<ToolBar Height="26" Name="ToolBar1" Width="575">
</ToolBar>
```

19. Add the following XAML code to create the toolbar buttons:

```
<ToolBar Height="26" Name="ToolBar1" Width="575">
    <Button Name="tbrClear" ToolTip="Clear">
        <Image Source="file:///C:/Program Files/Microsoft
        Visual Studio 10.0/Common7/VS2010ImageLibrary/1033/
        VS2010ImageLibrary/Actions/32bitcolor bitmaps/16x16/
        NewDocumentHS.BMP"></Image>
    </Button>
    <Separator Padding="1" />
    <Button Name="tbrRed" ToolTip="Red">
        <Image Source="file:///C:/Program Files/Microsoft
        Visual Studio 10.0/Common7/VS2010ImageLibrary/1033/
        VS2010ImageLibrary/Actions/32bitcolor bitmaps/16x16/
        Color_fontHS.bmp"></Image>
    </Button>
    <Button Name="tbrBlue" ToolTip="Blue">
        <Image Source="file:///C:/Program Files/Microsoft
```

```
                    Visual Studio 10.0/Common7/VS2010ImageLibrary/1033/
                    VS2010ImageLibrary/Actions/32bitcolor bitmaps/16x16/
                    Color_lineHS.bmp"></Image>
            </Button>
            <Separator/>
            <Button Name="tbrUpperCase" ToolTip="Upper Case">
                <Image Source="file:///C:/Program Files/Microsoft
                    Visual Studio 10.0/Common7/VS2010ImageLibrary/1033/
                    VS2010ImageLibrary/Actions/32bitcolor bitmaps/16x16/
                    FillUpHS.BMP"></Image>
            </Button>
            <Button Name="tbrLowerCase" ToolTip="Lower Case">
                <Image Source="file:///C:/Program Files/Microsoft
                    Visual Studio 10.0/Common7/VS2010ImageLibrary/1033/
                    VS2010ImageLibrary/Actions/32bitcolor bitmaps/16x16/
                    FillDownHS.BMP"></Image>
            </Button>
            <Separator/>
            <Button Name="tbrHelpAbout" ToolTip="About">
                <Image Source="file:///C:/Program Files/Microsoft
                    Visual Studio 10.0/Common7/VS2010ImageLibrary/1033/
                    VS2010ImageLibrary/Annotations&amp;Buttons/
                    bmp_format/Help.BMP"></Image>
            </Button>
        </ToolBar>
```

20. You need to ensure that your Startup URI is `TextEditor.xaml`. To do this, go to the Project menu and click WPF Text Editor Properties. On the Application tab, set the Startup URI to `TextEditor.xaml`.

21. Save your project by clicking the Save All button on the toolbar.

How It Works

For Windows Forms Application projects, the ToolStrip control docks to a particular position on the form. In this case, it docks itself to the top edge of the form.

The six buttons and three separators that you added to the toolbar actually appear as full members of the `TextEditor` class and have the usual events that you are accustomed to seeing. Later, you'll see how you can respond to the `Click` event for the various buttons.

A toolbar button can display text only, an image only, or both text and an image. Your project displays an image that is the default display style for toolbar buttons. Normally you would create your own images or have a graphics designer create the images, but for this Try It Out you used images that ship with Visual Studio 2010. At this point, your toolbar should look similar to the one shown in Figure 7-18.

FIGURE 7-18

The `ToolTipText` property enables Visual Basic 2010 to display a ToolTip for the button whenever the user hovers the mouse over it. You don't need to worry about actually creating or showing a ToolTip; Visual Basic 2010 does this for you.

For WPF Application projects, you use the ToolBarTray and ToolBar controls to create a toolbar. You have to position these controls manually and adjust their width in order to have the toolbar expand to fill the top of the window. Then you have to add some XAML to create the toolbar buttons and images.

The ToolBarTray control determines which buttons will fit in the toolbar and which buttons need to go into the overflow area as the form is resized smaller and larger. The ToolBarTray and ToolBar control work hand in hand to display a toolbar in a WPF application.

Each button on the toolbar is created using the `Button` class, as shown in the partial code listing below. The `Button` class contains the `Name` and `ToolTip` properties to set the name of the button that is used to access the button from code and to display the ToolTip when the user hovers a mouse over the button. The Separator control is created using the `Separator` class and contains no properties that need to be set. The remaining buttons for the toolbar are created in the same manner as the Clear button.

```
<Button Name="tbrClear" ToolTip="Clear">
    <Image Source="file:///C:/Program Files/Microsoft
Visual Studio 9.0/Common7/VS2010ImageLibrary/1033/VS2010ImageLibrary/ Actions/
        32bitcolor bitmaps/16x16/NewDocumentHS.BMP"></Image>
</Button>
<Separator />
```

The toolbar in your WPF Text Editor project looks very similar to the one shown previously in Figure 7-18.

CREATING THE STATUS BAR

The status bar is a panel that sits at the bottom of an application window and tells the user what's going on.

TRY IT OUT   Adding a Status Bar

Code file Text Editor.zip is available for download at Wrox.com

1. Return to your Windows Forms Text Editor project, drag a StatusStrip control from the Toolbox, and drop it onto your form. You'll notice that it automatically docks itself to the bottom edge of the form and you'll only be able to change the height portion of its `Size` property if desired.

2. You need to add one StatusStripLabel to the Items collection of the StatusStrip so that you can display text on the status bar. Use the drop-down in the StatusStrip and select StatusLabel to add one.

3. Set the following properties for the StatusStripLabel:

    ➤ Set `Name` to **sslStatus**.

    ➤ Set `DisplayStyle` to **Text**.

    ➤ Set `Text` to **Ready**.

4. You can also use the Items Collection Editor dialog for the Status Strip Label.

5. Open the Code Editor for the form and add the following code. You can quickly view the Code Editor by right-clicking the form and choosing View Code from the context menu or pressing F7:

```
'Get or set the text on the status bar
Public Property StatusText() As String
    Get
```

```
            Return sslStatus.Text
        End Get
        Set(ByVal value As String)
            sslStatus.Text = value
        End Set
    End Property
```

6. Switch over to your WPF Text Editor project. Drag a StatusBar control from the Toolbox onto the window. Position the control at the bottom left of the window and then expand the width of the control until it snaps to the right margin of the Grid.

7. In the properties window, click the button in the `Items` property to invoke the Items Collection Editor dialog. In the Collection Editor: Items dialog, click the Add button to add a StatusBarItem.

8. Set the `Content` property to **Ready** and then click the OK button to close the Collection Editor: Items dialog.

9. Click the StatusBarItem in the window. Then, in the Properties window, set the `Name` property to **sbiStatus**.

10. Right-click the window and choose View Code from the context menu and add the following code:

```
'Get or set the text on the status bar
Public Property StatusText() As String
    Get
        Return sbiStatus.Content.ToString
    End Get
    Set(ByVal value As String)
        sbiStatus.Content = value
    End Set
End Property
```

How It Works

There's no need to run the projects at this point, so let's just talk about what you've done here.

Visual Studio 2010 has some neat features for making form design easier. One thing that was always laborious in previous versions of Visual Basic and Visual C++ was creating a form that would automatically adjust itself when the user changed its size.

In Visual Studio 2010, controls have the capability to dock themselves to the edges of the form. By default, the StatusStrip control is set to dock to the bottom of the form, but you can change the docking location if so desired. That way, when someone resizes the form, either at design time or at runtime, the status bar (StatusStrip control) stays where you put it.

The StatusBar control in a WPF application behaves a little differently and does not automatically dock itself to the bottom of the window. You have to manually drag and position the control to the bottom, left corner of the window and then expand the width of the control in order to have it automatically stretch to fill the size of the window as it is resized.

You may be wondering why you built a `StatusText` property to get and set the text on the status bar. This comes back to abstraction. Ideally, you want to ensure that anyone using this class doesn't have to worry about how you've implemented the status bar. You might want to replace the .NET-supplied status bar with another control; and if you did, any users wanting to use your `TextEditor` class in their own applications (or developers wanting to add more functionality to this application later) would have to change their code to make sure it continued to work properly.

That's why you defined this property as `Public`. This means that others creating an instance of the `TextEditor` class to use its functionality in their own applications can change the status bar text if they want. If you don't want them to be able to change the text themselves, relying instead on other methods and properties on the form to change the text on their behalf, you would mark the property as `Private`.

As you work through this example, you'll see definitions of `Public` and `Private`. From this you'll be able to infer what functionality might be available to a developer using your `TextEditor` class.

CREATING AN EDIT BOX

The first thing you do in the next Try It Out is create a text box that can be used to edit the text entered. The text box has a `MultiLine` property, which by default is set to `False`. This property determines whether the text box should have only one line or can contain multiple lines. When you change this property to `True`, the text box control can be resized to any size that you want, and you can enter multiple lines of text in this control.

TRY IT OUT   Creating an Edit Box

Code file Text Editor.zip is available for download at Wrox.com

In this Try It Out, you will create an edit text box.

1. Return to the Forms Designer in the Windows Forms Text Editor project. Drag a TextBox control from the Toolbox and drop it onto your form.

2. Change the following properties of the TextBox control:
   - ➤ Set `Name` to **txtEdit.**
   - ➤ Set `Dock` to **Fill.**
   - ➤ Set `MultiLine` to **True.**
   - ➤ Set `ScrollBars` to **Vertical.**

   Your form should now look like Figure 7-19.

3. Switch over to the Forms Designer in your WPF Text Editor project. Drag a TextBox control from the Toolbox and drop it onto your form.

4. Align the text box to the left margin of the Grid directly beneath the toolbar. Expand the width of the text box until it snaps to the right border of the Grid. Then expand the height of the text box until it touches the status bar.

5. Change the following properties of the TextBox control:
   - ➤ Set `Name` to **txtEdit.**
   - ➤ Set `VerticalAlignment` to **Stretch.**

➤ Set VerticalScrollBarVisbility to **Visible**.

➤ Check AcceptsReturn.

➤ Set TextWrapping to **Wrap**.

FIGURE 7-19

Your form should now look like Figure 7-20.

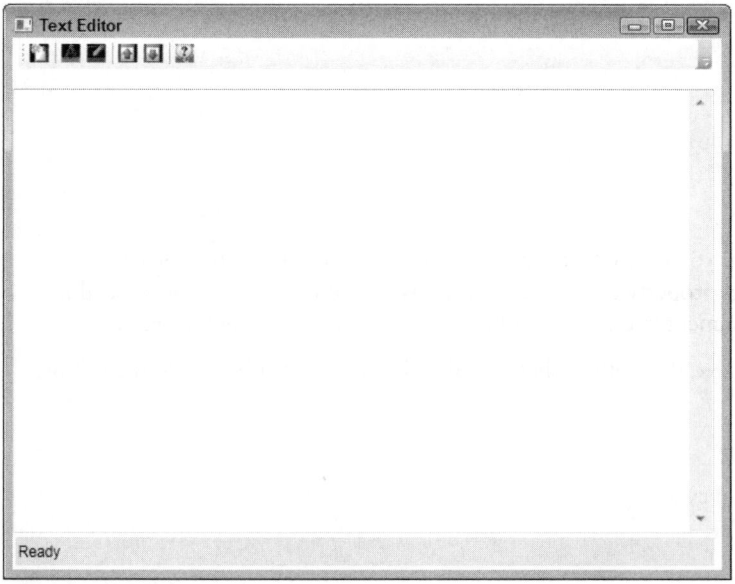

FIGURE 7-20

How It Works

By adding a textbox and changing a few properties, you now have an edit text box.

For the Windows Application, you turned on the vertical scrollbars by setting ScrollBars to Vertical. Setting Dock to Fill allows the textbox to resize with the form. The Multiline property set to true allows the user to type in and view multiple lines and text.

In the WPF application, setting the AcceptsReturn property to checked allows the user to press Enter to move the next line. To allow the text to wrap, you set the TextWrapping property to True. To allow the textbox to resize, you set the VerticalAlignment to Stretch. In case the user types more text than the screen can display, you changed the VerticalScrollBarVisiblity to Visible.

CLEARING THE EDIT BOX

To clear a textbox, you just need to set the text to "" or empty string. You will do this next.

TRY IT OUT   Clearing txtEdit

Code file Text Editor.zip is available for download at Wrox.com

In the following Try It Out, you're going to create a property called EditText that will get or set the text you're going to edit. Then, clearing the edit box will simply be a matter of setting the EditText property to an empty string.

1.   Switch to the Code Editor in your Windows Forms Text Editor project and add this code:

```
'Gets or sets the text that you're editing
Public Property EditText() As String
    Get
        Return txtEdit.Text
    End Get
    Set(ByVal value As String)
        txtEdit.Text = value
    End Set
End Property
```

As you have done earlier, when you created a property to abstract away the action of setting the status bar text, you created this property to give developers using the TextEditor form the ability to get or set the text of the document irrespective of how you actually implement the editor.

2.   You can now build ClearEditBox, the method that actually clears your text box. Add the following code:

```
'Clears the txtEdit control
Public Sub ClearEditBox()
    'Set the EditText property
    EditText = String.Empty

    'Reset the font color
    txtEdit.ForeColor = Color.Black
```

```
        'Set the status bar text
        StatusText = "Text box cleared"
    End Sub
```

3. Select txtEdit in the Class Name combo box and the TextChanged event in the Method Name combo box at the top of the Code Editor. Add this code:

```
Private Sub txtEdit_TextChanged(ByVal sender As Object, _
    ByVal e As System.EventArgs) Handles txtEdit.TextChanged

        'Reset the status bar text
        StatusText = "Ready"
    End Sub
```

4. Switch to the Code Editor in your WPF Text Editor project and add this code:

```
'Gets or sets the text that you're editing
Public Property EditText() As String
    Get
        Return txtEdit.Text
    End Get
    Set(ByVal value As String)
        txtEdit.Text = value
    End Set
End Property
```

5. Add the following code to create the ClearEditBox method:

```
'Clears the txtEdit control
Public Sub ClearEditBox()
    'Set the EditText property
    EditText = String.Empty

    'Reset the font color
    txtEdit.Foreground = Brushes.Black

    'Set the status bar text
    StatusText = "Text box cleared"
End Sub
```

6. Finally, select txtEdit in the Class Name combo box and the TextChanged event in the Method Name combo box at the top of the Code Editor. Add this code:

```
Private Sub txtEdit_TextChanged(ByVal sender As Object, _
    ByVal e As System.Windows.Controls.TextChangedEventArgs) _
    Handles txtEdit.TextChanged

        'Reset the status bar text
        StatusText = "Ready"
    End Sub
```

How It Works

The first thing you want to do is clear your text box. In the next Try It Out, you see how you can call ClearEditBox from the toolbar.

All this procedure does is set the EditText property to an empty string by using the Empty field of the String class. Then it sets the ForeColor property of the text box (which is the color of the actual text) to black and places the text **Text box `cleared`** in the status bar:

```
'Clears the txtEdit control
Public Sub ClearEditBox()
    'Set the EditText property
    EditText = String.Empty
    'Reset the font color
    txtEdit.ForeColor = Color.Black
    'Set the status bar text
    StatusText = "Text box cleared"
End Sub
```

The code in the EditText property of your WPF Text Editor project is slightly different in that you need to set the Foreground property of the text box using the Black property from the Brushes class:

```
'Reset the font color
txtEdit.Foreground = Brushes.Black
```

As mentioned, EditText abstracts the action of getting and setting the text in the box away from your actual implementation. This makes it easier for other developers down the line to use your TextEditor form class in their own applications. This code is the same for both projects:

```
'Gets or sets the text that you're editing
Public Property EditText() As String
    Get
        Return txtEdit.Text
    End Get
    Set(ByVal value As String)
        txtEdit.Text = value
    End Set
End Property
```

As you type, the TextChanged event handler will be repeatedly called.

Changing the status bar text at this point resets any message that might have been set in the status bar. For example, if users have to type a lot of text and look down to see "Text box cleared," they may be a little concerned. Setting it to "Ready" is a pretty standard way of informing the user that the computer is doing something or waiting. It does not mean anything specific.

RESPONDING TO TOOLBAR BUTTONS

TRY IT OUT   Responding to Toolbar Button Click Events

> *Code file Text Editor.zip is available for download at Wrox.com*

In the following Try It Out, you'll start implementing the Click events for the various toolbar buttons on your toolbar. When you look at building application menus in Chapter 9, you'll notice that most menus provide the same functionality as your toolbar buttons, and thus you'll want to implement the code in your menu item Click event procedures and have the corresponding toolbar button procedures call the menu item Click event procedures.

1. Return to the Code Editor in your Windows Forms Text Editor project and select `tbrClear` from the Class Name combo box; and in the Method Name combo box, select the `Click` event. Add the following bolded code to the `Click` event handler:

```
Private Sub tbrClear_Click(ByVal sender As Object, _
    ByVal e As System.EventArgs) Handles tbrClear.Click

    'Clear the edit box
    ClearEditBox()
End Sub
```

2. You need to create a procedure that will change the text in the edit box to red and update the status bar. Add the following code:

```
Public Sub RedText()
    'Make the text red
    txtEdit.ForeColor = Color.Red

    'Update the status bar text
    StatusText = "The text is red"
End Sub
```

3. Select `tbrRed` in the Class Name combo box, select the `Click` event in the Method Name combo box, and add the following bolded code to the `Click` event handler:

```
Private Sub tbrRed_Click(ByVal sender As Object, _
    ByVal e As System.EventArgs) Handles tbrRed.Click

    'Make the text red
    RedText()
End Sub
```

4. Run the project and enter some text. Click the Red button; the text's color will change from black to red. Note that if you continue typing in the edit box, the new text will also be red. Click the Clear button to remove the text and revert the color of any new text to black.

5. Switch to the Code Editor in your WPF Text Editor project. Select `tbrClear` from the Class Name combo box; and in the Method Name combo box, select the `Click` event and add the following bolded code:

```
Private Sub tbrClear_Click(ByVal sender As Object, _
    ByVal e As System.Windows.RoutedEventArgs) _
    Handles tbrClear.Click

    'Clear the edit box
    ClearEditBox()
End Sub
```

6. Add the following code to change the text in the edit box to red and update the status bar:

```
Public Sub RedText()
    'Make the text red
    txtEdit.Foreground = Brushes.Red

    'Update the status bar text
    StatusText = "The text is red"
End Sub
```

7. Select tbrRed in the Class Name combo box, select the Click event in the Method Name combo box, and add the following bolded code:

```
Private Sub tbrRed_Click(ByVal sender As Object, _
    ByVal e As System.Windows.RoutedEventArgs) _
    Handles tbrRed.Click

    'Make the text red
    RedText()
End Sub
```

8. Run the project and enter some text. Click the Red button; the text's color will change from black to red. Again, if you continue typing in the edit box, the new text will also be red. Click the Clear button to remove the text and revert the color of any new text to black.

9. Stop both projects if they are still running.

10. Return to the Code Editor in the Windows Forms Text Editor project and add the following BlueText procedure to change the text in the edit box to blue:

```
Public Sub BlueText()
    'Make the text blue
    txtEdit.ForeColor = Color.Blue

    'Update the status bar text
    StatusText = "The text is blue"
End Sub
```

11. Select tbrBlue in the Class Name combo box and the Click event in the Method Name combo box. Add the following bolded code to the Click event handler:

```
Private Sub tbrBlue_Click(ByVal sender As Object, _
    ByVal e As System.EventArgs) Handles tbrBlue.Click

    'Make the text blue
    BlueText()
End Sub
```

12. You now need to create a procedure to change the text in the edit box to all uppercase. Add the following code to your project:

```
Public Sub UpperCaseText()
    'Make the text uppercase
    EditText = EditText.ToUpper

    'Update the status bar text
    StatusText = "The text is all uppercase"
End Sub
```

13. Select tbrUpperCase in the Class Name combo box and the Click event in the Method Name combo box. Add the following bolded code to the Click event handler:

```
Private Sub tbrUpperCase_Click(ByVal sender As Object, _
    ByVal e As System.EventArgs) Handles tbrUpperCase.Click

    'Make the text uppercase
    UpperCaseText()
End Sub
```

14. Add the following procedure to change the text to all lowercase:

```
Public Sub LowerCaseText()
    'Make the text lowercase
    EditText = EditText.ToLower

    'Update the status bar text
    StatusText = "The text is all lowercase"
End Sub
```

15. Select tbrLowerCase in the Class Name combo box and the Click event in the Method Name combo box. Add the following code to the Click event handler:

```
Private Sub tbrLowerCase_Click(ByVal sender As Object, _
    ByVal e As System.EventArgs) Handles tbrLowerCase.Click

    'Make the text lowercase
    LowerCaseText()
End Sub
```

16. Run the project and enter some text into the box in a mixture of lowercase and uppercase. Then click the Uppercase button to make the text all uppercase, similar to the WPF Text Editor shown in Figure 7-21. Clicking the Lowercase button will convert the text to all lowercase, and clicking the Red or Blue buttons will cause the text to change color. Finally, clicking the Clear button will cause all text to be cleared and the color and case to be restored to the default.

FIGURE 7-21

17. Return to the Code Editor in the WPF Text Editor project. Add the following BlueText procedure to change the text in the edit box to blue:

```
Public Sub BlueText()
    'Make the text blue
    txtEdit.Foreground = Brushes.Blue
```

```
            'Update the status bar text
            StatusText = "The text is blue"
        End Sub
```

18. Select `tbrBlue` in the Class Name combo box and the `Click` event in the Method Name combo box and add the following bolded code:

```
Private Sub tbrBlue_Click(ByVal sender As Object, _
    ByVal e As System.Windows.RoutedEventArgs) _
    Handles tbrBlue.Click

        'Make the text blue
        BlueText()
End Sub
```

19. Add the following code to create a procedure to change the text in the edit box to all uppercase:

```
Public Sub UpperCaseText()
        'Make the text uppercase
        EditText = EditText.ToUpper

        'Update the status bar text
        StatusText = "The text is all uppercase"
End Sub
```

20. Select `tbrUpperCase` in the Class Name combo box and the `Click` event in the Method Name combo box. Add the following bolded code to the `Click` event handler:

```
Private Sub tbrUpperCase_Click(ByVal sender As Object, _
    ByVal e As System.Windows.RoutedEventArgs) _
    Handles tbrUpperCase.Click

        'Make the text uppercase
        UpperCaseText()
End Sub
```

21. Add the following procedure to change the text to all lowercase:

```
Public Sub LowerCaseText()
        'Make the text lowercase
        EditText = EditText.ToLower

        'Update the status bar text
        StatusText = "The text is all lowercase"
End Sub
```

22. Finally, select `tbrLowerCase` in the Class Name combo box and the `Click` event in the Method Name combo box. Add the following code to the `Click` event handler:

```
Private Sub tbrLowerCase_Click(ByVal sender As Object, _
    ByVal e As System.Windows.RoutedEventArgs) _
    Handles tbrLowerCase.Click

        'Make the text lowercase
        LowerCaseText()
End Sub
```

23. Run the project and again enter some text into the box in a mixture of lowercase and uppercase. Then click the Uppercase button to make the text all uppercase as shown in Figure 7-21. Exercise the code by clicking the Lowercase button to convert the text to all lowercase, and clicking on the Red and Blue buttons to change the color of the text.

How It Works

This Try It Out was quite simple. By this time, you are quite adept at creating the `Click` event handler for buttons on your form; creating the `Click` event handler for a toolbar button is no different. The first thing you did was create the `Click` event handler for the Clear toolbar button and add the code to call the `ClearEditBox` procedure:

```
Private Sub tbrClear_Click(ByVal sender As Object, _
    ByVal e As System.EventArgs) Handles tbrClear.Click

    'Clear the edit box
    ClearEditBox()
End Sub
```

Next, you created the `RedText` procedure to change the text in the edit box to red and to update the status bar with the appropriate information. To change the color of the text in the edit box, you set the `ForeColor` property of the edit box using the `Red` constant from the `Color` enumeration. (The `Color` enumeration contains an extensive list of named colors.) The `ForeColor` property remains red until you set it to something else — so clicking the Clear button turns it back to black:

```
Public Sub RedText()
    'Make the text red
    txtEdit.ForeColor = Color.Red

    'Update the status bar text
    StatusText = "The text is red"
End Sub
```

In your WPF Text Editor project you set the `Foreground` property to red using the `Red` property of the `Brushes` class:

```
'Make the text red
txtEdit.Foreground = Brushes.Red
```

You also change the text in the status bar using the `StatusText` property to display a message indicating the text color has changed. As soon as you start typing again, the message in the status bar is changed to "Ready," as set by the `TextChanged` event handler for the edit box.

In order to call the `RedText` procedure you added code to the `Click` event for the Red button on the toolbar:

```
'Make the text red
RedText()
```

The code for the Blue button on the toolbar works in the same manner. You create the `BlueText` procedure to set the `ForeColor` property of the edit box to `Blue` in your Windows Forms Text Editor project and to set the `Foreground` property to `Blue` in your WPF Text Editor project. Then update the status bar with the appropriate message. You then call the `BlueText` procedure from the `Click` event of the Blue toolbar button.

If the user clicks the Uppercase button on the toolbar, you call `UppercaseText`, which uses the `ToUpper` method to convert all the text held in `EditText` to uppercase text:

```
'Make the text uppercase
EditText = EditText.ToUpper
```

Likewise, if the user clicks the Lowercase button, you call `LowercaseText`, which uses the `ToLower` method to convert all the text held in `EditText` to lowercase text:

```
'Make the text lowercase
EditText = EditText.ToLower
```

Each of these procedures is called from the `Click` event of the appropriate toolbar buttons, and these procedures also update the message in the status bar to reflect whether the text has been changed to red, blue, uppercase, or lowercase.

USING MULTIPLE FORMS

All Windows applications have two types of windows: normal windows and dialog boxes, or dialogs. A normal window provides the main user interface for an application. For example, if you use Microsoft Word, you use a normal window for editing your documents.

On occasion, the application will display a dialog when you want to access a special feature. This type of window hijacks the application and forces the user to use just that window. For example, when you select the Print option in Word 2007, a dialog box appears, and from that point on, until you close the dialog by clicking OK, Cancel, or the close box, you can't go back and change the document — the only thing you can use is the Print dialog itself. Forms that do this are called *modal*. While they're up, you're in that mode.

Dialog boxes are discussed in more detail in Chapter 8. For now, you can focus on adding additional forms to your application. The form that you add in the next exercise is a simple modal form.

The About Dialog Box

Most applications have an About dialog box that describes the application's name and copyright information. As you already have a toolbar button for this feature, you'll want to create this form now.

TRY IT OUT   Adding an About Dialog Box

This Try It Out will apply only to your Windows Forms Text Editor project. You can add an About dialog in a similar manner for WPF applications in Visual Studio 2010.

1. To add a new form to the project, you need to use the Solution Explorer. Right-click the Windows Forms Text Editor project and select Add Windows Form. In the Add New Item–Windows Forms Text Editor dialog, shown in Figure 7-22, select the About Box in the Templates pane, enter **About.vb** in the Name field, and click the Add button to create the new form.

2. When the Form's Designer appears, you'll notice that all of the normal details that are shown in an About dialog box are already on the form. This includes such items as the product name, version number, copyright information, and so on.

3. Right-click the form and choose View Code from the context menu. You'll notice that the `Load` event for the form already contains a significant amount of code to populate the details on the About form. There is a `TODO` comment in the code that informs you that you need to update the assembly information for the application.

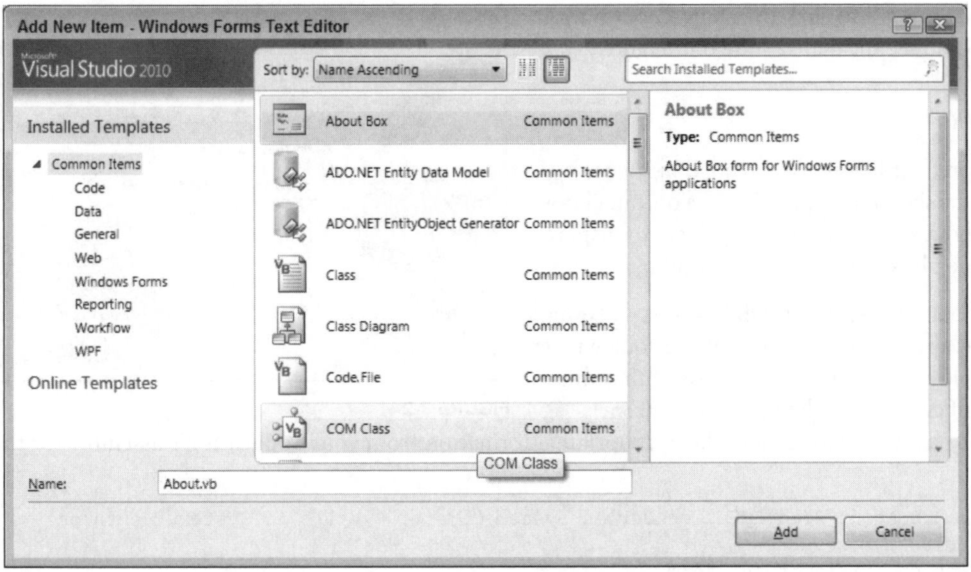

FIGURE 7-22

4. In the Solution Explorer, double-click My Project. Click the Assembly Information button in the Application pane of the Windows Forms Text Editor properties to display the Assembly Information dialog box. Edit the information in this dialog as shown in Figure 7-23 and then click OK to close this dialog.

5. You need to write a procedure that will display the About dialog box, so add this code to the TextEditor form:

```
Public Sub ShowAboutBox()
    'Display the About dialog box
    Using objAbout As New About
        objAbout.ShowDialog(Me)
    End Using
End Sub
```

FIGURE 7-23

6. Finally, you need to call ShowAboutBox when the Help About button on the toolbar is clicked. In the Class Name combo box at the top of the Code Editor, select tbrHelpAbout; and in the Method Name combo box, select the Click event. Add the following bolded code to the Click event handler:

```
Private Sub tbrHelpAbout_Click(ByVal sender As Object, _
    ByVal e As System.EventArgs) Handles tbrHelpAbout.Click

    'Display the About dialog box
    ShowAboutBox()
End Sub
```

7. Run the project and click the Help About button. You should see the dialog shown in Figure 7-24.

How It Works

A variety of prebuilt forms are provided in Visual Studio 2010, as shown in Figure 7-22. You can choose to add the About Box form to your project to display an About dialog box from your application.

When the About form starts, it will fire the Load event, and this event already has the appropriate code written to load the fields on the form. You'll notice that this code makes efficient use of the My.Application.

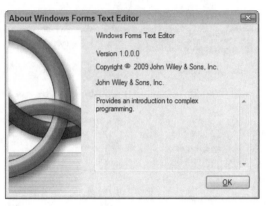

FIGURE 7-24

AssemblyInfo namespace to retrieve the appropriate information from your application's assembly for the About form:

```
Private Sub About_Load(ByVal sender As System.Object, ByVal e As System.EventArgs)
    Handles MyBase.Load
    ' Set the title of the form.
    Dim ApplicationTitle As String
    If My.Application.Info.Title <> "" Then
        ApplicationTitle = My.Application.Info.Title
    Else
        ApplicationTitle = System.IO.Path.GetFileNameWithoutExtension(My.Application.
        Info.AssemblyName)
    End If
    Me.Text = String.Format("About {0}", ApplicationTitle)
    ' Initialize all of the text displayed on the About Box.
    ' TODO: Customize the application's assembly information in the "Application" pane

          of the project
    '     properties dialog (under the "Project" menu).
    Me.LabelProductName.Text = My.Application.Info.ProductName
    Me.LabelVersion.Text = String.Format("Version {0}", My.Application.Info.
    Version.ToString)
    Me.LabelCopyright.Text = My.Application.Info.Copyright
    Me.LabelCompanyName.Text = My.Application.Info.CompanyName
    Me.TextBoxDescription.Text = My.Application.Info.Description
End Sub
```

The assembly information that you modified in the Assembly Information dialog box is used to populate the fields on your About form. If you added the text **John Wiley && Sons, Inc.** to the Company and Copyright fields in the Assembly Information dialog as shown in Figure 7-23, you'll have noticed that two consecutive ampersands were used. That's because the labels on your About form treat a single ampersand as the start of code representing a special character. Two consecutive ampersands is the code for the ampersand character itself.

To display another form, you have to create a new instance of it. That's exactly what you do in the ShowAboutBox procedure. A Using ... End Using block will create a new instance of an object (in this case the `About` form), enabling you to use the `ShowDialog` method to show the About form modally. When you pass the `Me` keyword as a parameter to the `ShowDialog` method, you are specifying that the `TextEditor` form is the owner of the dialog being shown — in this case, the `About` form:

```
Public Sub ShowAboutBox()
    'Display the About dialog box
    Using objAbout As New About
        objAbout.ShowDialog(Me)
    End Using
End Sub
```

To call the `ShowAboutBox` procedure, you had to add code to the `Click` event of the HelpAbout button on the toolbar:

```
Private Sub tbrHelpAbout_Click(ByVal sender As Object, _
    ByVal e As System.EventArgs) Handles tbrHelp.Click

    'Display the About dialog box
    ShowAboutBox()
End Sub
```

With very little effort and a minimal amount of code, you have added a lot of functionality to your Windows Form Text Editor project. You can see firsthand how Visual Studio 2010 provides productivity and time-saving features such as prebuilt forms.

SUMMARY

This chapter discussed some of the more advanced features of Windows forms and WPF Windows, as well as the commonly used controls. It discussed the event-driven nature of Windows and showed three events that can happen to a button — namely, `Click`, `MouseEnter`, and `MouseLeave`.

You created a simple application that enables you to enter some text and then, using radio buttons, choose between counting the number of characters or counting the number of words.

You then turned your attention to building a more complex application that enables you to edit text by changing its color or its case. This application demonstrated how easy it is to build an application with toolbars and status bars. You even added an About dialog box to display basic information about your application, such as the application title, description, version number, and copyright information.

To summarize, you should now know how to:

➤ Write code to respond to control events

➤ Set properties on controls to customize their look and behavior

➤ Use the ToolStrip and StatusStrip controls

➤ Display other forms in your application

EXERCISES

1. Name two controls you can use when adding a toolbar to your form.

2. What property do you set to display text to users when they hover over a button on a toolbar?

3. When you create a WPF and Windows application, you design different objects that are very similar. In a Windows application, you design a form. What do you design in a WPF application?

4. To work with a textbox so a user can add many lines of text, what property must be set to `true` in a Windows Forms application?

5. Why would you want to show a form using the `ShowDialog` method?

► WHAT YOU HAVE LEARNED IN THIS CHAPTER

TOPIC	CONCEPTS
Handling Click Events	You can create procedures that act as event handlers for control events. To do this, just double click a button and add your code to the procedure. The button is called the sender and the procedure is known as the handler.
Creating a Basic Menu	In a Windows Forms or WinForm application, you just need to add a ToolStrip control to your form and then add controls to it. You can add controls like Button, Separator, Label, TextBox, ComboBox and others. In a WPF application, add a ToolBarPanel and then a ToolBar control. Next, you can add the controls you want on your menu.
Adding a Status Bar	To provide feedback to the user, you can use a status bar. In a WinForm application, you can add a StatusTrip control to the bottom of the form. Next you can add a StatusStripLabel and other controls to provide feedback. In WPF, you can add a StatusBar and then a StatusBarItem to provide feedback to the application users.
About Box (Built in forms)	You can save a lot of time by using pre-built common forms like the About Box. You can quickly have an About the Program form using this form.

8

Displaying Dialog Boxes

WHAT YOU WILL LEARN IN THIS CHAPTER:

➤   Creating a message box using different buttons and icons

➤   Creating an Open dialog box that enables you to open files

➤   Creating a Save dialog box that enables you to save files

➤   Creating a Font dialog box that enables you to apply the selected font to text

➤   Creating a Color dialog box that enables you to define and select custom colors

➤   Creating a Print dialog box that prints text from your application

➤   Creating a Browse dialog box that enables you to browse for folders

Visual Basic 2010 provides several built-in dialog boxes that help you provide a rich user interface in your front-end applications. These dialog boxes provide the same common user interface that is found in most Windows applications. They also provide many properties and methods that enable you to customize them to suit your needs while still maintaining the standard look of Windows Forms applications.

This chapter explores these dialog boxes in depth and shows how you can use them in your Visual Basic 2010 applications to help you build more professional-looking applications for your users.

THE MESSAGEBOX

`MessageBox` is one of those dialog boxes that you will use often as a developer. This dialog box enables you to display custom messages to your users and accept their input regarding the choice that they have made. This dialog box is very versatile; you can customize it to display a variety of icons with your messages and choose which buttons to display.

In your day-to-day operation of a computer, you have seen message boxes that display each of the icons shown in Figure 8-1. In this section, you learn how to create and display message boxes that use these icons.

FIGURE 8-1

The first icon in Figure 8-1 has two names: Asterisk and Information. The second icon also has two names: Exclamation and Warning. The third icon has three names: Error, Hand, and Stop. The final icon in Figure 8-1 has only one name: Question.

When building a Windows application, at times you need to prompt the user for information or display a warning that something expected did not happen or that something unexpected did. For example, suppose the user of your application modified some data and tried to close the application without saving the data. You could display a message box that carries an information or warning icon and an appropriate message — that all unsaved data will be lost. You could also provide OK and Cancel buttons to enable users to continue or cancel the operation.

This is where the MessageBox dialog box comes in: It enables you to quickly build custom dialog boxes that prompt the user for a decision while displaying your custom message, choice of icons, and choice of buttons. All of this functionality also enables you to display a message box informing users of validation errors, and to display formatted system errors that are trapped by error handling.

Before you jump into some code, take a look at the MessageBox class. The Show method is called to display the MessageBox. The title, message, icons, and buttons displayed are determined by the parameters you pass to this method. This may seem complicated, but actually using MessageBox is very simple — as you have seen and will see in the following sections.

Available Icons for MessageBox

You saw the four available icons in Figure 8-1. Table 8-1 outlines these standard icons that you can display in a message box. The actual graphic displayed is a function of the operating system constants, so there are four unique symbols with multiple field names assigned to them.

TABLE 8-1: Message Box Icon Enumeration

MEMBER NAME	DESCRIPTION
Asterisk	Specifies that the message box displays an information icon
Information	Specifies that the message box displays an information icon
Error	Specifies that the message box displays an error icon
Hand	Specifies that the message box displays an error icon
Stop	Specifies that the message box displays an error icon
Exclamation	Specifies that the message box displays an exclamation icon
Warning	Specifies that the message box displays an exclamation icon
Question	Specifies that the message box displays a question mark icon
None	Specifies the message box will not display any icon

Available Buttons for MessageBox

Table 8-2 outlines the several combinations of buttons that you can display in a message box.

TABLE 8-2: Message Box Button Enumeration

MEMBER NAME	DESCRIPTION
AbortRetryIgnore	Specifies that the message box displays Abort, Retry, and Ignore buttons
OK	Specifies that the message box displays an OK button
OKCancel	Specifies that the message box displays OK and Cancel buttons
RetryCancel	Specifies that the message box displays Retry and Cancel buttons
YesNo	Specifies that the message box displays Yes and No buttons
YesNoCancel	Specifies that the message box displays Yes, No, and Cancel buttons

Setting the Default Button

Along with displaying the appropriate buttons, you can instruct the message box to set a default button for you. This enables users to read the message and press the Enter key to invoke the action for the default button without having to click the button itself with the mouse. Table 8-3 outlines the available default button options.

TABLE 8-3: Default Message Box Button Enumeration

MEMBER NAME	DESCRIPTION
Button1	Specifies that the first button in the message box should be the default button
Button2	Specifies that the second button in the message box should be the default button
Button3	Specifies that the third button in the message box should be the default button

You set the default button relative to the MessageBox buttons, from left to right. Therefore, if you have the Yes, No, and Cancel buttons displayed and you choose the third button to be the default, Cancel will be the default button. Likewise, if you choose the third button to be the default and you have only OK and Cancel buttons, the first button becomes the default. The default button will be highlighted until you hover your mouse over another button.

Miscellaneous Options

A couple of other options are available in the MessageBoxOptions enumeration and can be used with the message box. These are shown in Table 8-4.

TABLE 8-4: Other Message Box Options

MEMBER NAME	DESCRIPTION
DefaultDesktopOnly	Specifies that the message box be displayed on the active desktop
RightAlign	Specifies that the text in a message box be right-aligned, as opposed to left-aligned, which is the default
RtlReading	Specifies that the text in a message box be displayed with the RTL (right-to-left) reading order; this applies only to languages that are read from right to left
ServiceNotification	Specifies that the message box be displayed on the active desktop. The caller is a Windows service notifying the user of an event.

The Show Method Syntax

You call the Show method to display the message box. The following code example displays the message box shown in Figure 8-2. Notice that the code specifies the text that is displayed in the message box as the first argument, followed by the text that is displayed in the title bar. Then you specify the buttons that should be displayed, followed by the type of icon that should be displayed beside the text. Lastly, you specify the button that you want to set as the default button — in this case Button1.

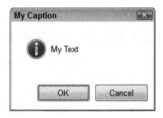

FIGURE 8-2

> ✏ **NOTE** *If you want to run this code, start a new Windows Application project, double-click the form in the Designer to generate the Form1_Load event, and place the following code inside that method:*
>
> ```
> MessageBox.Show("My Text", "My Caption", _
> MessageBoxButtons.OKCancel, MessageBoxIcon.Information, _
>     MessageBoxDefaultButton.Button1)
> ```

Now that you have seen the available icons, buttons, and default button fields, take a look at the Show method of the MessageBox class. You can specify the Show method in several ways; the more common syntaxes are shown in the following list:

➤ MessageBox.Show(*message text*)

➤ MessageBox.Show(*message text, caption*)

➤ MessageBox.Show(*message text, caption, buttons*)

➤ MessageBox.Show(*message text, caption, buttons, icon*)

➤ MessageBox.Show(*message text, caption, buttons, icon, default button*)

In the previous examples, *message text* represents the message that is displayed in the message box. This text can be static text (a literal string value) or supplied in the form of a string variable. The other parameters are optional:

➤ *caption* represents either static text or a string variable that will be used to display text in the title bar of the message box. If this parameter is omitted, no text is displayed in the title bar.

➤ *buttons* represents a value from the MessageBoxButtons enumeration. This parameter enables you to specify which of the available buttons to display in the message box. If you omit this parameter, the OK button is the only displayed button in the box.

➤ *icon* represents a value from the MessageBoxIcon enumeration. This parameter enables you to specify which of the available icons displays in the message box. If you omit this parameter, no icon is displayed.

➤ *default button* represents a value from the MessageBoxDefaultButton enumeration. This parameter enables you to specify which of the buttons is set as the default button in the message box. If you omit this parameter, the first button displayed becomes the default button.

All the syntax examples shown in the previous section return a value from the DialogResult enumeration, which indicates which button in the message box was chosen. Table 8-5 shows the available members in the DialogResult enumeration.

TABLE 8-5: DialogResult Enumeration Members

MEMBER NAME	DESCRIPTION
Abort	The return value is Abort and is the result of clicking the Abort button.
Cancel	The return value is Cancel and is the result of clicking the Cancel button.
Ignore	The return value is Ignore and is the result of clicking the Ignore button.
No	The return value is No and is the result of clicking the No button.
None	Nothing is returned, which means the dialog box continues running until a button is clicked.
OK	The return value is OK and is the result of clicking the OK button.
Retry	The return value is Retry and is the result of clicking the Retry button.
Yes	The return value is Yes and is the result of clicking the Yes button.

Example Message Boxes

Because multiple buttons can be displayed in a message box, there are multiple ways to display a dialog box and check the results. Of course, if you were displaying only one button using the message box for notification, you would not have to check the results at all and could use a very simple syntax.

Creating a Two-Button Message Box

Code file MessageBox Buttons.zip available for download at Wrox.com

This Try It Out demonstrates how to display two buttons in a message box and then check for the results from the message box to determine which button was clicked.

1.   Start Visual Studio 2010 and select File ⇨ New Project from the menu. In the New Project dialog box, select Windows Forms Application in the Templates pane and enter a project name of **MessageBox Buttons** in the Name field. Click OK to create this project.

2.   Click the form in the Forms Designer and then set its Text property to **MessageBox Buttons**.

3.   Add a Label control to the form to display results regarding which button in the message box a user clicks. Set the Name property to **lblResults** and the Text property to **Nothing Clicked**.

4.   Now add a Button control from the Toolbox to the form that will display a message box. Set its Name property to **btn2Buttons** and its Text property to **2 Buttons**.

5.   Double-click the button and add the bolded code in the Click event handler:

```
Private Sub btn2Buttons_Click(ByVal sender As System.Object, _
ByVal e As System.EventArgs) Handles btn2Buttons.Click
If MessageBox.Show("Your Internet connection will now be closed.", _
    "Network Notification", MessageBoxButtons.OKCancel, _
    MessageBoxIcon.Information, MessageBoxDefaultButton.Button1) _
    = Windows.Forms.DialogResult.OK Then

    lblResults.Text = "OK Clicked"
    'Call some method here
Else
    lblResults.Text = "Cancel Clicked"
    'Call some method here
End If
End Sub
```

6.   Save your project by clicking the Save All button on the toolbar.

7.   Run the project and then click the 2 Buttons button. You should see a message box dialog box like the one shown in Figure 8-3.

FIGURE 8-3

How It Works

The code uses the Show method of the MessageBox class and uses an If.End If statement to determine whether the user clicked the OK button:

```
If MessageBox.Show("Your Internet connection will now be closed.", _
    "Network Notification", MessageBoxButtons.OKCancel, _
    MessageBoxIcon.Information, MessageBoxDefaultButton.Button1) _
    = Windows.Forms.DialogResult.OK Then
```

The code specifies that the OK and Cancel buttons are to be displayed in the dialog box and that the OK button is to be the default button.

You have to specify something for the icon parameter, because this is required when you want to set the default button parameter. If you did not want to display an icon, you could use the Nothing keyword for that parameter.

Also notice that you check the results returned from MessageBox using `Windows.Forms.DialogResult.OK`. You could have just as easily have checked for `Windows.Forms.DialogResult.Cancel` and written the `If.End If` statement around that.

This is great if you want to test the results of only one or two buttons, but what if you want to test the results from a message box that contains three buttons? The following Try It Out demonstrates just that.

TRY IT OUT   Testing a Three-Button MessageBox

Code file MessageBox Buttons.zip available for download at Wrox.com

This Try It Out demonstrates how to display three buttons in a message box and then find out which button is pressed.

1. Stop your project if it is still running and open the Forms Designer for Form1.

2. Add another Button control and set its `Name` property to **btn3Buttons** and its `Text` property to **3 Buttons**. Double-click the button and add the bolded code to its `Click` event handler:

```
Private Sub btn3Buttons_Click(ByVal sender As System.Object, _
    ByVal e As System.EventArgs) Handles btn3Buttons.Click
    'Declare local variable
    Dim intResult As DialogResult

    'Get the results of the button clicked
    intResult = _
        MessageBox.Show("Do you want to save changes to New Document?", _
        "My Word Processor", MessageBoxButtons.YesNoCancel, _
        MessageBoxIcon.Warning, MessageBoxDefaultButton.Button3)

    'Process the results of the button clicked
    Select Case intResult
        Case Windows.Forms.DialogResult.Yes
            lblResults.Text = "Yes Clicked"
            'Do yes processing here
        Case Windows.Forms.DialogResult.No
            lblResults.Text = "No Clicked"
            'Do no processing here
        Case Windows.Forms.DialogResult.Cancel
            lblResults.Text = "Cancel Clicked"
            'Do cancel processing here
    End Select
End Sub
```

3. Run the project and click the 3 Buttons button. The message box dialog box shown in Figure 8-4 will be displayed, showing an icon and three buttons. Note that the third button is the default now.

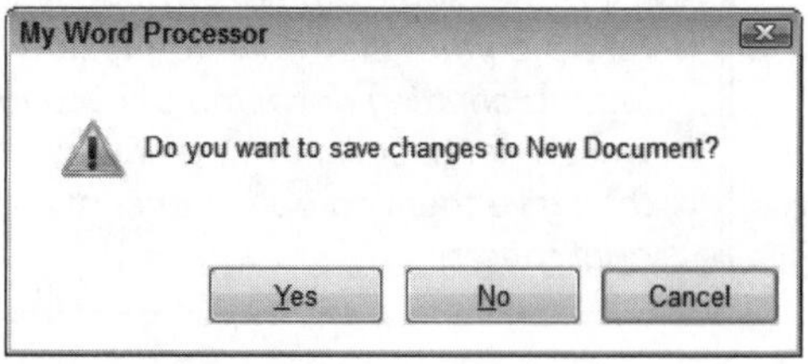

FIGURE 8-4

How It Works

The `Show` method returns a `DialogResult`, which is an `Integer` value. What you need to do when there are three buttons is capture the `DialogResult` in a variable and then test that variable.

In the following code, the first thing you do is declare a variable as a `DialogResult` to capture the `DialogResult` returned from the message box. Remember that the results returned from the dialog box are nothing more than an enumeration of `Integer` values. Next, you set the `DialogResult` in the variable:

```
'Declare local variable
Dim intResult As DialogResult

'Get the results of the button clicked
intResult = _
    MessageBox.Show("Do you want to save changes to New Document?", _
    "My Word Processor", MessageBoxButtons.YesNoCancel, _
    MessageBoxIcon.Warning, MessageBoxDefaultButton.Button3)
```

Finally, you test the value of the `intResult` in a `Select Case` statement and act on it accordingly:

```
'Process the results of the button clicked
Select Case intResult
    Case Windows.Forms.DialogResult.Yes
        lblResults.Text = "Yes Clicked"
        'Do yes processing here
    Case Windows.Forms.DialogResult.No
        lblResults.Text = "No Clicked"
        'Do no processing here
    Case Windows.Forms.DialogResult.Cancel
        lblResults.Text = "Cancel Clicked"
        'Do cancel processing here
End Select
```

In each of the `Case` statements, you write the name of the button selected in the label to indicate which button was clicked.

Now you have a better understanding of how the `MessageBox` dialog box works and you have a point of reference for the syntax. To familiarize yourself further with the `MessageBox`, try altering the values of the message text, caption, buttons, icon, and default button parameters in the previous examples.

> **WARNING** *Be careful not to overuse the `MessageBox` and display a message box for every little event. This can be a real annoyance to users. Use common sense and good judgment when deciding whether a message box is appropriate. You should display a `MessageBox` dialog box only when you absolutely need to inform users that some type of error has occurred or when you need to warn users that an action that they have requested is potentially damaging. An example of the latter is shutting down the application without saving their work. In this case, you want to let users know that if they continue they will lose all unsaved work, and then give them an option to continue or cancel the action of shutting down the application.*

THE OPENFILEDIALOG CONTROL

Many Windows applications process data from files, so you need an interface to select files to open and save. The .NET Framework provides the `OpenFileDialog` and `SaveFileDialog` classes to do just that. In this section you'll take a look at the OpenFileDialog control, and in the next section you'll look at the SaveFileDialog control.

When you use Windows applications, such as Microsoft Word or Paint, you see the same basic Open dialog box. This does not happen by accident. Available to all developers is a standard set of application programming interfaces (APIs) that enable the provision of this type of standard interface; however, using the APIs can be cumbersome and difficult for a beginner. Fortunately, all of this functionality is already built into the .NET Framework, so you can use it as you develop with Visual Basic 2010.

The OpenFileDialog Control

You can use OpenFileDialog as a .NET class by declaring a variable of that type in your code and modifying its properties in code, or as a control by dragging the control from the Toolbox onto the form at design time. In either case, the resulting objects will have the same methods, properties, and events.

You can find the OpenFileDialog control in the Toolbox under the Dialogs tab, where you can drag and drop it onto your form. Then, all you need to do is set the properties and execute the appropriate method. To use `OpenFileDialog` as a class, you declare your own objects of this type in order to use the dialog box. Then you have control over the scope of the dialog box and can declare an object for it when needed, use it, and then destroy it, thereby using fewer resources.

This section focuses on using OpenFileDialog as a control. Once you have a better understanding of this dialog box and feel comfortable using it, you can then expand your skills and use `OpenFileDialog` as a class by declaring your own objects for it. Using classes and objects is discussed in greater detail in Chapter 11.

You can use `OpenFileDialog` by simply invoking its `ShowDialog` method, producing results similar to those shown in Figure 8-5.

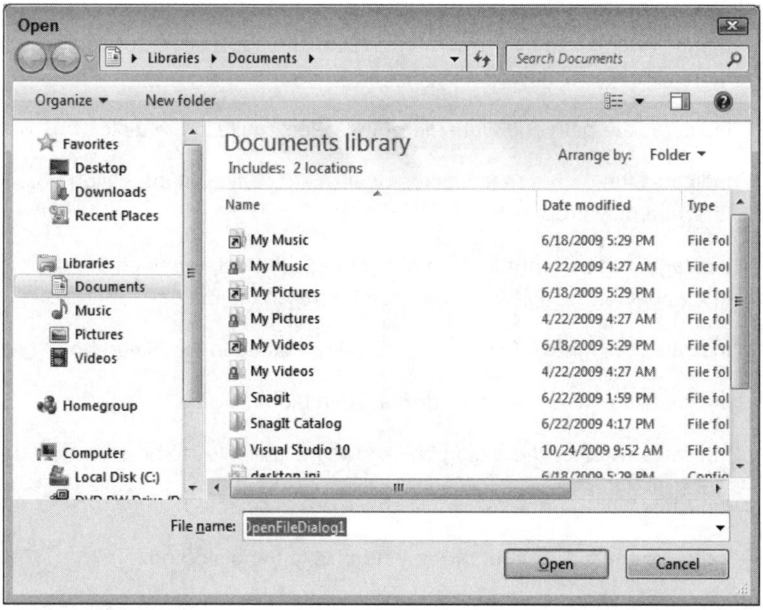

FIGURE 8-5

The Properties of OpenFileDialog

Although the dialog box shown in Figure 8-5 is the standard Open dialog displayed in Windows Vista, it provides no filtering. All file types are listed in the window and you cannot specify a file type for filtering because no filters exist. This is where the properties of OpenFileDialog come in. You can set some of the properties before the Open dialog box is displayed, thereby customizing the dialog box to your needs.

Table 8-6 lists some of the available properties for the OpenFileDialog control.

TABLE 8-6: Common OpenFileDialog Control Properties

PROPERTY	DESCRIPTION
AddExtension	Indicates whether an extension is automatically added to a filename if the user omits the extension. This is mainly used in the SaveFileDialog, described in the next section.
AutoUpgradeEnabled	Indicates whether this dialog should automatically upgrade its appearance and behavior when running on different versions of Windows. When false, it will appear with XP styles.
CheckFileExists	Indicates whether the dialog box displays a warning if the user specifies a filename that does not exist.
CheckPathExists	Indicates whether the dialog box displays a warning if the user specifies a path that does not exist.
DefaultExt	Indicates the default filename extension.
DereferenceLinks	Used with shortcuts. Indicates whether the dialog returns the location of the file referenced by the shortcut (True) or whether it returns only the location of the shortcut itself (False).
FileName	Indicates the path and filename of the selected file in the dialog box.
FileNames	Indicates the path and filenames of all selected files in the dialog box. This is a read-only property.
Filter	Indicates the current filename filter string, which determines the options that appear in the Files of Type: combo box in the dialog
FilterIndex	Indicates the index of the filter currently selected in the dialog box.
InitialDirectory	Indicates the initial directory displayed in the dialog box.
Multiselect	Indicates whether the dialog box allows multiple files to be selected.
ReadOnlyChecked	Indicates whether the read-only check box is selected.
SafeFileName	Indicates the filename of the selected file in the dialog box.

TABLE 8-6 *(continued)*

PROPERTY	DESCRIPTION
SafeFileNames	Indicates the filenames of all selected files in the dialog box. This is a read-only property.
ShowHelp	Indicates whether the Help button is displayed in the dialog box.
ShowReadOnly	Indicates whether the dialog box contains a read-only check box.
SupportMultiDotted Extensions	Indicates whether the dialog box supports displaying and saving files that have multiple filename extensions
Title	Indicates the title that is displayed in the title bar of the dialog box.
ValidateNames	Indicates whether the dialog box should only accept valid WIN32 filenames.

OpenFileDialog Methods

Although many methods are available in the `OpenFileDialog` class, you will be concentrating on the `ShowDialog` method in these examples. The following list contains some of the other available methods in `OpenFileDialog`:

➤ `Dispose` releases the resources used by the Open dialog box.

➤ `OpenFile` opens the file selected by the user with read-only permission. The file is specified by the `FileName` property.

➤ `Reset` resets all properties of the Open dialog box to their default values.

➤ `ShowDialog` shows the dialog box.

The `ShowDialog` method is straightforward, as it accepts either no parameters or the owner of the dialog box in the form of the `Me` keyword. Therefore, before calling the `ShowDialog` method, you must set all the properties that you want to set. After the dialog box returns, you can query the properties to determine which file was selected, the directory, and the type of file selected. An example of the `ShowDialog` method is shown in the following code fragment:

```
OpenFileDialog1.ShowDialog()
```

The OpenFileDialog control returns a `DialogResult` of `OK` or `Cancel`, with `OK` corresponding to the Open button on the dialog box. This control does not actually open and read a file for you; it is merely a common interface that enables users to locate and specify the file or files to be opened by the application. You need to query the OpenFileDialog properties that have been set by the control after the user clicks the Open button to determine which file or files should be opened.

Using the OpenFileDialog Control

Now that you have had a look at the OpenFileDialog control, you can put this knowledge to use by writing a program that uses this control.

TRY IT OUT   Working with OpenFileDialog

Code file Windows Forms Dialogs.zip available for download at Wrox.com

The program in the next Try It Out uses the OpenFileDialog control to display the Open File dialog box. You use the dialog box to locate and select a text file, and then you'll read the contents of the file into a text box on your form using the `My.Computer.FileSystem` namespace.

1.   Create a new Windows Forms Application project called **Windows Forms Dialogs.**

2.   To give your form a new name, in the Solution Explorer, right-click Form1.vb and choose Rename from the context menu. Then enter a new name of **Dialogs.vb.** Set the properties of the form as shown in the following list:

> ➤   Set `Size` to **460, 300.**

> ➤   Set `StartPosition` to **CenterScreen.**

> ➤   Set `Text` to **Dialogs.**

3.   Because you are going to read the contents of a file into a text box, you want to add a text box to the form. You also want to add a button to the form so that you can invoke the Open File dialog box at will. Add these two controls to the form and set their properties according to the following list:

> ➤   Name the text box **txtFile** and set the following properties: Anchor = **Top, Bottom,Left,Right**; Location = **13, 13**; MultiLine = **True**; ScrollBars = **Vertical**; Size = **330, 232.**

> ➤   Name the Button control **btnOpen** and set the following properties: Anchor = **Top, Right**; Location = **349, 13**; Text = **Open.**

4.   When you have finished placing the controls on your form and setting their properties, the form should look similar to Figure 8-6.

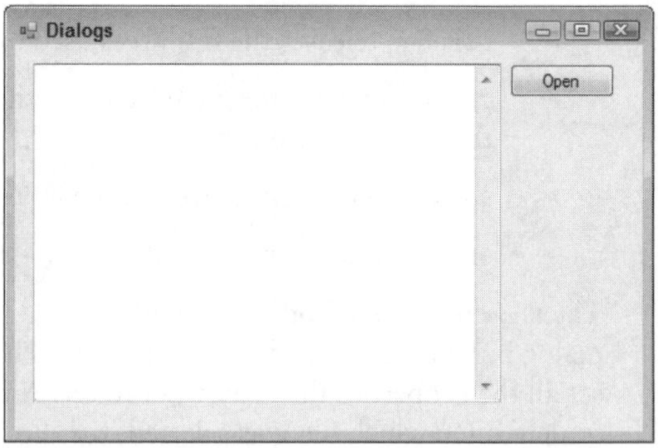

FIGURE 8-6

> ✎   **NOTE** *You anchored your controls in this example because when you resize or maximize your form, the text box is resized appropriately to the size of the form, and the button stays in the upper-right corner. You can test this at this point by running your project and resizing the form.*

5.   In the Toolbox, scroll down until you see the OpenFileDialog control in the Dialogs tab and then drag it onto your form and drop it. The control will actually be added to the bottom of the workspace in the IDE.

At this point, you could click the control in the workspace and then set the various properties for this control in the Properties window. However, accept the default name and properties for this control for now, as you'll set the various properties in code later.

6. Switch to the Code Editor for the form. Declare a string variable that will contain a filename. You set this variable later in your code to the actual path and filename from the Open File dialog box:

```
Public Class Dialogs
    'Declare variable
    Private strFileName As String
```

7. Now you need to write some code in the Click event for the btnOpen button. In the Class Name combo box at the top of the Code Editor, select btnOpen, and in the Method Name combo box select the Click event. Add the following bolded code to the Click event handler:

```
Private Sub btnOpen_Click(ByVal sender As Object, _
    ByVal e As System.EventArgs) Handles btnOpen.Click
    'Set the Open dialog properties
    With OpenFileDialog1
        .Filter = "Text Documents (*.txt)|*.txt|All Files (*.*)|*.*"
        .FilterIndex = 1
        .Title = "Demo Open File Dialog"
    End With

    'Show the Open dialog and if the user clicks the Open button,
    'load the file
    If OpenFileDialog1.ShowDialog = Windows.Forms.DialogResult.OK Then
        Try
            'Save the file path and name
            strFileName = OpenFileDialog1.FileName


        Catch ex As Exception
            MessageBox.Show(ex.Message, My.Application.Info.Title, _
                MessageBoxButtons.OK, MessageBoxIcon.Error)
        End Try
    End If
End Sub
```

8. Now it's time to use some of the prebuilt code snippets that come with Visual Studio 2010. Right-click in the blank space inside the Try block statement right before the Catch block statement and choose Insert Snippet from the context menu. In the drop-down menu that appears, double-click Fundamentals-Collections, Data Types, File System, Math and then in the new list double-click File System-Processing Drives, Folders, and Files. Finally, scroll down the list and double-click Read Text from a File. Your code should now look like this, and you'll notice that the filename C:\Test.txt is bolded, indicating that this code needs to be changed:

```
Try
    'Save the file path and name
    strFileName = OpenFileDialog1.FileName

    Dim fileContents As String
    fileContents = My.Computer.FileSystem.ReadAllText("C:\Test.txt")
Catch ex As Exception
```

9. Modify the code in the `Try` block as shown here. Replace `"C:Test.txt"` with **strFileName** and add the following code to display the contents of the text file:

```
Try
      'Save the file path and name
      strFileName = OpenFileDialog1.FileName

      Dim fileContents As String
      fileContents = My.Computer.FileSystem.ReadAllText(strFileName)

      'Display the file contents in the text box
      txtFile.Text = fileContents
Catch ex As Exception
```

10. Save your project by clicking the Save All button on the toolbar.

11. Run your project. When your form is displayed, click the Open button to have the Open File dialog box displayed. Notice the custom caption in the title bar of the dialog box; you specified this in your code. If you click the File filter combo box, you will see two filters. Click the second filter to see all of the files in the current directory.

12. Now locate a text file on your computer and select it. Then click the Open button to have the file opened and the contents of that file placed in the text box on the form, as shown in Figure 8-7.

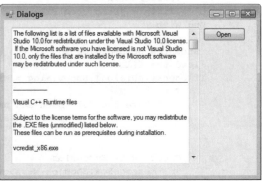

13. For the final test, close your application and then start it again. Click the Open button on the form and notice that the Open File dialog box has opened in the same directory from which you selected the last file. You didn't need to write any code to have the Open File dialog box do this.

FIGURE 8-7

How It Works

Before displaying the Open File dialog box, you need to set some properties of OpenFileDialog1 so that the dialog box is customized for your application. You can do this with a `With . . . End With` statement. The `With . . . End With` statement enables you to make repeated references to a single object without having to repeatedly specify the object name. You specify the object name once on the line with the `With` statement and then add all references to the properties of that object before the `End With` statement.

```
With OpenFileDialog1
```

The first property that you set is the `Filter` property. This property enables you to define the filters that are displayed in the File filter combo box in the bottom right corner of the dialog. When you define a file extension filter, you specify the filter description followed by a vertical bar (|) followed by the file extension. When you want the `Filter` property to contain multiple file extensions, as shown in the following code, you separate each file filter with a vertical bar as follows:

```
.Filter = "Text Documents (*.txt)|*.txt|All Files (*.*)|*.*"
```

The next property that you set is `FilterIndex`. This property determines which filter is shown in the File filter combo box. The default value for this property is 1, which is the first filter:

```
.FilterIndex = 1
```

Finally, you set the `Title` property. This is the caption that is displayed in the title bar of the dialog box:

```
.Title = "Demo Open File Dialog"
```

To show the Open File dialog box, you use the `ShowDialog` method. Remember that this method returns a `DialogResult` value, there are only two possible results, and you can compare the results from the `ShowDialog` method to `Windows.Forms.DialogResult.OK` and `Windows.Forms.DialogResult.Cancel`. If the user clicks the Open button in the dialog box, then the `ShowDialog` method returns a value of `OK`; if the user clicks the Cancel button, the `ShowDialog` method returns `Cancel`:

```
If OpenFileDialog1.ShowDialog = Windows.Forms.DialogResult.OK Then
```

Next, you add a `Try.Catch` block to handle any errors that may occur while opening a file. Inside the `Try` block you retrieve the path and filename that the user has chosen in the Open File dialog box and set it in your `strFileName` variable. The path and filename are contained in the `FileName` property of the OpenFileDialog control:

```
'Save the file name
strFileName = OpenFileDialog1.FileName
```

Next, you use the built-in code snippets provided by Visual Studio 2010 to simplify your programming tasks by using the Read Text from a File code snippet. This code snippet contains the necessary code to read the contents from a text file and to place those contents in a string variable.

Then, you modify the code from the code snippet, supplying the `strFileName` variable in the bolded section of code. This code will read the entire contents of the text file into the `fileContents` variable:

```
Dim fileContents As String
fileContents = My.Computer.FileSystem.ReadAllText(strFileName)
```

The final line of code that you wrote takes the contents of the `allText` variable and sets it in the `Text` property of the TextBox control, thereby populating the text box with the contents of your text file:

```
'Display the file contents in the text box
txtFile.Text = fileContents
```

The code in the `Catch` block uses the `MessageBox` class to display the contents of the `Message` property of the exception thrown should an error occur. The `caption` parameter of the `MessageBox` class retrieves the title of your application from the `Title` property of the `My.Application.Info` object:

```
Catch ex As Exception
    MessageBox.Show(ex.Message, My.Application.Info.Title, _
        MessageBoxButtons.OK, MessageBoxIcon.Error)
End Try
```

Many other properties in the OpenFileDialog control haven't been covered in this chapter, and you should feel free to experiment on your own to see all of the possibilities that this dialog box has to offer.

THE SAVEDIALOG CONTROL

Now that you can open a file with the OpenFileDialog control, take a look at the SaveFileDialog control so that you can save a file. Like the OpenFileDialog, the SaveFileDialog can be used as a control or a class. Once you have mastered the SaveFileDialog as a control, you will not have any problems using `SaveFileDialog` as a class.

After you open a file, you may need to make some modifications to it and then save it. The SaveFile-Dialog control provides the same functionality as the OpenFileDialog control, except in reverse. It enables you to choose the location and filename as you save a file. It is important to note that the SaveFileDialog control does not actually save your file; it merely provides a dialog box that enables the user to locate where the file should be saved and to provide a name for the file.

The Properties of SaveFileDialog

Table 8-7 lists some of the properties that are available in the SaveFileDialog control. As you can see, this control, or class if you will, contains a wealth of properties that can be used to customize how the dialog box will behave.

TABLE 8-7: Common SaveFileDialog Control Properties

PROPERTY	DESCRIPTION
AddExtension	Indicates whether an extension is automatically added to a filename if the user omits the extension
AutoUpgradeEnabled	Indicates whether this dialog box should automatically upgrade its appearance and behavior when running on different versions of Windows. When false, it will appear with XP styles.
CheckFileExists	Indicates whether the dialog box displays a warning if the user specifies a filename that does not exist. This is useful when you want the user to save a file to an existing name.
CheckPathExists	Indicates whether the dialog box displays a warning if the user specifies a path that does not exist.
CreatePrompt	Indicates whether the dialog box prompts the user for permission to create a file if the user specifies a file that does not exist.
DefaultExt	Indicates the default file extension
DereferenceLinks	Indicates whether the dialog box returns the location of the *file* referenced by the shortcut or whether it returns the location of the *shortcut itself.*
FileName	Indicates the filename of the selected file in the dialog box. This is a read-only property.

TABLE 8-7

PROPERTY	DESCRIPTION
FileNames	Indicates the filenames of all selected files in the dialog box. This is a read-only property that is returned as a string array.
Filter	Indicates the current filename filter string, which determines the options that appear in the Files of Type: combo box in the dialog box.
FilterIndex	Indicates the index of the filter currently selected in the dialog box
InitialDirectory	Indicates the initial directory displayed in the dialog box
OverwritePrompt	Indicates whether the dialog box displays a warning if the user specifies a filename that already exists.
ShowHelp	Indicates whether the Help button is displayed in the dialog box
SupportMultiDotted Extensions	Indicates whether the dialog box supports displaying and saving files that have multiple filename extensions
Title	Indicates the title that is displayed in the title bar of the dialog box
ValidateNames	Indicates whether the dialog box should accept only valid Win32 filenames

SaveFileDialog Methods

The SaveFileDialog control exposes the same methods as the OpenFileDialog. If you want to review these methods, go back to the section "OpenFileDialog Methods." All the examples use the `ShowDialog` method to show the Save File dialog.

Using the SaveFileDialog Control

In this exercise, you want to save the contents of the text box to a file.

You use the SaveFileDialog control to display a Save File dialog box that enables you to specify the location and name of the file. Then you write the contents of the text box on your form to the specified file, again using a built-in code snippet provided by Visual Studio 2010.

TRY IT OUT   Working with SaveFileDialog

Code file Windows Forms Dialogs.zip available for download at Wrox.com

To see how to include the SaveFileDialog control in your project, you begin with the Windows Forms Dialogs project from the previous Try It Out as a starting point and build upon it.

1. Return to the Forms Designer in the Windows Forms Dialogs project.

2. Drag another Button control from the Toolbox and drop it beneath the Open button and set its properties as follows:

   ➤ Set Name to **btnSave.**

   ➤ Set Anchor to **Top, Right.**

   ➤ Set Location to **349, 43.**

   ➤ Set Text to **Save.**

3. In the Toolbox, scroll down until you see the SaveFileDialog control and then drag and drop it onto your form. The control will be added to the bottom of the workspace in the IDE.

4. Double-click the Save button to bring up its Click event and add the bolded code:

```
Private Sub btnSave_Click(ByVal sender As System.Object, _
    ByVal e As System.EventArgs) Handles btnSave.Click
    'Set the Save dialog properties
    With SaveFileDialog1
        .DefaultExt = "txt"
        .FileName = strFileName
        .Filter = "Text Documents (*.txt)|*.txt|All Files (*.*)|*.*"
        .FilterIndex = 1
        .OverwritePrompt = True
        .Title = "Demo Save File Dialog"
    End With

    'Show the Save dialog and if the user clicks the Save button,
    'save the file
    If SaveFileDialog1.ShowDialog = Windows.Forms.DialogResult.OK Then
        Try
            'Save the file path and name
            strFileName = SaveFileDialog1.FileName

        Catch ex As Exception
            MessageBox.Show(ex.Message, My.Application.Info.Title, _
                MessageBoxButtons.OK, MessageBoxIcon.Error)
        End Try
    End If
End Sub
```

5. Right-click in the blank space inside the Try block statement right before the Catch block statement and choose Insert Snippet from the context menu. In the drop-down menu that appears, double-click Fundamentals-Collections, Data Types, File System, Math, and then in the new list double-click File System-Processing Drives, Folders, and Files. Finally, scroll down the list and double-click Write Text to a File. Your code should now look as follows, and you'll notice that the filename C:\Test.txt is bolded, as is the text string Text, indicating that this code needs to be changed:

```
Try
    'Save the file path and name
    strFileName = SaveFileDialog1.FileName

    My.Computer.FileSystem.WriteAllText("C:\Test.txt", "Text", True)
Catch ex As Exception
```

6. Modify the code in the `Try` block as shown here:

```
Try
    'Save the file path and name
    strFileName = SaveFileDialog1.FileName
    My.Computer.FileSystem.WriteAllText(strFileName, txtFile.Text, False)
Catch ex As Exception
```

7. At this point, you are ready to test this code, so run your project. Start with a simple test. Type some text into the text box on the form and then click the Save button. The Save dialog box will be displayed. Notice that the File name combo box already has the complete path and filename in it. This is the path filename that was set in the `strFileName` variable when you declared it in the previous Try It Out.

8. Enter a new filename but don't put a file extension on it. Then click the Save button and the file will be saved. To verify this, click the Open button on the form to invoke the Open File dialog box; you will see your new file.

9. To test the `OverwritePrompt` property of the SaveFile-Dialog control, enter some more text in the text box on the form and then click the Save button. In the Save File dialog box, choose an existing filename and then click the Save button. You will be prompted to confirm replacement of the existing file as shown in Figure 8-8.

FIGURE 8-8

If you choose Yes, the dialog box will return a `DialogResult` of `OK`, and the code inside your `If`. `End If` statement will be executed. If you choose No, you will be returned to the Save File dialog box so that you can enter another filename.

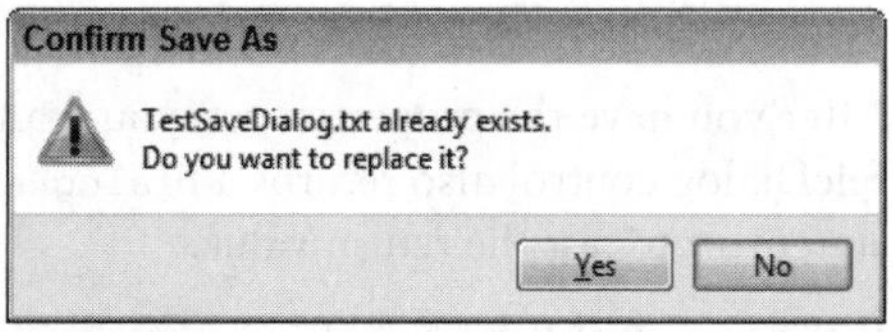

> **NOTE** When the Open File or Save File dialog box is displayed, the context menu is fully functional and you can cut, copy, and paste files, as well as rename and delete them. Other options may appear in the context menu depending on what software you have installed. For example, if you have WinZip installed, you will see the WinZip options on the context menu.

How It Works

Before displaying the Save File dialog box, you need to set some properties to customize the dialog to your application. The first property you set is the `DefaultExt` property. This property automatically sets the file extension if one has not been specified. For example, if you specify a filename of **NewFile** with no extension, the dialog box will automatically add .txt to the filename when it returns, so that you end up with a filename of NewFile.txt.

```
.DefaultExt = "txt"
```

The `FileName` property is set to the same path and filename as that returned from the Open File dialog. This enables you to open a file, edit it, and then display the same filename when you show the Save File dialog box. Of course, you can override this filename in the application's Save File dialog box.

```
.FileName = strFileName
```

The next two properties are the same as in the OpenFileDialog control. They set the file extension filters to be displayed in the Save as Type: combo box and set the initial filter:

```
.Filter = "Text Documents (*.txt)|*.txt|All Files (*.*)|*.*"
.FilterIndex = 1
```

The `OverwritePrompt` property accepts a Boolean value of `True` or `False`. When set to `True`, this property prompts you with a MessageBox dialog box if you choose an existing filename. If you select Yes, the Save File dialog box returns a `DialogResult` of `OK`; if you select No, you are returned to the Save File dialog box to choose another filename. When the `OverwritePrompt` property is set to `False`, the Save File dialog box does not prompt you to overwrite an existing file, and your code will overwrite it without asking for the user's permission.

```
.OverwritePrompt = True
```

The `Title` property sets the caption in the title bar of the Save File dialog box:

```
.Title = "Demo Save File Dialog"
```

After you have the properties set, you want to show the dialog box. The `ShowDialog` method of the SaveFileDialog control also returns a `DialogResult`, so you can use the SaveFileDialog control in an `If.End If` statement to test the return value.

If the user clicks the Save button in the Save File dialog box, the dialog box returns a `DialogResult` of `OK`. If the user clicks the Cancel button in the dialog box, the dialog box returns a `DialogResult` of `Cancel`. The following code tests for `Windows.Forms.DialogResult.OK`:

```
If SaveFileDialog1.ShowDialog = Windows.Forms.DialogResult.OK Then
```

The first thing that you do here is save the path and filename chosen by the user in your `strFileName` variable. This is done in case the user has chosen a new filename in the dialog box:

```
Try
    'Save the file path and name
    strFileName = SaveFileDialog1.FileName
```

Then you modify the code snippet generated by Visual Studio 2010 by replacing the bolded text with your variables. First, you replace the text `"C:\Test.txt"` with your variable, `strFileName`. This part of the code opens the file for output. Then you replace the text `"Text"` with the `Text` property of the text box on your form. This part of the code reads the contents of your text box and writes it to the file. The `False` parameter at the end of this line of code indicates whether text should be appended to the file. A value of `False` indicates that the file contents should be overwritten.

```
My.Computer.FileSystem.WriteAllText(strFileName,txtFile.Text, False)
```

The final bit of code in this `If.End If` block merely wraps up the `Try.Catch` block and the `If.End If` statement:

```
    Catch ex As Exception
        MessageBox.Show(ex.Message, My.Application.Info.Title, _
            MessageBoxButtons.OK, MessageBoxIcon.Error)
    End Try
End If
```

THE FONTDIALOG CONTROL

Sometimes you may need to write an application that allows users to choose the font in which they want their data to be displayed or entered. Or perhaps you may want to see all available fonts installed on a particular system. This is where the FontDialog control comes in; it displays a list of all available fonts installed on your computer in a standard dialog that your users have become accustomed to seeing.

Like the OpenFileDialog and SaveFileDialog controls, the `FontDialog` class can be used as a control by dragging it onto a form, or as a class by declaring it in code.

The FontDialog control is very easy to use; you just set some properties, show the dialog box, and then query the properties that you need.

The Properties of FontDialog

Table 8-8 lists some of its available properties.

TABLE 8-8: Common FontDialog Control Properties

PROPERTY	DESCRIPTION
AllowScriptChange	Indicates whether the user can change the character set specified in the Script drop-down box to display a character set other than the one currently displayed
Color	Indicates the selected font color
Font	Indicates the selected font
FontMustExist	Indicates whether the dialog box specifies an error condition if the user attempts to enter a font or style that does not exist
MaxSize	Indicates the maximum size (in points) a user can select
MinSize	Indicates the minimum size (in points) a user can select
ShowApply	Indicates whether the dialog box contains an Apply button
ShowColor	Indicates whether the dialog box displays the color choice
ShowEffects	Indicates whether the dialog box contains controls that allow the user to specify strikethrough, underline, and text color options
ShowHelp	Indicates whether the dialog box displays a Help button

The Methods of FontDialog

You will be using only one method (`ShowDialog`) of FontDialog in the following Try It Out. Other methods available include `Reset`, which enables you to reset all the properties to their default values.

Using the FontDialog Control

You can display the FontDialog control without setting any properties:

```
FontDialog1.ShowDialog()
```

The dialog box would then look like Figure 8-9.

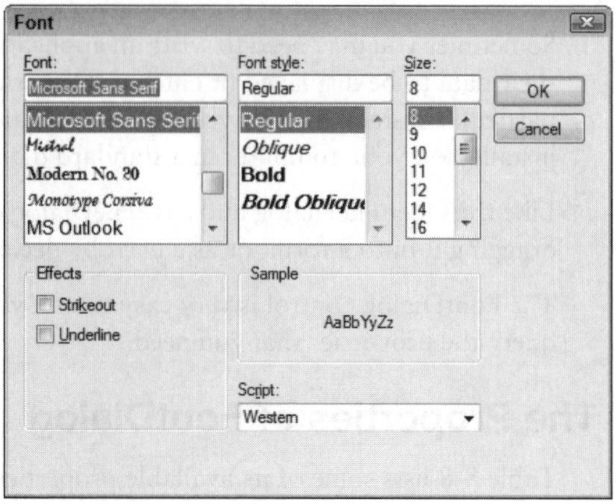

Note that the Font dialog box contains an Effects section that enables you to check the options for Strikeout and Underline. However, color selection of the font is not provided by default. If you want this, you must set the `ShowColor` property before calling the `ShowDialog` method on the dialog box:

```
FontDialog1.ShowColor = True
FontDialog1.ShowDialog()
```

FIGURE 8-9

The `ShowDialog` method of this dialog box, like all of the ones that you have examined thus far, returns a `DialogResult`. This will be either `DialogResult.OK` or `DialogResult.Cancel`.

When the dialog box returns, you can query for the `Font` and `Color` properties to see what font and color the user has chosen. You can then apply these properties to a control on your form or store them to a variable for later use.

TRY IT OUT **Working with FontDialog**

Code file Windows Forms Dialogs.zip available for download at Wrox.com

Now that you know what the Font dialog box looks like and how to call it, you can use it in a Try It Out. Using the program from the last two Try It Outs to open a file, you will have the contents of the file read into the text box on the form. You then use the FontDialog control to display the Font dialog box, which enables you to select a font. Then you change the font in the text box to the font that you have chosen.

1. Return to the Forms Designer in the Windows Forms Dialogs project.

2. Add another button from the Toolbox and set its properties according to the values shown in this list:

➤ Set `Name` to **btnFont**.

➤ Set `Anchor` to **Top, Right**.

➤ Set `Location` to **349, 73**.

➤ Set `Text` to **Font**.

3. You now need to add the FontDialog control to your project, so locate this control in the Toolbox and drag and drop it onto the form or in the workspace below the form; the control will be automatically placed in the workspace below the form if dragged onto the form. Accept all default properties for this control.

4. You want to add code to the Click event of the Font button, so double-click it and add the following bolded code:

```
Private Sub btnFont_Click(ByVal sender As System.Object, _
    ByVal e As System.EventArgs) Handles btnFont.Click

    'Set the Font dialog properties
    FontDialog1.ShowColor = True

    'Show the Font dialog and if the user clicks the OK button,
    'update the font and color in the text box
    If FontDialog1.ShowDialog = Windows.Forms.DialogResult.OK Then
        txtFile.Font = FontDialog1.Font
        txtFile.ForeColor = FontDialog1.Color
    End If
End Sub
```

5. Run your project. Once your form has been displayed, click the Font button to display the Font dialog box as shown in Figure 8-10. Choose a new font and color and then click OK.

6. Add some text in the text box on your form. The text will appear with the new font and color that you have chosen.

7. This same font and color will also be applied to the text that is loaded from a file. To demonstrate this, click the Open button on the form and open a text file. The text from the file is displayed in the same font and color that you chose in the Font dialog box.

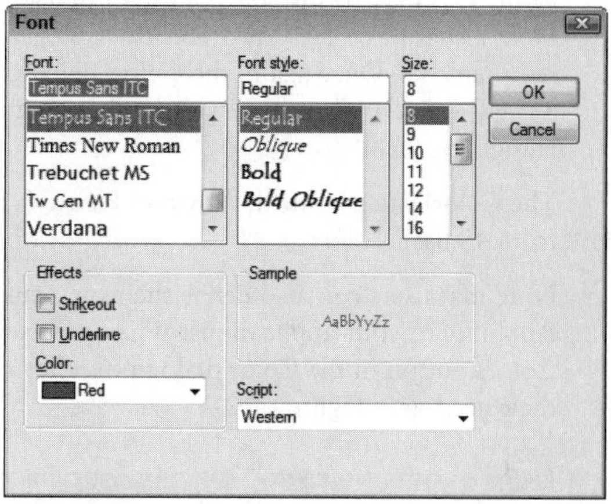

FIGURE 8-10

How It Works

You know that the Font dialog box does not show a Color box by default, so you begin by setting the ShowColor property of the FontDialog control to True so that the Color box is displayed:

```
'Set the Font dialog properties
FontDialog1.ShowColor = True
```

Next, you actually show the Font dialog box. Remember that the DialogResult returns a value of OK or Cancel, so that you can compare the return value from the FontDialog control to Windows.Forms.DialogResult.OK. If the button that the user clicked was OK, you execute the code within the If..End If statement:

```
'Show the Font dialog and if the user clicks the OK button,
'update the font and color in the text box
If FontDialog1.ShowDialog = Windows.Forms.DialogResult.OK Then
```

```
      txtFile.Font = FontDialog1.Font
      txtFile.ForeColor = FontDialog1.Color
   End If
```

You set the `Font` property of the text box (`txtFile`) equal to the `Font` property of the FontDialog control. This is the font that the user has chosen. Then you set the `ForeColor` property of the text box equal to the `Color` property of the FontDialog control, as this will be the color that the user has chosen. After these properties have been changed for the text box, the existing text in the text box is automatically updated to reflect the new font and color. If the text box does not contain any text, then any new text that is typed or loaded into the text box will appear in the new font and color.

THE COLORDIALOG CONTROL

Sometimes you may need to allow users to customize the colors on their form. This may be the color of the form itself, a control, or text in a text box. Visual Basic 2010 provides the ColorDialog control for all such requirements. Once again, the ColorDialog control can also be used as a class — declared in code without dragging a control onto the Forms Designer.

The ColorDialog control, shown in Figure 8-11, allows the user to choose from 48 basic colors.

Note that users can also define their own custom colors, adding more flexibility to your applications. When the users click the Define Custom Colors button in the Color dialog box, they can adjust the color to suit their needs (see Figure 8-12).

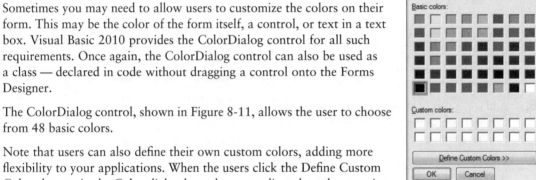

FIGURE 8-11

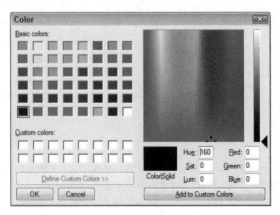

FIGURE 8-12

Having this opportunity for customization and flexibility in your applications gives them a more professional appearance, plus your users are happy because they are allowed to customize the application to suit their own personal tastes.

The Properties of ColorDialog

Before you dive into more code, take a look at some of the available properties for the ColorDialog control, shown in Table 8-9.

TABLE 8-9: Common ColorDialog Control Properties

PROPERTY	DESCRIPTION
AllowFullOpen	Indicates whether users can use the dialog box to define custom colors
AnyColor	Indicates whether the dialog box displays all available colors in the set of basic colors
Color	Indicates the color selected by the user
CustomColors	Indicates the set of custom colors shown in the dialog box
FullOpen	Indicates whether the controls used to create custom colors are visible when the dialog box is opened
ShowHelp	Indicates whether a Help button appears in the dialog box
SolidColorOnly	Indicates whether the dialog box will restrict users to selecting solid colors only

There aren't many properties that you need to worry about for this dialog box, which makes it even simpler to use than the other dialogs you have examined so far.

As with the other dialog box controls, ColorDialog contains a ShowDialog method. Because you have already seen this method in the previous examples, it is not discussed again.

Using the ColorDialog Control

All you need to do to display the Color dialog box is to execute its ShowDialog method:

```
ColorDialog1.ShowDialog()
```

The ColorDialog control will return a DialogResult of OK or Cancel. Hence, you can use the previous statement in an If..End If statement and test for a DialogResult of OK, as you have done in the previous examples that you coded.

To retrieve the color that the user has chosen, you simply retrieve the value set in the `Color` property and assign it to a variable or any property of a control that supports colors, such as the `ForeColor` property of a text box:

```
txtFile.ForeColor = ColorDialog1.Color
```

TRY IT OUT **Working with the ColorDialog Control**

Code file Windows Forms Dialogs.zip available for download at Wrox.com

In this Try It Out, you continue using the same project and make the ColorDialog control display the Color dialog box. Then, if the dialog box returns a `DialogResult` of `OK`, you change the background color of the form.

1. Return to the Forms Designer in the Windows Forms Dialogs project.

2. On the form, add another Button control from the Toolbox and set its properties according to the values shown:

➤ Set `Name` to **btnColor.**

➤ Set `Anchor` to **Top, Right.**

➤ Set `Location` to **349, 103.**

➤ Set `Text` to **Color.**

3. Add a ColorDialog control to your project from the Toolbox. It will be added to the workspace below the form. Accept all default properties for this control.

4. Double-click the Color button to bring up its `Click` event handler and add the following bolded code:

```
Private Sub btnColor_Click(ByVal sender As System.Object, _
    ByVal e As System.EventArgs) Handles btnColor.Click
    'Show the Color dialog and if the user clicks the OK button,
    'update the background color of the form
    If ColorDialog1.ShowDialog = Windows.Forms.DialogResult.OK Then
        Me.BackColor = ColorDialog1.Color
    End If
End Sub
```

5. That's all the code you need to add. Start your project to test your changes.

6. Once the form is displayed, click the Color button to display the Color dialog box. Choose any color that you want, or create a custom color by clicking the Define Custom Colors button. After you have chosen a color, click the OK button in the Color dialog box. The background color of the form will be set to the color that you selected.

7. As with the Font dialog box, you do not have to set the `Color` property of the ColorDialog control before displaying the Color dialog box again. It automatically remembers the color chosen, and this will be the color that is selected when the dialog box is displayed again. To test this, click the Color button again; the color that you chose will be selected.

How It Works

This time you did not need to set any properties of the ColorDialog control, so you jumped right in and displayed it in an If.End If statement to check the `DialogResult` returned by the `ShowDialog` method of this dialog box:

```
If ColorDialog1.ShowDialog = Windows.Forms.DialogResult.OK Then
```

Within the If.End If statement, you added the code necessary to change the `BackColor` property of the form. If the user clicks OK in the Color dialog box, the background color of the form is changed with the following line of code:

```
Me.BackColor = ColorDialog1.Color
```

THE PRINTDIALOG CONTROL

Any application worth its salt will incorporate some kind of printing capabilities, whether it is basic printing or more sophisticated printing, such as allowing a user to print only selected text or a range of pages. In this section you explore basic printing, looking at several classes that help you to print text from a file.

Visual Basic 2010 provides the PrintDialog control. It does not actually do any printing, but enables you to select the printer that you want to use and set the printer properties such as page orientation and print quality. It also enables you to specify the print range. You will not be using these features in this next example, but it is worth noting that this functionality is available in the PrintDialog control, as shown in Figure 8-13.

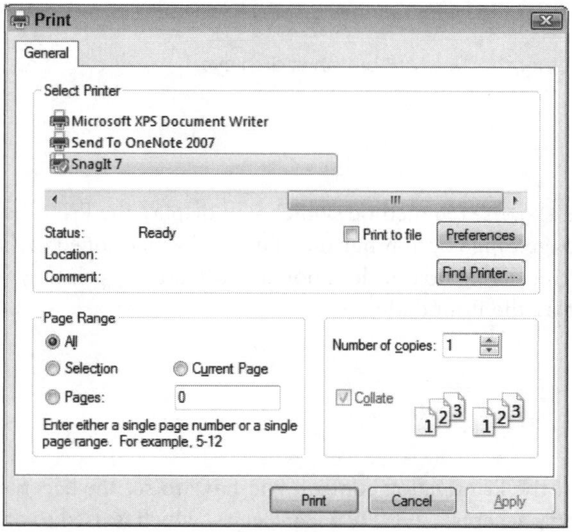

FIGURE 8-13

Like the previous dialog boxes that you have examined, the Print dialog provides Print (corresponding to the OK buttons in the other dialogs) and Cancel buttons; thus, its ShowDialog method returns a DialogResult of OK or Cancel. You can then use this result in an If..End If statement and test for the DialogResult. The Apply button merely applies changes made in the Print dialog but does not close the dialog.

The Properties of PrintDialog

Table 8-10 shows some of the properties provided in PrintDialog. Just like the other dialog boxes, PrintDialog exposes a ShowDialog method.

TABLE 8-10: Common PrintDialog Control Properties

PROPERTY	DESCRIPTION
AllowCurrentPage	Indicates whether the Current Page option button is enabled
AllowPrintToFile	Indicates whether the Print to File check box is enabled
AllowSelection	Indicates whether the Selection option button is enabled
AllowSomePages	Indicates whether the Pages option button is enabled
Document	Indicates the print document used to obtain the printer settings
PrinterSettings	Indicates the printer settings that the dialog box will be modifying
PrintToFile	Indicates whether the Print to File check box is checked
ShowHelp	Indicates whether the Help button is displayed
ShowNetwork	Indicates whether the Network button is displayed

Using the PrintDialog Control

The only method that you will be using is the ShowDialog method, which will display the Print dialog box shown in Figure 8-13 with only the All page range option button enabled. As mentioned earlier, the PrintDialog control merely displays the Print dialog box; it does not actually do any printing. The following code fragment shows how you display the Print dialog box:

```
PrintDialog1.ShowDialog()
```

The PrintDocument Class

Before you can call the ShowDialog method of the PrintDialog control, you have to set the Document property of the PrintDialog class. This property accepts a PrintDocument class, which is used to obtain the printer settings and can send output to the printer. This class requires the System.Drawing.Printing namespace, so you must include this namespace before attempting to define an object that uses the PrintDocument class.

The Properties of the PrintDocument Class

Before continuing, take a look at some of the important properties of the `PrintDocument` class, listed in Table 8-11.

TABLE 8-11: Common PrintDocument Class Properties

PROPERTY	DESCRIPTION
DefaultPageSettings	Indicates the default page settings for the document.
DocumentName	Indicates the document name that is displayed while printing the document. This is also the name that appears in the Print Status dialog box and printer queue.
PrintController	Indicates the print controller that guides the printing process.
PrinterSettings	Indicates the printer that prints the document.

Printing a Document

The `Print` method of the `PrintDocument` class prints a document to the printer specified in the `PrinterSettings` property. When you call the `Print` method of the `PrintDocument` class, the `PrintPage` event is raised for each page as it prints. Therefore, you need to create a method for that event and add an event handler for it. The method that you would create for the `PrintPage` event does the actual reading of the data to be printed.

Printing using the `PrintDocument` class requires a lot of coding and knowledge of how actual printing works. Fortunately, the help documentation provides some sample code in the `PrintDocument` class. This can be used as a starting point to help you gain an understanding of the basics of printing. Note that the sample code in the help documentation assumes that a single line in the file to be printed does not exceed the width of a printed page.

The sample code in the help documentation demonstrates how to print from a file.

TRY IT OUT   Working with the PrintDialog Control

Code file Windows Forms Dialogs.zip available for download at Wrox.com

In this Try It Out, you'll examine how to print the contents of a text box.

1. Return to the Forms Designer in the Windows Forms Dialogs project.

2. Drag a Button control from the Toolbox. Position it beneath the Color button and set the following properties of the new button:

➤ Set Name to **btnPrint**.

➤ Set Anchor to **Top, Right**.

➤ Set Location to **349, 133**.

➤ Set Text to **Print**.

3. Add a PrintDialog control to the project, dragging and dropping it from the Toolbox onto the form. It will be added to the workspace below the form. Accept all default properties for this control. You will find it under the Printing tab.

4. Switch to the Code Editor so that you can add the required namespace for printing. Add this namespace to the top of your class:

```
Imports System.Drawing.Printing

Public Class Dialogs
```

5. Add the following variable declarations to the top of your class:

```
'Declare variables and objects
Private strFileName As String
Private strPrintRecord As String

Private WithEvents DialogsPrintDocument As PrintDocument
```

6. Select `DialogsPrintDocument` in the Class Name combo box and the `PrintPage` event in the Method Name combo box. Add the following bolded code to the `DialogsPrintDocument_PrintPage` event handler:

```
Private Sub DialogsPrintDocument_PrintPage(ByVal sender As Object, _
    ByVal e As System.Drawing.Printing.PrintPageEventArgs) _
    Handles DialogsPrintDocument.PrintPage
    'Declare variables
    Dim intCharactersToPrint As Integer
    Dim intLinesPerPage As Integer
    Dim strPrintData As String
    Dim objStringFormat As New StringFormat
    Dim objPrintFont As New Font("Arial", 10)
    Dim objPageBoundaries As RectangleF
    Dim objPrintArea As SizeF

    'Get the page boundaries
    objPageBoundaries = New RectangleF(e.MarginBounds.Left, _
        e.MarginBounds.Top, e.MarginBounds.Width, e.MarginBounds.Height)

    'Get the print area based on page margins and font used
    objPrintArea = New SizeF(e.MarginBounds.Width, _
        e.MarginBounds.Height - objPrintFont.GetHeight(e.Graphics))

    'Break in between words on a line
    objStringFormat.Trimming = StringTrimming.Word

    'Get the number of characters to print
    e.Graphics.MeasureString(strPrintRecord, objPrintFont, objPrintArea, _
        objStringFormat, intCharactersToPrint, intLinesPerPage)

    'Get the print data from the print record
    strPrintData = strPrintRecord.Substring(0, intCharactersToPrint)

    'Print the page
        e.Graphics.DrawString(strPrintData, objPrintFont, Brushes.Black, _
        objPageBoundaries, objStringFormat)
    'If more lines exist, print another page
```

```
        If intCharactersToPrint < strPrintRecord.Length Then
            'Remove printed text from print record
            strPrintRecord = strPrintRecord.Remove(0, intCharactersToPrint)
            e.HasMorePages = True
        Else
            e.HasMorePages = False
        End If
End Sub
```

7. Select btnPrint in the Class Name combo box and the Click event in the Method Name combo box. Add the following bolded code to the btnPrint_Click event handler:

```
Private Sub btnPrint_Click(ByVal sender As System.Object, _
    ByVal e As System.EventArgs) Handles btnPrint.Click
    'Instantiate a new instance of the PrintDocument
    DialogsPrintDocument = New PrintDocument

    'Set the PrintDialog properties
    With PrintDialog1
        .AllowCurrentPage = False
        .AllowPrintToFile = False
        .AllowSelection = False
        .AllowSomePages = False
        .Document = DialogsPrintDocument
        .PrinterSettings.DefaultPageSettings.Margins.Top = 25
        .PrinterSettings.DefaultPageSettings.Margins.Bottom = 25
        .PrinterSettings.DefaultPageSettings.Margins.Left = 25
        .PrinterSettings.DefaultPageSettings.Margins.Right = 25
    End With

    If PrintDialog1.ShowDialog = DialogResult.OK Then
        'Set the selected printer settings in the PrintDocument
        DialogsPrintDocument.PrinterSettings = _
            PrintDialog1.PrinterSettings

        'Get the print data
        strPrintRecord = txtFile.Text

        'Invoke the Print method on the PrintDocument
        DialogsPrintDocument.Print()
    End If
End Sub
```

8. You are now ready to test your code, so run the project.

9. Click the Open button to open a file, and then click the Print button to display the Print dialog box shown in Figure 8-14.

> **NOTE** The Print to File check box as well as the Selection, Current Page, and Pages radio buttons are disabled. This is because you set the AllowCurrentPage, AllowPrintToFile, AllowSelection, and AllowSomePages properties in the PrintDialog control to False.

If you have more than one printer installed (refer to Figure 8-14), you can choose the printer name that you want from the list.

10. Click the Print button in the Print dialog box to have your text printed.

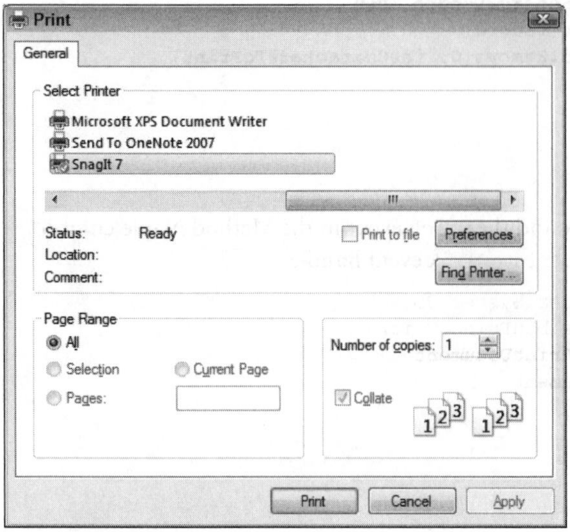

FIGURE 8-14

How It Works

You begin by importing the `System.Drawing.Printing` namespace, which is needed to support printing. This is the namespace in which the `PrintDocument` class is defined.

You then declare a variable and object needed for printing. The `strPrintRecord` variable is a string variable that will contain the data from the text box to be printed. The `DialogsPrintDocument` object will actually be responsible for printing the text.

Notice the `WithEvents` keyword. This keyword is used to refer to a class that can raise events, and will cause Visual Studio 2010 to list those events in the Method Name combo box at the top of the Code Editor:

```
Private strPrintRecord As String

Private WithEvents DialogsPrintDocument As PrintDocument
```

The `DialogsPrintDocument_PrintPage` event handler handles printing a page of output. This event is initially called after you call the `Print` method on the object defined as the `PrintDocument` class — in this case, the `DialogsPrintDocument`.

This event handler is where you have to provide the code for actually printing a document, and you must determine if more pages exist to be printed. This method starts off with a number of variable declarations. The first two variables are `Integer` data types and contain the number of characters to print to a page and the number of lines that can be printed on a page.

The `strPrintData` variable is a `String` data type that contains all of the data to be printed on a single page. The `objStringFormat` variable is declared as a `StringFormat` class, and this class encapsulates text layout information used to format the data to be printed. The `StringFormat` class is used to trim the data on word boundaries so that the text does not overflow the print area of a page.

The `objPrintFont` object is defined as a `Font` class and sets the font used for the printed text, while the `objPageBoundaries` object is defined as a `RectangleF` structure. The `RectangleF` structure contains four floating-point numbers defining the location and size of a rectangle and is used to define the top and left coordinates of a page, as well as its width and height. The `objPrintArea` object is defined as a `SizeF` structure and contains the height and width of the print area of a page. This is the actual area that you can print in, not the actual size of the page:

```
Private Sub DialogsPrintDocument_PrintPage(ByVal sender As Object, _
    ByVal e As System.Drawing.Printing.PrintPageEventArgs) _
    Handles DialogsPrintDocument.PrintPage

    'Declare variables
    Dim intCharactersToPrint As Integer
    Dim intLinesPerPage As Integer
    Dim strPrintData As String
    Dim objStringFormat As New StringFormat
    Dim objPrintFont As New Font("Arial", 10)
    Dim objPageBoundaries As RectangleF
    Dim objPrintArea As SizeF
```

The code in this method starts off by getting the page boundaries. The `PrintPageEventArgs` passed to this method in the `e` parameter contains the top and left coordinates of the page as well as the height and width of the page. These values are used to set the data in the `objPageBoundaries` object.

The print area of the page is contained in the `Width` and `Height` properties of the `PrintPageEventArgs`. The actual height of the page is calculated using the `GetHeight` method of the `Font` class in the `objPrintFont` object, as each font size requires more or less vertical space on a page:

```
'Get the page boundaries
objPageBoundaries = New RectangleF(e.MarginBounds.Left, _
    e.MarginBounds.Top, e.MarginBounds.Width, e.MarginBounds.Height)

'Get the print area based on page margins and font used
objPrintArea = New SizeF(e.MarginBounds.Width, _
    e.MarginBounds.Height — objPrintFont.GetHeight(e.Graphics))
```

You now set the `Trimming` property of the `objStringFormat` object to instruct it to break the data on a single line using word boundaries. This is done using the `StringTrimming` enumeration, which contains the `Word` constant. This ensures that a print line does not exceed the margins of a printed page.

You then need to determine the number of characters that will fit on a page based on the print area of the page, the font size used, and the data to be printed. This is done using the `MeasureString` method of the `Graphics` class. This method will take the data to be printed, the font used on the page, the print area of the page and the formatting to be applied, and then determine the number of characters that can be printed and the number of lines that will fit on a printed page. The number of print characters and the number of lines will be set in the `intCharactersToPrint` and `intLinesPerPage` variables, which are passed to the `MeasureString` method.

Once you know the number of characters that will fit on a page, you get that data from the `strPrintRecord` variable and set the data to be printed in the `strPrintData` variable. This is the variable that will contain the data to actually be printed:

```
'Break in between words on a line
objStringFormat.Trimming = StringTrimming.Word

'Get the number of characters to print
e.Graphics.MeasureString(strPrintRecord, objPrintFont, objPrintArea, _
    objStringFormat, intCharactersToPrint, intLinesPerPage)
```

```
'Get the print data from the print record
strPrintData = strPrintRecord.Substring(0, intCharactersToPrint)
```

Now that you have the appropriate data to be printed in the `strPrintData` variable, you are ready to actually send the data to be printed to the printer. This time you are going to use the `DrawString` method of the `Graphics` class. This method will actually format and send the data to the printer.

The parameters that you pass to the `DrawString` method are the data to be printed, the font to be used in printing, a `Brushes` object representing the font color of the text to print, the page boundaries, and a `StringFormat` object used to format the printed output:

```
'Print the page
e.Graphics.DrawString(strPrintData, objPrintFont, Brushes.Black, _
    objPageBoundaries, objStringFormat)
```

The last section of code in this method determines if more data exists to be printed. You want to compare the value contained in the `intCharactersToPrint` variable to the length of the `strPrintRecord` variable using the `Length` property of the `String` class. The `Length` property returns the number of characters in the string.

If the value contained in the `intCharactersToPrint` variable is less than the length of the `strPrintRecord` variable, then more data exists to be printed. In this case, you first want to remove the data from the `strPrintRecord` that has already been printed using the `Remove` method of the `String` class. The `Remove` method accepts the starting position from which to remove data and the amount of data to remove. The amount of data to be removed is contained in the `intCharactersToPrint` variable, the data that has already been printed.

Finally, you set the `HasMorePages` property of the `PrintPageEventArgs` parameter to `True`, indicating more data exists to be printed. Setting this property to `True` will cause the `PrintPage` event of the `DialogsPrintDocument` object to be raised once more, and this event handler will be executed again to continuing printing until all data has been printed.

If no more data exists to be printed, you set the `HasMorePages` property to `False`:

```
        'If more lines exist, print another page
        If intCharactersToPrint < strPrintRecord.Length Then
            'Remove printed text from print record
            strPrintRecord = strPrintRecord.Remove(0, intCharactersToPrint)
            e.HasMorePages = True
        Else
            e.HasMorePages = False
        End If
End Sub
```

The code in the `Click` event of the Print button is less complicated than the code in the `DialogsPrint Document_PrintPage` event handler. This method starts out by instantiating a new instance of the `PrintDocument` class in the `DialogsPrintDocument` object.

You then want to set the properties of the `PrintDialog` control before showing it. Since you have only a simple method to print all pages in a document, you want to disable the features that allow printing only the current page, printing to a file, printing a selection of text, and printing specific pages. This is all done by setting the first four properties in the following code to `False`.

Next, you need to set `Document` property of the `PrintDialog` to your `PrintDocument` object so that the dialog can obtain the printer settings. The printer settings are set and retrieved in the `PrintDocument` object and can be changed through the `PrintDialog` through its `PrinterSettings` property.

Finally, you set the default margins to be used when printing a document in the `PrinterSettings` property. This can be set before the `PrintDialog` is shown, to initially set the print margins for the printer:

```
'Instantiate a new instance of the PrintDocument
DialogsPrintDocument = New PrintDocument

'Set the PrintDialog properties
With PrintDialog1
    .AllowCurrentPage = False
    .AllowPrintToFile = False
    .AllowSelection = False
    .AllowSomePages = False
    .Document = DialogsPrintDocument
    .PrinterSettings.DefaultPageSettings.Margins.Top = 25
    .PrinterSettings.DefaultPageSettings.Margins.Bottom = 25
    .PrinterSettings.DefaultPageSettings.Margins.Left = 25
    .PrinterSettings.DefaultPageSettings.Margins.Right = 25
End With
```

The last thing you want to do in this method is actually display the `PrintDialog` and check for a `DialogResult` of `OK`. If the user clicks the Print button, the `PrintDialog` will return a `DialogResult` of `OK` and you want to actually invoke the printing of the data.

The first thing that you do in the `If ... Then` block is capture the printer settings from the `PrintDialog` and set them in the `DialogsPrintDocument`. If the user changed any of the margins or other printer settings, you want to pass them on to the `PrintDocument` that is used to print the data.

You also want to set the data to be printed from the text box in the `strPrintRecord` variable. Finally, you call the `Print` method on the `DialogsPrintDocument` object to start the printing process. Calling the `Print` method will raise the `PrintPage` event on the `DialogsPrintDocument` object, thus causing your code in the `DialogsPrintDocument_PrintPage` event handler to be executed:

```
If PrintDialog1.ShowDialog = DialogResult.OK Then
    'Set the selected printer settings in the PrintDocument
    DialogsPrintDocument.PrinterSettings = _
        PrintDialog1.PrinterSettings

    'Get the print data
    strPrintRecord = txtFile.Text

    'Invoke the Print method on the PrintDocument
    DialogsPrintDocument.Print()
End If
```

THE FOLDERBROWSERDIALOG CONTROL

Occasionally, you'll need to allow your users to select a folder instead of a file. Perhaps your application performs backups, or perhaps you need a folder to save temporary files. The FolderBrowserDialog control displays the Browse For Folder dialog box, which enables users to select a folder. This dialog box does not display files — only folders, which provides an obvious way to allow users to select a folder needed by your application.

Like the other dialog boxes that you have examined thus far, the FolderBrowserDialog control can also be used as a class declared in code. The Browse For Folder dialog box, shown in Figure 8-15 without any customization, enables users to browse for and select a folder. Notice that there is also a Make New Folder button that enables users to create and select a new folder.

The Properties of FolderBrowserDialog

FIGURE 8-15

Before you dive into some code, take a look at some of the available properties for the FolderBrowserDialog control, shown in Table 8-12.

TABLE 8-12: Common FolderBrowserDialog Control Properties

PROPERTY	DESCRIPTION
Description	Provides a descriptive message in the dialog box.
RootFolder	Indicates the root folder from which the dialog box should start browsing.
SelectedPath	Indicates the folder selected by the user.
ShowNewFolderButton	Indicates whether the Make New Folder button is shown in the dialog box

This is one dialog control for which you'll want to use all of the most common properties, as shown in the preceding table, to customize the dialog box displayed.

As with the other dialog controls, the FolderBrowserDialog contains a ShowDialog method. You have already seen this method in the previous examples, and since it is the same it does not need to be discussed again.

Using the FolderBrowserDialog Control

Before showing the Browse For Folder dialog box, you'll want to set some basic properties. The three main properties that you are most likely to set are shown in the following code snippet. The first of these properties is the Description property. This property enables you to provide a description or instructions for your users.

The next property is RootFolder, which specifies the starting folder for the Browse For Folder dialog box. This property uses one of the constants from the Environment.SpecialFolder enumeration. Typically, you would use the MyComputer constant to specify that browsing should start at the My

Computer level, or sometimes you may want to use to the `MyDocuments` constant to start browsing at the My Documents level.

The final property shown in the code snippet is the `ShowNewFolderButton` property. This property has a default value of `True`, which indicates that the Make New Folder button should be displayed. However, if you do not want this button displayed, you need to specify this property and set it to a value of `False`:

```
With FolderBrowserDialog1
    .Description = "Select a backup folder"
    .RootFolder = Environment.SpecialFolder.MyComputer
    .ShowNewFolderButton = False
End With
```

After you have set the necessary properties, you execute the `ShowDialog` method to display the dialog box:

```
FolderBrowserDialog1.ShowDialog()
```

The FolderBrowserDialog control will return a `DialogResult` of `OK` or `Cancel`. Hence, you can use the previous statement in an `If.End If` statement and test for a `DialogResult` of `OK`, as you have done in the previous examples that you have coded.

To retrieve the folder that the user has chosen, you simply retrieve the value set in the `SelectedPath` property and assign it to a variable. The folder that is returned is a fully qualified path name. For example, if you chose a folder named `Temp` at the root of your C drive, the path returned would be `C:\Temp`:

```
strFolder = FolderBrowserDialog1.SelectedPath
```

TRY IT OUT   **Working with the FolderBrowserDialog Control**

Code file Windows Forms Dialogs.zip available for download at Wrox.com

In this Try It Out, you continue using the same Windows Forms Dialogs project and have the Folder-BrowserDialog control display the Browse For Folder dialog box. Then, if the dialog box returns a `DialogResult` of `OK`, you'll display the selected folder in the text box on your form.

1.   Return to the Forms Designer in the Windows Forms Dialog project.

2.   Add another Button control from the Toolbox to the form beneath the Print button and set its properties as follows:

> ➤   Set `Name` to **btnBrowse.**

> ➤   Set `Anchor` to **Top, Right.**

> ➤   Set `Location` to **349, 163.**

> ➤   Set `Text` to **Browse.**

3.   Add a FolderBrowserDialog control to your project from the Toolbox. It will be added to the workspace below the form. Accept all default properties for this control, because you'll set the necessary properties in your code.

4. Double-click the Browse button to bring up its Click event handler, and add the following bolded code:

```
Private Sub btnBrowse_Click(ByVal sender As System.Object, _
    ByVal e As System.EventArgs) Handles btnBrowse.Click
    'Set the FolderBrowser dialog properties
    With FolderBrowserDialog1
        .Description = "Select a backup folder"
        .RootFolder = Environment.SpecialFolder.MyComputer
        .ShowNewFolderButton = False
    End With


    'Show the FolderBrowser dialog and if the user clicks the
    'OK button, display the selected folder
    If FolderBrowserDialog1.ShowDialog = Windows.Forms.DialogResult.OK Then
        txtFile.Text = FolderBrowserDialog1.SelectedPath
    End If
End Sub
```

5. That's all the code you need to add. To test your changes to your project, click the Start button on the toolbar.

6. When your form displays, click the Browse button, and you'll see a Browse For Folder dialog similar to the one shown in Figure 8-16.

7. Now browse your computer and select a folder. When you click the OK button, the selected folder will be displayed in the text box on your form. Notice that the folder returned contains a fully qualified path name.

How It Works

FIGURE 8-16

Before displaying the Browse For Folder dialog box, you needed to set some basic properties of the FolderBrowserDialog control to customize the look for this dialog box. You start by setting the Description property to provide some basic instructions for the user. Then you select the root folder at which the Browse For Folder dialog box should start browsing. In this instance, you use the MyComputer constant, which displayed all drives on your computer (refer to Figure 8-16). Finally, you set the ShowNewFolderButton property to False in order to not display the Make New Folder button:

```
'Set the FolderBrowser dialog properties
With FolderBrowserDialog1
    .Description = "Select a backup folder"
    .RootFolder = Environment.SpecialFolder.MyComputer
    .ShowNewFolderButton = False
End With
```

You display the dialog box in an If ... End If statement to check the DialogResult returned by the ShowDialog method of the FolderBrowserDialog control. Within the If ... End If statement, you add the code necessary to display the folder selected in the text box on your form, using the SelectedPath property:

```
'Show the FolderBrowser dialog and if the user clicks the
'OK button, display the selected folder
```

```
If FolderBrowserDialog1.ShowDialog = Windows.Forms.DialogResult.OK Then
    txtFile.Text = FolderBrowserDialog1.SelectedPath
End If
```

SUMMARY

This chapter has taken a look at some of the dialog boxes that are provided in Visual Basic 2010. You examined the MessageBox dialog box, and the OpenFileDialog, SaveFileDialog, FontDialog, ColorDialog, PrintDialog, and FolderBrowserDialog controls. Each of these dialog boxes help you provide a common interface in your applications for their respective functions. They also hide a lot of the complexities required to perform their tasks, enabling you to concentrate on the logic needed to make your application functional and feature-rich.

Although you used the controls from the Toolbox for all of these dialog boxes, except the Message-Box dialog box, remember that these controls can also be used as normal classes. This means that the classes that these dialog boxes expose the same properties and methods that you've seen, whether you are selecting a control visually or writing code using the class. You can define your own objects and set them to these classes, and then use the objects to perform the tasks that you performed using the controls. This provides better control over the scope of the objects. For example, you could define an object, set it to the OpenDialog class, use it, and then destroy it all in the same method. This uses resources only in the method that defines and uses the OpenDialog class, and reduces the size of your executable.

To summarize, you should now know how to:

➤ Use the MessageBox dialog box to display messages

➤ Display icons and buttons in the MessageBox dialog box

➤ Use the OpenFileDialog control and read the contents of a file

➤ Use the SaveFileDialog control and save the contents of a text box to a file

➤ Use the FontDialog control to set the font and color of text in a text box

➤ Use the ColorDialog control to set the background color of your form

➤ Use the PrintDialog control to print text

➤ Use the FolderBrowserDialog control to get a selected folder

EXERCISES

1. To display a dialog box to the user, what method do you use?

2. What method do you call to display a message box?

3. Name the five different ways to display an icon to the user on a message box.

4. How do you determine which button was pressed on a message box?

5. If you need to write basic code, where should you look for a simple example inside of Visual Studio?

▶ **WHAT YOU HAVE LEARNED IN THIS CHAPTER**

TOPIC	CONCEPTS
MessageBox	How to display and determine the button clicked on a message box
OpenFileDialog	How to use the OpenFileDialog control to find a file to open and read the text contents.
SaveFileDialog	How to use the SaveFileDialog control to save text to a file.
FontDialog	Displaying the FontDialog and using the selected font to change the font in a program.
ColorDialog	Displaying the ColorDialog and using the selected font to change the color in a program.
PrintDialog	What classes to use and how to use them to print text.
FolderBrowserDialog	How to setup the control to be shown and determine which folder was selected.

Creating Menus

➤   How to create menus

➤   How to create submenus

➤   How to create context menus

Menus are a part of every good application and provide not only an easy way to navigate within an application but also useful tools for working with that application. Take, for example, Visual Studio 2010. It provides menus for navigating the various windows that it displays and useful tools for making the job of development easier through menus and context menus (also called pop-up menus) for cutting, copying, and pasting code. It also provides menu items for searching through code.

This chapter takes a look at creating menus in your Visual Basic 2010 applications. You explore how to create and manage menus and submenus and how to create context menus and override the default context menus. Visual Studio 2010 provides two menu controls in the Toolbox, and you explore both of these.

UNDERSTANDING MENU FEATURES

The MenuStrip control in Visual Studio 2010 provides several key features. First and foremost, it provides a quick and easy way to add menus, menu items, and submenu items to your application. It also provides a built-in editor that enables you to add, edit, and delete menu items at the drop of a hat.

The menu items that you create may contain images, access keys, shortcut keys, and check marks as well as text labels.

Images

Nearly everyone is familiar with the images on the menus in applications such as Microsoft Outlook or Visual Studio 2010. In earlier versions of Visual Basic, developers were unable to create menu items with images without doing some custom programming or purchasing a third-party control. Visual Basic has come a long way and now provides an Image property for a menu item that makes adding an image to your menu items a breeze.

Access Keys

An *access key* (also known as an *accelerator key*) enables you to navigate the menus using the Alt key and a letter that is underlined in the menu item. When the access key is pressed, the menu appears on the screen, and the user can navigate through it using the arrow keys or the mouse.

Shortcut Keys

Shortcut keys enable you to invoke the menu item without displaying the menus at all. Shortcut keys usually consist of a control key and a letter, such as Ctrl+X to cut text.

Check Marks

A *check mark* symbol can be placed next to a menu item in lieu of an image, typically to indicate that the menu item is being used. For example, if you click the View menu in Visual Studio 2010 and then select the Toolbars menu item, you see a submenu that has many other submenu items, some of which have check marks. The submenu items that have check marks indicate the toolbars that are currently displayed.

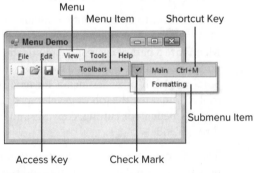

FIGURE 9-1

Figure 9-1 shows many of the available features that you can incorporate into your menus. As you can see, this sample menu provides all the features that were just mentioned plus a *separator*. A separator looks like a raised ridge and provides a logical separation between groups of menu items.

Figure 9-1 shows the menu the way it looks when the project is being run. Figure 9-2 shows how the menu looks in design mode.

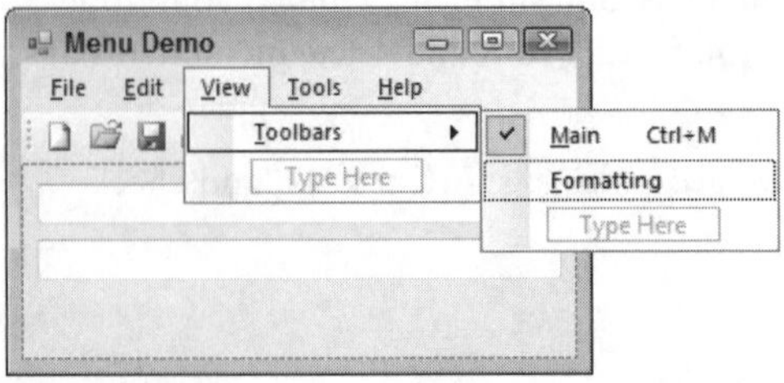

FIGURE 9-2

The first thing you'll notice when using the MenuStrip control is that it provides a means to add another menu, menu item, or submenu item quickly. Each time you add one of these, another blank text area is added.

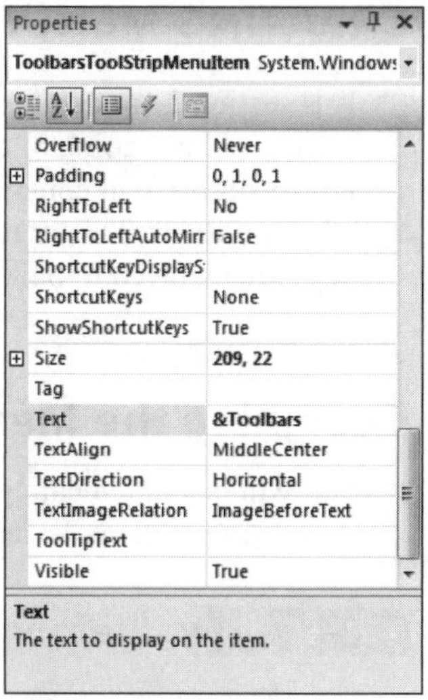

The Properties Window

While you are creating or editing a menu, the Properties window displays the available properties that can be set for the menu being edited, as shown in Figure 9-3, which shows the properties for the Toolbars menu item.

You can create as many menus, menu items, and submenu items as you need. You can even go as deep as you need to when creating submenu items by creating another submenu within a submenu.

Properties

ToolbarsToolStripMenuItem System.Windows

Overflow	Never
Padding	0, 1, 0, 1
RightToLeft	No
RightToLeftAutoMirr	False
ShortcutKeyDisplayS	
ShortcutKeys	None
ShowShortcutKeys	True
Size	209, 22
Tag	
Text	&Toolbars
TextAlign	MiddleCenter
TextDirection	Horizontal
TextImageRelation	ImageBeforeText
ToolTipText	
Visible	True

Text
The text to display on the item.

FIGURE 9-3

> **NOTE** *Keep in mind that if the menus are hard to navigate, or if it is hard for users to find the items they are looking for, they will rapidly lose interest in your application.*

You should stick with the standard format for menus that you see in most Windows applications today. These are the menus that you see in Visual Studio 2010. For example, you always have a File menu, and an Exit menu item in the File menu to exit from the application. If your application provides cut, copy, and paste functionality, you would place these menu items in the Edit menu, and so on.

> **NOTE** *The MSDN library contains a section on Windows User Experience Interaction Guidelines. A search for this on Google will return a link to* http://msdn.microsoft.com/en-us/library/aa511258.aspx. *The menu guidelines can be found at* http://msdn.microsoft.com/en-us/library/aa511502.aspx. *This section contains many topics that address the user interface and the Windows user interface. You can explore these topics for more details on Windows UI design–related topics.*

The key is to make your menus look and feel like the menus in other Windows applications so that the users feel comfortable using your application. This way, they don't feel like they have to learn the basics of Windows all over again. Some menu items will be specific to your application, but the key to incorporating them is to ensure that they fall into a general menu category that users are familiar with or to place them in your own menu category. You would then place this new menu in the appropriate place in the menu bar, generally in the middle.

CREATING MENUS

This section demonstrates how easy it is to create menus in your applications. In the following Try It Out, you are going to create a form that contains a menu bar, two toolbars, and two text boxes. The menu bar will contain five menus: File, Edit, View, Tools, and Help, and a few menu items and submenu items. This enables you to fully exercise the features of the menu controls. Because several steps are involved in building this application, the process is broken down into several sections.

Designing the Menus

You will be implementing code behind the menu items to demonstrate the menu and how to add code to your menu items, so let's get started.

TRY IT OUT   Creating Menus

Code file Windows Forms Menus.zip available for download at Wrox.com

In the first example, you will learn how to create menus and submenus.

1. Start Visual Studio 2010 and click File ⇨ New Project. In the New Project dialog, select Windows Forms Application in the Templates pane and enter the project name **Windows Forms Menus** in the Name field. Click the OK button to have the project created.

2. Click the form in the Forms Designer and set the following properties of the form:

> ➤ Set `Size` to **300, 180**.

> ➤ Set `StartPosition` to **CenterScreen**.

> ➤ Set `Text` to **Menu Demo**.

3. Drag a MenuStrip control from the Toolbox and drop it on your form. It is automatically positioned at the top of your form. The control is also added to the bottom of the development environment, just like the dialog box controls discussed in Chapter 8.

4. In the Properties window, set `Font Size` to **8**.

5. Right-click the MenuStrip1 control on the form and select the Insert Standard Items context menu item to have the standard menu items automatically inserted.

6. In the Properties window, click the items button with the ellipses next to the `Items` property or right-click on the MenuStrip control in your form and choose Edit Items from the context menu. In the Items Collection Editor dialog box, click the Add button to add a new menu item.

To be consistent with the current naming standard already in use with the other menu items, set the `Name` property for this new menu item to **ViewToolStripMenuItem**.

Now set the `Text` property to **&View**. An ampersand (`&`) in the menu name provides an access key for the menu or menu item. The letter before which the ampersand appears is the letter used to access this menu item in combination with the Alt key, so for this menu you can access and expand the View menu by pressing Alt+V. You'll see this when you run your project later.

You want to position this menu between the Edit and Tools menus so click the up arrow to the right of the menu items until the View menu is positioned between EditToolStripMenuItem and ToolsToolStripMenuItem in the list.

7. Now locate the `DropDownItems` property and click the ellipses button next to it so that you can add menu items beneath the View menu. A second Items Collection Editor appears; its caption reads "Items Collection Editor (ViewToolStripMenuItem.DropDownItems)."

There is only one menu item, Toolbars, under the View menu. Click the Add button in the Item Collections Editor to add a MenuItem.

Again, you want to be consistent with the naming standard already being used so set the `Name` property to **ToolbarToolStripMenuItem**. Then set the `Text` property to **&Toolbars**.

8. To add two submenu items under the Toolbars menu item, locate the `DropDownItems` property and click the button next to it to add items.

In the Item Collections Editor, click the Add button to add a new menu item. Set the `Name` property for this submenu item to **MainToolStripMenuItem** and the `Text` property to **&Main**. Set the `ShortcutKeys` property to Ctrl+M. To do this, check the box for **Ctrl** and then select **M** from the Key drop-down list. Next, make sure the `ShowShortcutKeys` property is set to **True**.

When you add the Main toolbar to this project in the next example, it is displayed by default, so this submenu item should be checked to indicate that the toolbar is displayed. Set the `Checked` property to **True** to cause this submenu item to be checked by default, and set the `CheckOnClick` property to **True** to allow the check mark next to this submenu item to be toggled on and off.

9. The next submenu item that you add is Formatting. Click the Add button to add a new menu item and set the `Name` property for this submenu item to **FormattingToolStripMenuItem** and the `Text` property to **&Formatting**.

Because the Formatting menu you add in the next example will not be shown by default, you need to leave the `Checked` property set to `False`. You do, however, need to set the `CheckOnClick` property to `True` so that the submenu item can toggle the check mark on and off.

Keep clicking the OK button in the Items Collection Editors until all of the editors are closed.

10. Save your project by clicking the Save All button on the toolbar.

11. If you run your project at this point and then enter Alt+V and Alt+T (without releasing the Alt key), you will see the submenu items, as shown in Figure 9-4. You can also click the other menus and see their menu items.

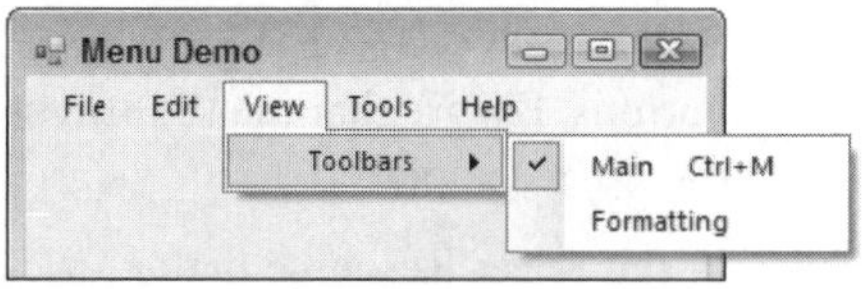

FIGURE 9-4

How It Works

Visual Studio 2010 takes care of a lot of the details for you by providing the Insert Standard Items context menu item in the MenuStrip control. You click this menu item to have Visual Studio 2010 create the standard menus and menu items found in most common applications. This enables you to concentrate on only the menus and menu items that are custom to your application, which is what you did by adding the View menu, Toolbars menu item, and Main and Formatting submenu items.

Adding Toolbars and Controls

In this section you add the toolbars and buttons for the toolbars that the application needs. The menus created in the previous section will control the displaying and hiding of these toolbars. You also add a couple of TextBox controls that are used in the application to cut, copy, and paste text using the toolbar buttons and menu items.

TRY IT OUT Adding Toolbars and Controls

Code file Windows Forms Menus.zip available for download at Wrox.com

You have certainly worked with toolbars before. In MS Word, you probably click on the print toolbar button when you need to print. In the next example, you will create similar toolbars.

1. Return to the Forms Designer in your Windows Forms Menus project. You need to add two toolbars to the form, so locate the ToolStrip control in the Toolbox and drag and drop it onto your form; it automatically aligns itself to the top of the form below the menu. Set the Name property to **tspMain**.

2. The default toolbar buttons will be fine for this project, so right-click the ToolStrip control on the form and select Insert Standard Items from the context menu to have the standard toolbar buttons added.

3. Next, add a second toolbar to the form in the same manner. It aligns itself below the first toolbar. Set its Name property to **tspFormatting** and its Visible property to **False**, because you don't want this toolbar to be shown by default.

4. You want to add three buttons to this toolbar, so click the ellipses button next to the Items property in the Properties window or right-click the ToolStrip control on the form and select Edit Items from the context menu.

In the Items Collection Editor dialog box, click the Add button to add the first button. Since you really won't be using these buttons, you can accept the default name and ToolTip text for these buttons. Ensure that the DisplayStyle property is set to **Image,** and then click the button next to the Image property.

In the Select Resource dialog, click the Import button and browse to the C:\Program Files\Microsoft Visual Studio 10.0\Common7\VS2010ImageLibrary\1033\VS2010ImageLibrary\ Actions\pngformat folder. This path assumes a default installation of Visual Studio 2010 and that you extracted the contents of the VS2008ImageLibrary zip file. In the Open dialog box, select AlignTableCellMiddleLeftJustHS.PNG and then click the Open button. Next, click the OK button in the Select Resource dialog box to close it.

5. In the Items Collection Editor dialog box, click the Add button again to add the second button. Ensure that the DisplayStyle property is set to **Image** and then set the Image property to the AlignTableCellMiddleCenterHS.png file.

6. In the Items Collection Editor dialog, click the Add button again to add the next button. Ensure that the `DisplayStyle` property is set to **Image** and then set the `Image` property to the `AlignTableCellMiddleRightHS.png` file.

7. Click the OK button in the Items Collection Editor dialog box to close it.

8. Add a Panel control from the Toolbox to your form and set its `Dock` property to **Fill**.

9. Add two TextBox controls to the Panel control and accept their default properties. Their location and size are not important, but they should be wide enough to contain text. Your completed form should look similar to the one shown in Figure 9-5. Notice that your second toolbar is not visible, as you set its `Visible` property to `False`.

If you run your project at this point you will see the menus, the main toolbar, and two text boxes. The formatting toolbar is not visible at this point because the `Visible` property is set to `False`.

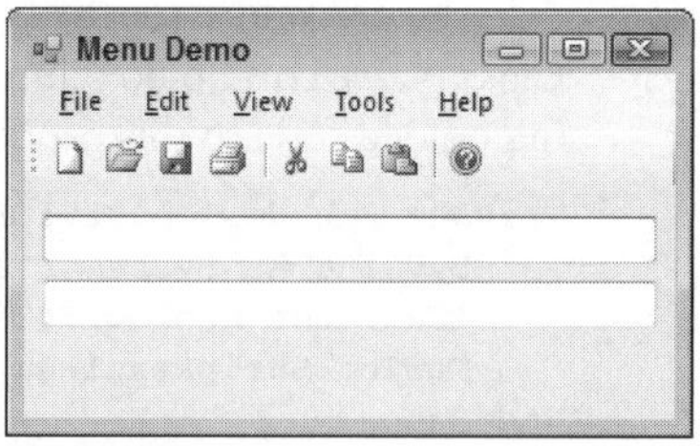

FIGURE 9-5

How It Works

You took a look at toolbars in Chapter 7, so review the Text Editor project for details on how the ToolStrip control works. The ToolStrip control, like the MenuStrip control, provides the Insert Standard Items context menu item, which does a lot of the grunt work for you by inserting the standard toolbar buttons, as was shown in Figure 9-5. This provides the most efficient means of having the standard toolbar buttons added to the ToolStrip control. You can, of course, rearrange the buttons that have been added and even add new buttons and delete existing buttons.

Because you set the `Visible` property to `False` for the tspFormatting ToolStrip control, that control does not take up any space on your form at design time after the control loses focus.

Coding Menus

Now that you have finally added all of your controls to the form, it's time to start writing some code to make these controls work. First, you have to add functionality to make the menus work. Then you add code to make some of the buttons on the main toolbar work.

TRY IT OUT Coding the File Menu

Code file Windows Forms Menus.zip available for download at Wrox.com

Next, you will put the code behind the menus so they actually do something.

1. Start by switching to the Code Editor for the form. In the Class Name combo box at the top of the Code Editor, select NewToolStripMenuItem and select the `Click` event in the Method Name combo box. Add the following bolded code to the `Click` event handler:

```
Private Sub NewToolStripMenuItem_Click(ByVal sender As Object, _
    ByVal e As System.EventArgs) Handles NewToolStripMenuItem.Click
```

```
        'Clear the text boxes
        TextBox1.Text = String.Empty
        TextBox2.Text = String.Empty

        'Set focus to the first text box
        TextBox1.Focus()
    End Sub
```

2. Add the procedure for the New button on the toolbar by selecting NewToolStripButton from the Class Name combo box and the Click event from the Method Name combo box. Add the following bolded code to this procedure:

```
    Private Sub NewToolStripButton_Click(ByVal sender As Object, _
        ByVal e As System.EventArgs) Handles NewToolStripButton.Click
        'Call the NewToolStripMenuItem_Click procedure
        NewToolStripMenuItem_Click(sender, e)
    End Sub
```

3. Select ExitToolStripMenuItem from the Class Name combo box and the Click event from the Method Name combo box and add the following bolded code to the procedure:

```
    Private Sub ExitToolStripMenuItem_Click(ByVal sender As Object, _
        ByVal e As System.EventArgs) Handles ExitToolStripMenuItem.Click
        'Close the form and end
        Me.Close()
    End Sub
```

How It Works

To clear the text boxes on the form in the NewToolStripMenuItem_Click procedure, add the following code. All you are doing here is setting the Text property of the text boxes to an empty string. The next line of code sets the focus to the first text box by calling the Focus method of that text box:

```
    'Clear the text boxes
    TextBox1.Text = String.Empty
    TextBox2.Text = String.Empty

    'Set focus to the first text box
    TextBox1.Focus()
```

When you click the New menu item under the File menu, the text boxes on the form are cleared of all text, and TextBox1 has the focus and is ready to accept text.

The New button on the toolbar should perform the same function, but you don't want to write the same code twice. You could put the text in the previous procedure in a separate procedure and call that procedure from both the newToolStripMenuItem_Click and newToolStripButton_Click procedures. Instead, you have the code in the newToolStripMenuItem_Click procedure and simply call that procedure from within the newToolStripButton_Click procedure. Since both procedures accept the same parameters, you simply pass the parameters received in this procedure to the procedure you are calling:

```
    'Call the newToolStripMenuItem_Click procedure
    newToolStripMenuItem_Click(sender, e)
```

Now you can click the New button on the toolbar or click the New menu item on the File menu and have the same results, clearing the text boxes on your form.

When you click the Exit menu item, you want the program to end. In the exitToolStripMenuItem_Click procedure, you added the following code. The Me keyword refers to the class where the code is executing, and in this case refers to the form class. The `Close` method closes the form, releases all resources, and ends the program:

```
'Close the form and end
Me.Close()
```

That takes care of the code for the File menu and its corresponding toolbar button. Now you can move on to the Edit menu and add the code for those menu items.

TRY IT OUT Coding the Edit Menu

Code file Windows Forms Menus.zip available for download at Wrox.com

In this example, you add code to make the edit menu and toolbar buttons work.

1. The first menu item in the Edit menu is the Undo menu item. Select UndoToolStripMenuItem in the Class Name combo box and select the `Click` event in the Method Name combo box. Add the following bolded code to the `Click` event handler:

```
Private Sub UndoToolStripMenuItem_Click(ByVal sender As Object, _
    ByVal e As System.EventArgs) Handles UndoToolStripMenuItem.Click
    'Undo the last operation
    If TypeOf Me.ActiveControl Is TextBox Then
        CType(Me.ActiveControl, TextBox).Undo()
    End If
End Sub
```

2. The next menu item that you want to add code for is the Cut menu item. Select CutToolStrip-MenuItem in the Class Name combo box and the `Click` event in the Method Name combo box. Add the bolded code here:

```
Private Sub CutToolStripMenuItem_Click(ByVal sender As Object, _
    ByVal e As System.EventArgs) Handles CutToolStripMenuItem.Click
    'Copy the text to the clipboard and clear the field
    If TypeOf Me.ActiveControl Is TextBox Then
        CType(Me.ActiveControl, TextBox).Cut()
    End If
End Sub
```

3. You'll want the Cut button on the toolbar to call the code for the Cut menu item. Select CutTool-StripButton in the Class Name combo box and the `Click` event in the Method Name combo box. Add the following bolded code:

```
Private Sub CutToolStripButton_Click(ByVal sender As Object, _
    ByVal e As System.EventArgs) Handles CutToolStripButton.Click
    'Call the CutToolStripMenuItem_Click procedure
    CutToolStripMenuItem_Click(sender, e)
End Sub
```

4. The next menu item that you need to code is the Copy menu item. Select CopyToolStripMenuItem in the Class Name combo box and the `Click` event in the Method Name combo box and then add the following bolded code:

```
Private Sub CopyToolStripMenuItem_Click(ByVal sender As Object, _
    ByVal e As System.EventArgs) Handles CopyToolStripMenuItem.Click
    'Copy the text to the clipboard
```

```
    If TypeOf Me.ActiveControl Is TextBox Then
        CType(Me.ActiveControl, TextBox).Copy()
    End If
End Sub
```

5. You want the Copy button on the toolbar to call the procedure you just added. Select CopyTool-StripButton in the Class Name combo box and the `Click` event in the Method Name combo box and then add the following bolded code:

```
Private Sub CopyToolStripButton_Click(ByVal sender As Object, _
    ByVal e As System.EventArgs) Handles CopyToolStripButton.Click
    'Call the CopyToolStripMenuItem_Click procedure
    CopyToolStripMenuItem_Click(sender, e)
End Sub
```

6. The Paste menu item is next so select PasteToolStripMenuItem in the Class Name combo box and the `Click` event in the Method Name combo box. Add the following bolded code to the `Click` event handler:

```
Private Sub PasteToolStripMenuItem_Click(ByVal sender As Object, _
    ByVal e As System.EventArgs) Handles PasteToolStripMenuItem.Click
    'Copy the text from the clipboard to the text box
    If TypeOf Me.ActiveControl Is TextBox Then
        CType(Me.ActiveControl, TextBox).Paste()
    End If
End Sub
```

7. The Paste toolbar button should execute the code in the `PasteToolStripMenuItem_Click` procedure. Select PasteToolStripButton in the Class Name combo box and the `Click` event in the Method Name combo box and add the following bolded code:

```
Private Sub PasteToolStripButton_Click(ByVal sender As Object, _
    ByVal e As System.EventArgs) Handles PasteToolStripButton.Click
    'Call the PasteToolStripMenuItem_Click procedure
    PasteToolStripMenuItem_Click(sender, e)
End Sub
```

8. The last menu item under the Edit menu that you'll write code for is the Select All menu item. Select SelectAllToolStripMenuItem in the Class Name combo box and the `Click` event in the Method Name combo box and add the following bolded code:

```
Private Sub SelectAllToolStripMenuItem_Click(ByVal sender As Object, _
    ByVal e As System.EventArgs) Handles SelectAllToolStripMenuItem.Click
    'Select all the text in the text box
    If TypeOf Me.ActiveControl Is TextBox Then
        CType(Me.ActiveControl, TextBox).SelectAll()
    End If
End Sub
```

How It Works

You added the code for the Edit menu starting with the Undo menu item. Since you have two text boxes on your form, you need a way to determine which text box you are dealing with or a generic way of handling an undo operation for both text boxes. In this example, you go with the latter option and provide a generic way to handle both text boxes.

You do this by first determining whether the active control you are dealing with is a TextBox control. The `ActiveControl` property of the `Form` class returns a reference to the active control on the form, the control that has focus.

Then you want to check the active control to see if it is a TextBox control. This is done using the `TypeOf` operator. This operator compares an object reference to a data type, and in the code shown below you are comparing the object reference returned in the `ActiveControl` property to a data type of `TextBox`.

When you know you are dealing with a TextBox control, you use the `CType` function to convert the object contained in the `ActiveControl` property to a TextBox control. This exposes the properties and methods of the TextBox control in IntelliSense allowing you to choose the `Undo` method:

```
If TypeOf Me.ActiveControl Is TextBox Then
    CType(Me.ActiveControl, TextBox).Undo()
End If
```

The menu and toolbar are never set as the active control. This enables you to use the menus and toolbar buttons and always reference the active control.

> **NOTE** The `ActiveControl` property works fine in this small example because you are only dealing with two text boxes. However, in a real-world application, you would need to test the active control to see whether it supports the method you were using (for example, `Undo`).

You use the same logic for the rest of the menu item procedures as the Undo menu item, checking the type of active control to see if it is a TextBox control. Then you call the appropriate method on the TextBox control to cut, copy, paste, and select all text.

Coding the View Menu and Toolbars

Now that you have added the code to make the Edit menu items and the corresponding toolbar buttons functional, the next step is to make the menu items under the View menu functional.

TRY IT OUT Coding the View Menu

Code file Windows Forms Menus.zip available for download at Wrox.com

Next, add the code to hide and show the toolbars.

1. Return to the Code Editor in the Windows Forms Menus project and in the Class Name combo box, select MainToolStripMenuItem. In the Method Name combo box, select the `Click` event. Add the following bolded code to the `Click` event handler:

```
Private Sub MainToolStripMenuItem_Click(ByVal sender As Object, _
    ByVal e As System.EventArgs) Handles MainToolStripMenuItem.Click
```

```
        'Toggle the visibility of the Main toolbar
        'based on the menu item's Checked property
        If MainToolStripMenuItem.Checked Then
            tspMain.Visible = True
        Else
            tspMain.Visible = False
        End If
    End Sub
```

2. You need to add the same type of code that you just added to the Formatting submenu item. Select FormattingToolStripMenuItem in the Class Name combo box and the Click event in the Method Name combo box and add the following bolded code:

```
Private Sub FormattingToolStripMenuItem_Click(ByVal sender As Object, _
    ByVal e As System.EventArgs) Handles FormattingToolStripMenuItem.Click
    'Toggle the visibility of the Formatting toolbar
    'based on the menu item's Checked property
    If FormattingToolStripMenuItem.Checked Then
        tspFormatting.Visible = True
    Else
        tspFormatting.Visible = False
    End If
End Sub
```

How It Works

When the Main submenu item under the Tools menu item is clicked, the submenu item either displays a check mark or removes it based on the current state of the Checked property of the submenu item. You add code in the Click event of this submenu item to either hide or show the Main toolbar by setting its Visible property to True or False:

```
'Toggle the visibility of the Main toolbar
'based on this menu item's Checked property
If MainToolStripMenuItem.Checked Then
    tspMain.Visible = True
Else
    tspMain.Visible = False
End If
```

The same principle works for the Formatting submenu item, and its code is very similar to that of the Main submenu item:

```
'Toggle the visibility of the Formatting toolbar
'based on this menu item's Checked property
If FormattingToolStripMenuItem.Checked Then
    tspFormatting.Visible = True
Else
    tspFormatting.Visible = False
End If
```

Testing Your Code

As your applications become more complex, testing your code becomes increasingly important. The more errors that you find and fix during your testing, the better able you will be to implement an application that is both stable and reliable for your users. This translates into satisfied users and earns you a good reputation for delivering a quality product.

You need to test not only the functionality of your application, but also various scenarios that a user might encounter or perform. For example, suppose you have a database application that gathers user input from a form and inserts it into a database. A good application validates all user input before trying to insert the data into the database, and a good test plan tries to break the data validation code. This ensures that your validation code handles all possible scenarios and functions properly.

TRY IT OUT   Testing Your Code

Code file Windows Forms Menus.zip available for download at Wrox.com

You can treat this Try It Out as your test plan. Follow these steps to test your code.

1. It's time to test your code. Click the Run toolbar button. When your form loads, the only toolbar that you should see is the main toolbar, as shown in Figure 9-6.

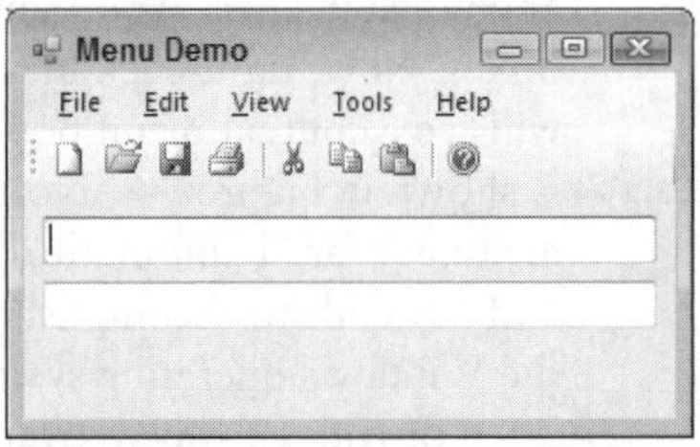

2. Click the View menu and then click the Toolbars menu item. Note that the Main submenu item is selected and the main toolbar is visible. Go ahead and click the Formatting submenu item. The Formatting toolbar is displayed along with the main toolbar.

Note also that the controls on your form shifted down when the Formatting toolbar was displayed. This happened because you placed a Panel control on your form, set its `Dock` property to `Fill`, and then placed your TextBox controls on the Panel control. Doing this allows the controls on your form to be repositioned, either to take up the space when a toolbar is hidden or to make room for the toolbar when it is shown; much like the behavior in Microsoft Outlook or Visual Studio 2010.

FIGURE 9-6

3. If you click the View menu again and then click the Toolbars menu item, you will see that both the Main and Formatting submenu items are checked. The selected submenu items indicate that the toolbar is visible, and an unchecked submenu item indicates that the toolbar is not visible.

4. Now test the functionality of the Edit menu. Click in the first text box and type some text. Then click the Edit menu and select the Select All menu item. Once you select the Select All menu item, the text in the text box is highlighted.

5. You now want to copy the text in the first text box while the text is highlighted. Hover your mouse over the Copy button on the toolbar to view the ToolTip. Now either click the Copy button on the toolbar or select the Edit ⇨ Copy menu item.

Place your cursor in the second text box and then either click the Paste button on the toolbar or select Edit ⇨ Paste. The text is pasted into the second text box, as shown in Figure 9-7.

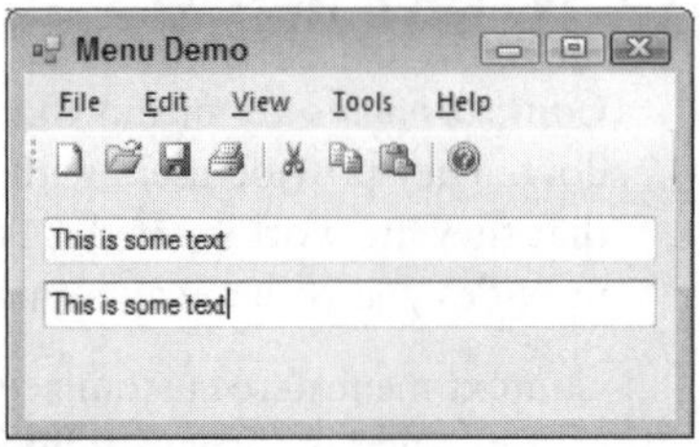

FIGURE 9-7

6. Click the first text box and then click Edit ⇨ Undo. Note that the changes you made to the first text box have been undone. You might have expected that the text in the second text box would be removed, but Windows keeps track of the cut, copy, and paste operations for each control individually, so there's nothing you need to do.

7. The last item on the Edit menu to test is the Cut menu item. Type some more text in the first text box, and then highlight the text in the first text box by clicking the Edit menu and selecting the Select All menu item. Then either click the Cut icon on the toolbar or select Edit ⇨ Cut. The text is copied to the Clipboard and is then removed from the text box.

Place your cursor in the second text box at the end of the text there. Then paste the text in this text box using the Paste shortcut key, Ctrl+V. The text has been placed at the end of the existing text in the text box. This is how Windows' cut, copy, and paste operations work, and, as you can see, there was very little code required to implement this functionality in your program.

8. Now click the File menu and choose the New menu item. The text in the text boxes is cleared. The only menu item left to test is the Exit menu item under the File menu.

9. Before testing the Exit menu item, take a quick look at context menus. Type some text in one of the text boxes. Now, right-click in that text box, and you will see a context menu pop up, similar to what is shown in Figure 9-8. Notice that this context menu appeared automatically; you didn't need to add any code to accomplish this. This is a feature of the Windows operating system, and Visual Studio 2010 provides a way to override the default context menus, as you will see in the next section.

10. To test the last bit of functionality of your program, select File ⇨ Exit, and your program ends.

How It Works

FIGURE 9-8

This example showed you how to walk through a test plan to test your code. You should create test plans similar to this to be followed during testing of your code.

CONTEXT MENUS

Context menus are menus that pop up when a user clicks the right mouse button on a control or window. They provide users with quick access to the most commonly used commands for the control that they are working with. As you just saw in the preceding section, the context menu that appeared provides you with a way to manage the text in a text box.

Context menus are customized for the control that you are working with; and in more complex applications, such as Visual Studio 2010 or Microsoft Word, they provide quick access to the commands for the task that is being performed.

You saw that Windows provides a default context menu for the TextBox control that you are working with, and you can override the default context menu if your application's needs dictate that. For example, suppose you have an application in which you want users to be able to copy the text in a text box but not actually cut or paste text in that text box. This would be an ideal situation to provide your own context menu to allow only the operations that you want.

Visual Studio 2010 provides a ContextMenuStrip control that you can place on your form and customize, just as you did the MenuStrip control. However, the main difference between the MenuStrip control and the ContextMenuStrip control is that you can create only one top-level menu with the ContextMenuStrip control. You can still create submenu items with the ContextMenuStrip if needed.

Most controls in the toolbox have a `ContextMenuStrip` property that can be set to the context menu that you define. When you right-click that control, the context menu that you defined is displayed instead of the default context menu.

Some controls, such as the ComboBox and ListBox controls, do not have a default context menu because they contain a collection of items, not a single item like simple controls such as the TextBox. They do, however, have a `ContextMenuStrip` property that can be set to a context menu that you define.

> **NOTE** *The ComboBox control does not provide a context menu when its* `DropDownStyle` *property is set to* `DropDownList`, *but it does provide a context menu when its* `DropDownStyle` *property is set to* `Simple` *or* `DropDown`

Creating Context Menus

Now that you know what context menus are, you are ready to learn how to create and use them in your Visual Basic 2010 applications.

TRY IT OUT   Creating Context Menus

Code file Windows Forms Menus.zip available for download at Wrox.com

In this Try It Out, you expand the code from the previous Try It Out example by adding a context menu to work with your text boxes. You add one context menu and use it for both text boxes. You could just as easily create two context menus, one for each text box, and have the context menus perform different functions.

1.   Return to the Forms Designer in your Windows Forms Menus project and then click the Toolbox to locate the ContextMenuStrip control. Drag and drop it onto your form, where it is added at the bottom of the development environment just as the MenuStrip control was.

2.   In the Properties window, click the button next to the `Items` property. You'll be adding five menu items in your context menu in the next several steps.

3.   Click the Add button in the Items Collection Editor dialog to add the first menu item and set the `Name` property to **ContextUndoToolStripMenuItem**. Click the ellipsis button next to the `Image` property and then click the Import button in the Select Resource dialog. Locate an Undo bitmap or portable network graphics (png) file on your computer and click the Open button. Click OK in the Select Resource dialog to close it and to return to the Items Collection Editor. Locate the Text property and set it to **Undo**.

4. You want to add a separator between the Undo menu item and the next menu item. Select Separator in the List combo box in the Items Collection Editor dialog and then click the Add button. Accept all default properties for the separator.

5. Select MenuItem in the combo box and click the Add button again to add the next menu item. Set the Name property to **ContextCutToolStripMenuItem**. Click the button next to the Image property and, in the Select Resource dialog, locate a Cut bitmap or png file. Finally, set the Text property to **Cut**.

6. Click the Add button again to add the next menu item and set the Name property to **ContextCopyToolStripMenuItem**. Click the ellipsis button next to the Image property and, in the Select Resource dialog, locate a Copy bitmap or icon file. Finally, set the Text property to **Copy**.

7. Click the Add button once again to add the next menu item and set the Name property to **ContextPasteToolStripMenuItem**. Click the ellipse button next to the Image property and in the Select Resource dialog, import a file to use for Paste. Then set the Text property to **Paste**.

8. Now you want to add a separator between the Paste menu item and the next menu item. Select Separator in the combo box in the Items Collection Editor dialog and then click the Add button. Again, accept all default properties for the separator.

9. Select MenuItem in the combo box and click the Add button to add the final menu item. Set the Name property to **ContextSelectAllToolStripMenuItem** and the Text property to **Select All**. There is no image for this menu item. Finally, click OK in the Items Collection Editor dialog to close it.

10. When you are done, click any part of the form to make the context menu disappear. (You can always make it reappear by clicking the ContextMenuStrip1 control at the bottom of the development environment.)

11. Click the first text box on your form. In the Properties window, select ContextMenuStrip1 in the drop-down list for the ContextMenuStrip property. Repeat the same action for the second text box to assign a context menu in the ContextMenuStrip property.

12. Test your context menu for look and feel. At this point, you haven't added any code to it, but you can ensure that it looks visually correct. Run the application and then right-click in the first text box; you will see the context menu that you have just added, shown in Figure 9-9. The same context menu appears if you also right-click in the second text box.

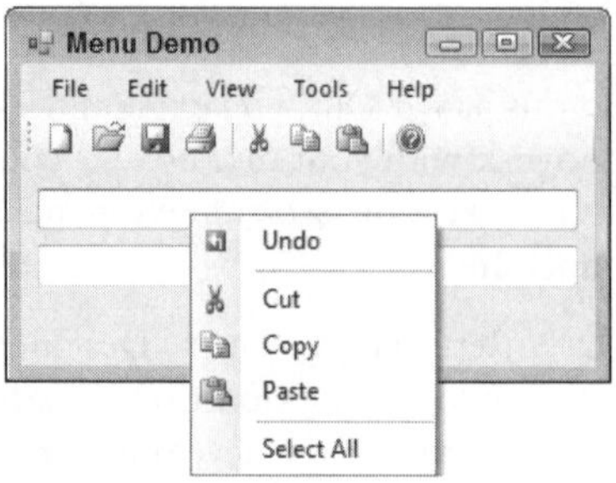

FIGURE 9-9

13. Stop your program and switch to the Code Editor for your form so that you can add the code for the context menus. The first procedure that you want to add is that for the Undo context menu item. Select ContextUndoToolStripMenuItem in the Class Name combo box and the Click event in the Method Name combo box and add the following bolded code:

```
Private Sub ContextUndoToolStripMenuItem_Click(ByVal sender As Object, _
    ByVal e As System.EventArgs) Handles ContextUndoToolStripMenuItem.Click
```

```
        'Call the UndoToolStripMenuItem_Click procedure
        UndoToolStripMenuItem_Click(sender, e)
    End Sub
```

14. Select ContextCutToolStripMenuItem in the Class Name combo box and the `Click` event in the Method Name combo box. Add the following bolded code to the `Click` event handler:

```
Private Sub ContextCutToolStripMenuItem_Click(ByVal sender As Object, _
    ByVal e As System.EventArgs) Handles ContextCutToolStripMenuItem.Click
    'Call the CutToolStripMenuItem_Click procedure
    CutToolStripMenuItem_Click(sender, e)
End Sub
```

15. For the Copy context menu item, select ContextCopyToolStripMenuItem in the Class Name combo box and the `Click` event in the Method Name combo box and then add the following bolded code:

```
Private Sub ContextCopyToolStripMenuItem_Click(ByVal sender As Object, _
    ByVal e As System.EventArgs) Handles ContextCopyToolStripMenuItem.Click
    'Call the CopyToolStripMenuItem_Click procedure
    CopyToolStripMenuItem_Click(sender, e)
End Sub
```

16. Select ContextPasteToolStripMenuItem in the Class Name combo box for the Paste context menu item and the `Click` event in the Method Name combo box. Then add the following bolded code:

```
Private Sub ContextPasteToolStripMenuItem_Click(ByVal sender As Object, _
    ByVal e As System.EventArgs) Handles ContextPasteToolStripMenuItem.Click
    'Call the PasteToolStripMenuItem_Click procedure
    PasteToolStripMenuItem_Click(sender, e)
End Sub
```

17. The last procedure that you need to perform is for the Select All context menu item. Select ContextSelectAllToolStripMenuItem in the Class Name combo box and the `Click` event in the Method Name combo box and then add the following bolded code:

```
Private Sub ContextSelectAllToolStripMenuItem_Click(ByVal sender As Object, _
    ByVal e As System.EventArgs) _
    Handles ContextSelectAllToolStripMenuItem.Click
    'Call the SelectAllToolStripMenuItem_Click procedure
    SelectAllToolStripMenuItem_Click(sender, e)
End Sub
```

18. That's all the code that you need to add to implement your own context menu. Pretty simple, no? Now run your project to see your context menu in action and test it. You can test the context menu by clicking each of the context menu items shown. They perform the same functions as their counterparts in the toolbar and Edit menu.

Do you see the difference in your context menu from the one shown in Figure 9-8? Your context menu has a cleaner look and shows the icons for the various menu items. There is one other subtle difference: Your menu items are all enabled, although some of them shouldn't be. You'll rectify this in the next Try It Out.

How It Works

The ContextMenuStrip works in the same manner as the MenuStrip, and you should have been able to follow along and create a context menu with ease. You may have noticed that you use a prefix of `Context` for your context menu names in this exercise. This distinguishes these menu items as context menu items, and groups these menu items in the Class Name combo box in the Code Editor, as you probably noticed.

The code you added here was a no-brainer, as you have already written the code to perform undo, cut, copy, paste, and select all operations. In this exercise, you merely call the corresponding menu item procedures in your `Click` event handlers for the context menu items.

Enabling and Disabling Menu Items and Toolbar Buttons

Now that you have implemented a context menu and have it functioning, you are ready to write some code to complete the functionality in your application.

TRY IT OUT Enabling and Disabling Menu Items and Toolbar Buttons

Code file Windows Forms Menus.zip available for download at Wrox.com

In this Try It Out, you implement the necessary code to enable and disable menu items, context menu items, and toolbar buttons.

1. You need to create a procedure that can be called to toggle all of the Edit menu items, toolbar buttons, and context menu items, enabling and disabling them as needed. They are enabled and disabled based upon what should be available to the user. You should call this procedure `ToggleMenus`, so stop your program and add the following procedure at the end of your existing code:

```
Private Sub ToggleMenus()
    'Declare a TextBox object and set it to the ActiveControl
    Dim objTextBox As TextBox = CType(Me.ActiveControl, TextBox)

    'Declare and set a Boolean variable
    Dim blnEnabled As Boolean = CType(objTextBox.SelectionLength, Boolean)

    'Toggle the Undo menu items
    UndoToolStripMenuItem.Enabled = objTextBox.CanUndo
    ContextUndoToolStripMenuItem.Enabled = objTextBox.CanUndo

    'Toggle the Cut toolbar button and menu items
    CutToolStripButton.Enabled = blnEnabled
    CutToolStripMenuItem.Enabled = blnEnabled
    ContextCutToolStripMenuItem.Enabled = blnEnabled

    'Toggle the Copy toolbar button and menu items
    CopyToolStripButton.Enabled = blnEnabled
    CopyToolStripMenuItem.Enabled = blnEnabled
    ContextCopyToolStripMenuItem.Enabled = blnEnabled

    'Reset the blnEnabled variable
    blnEnabled = My.Computer.Clipboard.ContainsText

    'Toggle the Paste toolbar button and menu items
    PasteToolStripButton.Enabled = blnEnabled
    PasteToolStripMenuItem.Enabled = blnEnabled
    ContextPasteToolStripMenuItem.Enabled = blnEnabled
```

```
'Reset the blnEnabled variable
If objTextBox.SelectionLength < objTextBox.TextLength Then
    blnEnabled = True
Else
    blnEnabled = False
End If

'Toggle the Select All menu items
SelectAllToolStripMenuItem.Enabled = blnEnabled
ContextSelectAllToolStripMenuItem.Enabled = blnEnabled
End Sub
```

That's it! All of that code will toggle the Edit menu items, the context menu items, and the toolbar buttons. Now you need to figure out when and where to call this procedure.

2. Return to the Forms Designer and locate the Timer control in the Toolbox. Drag this control onto your form, where it is positioned at the bottom of the IDE. In the Properties window, set the Enabled property to **True** and the Interval property to **250**.

3. Double-click the Timer control at the bottom of the IDE to create the Tick event handler and add this code:

```
Private Sub Timer1_Tick(ByVal sender As Object, _
    ByVal e As System.EventArgs) Handles Timer1.Tick
    'Toggle toolbar and menu items
    ToggleMenus()
End Sub
```

4. Run your project again. After the form has been displayed, click in the first text box and enter some text. Then, right-click in the text box to display your context menu. Now the context menu has the appropriate menu items enabled, as shown in Figure 9-10, as do the toolbar buttons and Edit menu items.

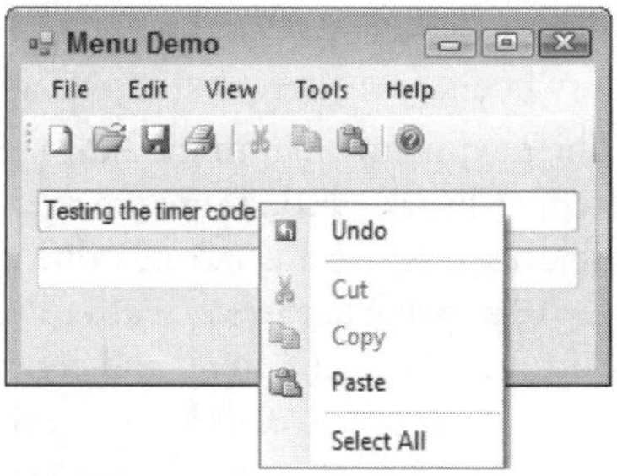

How It Works

FIGURE 9-10

The first thing that you do in the ToggleMenus procedure is declare an object and set it equal to the active TextBox control. You saw the ActiveControl property in the "Coding the Edit Menu" Try It Out exercise:

```
'Declare a TextBox object and set it to the ActiveControl
Dim objTextBox As TextBox = CType(Me.ActiveControl, TextBox)
```

Next you declare a Boolean variable that will be used to determine whether a property should set to True or False, and initially set it based on the SelectionLength property of the active text box. The SelectionLength property returns the number of characters selected in a text box. You can use this number to act as a True or False value because a value of False in Visual Basic 2010 is zero and a value of True is one. Since the value of False is always evaluated first, any number other than zero evaluates to True.

In order to make this happen, you need to convert the SelectionLength property from an Integer data type to a Boolean data type using the CType function, as shown here:

```
'Declare and set a Boolean variable
Dim blnEnabled As Boolean = CType(objTextBox.SelectionLength, Boolean)
```

The first Edit menu item is Undo, so you start with that one. The `TextBox` class has a property called `CanUndo`, which returns a `True` or `False` value indicating whether or not the last operation performed in the text box can be undone.

You use the `CanUndo` property to set the `Enabled` property of the Edit menu item. The `Enabled` property is set using a `Boolean` value, which works out great because the `CanUndo` property returns a `Boolean` value. The following code shows how you set the `Enabled` property of the Undo menu item and context menu item:

```
'Toggle the Undo menu items
undoToolStripMenuItem.Enabled = objTextBox.CanUndo
contextUndoToolStripMenuItem.Enabled = objTextBox.CanUndo
```

The next menu item in the Edit menu that you wrote code for is the Cut menu item. You have already set the `blnEnabled` variable, so the following code merely uses the value contained in that variable to set the `Enabled` property of the Cut menu item, toolbar button, and context menu item:

```
'Toggle the Cut toolbar button and menu items
CutToolStripButton.Enabled = blnEnabled
CutToolStripMenuItem.Enabled = blnEnabled
ContextCutToolStripMenuItem.Enabled = blnEnabled
```

The next menu item in the Edit menu is the Copy menu item. Again, you use the `blnEnabled` variable to set the `Enabled` property appropriately:

```
'Toggle the Copy toolbar button and menu items
CopyToolStripButton.Enabled = blnEnabled
CopyToolStripMenuItem.Enabled = blnEnabled
ContextCopyToolStripMenuItem.Enabled = blnEnabled
```

The next menu item in the Edit menu is the Paste menu item. Setting the `Enabled` property of this menu item requires a little more work. You query the `ContainsText` property of the `My.Computer.Clipboard` object to receive a `Boolean` value indicating whether the Clipboard contains any text. You then set that `Boolean` value in the `blnEnabled` variable, which is used to set the `Enabled` property of the Paste toolbar button, Paste menu item, and context menu item, as shown in the following code:

```
'Reset the blnEnabled variable
blnEnabled = My.Computer.Clipboard.ContainsText
'Toggle the Paste toolbar button and menu items
PasteToolStripButton.Enabled = blnEnabled
PasteToolStripMenuItem.Enabled = blnEnabled
ContextPasteToolStripMenuItem.Enabled = blnEnabled
```

The last Edit menu item is the Select All menu item. You again use the `SelectionLength` property to determine whether any or all text has been selected. If the `SelectionLength` property is less than the `TextLength` property, you set the `blnEnabled` variable to `True`, as not all text in the text box has been selected; otherwise, you set it to `False`. After the `blnEnabled` variable has been appropriately set, you use that variable to set the `Enabled` property of the Select All menu item and context menu item:

```
'Reset the blnEnabled variable
If objTextBox.SelectionLength < objTextBox.TextLength Then
    blnEnabled = True
Else
    blnEnabled = False
End If

'Toggle the Select All menu items
SelectAllToolStripMenuItem.Enabled = blnEnabled
ContextSelectAllToolStripMenuItem.Enabled = blnEnabled
```

To enable and disable the menu items, context menu items, and toolbar buttons, you have to call the `ToggleMenus` procedure. The best place to do this is in the `Tick` event of the Timer control that you placed on your form. The `Tick` event is fired using the `Interval` property that you set to a value of `250`. The `Interval` property is expressed in milliseconds, where 1,000 milliseconds equals one second — so basically the `Tick` event of the Timer control is fired every quarter-second:

```
Private Sub Timer1_Tick(ByVal sender As Object, _
    ByVal e As System.EventArgs) Handles Timer1.Tick

    'Toggle toolbar and menu items
    ToggleMenus()
End Sub
```

SUMMARY

This chapter explained how to implement menus, menu items, and submenu items. You also learned how to implement multiple toolbars, although that was not the focus of the chapter. Through practical hands-on exercises, you have seen how to create menus, menu items, and submenu items. You have also seen how to add access keys, shortcut keys, and images to these menu items.

Because you used the Edit menu in the Try It Outs, you have also seen how easy it is to implement basic editing techniques in your application by using the properties of the TextBox control and the `Clipboard` object. Now you know how easy it is to provide this functionality to your users — something users have come to expect in every good Windows application.

You also explored how to create and implement context menus and how to override the default context menus provided by Windows. As you already coded the procedure to implement undo, cut, copy, and paste operations, you simply reused that code in your context menus.

Now that you have completed this chapter, you should know how to do the following:

➤ Add a MenuStrip control to your form and add menus, menu items, and submenu items

➤ Customize the menu items with a check mark

➤ Add access keys and shortcut keys to your menu items

➤ Add a ContextMenuStrip control to your form and add menu items

➤ Use the properties of the TextBox control to toggle the `Enabled` property of menu items

EXERCISES

1. How do you add the commonly used menus and toolbars to either a MenuStrip or ToolStrip control?

2. How do you add a custom context menu to a TextBox control?

3. How do you add a shortcut to a menu item, such as Alt+F?

4. How do you add a shortcut to a menu item, such as Ctrl+C?

▶ **WHAT YOU HAVE LEARNED IN THIS CHAPTER**

TOPIC	CONCEPTS
Work with menus and submenus	Add images, access keys, shortcut keys and checkboxes to menus. When needed, you should disable menu items that cannot be used.
Add toolbars	Add custom buttons and images or choose standard items to have common buttons inserted for you.
Use context menus	How to add a custom context menu to a control.

10

Debugging and Error Handling

WHAT YOU WILL LEARN IN THIS CHAPTER:

➤ How to correct the major types of errors you may encounter

➤ How to debug a program

➤ How to implement error handling in a program

Debugging is an essential part of any development project, as it helps you find errors both in your code and in your logic. Visual Studio 2010 has a sophisticated debugger built right into the development environment. This debugger is the same for all languages that Visual Studio 2010 supports. When you have mastered debugging in one language, you can debug in any language that you can write in Visual Studio 2010.

No matter how good your code is, there are always going to be some unexpected circumstances that will cause your code to fail. If you do not anticipate and handle errors, your users will see a default error message about an unhandled exception, which is provided by the common language runtime package. This is not a user-friendly message and usually does not clearly inform the user about what is going on or how to correct it.

This is where error handling comes in. Visual Studio 2010 also provides common structured error-handling functions that are used across all languages. These functions enable you to test a block of code and catch any errors that may occur. If an error does occur, you can display your own user-friendly message that informs the user of what happened and how to correct it, or you can simply handle the error and continue processing.

This chapter looks at some of the debugging features available in Visual Studio 2010 and provides a walk-through of debugging a program. You examine how to set breakpoints in your code to stop execution at any given point, how to watch the value of a variable change, and how to control the number of times a loop can execute before stopping. All of these can help you determine just what is going on inside your code. Finally, this chapter takes a look at the structured error-handling functions provided by Visual Studio 2010.

MAJOR ERROR TYPES

Error types can be broken down into three major categories: syntax, execution, and logic. This section shows you the important differences among these three types of errors and how to correct them.

> **NOTE** *Knowing what type of errors are possible and how to correct them will significantly speed up the development process. Of course, sometimes you just can't find the error on your own. Don't waste too much time trying to find errors in your code by yourself in these situations. Coming back to a nagging problem after a short coffee break can often help you crack it. Otherwise, ask a colleague to have a look at your code with you; two pairs of eyes are often better than one in these cases.*

Syntax Errors

Syntax errors, the easiest type of errors to spot and fix, occur when the code you have written cannot be understood by the compiler because instructions are incomplete, supplied in unexpected order, or cannot be processed at all. An example of this would be declaring a variable of one name and misspelling this name in your code when you set or query the variable.

The development environment in Visual Studio 2010 has a very sophisticated syntax-checking mechanism, making it hard, but not impossible, to have syntax errors in your code. It provides instant syntax checking of variables and objects and lets you know immediately when you have a syntax error.

Suppose you try to declare a variable as `Private` in a procedure. Visual Studio 2010 underlines the declaration with a blue wavy line indicating that the declaration is in error. If the integrated development environment (IDE) can automatically correct the syntax error, you'll see a little orange rectangular box at the end of the blue wavy line, as shown in Figure 10-1 (minus the color), indicating that AutoCorrect options are available for this syntax error. AutoCorrect is a feature of Visual Studio 2010 that provides error-correction options that the IDE will suggest to correct the error.

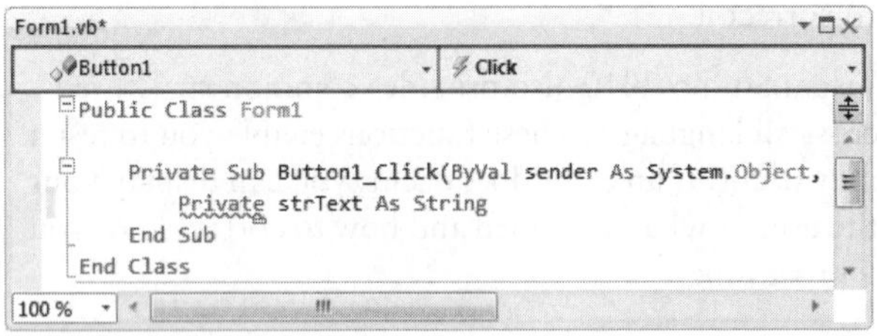

FIGURE 10-1

When you hover your mouse over the code in error, you'll receive a ToolTip, telling you what the error is, and a small gray box with a red circle and a white exclamation point. If you then move your mouse into the gray box, a down arrow appears, as shown in Figure 10-2, to let you know that a dialog box is available with some suggested error-correction options.

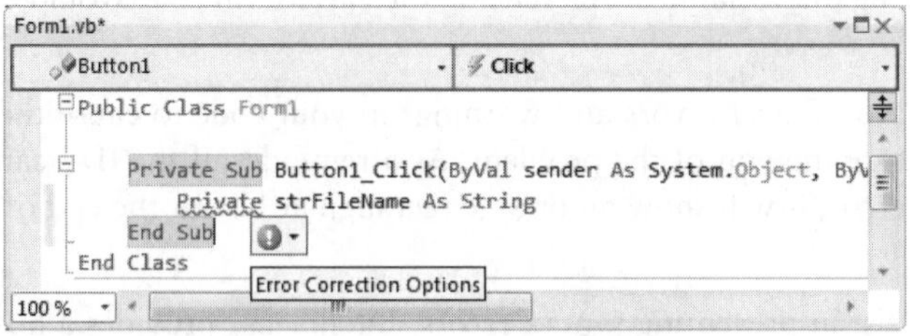

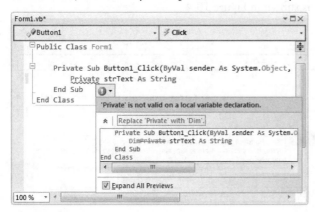

FIGURE 10-2

Clicking the down arrow or pressing Shift+Alt+F10 causes the Error Correction Options dialog to appear, as shown in Figure 10-3. This dialog presents one or more options for correcting the error. In this instance, there is only one option to correct the syntax error.

FIGURE 10-3

Note that the dialog box shows you how your code can be corrected: by replacing the `Private` keyword with the `Dim` keyword. The sample code displayed in the dialog box has your offending statement in strikethrough and the suggested correction preceding it. Above the code in the dialog is a hyperlink that will replace the `Private` keyword with the `Dim` keyword. Click this link to apply the fix to your code.

Another option available for reviewing all the errors in your code is the Error List window. This window displays a grid with all the errors' descriptions, the files they exist in, and the line numbers and column numbers of the error. If your solution contains multiple projects, it also displays the project in which each error occurs.

The Error List can be accessed by clicking the Error List tab at the bottom of the IDE if it is already displayed in the IDE or by clicking the Error List item on the View menu. When the Error List window is displayed, you can double-click any error to be taken to that specific error in your code.

Sometimes you'll receive warnings, displayed with a green wavy line under the code in question. These are just warnings and your code will compile. However, you should heed these warnings and try to correct these errors if possible, because they may produce undesirable results at runtime.

For example, a warning would occur in the line of code shown in Figure 10-3 once the `Private` keyword was replaced with the `Dim` keyword. The IDE would give you a warning that the variable, `strText`, is unused in the procedure. Simply initializing the variable or referencing the variable in code would cause this warning to go away.

Keep in mind that you can hover your mouse over errors and warnings in your code to cause the appropriate ToolTip to be displayed informing you of the problem. As a reminder, if the IDE can provide the AutoCorrect feature for an error, it will show an orange rectangular box at the end of the blue wavy line.

The IDE also provides IntelliSense to assist in preventing syntax errors. IntelliSense provides a host of features such as providing a drop-down list of members for classes, structures, and namespaces, as shown in Figure 10-4. This enables you to choose the correct member for the class, structure, or namespace that you are working with. It also provides ToolTip information for the selected member or method, also shown in Figure 10-4. IntelliSense initially displays a list of all members for the object being worked with; and as soon as you start typing one or more letters, the list of members is shortened to match the letters that you have typed, as shown in Figure 10-4.

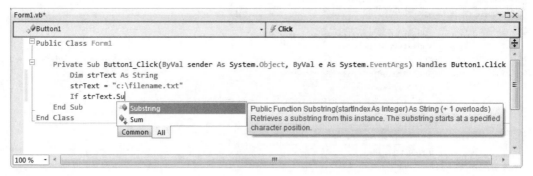

FIGURE 10-4

These IntelliSense features provide two major benefits. First, you do not have to remember all the available members for the class. You simply scroll through the list to find the member that you want to work with or you type the first letter or two of the member to see a list reduced to the relevant members. To select the member in the list that you want to work with, you press the Tab or Enter key or double-click the member. Second, the features help you prevent syntax errors because you are less likely to misspell member names or try to use members that do not exist in the given class.

Another great feature of IntelliSense is that it provides a parameter list for the method you are working with. IntelliSense lists the number, names, and types of the parameters required by the function, as shown in Figure 10-4. This is also a time saver, as you do not have to remember the required parameters for every class member that you work with, or indeed search the product documentation for what you need.

If the method is overloaded — that is, there are several methods with the same name but different parameters — the ToolTip indicates this, as shown in Figure 10-4 with the text "(+ 1 overloads)." Also, when you start to work with the member, a pop-up list enables you to scroll through the different overloaded methods, as shown in Figure 10-5 for the Substring method of the String class, by simply clicking the up and down arrows to view the different overloaded methods.

Another IntelliSense list appears for the parameter that you are working with, and this large list of all classes and members is also reduced to only those that might be relevant after you start typing one or more letters, as indicated in Figure 10-5. In this case, I started typing the letters my to have the list of available classes and namespaces reduced to only those that begin with the letters my.

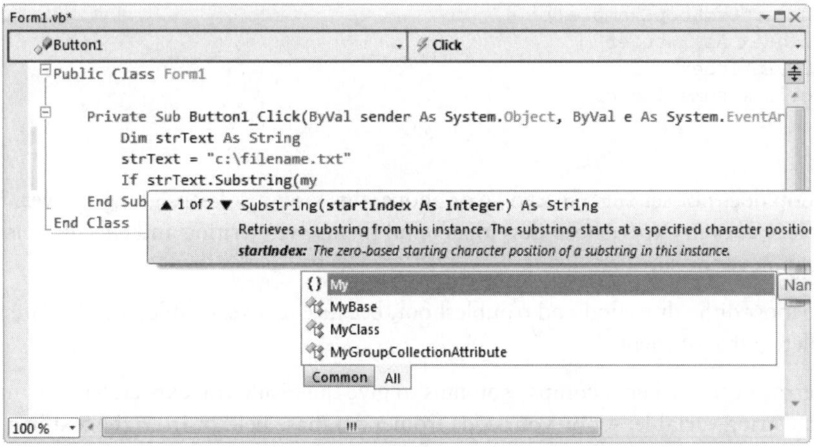

FIGURE 10-5

Plenty of built-in features in the development environment can help prevent syntax errors. All you need to do is be aware of these features and take advantage of them to help prevent syntax errors in your code.

Execution Errors

Execution errors (or *runtime errors*) occur while your program is executing. These errors are often caused because something outside of the application, such as a user, database, or hard disk, does not behave as expected. In .NET, you will read about error handling or exception handling. If you talk to a programmer who has not worked in prior languages, they will use the term exception versus error. For programmers who have worked in earlier versions of VB, they will likely use error versus exception. You should treat them as the same. In this chapter, you will see both used.

Developers need to anticipate the possibility of execution errors and build appropriate error-handling logic. Implementing the appropriate error handling does not prevent execution errors, but it does enable you to handle them by either gracefully shutting down your application or bypassing the code that failed and giving the user the opportunity to perform that action again. Error handling is covered later in this chapter.

One way to prevent execution errors is to anticipate the error before it occurs, and then use error handling to trap and handle it. You must also thoroughly test your code before deploying it.

Most execution errors can be found while you are testing your code in the development environment. This enables you to handle the errors and debug your code at the same time. You can then see what type of errors may occur and implement the appropriate error-handling logic. Debugging, whereby you find and handle any execution errors that may crop up, is covered later in the "Debugging" section.

Logic Errors

Logic errors (or *semantic errors*) lead to unexpected or unwanted results because you did not fully understand what the code you were writing would do. Probably the most common logic error is an infinite loop:

```
Private Sub PerformLoopExample()
    Dim intIndex As Integer
    Do While intIndex < 10
        ..perform some logic
    Loop
End Sub
```

If the code inside the loop does not set intIndex to 10 or above, this loop just keeps going forever. This is a very simple example, but even experienced developers find themselves writing and executing loops whose exit condition can never be satisfied.

Logic errors can be the most difficult to find and troubleshoot, because it is very difficult to be sure that your program is completely free of them.

Another type of logic error occurs when a comparison fails to give the result you expect. Say you made a comparison between a string variable, set by your code from a database field or from the text in a file, and the text entered by the user. You do not want the comparison to be case sensitive, so you might write code like this:

```
If strFileName = txtInput.Text Then
    ..perform some logic
End If
```

However, if strFileName is set to Index.HTML and txtInput.Text is set to index.html, the comparison fails. One way to prevent this logic error is to convert both fields being compared to either uppercase or lowercase. This way, the results of the comparison would be True if the user entered the same text as that contained in the variable, even if the case were different. The next code fragment shows how you can accomplish this:

```
If strFileName.ToUpper = txtInput.Text.ToUpper Then
    ..perform some logic
End If
```

The ToUpper method of the String class converts the characters in the string to all uppercase and returns the converted results. Because the Text property of a text box is also a string, you can use the same method to convert the text to all uppercase. This would make the comparison in the previous example equal.

An alternative to using either the ToUpper or ToLower methods of the String class is to use the Compare method of the String class, as shown in the next example. This enables you to compare the two strings while ignoring the case of the strings. This is covered in the section "String Comparison" in Chapter 4.

```
If String.Compare(strFileName, txtInput.Text, True) Then
    .. perform some logic
End If
```

> **NOTE** *Because logic errors are the hardest errors to troubleshoot and can cause applications to fail or give unexpected and unwanted results, you must check the logic carefully as you code and try to plan for all possible errors that may be encountered by a user. As you become more experienced, you will encounter and learn from the common errors that you and your users make.*

One of the best ways to identify and fix logic errors is to use the debugging features of Visual Studio 2010. Using these features, you can find loops that execute too many times or comparisons that do not provide the expected result.

DEBUGGING

Debugging code is a part of life — even experienced developers make mistakes and need to debug their code. Knowing how to efficiently debug your code can make the difference between enjoying your job as a developer and hating it.

In the following sections, you'll create and debug a sample project while learning about the Exception Assistant, breakpoints, and how to step through your code and use the Watch, Autos, and Locals windows to examine variables and objects.

Creating a Sample Project

In this section, you take a look at some of the built-in debugging features in the Visual Studio 2010 development environment through various Try It Out exercises. You write a simple program and learn how to use the most common and useful debugging features available.

TRY IT OUT   Creating a Sample Project to Debug

Code file Debugging.zip available for download at Wrox.com

You begin the debugging process by creating a program that uses three classes that you create. Classes and objects are covered in greater detail in the next chapter, but by creating and using these classes, you'll learn about some of the other features in Visual Basic 2010, as well as how to debug your programs. These classes are used to provide data to be displayed in a list box on your form. The classes introduce two powerful concepts in particular: the generic class with type constraints and the interface. These concepts are explained after the example in the "How It Works" section.

1. Create a new Windows Forms Application project and name it **Debugging**.

2. In the Solution Explorer window, rename the form to Debug.vb by right-clicking the form and choosing Rename from the context menu. Click the form in the Forms Designer and then set the form's properties in the Properties window as shown:

➤ Set Size to **440, 300**.

➤ Set StartPosition to **CenterScreen**.

➤ Set Text to **Debug Demo**.

3. Add some basic controls to the form and set their properties as shown in the following list:

➤ Create a Button control named **btnStart** and set these properties: Anchor = **Top, Right,** Location = **329, 12**; Text = **Start.**

➤ Create a ListBox control named **lstData**, and set these properties: Anchor = **Top, Bottom, Left, Right**; Integral Height = False; Location = **12, 41**; Size = **391, 204.**

4. Right-click the Debugging project in the Solution Explorer, choose Add from the context menu, and then choose the Class submenu item. In the Add New Item - Debugging dialog box, enter a class name of **Customer** in the Name field and then click the Add button. Add the following highlighted code to the class:

```
Public Class Customer
    Private intCustomerID As Integer
    Private strName As String

    Public Sub New(ByVal customerID As Integer, ByVal name As String)
        intCustomerID = customerID
        strName = name
    End Sub

    Public ReadOnly Property CustomerID() As Integer
        Get
            Return intCustomerID
        End Get
    End Property

    Public Property CustomerName() As String
        Get
            Return strName
        End Get
        Set(ByVal value As String)
            strName = value
        End Set
    End Property
End Class
```

5. Before moving on to create the next class, take a quick look at the AutoCorrect option in Visual Studio 2010 so that you can get firsthand experience with this feature. The CustomerName property that you just created should really be a ReadOnly property. Insert the ReadOnly keyword between Public and Property and then click the next line of code.

6. You'll notice that the Set statement in this property has a blue wavy line underneath it indicating an error. If you hover your mouse over the line of code in error, you get a ToolTip informing you that a ReadOnly property cannot have a Set statement.

7. Click the small gray box with a red circle and white exclamation point to display the Error Correction Options dialog box, shown in Figure 10-6.

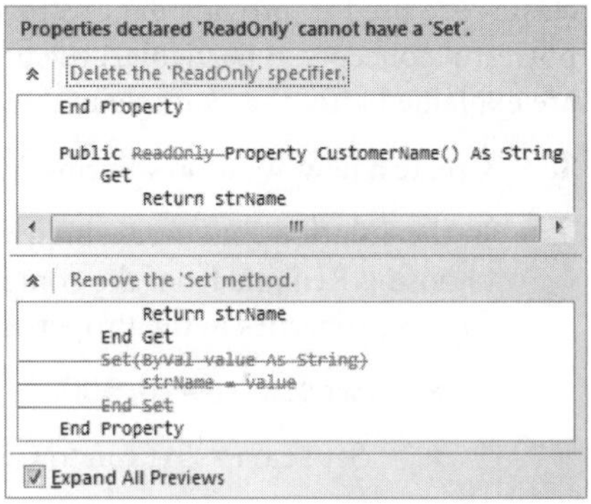

FIGURE 10-6

8. You have two options to choose from. The option that you want is the second one, which is to remove the `Set` method. Click the hyperlink to have the AutoCorrect feature remove the `Set` statement from this property.

9. Add another class to the Debugging project, called **Generics**. Then modify the `Class` statement as highlighted here:

```
Public Class Generics(Of elementType)

End Class
```

10. Add the following highlighted code to the `Generics` class:

```
Public Class Generics(Of elementType)
    'This class provides a demonstration of Generics

    'Declare Private variables
    Private strKey() As String
    Private elmValue() As elementType

    Public Sub Add(ByVal key As String, ByVal value As elementType)
        'Check to see if the objects have been initialized
        If strKey IsNot Nothing Then
            'Objects have been initialized
            ReDim Preserve strKey(strKey.GetUpperBound(0) + 1)
            ReDim Preserve elmValue(elmValue.GetUpperBound(0) + 1)
        Else
            'Initialize the objects
            ReDim strKey(0)
            ReDim elmValue(0)
        End If

        'Set the values
        strKey(strKey.GetUpperBound(0)) = key
        elmValue(elmValue.GetUpperBound(0)) = value
    End Sub

    Public ReadOnly Property Key(ByVal Index As Integer) As String
        Get
            Return strKey(Index)
        End Get
    End Property

    Public ReadOnly Property Value(ByVal Index As Integer) As elementType
        Get
            Return elmValue(Index)
        End Get
    End Property
End Class
```

11. Add one more class to the Debugging project, called **Computer**. This is an example of a class that *implements* the `IDisposable` interface, which is explained in the "How It Works" section. Enter the following highlighted code. Once you press the Enter key, Visual Studio 2010 inserts the remaining code listed here automatically:

```
Public Class Computer
    Implements IDisposable
```

```vbnet
#Region "IDisposable Support"
    Private disposedValue As Boolean ' To detect redundant calls

    ' IDisposable
    Protected Overridable Sub Dispose(ByVal disposing As Boolean)
        If Not Me.disposedValue Then
            If disposing Then
                ' TODO: dispose managed state (managed objects).
            End If

            ' TODO: free unmanaged resources (unmanaged objects)
            'and override Finalize() below.
            ' TODO: set large fields to null.
        End If
        Me.disposedValue = True
    End Sub

    ' TODO: override Finalize() only if Dispose(ByVal disposing As
    ' Boolean) above has code to free unmanaged resources.
    'Protected Overrides Sub Finalize()
    '    ' Do not change this code.  Put cleanup code in Dispose
    ' (ByVal disposing As Boolean) above.
    '    Dispose(False)
    '    MyBase.Finalize()
    'End Sub

    ' This code added by Visual Basic to correctly implement the
    'disposable pattern.
    Public Sub Dispose() Implements IDisposable.Dispose
        ' Do not change this code.  Put cleanup code
        'in Dispose(ByVal disposing As Boolean) above.
        Dispose(True)
        GC.SuppressFinalize(Me)
    End Sub
#End Region

End Class
```

12. Add the following two properties to the end of the `Computer` class:

```vbnet
Public ReadOnly Property FreeMemory() As String
    Get
        'Using the My namespace
        Return Format(( _
            My.Computer.Info.AvailablePhysicalMemory.ToString \ 1024), _
            "#,###,##0") & " K"
    End Get
End Property

Public ReadOnly Property TotalMemory() As String
    Get
        'Using the My namespace
        Return Format(( _
```

```
              My.Computer.Info.TotalPhysicalMemory.ToString \ 1024), _
              "#,###,##0") & " K"
      End Get
  End Property
```

13. Switch to the code for the Debug form and add the following highlighted Imports statement:

Imports System.Collections.Generic

```
Public Class Debug
```

14. You need to add a few private variable declarations next. Add the following code:

```
Public Class Debug
    'Using the Generics class
    Private objStringValues As New Generics(Of String)
    Private objIntegerValues As New Generics(Of Integer)

    'Using the List(Of T)(Of T) class
    Private objCustomerList As New List(Of Customer)
```

15. Add the following ListCustomer procedure to add customers to the list box on your form:

```
      Private Sub ListCustomer(ByVal customerToList As Customer)
          lstData.Items.Add(customerToList.CustomerID & _
              "-" & customerToList.CustomerName)
      End Sub
```

16. Next, you need to add the rest of the code to the Start button Click event handler. Select btnStart in the Class Name combo box at the top of the Code Editor and then select the Click event in the Method Name combo box. Add the following highlighted code to the Click event handler:

```
      Private Sub btnStart_Click(ByVal sender As Object, _
          ByVal e As System.EventArgs) Handles btnStart.Click
          'Declare variables
          Dim strData As String

          lstData.Items.Add("String variable data:")
          If strData.Length > 0 Then
              lstData.Items.Add(strData)
          End If

          'Add an empty string to the ListBox
          lstData.Items.Add(String.Empty)

          'Demonstrates the use of the List(Of T) class
          lstData.Items.Add("Customers in the Customer Class:")
          objCustomerList.Add(New Customer(1001, "Henry For"))
          objCustomerList.Add(New Customer(1002, "Orville Wright"))
          For Each objCustomer As Customer In objCustomerList
              ListCustomer(objCustomer)
          Next

          'Add an empty string to the ListBox
          lstData.Items.Add(String.Empty)
```

```
            'Demonstrates the use of Generics
            lstData.Items.Add("Generics Class Key/Value Pairs using String Values:")
            objStringValues.Add("1001", "Henry Ford")
            lstData.Items.Add(objStringValues.Key(0) & " = " & _
                objStringValues.Value(0))

            'Add an empty string to the ListBox
            lstData.Items.Add(String.Empty)

            'Demonstrates the use of Generics
            lstData.Items.Add("Generics Class Key/Value Pairs using Integer Values:")
            objIntegerValues.Add("Henry Ford", 1001)
            lstData.Items.Add(objIntegerValues.Key(0) & " = " & _
                objIntegerValues.Value(0))

            'Add an empty string to the ListBox
            lstData.Items.Add(String.Empty)

            'Demonstrates the use of the Using statement
            'Allows acquisition, usage and disposal of the resource
            lstData.Items.Add("Computer Class Properties:")
            Using objMemory As New Computer
                lstData.Items.Add("FreeMemory = " & objMemory.FreeMemory)
                lstData.Items.Add("TotalMemory = " & objMemory.TotalMemory)
            End Using

            'Add an empty string to the ListBox
            lstData.Items.Add(String.Empty)

            'Demonstrates the use of the Continue statement
            Dim strPassword As String = "POpPassword"
            Dim strLowerCaseLetters As String = String.Empty
            'Extract lowercase characters from string
            For intIndex As Integer = 0 To strPassword.Length-1
                'Demonstrates the use of the Continue statement
                'If no uppercase character is found, continue the loop
                If Not strPassword.Substring(intIndex, 1) Like "[a-z]" Then
                    'No upper case character found, continue loop
                    Continue For
                End If
                'Lowercase character found, save it
                strLowerCaseLetters &= strPassword.Substring(intIndex, 1)
            Next

        'Display lowercase characters
        lstData.Items.Add("Password lower case characters:")
        lstData.Items.Add(strLowerCaseLetters)
    End Sub
```

17. Before examining how the code works, hover your mouse over the Error List tab at the bottom of the IDE so that the Error List window appears (see Figure 10-7). If the Error List tab is not visible, select View Error List from the menu bar. You have one warning about a potential error in your code. The line in question causes an error when you run your project; however, this is deliberate and is intended to demonstrate some of the debugging capabilities of Visual Studio 2010. You can ignore this warning for now because you'll be correcting it shortly.

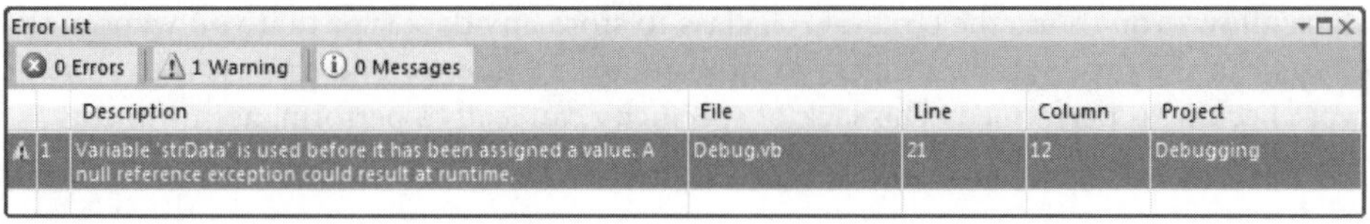

FIGURE 10-7

18. Save your project by clicking the Save All button on the toolbar.

How It Works

After building the user interface for the Debugging project, you add the `Customer` class. This class is also straightforward and contains two private variables, a constructor, and two properties.

The two variables in the `Customer` class are declared as `Private`, which means that these variables are accessible only to the procedures in the class:

```
Public Class Customer
    Private intCustomerID As Integer
     Private strName As String
```

The *constructor* for this class — a method called whenever a new object of this class is to be created — is defined as a `Public` procedure with a procedure name of `New`. In VB, all constructors for classes in the .NET Framework must be declared with a procedure name of `New`.

This constructor accepts two input parameters: `customerID` and `name`. The parameters are used to set the values in the private variables defined for this class:

```
Public Sub New(ByVal customerID As Integer, ByVal name As String)
    intCustomerID = customerID
    strName = name
End Sub
```

Two properties are defined: `CustomerID` and `CustomerName`. These are read-only properties, meaning that the consumer of this class can use these properties only to read the customer ID and customer name; consumers cannot change them:

```
Public ReadOnly Property CustomerID() As Integer
    Get
        Return intCustomerID
    End Get
End Property

    Public Property CustomerName() As String
        Get
            Return strName
        End Get
    End Property
End Class
```

The next class that you added to the Debugging project is the `Generics` class. This class is used to demonstrate the use of generics in Visual Basic 2010.

The `Collections` class in the .NET Framework enables you to store data in the collection in a key/value pair. The key is always a string value that identifies the value, also known as an *item*. The item is defined as an object, which allows you to use the Collection class to store any data type that you want in the item. For example, you can use the Collection class to store Integer values or you can use it to store String values. No type checking is performed. This lack of specificity can lead to performance problems as well as run-time problems.

Suppose you intend to use the Collection class to store Integer values. If (through poor coding practices) you allowed a String value to be added to the collection, you would not receive a run-time error when adding the item, but you could receive one when you tried to access the item.

The performance problems that you will encounter are the conversion of the data going into the collection and the data coming out of the collection. When you add an item to the collection, the data must be converted from its native data type to an Object data type, as that is how the Item property is defined. Likewise, when you retrieve an item from the collection, the item must be converted from an Object data type to the data type that you are using.

In Chapter 5, when working with ArrayLists (which are a kind of collection), you solved the problem of being able to store items of the wrong type by creating a strongly typed collection class. This did not solve the performance problem. Both problems are solved through generics and through the introduction of *type constraints*. A type constraint is specified on a class such as Collection by using the Of keyword followed by a list of type name placeholders that are replaced by actual type names when an object of the class is created. This provides type safety by not allowing you to add an item that is not of the same data type that was defined for the class. It also improves performance because the item does not have to be converted to and from the Object data type. The data type for the item is defined using the data type that was defined for the class. You'll see how all of this works in more detail as you explore the rest of the code and as you go through the debugging process.

After adding the Generics class, you modify the class by adding a type constraint using the Of keyword and defining a type list, which in this case contains only one type. This type name is a placeholder that will be used throughout the class to represent the data type that this class is working with. The actual data type is defined when an object of the class is created, as you'll see later in your code:

```
Public Class Generics(Of elementType)

End Class
```

You add two private variables to this class, with both of these variables being defined as arrays. The first variable is defined as a String data type, while the second variable is defined as a generic data type, which is set when an object of the class is created. Note that you have used the type name elementType, which was defined at the class level. This type name is replaced automatically by the data type that is used to create the Generics object:

```
Public Class Generics(Of elementType)
    'This class provides a demonstration of Generics

    'Declare Private variables
    Private strKey() As String
    Private elmValue() As elementType
```

The Add method enables you to add items to your collection. This method accepts two parameters: one for the key and the other for the value, making a key/value pair. The key parameter is always a string value, and the value parameter is defined using the data type that is used when a Generics object is created.

The first thing that you want to do in this procedure is see whether the variable arrays have been initialized. You do this by using the IsNot operator and comparing the strKey array to a value of Nothing. If the array is not equal to a value of Nothing, the array has already been initialized, and you simply need to increment the array dimension by one. This is done by first getting the current upper bounds of the array and then adding 1 to it.

If the variable arrays have not been initialized, you need to initialize them using the ReDim statement as shown in the Else statement in the code that follows. After the arrays have been expanded or initialized, you add the key and value to the arrays:

```
Public Sub Add(ByVal key As String, ByVal value As elementType)
    'Check to see if the objects have been initialized
    If strKey IsNot Nothing Then
        'Objects have been initialized
        ReDim Preserve strKey(strKey.GetUpperBound(0) + 1)
        ReDim Preserve elmValue(elmValue.GetUpperBound(0) + 1)
    Else
        'Initialize the objects
        ReDim strKey(0)
        ReDim elmValue(0)
    End If

    'Set the values
    strKey(strKey.GetUpperBound(0)) = key
    elmValue(elmValue.GetUpperBound(0)) = value
End Sub
```

You add two read-only properties to this class to return the key and the value for a key/value pair. Notice that the Value property is defined to return the data type that will be used when a Generics object is created:

```
Public ReadOnly Property Key(ByVal Index As Integer) As String
    Get
        Return strKey(Index)
    End Get
End Property

Public ReadOnly Property Value(ByVal Index As Integer) As elementType
    Get
        Return elmValue(Index)
    End Get
End Property
End Class
```

The final class that you added was the Computer class. This class implements the IDisposable interface. An interface in this sense is a set of methods and properties common to all classes that implement it. In this case, the IDisposable interface contains methods for releasing memory resources when an object of the class is disposed of. Methods that use this class should call the Dispose method when they are through with a Computer object.

To implement the interface, you add the Implements statement and specify the IDisposable interface. When you press the Enter key, Visual Studio 2010 adds the code from the IDisposable interface to your class, as shown in the following code:

```
Public Class Computer
    Implements IDisposable

#Region "IDisposable Support"
    Private disposedValue As Boolean ' To detect redundant calls
```

```
    ' IDisposable
    Protected Overridable Sub Dispose(ByVal disposing As Boolean)
        If Not Me.disposedValue Then
            If disposing Then
                ' TODO: dispose managed state (managed objects).
            End If

            ' TODO: free unmanaged resources (unmanaged objects)
            'and override Finalize() below.
            ' TODO: set large fields to null.
        End If
        Me.disposedValue = True
    End Sub

    ' TODO: override Finalize() only if Dispose(ByVal disposing As Boolean)
    ' above has code to free unmanaged resources.
    'Protected Overrides Sub Finalize()
    '    ' Do not change this code.  Put cleanup code in Dispose(ByVal
    '    'disposing As Boolean) above.
    '    Dispose(False)
    '    MyBase.Finalize()
    'End Sub

    ' This code added by Visual Basic to correctly implement the disposable pattern.
    Public Sub Dispose() Implements IDisposable.Dispose
        ' Do not change this code.  Put cleanup code in Dispose
        ' (ByVal disposing As Boolean) above.
        Dispose(True)
        GC.SuppressFinalize(Me)
    End Sub
#End Region

End Class
```

You add two read-only properties to this class: `FreeMemory` and `TotalMemory`. These properties return the available memory on your computer as well as the total amount of memory on your computer. These properties use the `My.Computer.Info` namespace to access the amount of available memory and the total amount of memory.

The `AvailablePhysicalMemory` and `TotalPhysicalMemory` properties of the `My.Computer.Info` namespace return the available and total memory in bytes. However, as users we are used to seeing these numbers in kilobytes. Therefore, you convert the number of bytes into kilobytes and then have that number formatted using commas.

> **NOTE** Remember that there are 1,024 bytes to a kilobyte, 1,024 kilobytes to a megabyte, and so on. The number that you pass to the `Format` function will be in kilobytes after you divide the number of bytes by 1,024.

You then add a space to the formatted number and then the letter K, indicating that the available and total memory figures are in kilobytes:

```
Public ReadOnly Property FreeMemory() As String
    Get
        'Using the My namespace
```

```
            Return Format(( _
                My.Computer.Info.AvailablePhysicalMemory.ToString \ 1024), _
                "#,###,##0") & " K"
        End Get
    End Property

    Public ReadOnly Property TotalMemory() As String
        Get
            'Using the My namespace
            Return Format(( _
                My.Computer.Info.TotalPhysicalMemory.ToString \ 1024), _
                "#,###,##0") & " K"
        End Get
    End Property
```

You add code to the `Debug` form class next. This class uses `List(Of T)` a generic list class, `List(Of T)`. You'll be using this class to hold a list of `Customer` objects created from your `Customer` class. The `List(Of T)` class uses a collection to hold the objects of the type that you specify: You need to import the `System.Collections.Generic` namespace in order to access the `List(Of T)` class. You accomplish that requirement by using an `Imports` statement:

```
Imports System.Collections.Generic
```

Next you define three private objects at the class level; these objects are available to all procedures in this class. The first two objects use your `Generics` class. Remember that the `Generics` class used the `Of` keyword to define a type list. In the declaration of your objects, you use similar `Of` clauses to specify that the `Generics` class should be using a `String` data type in the type list for the first object and an `Integer` data type for the second object. The data type specified here will be applied throughout the `Generics` class. Even when you compile your code, any instances where you try and add the wrong type to the collection you will get a message from the compiler.

The last object that you define here is an object that holds an array of `Customer` objects created from your `Customer` class:

```
    'Using the Generics class
    Private objStringValues As New Generics(Of String)
    Private objIntegerValues As New Generics(Of Integer)

    'Using the List(Of T) class
    Private objCustomerList As New List(Of Customer)
```

The `ListCustomer` procedure simply accepts a `Customer` object as input and adds the `CustomerID` and `CustomerName` to the list box on your form:

```
    Private Sub ListCustomer(ByVal customerToList As Customer)
        lstData.Items.Add(customerToList.CustomerID & _
            "-" & customerToList.CustomerName)
    End Sub
```

The `Click` event handler for the Start button contains the rest of the code for your project. You start this procedure by declaring a local `String` variable that will be used to demonstrate checking to see whether a variable has been initialized.

The code following the variable declaration checks the length of the variable and then adds the contents of the variable to the list box on the form:

```
    Private Sub btnStart_Click(ByVal sender As Object, _
        ByVal e As System.EventArgs) Handles btnStart.Click
```

```
'Declare variables
Dim strData As String

lstData.Items.Add("String variable data:")
If strData.Length > 0 Then
    lstData.Items.Add(strData)
End If
```

Since you will be writing the various results of your processing to the list box on your form, you'll want to add a blank entry to the list box to separate your results for aesthetic reasons, which is what the next line of code does. Here you simply use the `Empty` method of the `String` class to return an empty string to be added to the list box:

```
'Add an empty string to the ListBox
lstData.Items.Add(String.Empty)
```

This next section of code demonstrates the use of the `List(Of T)` class, as the comment in the code indicates. You add two new `Customer` objects to the `objCustomerList` object and then display those customers in the list box. Using a `For Each . . . Next` loop to iterate through the collection of `Customer` objects, you add each customer to the list box by calling the `ListCustomer` function, passing that function the `Customer` object:

```
'Demonstrates the use of the List(Of T) class
lstData.Items.Add("Customers in the Customer Class:")
objCustomerList.Add(New Customer(1001, "Henry For"))
objCustomerList.Add(New Customer(1002, "Orville Wright"))
For Each objCustomer As Customer In objCustomerList
    ListCustomer(objCustomer)
Next
```

Again you add a blank entry to the list box and use the objects that were defined using your `Generics` class. The first object, `objStringValues`, uses the `Generics` class with a `String` data type, as the object name indicates. Remember that the `Add` method in this class accepts a key/value pair and that the `key` parameter is always a `String` value. The `value` parameter uses the data type that was used to initialize this class, which in this case is also a `String`.

When you add a key/value pair to your `objStringValues` object, you want to display that data in the list box on your form. You do this by accessing the `Key` and `Value` properties in the `Generics` class from which this object was derived:

```
'Add an empty string to the ListBox
lstData.Items.Add(String.Empty)

'Demonstrates the use of Generics
lstData.Items.Add("Generics Class Key/Value Pairs using String Values:")
objStringValues.Add("1001", "Henry Ford")
lstData.Items.Add(objStringValues.Key(0) & " = " & _
    objStringValues.Value(0))
```

Again you add another blank line to the list box and then add a key/value pair that uses an `Integer` data type for the `value` parameter to the `objIntegerValues` object. Then you add that key/value pair to the list box:

```
'Add an empty string to the ListBox
lstData.Items.Add(String.Empty)
```

```
'Demonstrates the use of Generics
lstData.Items.Add("Generics Class Key/Value Pairs using Integer Values:")
objIntegerValues.Add("Henry Ford", 1001)
lstData.Items.Add(objIntegerValues.Key(0) & " = " & _
    objIntegerValues.Value(0))
```

After you add another blank line to the list box, you use a `Using ... End Using` block to create a new object of the `Computer` class, add the free memory and total memory of your computer to the list box, and then dispose of the `Computer` class.

When you use a class, you typically instantiate it using the `New` keyword as you did with your `Generics` class, use the class, and then dispose of the class by calling its `Dispose` method if it implements one. The problem with that scenario is that when an exception occurs, the resource may or may not be disposed of. Even if you implement the code using structured error handling, a topic discussed later in this chapter, you are not always guaranteed to be able to dispose of the class.

The `Using` statement is an efficient means of acquiring a resource, using it, and then disposing of it, regardless of whether an exception occurs. There is one caveat to this: The class that you use in a `Using ... .End Using` block must implement the `IDisposable` interface, which is why you added this interface to your `Computer` class.

In the following code, the object name, `objMemory`, has not been defined anywhere except in the `Using` statement. The `Using` statement takes care of declaring this object for you and sets it to a new instance of the class that you specify, which in this case is the `Computer` class. Keep in mind that the object, `objMemory`, is local to the `Using ... End Using` block and you can reference it only within this block.

When the `End Using` statement is reached, the Common Language Runtime (CLR) automatically calls the `Dispose` method on the `Computer` class, thereby releasing its reference to it, and the `Computer` class executes any cleanup code that has been implemented in the `Dispose` method:

```
'Add an empty string to the ListBox
lstData.Items.Add(String.Empty)

'Demonstrates the use of the Using statement
'Allows acquisition, usage and disposal of the resource
lstData.Items.Add("Computer Class Properties:")
Using objMemory As New Computer
    lstData.Items.Add("FreeMemory = " & objMemory.FreeMemory)
    lstData.Items.Add("TotalMemory = " & objMemory.TotalMemory)
End Using
```

Once again you add another blank line to the list box, and then you get to the final bit of code in this procedure. In this section of code we wanted to demonstrate the use of the `Continue` statement. The `Continue` statement is an efficient means of immediately transferring control to the next iteration of a loop. Instead of coding a lot of `If ... Then` statements in a loop, you can merely test to see whether a condition is what you want and if it is not, you can call the `Continue` statement to pass control to the next iteration of a `Do`, `For`, or `While` loop.

Take a look at the code that you have here. First you declare a couple of variables and set their values. The first variable, `strPassword`, is declared and set to a password that contains uppercase and lowercase letters. The second variable, `strLowerCaseLetters`, is declared and set to an empty string so that the variable is initialized.

Next, you set up a For . . . Next loop to check each character in the strPassword variable. The If . . . Then statement uses the Like operator to compare a character in the password variable to a pattern of letters. If a match is found, the Like operator returns a value of True. However, you are using a negative comparison here, because you have included the Not keyword in the If . . . Then statement, so if the character in the password variable is not like one of the letters in the pattern, [a-z], you execute the next statement, which is the Continue statement.

If the character in the password variable is a lowercase letter, then you concatenate the character to the strLowerCaseLetters variable, which is why you needed to initialize this variable to an empty string when you declared it.

Finally, after all lowercase letters have been extracted from the password variable, you display the results of the strLowerCaseLetters variable in the list box on your form:

```
'Add an empty string to the ListBox
lstData.Items.Add(String.Empty)

'Demonstrates the use of the Continue statement
Dim strPassword As String = "POpPassword"
Dim strLowerCaseLetters As String = String.Empty
'Extract lowercase characters from string
For intIndex As Integer = 0 To strPassword.Length - 1
    'Demonstrates the use of the Continue statement
    'If no uppercase character is found, continue the loop
    If Not strPassword.Substring(intIndex, 1) Like "[a-z]" Then
        'No uppercase character found, continue loop
        Continue For
    End If
    'Lowercase character found, save it
    strLowerCaseLetters &= strPassword.Substring(intIndex, 1)
Next

'Display lowercase characters
lstData.Items.Add("Password lower case characters:")
lstData.Items.Add(strLowerCaseLetters)
End Sub
```

At this point, you are probably pretty eager to run your project and test your code.

TRY IT OUT   **Using the Exception Assistant**

Code file Debugging.zip available for download at Wrox.com

In this Try It Out, you examine the Exception Assistant in Visual Studio 2010. This useful assistant provides help when an unhandled exception occurs in your code.

1. Start your project by clicking the Start button on the toolbar or by clicking the Debug menu and choosing the Start menu item.

2. When your form is displayed, click the Start button on your form to have your code in the Click event handler for the Start button executed. You'll immediately see the Exception Assistant, shown in Figure 10-8.

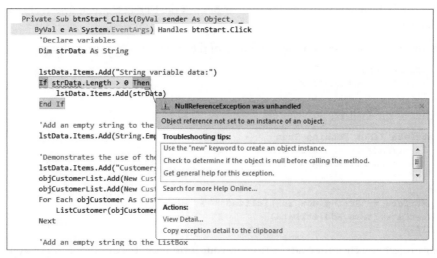

```vb
Private Sub btnStart_Click(ByVal sender As Object, _
    ByVal e As System.EventArgs) Handles btnStart.Click
    'Declare variables
    Dim strData As String

    lstData.Items.Add("String variable data:")
    If strData.Length > 0 Then
        lstData.Items.Add(strData)
    End If

    'Add an empty string to the
    lstData.Items.Add(String.Emp

    'Demonstrates the use of th
    lstData.Items.Add("Customer
    objCustomerList.Add(New Cus
    objCustomerList.Add(New Cus
    For Each objCustomer As Cus
        ListCustomer(objCustome
    Next

    'Add an empty string to the ListBox
```

NullReferenceException was unhandled

Object reference not set to an instance of an object.

Troubleshooting tips:

Use the "new" keyword to create an object instance.

Check to determine if the object is null before calling the method.

Get general help for this exception.

Search for more Help Online...

Actions:

View Detail...

Copy exception detail to the clipboard

FIGURE 10-8

NOTE *The Exception Assistant dialog box displays the type of exception that occurred in the title bar of the dialog box. It also provides links to some basic troubleshooting tips and a link at the bottom that provides details about the exception.*

3. Click the View Detail link in the Exception Assistant dialog box to view the View Detail dialog box shown in Figure 10-9. You are mainly interested in the exception message, and, as you can see, it informs you that the object reference has not been set to an instance of an object. Basically, you have not initialized the variable strData. This is also a warning during compilation.

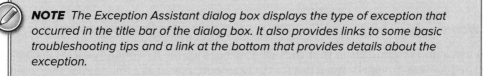

View Detail

Exception snapshot:

System.NullReferenceException	{"Object reference not set to an instance of an
▷ Data	{System.Collections.ListDictionaryInternal}
HelpLink	Nothing
InnerException	Nothing
Message	Object reference not set to an instance of an o
Source	Debugging
StackTrace	at Debugging.Debug.btnStart_Click(Object s
▷ TargetSite	{Void btnStart_Click(System.Object, System.Eve

OK

FIGURE 10-9

4. Click the OK button to close the View Detail dialog box and then click the Close button in the upper right-hand corner of the Exception Assistant dialog box to close it.

5. Now click the Stop Debugging button on the toolbar or click the Debug menu and select the Stop Debugging menu item.

6. Locate the following section of code at the beginning of the btnStart_Click procedure:

```
If strData.Length > 0 Then
    lstData.Items.Add(strData)
End If
```

7. Modify that code as shown here:

```
If strData IsNot Nothing Then
    If strData.Length > 0 Then
        lstData.Items.Add(strData)
    End If
Else
    strData = "String now initialized"
    lstData.Items.Add(strData)
End If
```

8. Now run your project and click the Start button on your form once it is displayed. All of your code should have executed, and the list box should be populated with the various results of the processing that took place in the btnStart_Click procedure.

How It Works

When an unhandled error occurs in your code while debugging, the Exception Assistant dialog box is displayed and provides troubleshooting tips for the exception, as well as a link to view the details of the exception as shown in Figure 10-8. Figure 10-9 displayed the View Detail dialog, which provides detailed information about the exception, which can also be an invaluable tool for determining its exact cause.

You modified the code that caused the error as shown here. Because the string variable strData was declared but never initialized, the variable is Nothing. This means that it has not been set to an instance of the String class and therefore the properties and methods of the variable cannot be referenced without causing a NullReferenceException (refer to Figure 10-8).

To rectify this problem, you first test the strData variable to see if it is not equal to Nothing by using the IsNot operator, as shown in the first line of the code that follows. If the variable has been initialized, then you can execute the code in the If statement. Otherwise, processing falls through to the Else statement, where you set the variable to a String constant and then display the contents of the variable in the list box:

```
If strData IsNot Nothing Then
    If strData.Length > 0 Then
        lstData.Items.Add(strData)
    End If
Else
    strData = "String now initialized"
    lstData.Items.Add(strData)
End If
```

An alternative to the previous code example would be to use a Try . . . Catch block to handle the exception. This technique is demonstrated later in this chapter.

Setting Breakpoints

When trying to debug a large program, you may find that you want to debug only a section of code; that is, you want your code to run up to a certain point and then stop. This is where *breakpoints* come in handy; they cause execution of your code to stop anywhere they are set. You can set breakpoints anywhere in your code and your code executes to that point and stops.

Execution of the code stops *before* executing the code on which the breakpoint is set.

You can set breakpoints when you write your code, or you can set them at runtime by switching to your code and setting the breakpoint at the desired location. You cannot set a breakpoint while your program is actually executing a section of code such as the code in a loop, but you can do so when the program is idle and waiting for user input.

When the development environment encounters a breakpoint, execution of your code halts, and your program is considered to be in *break mode*. While your program is in break mode, a lot of debugging features are available. In fact, a lot of debugging features are available to you only when your program is in break mode.

You can set breakpoints by clicking the gray margin next to the line of code on which you want to set the breakpoint or by pressing F9 while on the line you want to set a breakpoint on or take one off. When the breakpoint is set, you can see a solid red circle in the gray margin, and the line is highlighted in red. When you are done with a particular breakpoint, you can remove it by clicking the solid red circle. You see more of this in the Try It Out exercise in this section.

Sometimes you'll want to debug code in a loop, such as one that reads data from a file. You know that the first *x* number of records are good, and it is time-consuming to step through all the code repetitively until you get to what you suspect is the bad record. A breakpoint can be set inside the loop and you can set a hit counter on it. The code inside the loop executes the number of times that you specified in the hit counter and then stops and places you in break mode. This can be a real time saver, and you will take a look at breakpoint hit counts later in this section.

You can also set a condition on a breakpoint, such as when a variable contains a certain value or when the value of a variable changes. This is also examined later in this section.

TRY IT OUT   Working with Breakpoints

In this example, you begin with some breakpoint work. Next, some discussion on the IDE and then finally you complete the example.

Code file Debugging.zip is available for download at Wrox.com

1.   The first thing you want to do is set a breakpoint in your code. Using Figure 10-10 as a guide, set the breakpoint in your code by clicking the gray margin to the left of the line of code shown.

2.   Run the project.

3.   To get to the code where the breakpoint is set, click the Start button on your form. The code executes up to the breakpoint, and the development environment window receives focus, making it the topmost window. The entire line should be highlighted in yellow and the breakpoint circle in the margin should now contain a yellow arrow in it pointing to the line of code where execution has been paused, which in this case is the End If statement shown in Figure 10-10.

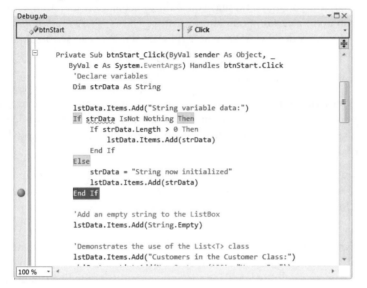

FIGURE 10-10

> ***NOTE*** *A few new windows appear at the bottom of the development environment. What you see will vary depending on which windows you have specified to be shown — you can choose different ones using the tabs at the bottom.*
>
> *This Try It Out pauses at this point so you can learn about some of the features of the IDE in debug mode. The Try It Out picks up again with step 4.*

The Breakpoints Window

You can display the Breakpoints window, if the tab is not shown, in the bottom-right corner of the IDE by clicking the Breakpoints icon on the Debug toolbar or by selecting Debug Windows Breakpoints. The Breakpoints window shows what line of code the current breakpoint is at, any conditions it has, and the hit count if applicable, as shown in Figure 10-11.

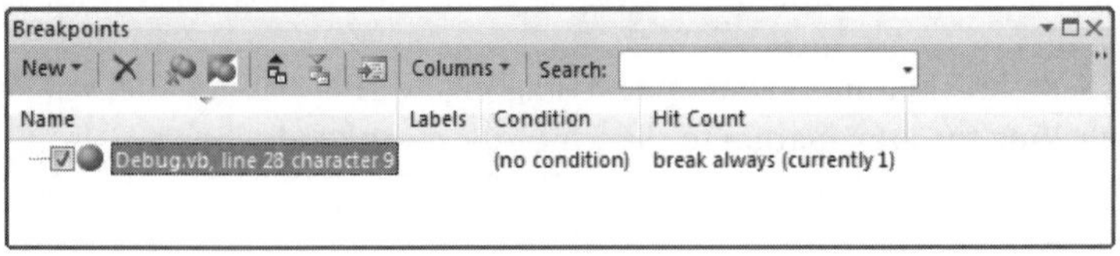

FIGURE 10-11

The Breakpoints window shows all the breakpoints you have set in your code. When a breakpoint is encountered, it is highlighted in both the code and the Breakpoints window, as shown in Figure 10-11. In this window, you can set new breakpoints, delete existing breakpoints, and change the properties of the breakpoints. You will see more of this later in the chapter.

Useful Icons on the Toolbar

In this Try It Out, you want to step through your code line by line. The Standard toolbar in the IDE contains three icons of particular interest to you, shown in Figure 10-12.

FIGURE 10-12

➤ The first icon is the Step Into icon. When you click this icon, you can step through your code line by line. This includes stepping into any function or procedure that the code calls and working through it line by line.

➤ The second icon is the Step Over icon. This works in a similar way to Step Into, but you pass straight over the procedures and functions — they still execute, but all in one go. You then move straight on to the next line in the block of code that called the procedure.

➤ Last is the Step Out icon. This icon enables you to jump to the end of the procedure or function that you are currently in and to move to the line of code *after* the line that called the procedure or function. This is handy when you step into a long procedure and want to get out of it. The rest of the code in the procedure is still executed, but you do not step through it.

There is one more really useful button worth adding to the toolbar: Run To Cursor. The Run To Cursor icon enables you to place your cursor anywhere in the code following the current breakpoint where execution has been paused and then click this icon. The code between the current breakpoint and where the cursor is positioned is executed, and execution stops on the line of code where the cursor is located.

To add this button to the Standard toolbar, right-click any empty area of the toolbar and choose Customize from the context menu. In the Customize dialog box, click the Add Commands button in the Commands tab, and then select Debug in the Categories list. In the Commands list, select Run To Cursor and then click OK. Move the icon down in the Controls list, to form a group of icons as shown in Figure 10-13, and then click the Close button to close the Customize dialog box.

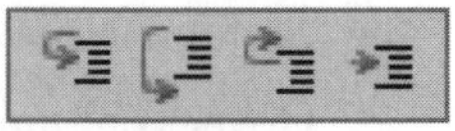

FIGURE 10-13

> **NOTE** *Most of your menu items and toolbar buttons have keyboard shortcuts that are easy to use. For debugging, you can use F8 to Step Into and Shift+F8 to Step Over. The shortcut for Run To Cursor is Ctrl+8.*

You are now ready to continue working through the Try It Out.

Code file Debugging.zip available for download at Wrox.com

4. You ended the last step of the Try It Out at the breakpoint. Before continuing, you want to examine the contents of the string variable, strData. Hover your mouse over the variable to view a Data Tip, as shown in Figure 10-14. Notice that the variable name is listed along with its contents, a magnifying glass, and a down arrow.

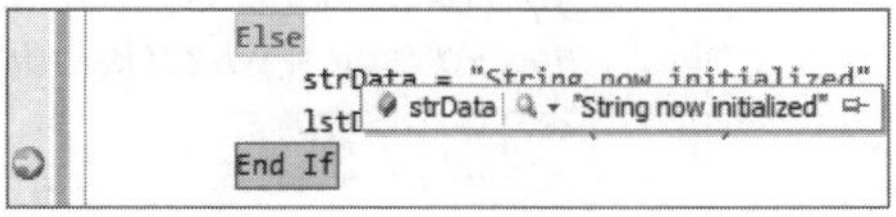

```
        Else
            strData = "String now initialized"
            lstd  strData  🔍 ▾  "String now initialized"  ⊡
        End If
```

FIGURE 10-14

5.   Clicking the contents of the variable in the Data Tip puts you in edit mode for the variable, and you can actually change the contents of that variable. Clicking the magnifying glass will cause the contents of the variable to be displayed automatically in the Text Visualizer dialog box, which is a useful tool for displaying the data for string variables that contain a significant amount of data. Clicking the down arrow provides you with a drop-down list of options for viewing the contents of the variable, including options for Text Visualizer, XML Visualizer, and HTML Visualizer.

6.   At this point, you'll want to test the debugging icons on the toolbar, starting with the Run To Cursor icon first. Place your cursor on the line of code that calls the `ListCustomer` procedure.

Click the Run To Cursor icon on the toolbar. The code between the breakpoint at the `End If` statement shown in Figure 10-14 and the line of code that calls the `ListCustomer` procedure is executed. Your project stops execution on the line of code on which you have your cursor, as shown in Figure 10-15.

```
objCustomerList.Add(New Customer(1001, "Henry For"))
objCustomerList.Add(New Customer(1002, "Orville Wright"))
For Each objCustomer As Customer In objCustomerList
    ListCustomer(objCustomer)
Next
```

FIGURE 10-15

7.   Click the Step Into icon next, and you should now be at the beginning of the `ListCustomer` procedure. Data Tips can be displayed for objects that contain multiple values as well as variables that contain only a single value.

Hover your mouse over the `customerToList` parameter for this procedure to display the Data Tip for this object. You'll see a plus sign next to the object name in the Data Tip. Click the plus sign, or simply hover your mouse over it, and the contents of the object are displayed, as shown in Figure 10-16.

```
Private Sub ListCustomer(ByVal customerToList As Customer)
    lstData.Items.Add(customerToList.Cus
        "-" & customerToList.CustomerN
End Sub

Private Sub btnStart_Click(ByVal sender As Object, _
```

✓ customerToList	{Debugging.Customer}	
CustomerID		1001
CustomerName	⚲ ▾	"Henry For"
intCustomerID		1001
strName	⚲ ▾	"Henry For"

FIGURE 10-16

 NOTE *This Data Tip displays not only the properties in the* `Customer` *class, the class from which the* `customerToList` *object is derived, but also the private variables in that class. You also have the same options for viewing the contents of string variables, which is indicated by the presence of the magnifying glass and down arrow icons.*

Because the text, which is supposed to read `"Henry Ford"`, is misspelled, you want to correct it in the Data Tip. This can be done by editing the `strName` variable in the Data Tip. Click the text `"Henry For"` in the Data Tip to put it into edit mode. Correct the text by adding the letter **d** at the end of the text and then click the name or variable name in the Data Tip. Note that the text for both the property and variable has been updated with your corrections. In addition, note that you can change the contents of `Integer` data types in the Data Tip as well.

8. Click the Step Into icon once more and you should be at the first line of code in the `ListCustomer` procedure.

9. Because you do not want to see any of this code at this time, you are going to step out of this procedure. This places you back at the line of code that called the procedure. Click the Step Out icon. Note that you are taken out of the `ListCustomer` procedure and back to where the call originated.

10. Now click the Step Into icon twice more so that you are back at the call to the `ListCustomer` procedure once again.

11. The final icon to be tested is the Step Over icon. Click this icon now and note that you have totally stepped over the execution of the `ListCustomer` procedure. The procedure was actually executed, but because you chose to step over it, the debugger does not indicate that the procedure was executed.

12. Continue processing as normal and execute the rest of the code without interruption. If you hover your mouse over the Start icon on the toolbar, you will notice that the ToolTip has been changed from Start to Continue. Click this icon to let the rest of the code run or press F5. You should now see your completed form as shown in Figure 10-17.

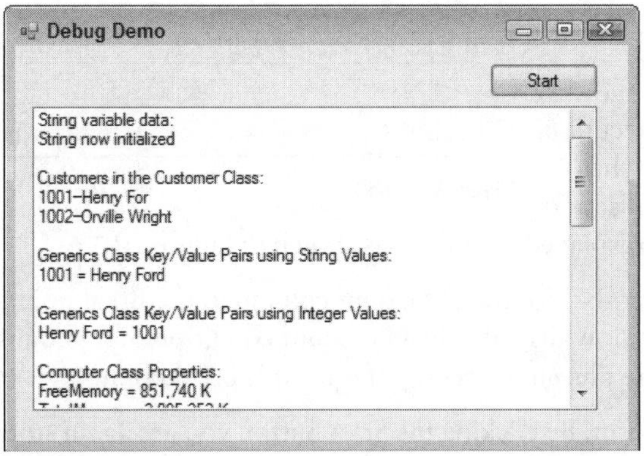

FIGURE 10-17

TRY IT OUT Using the Breakpoint's Hit Count

Code file Debugging.zip available for download from Wrox.com

In this Try It Out, you examine the Breakpoint Hit Count dialog box. The Breakpoint Hit Count dialog box allows you to define the number of executions of a loop that should be performed before the IDE stops execution of your code and puts it into break mode. As previously described, this is useful for processing loops, because you can specify how many iterations the loop should make before you encounter a breakpoint.

1. Stop your project and set a breakpoint in the For loop as shown in Figure 10-18. Remember that to set a breakpoint, you need to click in the gray margin on the line of code where the breakpoint should be.

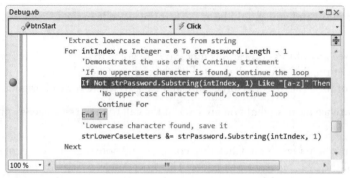

```
Debug.vb
btnStart                              Click
                'Extract lowercase characters from string
                For intIndex As Integer = 0 To strPassword.Length - 1
                    'Demonstrates the use of the Continue statement
                    'If no uppercase character is found, continue the loop
                    If Not strPassword.Substring(intIndex, 1) Like "[a-z]" Then
                        'No upper case character found, continue loop
                        Continue For
                    End If
                    'Lowercase character found, save it
                    strLowerCaseLetters &= strPassword.Substring(intIndex, 1)
                Next
```

FIGURE 10-18

2. Start your project again by clicking the Start icon on the toolbar.

3. In the Breakpoints window, right-click the second breakpoint and choose Hit Count from the context menu to invoke the Breakpoint Hit Count dialog box.

4. The breakpoint that you currently have set halts execution every time it is encountered. Change it to break only when the loop enters its third execution. You do this by selecting the option "break when the hit count is equal to" in the drop-down list and then entering the number **3** in the text box displayed next to it, as shown in Figure 10-19.

Breakpoint Hit Count

A breakpoint is hit when the breakpoint location is reached and the condition is satisfied. The hit count is the number of times the breakpoint has been hit.

When the breakpoint is hit:

break when the hit count is equal to   [3]

Current hit count: 0

[Reset]   [OK]   [Cancel]

FIGURE 10-19

Click the OK button to close this dialog box. Notice the Hit Count column in the Breakpoints window in the IDE. The second breakpoint now displays the Hit Count condition that you just defined. The red circle will now have a white plus in the center of it for this breakpoint.

5. At this point, click the Start button on the form. By clicking the Start button you are again stopped at your first breakpoint.

6. This breakpoint is highlighted in the Breakpoints window. You no longer need this breakpoint, so click it and then click the Delete icon in the Breakpoints window; the breakpoint will be deleted. Your code is still paused at this point, so click the Continue button on the Debug toolbar.

7. You are now stopped at your breakpoint in the For loop as it enters its third execution. Notice that the Breakpoints window shows both the hit count criteria that you selected and the current hit count.

As you can see, this is a handy way to have a loop execute a definite number of iterations before breaking at a defined breakpoint.

8. Now let your code continue executing by clicking the Continue button on the Debug toolbar.

9. Stop your project once the form has been displayed.

TRY IT OUT Changing Breakpoint Properties

Code file Debugging.zip available for download at Wrox.com

In this Try It Out, you modify the properties of the only breakpoint that you have left.

1. In the previous Try It Out, you modified the breakpoint while the project was running. This time you will modify the breakpoint while the project is stopped. To view the Breakpoints window, select Debug ⇨ Windows ⇨ Breakpoints.

2. In the Breakpoints window, right-click the breakpoint and choose Hit Count from the context menu to display the Breakpoint Hit Count dialog box. Notice the Reset button. When you click this button, you reset the hit counter for the next execution, but this is not what you'll do at this point.

3. Change the hit count back to its original setting. Select Break Always in the drop-down box and then click the OK button to close this dialog.

4. To set a specific condition for this breakpoint, right-click the breakpoint and choose Condition from the context menu to invoke the Breakpoint Condition dialog box. Enter the condition as shown in Figure 10-20. This causes this breakpoint to break only when the variable intIndex is equal to 3. Note that you could also specify that the breakpoint be activated when the value of a variable changes. Click the OK button to close the dialog box and then start your project.

5. Click the Start button on your form. Once the intIndex variable is equal to 3, the breakpoint is activated and execution of the code is paused at the line where the breakpoint is specified. This is actually your fourth time into the loop, as the For ... Next loop specifies a starting index of 0 for the variable intIndex.

6. Finally, let your code finish executing by clicking the Continue button on the Debug toolbar. Once your form is displayed, stop your project.

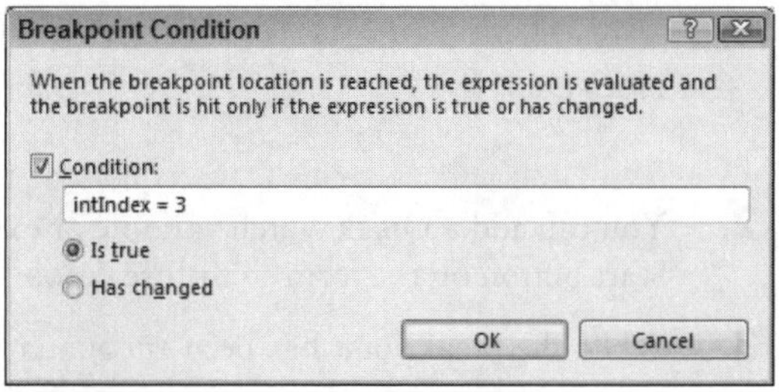

FIGURE 10-20

Debugging Using the Watch Window and QuickWatch Dialog Box

The Watch window provides a method for you to observe variables and expressions easily while the code is executing — this can be invaluable when you are trying to debug unwanted results in a variable. You can even change the values of variables in the Watch window. You can also add as many variables and expressions as needed to debug your program. This provides a mechanism for watching the values of your variables change without any intervention on your part. This is an easy place to watch many variables.

The QuickWatch dialog box is best for watching a single variable or expression. You can add or delete variables or expressions in the QuickWatch dialog box only when your program is in break mode.

Therefore, before you run your program, you need to set a breakpoint before the variable or expression that you want to watch. When the breakpoint has been reached, you can add as many Watch variables or expressions as needed.

TRY IT OUT **Using QuickWatch**

Code file Debugging.zip available from Wrox.com

In this Try It Out, you add the `intIndex` variable to the Watch window and add an expression using the `intIndex` variable. This enables you to observe this variable and expression as you step through your code.

1. Start your program again. When your form displays, switch to the IDE and clear the current breakpoint by deleting it in the Breakpoints window or by clicking it in the gray margin where it is set. Then set a new breakpoint, as shown in Figure 10-21.

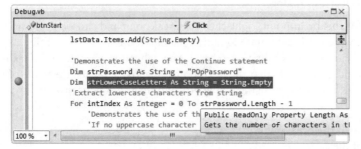

```
Debug.vb
btnStart                          Click

        lstData.Items.Add(String.Empty)

        'Demonstrates the use of the Continue statement
        Dim strPassword As String = "POpPassword"
        Dim strLowerCaseLetters As String = String.Empty
        'Extract lowercase characters from string
        For intIndex As Integer = 0 To strPassword.Length - 1
            'Demonstrates the use of th   Public ReadOnly Property Length As
            'If no uppercase character    Gets the number of characters in t
100 %
```

FIGURE 10-21

2. You can add a QuickWatch variable or expression only while your program is paused. Click the Start button on the form so the breakpoint will be encountered and your program paused.

3. When the breakpoint has been encountered, right-click the variable, `intIndex`, in the `For ... Next` loop and choose Expression: 'intIndex' and then QuickWatch from the context menu to invoke the QuickWatch dialog box. Note that this variable has not only been added to the Expression drop-down box but has also been placed in the current value grid in the dialog, as shown in Figure 10-22. Click the Add Watch button to add this variable to the Watch window.

QuickWatch

Expression:
intIndex

Reevaluate

Add Watch

Value:

Name	Value	Type
intIndex	Name 'intIndex' is not declared.	

Close   Help

FIGURE 10-22

> **NOTE** *Because the variable is declared in the* For ... Next *loop, you see an error here. You can safely ignore this error because once the loop has started processing, the variable will be declared.*

4. While you have the QuickWatch dialog open, set an expression to be evaluated. Type the expression **intIndex = 1** in the Expression drop-down box. Then click the Add Watch button to have this expression added to the Watch window. Close the QuickWatch dialog by clicking the Close button.

5. If you do not see the Watch window at the bottom of the IDE, select Debug ➪ Windows ➪ Watch ➪ Watch 1. You should see a variable and an expression in the Watch window, as shown in Figure 10-23.

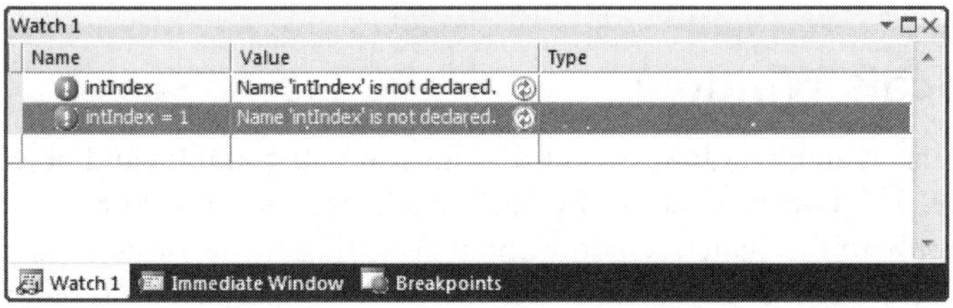

FIGURE 10-23

The second watch expression that you added here returns a value of `True` when the `intIndex` variable equals 1, so Visual Studio 2010 sets the type to `Boolean` once you enter the `For . . . Next` loop.

6. Step through your code line by line so that you can watch the value of the variable and expression change. Click the Step Into icon on the Debug toolbar to step to the next line of code. Keep clicking the Step Into icon to see the values of the variable and expression in the Watch window change.

> **NOTE** *As you step through the loop in your code, you continue to see the value for the `intIndex` variable change in the Watch window. When the value of the variable in the Watch window turns the color red, as shown in Figure 10-24 (although you will not see it in the black and white image well), the value has just been changed. You can manually change the value at any time by entering a new value in the Value column in the Watch window.*

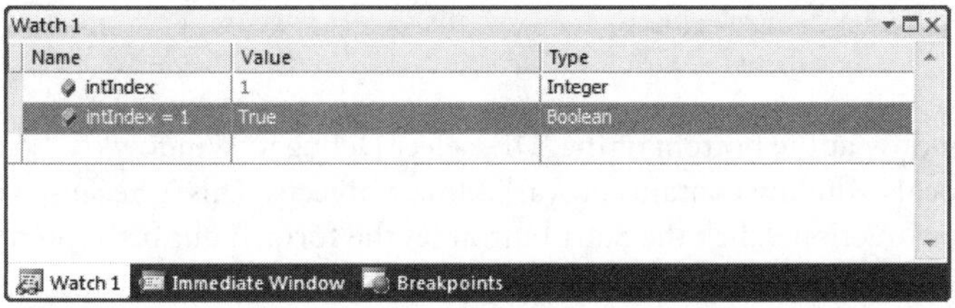

FIGURE 10-24

7. When you are done, click the Continue icon on the Debug toolbar to let your code finish executing. Then stop your project once the form has been displayed.

Debugging with the Autos Window

The Autos window is similar to the Watch window, except that it shows all variables and objects, the current statement and the three statements before and after the current statement. The Autos window also lets you change the value of a variable or object, and the same rules that apply to the Watch window apply here (that is, the program must be paused before a value can be changed). The text for a value that has just changed also turns red, making it easy to spot the variable or object that was changed.

Debugging with the Locals Window

The Locals window is similar to the Watch window, except that it shows all variables and objects for the current function or procedure. The Locals window also lets you change the value of a variable or object, and the same rules that apply to the Watch window apply here (that is, the program must be paused before a value can be changed). The text for a value that has just changed also turns red, making it easy to spot the variable or object that was changed.

The Locals window is great if you want a quick glance at everything that is going on in a function or procedure, but it is not very useful for watching the values of one or two variables or expressions. That's because the Locals window contains all variables and objects in a procedure or function. Therefore, if you have a lot of variables and objects, you have to scroll through the window constantly to view them. This is where the Locals window comes in handy; it enables you to observe just the variables that you need. You learned about the Watch window in the previous example.

> **TRY IT OUT** Using the Locals Window

Code file Debugging.zip available for download at Wrox.com

In this Try It Out, you examine the contents of the Locals window in two different procedures. This demonstrates how the contents of the Locals window changes from one procedure to the next.

1. To prepare for this exercise, you need to have the current breakpoint set and set a new breakpoint in the `ListCustomer` procedure. Locate the `ListCustomer` procedure and set a breakpoint on the one line of code in that procedure:

```
lstData.Items.Add(customerToList.CustomerID & _
    "-" & customerToList.CustomerName)
```

2. Now start your program.

3. If you do not see the Locals window at the bottom of the IDE, select Debug ➪ Windows ➪ Locals. Notice that at this point the Locals window contains no variables or objects. This is because you have not entered a procedure or function. Click the Start button on the form. Your breakpoint in the `ListCustomer` procedure is encountered first and execution is paused.

4. Notice the various objects and their types listed in the Locals window. The first item in the list is `Me`, which is the form itself. If you expand this item, you see all the objects and controls associated with your form. If you expand the `customerToList` object, you'll see the properties and variables defined in the `Customer` class, as shown in Figure 10-25.

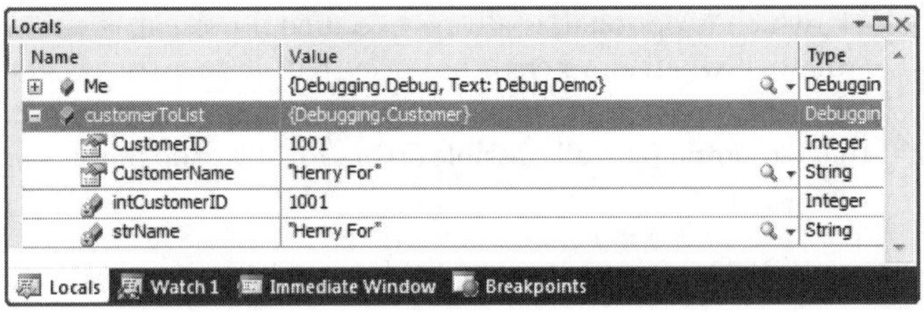

FIGURE 10-25

5. Click the Continue icon on the Debug toolbar until you encounter your second breakpoint.

6. Take a look at the Locals window. You should see a different set of objects and variables. The one constant item in both procedures is Me, which is associated with the form.

7. If you step through a couple of lines of code in the loop where the breakpoint has paused your program, you see the values in the Locals window change. You can continue to step through your code, or you can click the Continue icon on the Debug toolbar to let your program run to completion.

> **NOTE** *After you change your build configuration from Debug to Release, debugging is no longer available; even if you have breakpoints set in your code, they will not be encountered.*

8. To clear all breakpoints in your code, you can delete each breakpoint in the Breakpoints window or you can click the Debug menu and choose Delete All Breakpoints. When you are done, stop your project.

ERROR HANDLING

Error handling is an essential part of any good code. In Visual Basic 2010, the error mechanism is based on the concept of *exceptions* that can be *thrown* to raise an error and *caught* when the error is handled. If you do not provide any type of error handling and an error occurs, your user receives a message about an unhandled exception, which is provided by the CLR, and then the program may terminate, depending on the type of error encountered. This is not a user-friendly message and does not inform the user about the true nature of the error or how to resolve it. The unhandled exception could also cause users to lose the data that they were working with or leave the user and the data in an unknown state.

Visual Studio 2010 provides *structured error-handling* statements that are common across all languages. Structured error handling is a way to organize blocks of code in a structure that handles errors. In this section you examine structured error handling and how it can be incorporated into your programs with very little effort.

Structured error handling in Visual Basic 2010 is incorporated with the Try... Catch... Finally block. You execute the code that might throw an exception in the Try block, and you handle anticipated errors in the `Catch` block. The `Finally` block, which is optional, is always executed if present; it enables you to place any cleanup code there regardless of whether an error has occurred. If an error occurs that was not handled in the `Catch` block, the CLR displays its standard error message and terminates your program. Therefore, it is important to try to anticipate all possible errors for the code that is contained in the `Try` block.

Take a look at the syntax for the `Try ... Catch ... Finally` statement:

```
Try
    [try statements]
    [Exit Try]
Catch exceptionvariable As exceptiontype
    [catch statements]
    [Exit Try]
  [Additional Catch blocks]
Finally
    [finally statements]
End Try
```

➤   The [try statements] are the statements to be executed that may cause an error.

➤   The exceptionvariable can be any variable name. It will be set to contain the value of the error that is thrown.

➤   The exceptiontype specifies the exception class type to which the exception belongs. If this type is not supplied, your `Catch` block handles any exception defined in the `System.Exception` class. This argument enables you to specify the type of exception that you may be looking for. An example of a specific exception is `IOException`, which is used when performing any type of I/O (input/output) against a file.

➤   The [catch statements] handle and process the error that has occurred.

➤   The [finally statements] are executed after all other processing has occurred.

➤   The optional `Exit Try` statement enables you to completely break out of a `Try ... Catch ... Finally` block and resume execution of code immediately following the `Try ... Catch ... Finally` block. You can have multiple `Catch` blocks, meaning that you can test for multiple errors with different exception types within the same `Try` block. When an error occurs among the `Try` statements, control is passed to the appropriate `Catch` block for processing.

When you define a `Catch` block, you can specify a variable name for the exception and define the type of exception you want to catch, as shown in the following code fragment. This code defines an exception variable named `IOExceptionErr`, and the type of exception is an `IOException`. This example traps any type of I/O exception that may occur when processing files, and stores the error information in an object named `IOExceptionErr`:

```
Catch IOExceptionErr As IOException
    ..
    code to handle the exception goes here
    ..
```

When dealing with mathematical expressions, you can define and catch the various errors that you may encounter, such as a divide-by-zero exception. You can also catch errors such as overflow errors, which may occur when multiplying two numbers and trying to place the result in a variable that is too small for the result. However, in cases such as these it may be better to check for problems in advance — you should use exceptions only in exceptional circumstances.

When testing `Try ... Catch` statements, you can cause an error by using the `Throw` keyword inside the `Try` statement. To throw a new error, use the following syntax:

```
Throw New FileNotFoundException()
```

Inside of `Catch` statements, you can raise an error that has occurred back up to the caller. To throw an error back up to the caller, use the following syntax, which will allow the caller to handle the actual error:

```
Throw
```

Using Structured Error Handling

In the following Try It Out you add some structured error handling to the sample program with which you have been working. When you first ran the Debugging project, you received the `NullReferenceException` that was shown in Figure 10-8 because you tried to access the properties of the `strData` string variable before it had been set. This code is a prime candidate for structured error handling. You temporarily bypassed the problem at that point by using an `If ... Then ... Else` statement to first see whether the variable had been initialized. Another way to handle such a case is in a `Try ... Catch` block.

TRY IT OUT Structured Error Handling

In this example, you will update your code to handle the null check with a `Try...Catch` statement versus an `If...Then` statement.

Code file Debugging.zip available for download at Wrox.com

1. Modify the code for the `strData` variable in the `btnStart_Click` procedure as shown:

```
lstData.Items.Add("String variable data:")
Try
    If strData.Length > 0 Then
        lstData.Items.Add(strData)
    End If
Catch NullReferenceExceptionErr As NullReferenceException
    strData = "String now initialized"
    lstData.Items.Add(strData)
End Try
```

How It Works

The code you entered contains a `Try` block and a `Catch` block. You opt not to use the `Finally` block in this error-handling routine because the `Catch` block performs the necessary code to set the `strData` variable, and have the contents of that variable added to the list box on your form:

```
Try
    If strData.Length > 0 Then
```

```
            lstData.Items.Add(strData)
        End If
    Catch NullReferenceExceptionErr As NullReferenceException
        strData = "String now initialized"
        lstData.Items.Add(strData)
    End Try
```

When you try to access the `Length` property of the `strData` variable in the `Try` block, a `NullReference Exception` exception is thrown because the variable has been declared but not set.

The error that you want to trap is a `NullReferenceException`, and that exception is specified in the `Catch` block. You defined the variable `NullReferenceExceptionErr` for the exception variable argument; the standard practice among most developers is to use the exception name along with a suffix of `Err`. You then defined the type of exception that you want to test for and trap.

You place your error-handling code within the `Catch` block, as you have done here. When a `NullReferenceException` occurs, you set the `strData` variable to a string constant and then add the contents of that variable to the list box on your form.

TRY IT OUT **Testing Your Error Handler**

In the final example for this chapter, you use the `Watch Window` to make sure your `Try ... Catch` statement is working.

Code file Debugging.zip available for download at Wrox.com

1. Set a breakpoint on the `Try` statement and then run your project. Once the form is displayed, click the Start button.

2. Once the breakpoint is encountered, right-click the variable `strData` and add a Watch from the context menu. Click the Watch1 window so that you can view the contents of the variable.

3. At this point, the `strData` variable has a value of `Nothing`. Click the Step Into icon on the toolbar; you'll be taken to the first line of code in the `Try` block.

4. Click the Step Into icon again. A `NullReferenceException` is thrown, and you are taken to the `Catch` block.

5. Note the value of the variable in the Watch1 window, click the Step Into icon twice more, and note the value of the variable in the Watch1 window (see Figure 10-26).

6. Click the Continue icon on the toolbar to allow the rest of your code to run.

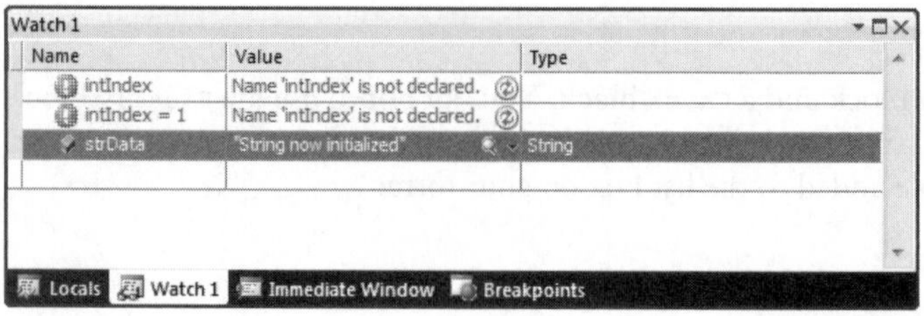

Name	Value	Type
intIndex	Name 'intIndex' is not declared. ②	
intIndex = 1	Name 'intIndex' is not declared. ②	
strData	"String now initialized"	String

Locals | Watch 1 | Immediate Window | Breakpoints

FIGURE 10-26

How It Works

As you become more familiar with the types of errors that can occur, you will be able to write more sophisticated structured error handlers. This comes only with experience and testing. You will discover more errors and will be able to handle them only by thoroughly testing your code. The online documentation for most methods that you use in Visual Studio 2010 will have Exceptions sections that list and explain the possible exceptions that could occur by using the method.

SUMMARY

This chapter covered some useful debugging tools that are built into the Visual Studio 2010 development environment. You saw how easy it is to debug your programs as you stepped through the various Try It Out sections.

In the discussion of breakpoints, you learned how to stop the execution of your program at any given point. As useful as this is, setting breakpoints with a hit counter in a loop is even more useful, because you can execute a loop several times before encountering a breakpoint in the loop.

You also examined some of the various windows available while debugging your program, such as the Watch window and the Locals window. These windows provide you with valuable information about the variables and expressions in your program. You can watch the values change and are able to change the values to control the execution of your code.

You should know what types of major errors you may encounter while developing and debugging your code, and you should be able to recognize syntax and execution errors, correcting them if possible. Although debugging a program for logic errors may be difficult at first, it does become easier with time and experience.

This chapter also covered structured error handling, and you should incorporate this knowledge into your programs at every opportunity. Structured error handling provides you with the opportunity to handle and correct errors at runtime.

To summarize, you should know:

- ➤ How to recognize and correct major types of errors
- ➤ How to use breakpoints successfully to debug your program
- ➤ How to use the Locals and Watch windows to see and change variables and expressions
- ➤ How to use structured error handling

1. What window do you use to track a specific variable while debugging?

2. How do you look at all of the variables in scope while debugging?

3. How do you best add error handling to your code?

4. Sometimes you need to cause errors to happen in your code. What keyword do you use to cause errors?

5. While debugging, how do you move to the very next statement?

► **WHAT YOU HAVE LEARNED IN THIS CHAPTER**

TOPIC	CONCEPTS
Major Types of Errors	Syntax, Execution and Logic Errors
Error handling	Use `Try ... Catch ... Finally` statements to handle exceptions that are raised or thrown from your code. The `Finally` block always executes.
Breakpoints	Use breakpoints to stop execution of your code at a certain spot to debug.
Debugging	Step Into, Step Over, Step Out, Run, and Run To Cursor are common commands you will use to debug your program. You will use the Watch Window, QuickWatch Dialog, Locals Window and Autos Windows to aid your debugging.

11

Building Objects

WHAT YOU WILL LEARN IN THIS CHAPTER:

➤ Building a reusable object with methods and properties

➤ Inheriting the object that you build in another object

➤ Overriding methods and properties in your base object

➤ Creating your own namespace

You may have heard the term *object oriented* a lot since you first started using computers. You may also have heard that it is a scary and tricky subject to understand. In its early years it was, but today's modern tools and languages make object orientation (OO) a wonderfully easy-to-understand concept that brings massive benefits to software developers. This is mainly because languages such as Visual Basic and C# have matured to a point where they make creating objects and the programs that use them very easy indeed. With these languages, you will have no problem understanding even the most advanced object-oriented concepts and will be able to use them to build exciting object-based applications.

You have been using objects and classes throughout this book, but in this chapter you look at object orientation in detail and build on the foundations of the previous chapters to start producing some cool applications using Visual Basic 2010.

UNDERSTANDING OBJECTS

An object is almost anything you can think of. We work with physical objects all the time: televisions, cars, customers, reports, light bulbs — anything. In computer terms, an object is a representation of a thing that you want to manipulate in your application. Sometimes, the two definitions map exactly onto each other. So, if you have a physical car object sitting in your driveway and want to describe it in software terms, you build a software Car object that sits in your computer.

Likewise, if you need to write a piece of software that generates a bill for a customer, you may well have a `Bill` object and a `Customer` object. The `Customer` object represents the customer and may be capable of having a name, address, and also have the capability to generate the bill. The `Bill` object would represent an instance of a bill for a customer and would be able to impart the details of the bill and may also have the capability to print itself.

What is important here is the concept that the object has the intelligence to produce actions related to it — the `Customer` object can generate the bill. In effect, if you have a `Customer` object representing a customer, you can simply say to it: "Produce a bill for me." The `Customer` object would then go away and do all the hard work related to creating the bill. Likewise, when you have a `Bill` object, you can say to it: "Print yourself." What you have here are two examples of object *behavior*.

Objects are unbelievably useful because they turn software engineering into something conceptually similar to wooden building blocks. You arrange the blocks (the objects) to build something greater than the sum of the parts. The power of objects comes from the fact that, as someone using objects, you don't need to understand how they work behind the scenes. You're familiar with this concept with real-world objects too. When you use a mobile phone, you don't need to understand how it works inside. Even if you do understand how a mobile phone works inside — even if you made it yourself — it's still much easier to use the mobile phone's simple interface. The interface can also prevent you from accidentally doing something that breaks the phone. The same is true with computer objects. Even if you build all the objects yourself, having the complicated workings hidden behind a simple interface can make your life much easier and safer.

Object orientation is perhaps best explained by using a television metaphor. Look at the television in your home. There are several things you know how to do with it:

➤   Watch the image on the screen

➤   Change channel

➤   Change volume

➤   Switch it on or off

What you don't have to do is understand how everything works to allow you to carry out these activities. If asked, most people couldn't put together the components needed to make a modern television. We could, with a little research and patience, come up with something fairly basic, but nothing as complex as the one sitting in my home. However, we do understand how to use a television. We know how to change the channel, change the volume, switch it on and off, and so on.

Objects in software engineering work in basically the same way. When you have an object, you can use it and ask it do things without having to understand how the internals of it actually work. This is phenomenally powerful, as you'll see soon.

Software objects typically have the following characteristics:

➤   **Identity:** *User:* "What are you?" *TV:* "I'm a TV."

➤   **State:** *User:* "What channel am I watching?" *TV:* "You're watching Channel 4."

➤   **Behavior:** User: "Please turn up the volume to 50%." Then, we can use the State again. User: "How loud is the volume?" TV: "50%."

Encapsulation

The core concept behind object oriented programming (OO) is *encapsulation*. This is a big word, but it's very simple to understand. What this means is that the functionality is wrapped up in a self-contained manner and that you don't need to understand what it's actually doing when you ask it to do something.

If you remember from Chapter 3, you built a function that calculated the area of a circle. In that function, you encapsulated the logic of calculating the area in such a way that anyone using the function could find the area without having to know how to perform the operation. This is the same concept but taken to the next level.

Methods and Properties

You interact with objects through methods and properties. These can be defined as follows:

➤ *Methods* are ways of instructing an object to do something.

➤ *Properties* are things that describe features of an object.

A method was defined previously as a self-contained block of code that does something. This is true, but it is a rather simplistic definition. In fact, the strict definition of a method applies only to OO and is a way to manipulate an object — a way to instruct it to perform certain behaviors. In previous chapters you created methods that instructed an object — in most cases a form — to do something. When you create a form in Visual Basic 2010, you are actually defining a new type of Form object.

So, if you need to turn on the TV, you need to find a method that does this, because a method is something you get the object to do. When you invoke the method, the object itself is supposed to understand what to do to satisfy the request. To drive the point home, you don't care what it actually does; you just say, "Switch on." It's up to the TV to switch on relays to deliver power, boot up the circuitry, warm up the electron gun, and all the other things that you don't need to understand!

> **NOTE** *On the other hand, if you need to change the channel, you might set the* Channel *property. If you want to tune into Channel 10, you set the* Channel *property to the value 10. Again, the object is responsible for reacting to the request; you don't care about the technical hoops it has to go through to do that.*

Events

In Visual Basic 2010 you listen for events to determine when something has happened to a control on a form. You can consider an event as something that an object does. In effect, someone using an object can listen to events, like a Click event on a button or a PowerOn event on a TV. When the event is received, the developer can take some action. In OO terms, there is the SwitchOn method that gets invoked on the TV object; when the TV has warmed up (some old TVs take ages to warm up), it raises a PowerOn event. You could then respond to this event by adjusting the volume to the required level.

An event might also be used when the performer of an action is not the only entity interested in the action taking place. For example, when you have the TV on, you might go and get a drink during a commercial break. However, while you're in the kitchen, you keep your ears open for when the program starts again. Effectively, you are listening for a `ProgramResume` event. You do not cause the program to resume, but you do want to know when it does.

Visibility

To build decent objects you have to make them easy for other developers to use. For example, internally it might be really important for your TV object to know what frequency the tuner needs, but does the person using the TV care? More important, do you actually want the developer to be able to change this frequency directly? What you're trying to do is make the object more *abstract*.

Some parts of your object will be private, whereas other parts will be public. The public interface is available for others to use. The private parts are what you expect the object itself to use internally. The logic for the object exists in the private parts, and may include methods and properties that are important but won't get called from outside the object. For example, a TV object might have methods for `ConnectPower`, `WarmUp`, and so on. These would be private and would all be called from the public `SwitchOn` method. Similarly, while there is a public `Channel` property, there will probably be a private `Frequency` property. The TV could not work without knowing the signal frequency it was receiving, but the users are only interested in the channel.

Now that you understand the basics of object orientation, take a look at how you can use objects within an application.

You'll notice that some of the code samples you saw in previous chapters included a line that looked similar to this:

```
lstData.Items.Add(strData)
```

That's a classic example of object orientation! `lstData` is, in fact, an object. `Items` is a property of the `lstData` object. The `Items` property is an object in its own right and has an `Add` method. The period (`.`) tells Visual Basic 2010 that the word to the right is a *member* of the word to the left. So, `Items` is a member of `lstData`, and `Add` is a member of `Items`. Members are either properties or methods of an object.

`lstData` is an instance of a class called `System.Windows.Forms.ListBox` (or just `ListBox`). This class is part of the .NET Framework you learned about in Chapter 2.

The `ListBox` class can display a list of items on the form and let a user choose a particular one. Again, here's the concept of encapsulation. As a user of `ListBox`, you don't need to know anything about the technologies involved in displaying the list or listening for input. You may not have even heard of GDI+, stdin, keyboard drivers, display drivers, or anything else that's part of the complex action of displaying a list on a form, yet you still have the capability to do it.

The `ListBox` is an example of an object that you can see. Users can look at a program running and know that a `ListBox` is involved. Most objects in OO programming are invisible and represent something in memory.

What Is a Class?

A *class* is the definition of a particular kind of object. The class is made up of the software code needed to store and retrieve the values of the properties, carry out the methods, and undergo the events pertaining to that kind of object. This is effectively the circuitry inside the black box. If you want to build a software object, you have to understand how the internals work. You express those internals with Visual Basic 2010 code. So, when the software developer using your object says, "Turn up the volume," you have to know how to instruct the amplifier to increase the output. (As a side note, remember that the amplifier is just another object. You don't necessarily need to know how it works inside. In OO programming, you will often find that one object is made up of other objects with some code to link them — just as a TV is made of standard components and a bit of custom circuitry.)

Each object belonging to a class is an *instance* of the class. So, if you have 50 TV objects, you have 50 instances of the TV class. The action of creating an instance is called *instantiation*. From now on, we won't say that you *create classes* but that you *instantiate objects*. The difference is used to reduce ambiguity. Creating a class is done at design time when you're building your software and involves writing the actual code. Instantiating an object is done at run time, when your program is being used.

A classic analogy is the cookie cutter. You can go out to your workshop and form a piece of metal into the shape of a Christmas tree. You do this once and put the cutter in a drawer in your kitchen. Whenever you need to create Christmas tree cookies, you roll some dough (the computer's memory) and stamp out however many you need. In effect you're instantiating cookies. You can reuse the cutter later to create more cookies, each the same shape as the ones before.

When you've instantiated the objects, you can manipulate each object's properties defined for the class, and you can invoke the methods defined for the class on the object. For example, suppose you build a class once at design time that represents a television. You can instantiate the class twice to make two objects from that class — say, one to represent the TV in the living room and one to represent the TV in the bedroom. Because both instances of the object share the same class, both instances have the same properties and methods. To turn on either TV you invoke the `SwitchOn` method on it. To change the channel you set its `Channel` property, and so on.

BUILDING CLASSES

You have already started building classes, particularly in Chapters 5 and 10. In general, when you design an algorithm, you will discover certain objects described. You need to abstract these real-world objects into a software representation. Here's an example:

1. Select a list of 10 customers from the database.

2. Go through each customer and prepare a bill for each.

3. When each bill has been prepared, print it.

For a pure object-oriented application (and with .NET you end up using objects to represent everything) every real-world object needs a software object. For example:

➤ `Customer`: An object that represents a customer.

➤ `Bill`: An object that represents a bill that is produced.

➤ `Printer`: An object that represents a hardware printer that can be used to print the bill.

When you write software in Visual Basic 2010, you are given a vast set of classes called the Microsoft .NET Framework classes. These classes describe virtually everything about the computing environment for which you're trying to write software. Writing object-oriented software for .NET is simply a matter of using objects that fit your needs and creating new objects if required. Typically, while building an application, some of the classes you need are included in the .NET Framework, whereas you have to build others yourself.

For example, some objects in the .NET Framework provide printing functionality and database access functionality. As your algorithm calls for both kinds of functionality, you don't need to write your own. If you need to print something, you create an object that understands how to print, tell it what you want to print, and then tell it to print it. Again, this is encapsulation — you don't care how to turn your document into PostScript commands and send it down the wire to the printer; the object knows how to do this for itself. In this example, there are classes that deal with printing that you can use to print bills, although there's no specific `Printer` object.

In some cases, objects that you need to represent do not exist in the .NET Framework. In this example, you need a `Customer` object and a `Bill` object.

REUSABILITY

Perhaps the hardest aspect of object-oriented programming is understanding how to divide responsibility for the work. One of the most beautiful aspects of object orientation is *code reuse*. Imagine that your company needs several different applications: one to display customer bills, one to register a new customer, and one to track customer complaints. In each of those applications, you need to have a `Customer` object.

To simplify the issue, those three projects are not going to be undertaken simultaneously. You start by doing the first; when finished, you move on to the second; when you've finished that, you move on to the third. Do you want to build a new `Customer` class for each project, or do you want to build the class once and reuse it in each of the other two projects?

Reuse is typically regarded as something that's universally good, although there is a trade-off. Ideally, if you build a `Customer` class for one project, and another project you're working on calls for another `Customer` class, then you should use the same one. However, it may well be that you can't just plug the class into another project for some reason. We say "for some reason" because there are no hard-and-fast rules when it comes to class design and reuse. It may also be easier or more cost-effective to build simple classes for each project, rather than try to create one complex object that does everything. This might sound like it requires a degree in clairvoyance, but luckily it comes with experience! As you develop more and more applications, you'll gain a better understanding of how to design great, reusable objects.

Each object should be responsible for activities involving itself and no more. We've discussed only two objects — `Bill` and `Customer` — so you'll look only at those.

The activity of printing a bill (say, for telephone charges) follows this algorithm:

➤ For a given customer, find the call details for the last period.

➤ Go through each call and calculate the price of each one.

➤ Aggregate the cost of each call into a total.

➤ Apply tax charges.

➤ Print out the bill with the customer's name, address, and bill summary on the first page, and then the bill details on subsequent pages.

You have only two places where you can code this algorithm: the `Bill` object or the `Customer` object. Which one do you choose?

The calls made are really a property of the `Customer`. Basically, you are using these details to create a bill. Most of the functionality would be placed in the `Bill` object. A `Customer` is responsible for representing a customer, not representing a bill. When you create a `Bill` object, you would associate it with a particular customer by using a `Cust` property, like this:

```
myBill.Cust = myCustomer
```

The `Bill` object would then know that it was a bill for a given customer (represented by the `myCustomer` object) and could use the customer's details when creating a bill. You might want to change some other properties of the `Bill`, such as to where it will be mailed, whether it should contain a warning because it is overdue, and so on. Finally, the `Bill` would have a `Print` method:

```
myBill.Print()
```

The `Bill` object would then *use* a `Printer` object in order to print the bill. The `Bill` object would be said to be the user or *consumer* of the `Printer` object. It would even be said to consume the `Printer` object, even though (at least you hope) the printer is not used up or destroyed in printing the bill.

DESIGNING AN OBJECT

Contrary to what's been said so far, in this first project you're not going to define an algorithm and then build objects to support it. For this rather academic example, you're going to walk through some of the features of a typical object — in this case, a car.

There are certain facts you might want to know about the object:

What it looks like: A car includes things like make, model, color, number of doors, and so on. These aspects of the car rarely change during the object's lifetime.

Its capabilities: Horsepower, engine size, cylinder configuration, and so on

What it's doing: Whether it's stationary, moving forward or backward, and its speed and direction

Where it is: The Global Positioning System (GPS) coordinates of its current position. This is effectively its position relative to another object (the planet Earth).

> **NOTE** *Controls on forms have coordinates that describe their location relative to the form (say, in pixels to the right of and below the top left corner).*

You might also want to be able to control the object — for example:

➤ Tell it to accelerate.

➤ Tell it to decelerate.

➤ Tell it to turn left.

➤ Tell it to turn right.

➤ Tell it to straighten out of a turn.

➤ Tell it to do a three-point turn.

➤ Tell it to stop completely.

As described earlier, there are three concepts about objects that you need to be aware of: identity, state, and behavior. You should assume that identity is covered because you know what the class is, so the state and behavior are of interest here.

State

State describes facts about the object now. For example, a car's location and speed are part of its state. When designing objects, you need to think about what aspects of state you need to handle. It might not be useful to know a customer's speed, for example, but you might well want to know that customer's current address.

State tends to be implemented as values inside an object. Some of these values are publicly available through properties, and some are private. Also, some aspects of state might be publicly readable but not changeable. For example, cars have a speedometer that is readable to anybody using the car. But you can't change the car's speed by playing with the speedometer — you need to alter the car's behavior by using the brake or accelerator.

Behavior

While a car might have a read-only Speed property, it would have methods to accelerate and decelerate. When you invoke an object's method, you are telling your object to do something — so behavior is usually associated with methods. Properties can also be associated with behavior. When you set a property to a particular value (such as by changing the setting of a control), you can trigger behavior.

Behavior is implemented as a set of Visual Basic 2010 statements that do something. This usually involves one or both of the following:

Changing its own state: When you invoke the Accelerate method on a car, it should get faster if it is capable of doing so.

Somehow affecting the world outside the object: This could be manipulating other objects in the application, displaying something to the user, saving something to a disk, or printing a document.

In this chapter, you won't build all of the properties and methods discussed. Instead, you'll build a handful of the more interesting ones. You begin in the following Try It Out by creating a new class.

TRY IT OUT   Creating a New Project and the Car Class

Code file Objects.zip is available for download at Wrox.com

In this example, you will create a simple Car class.

To learn how to add a class to a project, follow these simple steps:

1.   Start Visual Basic 2010 and select File ⇨ Add ⇨ New Project from the menu.

2. When the Add New Project dialog box appears, select the Console Application template and enter the name of the project as **Objects**. Click OK to create the project.

3. You now need to create a new class. This is done through the Solution Explorer, so right-click the Objects project and select Add ⇨ Class. When prompted for a new class name, enter **Car.vb** and click Add. The new class is added to the Solution Explorer and the editor now shows the code listing for it, albeit empty.

How It Works

In this example you learned how to add a class to a project. This is the first step in creating your own custom objects.

Storing State

State describes what the object understands about itself, so if you give a Car object some state — for example, "You are blue" — you're giving the car object a fact: "The car I represent is blue."

How do you actually manage state in your classes? State is typically held in variables, and you define those variables within the class. You will see how to do this in a moment.

Usually, the methods and properties you build will either affect or use the state in some way. Imagine you've built a property that changes the color of the car. When you *set* that property, the variable that's responsible for storing the state is changed to reflect the new value that it has been given. When you retrieve (*get*) that property, the variable responsible for storing the state is read and the current value is returned to the caller.

In a way, then, properties *are* behaviors. Under the hood, a public property has two methods: a Get method and a Set method (defined by Get ... End Get and Set ... End Set blocks of code, as you have already encountered in Chapter 5). A simple Get method for the Color property contains code to tell the caller the color of the car. A simple Set method for the Color property sets a value that represents the car's color. In a real application, though, Color would probably mean something more than just remembering a value. In a driving game, for example, the Set method of the Color property would need to make the screen display change the color in which the car is shown on the screen.

When a property has no behavior at all, you can cheat. In the next Try It Out, you create a Color property by declaring a Color variable and making it public. When a property is implemented like this, it is also called a *field*. Although this can be a useful and very fast technique for adding properties, declaring a field instead of the Property, Get, and Set blocks is not actually recommended, but for this small example it is just fine.

TRY IT OUT   Creating an Object and Adding a Color Property

Code file Objects.zip is available for download at Wrox.com

This example will teach you how to create a field or a property without a Get and Set block. Be sure to use the class you created in the preceding example.

1. In the `Car` class, add this code below the `Public Car Class` statement:

   ```
   Public Color As String
   ```

2. That's it! However, you do need a way to consume the class so that you can see it working. Open `Module1.vb` and add this code:

   ```
   Sub Main()
           `Create a new car object
           Dim objCar As New Car

           `Set the Color property to Red
           objCar.Color = `Red"

           `Show what the value of the property is
           Console.WriteLine(`My car is this color:")
           Console.WriteLine(objCar.Color)

           `Wait for input from the user
           Console.ReadLine()
   End Sub
   ```

3. Save your project by clicking the Save All button on the toolbar.

4. Now run the project. A new window similar to Figure 11-1 will appear.

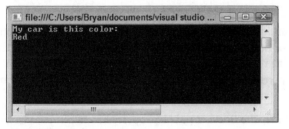

FIGURE 11-1

5. Press Enter to end the program.

How it Works

This example illustrates that defining a field is easy. The line of code

```
Public Color As String
```

tells the class that you want to create a variable called `Color` and you want the field to hold a string of text characters. The use of the `Public` keyword when you declare the `Color` variable tells the class that the variable is accessible to developers using the `Car` class, not only from within the class itself.

Using the object is simple, and you do this from within `Module1.vb`. This process actually takes two steps:

1. Declare a variable to refer to an object for the class.

2. Instantiate the object. The following line of code creates an object variable called `objCar` and specifies that it's going to hold exclusively any objects created using the `Car` class:

   ```
   Dim objCar As Car
   ```

When you define the variable, it doesn't yet have an object instance associated with it; you are simply identifying the type of object. It's a bit like telling the computer to give you a hook that you can hang a Car object on, and calling the hook objCar. You haven't hung anything on it yet — to do that you have to create an instance of the class. This is done using the New keyword:

```
Set objCar = New Car
```

But Visual Basic 2010 allows you to combine both steps into one line of code:

```
`Create a new car object
Dim objCar As New Car
```

What you're saying here is, "Let objCar refer to a newly created object instantiated from the class Car." In other words, "Create a new car and hang it on the hook called objCar." You now have a Car object and can refer to it with the name objCar.

After you have an object instance, you can set its properties and call its methods. Here is how you set the Color property:

```
`Set the Color property to Red
objCar.Color = `Red"
```

After the property has been set, it can be retrieved as many times as you want or its value changed at a later point. Here, retrieval is illustrated by passing the Color property to the WriteLine method on the Console class:

```
`Show what the value of the property is
Console.WriteLine(`My car is this color:")
Console.WriteLine(objCar.Color)
```

The Console.ReadLine line means that the program does not continue until you press Enter. Basically, the console window is waiting for input from you:

```
`Wait for input from the user
Console.ReadLine()
```

Even though this is not really a property from the point of view of a developer using the class, it works just like one. In fact, real properties are methods that look like variables to users of the class. Whether you use a method or a property really depends on what the users of your class find easier. You'll start to see this in the next section.

Real Properties

Now that you've seen how to cheat, let's see how to do things properly. The property you saw can be set to pretty much anything. As long as it's a string, it will be accepted. Also, setting the property doesn't do anything except change the object's internal state. Often you want to control what values a property can be set to; for example, you might have a list of valid colors that a car can be. You might also want to associate a change to a property with a particular action. For example, when you change a channel on the TV, you want it to do a bit more than just change its mind about what channel it's displaying. You want the TV to show a different picture! Just changing the value of a variable won't help here.

Another reason to use real properties is that you want to prevent the user of the class from directly changing the value. This is called a *read-only property*. The car's speed is a good example of how a class that models a real-world object should behave like that real-world object. If you are going 60 mph, you cannot simply change the speed to a value you prefer. You can read the speed of a car from the speedometer, but you cannot change (write) the speed of the car by physically moving the needle around the dial with your finger. You have to control the car in another fashion, which you do by stepping on the gas pedal or the brake to either accelerate or decelerate, respectively. To model this feature in the Car class, you use methods (Accelerate, Decelerate) that affect the speed, and keep a read-only property around called Speed that will report on the current speed of the vehicle.

You'll still need to keep the speed around in a member variable, but what you need is a member variable that can be seen or manipulated only by the class itself. You accomplish this by using the Private keyword:

```
Private intSpeed As Integer
```

The intSpeed variable is marked as Private and can, therefore, be accessed only by functions defined inside the class itself. Users of Car will not even be aware of its presence.

TRY IT OUT   Adding a Speed Property

Code file Objects.zip is available for download at Wrox.com

Now you'll see how you can build a property that gives the user of the object read-only access to the car's speed.

1. To define a private variable, use the Private instead of the Public keyword. Add this statement to the Car class:

```
Public Color As String
Private intSpeed As Integer
```

2. To report the speed, you need to build a read-only property. Add this code to your Car class:

```
`Speed—read-only property to return the speed
Public ReadOnly Property Speed() As Integer
    Get
        Return intSpeed
    End Get
End Property
```

3. Now build a method called Accelerate that adjusts the speed of the car by however many miles per hour you specify. Add this code after the Speed property:

```
`Accelerate—add mph to the speed
Public Sub Accelerate(ByVal accelerateBy As Integer)
    `Adjust the speed
    intSpeed += accelerateBy
End Sub
```

4. To test the object, you need to make some changes to the Main procedure in Module1. Open the file and modify the code as shown:

```
Sub Main()
    `Create a new car object
    Dim objCar As New Car

    `Report the speed
```

```
        Console.WriteLine("The car's speed is:")
        Console.WriteLine(objCar.Speed)

        `Accelerate
        objCar.Accelerate(5)

        `Report the new speed
        Console.WriteLine("The car's speed is now:")
        Console.WriteLine(objCar.Speed)

        `Wait for input from the user
        Console.ReadLine()
    End Sub
```

5. Now run the project. A new window similar to Figure 11-2 appears.

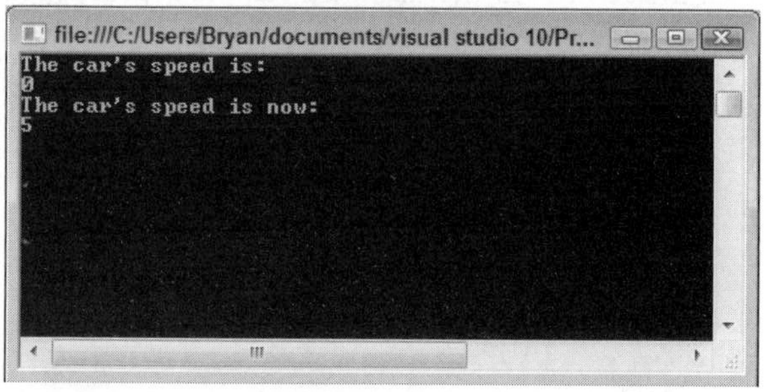

FIGURE 11-2

How It Works

The first thing you do in this example is define a private member variable called `intSpeed` in the `Car` class:

```
Private intSpeed As Integer
```

By default, when the object is created, `intSpeed` has a value of zero because this is the default value for the `Integer` data type.

You then define a read-only property that returns the current speed:

```
`Speed—readonly property to return the speed
Public ReadOnly Property Speed() As Integer
    Get
        Return intSpeed
    End Get
End Property
```

When you define properties, you can set them to be read-only (through the `ReadOnly` keyword), write-only (through the `WriteOnly` keyword), or both readable and writable by using neither. Reading a property is known as *getting* the value, whereas writing to a property is known as *setting* the value. The code between `Get` and `End Get` is executed when the property is read. In this case, the only thing you're doing is returning the value currently stored in `intSpeed`.

You also created a method called `Accelerate`. This method doesn't have to return a value, so you use the `Sub` keyword:

```
`Accelerate—add mph to the speed
```

```
Public Sub Accelerate(ByVal accelerateBy As Integer)
    `Adjust the speed
    intSpeed += accelerateBy
End Sub
```

The method takes a single parameter called `accelerateBy`, which you use to tell the method how much to increase the speed by. The only action of the method is to adjust the internal member `intSpeed`. In real life, the pressure on the accelerator pedal, along with factors such as wind speed and road surface, affect the speed. The speed is an outcome of several factors — not something you can just change. You need some complex code to simulate this. Here you are just keeping things simple and incrementing the `intSpeed` variable with the value passed to the method.

Accelerating a car is another example of encapsulation. To accelerate the car in a real-world implementation you need an actuator of some kind to open the throttle further until the required speed is reached. As consumers of the object, you don't care how this is done. All you care about is how to tell the car to accelerate.

Consuming this new functionality is simple:

1. Create the variable and instantiate the object as you did in the previous exercise:

```
`Create a new car object
Dim objCar As New Car
```

2. Write the current speed:

```
`Report the speed
Console.WriteLine("The car's speed is:")
Console.WriteLine(objCar.Speed)
```

Notice how you're using the read-only `Speed` property to get the current speed of the car. When the object is first created, the internal _speed member will be set at `0`.

3. Call `Accelerate` and use it to increase the speed of the car:

```
`Accelerate
objCar.Accelerate(5)
```

4. Write out the new speed:

```
`Report the new speed
Console.WriteLine("The car's speed is now:")
Console.WriteLine(objCar.Speed)
```

Read/Write Properties

Why would you need to use the `Property` keyword to define properties that are both readable and writable if you can achieve the same effect with a line like this:

```
Public Color As String
```

If you build the property manually using the `Property` keyword, you can write code that is executed whenever the property is set or read. This is extremely powerful!

For example, the `Property` keyword allows you to provide validation for new values. Imagine you had a property called `NumberOfDoors`. You wouldn't want this to be set to nonsense values like `0` or `23453`. Rather, you would have a possible range. For modern cars this is going to range from `2` to `5`.

> **NOTE** *This is an important consideration for developers building objects. It's imperative that you make life as easy as possible for a developer to consume your object. Dealing with problems like making sure a car can't have 10 million doors is an important aspect of object design.*

Likewise, you might not have the information to return to the consumer of your object when you are asked to return the property; you might have to retrieve the value from somewhere, or otherwise calculate it. You might have a property that describes the total number of orders a customer has ever made or the total number of chew toys a dog has destroyed in its life. If you build this as a property, you can intercept the instruction to get the value and find the actual value you require on demand from some other data store, such as a database or a web service. You'll see this in later chapters.

For now, let's deal with the number of doors problem.

TRY IT OUT Adding a NumberOfDoors Property

Code file Objects.zip is available for download at Wrox.com

You have already seen how to add a property and this example will help you reinforce that knowledge.

1. The first thing you need to do is build a private member that will hold the number of doors. You're going to define this member as having a default of 5. Add this code in the `Car` class as bolded here:

```
Public Color As String
Private intSpeed As Integer
Private intNumberOfDoors As Integer = 5
```

2. Now you can build a property that gets and sets the number of doors, provided the number of doors is always between 2 and 5. Add this code to your `Car` class directly beneath the `Accelerate` method:

```
`NumberOfDoors—get/set the number of doors
Public Property NumberOfDoors() As Integer
    `Called when the property is read
    Get
        Return intNumberOfDoors
    End Get
    `Called when the property is set
    Set(ByVal value As Integer)
        `Is the new value between two and five
        If value >= 2 And value <= 5 Then
            intNumberOfDoors = value
        End If
    End Set
End Property
```

In this chapter, you're going to ignore the problem of telling the developer if the user has provided an invalid value for a property. Ideally, whenever this happens, you need to throw an exception. The developer will be able to detect this exception and behave accordingly. (For example, if the user types the number of doors as 9999 into a text box, the program could display a message box indicating that an invalid value has been provided for the number of doors, as no car has that many.) You learned about exception handling in Chapter 10.

3. To test the property, you need to change the `Main` procedure in Module1 by modifying the code as indicated here:

```
Sub Main()
    `Create a new car object
    Dim objCar As New Car

    `Report the number of doors
    Console.WriteLine("The number of doors is:")
    Console.WriteLine(objCar.NumberOfDoors)

    `Try changing the number of doors to 1000
    objCar.NumberOfDoors = 1000

    `Report the number of doors
    Console.WriteLine("The number of doors is:")
    Console.WriteLine(objCar.NumberOfDoors)

    `Now try changing the number of doors to 2
    objCar.NumberOfDoors = 2

    `Report the number of doors
    Console.WriteLine("The number of doors is:")
    Console.WriteLine(objCar.NumberOfDoors)

    `Wait for input from the user
    Console.ReadLine()
End Sub
```

4. Now run the project. You should see a screen like the one in Figure 11-3.

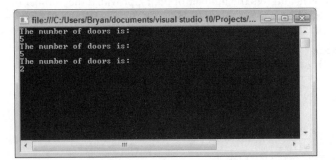

FIGURE 11-3

How It Works

In this example, you define a private member variable called `intNumberOfDoors`. You also assign the default value of 5 to this variable.

```
Private intNumberOfDoors As Integer = 5
```

The motivation behind setting a value at this point is simple: You want `intNumberOfDoors` to always be between 2 and 5. When the object is created, the `intNumberOfDoors` will be assigned a value of 5. Without this assignment, `intNumberOfDoors` would have a default value of 0. This would be inconsistent with the understanding that the number of doors must always be between 2 and 5, so you guard against it.

Next is the property itself. The `Get` portion is simple. Just return the value held in `intNumberOfDoors`. The `Set` is more complex. `Set` involves a check to ensure that the new value is valid. The new value is passed in through a parameter called `value`:

```
`NumberOfDoors—get/set the number of doors
Public Property NumberOfDoors() As Integer
    `Called when the property is read
    Get
        Return intNumberOfDoors
    End Get
    `Called when the property is set
    Set(ByVal value As Integer)
        `Is the new value between two and five
        If value >= 2 And value <= 5 Then
            intNumberOfDoors = value
        End If
    End Set
End Property
```

The test code you add to Module1 is not very complex. You simply display the initial value of `intNumberOfDoors` and then try to change it to `1000`. The validation code in the `NumberOfDoors` property won't change the `intNumberOfDoors` member variable if an inconsistent number is used, so when you report the number of doors again, you find it hasn't changed from 5. Lastly, you try setting it to 2, which is a valid value; and this time, when you report the number of doors, you get an output of 2.

Even though read-write properties and public variables seem to work the same way, they are very different. When your Visual Basic 2010 code is compiled, the compiled code treats property calls as calls to a method. Always using properties instead of public variables makes your objects more flexible and extendable. Of course, using public variables is easier and quicker. You need to decide what is most important in each case.

The IsMoving Method

When building objects, you should always have the following question in the back of your mind: "How can I make this object easier to use?" For example, if the consumer needs to know whether the car is moving, what would be the easiest way to determine this?

One way would be to look at the `Speed` property. If this is zero, it can be assumed that the car has stopped. (On most cars the speed is not reported when the car is moving in reverse, so assume for now that you have only forward gears!) However, relying on the developers using the object to understand this relies on their having an understanding of whatever is being modeled. Common sense tells us that an object with a speed of "zero mph" is stationary, but should you assume anyone consuming the object shares your idea of common sense?

Instead, it's good practice to create methods that deal with these eventualities. One way you can solve this problem is by creating an `IsMoving` method, as shown in the next exercise.

Adding an IsMoving Method

Code file Objects.zip is available for download at Wrox.com

The `IsMoving` method will return a Boolean value. Either the car is moving or not.

1. All the `IsMoving` method needs in order to work is a simple test to look at the speed of the car and make a `True` or `False` determination as to whether it's moving. Add this code to the `Car` class after the `NumberOfDoors` property:

```
`IsMoving—is the car moving?
Public Function IsMoving() As Boolean
    `Is the car's speed zero?
    If Speed = 0 Then
        Return False
    Else
        Return True
    End If
End Function
```

2. To test this method, make the following changes to the `Main` procedure in Module1 with this new code as indicated:

```
Sub Main()
    `Create a new car object
    Dim objCar As New Car

    `Accelerate the car to 25mph
    objCar.Accelerate(25)

    `Report whether or not the car is moving
    If objCar.IsMoving = True Then
        Console.WriteLine("The car is moving.")
    Else
        Console.WriteLine("The car is stopped.")
    End If

    `Wait for input from the user
    Console.ReadLine()
End Sub
```

3. Now try running the project. A new window similar to Figure 11-4 will appear.

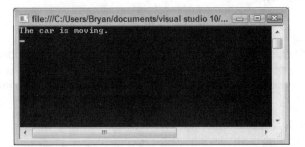

FIGURE 11-4

How It Works

In this example you created a simple method that examines the value of the `Speed` property and returns `True` if the speed is not zero, or `False` if it is:

```
`IsMoving—is the car moving?
Public Function IsMoving() As Boolean
    `Is the car's speed zero?
    If Speed = 0 Then
        Return False
    Else
        Return True
    End If
End Function
```

Although this method is simple, it removes the conceptual leap required on the part of the consumer to understand whether the object is moving. There's no confusion as to whether the car is moving based on interpreting the value of one or more properties; one simple method returns a definitive answer.

Of course, before you go off and build hundreds of methods for every eventuality, remember that, ironically, the more methods and properties an object has, the harder it is to understand. Take care while designing the object and try to strike the right balance between too few and too many methods and properties.

You may be wondering why you used a method here when this is actually a property. All you are doing is reporting the object's state, without affecting its behavior. There is no reason for not using a property here. However, using a method does remind users of the object that this value is calculated and is not a simple report of an internal variable. It also adds a bit of variety to your examples and reminds you how easy it is to add a method!

CONSTRUCTORS

One of the most important aspects of object design is the concept of a *constructor*. As mentioned in Chapter 10, this is a piece of initialization code that runs whenever an object is instantiated. It's extremely useful when you need the object to be set up in a particular way before you use it. For example, it can be used to set up default values, just as you did for the number of doors earlier.

In this Try It Out, you take a look at a simple constructor.

TRY IT OUT Creating a Constructor

Code file Objects.zip is available for download at Wrox.com

You need to set a few properties whenever the object is instantiated. You will set three properties with default values in this example.

1. For the sake of this discussion, you're going to remove the default value of 5 from the `intNumberOfDoors` member. Make this change to the `Car` class:

```
Public Color As String
Private intSpeed As Integer

Private intNumberOfDoors As Integer
```

2. Add this method, which forms the constructor. Any code within this method is executed whenever an object is created from the Car class:

```
`Constructor
Public Sub New()
    `Set the default values
    Color = "White"
    intSpeed = 0
    intNumberOfDoors = 5
End Sub
```

3. To test the action of the constructor, you create a separate procedure that displays the car's details. Add the DisplayCarDetails procedure in Module1:

```
`DisplayCarDetails—procedure that displays a car's details
Sub DisplayCarDetails(ByVal theCar As Car)
    `Display the details of the car
    Console.WriteLine("Color: " & theCar.Color)
    Console.WriteLine("Number of doors: " & theCar.NumberOfDoors)
    Console.WriteLine("Current speed: " & theCar.Speed)
End Sub
```

4. Modify the Main procedure in Module1 to call the DisplayCarDetails procedure:

```
Sub Main()
    `Create a new car object
    Dim objCar As New Car

    `Display the details of the car
    DisplayCarDetails(objCar)

    `Wait for input from the user
    Console.ReadLine()
End Sub
```

5. Try running the project. You should see output similar to Figure 11-5.

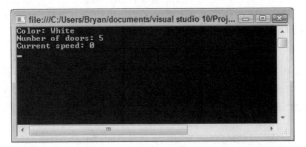

FIGURE 11-5

How It Works

In this example, the code in the constructor is called whenever an object is created. This is where you take an opportunity to set the default values for the members:

```
`Constructor
Public Sub New()
```

```
         `Set the default values
         Color = "White"
         intSpeed = 0
         intNumberOfDoors = 5
    End Sub
```

You see the results of the changes made to the properties when you run the project and see the details of the car displayed in the window. A constructor must always be a subroutine (defined with the Sub keyword) and must always be called New. This provides consistency in the .NET Framework for all class constructors, and the framework will always execute this procedure when a class is instantiated.

When you test the object, you use a separate function called DisplayCarDetails in Module1. This is useful when you need to see the details of more than one Car object or want to see the details of the Car object multiple times in your code.

INHERITANCE

Although the subject of *inheritance* is quite an advanced object-oriented programming topic, it is really useful. In fact, the .NET Framework itself makes heavy use of it, and you have already created classes that inherit from another class — every Windows Form that you write is a new class inherited from a simple blank form (the starting point when you create a form).

Inheritance is used to create objects that have everything another object has, but also some of their own bits and pieces. It's used to extend the functionality of objects, but it doesn't require you to have an understanding of how the internals of the object work. This is in line with your quest of building and using objects without having to understand how the original programmers put them together.

Inheritance enables you to, in effect, take another class and bolt on your own functionality, either by adding new methods and properties or by replacing existing methods and properties. For example, you can move from a general car class to more specific variations — for example, sports car, SUV, van, and so on.

For example, if you wanted to model a sports car, you would likely want the default number of doors to be 2 instead of 5, and you might also like to have properties and methods that help you understand the performance of the car, such as Weight and PowerToWeightRatio, as shown in Figure 11-6.

One thing that you need to understand about inheritance is the way that access to public and private members is controlled. Any public member, such as Color, is accessible to inheriting classes. However, private members such as intSpeed are not. This means that if SportsCar has to change the speed of the car, it has to do so through the properties and methods provided in the Car class itself.

In other commonly encountered terminology, the inheriting class is called a *derived class*, and the class it inherits from is its *base class*. Car is the base class from which SportsCar is derived. The terms *subclass* and *superclass* are also used. SportsCar is a subclass of Car; Car is the superclass of SportsCar. The sub and super prefixes mean the same as they do when speaking of subsets and supersets in mathematics.

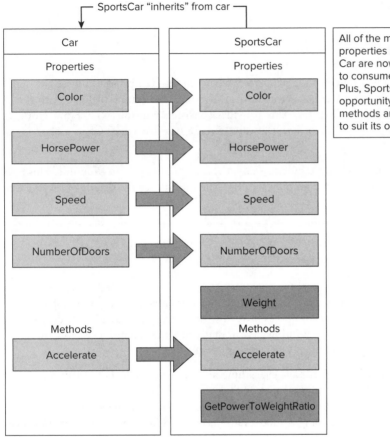

SportsCar "inherits" from car

All of the methods and properties implemented on Car are now available to consumers of SportsCar. Plus, SportsCar has the opportunity to add its own methods and properties to suit its own needs.

FIGURE 11-6

Adding New Methods and Properties

To illustrate inheritance, you will inherit from a base class next.

TRY IT OUT Inheriting from Car

Code file Objects.zip is available for download at Wrox.com

In the next Try It Out, you create a new class called SportsCar, which inherits from Car and enables you to see the power-to-weight ratio of your sports car.

1. For this demonstration, you need to add an additional public variable to the Car class that represents the horsepower of the car. Of course, if you want to make it really robust, you would use a property and ensure a sensible range of values. But here, simplicity and speed win out. Open the Car class and add this line of code as indicated:

```
Public Color As String
Public HorsePower As Integer
Private intSpeed As Integer
Private intNumberOfDoors As Integer
```

2. Create a new class in the usual way by right-clicking the Objects project in the Solution Explorer and selecting Add ➪ Class. Enter the name of the class as **SportsCar.vb** and click Add.

3. To tell SportsCar that it inherits from Car, you need to use the Inherits keyword. Add this code to SportsCar:

```
Public Class SportsCar
    Inherits Car
End Class
```

4. At this point, SportsCar has all the methods and properties that Car has. What you want to do now is add a new public variable called Weight to the SportsCar class:

```
        Public Weight As Integer
```

5. To test the new class you need to add a new procedure to Module1:

```
`DisplaySportsCarDetails—procedure that displays a sports car's details
Sub DisplaySportsCarDetails(ByVal theCar As SportsCar)
    `Display the details of the sports car
    Console.WriteLine()
    Console.WriteLine("Sports Car Horsepower: " & theCar.HorsePower)
    Console.WriteLine("Sports Car Weight: " & theCar.Weight)
End Sub
```

6. Modify the Main procedure in Module1. Pay close attention to the fact that you need to create a SportsCar object, not a Car object, in order to get at the Weight property. Add the new code as indicated:

```
Sub Main()
    `Create a new sports car object
    Dim objCar As New SportsCar

    `Modify the number of doors
    objCar.NumberOfDoors = 2

    `Set the horsepower and weight(kg)
    objCar.HorsePower = 240
    objCar.Weight = 1085

    `Display the details of the car
    DisplayCarDetails(objCar)
    DisplaySportsCarDetails(objCar)

    `Wait for input from the user
    Console.ReadLine()
End Sub
```

7. Run the project. You should see output similar to that shown in Figure 11-7.

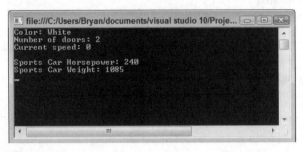

FIGURE 11-7

How It Works

The directive to make `SportsCar` inherit from `Car` is done with the `Inherits` keyword in this example:

```
Public Class SportsCar
    Inherits Car
```

At this point, the new `SportsCar` class contains all the methods and properties of the `Car` class, but it cannot see or modify the private member variables. When you add your new property:

```
Public Weight As Integer
```

you have a property that's available only when you create instances of `SportsCar`, and not available to you if you are creating plain instances of `Car`. This is an important point: If you don't create an instance of `SportsCar`, you'll get a compile error if you try to access the `Weight` property. `Weight` isn't, and never has been, a property of `Car` (refer to Figure 11-6 for a clarification of this).

The new `DisplaySportsCarDetails` procedure displays the `Horsepower` property from the `Car` class and the `Weight` property from the `SportsCar` class. Remember that because the `SportsCar` class inherits from the `Car` class, it contains all of the methods and properties in the `Car` class:

```
`DisplaySportsCarDetails—procedure that displays a sports car's details
Sub DisplaySportsCarDetails(ByVal theCar As SportsCar)
    `Display the details of the sports car
    Console.WriteLine()
    Console.WriteLine("Sports Car Horsepower: " & theCar.HorsePower)
    Console.WriteLine("Sports Car Weight: " & theCar.Weight)
End Sub
```

You instantiate a new `SportsCar` object in your `Main` procedure, and this allows you to get and set the value for the `Weight` property:

```
`Create a new sports car object
Dim objCar As New SportsCar
```

You are able to call the `DisplayCarDetails` procedure and pass it a `SportsCar` object because `SportsCar` is a subclass of `Car` — that is, every `SportsCar` is also a `Car`. The `DisplayCarDetails` procedure does not access any of the properties of the `SportsCar` class, so call this procedure, passing it the `SportsCar` object that you created. You then call the `DisplaySportsCarDetails` procedure to display the properties of both the `Car` class and the `SportsCar` class:

```
`Display the details of the car
DisplayCarDetails(objCar)
DisplaySportsCarDetails(objCar)
```

Adding a GetPowerToWeightRatio Method

The `GetPowerToWeightRatio` method will determine how much horsepower per pound is produced. You will add it next.

TRY IT OUT Adding a GetPowerToWeightRatio Method

Code file Objects.zip is available for download at Wrox.com

A `GetPowerToWeightRatio` method could be implemented as a read-only property (in which case you would probably call it `PowerToWeightRatio` instead), but for this discussion you'll add it as a method in the next Try It Out.

1. For this method, all you need to do is divide the horsepower by the weight. Add this code to the `SportsCar` class:

```
`GetPowerToWeightRatio-work out the power to weight
Public Function GetPowerToWeightRatio() As Double
    `Calculate the horsepower
    Return CType(HorsePower, Double) / CType(Weight, Double)
End Function
```

2. To see the results, add the bolded code to the `DisplaySportsCarDetails` procedure in Module1:

```
'DisplaySportsCarDetails-procedure that displays a sports car's details
Sub DisplaySportsCarDetails(ByVal theCar As SportsCar)
  `Display the details of the sports car
  Console.WriteLine()
  Console.WriteLine("Sports Car Horsepower: " & theCar.HorsePower)
  Console.WriteLine("Sports Car Weight: " & theCar.Weight)
  Console.WriteLine("Power to Weight Ratio: " & theCar.GetPowerToWeightRatio)
End Sub
```

3. Run the project and you'll see something similar to Figure 11-8.

How It Works

Again, all you've done in this example is add a new method to the new class called `GetPowerToWeightRatio`. This method then becomes available to anyone working with an instance of `SportsCar`, as shown in Figure 11-9.

FIGURE 11-8

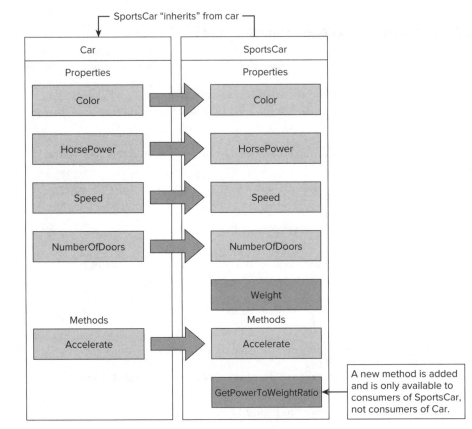

FIGURE 11-9

The only thing you have to be careful of is that if you divide an integer by an integer, you get an integer result, but what you actually want here is a floating-point number. You have to convert the integer `HorsePower` and `Weight` properties to `Double` values in order to see the results:

```
`Calculate the horsepower
Return CType(HorsePower, Double) / CType(Weight, Double)
```

Changing Defaults

In addition to adding new properties and methods, you might want to change the way an existing method or property works from that of the base class. To do this, you need to create your own implementation of the method or property.

Think back to the discussion on constructors. These are methods that are called whenever the object is created and they enable you to get the object into a state where it can be used by a developer. In this constructor you set the default `intNumberOfDoors` value to be 5. However, in a sports car, this number should ideally be 2, which is what you set using the `NumberOfDoors` property. But wouldn't it be nice to have this automatically done in the constructor of the `SportsCar` class?

If you are creating a derived class and want to replace a method or property existing in the base class with your own, the process is called *overriding*. In this next Try It Out, you learn how to override the base class's constructor.

TRY IT OUT Overriding a Constructor

Code file Objects.zip is available for download at Wrox.com

The `SportsCar` class does not need the same default values as the `Car` class. You will set the correct default values by overriding the constructor of the `Car` class.

1. To override the constructor in the base class, all you have to do is create your own constructor in the `SportsCar` class. Add this code to `SportsCar`:

```
`Constructor
Public Sub New()
    `Change the default values
    Color = `Green"
    NumberOfDoors = 2
End Sub
```

2. Remove the following code from the `Main` procedure in Module1.

```
`Modify the number of doors
objCar.NumberOfDoors = 2
```

3. Run your project to test your constructor in the `SportsCar` class. You should see output similar to Figure 11-10.

FIGURE 11-10

How It Works

The new constructor that you added to `SportsCar` in this example runs after the existing one in `Car`. The .NET Framework knows that it's supposed to run the code in the constructor of the base class before running the new constructor in the class that inherits from it, so in effect it runs this code first:

```
`Constructor
Public Sub New()
    `Set the default values
    Color = `White"
    intSpeed = 0
    intNumberOfDoors = 5
End Sub
```

Then it runs this code:

```
`Constructor
Public Sub New()
    `Change the default values
    Color = `Green"
    NumberOfDoors = 2
End Sub
```

To summarize what happens:

1. The constructor on the base class `Car` is called.

2. `Color` is set to `White`.

3. `intSpeed` is set to `0`.

4. `intNumberOfDoors` is set to `5`.

5. The constructor on the new class `SportsCar` is called.

6. `Color` is set to `Green`.

7. `NumberOfDoors` is set to `2`.

Because you defined `intNumberOfDoors` as a private member in `Car`, you cannot directly access it from inherited classes, just as you wouldn't be able to access it directly from a consumer of the class. Instead, you rely on being able to set an appropriate value through the `NumberOfDoors` property.

Polymorphism: Scary Word, Simple Concept

Another very common word mentioned when talking about object-oriented programming is *polymorphism*. This is, perhaps, the scariest term, but one of the easiest to understand! In fact, you have already done it in the previous example.

Look again at the code for `DisplayCarDetails`:

```
`DisplayCarDetails—procedure that displays a car's details
Sub DisplayCarDetails(ByVal theCar As Car)
    `Display the details of the car
    Console.WriteLine("Color: " & theCar.Color)
    Console.WriteLine("Number of doors: " & theCar.NumberOfDoors)
    Console.WriteLine("Current speed: " & theCar.Speed)
End Sub
```

The first line says that the parameter you want to accept is a `Car` object; but when you call the object, you're actually passing it a `SportsCar` object.

Look at how you create the object and call `DisplayCarDetails`:

```
'Create a new sportscar object
Dim objCar As New SportsCar

'Display the details of the car
DisplayCarDetails(objCar)
```

How can it be that if the function takes a `Car` object, you're allowed to pass it as a `SportsCar` object?

Well, *polymorphism* (which comes from the Greek for *many forms*) means that an object can be treated as if it were a different kind of object, provided common sense prevails. In this case, you can treat a `SportsCar` object like a `Car` object because `SportsCar` inherits from `Car`. This act of inheritance dictates that what a `SportsCar` object can do must include everything that a `Car` object can do; therefore, you can treat the two objects in the same way. If you need to call a method on `Car`, `SportsCar` must also implement the method.

This does not hold true the other way around. Your `DisplaySportsCarDetails` function, defined like this:

```
Sub DisplaySportsCarDetails(ByVal theCar As SportsCar)
```

cannot accept a `Car` object. `Car` is not guaranteed to be able to do everything a `SportsCar` can do, because the extra methods and properties you add to `SportsCar` won't exist on `Car`. `SportsCar` is a more specific type of `Car`.

To summarize, when people talk about polymorphism, this is the action they are referring to — the principle that an object can behave as if it were another object without the developer having to go through too many hoops to make it happen.

Overriding More Methods

Although you've overridden `Car`'s constructor, for completeness you should look at how to override a normal method.

To override a method, you need to have the method in the base `Car` class. Because `Accelerate` shouldn't change depending on whether you have a sports car or a normal car, and `IsMoving` was added for ease of use — and hence doesn't really count in this instance, as it isn't a behavior of the object — you need to add a new method called `CalculateAccelerationRate`. Assume that on a normal car this is a constant, and on a sports car you change it so that it takes the power-to-weight ratio into consideration. In the following Try It Out, you add another method to override.

TRY IT OUT   **Adding and Overriding Another Method**

Code file Objects.zip is available for download at Wrox.com

This example will reinforce the concept of overriding.

1.   Add this method to the `Car` class:

```
'CalculateAccelerationRate—assume a constant for a normal car
Public Function CalculateAccelerationRate() As Double
```

```
      `If we assume a normal car goes from 0-60 in 14 seconds,
      `that's an average rate of 4.2 mph/s
      Return 4.2
End Function
```

2. To test the method, change the `DisplayCarDetails` procedure in Module1 to read like this:

```
`DisplayCarDetails—procedure that displays a car's details
Sub DisplayCarDetails(ByVal theCar As Car)
    `Display the details of the car
    Console.WriteLine(`Color: ` & theCar.Color)
    Console.WriteLine(`Number of doors: ` & theCar.NumberOfDoors)
    Console.WriteLine(`Current speed: ` & theCar.Speed)
    Console.WriteLine(`Acceleration rate: ` & _
        theCar.CalculateAccelerationRate)
End Sub
```

3. Run the project. You should get output similar to Figure 11-11.

```
file:///C:/Users/Bryan/documents/visual studio 10/...
Color: Green
Number of doors: 2
Current speed: 0
Acceleration rate: 4.2

Sports Car Horsepower: 240
Sports Car Weight: 1085
Power to Weight Ratio: 0.221198156682028
```

FIGURE 11-11

You've built a method on `Car` as normal. This method always returns a value of 4.2 mph/s for the acceleration rate.

4. To override the method, you just have to provide a new implementation in `SportsCar`. However, there's one thing you need to do first. To override a method you have to mark it as `Overridable`. To do this, open the `Car` class again and add the `Overridable` keyword to the method:

```
Public Overridable Function CalculateAccelerationRate() As Double
```

5. Now you can create a method with the same name in the `SportsCar` class. To override the method in the base class, you must add the `Overrides` keyword before the method type (`Function` or `Procedure`):

```
`CalculateAccelerationRate—take the power/weight into consideration
Public Overrides Function CalculateAccelerationRate() As Double
    `You'll assume the same 4.2 value, but you'll multiply it
    `by the power/weight ratio
    Return 4.2 * GetPowerToWeightRatio()
End Function
```

6. Run the project; you get an adjusted acceleration rate, as shown in Figure 11-12.

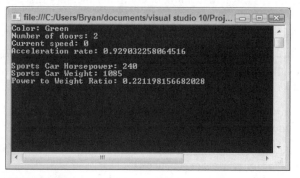

FIGURE 11-12

How It Works

In this example you learned that overriding the method enables you to create your own implementation of an existing method on the object. Returning to the concept of encapsulation, the object consumers don't have to know that anything is different about the object — they just call the method in the same way as they would for a normal `Car` object. This time, however, they get a result rather different from the constant value they always got on the normal `Car` object.

Inheriting from the Object Class

With respect to inheritance, the final thing to look at is that if you create a class without using the `Inherits` clause, then the class automatically inherits from a class called `Object`. This object provides you with a few methods that you can guarantee are supported by every object you'll ever have. Most of these methods are beyond the scope of this book, but the two most useful methods at this level are as follows:

➤ `ToString`: This method returns a string representation of the object. You can override this to provide a helpful string value for any object; for example, you might want a person object to return that person's name. If you do not override it, it will return the name of the class.

➤ `GetType`: This method returns a `Type` object that represents the data type of the object.

Remember, you do not have to inherit explicitly from `Object`. This happens automatically.

OBJECTS AND STRUCTURES

You created a structure in Chapter 5. Like a class, a structure provides a way to group several pieces of information together that all refer to one thing. A structure can even have methods and properties as well as member variables, just as a class can. Here are some of the differences between structures and classes.

In terms of semantics, structures are known as *value types* and classes are known as *reference types*. That is, a variable representing a structure means the actual chunk of computer memory that stores the contents of the structure itself, whereas a variable representing a class instance is actually, as you have seen, a "hook" on which the object hangs.

This explains the difference in instantiation — you don't need to use the New keyword to instantiate a structure before you use it because it is a value type, just like an integer. You do have to use the New keyword with a form or other complex object because it is a class instance — a reference type.

You have seen that two different object variable hooks can be used to hang up the same object. If you set a property in the object using either of the hooks, both objects will have the same value.:

```
Dim objMyCar As New Car       `objMyCar.Color is "White"
Set objThisCar = objMyCar     `same object, different hooks
objThisCar.Color = "Beige"    `now objMyCar.Color is also "Beige"
```

Two different structure variables, on the other hand, always refer to different groups of pieces of information:

```
Dim structMyCustomer As Customer, structThisCustomer As Customer
structMyCustomer.FirstName = "Victor"
structThisCustomer = structMyCustomer   `different structures
structThisCustomer.FirstName = "Victoria"
'structMyCustomer.FirstName is still "Victor"
```

Also, you cannot inherit from a structure — another important consideration when choosing whether to use a class or a structure.

THE FRAMEWORK CLASSES

Although Chapter 2 included a general discussion of the .NET Framework in general, a more in-depth look at some aspects of the .NET Framework's construction can help you when building objects. In particular, you want to take a look at namespaces and how you can create your own namespaces for use within your objects.

Namespaces

The .NET Framework is actually a vast collection of classes. There are over 4,000 classes in the .NET Framework all told, so how are you, as a developer, supposed to find the ones that you want?

The .NET Framework is divided into a broad set of namespaces that group similar classes together. This limits the number of classes that you have to hunt through when you're looking for a specific piece of functionality.

These namespaces are also hierarchical in nature, meaning that a namespace can contain other namespaces that further group classes together. Each class must belong to exactly one namespace — it can't belong to multiple namespaces.

Most of the .NET Framework classes are lumped together in a namespace called System, or namespaces that are also contained within System. For example:

➤ System.Data: Contains classes related to accessing data stored in a database.

➤ `System.Xml`: Contains classes used to read and write XML documents.

➤ `System.Windows.Forms`: Contains classes for drawing windows on the screen.

➤ `System.Net`: Contains classes for communicating over a network.

The existence of namespaces means that all of the objects you've been using actually have longer names than the ones used in your software code. Until this point, you've been using a shorthand notation to refer to classes.

In fact, when we said earlier that everything has to be derived from `Object`, we were stretching it a bit. Because `Object` is contained within the `System` namespace, its full name is `System.Object`. Likewise, `Console` is actually shorthand for `System.Console`, meaning the following two lines refer to the same thing:

```
Console.ReadLine()

System.Console.ReadLine()
```

> **NOTE** *This can get a little silly, especially when you end up with object names like* `System.Web.Services.Description.ServiceDescription`.

.NET automatically creates a shorthand version of all the classes within `System`, so you don't have to type `System` all the time. Later, you'll see how you can add shorthand references to other namespaces.

There is also the `My` namespace, which you've already seen in use in some of the earlier chapters. This namespace provides access to the common classes that you're most likely to need in your everyday programming tasks.

Like the `System` namespace, the `My` namespace contains a collection of other classes, which in turn contain classes of their own. At the top level, there is the `My.Application` class, which provides a wealth of information related to the currently executing application, such as the application's assembly name, the current path to the application's executable file, and so on. There is also the `My.Computer` class, which provides detailed information about the computer on which the application is executing, such as the amount of free space on the hard drive and the amount of available memory.

The `My.Forms` class provides access to the various forms in the application and allows you to manipulate those forms easily; for example, you can show, hide, and close them. There is also the `My.Resources` class, which provides quick and easy access to an application's resource files if it contains them. You can place localized text strings and images in a resource file and use the `My.Resources` class to gain access to these resources for use in your application.

The `My.Settings` class provides access to an application's configuration file if it has one and allows you to quickly read the settings needed by your application, such as startup settings or database connection information. It also allows you to create, persist, and save user settings for your application. Finally, there is the `My.User` class, which provides a wealth of information related to the current user of your application, such as login name and the domain name that the user is logged into.

Finding the Name of the Current Namespace

Code file Objects.zip is available for download at Wrox.com

Every class must be in exactly one namespace, but what about the classes we've made so far? Well, this project has a default namespace, and your new classes are placed into this namespace. In the next Try It Out, you discover a current namespace.

1. To see the namespace that you're using, double-click My Project in the Solution Explorer.

2. The Root Namespace entry in the Objects Property Pages window gives the name of the namespace that will be used for new classes, as shown in Figure 11-13.

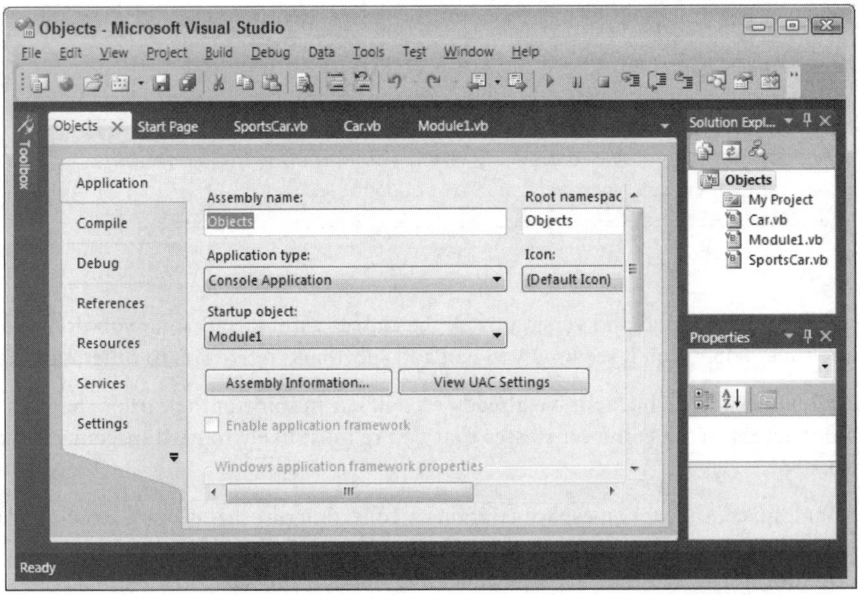

FIGURE 11-13

How It Works

What this means is that your classes have the text `Objects` prefixed to them, like this:

➤ The `Car` class is actually called `Objects.Car`.

➤ The `SportsCar` class is actually called `Objects.SportsCar`.

As you may have guessed, .NET automatically creates a shorthand version of your classes too, so you can refer to **SportsCar** instead of having to type **Objects.SportsCar**.

The motivation behind using namespaces is to make life easier for developers using your classes. Imagine that you give this project to another developer for use and they have already built their own class called `Car`. How do they tell the difference between their class and your class?

Yours will actually be called `Objects.Car`, whereas theirs will have a name like `MyOwnProject.Car` or `YaddaYadda.Car`. Namespaces remove the ambiguity of class names. (Of course, we didn't choose a very good namespace, because it doesn't really describe the classes that the namespace contains — we just chose a namespace that illustrates the purpose of the chapter.)

The Imports Statement

Now you know you don't need to prefix your classes with `Car` or `System` because .NET automatically creates a shorthand version, but how do you do this yourself? The answer is the `Imports` statement!

If you go back to Chapter 10, you might remember this code from the top of the Debug form:

```
Imports System.Collections.Generic

Public Class Debug
```

You may recall this code as well:

```
'Using the List<T> class
Private objCustomerList As New List(Of Customer)
```

You used the `Imports` statement to import the `System.Collections.Generic` namespace into your project. You needed to do this for access to the `List<T>` class. The full name of this class is `System.Collections.Generic.List(Of T)`, but because you added a namespace import declaration, you could just write `List(Of Customer)` instead, substituting the `Customer` class in place of the `T` parameter.

All `Imports` statements must be written at the top of the code file in which you want to use them, before any other code, including the `Class` declaration.

However, if you import two namespaces that have an identically named class or child namespace, Visual Basic 2010 cannot tell what you are after (such as `Car.Car` and `MyOwnProject.Car`). If this happens, Visual Basic 2010 informs you that the name is ambiguous — in which case the quickest and easiest thing to do is to specify the full name.

Creating Your Own Namespace

Namespaces are defined by wrapping the `Class ... End Class` definition in a `Namespace ... End Namespace` definition. By default, classes created in Visual Basic 2010 are automatically assigned to a root namespace. Visual Studio 2010 automatically names this root namespace based on the project name.

TRY IT OUT   Creating a Namespace

Code file Objects.zip is available for download at Wrox.com

In the next Try It Out, you learn to create a namespace.

1. Using the Solution Explorer, double-click My Project. The Root Namespace field tells you the name. In this case, the root namespace name is `Objects`.

2. It's often recommended that you build your namespaces such that the full names of the classes you develop are prefixed with the name of your company. For example, if your company were called MyCodeWidgets, ideally you would want the `Car` class called `MyCodeWidgets.Car`. To do this, change the Root Namespace field from Objects to **MyCodeWidgets** (see Figure 11-14). Then click the Save button on the toolbar to have this change applied to your project.

FIGURE 11-14

3. The Visual Studio 2010 Object Browser is a useful tool that enables you to see what classes are available in your project. You can find it by selecting View ⇨ Object Browser from the menu bar. When the Object Browser is displayed, the first item is usually All Components. You can click My Solution in the Browse combo box and then navigate to find your `Car` class (see Figure 11-15).

4. Note that you can also see the methods, properties, and member variables listed for the class. Pertinent to this discussion, however, is the namespace. This is immediately above the class and is indicated by the icon containing the open and close brace symbols (`{}`).

That's fine, but imagine now that you have two projects both containing a class called `Car`. You need to use namespaces to separate the `Car` class in one project from the `Car` class in the other. Open the Code Editor for `Car` and add `Namespace CarPerformance` before the class definition, and `End Namespace` after it (I've omitted the code for brevity):

```
Namespace CarPerformance
    Public Class Car

        .
    End Class
End Namespace
```

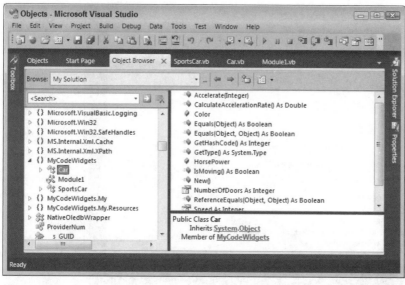

FIGURE 11-15

5.   Open the Object Browser again and you'll see a screen like the one shown in Figure 11-16.

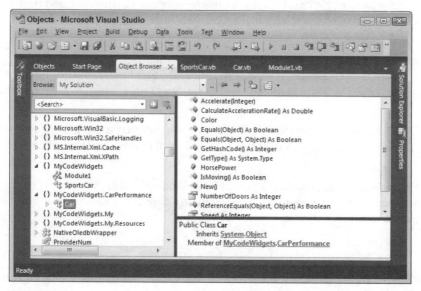

FIGURE 11-16

6.   Because you added the `CarPerformance` namespace to the `Car` class, any code that references the `Car` class needs to import that namespace in order to access the shorthand methods of the `Car` class.

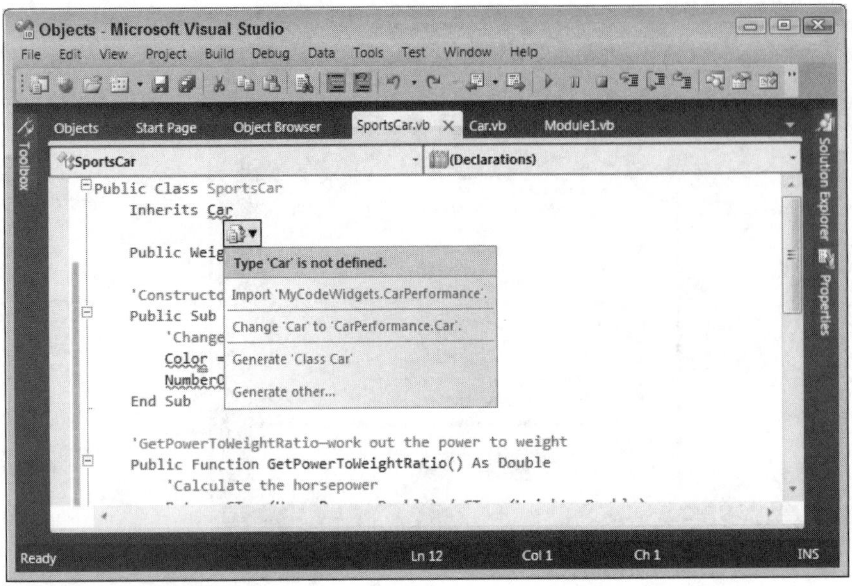

FIGURE 11-17

If you take a look at the SportsCar class, you'll notice that Visual Studio 2010 is reporting an error on the Inherits statement for Car. Hover your mouse over Car in your code and then move your mouse into the gray box and click it. This can be a little tricky to click in the right place.

As shown in Figure 11-17, you have two options: Import the namespace or prefix Car in the Inherits statement with the namespace. You want to choose the first option, so click Import MyCodeWidget.CarPerformance. This causes the Imports statement to be added to the top of the SportsCar class.

7. If you click the Error List tab at the bottom of the IDE, you'll notice that it is reporting one remaining error. Double-click the error in the Error List, and the IDE takes you to the line of code in error.

8. You should now be at the DisplayCarDetails procedure in Module1, where the error is on the Car class in the parameter to the procedure. Hover your mouse over Car in your code, move your mouse into the gray box, and then click it.

How It Works

This time you have three options for correcting the error. Choose the second option, Change Car to CarPerformance.Car. That's it for this example.

In this example you've put Car inside a namespace called CarPerformance. Because this namespace is contained within MyCodeWidgets, the full name of the class becomes MyCodeWidgets.CarPerformance.Car. If you put the classes of the other (imaginary) project into CarDiagnostics, it would be called MyCodeWidgets.CarDiagnostics.Car.

> **NOTE** `Module1` *still appears directly inside* `MyCodeWidgets`. *That's because you haven't wrapped the definition for* `Module1` *in a namespace as you did with* `Car`. *Running your project at this point will produce the same results as before.*

Inheritance in the .NET Framework

Inheritance is an advanced object-oriented topic, but it's very important to include this here because the .NET Framework makes heavy use of inheritance.

One thing to understand about inheritance in .NET is that no class can inherit directly from more than one class. As everything must inherit from `System.Object`, if a class does not specifically state that it inherits from another class, it inherits directly from `System.Object`. The upshot of this is that everything must inherit directly from exactly one class (everything, that is, except `System.Object` itself).

When we say that each class must inherit directly from exactly one class, we mean that each class can mention only one class in its `Inherits` statement. The class that it's inheriting from can also inherit from another class. So, for example, you could create a class called `Porsche` that is inherited from `SportsCar`. You could then say that it *indirectly* inherits from `Car`, but it *directly* inherits from only one class — `SportsCar`. In fact, many classes indirectly inherit from many classes — but there is always a direct ancestry, where each class has exactly one parent.

You may want to have some functionality in different classes that are not related to each other by inheritance. You can solve the problem by putting that functionality in an interface that both classes implement, like the `IDisposable` interface you encountered in Chapter 10.

SUMMARY

In this chapter, you looked at how to start building your own objects. You kicked off by learning how to design an object in terms of the properties and methods that it should support and then built a class that represented a car. You then started adding properties and methods to that class and used it from within your application.

Before moving on to the subject of inheritance, you looked at how an object can be given a constructor — a block of code that's executed whenever an object is created. The discussion of inheritance demonstrated a number of key aspects of object-oriented design, including polymorphism and overriding.

To summarize, you should know how to:

➤ Create properties and methods in a class

➤ Provide a constructor for your class to initialize the state of your class

➤ Inherit another class

➤ Override properties and methods in the inheriting class

➤ Create your own namespace for a class

1. Modify your Car class to implement the IDisposable interface. In the Main procedure in Module1, add code to dispose of the objCar object after calling the DisplaySportsCarDetails procedure.

2. Modify the code in the Main procedure in Module1 to encapsulate the declaration and usage of the SportsCar class in a Using ... End Using statement. Remember that the Using ... End Using statement automatically handles disposal of objects that implement the IDisposable interface.

► **WHAT YOU HAVE LEARNED IN THIS CHAPTER**

TOPIC	CONCEPTS
Creating classes	Use properties and methods to represent an object. You can use a Constructor to setup default values.
Inheritance	You can create a class with the same properties of another by inheriting it. When you inherit a class, you can change the way the new class works by overriding its properties and methods.
Polymorphism	Treating an object as another. So, when you inherit a class the new class can be treated as the inherited one.
Encapsulation	The complex code is hidden inside the class. To use the class, you do not need to understand how it does what it does.

12

Advanced Object-Oriented Techniques

WHAT YOU WILL LEARN IN THIS CHAPTER:

➤ Creating classes that can be used by multiple applications

➤ Learning about shared properties and methods

➤ Learning about memory management in the .NET Framework

In Chapter 11, you looked at how you can build your own objects. Prior to that, you had been mostly using objects that already existed in the .NET Framework to build your applications. In this chapter, you'll take a look at some more object-oriented software development techniques.

In the first half of this chapter, you create your own classes. You will create a single-tier application like the others discussed so far in this book. The idea of creating two-tier applications, as opposed to single-tier applications, is introduced in Chapter 15. You then learn about creating your own shared properties and methods. These are very useful when you want a method or property to apply to a class as a whole, rather than a specific instance of that class. Finally, you look at memory management in Visual Studio 2010 and what you can do to clean up your objects properly.

BUILDING A FAVORITES VIEWER

In the first half of this chapter, you're going to build a simple application that displays all your Internet Explorer favorites and provides a button that you can click to open the URL in Internet Explorer. This application illustrates a key point regarding code reuse and some of the reasons why building code in an object-oriented fashion is so powerful.

Internet Shortcuts and Favorites

You're most likely familiar with the concept of favorites in Internet Explorer. What you may not know is how Internet Explorer stores those favorites. In fact, the Favorites list is available to all other applications — provided you know where to look.

Windows applications have the option of storing data in separate user folders within a main folder. On earlier Windows systems such as Windows XP, this folder is called `C:\Documents and Settings`. On Windows Vista and Windows 7, this folder is called `C:\Users`. In Figure 12-1 you can see that my computer has three user folders: `Public`, `Administrator2`, and `Bryan`.

> **NOTE** *Administrator2 is the default user that was specified on this computer when Windows 7 was set up. This will most likely be different for you. For users who are using Windows XP, Administrator is the default administrator on your computer and a folder called Administrator will be displayed. If you see a Default folder, it is a special folder that Windows uses whenever a new user logs onto the computer for the first time. The Public folder is where public documents, downloads, music, videos, and pictures are stored that are accessible to all users of that computer.*

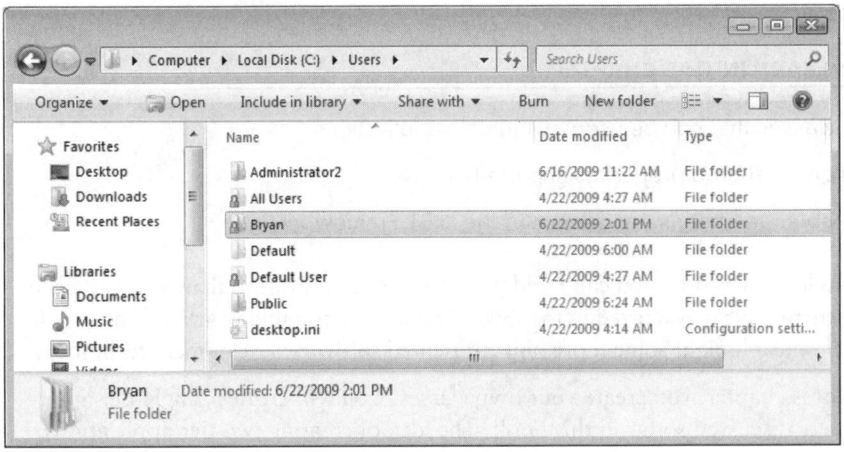

FIGURE 12-1

Depending on how the security of your computer is configured, you may not be able to access the `C:\Users` folder. If you can, open the folder whose name matches the name that you supply when you log on. In the screenshots throughout this chapter, I've used `Bryan`. (If you cannot consistently open the folder, ask your system administrator to help you log in as a different user or give you the appropriate permissions.) If you open this folder, you'll find another group of folders. You'll see something like what is shown in Figure 12-2 (though it may look different depending upon how your login is configured).

You'll notice that in Figure 12-1 some of these folder icons appear as faint icons, whereas others appear as normal folder icons. The computer is configured to show all folders, so you may find that on your machine the faint folders do not appear because these are normally hidden. This doesn't matter, because the one you're specifically looking for — `Favorites` — will appear whatever your system settings are.

This folder (`Bryan` on this computer) is where Windows stores a lot of folders that are related to the operation of your computer for your login account, for example:

➤ AppData stores application data related to the applications that you use.

➤ Contacts stores the Windows contacts, similar to the contacts stored in Microsoft Outlook.

➤ Desktop stores the folders and links that appear on your desktop.

➤ My Documents stores any folders or documents that you create.

➤ Favorites stores a list of Internet Explorer favorites.

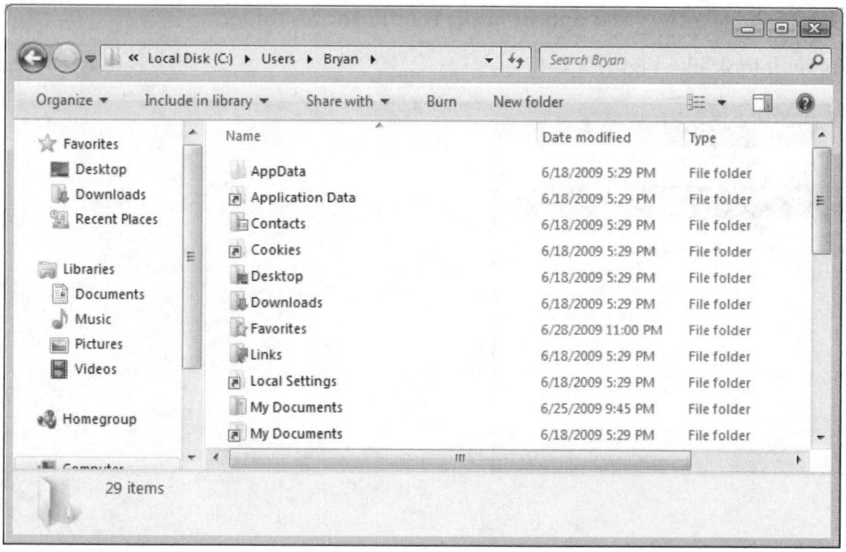

FIGURE 12-2

It's the Favorites folder that you're interested in here, so open it. You'll see something like Figure 12-3 (obviously, this list will be different on your computer because you'll have different favorites).

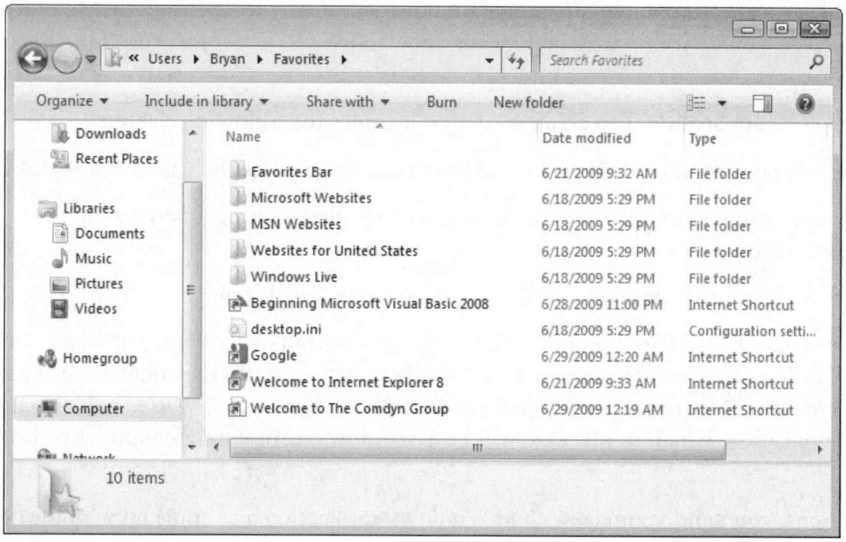

FIGURE 12-3

You'll notice that the links inside this folder relate to the links that appear in the Favorites menu in your browser. If you double-click one of those links, you'll see that Internet Explorer opens and navigates to the URL that the favorite points to.

You can be fairly confident at this stage that if you have a folder of links that appear to be favorites, you can create an application that opens this folder and can do something with the links — namely, iterate through all of them, add each of them to a list, find out what URL it belongs to, and provide a way to open that URL from your application. In the example that follows, you're going to ignore the folders and just deal with the favorites that appear in the root Favorites folder.

Your final application will look like Figure 12-4.

FIGURE 12-4

Using Classes

So far in this book, you've built basic applications that do something, but most functionality that they provide has been coded into the applications' forms. Here, you're about to build some functionality that can load a list of favorites from a user's computer and provide a way to open Internet Explorer to show the URL. However, you do it in a way that means you can use the *list of favorites* functionality elsewhere.

The best way to build this application is to create a set that includes the following classes:

➤   `WebFavorite`: Represents a single favorite and has member variables such as `Name` and `Url`

➤   `Favorites`: Can scan the favorites list on the user's computer, creating a new `WebFavorite` object for each favorite

➤   `WebFavoriteCollection`: Contains a collection of `WebFavorite` objects

These three classes provide the *back-end* functionality of the application — in other words, all classes that do something but do not present the user with an interface. This isolates the code in the classes and allows you to reuse the code from different parts of the application — *code reuse*. You also need a *front end* to this application, which in this case will be a Windows form with a couple of controls on it.

In the following sections, you build your classes and Windows application and come up with the application shown in Figure 12-4.

Code file Favorites.zip is available for download at Wrox.com

In the first Try It Out, you start by building the Windows Application project.

1. Open Visual Studio 2010 and create a new Windows Forms Application project called **Favorites Viewer**.

2. Rename Form1.vb in the Solution Explorer to **Viewer.vb** and then modify the form properties as follows:

> **NOTE** *You may have to unzip the image library. To do so, navigate to* C:\Program Files\Microsoft Visual Studio 10.0\Common7\VS2010ImageLibrary\ 1033 *and unzip* VS2010ImageLibrary.zip. *Extract the files in the folder* 1033.

> ➤ Set Font to **Segoe UI, Regular, 8pt.**

> ➤ Set Icon to C:\Program Files\Microsoft Visual Studio 10.0\Common7\ VS2010ImageLibrary\1033\VS2010ImageLibrary\Objects\ico_format\WinVista\ Favorites.ico.

> ➤ Set Size to **470, 300.**

> ➤ Set StartPosition to **CenterScreen.**

> ➤ Set Text to **My Favorites.**

3. Add a ListView control to the form and size it to look similar to Figure 12-5 and set these properties:

> ➤ Set Name to **lvwFavorites.**

> ➤ Set Anchor to **Top, Bottom, Left, Right.**

> ➤ Set FullRowSelect to **True.**

> ➤ Set View to **Details.**

4. Select the Columns property in the Properties window for the lvwFavorites control. Click the ellipsis dots (. . .) button to display the ColumnHeader Collection Editor dialog box.

5. Click the Add button. Set these properties on the new column header:

> ➤ Set Name to **hdrName.**

> ➤ Set Text to **Name.**

> ➤ Set Width to **220.**

6. Click the Add button again to add a second column. Set these properties on the new column header:

> ➤ Set Name to **hdrUrl.**

> ➤ Set Text to **URL.**

> ➤ Set Width to **220.**

7. Click OK to close the editor.

8. Add a LinkLabel control to the bottom of the form and set these properties:

> ➤ Set Name to **lnkUrl**.

> ➤ Set Anchor to **Bottom, Left, Right**.

> ➤ Set TextAlign to **MiddleLeft**.

9. Your completed form should now look similar to the one shown in Figure 12-5.

10. Save your project by clicking the Save All button on the toolbar.

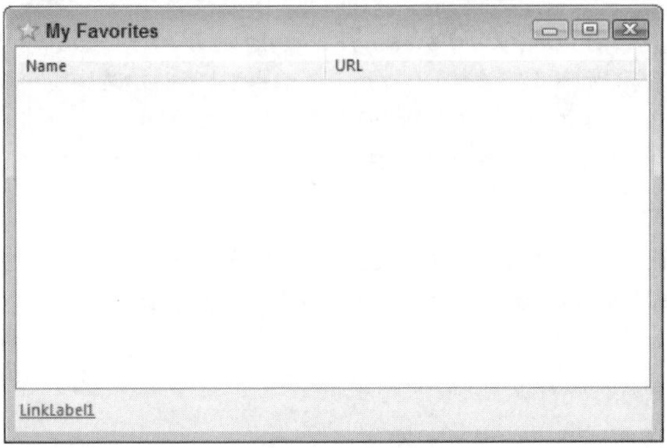

FIGURE 12-5

How It Works

All that you've done here is to build the basic shell of the application, the form that will display the results of the processing. You started by modifying some basic properties of the form and then added two controls: a list view and a link label. The ListView control will be used to display the name and URL of each favorite in your Favorites folder. The LinkLabel control will be used to launch a browser with the selected favorite URL in the list.

That's the basics of the form put together.

TRY IT OUT **Building WebFavorite**

Code file Favorites.zip is available for download at Wrox.com

In the next Try It Out, you look at how you can add the back-end classes. In previous chapters, you learned how to add classes to a Visual Studio 2010 project, so you will use this knowledge to create the back end of your application.

1. Using the Solution Explorer, right-click Favorites Viewer. Select Add ⇨ Class from the menu to display the Add New Item–Favorites Viewer dialog box. Enter a name of **WebFavorite.vb** and then click the Add button.

2. Add this namespace import declaration to the top of the code listing:

```
Imports System.IO

Public Class WebFavorite
```

3. This class will need to implement the `IDisposable` interface, so add this `Implements IDisposable` statement. When you press Enter, Visual Studio 2010 inserts the members and methods associated with the `IDisposable` interface:

```
Public Class WebFavorite
    Implements IDisposable
```

4. Now add the following two members after the `IDisposable` interface code inserted by Visual Studio 2010:

```
#End Region

    'Public Members
    Public Name As String
    Public Url As String
```

5. Now add the `Load` method, which will load the member variables in this class:

```
Public Sub Load(ByVal fileName As String)
    'Declare variables
    Dim strData As String
    Dim strLines() As String
    Dim strLine As String
    Dim objFileInfo As New FileInfo(fileName)

    'Set the Name member to the file name minus the extension
    Name = objFileInfo.Name.Substring(0, _
        objFileInfo.Name.Length - objFileInfo.Extension.Length)

    Try
        'Read the entire contents of the file
        strData = My.Computer.FileSystem.ReadAllText(fileName)

        'Split the lines of data in the file
        strLines = strData.Split(New String() {ControlChars.CrLf}, _
            StringSplitOptions.RemoveEmptyEntries)

        'Process each line looking for the URL
        For Each strLine In strLines
            'Does the line of data start with URL=
            If strLine.StartsWith("URL=") Then
                'Yes, set the Url member to the actual URL
                Url = strLine.Substring(4)
                'Exit the For..Next loop
                Exit For
            End If
        Next
    Catch IOExceptionErr As IOException
        'Return the exception to the caller
        Throw New Exception(IOExceptionErr.Message)
    End Try
End Sub
```

How It Works

In this example, you created the `WebFavorite` class. It will be useful to examine how the `WebFavorite` class populates itself when the `Load` method is invoked.

The first thing you do is declare the variables needed by this method. The `strData` variable is used to receive the entire contents of the favorite's shortcut file. The `strLines()` variable is used to create an array containing each individual line of data from the `strData` variable, and the `strLine` variable is used to iterate through the array of lines. Finally, the `objFileInfo` object gets the file information from the full path and file name passed to this method:

```
Public Sub Load(ByVal fileName As String)
    'Declare variables
    Dim strData As String
    Dim strLines() As String
    Dim strLine As String
    Dim objFileInfo As New FileInfo(fileName)
```

Next, the `Name` member is set to just the file name of the favorite's shortcut file; for example, `Google`. This is the name of the favorite that shows up on the Favorites list in the browser. The `fileName` parameter passed to this method will contain the complete path to the file, the filename, and the file extension (for example, `C:\Users\Bryan\Favorites\Google.url`). What you have to do is extract only the file name from the complete path.

You do this by using the `objFileInfo` object, which has been initialized to an instance of the `FileInfo` class with the `fileName` variable passed to it. The `FileInfo` class provides several methods that return the various parts of the complete file path and name, such as only the file name and only the file extension.

You use the `Name` property of the `objFileInfo` object to get just the filename and extension of the file without the path, and you use the `Substring` method of the `Name` property to extract the filename minus the file extension. To supply the parameters to the `Substring` method, you also use the `Length` property of the `Name` property in the `objFileInfo` object to determine how long the file name is, and the `Length` property of the `Extension` property to determine how long the file extension is.

So basically what you're saying here is, "Take a substring, starting at the first character, and continue for the complete length of the string minus the length of the `Extension` property." This, in effect, removes the `.url` from the end. Remember that the array of characters that make up a string is zero-based; thus, you specify a starting position of `0` for the `SubString` method:

```
'Set the Name member to the file name minus the extension
Name = objFileInfo.Name.Substring(0, _
    objFileInfo.Name.Length—objFileInfo.Extension.Length)
```

You read the entire contents of the file next into the `strData`. Because you are reading from a file, you'll want to encapsulate the logic in a `Try ... Catch` block to handle any IO exceptions that might occur.

The first thing that you do in this `Try ... Catch` block is read the entire contents of the file into the `strData` variable. This is done using the `My.Computer` namespace and the `ReadAllText` method of the `FileSystem` class. This method handles all the details of opening the file, reading the entire contents, closing the file, and releasing the resources used to perform these operations:

```
Try
    'Read the entire contents of the file
    strData = My.Computer.FileSystem.ReadAllText(fileName)
```

After the contents of the file have been read, the `strData` variable will contain something similar to the data shown here. This is the data from the `C:\Users\Bryan\Favorites\Google.url` shortcut file:

```
[DEFAULT]
BASEURL=http://www.google.com/
[InternetShortcut]
URL=http://www.google.com/
IDList=
IconFile=http://www.google.com/favicon.ico
IconIndex=1
[{000214A0-0000-0000-c120-000000000046}]
Prop3=19,2
```

Now that you have the entire contents of the favorite's shortcut file in a single string variable, you split the contents of the `strData` variable into separate lines. This is done using the `Split` method of the `String` class, from which the `strData` variable is derived. The `Split` method is an overloaded method, and the version that you are using here accepts an array of strings as the first parameter and the split options as the second parameter.

The data in the `strData` variable is separated with a carriage return and line feed character combination, and thus you provide a string array containing only one entry, `ControlChars.CrLf`, as the first parameter of the `Split` method. The split options parameter of the `Split` method is a value in the `StringSplitOptions` enumeration that lets you specify how empty elements are handled. Here you specify the `RemoveEmptyEntries` constant of that enumeration, to remove any empty entries in the array that are returned:

```
'Split the lines of data in the file
strLines = strData.Split(New String() {ControlChars.CrLf}, _
    StringSplitOptions.RemoveEmptyEntries)
```

Next you need to process each line of data in the `strLines` array using a For . . . Next loop. You are looking for the line of data that begins with "`URL=`". Using an `If . . . Then` statement, you check the `strLine` variable to see whether it begins with the specified text. The `StartsWith` method of the `String` class, the class from which the `strLine` variable is derived, returns a `Boolean` value of `True` if the string that is being tested contains the string that is passed to this method, and a value of `False` if it does not.

If the line of data being tested starts with the text "`URL=`", then it is the actual URL that you want to save in the `Url` member of the class. To do so, you use the `SubString` method to get the URL in the `strLine` variable minus the beginning text. In order to do this, you pass a starting position of 4 to the `SubString` method, telling it to start extracting data at position 4, because positions 0 – 3 contain the text "`URL=`". Once you find the data that you are looking for and set the `Url` member, there's no need to process the rest of the `strLines` array, so you exit the For . . . Next loop:

```
'Process each line looking for the URL
For Each strLine In strLines
    'Does the line of data start with URL=
    If strLine.StartsWith("URL=") Then
        'Yes, set the Url member to the actual URL
        Url = strLine.Substring(4)
        'Exit the For..Next loop
        Exit For
    End If
Next
```

The `Catch` block handles any IO exception that might be thrown. Here you want to return the exception to the caller of this method, so you throw a new `Exception` and pass it the `Message` property of the `IOExceptionErr` variable. This gracefully handles any IO exceptions in this class and returns the message of the exception to the caller:

```
Catch IOExceptionErr As IOException
    'Return the exception to the caller
    Throw New Exception(IOExceptionErr.Message)
End Try
End Sub
```

Scanning Favorites

So that you can scan the favorites, in the next Try It Out you will add a couple of new classes to the project.

TRY IT OUT   Scanning Favorites

Code file Favorites.zip is available for download at Wrox.com

Next, add two new classes. The first, `WebFavoriteCollection`, holds a collection of `WebFavorite` objects. The second, `Favorites`, physically scans the Favorites folder on the computer, creates new `WebFavorite` objects, and adds them to the collection.

1. Using the Solution Explorer, create a new class called **WebFavoriteCollection**. This class will be instantiated to an object that can hold a number of `WebFavorite` objects.

2. Add the highlighted code in your class:

```
Public Class WebFavoriteCollection
    Inherits CollectionBase

    Public Sub Add(ByVal Favorite As WebFavorite)
        'Add item to the collection
        List.Add(Favorite)
    End Sub

    Public Sub Remove(ByVal Index As Integer)
        'Remove item from collection
        If Index >= 0 And Index < Count Then
            List.Remove(Index)
        End If
    End Sub

    Public ReadOnly Property Item(ByVal Index As Integer) As WebFavorite
        Get
            'Get an item from the collection by its index
            Return CType(List.Item(Index), WebFavorite)
        End Get
    End Property
End Class
```

3. Create another new class called **Favorites**. This will be used to scan the Favorites folder and return a `WebFavoriteCollection` containing a `WebFavorite` object for each favorite in the folder. Like the `WebFavorite` class, this class implements the `IDisposable` interface. Enter the following highlighted code and press Enter to add the properties and methods of the `IDisposable` interface to your class:

```
Public Class Favorites
    Implements IDisposable
```

4. Next, add this member below the code for the `IDisposable` interface:

```
'Public member
Public FavoritesCollection As WebFavoriteCollection
```

5. You need a read-only property that can return the path to the user's Favorites folder. Add the following code to the `Favorites` class:

```
Public ReadOnly Property FavoritesFolder() As String
    Get
        'Return the path to the user's Favorites folder
        Return Environment.GetFolderPath( _
            Environment.SpecialFolder.Favorites)
    End Get
End Property
```

6. Finally, you need a method that's capable of scanning through the Favorites folder looking for files. When it finds one, it creates a `WebFavorite` object and adds it to the Favorites collection. You provide two versions of this method — one that automatically determines the path of the favorites by using the `FavoritesFolder` property and one that scans through a given folder. To create this overloaded method, add the following code to the `Favorites` class:

```
Public Sub ScanFavorites()
    'Scan the Favorites folder
    ScanFavorites(FavoritesFolder)
End Sub

Public Sub ScanFavorites(ByVal folderName As String)
    'If the FavoritesCollection member has not been instantiated
    'then instantiate it
    If FavoritesCollection Is Nothing Then
        FavoritesCollection = New WebFavoriteCollection
    End If

    'Process each file in the Favorites folder
    For Each strFile As String In _
        My.Computer.FileSystem.GetFiles(folderName)

        'If the file has a url extension..
        If strFile.EndsWith(".url", True, Nothing) Then

            Try
                'Create and use a new instance of the
                'WebFavorite class
                Using objWebFavorite As New WebFavorite
                    'Load the file information
                    objWebFavorite.Load(strFile)
```

```
                        'Add the object to the collection
                        FavoritesCollection.Add(objWebFavorite)
                End Using
            Catch ExceptionErr As Exception
                'Return the exception to the caller
                Throw New Exception(ExceptionErr.Message)
            End Try

        End If

    Next
End Sub
```

To make all of this work, you need to have the Favorites Viewer project create an instance of a `Favorites` object, scan the favorites, and add each one it finds to the list. You do this in the next Try It Out.

How It Works

There's a lot to take in for this example, but a good starting point is the `WebFavoriteCollection` class. This illustrates an important best practice when working with lists of objects. As you saw in Chapter 5, you can hold lists of objects in one of two ways: in an array or in a collection.

When building classes that work with lists, the best practice is to use a collection. You should build collections that are also tied into using whatever types you're working with, so in this example you built a `WebFavoriteCollection` class that exclusively holds a collection of `WebFavorite` objects.

You derived `WebFavoriteCollection` from `CollectionBase`. This provides the basic list that the collection will use:

```
Public Class WebFavoriteCollection
    Inherits CollectionBase
```

To fit in with the .NET Framework's way of doing things, you need to define three methods on a collection that you build. The `Add` method adds an item to the collection:

```
Public Sub Add(ByVal Favorite As WebFavorite)
    'Add item to the collection
    List.Add(Favorite)
End Sub
```

The `List` property is a protected member of `CollectionBase` that only code within classes inheriting from `CollectionBase` can access. You access this property to add, remove, and find items in the list. You can see from the `Add` method here that you specified that the item must be a `WebFavorite` object. This is why you're supposed to build collections using this technique — because you can add objects only of type `WebFavorite`; anyone who has hold of a `WebFavoriteCollection` object knows that it will contain objects only of type `WebFavorite`. This makes life much easier for users, because they will not get nasty surprises when they discover it contains something else, and therefore it reduces the chance of errors. The `Remove` method that you built removes an item from the list:

```
Public Sub Remove(ByVal Index As Integer)
    'Remove item from collection
    If Index >= 0 And Index < Count Then
        List.Remove(Index)
    End If
End Sub
```

The `Item` method lets you get an item from the list when given a specific index:

```
Public ReadOnly Property Item(ByVal Index As Integer) As WebFavorite
    Get
        'Get an item from the collection by its index
        Return CType(List.Item(Index), WebFavorite)
    End Get
End Property
```

How do you populate this collection? Well, in the `Favorites` class you built an overloaded method called `ScanFavorites`. The second version of this method takes a folder and examines it for files that end in `.url`. But before you look at that, you need to look at the `FavoritesFolder` property.

Because the location of the Favorites folder can change depending on the currently logged-in user, you have to ask Windows where this folder actually is. To do this, you use the shared `GetFolderPath` method of the `System.Environment` class:

```
Public ReadOnly Property FavoritesFolder() As String
    Get
        'Return the path to the user's Favorites folder
        Return Environment.GetFolderPath( _
            Environment.SpecialFolder.Favorites)
    End Get
End Property
```

The `GetFolderPath` method uses one of the constants from the `Environment.SpecialFolder` enumeration. This enumeration provides constants for many different special folders that you are likely to need access to when writing applications.

When the application asks this class to load in the favorites from the Favorites folder, it calls `ScanFavorites`. The first version of this method accepts no parameters. It looks up the location of the user's Favorites folder and passes that to the second version of this overloaded method:

```
Public Sub ScanFavorites()
    'Scan the Favorites folder
    ScanFavorites(FavoritesFolder)
End Sub
```

The first thing that the second version of this overloaded method does is check to ensure that the `FavoritesCollection` member has been instantiated using the `WebFavoriteCollection` class. If it hasn't, it instantiates this member using that class:

```
Public Sub ScanFavorites(ByVal folderName As String)
    'If the FavoritesCollection member has not been instantiated
    'then instantiate it
    If FavoritesCollection Is Nothing Then
        FavoritesCollection = New WebFavoriteCollection
    End If
```

Next, you want to get a list of files in the Favorites folder and process them. You do this by calling the `GetFiles` method in the `FileSystem` class and passing it the path and name of the Favorites folder. This class exists in the `My.Computer` namespace, as indicated by the following `For Each` code.

The `GetFiles` method returns an array of filenames, and you process this array using a `For Each...Next` loop. You declare the variable, `strFile`, inline in the `For Each` loop, as indicated in the following code, and this variable will be set to a file name in the Favorites folder for each iteration of the loop:

```
'Process each file in the Favorites folder
For Each strFile As String In _
    My.Computer.FileSystem.GetFiles(folderName)
```

Within the loop, you first test the file name to see whether it is a Favorites file by checking to see whether it contains a `.url` file extension. The `strFile` variable is derived from the `String` class; thus, you can use the `EndsWith` method to determine whether the file name ends with the `.url` file extension.

The `EndsWith` method is an overloaded method, and the version that you are using here accepts three parameters. The first parameter accepts the value to be compared to the end of the string, and here you supply the text `.url`. The next parameter accepts a `Boolean` value indicating whether the `EndsWith` method should ignore the case of the text when making the comparison. You do want to ignore the case when making the comparison, so you pass a value of `True` for this parameter. The final parameter accepts the culture information that will be used when making the comparison. Passing a value of `Nothing` here indicates that you want to use the current culture information defined on the user's computer:

```
'If the file has a url extension..
If strFile.EndsWith(".url", True, Nothing) Then
```

If the file name being processed does contain the `.url` file extension, then you want to load the file information and have it added to the Favorites collection. Since you are using the `WebFavorite` class and this class reads the file, the potential for an exception exists. Therefore, you need to encapsulate the next block of code in a `Try...Catch` block to handle any exceptions that might be thrown by the `WebFavorite` class.

The first thing that you do in the `Try` block is use a `Using...End Using` block to declare, instantiate, use, and destroy the `WebFavorite` class. Remember that you can use the `Using` statement only with a class that implements the `IDisposable` interface, which is why you added that interface to the `WebFavorite` class.

The first thing that you do in the `Using...End Using` block is call the `Load` method on the `objWebFavorite` object, passing it the file name of the favorite's shortcut file. Then you add the `objWebFavorite` to the Favorites collection:

```
Try
    'Create and use a new instance of the
    'WebFavorite class
    Using objWebFavorite As New WebFavorite
        'Load the file information
        objWebFavorite.Load(strFile)

        'Add the object to the collection
        FavoritesCollection.Add(objWebFavorite)
    End Using
```

The `Catch` block contains the necessary code to handle an exception that might be thrown by the `WebFavorite` class and to return that exception to the caller of this method. This is done by throwing a new `Exception`, passing it the message received in the `ExceptionErr` variable:

```
Catch ExceptionErr As Exception
    'Return the exception to the caller
    Throw New Exception(ExceptionErr.Message)
End Try
```

```
            End If

      Next
   End Sub
```

In the following Try It Out, you implement the new functionality in your form.

TRY IT OUT Creating an Instance of a Favorites Object

Code file Favorites.zip is available for download at Wrox.com

In this Try It Out, you change the form to use the Favorites class to gather all of your Internet Favorites, and the WebFavorite class to load those shortcuts in the ListView control on your form.

1. View the code for the Viewer form and select (Viewer Events) in the Class Name combo box, and then select Load in the Method Name combo box. Add the highlighted code:

```
Private Sub Viewer_Load(ByVal sender As Object, _
    ByVal e As System.EventArgs) Handles Me.Load

    Try
        'Create and use a new instance of the Favorites class
        Using objFavorites As New Favorites

            'Scan the Favorites folder
            objFavorites.ScanFavorites()

            'Process each objWebFavorite object in the
            'favorites collection
            For Each objWebFavorite As WebFavorite In _
                objFavorites.FavoritesCollection

                'Declare a ListViewItem object
                Dim objListViewItem As New ListViewItem

                'Set the properties of the ListViewItem object
                objListViewItem.Text = objWebFavorite.Name
                objListViewItem.SubItems.Add(objWebFavorite.Url)

                'Add the ListViewItem object to the ListView
                lvwFavorites.Items.Add(objListViewItem)
            Next

        End Using
    Catch ExceptionErr As Exception
        'Display the error
        MessageBox.Show(ExceptionErr.Message, "Favorites Viewer", _
            MessageBoxButtons.OK, MessageBoxIcon.Warning)
    End Try
End Sub
```

2. Run the project and you should see something similar to Figure 12-6.

FIGURE 12-6

How It Works

In this example, you hooked up the form with the classes you created earlier. Since both the `Favorites` and `WebFavorite` classes can throw an exception, you must handle any exceptions that might be thrown. Therefore, all your code is encapsulated in a `Try...Catch` block. You use a `Using...End Using` statement to declare, instantiate, and destroy the object created with the `Favorites` class. Regardless of whether this class throws an exception, the `Using` statement destroys the `objFavorites` object that it declares:

```
Private Sub Viewer_Load(ByVal sender As Object, _
    ByVal e As System.EventArgs) Handles Me.Load

    Try
        'Create and use a new instance of the Favorites class
        Using objFavorites As New Favorites
```

Inside the `Using...End Using` block the `objFavorites` object scans the users Favorites folder by calling the `ScanFavorites` method. The effect here is that a new `WebFavoritesCollection` object is created and filled and will be accessible through the `FavoritesCollection` property:

```
'Scan the Favorites folder
objFavorites.ScanFavorites()
```

After the `ScanFavorites` method finishes, you take each `WebFavorite` in the `FavoritesCollection` and add it to the ListView control on your form. You do this by first declaring a `ListViewItem` and then setting the `Text` property to the Favorite name. Then you add the URL of the Favorite to the `SubItems` collection, and finally you add the `objListViewItem` to the `Items` collection of the ListView control:

```
'Process each objWebFavorite object in the
'favorites collection
For Each objWebFavorite As WebFavorite In _
    objFavorites.FavoritesCollection

    'Declare a ListViewItem object
    Dim objListViewItem As New ListViewItem

    'Set the properties of the ListViewItem object
    objListViewItem.Text = objWebFavorite.Name
        objListViewItem.SubItems.Add(objWebFavorite.Url)
```

```
            'Add the ListViewItem object to the ListView
            lvwFavorites.Items.Add(objListViewItem)
    Next

End Using
```

You wrap up this code with the Catch block, which handles any exceptions thrown and displays the exception message in a message dialog box:

```
    Catch ExceptionErr As Exception
        'Display the error
        MessageBox.Show(ExceptionErr.Message, "Favorites Viewer", _
            MessageBoxButtons.OK, MessageBoxIcon.Warning)
    End Try
End Sub
```

That's it! Now you can display a list of the favorites installed on the user's machine. However, you can't actually view favorites, so let's look at that now.

Viewing Favorites

You will add some code to view your favorite in the next Try It Out.

TRY IT OUT Viewing Favorites

Code file Favorites.zip is available for download at Wrox.com

Now that all of your code is in place to retrieve and display a list of favorites, in this Try It Out you add some code to display the selected favorite in the LinkLabel control on your form and then add some code to the control to process the selected link in Internet Explorer.

1. In the Code Editor for Viewer, click **lvwFavorites** in the Class Name combo box and the Click event in the Method Name combo box. Add the following highlighted code to the Click event handler:

```
Private Sub lvwFavorites_Click(ByVal sender As Object, _
    ByVal e As System.EventArgs) Handles lvwFavorites.Click

    'Update the link label control Text property
    lnkUrl.Text = "Visit " & lvwFavorites.SelectedItems.Item(0).Text

    'Clear the default hyperlink
    lnkUrl.Links.Clear()

    'Add the selected hyperlink to the LinkCollection
    lnkUrl.Links.Add(6, lvwFavorites.SelectedItems.Item(0).Text.Length, _
        lvwFavorites.SelectedItems.Item(0).SubItems(1).Text)
End Sub
```

2. Click **lnkUrl** in the Class Name combo box and select the LinkClicked event in the Method Name combo box. Add the following highlighted code to the LinkClicked event:

```
Private Sub lnkUrl_LinkClicked(ByVal sender As Object, _
```

```
       ByVal e As System.Windows.Forms.LinkLabelLinkClickedEventArgs) _
       Handles lnkUrl.LinkClicked

       'Process the selected link
       Process.Start(e.Link.LinkData)
   End Sub
```

3. Run the project. You should now see that when a URL is selected from the list, the LinkLabel control changes to reflect the name of the selected item (refer to Figure 12-4). When you click the link, Internet Explorer opens the URL in the LinkLabel control's LinkCollection.

How It Works

Now that you have the application working in this example, let's look at how it works. When you click an item in the ListView control, the Click event is fired for that control. You add code to the Click event to load the LinkLabel control with the selected link. You start by first setting the Text property of the LinkLabel control. This is the text that will be displayed on the form as shown in Figure 12-4.

You set the Text property using the static text Visit followed by the actual favorite name. The favorite name is retrieved from the ListView control's Item collection. Each row in the ListView control is called an *item*, and the first column contains the text of the item. Each column past the first column in a row is a subitem of the item (the text in the first column). The text that gets displayed in the link label is taken from the Text property of the Item collection:

```
   Private Sub lvwFavorites_Click(ByVal sender As Object, _
       ByVal e As System.EventArgs) Handles lvwFavorites.Click

       'Update the link label control Text property
       lnkUrl.Text = "Visit " & lvwFavorites.SelectedItems.Item(0).Text
```

The Links property of the LinkLabel control contains a LinkCollection that contains a default hyperlink consisting of the text that is displayed in the LinkLabel control. You clear this collection and set it using the correct hyperlink for the selected Favorite. You do this by calling the Clear method on the Links property:

```
       'Clear the default hyperlink
       lnkUrl.Links.Clear()
```

Finally, you add your hyperlink using the subitem of the selected item in the ListView control. The Add method of the Links property is an overloaded method, and the method that you are using here expects three parameters: start, length, and linkdata. The start parameter specifies the starting position of the text in the Text property that you want as the hyperlink, and the length parameter specifies how long the hyperlink should be.

You do not want the word *Visit* to be part of the hyperlink, so you specify the starting position to be 6, which takes into account the space after the word *Visit*. Then you specify the length parameter using the Length property of the Text property of the selected item in the ListView control. Finally, you specify the linkdata parameter by specifying the selected subitem from the ListViewlist view control. This subitem contains the actual URL for the favorite.

```
       'Add the selected hyperlink to the LinkCollection
       lnkUrl.Links.Add(6, lvwFavorites.SelectedItems.Item(0).Text.Length, _
           lvwFavorites.SelectedItems.Item(0).SubItems(1).Text)
   End Sub
```

When a hyperlink on the LinkLabel control is clicked, it fires the `LinkClicked` event, and this is where you place your code to process the hyperlink of the favorite being displayed in this control. The `LinkLabelLinkClickedEventArgs` class contains information about the link label and, in particular, the actual hyperlink in the `LinkCollection`.

To retrieve the hyperlink, you access the `LinkData` property of the `Link` property. Then you pass this data to the `Start` method of the `Process` class, which causes a browser to be open and display the selected hyperlink:

```
Private Sub lnkUrl_LinkClicked(ByVal sender As Object, _
    ByVal e As System.Windows.Forms.LinkLabelLinkClickedEventArgs) _
    Handles lnkUrl.LinkClicked

    'Process the selected link
    Process.Start(e.Link.LinkData)
End Sub
```

AN ALTERNATIVE FAVORITE VIEWER

You know that building separate classes promotes code reuse, but let's prove that. If code reuse is such a hot idea, without having to rewrite or change any of the code you should be able to build another application that can use the functionality in the classes to find and open favorites.

In this case, you might have given a colleague the `Favorites`, `WebFavorite`, and `WebFavoriteCollection` classes, and that colleague should be able to build a new application that uses this functionality without having to understand the internals of how Internet shortcuts work or how Windows stores the user's favorites.

Building a Favorites Tray

In this section, you build an application that displays a small icon on the system tray. Clicking this icon opens a list of the user's favorites as a menu, as shown in Figure 12-7. Clicking a favorite automatically opens the URL in Internet Explorer or whatever browser the user has set to be the default. Later, when you see Internet Explorer, it may be a different browser for you.

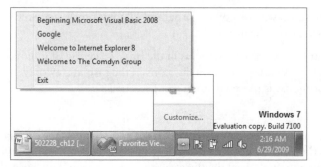

FIGURE 12-7

To demonstrate this principle of code reuse, you need to create a new Visual Basic 2010 project in this solution.

TRY IT OUT   Building a Favorites Tray

Code file Favorites.zip is available for download at Wrox.com

In this example, you will add a new project

1. Using Visual Studio 2010, select File ⇨ Add ⇨ New Project from the menu and create a new Visual Basic 2010 Windows Forms Application project called **Favorites Tray**. Now, you will see two projects in the Solution Explorer.

2. When the Designer for Form1 appears, click the form in the Forms Designer and then change the `WindowState` property to **Minimized** and change the `ShowInTaskbar` property to **False**. This, effectively, prevents the form from being displayed.

3. Using the Toolbox, drag a NotifyIcon control onto the form. It will drop into the component tray at the bottom of the form. Set the `Name` property of the new control to **icnNotify** and set the `Text` property to **Right-click me to view Favorites,** and set the `Icon` property to `C:\Program Files\Microsoft Visual Studio 10.0\Common7\VS2010ImageLibrary\1033\VS2010ImageLibrary\Objects\ico_format\WinVista\Favorites.ico`.

4. Next, open the Code Editor for Form1. In the Class Name combo box at the top of the Code Editor, select (Form1 Events), and in the Method Name combo box select **VisibleChanged**. Add the following highlighted code to the event handler:

```
Private Sub Form1_VisibleChanged(ByVal sender As Object, _
    ByVal e As System.EventArgs) Handles Me.VisibleChanged

        'If the user can see us, hide us
        If Me.Visible = True Then Me.Visible = False
End Sub
```

5. Right-click the Favorites Tray project in the Solution Explorer and select Set As Startup Project. Now try running the project. You should discover that the tray icon is added to your system tray as shown in Figure 12-8, but no form window will appear. If you hover your mouse over the icon, you'll see the message that you set in the `Text` property of the NotifyIcon control.

FIGURE 12-8

6. Also, you'll notice that there appears to be no way to stop the program! Flip back to Visual Studio 2010 and select Debug ⇨ Stop Debugging from the menu.

7. When you do this, although the program stops, the icon remains in the tray. To get rid of it, hover the mouse over it and it should disappear. Windows redraws the icons in the system tray only when necessary (for example, when the mouse is passed over an icon).

How It Works

You learn that setting a form to appear minimized (`WindowState = Minimized`) and telling it not to appear in the taskbar (`ShowInTaskbar = False`) has the effect of creating a window that's hidden in this example. You need a form to support the tray icon, but you don't need the form for any other reason. However, this is only half the battle, because the form could appear in the Alt+Tab application switching list, unless you add the following code, which you already did:

```
Private Sub Form1_VisibleChanged(ByVal sender As Object, _
    ByVal e As System.EventArgs) Handles Me.VisibleChanged
```

```
        'If the user can see us, hide us
        If Me.Visible = True Then Me.Visible = False
    End Sub
```

This event handler has a brute-force approach that says, "If the user can see me, hide me."

Displaying Favorites

In the next Try It Out, you look at how to display the favorites.

TRY IT OUT   Displaying Favorites

Code file Favorites.zip is available for download at Wrox.com

In this example, the first thing you need to do is include the classes built in `Favorites Viewer` in this Favorites Tray solution. You can then use the `Favorites` object to get a list of favorites back and build a menu.

1. To display favorites, you need to get hold of the classes defined in the Favorites Viewer project. To do this you add the `Favorites`, `WebFavorite`, and `WebFavoriteCollection` classes to this project.

Using the Solution Explorer, right-click the Favorites Tray project and select Add ⇨ Existing Item. Browse to the classes in your Favorites Viewer project and find the `Favorites` class. After clicking Add, the class appears in the Solution Explorer for this project. You can select multiple files at once by holding down the Ctrl key.

2. Repeat this for the `WebFavorite` and `WebFavoriteCollection` classes.

3. Create a new class in the Favorites Tray by clicking the project once more and selecting Add ⇨ Class. Call the new class **WebFavoriteMenuItem.vb** and then click the Add button to add this class to the project.

4. Set the new class to inherit from `System.Windows.Forms.MenuItem` by adding this code:

```
Public Class WebFavoriteMenuItem
    Inherits MenuItem
```

5. Add this member and method to the class:

```
'Public member
Public Favorite As WebFavorite

'Constructor
Public Sub New(ByVal newFavorite As WebFavorite)
    'Set the property
    Favorite = newFavorite

    'Update the text
    Text = Favorite.Name
End Sub
```

6. Unlike `ListViewItem`, `MenuItem` objects can react to themselves being clicked by overloading the `Click` method. In the Class Name combo box at the top of the Code Editor, select

(WebFavoriteMenuItem Events) and then select the Click event in the Method Name combo box. Add the following highlighted code to the Click event handler:

```
Private Sub WebFavoriteMenuItem_Click(ByVal sender As Object, _
    ByVal e As System.EventArgs) Handles Me.Click

        'Open the favorite
        If Not Favorite Is Nothing Then
            Process.Start(Favorite.Url)
        End If
End Sub
```

7. You need to do a similar trick to add an Exit option to your pop-up menu. Using the Solution Explorer, create a new class called **ExitMenuItem.vb** in the Favorites Tray project. Add the following highlighted code to this class:

```
Public Class ExitMenuItem
    Inherits MenuItem

    'Constructor
    Public Sub New()
        Text = "Exit"
    End Sub

    Private Sub ExitMenuItem_Click(ByVal sender As Object, _
        ByVal e As System.EventArgs) Handles Me.Click

        Application.Exit()
    End Sub
End Class
```

8. Finally, you're in a position where you can load the favorites and create a menu for use with the tray icon. Add these members to Form1:

```
Public Class Form1
    'Public member
    Public Favorites As New Favorites()

    'Private member
    Private blnLoadCalled As Boolean = False
```

9. In the Class Name combo select (Form1 Events), and in the Method Name combo box, select the Load event. Then add the following highlighted code to this event handler:

```
Private Sub Form1_Load(ByVal sender As Object, _
    ByVal e As System.EventArgs) Handles Me.Load

  'Load the favorites
  Favorites.ScanFavorites()

  'Create a new context menu
  Dim objMenu As New ContextMenu()

  'Process each favorite
  For Each objWebFavorite As WebFavorite In Favorites.FavoritesCollection
      'Create a menu item
      Dim objItem As New WebFavoriteMenuItem(objWebFavorite)
```

```
            'Add it to the menu
            objMenu.MenuItems.Add(objItem)
        Next

        'Add a separator menu item
        objMenu.MenuItems.Add("-")

        'Now add the Exit menu item
        objMenu.MenuItems.Add(New ExitMenuItem())

        'Finally, tell the tray icon to use this menu
        icnNotify.ContextMenu = objMenu

        'Set the load flag and hide ourselves
        blnLoadCalled = True
        Me.Hide()
    End Sub
```

10. Modify the `Form1_VisibleChanged` procedure as follows:

```
    Private Sub Form1_VisibleChanged(ByVal sender As Object, _
        ByVal e As System.EventArgs) Handles Me.VisibleChanged

        'Don't set the Visible property until the Load event has
        'been processed
        If blnLoadCalled = False Then
            Return
        End If

        'If the user can see us, hide us
        If Me.Visible = True Then Me.Visible = False
    End Sub
```

11. Run the project, and the icon will appear on the system tray. Right-click the icon, and you'll see a list of favorites as was shown in Figure 12-7. Clicking one opens Internet Explorer; clicking Exit closes the application. Depending on what applications you have open and your settings, the icon may be grouped in the hidden icon section on the taskbar.

How It Works

That completes this example. One thing to note is that because of the order of events that are fired for your form, you have to create a variable in Form1 called `blnLoadCalled`. This variable makes sure that your favorites get loaded in the form's `Load` event.

The `WebFavoriteMenuItem` class accepts a `WebFavorite` object in its constructor, and it configures itself as a menu item using the class. However, this class provides a `Click` method that you can overload, so when the user selects the item from the menu, you can immediately open the URL:

```
    Private Sub WebFavoriteMenuItem_Click(ByVal sender As Object, _
        ByVal e As System.EventArgs) Handles Me.Click

        'Open the favorite
        If Not Favorite Is Nothing Then
            Process.Start(Favorite.Url)
        End If
    End Sub
```

The `ExitMenuItem` class does a similar thing. When this item is clicked, you call the shared `Application.Exit` method to quit the program:

```
Private Sub ExitMenuItem_Click(ByVal sender As Object, _
    ByVal e As System.EventArgs) Handles Me.Click

    Application.Exit()
End Sub
```

The important thing here is not the construction of the application itself but rather the fact that you can reuse the functionality you built in a different project. This underlines the fundamental motive for reuse; it means you don't have to reinvent the wheel every time you want to do something.

The method of reuse described here was to add the existing classes to your new project, hence making a second copy of them. This isn't efficient, because it takes double the amount of storage needed for the classes; however, the classes are small, so the cost of memory is minimal. It did save you from having to create the classes from scratch, allowing you to reuse the existing code, and it was very easy to do.

An alternative way of reusing classes is to create them in a class library. This class library is a separate project that can be referenced by a number of different applications so that only one copy of the code is required. This is discussed in Chapter 13.

USING SHARED PROPERTIES AND METHODS

On occasion, you might find it useful to access methods and properties that are not tied to an instance of an object but are still associated with a class.

Imagine you have a class that stores the user name and password of a user for a computer program. You might have something that looks like this:

```
Public Class User
    'Public members
    Public Username As String

    'Private members
    Private strPassword As String
End Class
```

Now imagine that the password for a user has to be of a minimum length. You create a separate member to store the length and implement a property like this:

```
Public Class User
    'Public members
    Public Username As String
    Public MinPasswordLength As Integer = 6

    'Private members
    Private strPassword As String

    'Password property
    Public Property Password() As String
        Get
```

```
            Return strPassword
        End Get
        Set(ByVal value As String)
            If value.Length >= MinPasswordLength Then
                strPassword = value
            End If
        End Set
    End Property
End Class
```

That seems fairly straightforward. But now imagine that you have five thousand user objects in memory. Each `MinPasswordLength` variable takes up 4 bytes of memory, meaning that 20 KB of memory is being used to store the same value. Although 20 KB of memory isn't a lot for modern computer systems, it's extremely inefficient, and there is a better way.

Using Shared Properties

See how to use shared properties and understand them in the next example.

Code file Shared Demo.zip is available for download at Wrox.com

Ideally, you want to store the value for the minimum password length in memory against a specific class once and share that memory between all of the objects created from that class, as you'll do in the following Try It Out.

1. Close the existing solution if it is still open and create a new Windows Forms Application project called **Shared Demo**.

2. When the Designer for Form1 appears, change the `Text` property of the form to **Shared Demo** and then drag a ListBox, a Label, and a NumericUpDown control from the Toolbox onto the form. Set the `Text` property of the Label to **Password Length**. Arrange the controls as shown in Figure 12-9.

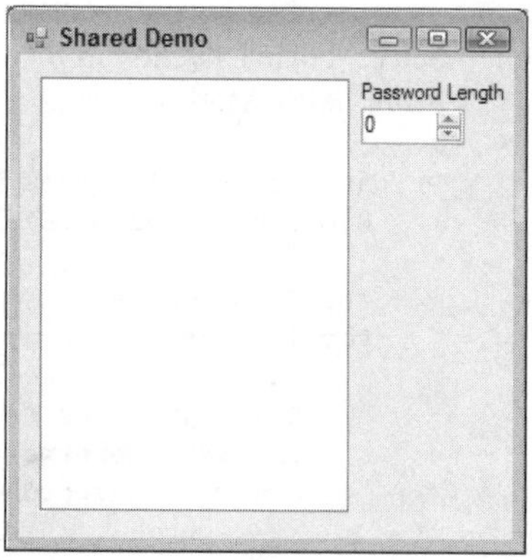

3. Set the `Name` property of the ListBox control to **lstUsers**.

4. Set the `Name` property of the NumericUpDown control to **nud-MinPasswordLength,** set the `Maximum` property to **10**, and set the `Value` property to **6**.

5. Using the Solution Explorer, create a new class named **User**. Add the highlighted code to the class:

FIGURE 12-9

```
Public Class User
    'Public members
    Public Username As String
    Public Shared MinPasswordLength As Integer = 6
```

```
    'Private members
    Private strPassword As String

    'Password property
    Public Property Password() As String
        Get
            Return strPassword
        End Get
        Set(ByVal value As String)
            If value.Length >= MinPasswordLength Then
                strPassword = value
            End If
        End Set
    End Property
End Class
```

6. View the code for Form1 and add this highlighted member:

```
Public Class Form1
    'Private member
    Private arrUserList As New ArrayList()
```

7. Add this method to the Form1 class:

```
Private Sub UpdateDisplay()
    'Clear the list
    lstUsers.Items.Clear()

    'Add the users to the list box
    For Each objUser As User In arrUserList
        lstUsers.Items.Add(objUser.Username & ", " & objUser.Password & _
            " (" & User.MinPasswordLength & ")")
    Next
End Sub
```

8. Select (Form1 Events) in the Class Name combo box at the top of the Code Editor and the Load event in the Method Name combo box. Add the highlighted code to the Load event:

```
Private Sub Form1_Load(ByVal sender As Object, _
    ByVal e As System.EventArgs) Handles Me.Load

    'Load 100 users
    For intIndex As Integer = 1 To 100
        'Create a new user
        Dim objUser As New User
        objUser.Username = "Stephanie" & intIndex
        objUser.Password = "password15"

        'Add the user to the array list
        arrUserList.Add(objUser)
    Next

    'Update the display
    UpdateDisplay()
End Sub
```

9. Select `nudMinPasswordLength` in the Class Name combo box at the top of the Code Editor and the `ValueChanged` event in the Method Name combo box. Add the highlighted code to the `ValueChanged` event:

```
Private Sub nudMinPasswordLength_ValueChanged(ByVal sender As Object, _
    ByVal e As System.EventArgs) Handles nudMinPasswordLength.ValueChanged

        'Set the minimum password length
        User.MinPasswordLength = nudMinPasswordLength.Value
        'Update the display
        UpdateDisplay()
    End Sub
```

10. Save your project by clicking the Save All button on the toolbar.

11. Run the project. You should see a screen like the one shown in Figure 12-10.

12. Scroll the NumericUpDown control up or down, and the list updates; the number in parentheses changes to correspond to the number shown in the NumericUpDown control.

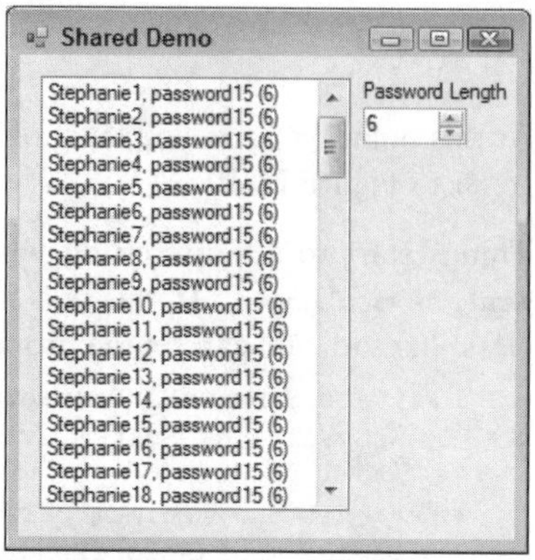

FIGURE 12-10

How It Works

To create a member variable, property, or method on an object that is shared, you use the `Shared` keyword as you did in this example.

```
Public Shared MinPasswordLength As Integer = 6
```

This tells Visual Basic 2010 that the item should be available to all instances of the class.

Shared members can be accessed from within nonshared properties and methods as well as from shared properties and methods. For example, here's the `Password` property, which can access the shared `MinPasswordLength` member:

```
'Password property
Public Property Password() As String
    Get
        Return strPassword
    End Get
    Set(ByVal value As String)
        If value.Length >= MinPasswordLength Then
            strPassword = value
        End If
    End Set
End Property
```

What's important to realize here is that although the `Password` property and `strPassword` member belong to the particular instance of the `User` class, `MinPasswordLength` does not; therefore, if it is changed the effect is felt throughout all the object instances built from the class in question.

In the form, `UpdateDisplay` is used to populate the list. You can gain access to `MinPasswordLength` as if it were a normal, nonshared public member of the `User` object:

```
Private Sub UpdateDisplay()
    'Clear the list
    lstUsers.Items.Clear()

    'Add the users to the list box
    For Each objUser As User In arrUserList
        lstUsers.Items.Add(objUser.Username & ", " & objUser.Password & _
            " (" & User.MinPasswordLength & ")")
    Next
End Sub
```

At this point, you have a listing of users that shows that the `MinPasswordLength` value of each is set to 6 (refer to Figure 12-10).

Things start to get interesting when you scroll the NumericUpDown control and change `MinPasswordLength`. As this is a shared member, you don't specifically *need* an instance of the class. Instead, you can set the property just by using the *class* name:

```
Private Sub nudMinPasswordLength_ValueChanged(ByVal sender As Object, _
    ByVal e As System.EventArgs) Handles nudMinPasswordLength.ValueChanged

    'Set the minimum password length
    User.MinPasswordLength = nudMinPasswordLength.Value

    'Update the display
    UpdateDisplay()
End Sub
```

When building this method, you may notice that after you type **User.**, Visual Studio 2010's IntelliSense pops up a list of members, including the `MinPasswordLength` property, as shown in Figure 12-11.

Shared members, properties, and methods can all be accessed through the class directly — you don't specifically need an instance of the class.

FIGURE 12-11

When you change this member with code in the `ValueChanged` event handler, you update the display, and this time you can see that the perceived value of `MinPasswordLength` has seemingly been changed for *all* instances of `User`, even though you changed it in only one place.

Using Shared Methods

Although you've seen how to make a public member variable shared, you haven't seen how to do this with a method. The main limitation with a shared method is that you can access other shared methods and shared properties only in the class in which it is defined.

> **NOTE** *This is a hypothetical example of using a shared method, as you could do the same job here with a customized constructor.*

TRY IT OUT   Using a Shared Method

Code file Shared Demo.zip is available for download at Wrox.com

In this Try It Out, you look at an example of how to build a shared method that can create new instances of User.

1. Open the Code Editor for User. Add the following code to the User class:

```
Public Shared Function CreateUser(ByVal userName As String, _
    ByVal password As String) As User

    'Declare a new User object
    Dim objUser As New User()

    'Set the User properties
    objUser.Username = userName
    objUser.Password = password

    'Return the new user
    Return objUser
End Function
```

2. Open the Code Editor for Form1 and locate the Load event handler. Change the code so that it looks like the following block. You'll notice that as you type in the code, as soon as you type **User.**, IntelliSense offers CreateUser as an option:

```
Private Sub Form1_Load(ByVal sender As Object, _
    ByVal e As System.EventArgs) Handles Me.Load

    'Load 100 users
    For intIndex As Integer = 1 To 100
        'Create a new user
        Dim objUser As New User
        objUser = User.CreateUser("Stephanie" & intIndex, "password15")

        'Add the user to the array list
        arrUserList.Add(objUser)
    Next

    'Update the display
    UpdateDisplay()
End Sub
```

3. If you run the project, you get the same results as the previous example.

How It Works

The important thing to look at in this example is the fact that CreateUser appears in the IntelliSense list after you type the class name. This is because it is shared and you do not need a specific instance of a class to access it. You create the method as a shared method by using the Shared keyword:

```
Public Shared Function CreateUser(ByVal userName As String, _
    ByVal password As String) As User
```

One thing to consider with shared methods is that you can access only members of the class that are also shared. You cannot access nonshared methods, simply because you don't know what instance of the class you're actually running on. Likewise, you cannot access Me from within a shared method for the same reason.

UNDERSTANDING OBJECT-ORIENTED PROGRAMMING AND MEMORY MANAGEMENT

Object orientation has an impact on how memory is used in an operating system. .NET is heavily object oriented, so it makes sense that .NET would have to optimize the way it uses memory to best suit the way objects are used.

Whenever you create an object, you're using memory. Most of the objects you use have *state,* which describes what an object knows. The methods and properties that an object has will either affect or work with that state. For example, an object that describes a file on disk will have state that describes its name, size, folder, and so on. Some of the state will be publicly accessible through properties. For example, a property called Size returns the size of the file. Some state is private to the object and is used to keep track of what the object has done or what it needs to do.

Objects use memory in two ways. First, something needs to keep track of the objects that exist on the system in memory. This is usually a task shared between you as an application developer and .NET's Common Language Runtime (CLR). If you create an object, you'll have to hold a reference to it in your program's memory so that you know where it is when you need to use its methods and properties. The CLR also needs to keep track of the object to determine when you no longer need it. Second, the CLR needs to allocate memory to the object so that the object can store its state. The more state an object has, the more memory it will need to use it.

The most expensive resource on a computer is the memory. *Expense* here means in terms of what you get for your money. For about $100, you can buy a 120GB hard drive, but for the same amount of money you can't buy 1GB of memory. Retrieving data from memory is thousands of times faster than retrieving it from disk, so there's a trade-off — if you need fast access, you have to store it in memory, but there isn't as much memory available as there is hard disk space.

When building an application, you want to use as little memory as possible, so there's an implication that you want to have as few objects as possible and that those objects should have as little state as possible. The upside is that, today, computers have a lot more memory than they used to have, so your programs can use more memory than their predecessors of 10 years ago. However, you still need to be cognizant of your application's memory usage.

The CLR manages memory in several distinct ways. First, it's responsible for creating objects at the request of the application. With a heavily object-oriented programming platform like .NET, this is going to happen all the time, so Microsoft has spent an enormous amount of time making sure that the CLR creates objects in the most efficient way. The CLR, for example, can create objects far faster than its Component Object Model (COM) predecessor could. Second, the CLR is responsible for cleaning up memory when it's no longer needed. In the developer community, the manner in which the CLR cleans up objects is one of the most controversial.

Imagine you're writing a routine that opens a file from disk and displays the contents on the screen. Well, with .NET you could use perhaps two .NET Framework objects to open the file and read its contents — namely, `System.IO.FileStream` and `System.IO.StreamReader`. However, after the contents have been read, do you need these objects anymore? Probably not, so you remove your references to the objects and make the memory the objects were using available for creating more objects.

Imagine now that you don't remove your references to the objects. In this situation, the memory that the objects were using can't be used by anyone else. Now imagine that happening several thousand times. The amount of memory that's being wasted keeps growing. In extreme circumstances, the computer runs out of memory, meaning that other applications wouldn't ever be able to create any objects. This is a pretty catastrophic state of affairs.

We describe an object that is no longer needed but that holds onto memory as a *leak*. Memory leaks are one of the biggest causes of reliability problems on Windows, because when a program is no longer able to obtain memory, it will crash.

With .NET this *should* never happen, or, at the very least, to leak memory you would have to go to some pretty extreme steps. This is because of a feature called *garbage collection*. When an object is no longer being used, the *garbage collector (GC)* automatically removes the object from memory and makes the memory it was using available to other programs.

Garbage Collection

The garbage collector (GC) works by keeping track of how many parts of a program have a reference to an object. If it gets to the point where there are no open references to the object, it is deleted.

To understand this, think back to the discussion of scope in Chapter 3. Imagine you create a method and at the top of that method you define a variable with local scope. That variable is used to store an object (it doesn't matter what kind of object is used for this discussion). At this point, one part of the program knows about the object's existence — that is, the variable is holding a reference to the object. When you return from the method, the variable goes out of scope, and therefore the variable forgets about the object's existence; in other words, the only reference to the object is lost. At this point, no one knows about the object, and so it can be safely deleted.

For an example, look at the following code:

```
Dim objObject As New MyObject
Console.WriteLine(objObject.GetType().FullName)
objObject = Nothing
```

This code snippet creates a new object from class `MyObject`, invokes a method on it, and then removes the reference to the object. In this case, when you create the object, the `objObject` variable is the only thing that holds a reference to it. In the last line, `objObject` is set to `Nothing`, hence removing the only reference to the object. The GC is then free to remove the reference to the object.

The GC does not run constantly. Instead, it runs periodically based on a complex algorithm that measures the amount of work the computer is doing and how many objects might need to be deleted. When the GC runs, it looks through the master list of all the objects the program has ever created for any that can be deleted at this point.

In old-school programming, programmers were responsible for deleting their own objects and had the freedom to say to an object, "You, now, clean yourself up and get out of memory." With .NET this ability is gone. Rather, an object will be deleted at some *indeterminate* time in the future.

Exactly when this happens is nondeterministic — in other words, as a developer you don't know when the GC is going to run. This means that there is no immediate connection between the removal of the last reference to an object and the physical removal of that object from memory. This is known as *nondeterministic finalization*.

Releasing Resources

In some cases, objects that you build may need access to certain system and network resources, such as files and database connections. Using these resources requires a certain discipline to ensure that you don't inadvertently cause problems.

Here's an example — if you create a new file, write some data to it, but forget to close it, no one else will be able to read data from that file. This is because you have an *exclusive lock* on the file; it doesn't make sense for someone to be able to read from a file when it's still being written to. You must take care to release system resources should you open them.

When an object has access to scarce system or network resources like this, it's important that the caller tell the object that it can release those resources as soon as they're no longer needed. For example, here's some code that creates a file:

```
'Open a file
Dim objFileStream As New FileStream("c:\myfile.txt", FileMode.Create)
'Do something with the file
..
'Close the file
objFileStream.Close()
'Release your reference to the object
objFileStream = Nothing
```

As soon as you finish working with the file, you call `Close`. This tells .NET that the consumer is finished with the file and Windows can make it available for other applications to use. This is known as *releasing the lock*. When you release the object reference in the next line by setting `objFileStream = Nothing`, this is an entirely separate action from calling `Close`.

The `FileStream` object releases the lock on the file when its `Finalize` method is called. However, as you've just learned, the time period between the instance of the `FileStream` object becoming a candidate for garbage collection (which happens when `objFileStream = Nothing`) and `Finalize` being called is nondeterministic. So, if you had not called `Close`, the file would have remained open for a period of time, which would have caused problems for anyone else who needed to use the file.

Another way to release resources within objects is to implement the `IDisposable` interface, which you did with the `WebFavorite` and `Favorites` classes. This interface provides a `Dispose` method for your objects, in which you can put code to clean up the resources used in that class.

Ideally, the consumer of these objects would call the `Dispose` methods on these objects when they are done using them, but if they do not, the `Finalize` method in these objects will, when the GC runs.

Defragmentation and Compaction

As the last item in its bag of tricks, the GC is able to defragment and compact memory. In much the same way that your computer's hard disk needs periodic defragmentation to make it run more efficiently, so does memory. Imagine you create 10 small objects in memory, each about 1 KB in size. Imagine that .NET allocates them all on top of each other, so you end up taking up one 10 KB piece of memory. (In reality, you don't usually care where objects exist in memory, so this discussion is a bit academic.)

Next, imagine you want to create another object and this object is of medium size, say about 3 KB. .NET has to create this object at the end of the 10 KB block. This means that you'll have allocated 13 KB in total.

Then imagine that you delete every other small object, so now your 10 KB block of memory has holes in it. Not much of a problem, but imagine you want to create another 3 KB object. Although there's 5 KB of space in the original block, you can't put it there because no gap is big enough. Instead, it has to go on the end, meaning your application is now taking up 16 KB of memory.

What the GC can do is defragment memory, which means that it removes the gaps when objects have been removed, as shown in Figure 12-12. The upshot of this is that your application uses memory more efficiently, so applications take up less memory.

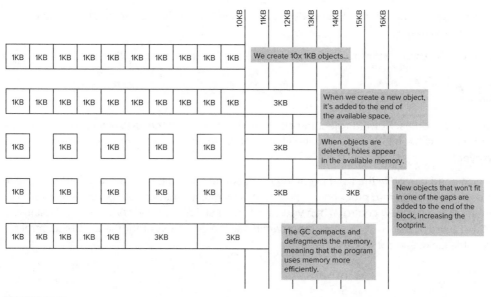

FIGURE 12-12

Although this may not seem like a big deal on a PC with 1 GB of memory available, consider that .NET could potentially be running on much smaller devices where memory usage is a big deal — for example, a mobile device with 32MB of memory in total. Besides, imagine making three thousand 5 KB savings in this example; then you've have saved over 15MB of memory! Chapter 25 introduces you to writing applications for mobile devices and to topics that you need to be aware of when coding for these devices.

SUMMARY

In this chapter, you took a look at some more valuable techniques that you are able to use to assist the building of object-oriented software. Initially, you examined the idea of reuse. Specifically, you looked at classes that allow you to examine the Internet Explorer Favorites stored on the user's computer. You consumed these classes from two applications — one standard desktop application and also a mini-application that exists on the system tray.

You then examined the idea of shared members, properties, and methods. Sharing these kinds of items is a powerful way to make common functionality available to all classes in an application.

Finally, you examined how consumers of objects should ensure that scarce systems resources are freed whenever an object is deleted by the garbage collector using the `Dispose` and `Finalize` methods.

To summarize, you should know how to:

➤ Build a class that inherits from the `System.Collections.CollectionBase` namespace, add methods that allow you to add and remove objects from the collection, and provide a property that allows an application to query for the number of items in the collection

➤ Use the `Collections` class in your own application to create objects and add them to the collection

➤ Use shared properties and methods in a class that can be shared among all instantiated instances of the class

➤ Properly dispose of resources to make efficient use of the garbage collector

EXERCISES

1. Modify the Favorites Viewer project to select the first favorite in the ListView control automatically after it has been loaded so that the LinkLabel control displays the first item when the form is displayed.

   You also need to modify the `Load` event in Form1, and ensure that the ListView control contains one or more items before proceeding. You do this by querying the `Count` property of the `Items` property of the ListView control. Then you select the first item in the ListView control using the `lstFavorites.Items(0).Selected` property and call the `Click` event for the ListBox control to update the LinkLabel control.

► **WHAT YOU HAVE LEARNED IN THIS CHAPTER**

TOPIC	CONCEPTS
Code reuse	You can access your classes by more than one application.
Shared methods and properties	You can mark these as shared to have them associated with the class and not each instance of the class.
Memory management	Understand that garbage collection happens automatically and you should release expensive resources as soon as the program is finished using them.

13

Building Class Libraries

WHAT YOU WILL LEARN IN THIS CHAPTER:

➤ Creating your own class libraries

➤ Learning how to retrieve information about existing libraries that are not part of the .NET Framework.

➤ Learning to assign strong-name assemblies (compiled files) so all assemblies have a unique identity.

➤ Registering assemblies in a repository called the Global Assembly Cache (GAC) to share them between applications on the same computer.

In this chapter, you're going to look at building libraries of classes, a process that gathers many of the concepts covered in this book, so here's a quick review. So far, you've learned a lot about developing Windows applications by dragging controls onto forms, editing their properties, and adding code. When you edit a form in the Forms Designer, you are actually designing a new class that inherits from the System.Windows.Forms.Form class.

When you make changes to the form in the designer, the designer works out what code needs to be added to the class. You can view this code by clicking the Show All Files icon in the Solution Explorer and then opening the designer-generated code for your form. When you run the program, an instance of this class is created — an object. Like most objects, the form has state and behavior — you can have variables and controls on the form (state) and you can perform actions when, for example, the user clicks a button on the form (behavior). In theory, you could write your forms without using the designer at all; very few programmers work this way while creating Windows forms.

Right from the start you've been creating classes. You've also looked at creating your own classes from scratch. Recall what you studied about building objects in Chapter 11, where you created a project called Objects, which contained the classes `Car` and `SportsCar`. These classes were used in a console application because it made the objects easier to test, but they would have worked just as well in a Windows application. You could even have used them in a web application or web service. In fact, one of the key benefits of using classes is that once you've designed a good one, you can use it over and over again in different applications.

UNDERSTANDING CLASS LIBRARIES

In Chapter 12 you used the same classes in two different applications. You built a favorites viewer in your application and a task-bar application using the same underlying classes. You did this by creating the class in one application and then adding a copy of that code to the second. This was a quick and easy way of reusing code, but there were some problems with it:

➤ To use the class you needed to have access to the source code file. One of the advantages of classes and objects is that they can be a black box. Developers should not need to know what goes on inside the classes they use. It is often a good thing if they don't. Also, if you've developed a class, you might want to keep your source code secret. You might be happy to let people use it, but not let them copy the way it works or improve it, or even claim it as their own work.

➤ Every time the program that uses the class is compiled, the class needs to be compiled too. This is not really a problem if the application uses a few simple classes, but if it's using a lot of complex classes, it will make compilation slower. It will also make the resulting program very big because one `.exe` file will include all of the classes.

➤ If you realize that there is a bug in the class or that there is a way to make it faster or more efficient, you need to make the change in lots of different places — in every application that uses the class.

The solution is class libraries. A *class library* is a collection of classes that compile to a file: a Windows Dynamic Link Library (DLL, or `.dll` file). You cannot run a class library by itself, but you can use the classes in it from your applications. You can use a class library without the source code; it does not need to be recompiled when the application is compiled, and if the library changes, the applications using it will automatically get the advantage of the improved code.

Creating a Class Library

These are instructions for creating a class library in Visual Studio.

TRY IT OUT   Creating a Class Library

Code file Internet Favorites.zip available for download at Wrox.com

1. In Visual Studio 2010, select File → New Project.

2. Select Visual Basic from the Project Types list on the left and then choose the Class Library icon from the Templates listed, as shown in Figure 13-1. Enter the name **Internet Favorites**.

3. Click OK. A new Class Library project will be created with a default class called `Class1.vb`. Right-click `Class1.vb` in the Solution Explorer and choose Delete.

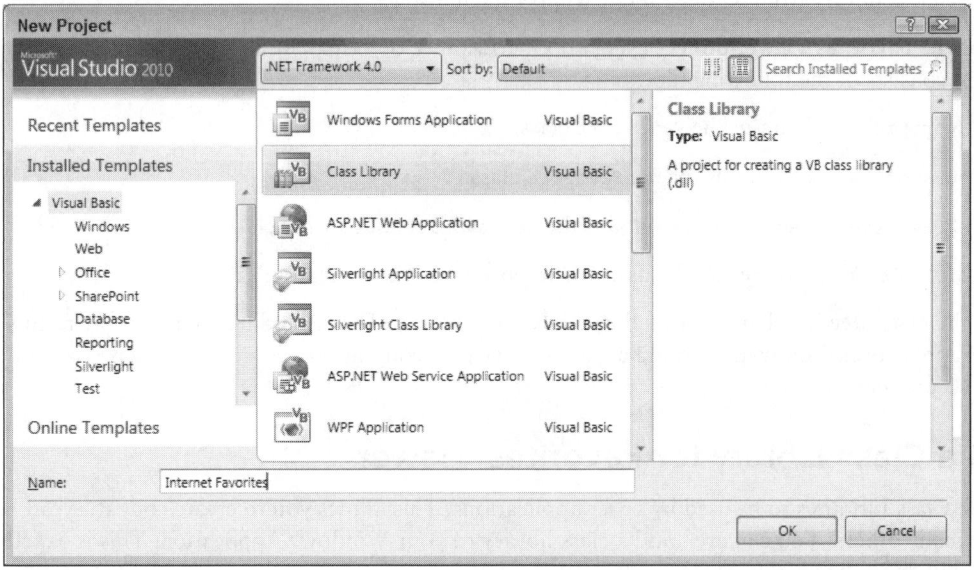

FIGURE 13-1

How It Works

This was a very easy example. Just think about what Visual Studio 2010 is doing during these two steps. First, you choose a Class Library project. The template that you choose controls how Visual Studio 2010 sets up the project and what type of file it compiles to. The most obvious difference is that when you start a Windows Forms application you get a blank form in the Forms Designer. The blank form is called `Form1.vb`. When you start a class library, you get no designer and a blank class called `Class1.vb`.

There are also more subtle differences. When you create a Windows Forms application, Visual Studio 2010 knows that you will be compiling it into a program that can run. When you choose a class library, Visual Studio 2010 knows that the resulting library will not be run on its own, so the choices you make here affect what Visual Studio 2010 does when you build the project. Selecting a class library means that Visual Studio 2010 will build the project into a `.dll` (dynamic-link library) file instead of an `.exe` (executable) file.

After clicking OK, you delete the blank class that Visual Studio 2010 generates. Having classes with the name `Class1` is not very helpful — it's much better to start from scratch with meaningful file and class names.

In the previous chapter you created classes and used the same class in two projects: Favorites Viewer and Favorites Tray. In the following sections you see how to convert these applications so that both of them use a copy of the same compiled class library. Of course, this is a somewhat unrealistic situation. Usually, you would build a class library and application, rather than create an application and then split it into a smaller application and a class library. However, this will give you a good idea of how you create a class library from scratch, and it will be much faster.

First, open the Favorites Viewer project using another instance of Visual Studio 2010. Remember that this project consists of the following files:

➤   `Favorites.vb`: Contains the `Favorites` class.

➤   `WebFavorite.vb`: Contains the `WebFavorite` class.

➤   `WebFavoriteCollection.vb`: Contains the `WebFavoriteCollection` class.

➤   `Form1.vb`: Contains the `Form1` class, which represents the application's main form.

Of these, the first three listed are also used in the Favorites Tray. The remaining file is specific to this particular application. You want to build a class library that contains `Favorites`, `WebFavorite`, and `WebFavoriteCollection`.

Building a Class Library for Favorites Viewer

You create Class Libraries to be used by other applications. This allows you to create code that can be reused by many others. You can even add a class library to your Windows Application. This is exactly what you will do in the next example.

TRY IT OUT   Adding a Class Library Project to an Existing Solution

Code file Internet Favorites.zip available for download at Wrox.com

---

When you're writing Visual Basic 2010 applications, a solution can contain multiple projects. At the moment you have two projects in the solution: the Favorites Viewer application and the Favorites Tray application. In the next Try It Out, you add a Class Library project to this solution and then move the classes from the Windows Forms Application project to the Class Library project.

1.   Switch to the instance of Visual Studio 2010 containing the Internet Favorites project.

2.   Save the project and then close Visual Studio 2010.

3.   Switch to the instance of Visual Studio 2010 containing the Favorites Viewer project.

4.   Click the File ⇨ Add ⇨ Existing Project.

5.   Navigate to where you saved your Internet Favorites project and then select the `Internet Favorites.vbproj` file. Click Open to add this project to the solution.

6.   Right-click the Favorites Viewer project in the Solution Explorer and select Set As StartUp Project.

7.   Right-click the Favorites Tray project in the Solution Explorer and select Remove.

How It Works

Now you have two projects within your solution. You have a Windows Forms application and a class library. Currently, the class library is empty; all the classes that you want to add to it are in the Favorites Viewer project.

You have already seen how to add a new class to a Windows Forms application, and you can add new classes to a class library in exactly the same way. Just right-click the Internet Favorites project and select Add → Class. You don't want to do that, though, because the classes already exist. The quickest way to move a class between two projects in the same solution is to drag and drop them, which is what you do in the next Try It Out.

TRY IT OUT   Moving Classes Between Projects

Code file Internet Favorites.zip available for download at Wrox.com

In this example, you will move classes from one project to another.

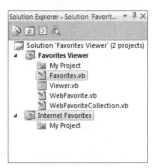

1. Select the `Favorites.vb` file in the Solution Explorer, as shown in Figure 13-2, and drag it onto the Internet Favorites project. This causes a copy of the `Favorites` class to be added to the Internet Favorites project.

2. Follow the same procedure for `WebFavorite.vb` and `WebFavoriteCollection.vb`.

3. Right-click the `Favorites.vb` file in the Favorites Viewer project and select Delete from the context menu to delete the file from that project.

FIGURE 13-2

4. Follow the same procedure for `WebFavorite.vb` and `WebFavoriteCollection.vb`.

How It Works

You now have a Class Library project and a Windows Forms Application project. However, even though they are both contained in the same solution, they cannot see each other. If you try running the application now, you will see an error that type `Favorites` is not defined.

These types of errors occur because the code in `Form1.vb` cannot see the classes in the class library. There are two stages to solving this problem:

1. Add a reference to the Class Library project, so that the Windows Forms application knows to look for the compiled `Internet Favorites.dll` file that contains the classes. Previously, all code was compiled into one file, so you didn't need to do this.

2. Add an `Imports` statement to Form1, so that it can see the classes in the `Internet_Favorites` namespace without giving a fully qualified name (that is, including the namespace as well as the class name). Previously, all classes were in the same namespace, so you didn't need to do this. As discussed in Chapter 4, classes are by default given their project name as their namespace. When a project contains a space in the name, Visual Studio 2010 replaces the blank space in the name with an underscore (_) character.

If this doesn't seem very clear — don't worry! Both of these things are easy to do.

TRY IT OUT   **Adding a Reference and Imports Statement**

Code file Internet Favorites.zip available for download at Wrox.com

Now, you will hook up the new Class Library so you can use it in the application.

1. Right-click the Favorites Viewer project in the Solution Explorer and select Add Reference.

2. Select the Projects tab in the Add Reference dialog box and you'll see that the Internet Favorites project is already populated in the list, as shown in Figure 13-3. Click OK to have this reference added to your Favorites Viewer project.

3. Right-click `Viewer.vb` in the Solution Explorer and select View Code. Add the following line at the very top of the code file:

```
Imports Internet_Favorites
```

How It Works

By adding a reference in steps 1 and 2, you tell Visual Studio 2010 that the `Favorites Viewer.exe` file will require the `Internet Favorites.dll` file to run. Visual Studio 2010 can use the classes exposed from Internet Favorites to check the syntax of the code, so the automatic underlining of errors and so on will work correctly.

> **NOTE** *Whenever you want to use a class library, you must add a reference to it. You can add references to projects within the solution or to compiled DLLs.*

However, if you try to run the application before you perform step 3, you still get errors because the classes in the Favorites Viewer application would be trying to use classes in the `Internet Favorites` class library without giving a fully qualified name. Unless you specify otherwise, classes are given the name of the project they are in as their namespace name. This means that the classes you moved from Favorites Viewer to Internet Favorites changed namespace too.

The easiest way to cope with this problem is to add an `Imports` statement to the top of the classes that rely on this class library. This is what you did in Step 3, but remember that you have two other choices:

You can use fully qualified names every time you want to access a class in the class library from a class in the application. This requires quite a few changes.

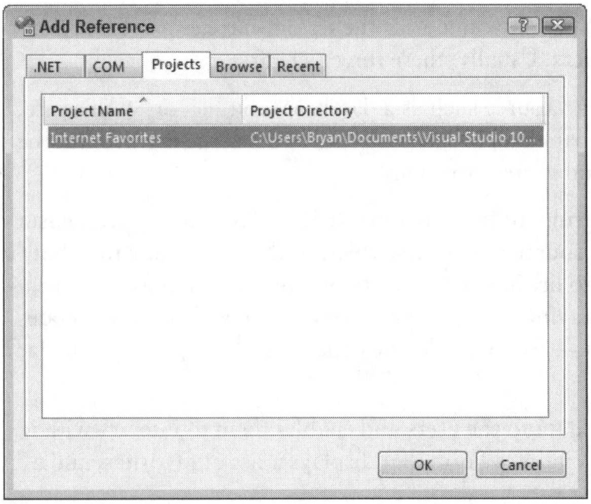

FIGURE 13-3

You can change the namespace of either the classes in the application or the classes in the class library. If the namespace was the same for both projects, then you don't need to use fully qualified names or have an `Imports` statement. However, because the two projects are quite different, it would not really be sensible to give both of them the same namespace.

The `Imports` statement means that any time there is a reference to a class that is not qualified with a namespace, the Visual Basic 2010 compiler will check the `Internet_Favorites` namespace to see whether a matching class exists there. Therefore, the compiler will be able to resolve the class name when you insert the `Imports` statement.

That's it! You have converted your Windows Forms application into a small client application and a class library. Run the application and it will work perfectly, and you'll see the same results you saw in the previous chapter; the application displays a list of your Internet Favorites shortcuts.

> **NOTE** When you run this application, Visual Studio 2010 compiles the class library to a DLL, then compiles the application to an EXE, and then runs the EXE. It needs to compile the DLL first because the compiler depends upon it while compiling the EXE.

A Multitiered Application

In the previous demonstration, you split your application into two *tiers,* or *layers.* The class library is a tier that handles the concept of a favorite and obtains a list of the users' favorites from their computer. The other tier presents the favorites to the user and enables the user to perform actions on them. Class libraries are a powerful tool for creating tiered applications, because they enable you to completely separate the code that exists in different tiers. You may often hear the term *n-tier design*. This refers to an application that has at least three separate tiers. Usually, these three tiers are:

➤ A *data tier* obtains raw data from a data source such as a database, text file, or, in this case, your Favorites folder, and then writes data back. It generally is not concerned with what the data means. It just enables data read and write operations.

➤ A *business tier* applies certain business rules to the data retrieved from the data source, ensuring that data being written to the data source obeys these rules. In this case, there may be certain sites that you would not want to list in your Favorites viewer, or you may want to ensure that URLs are valid before displaying them. The business tier may also contain code for manipulating or working with data — for example, the code needed to open a particular favorite.

➤ A *presentation tier,* which displays the data to the users and enables them to interact with it in some way. In this case, you have a Windows Form that displays a list of favorites, and a link button that lets users view them.

Your application is so small that there's no practical need to separate the data tier and the business tier. However, in a big application it can make the project far more manageable, even if it does mean spending a bit more time on design before the coding starts.

One of the great things about tiers is that you can mix and match them quite easily. For example, if a new browser became popular, you could change the data tier to read a different data format but still use the same presentation tier and business tier. This would be much easier if the data tier and business tier were separate.

Soon you are going to use your class library, which is really a combination of the business and data tiers, in conjunction with a different presentation tier — namely, the Favorites Tray application.

> **NOTE** *In this chapter, you are working with existing projects so that you can concentrate specifically on class libraries, rather than writing code. In most cases you would develop the class library first and then develop applications to use that library. Of course, as you are building the application, you might decide to modify the library slightly. Using Visual Studio 2010 you can do this very easily. When working in Visual Studio 2010 you can make any changes you like to the code in the library, and the change will instantly be available in the application.*

USING STRONG NAMES

Your complete solution now compiles to two files: a DLL and an EXE. You have written both files. Nobody else is writing applications that rely on the DLL, and nobody else is going to change the DLL. In real life, this is often not the case. Often you use off-the-shelf DLLs, or two separate developers are working on the DLL and the EXE.

For example, imagine that Matt is working on `Internet Favorites.dll` and Robbin is working on `Favorites Viewer.exe`. Matt decides that `ScanFavorites` is not a very good name for a method and changes it to `LoadFavorites`. Then he recompiles the DLL. Later, Robbin runs `Favorites Viewer .exe`. `Favorites Viewer.exe` tries to call `ScanFavorites` in the DLL, but the method no longer exists. This generates an error and the program doesn't work.

Of course, Matt shouldn't really have made the change to the DLL. He should have known that applications existed that required the `ScanFavorites` method. All too often, however, developers of libraries don't realize this. They make changes to DLLs that render existing software unusable.

Another possible scenario is that Jay is working on a system to manage favorites, and he creates a file called `Internet Favorites` that is different from the one that Matt developed. There is a danger that the two different DLLs will be confused, and once again Favorites Viewer won't work.

These DLL management problems have been a nightmare for Windows developers, and it spawned the expression "DLL Hell." However, Visual Basic 2010 goes a long way toward solving the problem. The problem is connected with two things:

➤ There can be several versions of a DLL, and these can all work in different ways. It is not possible to tell the version from the filename alone.

➤ Different people can write DLLs with the same filename.

Strongly named assemblies store information about their version and their author within the assembly itself. Because of this, it would be possible to tell the difference between the DLL used (when Favorites Viewer compiled) and the changed version. It would also be possible to tell the difference between Matt's `Internet Favorites.dll` and Jay's `Internet Favorites.dll`. Strong naming can also store information about other properties that helps uniquely identify an assembly (for example, the culture for which it was written), but you concentrate on version and author.

Signing Assemblies

One way to certify who wrote an assembly is to sign it. To do this, you generate a *key pair* and sign the assembly with it. A key pair is unique, and therefore can identify the person or company who wrote an assembly. The principles behind assembly signing are quite advanced, but the actual practice is quite simple.

> **NOTE** *A strongly named assembly cannot reference a simply named assembly, because it would lose the versioning control that it enjoys.*
>
> *Two steps are involved in creating a strongly named or signed assembly:*
>
> **1.** *Create a key pair that you can use to sign your assembly, as you do in the next Try It Out.*
>
> **2.** *Apply this key pair to your assembly so that it will be used to sign the assembly at the time of compilation.*

TRY IT OUT   Creating a Key Pair

Code file Internet Favorites.zip available for download at Wrox.com

---

In this example, you will complete the first step that is needed to sign an assembly: creating a key pair.

1.   First, you create a new key pair. From the Windows Start menu select All Programs ⇨ Microsoft Visual Studio 2010 ⇨ Visual Studio Tools ⇨ Visual Studio 2010 Command Prompt.

> **NOTE** *If you are running on Windows Vista or Windows 7, you will most likely need to run the command prompt with administrator privileges. To do this, instead of left-clicking the Visual Studio 2010 Command Prompt, right-click it and choose Run As Administrator from the context menu.*

2.   Type the following into the command prompt that appears:

```
sn -k InternetFavoriteskey.snk
```

How It Works

This generates a key pair in the folder where the command is run (in this case, `C:\Program Files\Microsoft Visual Studio 10.0\VC`). Check the command prompt window to verify the location. If you don't see the file in the location, make sure you chose to run as administrator in Vista and Windows 7.

In the preceding example, running the Visual Studio 2010 command prompt opens a DOS-style command window with the environment set up so that you can use the .NET command-line tools. You use this environment to run the Visual Studio 2010 strong naming command, `sn`. The k switch means that the command generates a new key pair and writes it to the specified file.

Now you have a key pair in the file `InternetFavoriteskey.snk`. If you want, you can move this to a more convenient location, such as your project folder for the Internet Favorites project. After this, in the next Try It Out, you use it to sign your assembly.

TRY IT OUT   Signing the FavoritesLib Assembly

Code file Internet Favorites.zip available for download at Wrox.com

---

In this example, you will sign the assembly.

1.   In the Solution Explorer, double-click the My Project file in the Internet Favorites project.

2.   Now click the Signing tab along the left side of the project file, as shown in Figure 13-4.

3.   Select the Sign the assembly check box.

4. In the Choose a Strong Name key file combo box, select <Browse> and then browse to the location of your key file and select it.

5. Build your project. The DLL will then be strongly named.

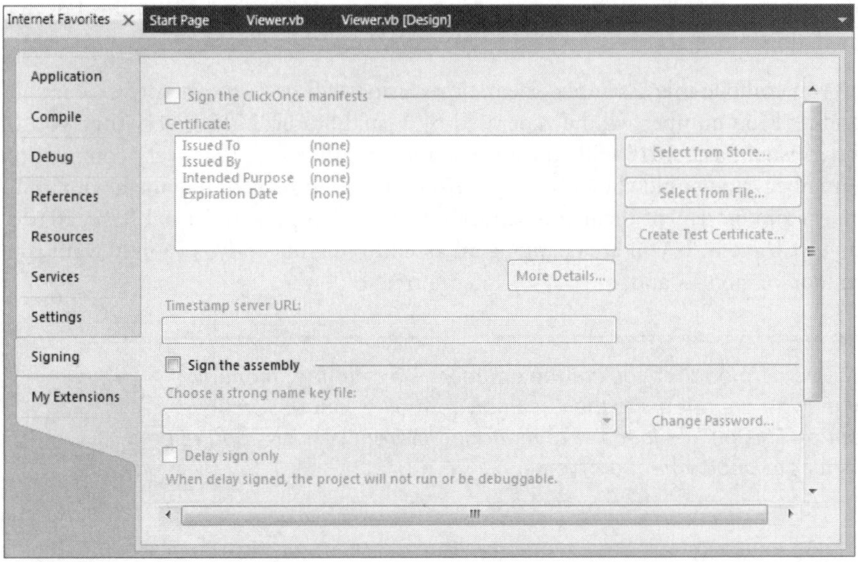

FIGURE 13-4

How It Works

When you compile an assembly with a key file, it adds a copy of your public key to the assembly. It also adds a hash of the whole assembly, encrypted using the private key.

With public-private key cryptography, a message encrypted with one key can be decrypted only with the other key. You can't use the same key to encrypt and decrypt. You can give a public key to a lot of people and they can encrypt messages with it. If you keep the private key secret, nobody else will be able to read the encrypted messages — even if they have a copy of the public key.

You can also make this work the other way around. If you encrypt a message with the private key, people can use the public key to decrypt it. If the decryption works and you haven't let somebody else get their hands on your private key, it proves that you wrote the message.

Part of the purpose of signing an assembly is to prove who wrote it and to prove that it has not been tampered with. This could be done by encrypting the whole assembly using the private key and then decrypting the whole assembly using the public key when it needs to be used. However, this would be very slow. Instead, the Visual Basic 2010 compiler takes a hash of the assembly and encrypts that using the private key. If anybody tries to tamper with the assembly, the hash will cease to be valid.

Assembly Versions

Visual Basic 2010 automatically keeps track of versions for you. When you build an assembly, a number signifying the version is automatically updated. There are four elements of this number: major version, minor version, build, and revision. If you click the Application tab of the project file and then click the Assembly Information button, the assembly version appears in the bottom third of the Assembly Information dialog.

This means that when you compile this assembly, the major version will be 1, the minor version will be 0, and the build and revision number will be generated by Visual Studio 2010. Every time you recompile the assembly, Visual Basic 2010 will adjust these numbers to ensure that every compilation has a unique version number. You could choose to replace the build and revision numbers with your own hard-coded numbers and increment them yourself, but if you're happy with Visual Basic 2010's decision, then you can just leave it. If you are changing an assembly significantly, you may want to change the major or minor version — and, of course, you are free to do that.

> **NOTE** It is recommended that you set the entire version number manually, especially when you are releasing the assembly formally, so that you have complete control. This makes it easier to manage different versions and to bring in fewer unfortunate deployment problems.

REGISTERING ASSEMBLIES

You've seen how an assembly can contain information proving who wrote it (in the sense that a unique identifier is unique per publisher), and information to prove its own version. This is very useful, because it means that executables using these assemblies know what assembly author and version to look for in place of just a filename. However, this doesn't prevent Matt from overwriting an existing DLL with a new version — it just means that applications using the DLL will be able to tell that it has changed.

This is where the Global Assembly Cache (GAC) comes in. The GAC can ensure that several versions of the same assembly are always available. If your application requires the `Internet Favorites` assembly version 1, and Matt's application requires the assembly version 2, both can go in the GAC and both can be available. Moreover, assemblies with the same name but written by different people can go in the GAC. You can guarantee that your applications will use the same assembly while running as they did when they were compiled, provided the required assembly is in the GAC.

To register an assembly into the GAC, you simply need to drag the relevant `.dll` file into the GAC (located in the `C:\windows\assembly` folder on Windows XP, Windows Vista, and Windows 7).

Gacutil Utility

`Gacutil.exe` is a utility provided with the .NET Framework for installing/uninstalling GAC assemblies via a command line.

From the Windows Start menu, select Programs → Microsoft Visual Studio 2010 ⇨ Visual Studio Tools ⇨ Visual Studio 2010 Command Prompt. Navigate to the bin folder for your Internet Favorites project. Be sure to check the output path in the Compile Tab in project properties. You will need to have administrator privileges to use the Gacutil. Then enter the following command to install your assembly into the GAC:

```
Gacutil -i "internet favorites.dll"
```

In the console window, you can use the i and u options to install and uninstall, respectively:

```
Gacutil -u "internet favorites"
```

Why Is My Assembly Not Visible in the References Dialog Box?

It is important to understand that the GAC is not shown in the References dialog within Visual Studio. Therefore, after you add your assembly to the GAC, you will not see it in the References dialog; you must browse for it.

DESIGNING CLASS LIBRARIES

By now, you should be aware of how useful class libraries are and have an understanding of the nature of classes, objects, and class libraries.

When designing an application, it is best to understand what you are dealing with. Much like an architect designing a house, you need to understand how things work (the rules, the regulations, and the recommendations) in order to know how to draw the best plan.

When software architects plan, draw out, and generate template code for components and applications, they may use a drawing tool such as Microsoft Visio, which integrates with Visual Studio 2010. Visio contains various types of symbol libraries that can be used for creating schematics, flowcharts, and other diagrams. A very well-known set of descriptive symbols and diagram types is Unified Modeling Language (UML), which has its own symbols and rules for drawing software and architecture models. UML has various types of symbol libraries, which contain symbols that have different meanings and functions. These symbols have been derived from previous modeling symbols to form something of a fusion of styles. UML also has many types of diagrams. These diagrams range from deployment-type diagrams to component definition diagrams.

> **NOTE** *If you want to learn more about UML, take a look at Tom Pender's* UML Bible *(Wiley, 2003).*

If the questions "How many parameters and methods should an object expose?" and "Should an object have properties rather than methods?" are not answered correctly, your object would not be rendered completely useless, but it may be ineffective. There are, however, some things to consider.

Imagine a class library that contains over 40 methods and properties on each of its 20 or so classes. Also imagine that each class's methods contain at least 15 parameters. This component might be a little daunting — in fact, a component should never be designed this way.

Instead, when designing your objects, try to follow the golden rule: simplicity. Simplicity is probably the most crucial element that you can have in your classes. While creating an extremely large class library is not necessarily a bad thing, using a small number of related classes, aided by a few other class libraries, is by far a better solution.

When you're dealing with a large, complex set of business rules for a large system, the code within the library can be extremely complicated, often leading to debugging and maintenance nightmares. In many situations, getting around the fact that many objects need to be created is a difficult task, but the point that needs to come across is that many situations lend themselves to reuse. The more reusable the classes are, the smaller the end-product will be and the easier it will be to create new applications that need the same functionality provided by the components.

Every developer who uses your class library should be able to do so successfully, without any major effort or a tremendous amount of reading. You can achieve this in the following ways:

➤ Try to keep your methods to five or six parameters *maximum*, unless completely necessary. This will make coding easier.

➤ Ensure that all parameters and methods have meaningful names. Try to spell out the function, rather than keep it short. For example, it is not easy to identify the meaning of StdNo as it is to identify the meaning of StudentNumber.

➤ Do not overexert yourself by adding every conceivable method and functional enhancement that an object can have; rather, think ahead but code later. You can easily complicate matters for your developers by granting them too many options; and, at the same time, you may be adding functionality that will never be used.

➤ Try to keep classes within your library to a minimum, because better reuse comes from keeping your libraries smaller.

➤ Properties are extremely useful in a class, and they enable it to be used more easily.

USING THIRD-PARTY CLASS LIBRARIES

A class library compiles to a .dll file. To use the class library you need only the DLL; you don't need the source code. This means that you can give your DLL to other people to use and you can use other people's DLLs in your own applications. To demonstrate how to use a DLL, you're going to use the Internet Favorites.dll file that you created in the previous Try It Out.

TRY IT OUT **Using Internet Favorites.dll in the Favorites Tray Application**

Code file Internet Favorites.zip available for download at Wrox.com

You've already seen how to create references to other projects in a solution. This is a really good way to develop and test class libraries and applications at the same time. In this example you're going to pretend that you didn't create Internet Favorites.dll. Instead, you'll modify the Favorites Tray application so that it uses Internet Favorites.dll. This is a very quick way to demonstrate the use of DLLs, but remember that in real life you would add a reference to the DLL early on in developing the application, and then write code to use the DLL.

1. Open the Favorites Tray project.

2. Delete the following files from the project: `Favorites.vb`, `WebFavorite.vb`, and `WebFavorite-Collection.vb`.

3. Now you need to add a reference to `Internet Favorites.dll`. Use Windows Explorer to copy the `Internet Favorites.dll` into a new folder, `C:\Developer Assemblies`. Right-click the Favorites Tray project and select Add Reference. Select the Browse tab and find Internet Favorites. Select it and then click the OK button to close the Add Reference dialog. (When you work in a team you will want to create a directory on every developer's machine where you keep DLLs to use in projects.)

4. Remember that the classes in the class library are in the `Internet_Favorites` namespace, so you need to tell your code to look in that namespace for class names you use. Add the following `Imports` statement to the top of `Form1.vb` and `WebFavoriteMenuItem.vb`:

```
Imports Internet_Favorites
```

You do not need to add it to `ExitMenuItem.vb` because this class does not use any of the classes in the library.

5. Run the program. It will work as normal, but will use the class library now instead of classes within the application's `.exe` file.

How It Works

This example shows how the process works more easily than adding a reference to another project does. You still use the classes in the class library in exactly the same way regardless of whether you reference the Class Library project or the compiled DLL. The main difference is that you cannot see or edit the class library's source code.

However, the Visual Studio 2010 environment can still tell a lot about the classes even without the source code. For example, IntelliSense still works. This is because Visual Studio 2010 can tell from the DLL itself what methods and properties are available on each class. You can investigate a class without using IntelliSense but using the Object Browser.

VIEWING CLASSES WITH THE OBJECT BROWSER

To view classes that can be used within Visual Basic 2010, you can use a quick and easy tool known as the Object Browser. You can also use the Object Browser to view class names and method names on objects. The Object Browser window can be viewed inside Visual Studio 2010 by pressing F2. It is also available by selecting View → Object Browser, or by clicking the Object Browser icon on the toolbar.

The Object Browser is basically used for a quick reference to the classes you need to see. It will show all assemblies that are used in the current solution, including Visual Basic projects and compiled DLLs.

The Object Browser shows all members, including methods, enumerations, and constants. Each member type is shown with a different icon. Figure 13-5 shows the `Internet_Favorites.Favorites` class. You select this class by first choosing the `Internet_Favorites` assembly. Within that you choose the `Internet_Favorites` namespace, and then within that the `Favorites` class.

> **NOTE** *Remember that an assembly can contain several namespaces and that the same namespace can be spread across several assemblies. It just happens that in Visual Basic 2010, you normally have a single namespace inside a single assembly of the same name.*

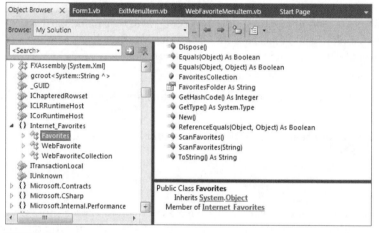

FIGURE 13-5

The MSDN Library documentation that gets installed with Visual Studio 2010 contains plenty of information about classes in the .NET Framework, so you don't often need to use the Object Browser when you're using only .NET Framework classes. It is really useful, however, when you are using a DLL from a third party that does not come with documentation. Often the method and property names can give you a clue about what's happening. Of course, this underlines why it is necessary to choose good names for your classes and their members.

On other occasions, the DLL will provide short descriptions of each of its classes and members. This is done using attributes, a subject outside the scope of this text.

SUMMARY

Class libraries are an integral part of Visual Basic 2010; they are important to all of the languages in the .NET Framework. They encompass what you use and what you need to know in terms of the common language runtime and within your development projects.

In this chapter, you have considered the nature of class libraries and how to view the properties and methods contained within them using the Object Browser. You have also seen how the .NET Framework allows developers to avoid DLL Hell through the use of keys and signatures, and you looked at some of the broad issues regarding designing your own components.

In Chapter 14, you learn how to create Windows Forms controls that are components with a user interface, as opposed to class library projects, which are purely code-based. There, too, you will see the importance of reusable and stable code.

EXERCISES

1. When you compile a Class Library project, what type of file is created?

2. Where are signed assemblies stored to be shared on a computer?

3. How do you install assemblies into the GAC?

4. When does the task bar redraw?

5. If you use a third-party DLL and do not have the documentation, how would you investigate the properties and methods available to you?

▶ **WHAT YOU HAVE LEARNED IN THIS CHAPTER**

TOPIC	CONCEPTS
To create a Class Library	Create a new Class Library Project and add your classes to create one.
To sign an assembly	Use *sn.exe* (Strong Name Tool).
To register an assembly in the GAC	Copy files or use *Gacutil.exe.*

14

Creating Windows Forms User Controls

WHAT YOU WILL LEARN IN THIS CHAPTER:

➤ Learning what a Windows Forms Control is and how it works

➤ Creating and using a Windows Forms Control

➤ Learning to add methods and events to your control

➤ Learning to code for design time and runtime

In this book, you have used many of the controls that come with the .NET Framework, from the Button and the TextBox controls to the ListBox control. You may even have used some of the more advanced controls such as the DataGrid and the TreeView. Although at first some of them may be hard to use, they offer a lot of functionality. These controls make it easy to create a user interface in your applications. Once you get to know how to use all their features, you will find that creating user interfaces also becomes a faster experience.

Another important aspect that makes controls so useful is that they are reusable. You can drag and drop a Button control onto any form in any new Windows project and it *works* as a button should. The reuse factor is an important reason why Visual Basic, in general, became one of the most popular and is one of the most powerful development languages in use today. Did you know that you owe much of what you experience today in Visual Studio 2010, like Windows Forms Controls, to Visual Basic? The history of Windows Forms Controls has roots in something known as Visual Basic Extension (VBX). This later became more widely known as ActiveX, and today, revitalized and reborn into the .NET Framework, it is known as *Windows Forms Controls*.

You will need Microsoft Visual Basic 2010 Professional Edition or above in order to complete the Try It Out exercises in this chapter.

WINDOWS FORMS CONTROLS

Today, there are several good reasons for wanting to create Windows Forms Controls:

➤ You can use the same control throughout an application or in a lot of different applications, thus saving on code (reuse).

➤ You can keep code relating to a control within the control's class, making the code cleaner and easier to understand. For example, you could write a button that handles its own click event — meaning you don't need to handle the event in your form's code.

There are two main ways to reuse controls between applications. The first is to add the control's source file to every project in which you need the control. Then, when you build the application, the control is compiled into the main executable. This is the approach you take in this chapter, because it is simpler and allows you to concentrate on how it works.

The second way is to build a control library. Control libraries are similar to the class libraries that you examined in the previous chapter. In fact, they *are* class libraries that happen to contain UI-driven classes. Like any other class library, a control library will compile to its own assembly, which you can use in your applications. This method is attractive, because it means you can distribute the assembly to other developers without giving away your source code. You can also make changes to the assembly, and these will be reflected in the applications that use it — even without the applications being recompiled. The techniques for building the controls are the same regardless of whether you are using a control library or using a control only within your application project.

CREATING AND TESTING A USER CONTROL

You might find, in the applications that you build, that you have a common need for a control that goes to a database to retrieve certain information, such as login information. If you want to build a robust control, you need to make it as useful as possible to developers using it down the line, while requiring the minimum amount of labor to get it working. You will probably want to encapsulate the functionality of connecting to the database, querying the results, and populating the control with information, so that subsequent developers using your control do not have to know how to do this. This is a key principle of encapsulation — to make life easier for the next developer. In this way, you can also benefit from the more tangible advantage of reducing costs through quality application development and code reuse.

Creating a user control from scratch is not difficult. From one perspective, it is similar to building Windows Forms. In this section, you create a Windows application that uses User Controls. In the first Try It Out, you create a simple control that has three basic Button controls inside of it.

> **NOTE** *When you create your own custom control that uses (hosts) existing controls inside of it, the control is known as a composite control.*

A different message is displayed when each button is clicked. You then see how this control can be used in a standard Windows Forms application.

TRY IT OUT Building Your First Control

Code file MyNamespaceControl.zip available for download at Wrox.com

In this first example, you will build your first User Control.

1. Open Visual Studio 2010 and then click File ⇨ New Project. In the New Project dialog box, select Visual Basic and then Windows under Installed Templates list and Windows Forms Control Library in the templates list. Enter **MyNamespaceControl** in the Name field and then click OK.

2. Right-click UserControl1.vb in the Solution Explorer, choose Rename from the context menu, and change the name to **MyNamespace.vb.** You will have something that looks very much like a Forms Designer without the title bar or borders. Usually, when building a control, you drag on other controls and define a way in which those controls interact. This extra behavior defines a control's purpose and makes it useful.

3. Drag three Button controls from the Toolbox and drop them onto the form and set their Text properties using Figure 14-1 as a guide. Also resize the control so that it also looks similar to Figure 14-1.

4. Set the Name properties of the Button controls to **btnApplicationCopyright, btnScreenBounds,** and **btnScreenWorkingArea,** respectively.

5. At the moment, this control won't do anything when the buttons are clicked — you need to wire up the event code behind the Click event for each button in order for it to work. Double-click the ApplicationCopyright button and add the bolded code:

FIGURE 14-1

```
Private Sub btnApplicationCopyright_Click(ByVal sender As System.Object, _
    ByVal e As System.EventArgs) Handles btnApplicationCopyright.Click

    MessageBox.Show(My.Application.Info.Copyright)
End Sub
```

6. Select btnScreenBounds in the Class Name combo box at the top of the Code Editor and select the Click event in the Method Name combo box. Add the following bolded code to the Click event handler:

```
Private Sub btnScreenBounds_Click(ByVal sender As Object, _
    ByVal e As System.EventArgs) Handles btnScreenBounds.Click

    MessageBox.Show(My.Computer.Screen.Bounds.ToString)
End Sub
```

7. Finally, select btnScreenWorkingArea in the Class Name combo box and select the Click event in the Method Name combo box. Add this code to the Click event handler:

```
Private Sub btnScreenWorkingArea_Click(ByVal sender As Object, _
    ByVal e As System.EventArgs) Handles btnScreenWorkingArea.Click

    MessageBox.Show(My.Computer.Screen.WorkingArea.ToString)
End Sub
```

8. Save your project by clicking the Save All button on the toolbar.

9. Now run your project. The user control will be displayed in a Test Container dialog box, as shown in Figure 14-2. From here, you can test your control by clicking each of the buttons, and the appropriate information will be displayed in a message box. When you are done, click the Close button.

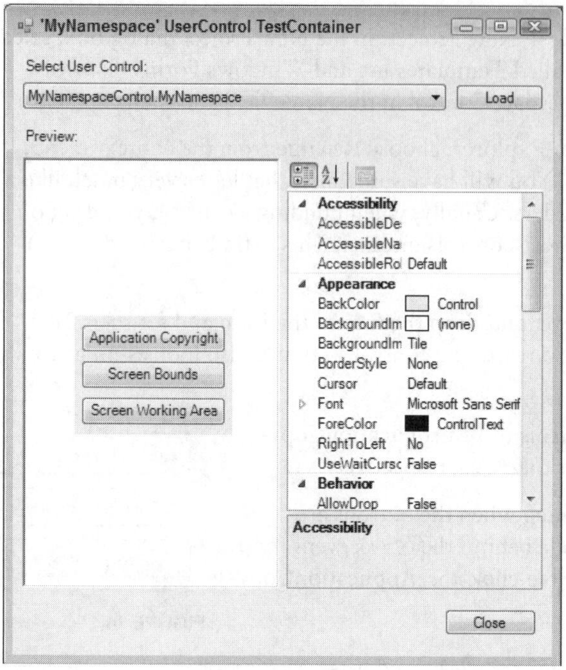

FIGURE 14-2

How It Works

You see that building the UI for the control is not at all different from building the UI for a Windows application in the preceding example. You simply drag the necessary controls from the Toolbox and drop them on the control designer. Then you wire up the events for the code using the same techniques that you've used all along when building Windows applications.

The code that you added for the btnApplicationCopyright button displays the copyright information for your application. This is done by using the My.Application namespace and retrieving the copyright information with the Copyright property of the Info class:

```
Private Sub btnApplicationCopyright_Click(ByVal sender As System.Object, _
    ByVal e As System.EventArgs) Handles btnApplicationCopyright.Click

    MessageBox.Show(My.Application.Info.Copyright)
End Sub
```

The code that you added for the btnScreenBounds button will display the current boundaries of the computer screen, which is determined from the screen resolution settings. This is done by using the

`My.Computer` namespace and retrieving the screen boundary information with the `Bounds` property of the `Screen` class:

```
Private Sub btnScreenBounds_Click(ByVal sender As Object, _
    ByVal e As System.EventArgs) Handles btnScreenBounds.Click

    MessageBox.Show(My.Computer.Screen.Bounds.ToString)
End Sub
```

The code that you added for the btnScreenWorkingArea button will display the current working area of the screen. This is the area of the screen that is available to your application's forms. This is done by using the `My.Computer` namespace and retrieving the screen working area information with the `WorkingArea` property of the `Screen` class:

```
Private Sub btnScreenWorkingArea_Click(ByVal sender As Object, _
    ByVal e As System.EventArgs) Handles btnScreenWorkingArea.Click

    MessageBox.Show(My.Computer.Screen.WorkingArea.ToString)
End Sub
```

When you built the solution, the control was automatically added to the Toolbox in the MyNamespace-Control Components tab. This will not become evident, however, until you add a Windows application to this solution. This will allow you to use your user control in your application just as you would with any other control in the toolbox.

To completely test the control, you can't just run the project. Instead, you have to put the control onto a form, which is covered in the following Try It Out.

TRY IT OUT Adding Your New User Control to a Form

Code file MyNamespaceControl.zip available for download at Wrox.com

You need to add your control to a form. In this example, you will create a new application to host your control.

1. Click File ⇨ Add New Project.

2. In the Add New Project dialog box, select Visual Basic and then Windows under Installed Templates list and Windows Forms Control Library in the templates list. Enter a project name of **Controls** and then click OK.

3. Click the MyNamespaceControl Components tab of the Toolbox and drag the MyNamespace control onto Form1.

4. Right-click the Controls project in the Solution Explorer and choose Set as Startup Project from the context menu.

5. Run your project. The control appears on the form and clicking the buttons has the same effects as when you tested the control in the TestContainer dialog box.

How It Works

In this example, a custom-built control works the same as any other control that you've used up until this point. You simply drag the control from the Toolbox, drop it on your form, and run your project. You didn't need to wire up any code for the `Click` events of the buttons because that functionality is part of the control itself.

EXPOSING PROPERTIES FROM USER CONTROLS

A user control is implemented as a class. Therefore, anything that you can do with a class you can also do with a user control. This means that you can add properties, methods, and events to the user control that can be manipulated by anyone consuming it. First, take a look at adding a new property to your control.

Your control can have two sorts of properties: those that can be manipulated from the Properties window at design time and those that have to be programmatically manipulated at runtime. For example, at design time you might want to change properties pertaining to the color or the font used to draw the control. But at runtime you might want to change properties that depend on the contents of a file that the user selected, and so on. Usually, if the property is a fairly simple type such as `String`, `Integer`, or `Boolean` and doesn't have parameters, it can be manipulated at design time. If the property is a complex object, such as a database or file connection, or if it has parameters, then you'll have to manipulate the property at runtime.

Adding Properties

When you build User Controls, you will want to give the end user some flexibility to change the way the control looks or behaves. You typically do this by adding Properties to your control. This is what you will do in the next Try It Out.

TRY IT OUT **Adding a New Property to the MyNamespace Control**

Code file MyNamespaceControl.zip available for download at Wrox.com

In the following Try It Out, you take a look at adding a property to your control. The property you're going to add is called `ApplicationName`. This property will contain the name of your application. When this property is changed, you'll want to display the text in the title bar of the message boxes on the control.

1. To add a new property you need a member variable that will store the value. Switch to the Code Editor for MyNamespace and add the following bolded code:

```
Public Class MyNamespace

    'Private members
    Private strApplicationName As String = String.Empty
```

2. When this property is set, you need to set the text in the private member that you just defined. Add this code directly after the lines you added in step 1:

```
Public Property ApplicationName() As String
    Get
        Return strApplicationName
    End Get
    Set(ByVal value As String)
        strApplicationName = value
    End Set
End Property
```

3. To have the message boxes display the application name in the title bar, you need to set the `caption` parameter of the `Show` method of the `MessageBox` class. Modify the `Click` events for each of the buttons as shown:

```
Private Sub btnApplicationCopyright_Click(ByVal sender As System.Object, _
    ByVal e As System.EventArgs) Handles btnApplicationCopyright.Click

    MessageBox.Show(My.Application.Info.Copyright, _
        strApplicationName)
End Sub

Private Sub btnScreenBounds_Click(ByVal sender As Object, _
    ByVal e As System.EventArgs) Handles btnScreenBounds.Click

    MessageBox.Show(My.Computer.Screen.Bounds.ToString, _
        strApplicationName)
End Sub

Private Sub btnScreenWorkingArea_Click(ByVal sender As Object, _
    ByVal e As System.EventArgs) Handles btnScreenWorkingArea.Click

    MessageBox.Show(My.Computer.Screen.WorkingArea.ToString, _
        strApplicationName)
End Sub
```

4. To expose the new property for this control to Form1, you need to build the project. Right-click the MyNamespaceControl project in the Solution Explorer and select Build from the context menu. The new property will now be exposed.

5. Switch to the Form Designer for Form1 and select the `MyNamespace1` control and delete it. Then drag a new MyNamespace control from the Toolbox and drop it on your form. In the Properties window the new `ApplicationName` property will appear under the Misc category (or in the usual place if you have the properties arranged alphabetically).

> **NOTE** *If you do not see the new property, close Visual Studio and reopen the solution.*

6. Set the `ApplicationName` property to **My Windows Application**.

7. Run your project and click any of the buttons on the form. Each message box will display the text `My Windows Application` in the title bar of the message box.

How It Works

Notice in this example that the default value of an empty string for the `ApplicationName` property has passed through to the designer. If you change the property in the Properties window, the text displayed in the title bar of the message boxes of the control will change.

When the designer needs to update the Properties window, it calls into the object and requests the `ApplicationName` property. Likewise, when you change the value, it calls into the object and sets the property. This also happens when the form is loaded from disk when you start up the designer.

Exposing Methods from User Controls

As you've probably guessed, if you can expose new properties for your control, you can also expose new methods. All that you need to do to make this happen is to add a public function or procedure to the control, and then you'll be able to call it from the form that's hosting the control, which you do in the next Try It Out.

TRY IT OUT Adding a Method to the MyNamespace Control

Code file MyNamespaceControl.zip available for download at Wrox.com

Here, you will add a public function to calculate the height of the taskbar.

1. Switch to the Code Editor for `MyNamespace.vb` and add this function:

```
Public Function TaskBarHeight() As Integer
    Return My.Computer.Screen.Bounds.Height-_
        My.Computer.Screen.WorkingArea.Height
End Function
```

2. Switch to the Forms Designer for Form1. Drag a Button control from the Toolbox and drop it on your form. Set the `Name` property to **btnTaskbarHeight** and the `Text` property to **Taskbar Height**.

3. Double-click the button and add the following bolded code to its `Click` event handler:

```
Private Sub btnTaskbarHeight_Click(ByVal sender As System.Object, _
    ByVal e As System.EventArgs) Handles btnTaskbarHeight.Click

    MessageBox.Show("Taskbar Height = " & _
        MyNamespace1.TaskBarHeight & " pixels", "Form1")
End Sub
```

4. Run your project and click the Taskbar Height button on Form1. You'll see a message box with the calculated height of the taskbar.

How It Works

Exposing a function or procedure from a user control is no different from exposing a function or procedure from a class, as you see in this example. You just need to mark the function or procedure as `Public` so that it is exposed to the user of the class.

The `TaskBarHeight` function calculates the height of the taskbar by subtracting the working area height from the screen bounds height and returning the calculated value:

```
Public Function TaskBarHeight() As Integer
    Return My.Computer.Screen.Bounds.Height-_
        My.Computer.Screen.WorkingArea.Height
End Function
```

When you call the `TaskBarHeight` function from your code in Form1, you specify the control name of `MyNamespace1` and then choose the `TaskBarHeight` function from the drop-down list in IntelliSense:

```
Private Sub btnTaskbarHeight_Click(ByVal sender As System.Object, _
    ByVal e As System.EventArgs) Handles btnTaskbarHeight.Click

    MessageBox.Show("Taskbar Height = " & _
        MyNamespace1.TaskBarHeight & " pixels", "Form1")
End Sub
```

There was no need to recompile the MyNamespaceControl control to expose this new function to Form1, as it did not affect the control's user interface or properties.

Exposing Events from User Controls

Now that you've seen how to expose your own properties and methods from your control, you need to take a look at how to expose your own events from the control. When you add events to one of your own controls, people who use your control can take action in their code when the event is raised.

TRY IT OUT Defining and Raising Events

Code file MyNamespaceControl.zip available for download at Wrox.com

In the this Try It Out, you add three events that return the data that is displayed in the message boxes that get displayed when the buttons are clicked.

1. Defining an event is as simple as adding an `Event` statement, the event name, and the parameters that the event will return. Add the following bolded code to the `MyNamespace.vb` file:

```
'Private members
Private strApplicationName As String = String.Empty

'Public Events
Public Event ApplicationCopyrightChanged(ByVal text As String)
Public Event ScreenBoundsChanged(ByVal bounds As Rectangle)
Public Event ScreenWorkingAreaChanged(ByVal bounds As Rectangle)
```

2. To raise an event you need to specify the RaiseEvent statement, passing it the event name as well as the parameters for the event being raised. Modify the code in MyNamespace.vb as follows:

```vb
Private Sub btnApplicationCopyright_Click(ByVal sender As System.Object, _
    ByVal e As System.EventArgs) Handles btnApplicationCopyright.Click

    RaiseEvent ApplicationCopyrightChanged( _
        My.Application.Info.Copyright)
    MessageBox.Show(My.Application.Info.Copyright, _
        strApplicationName)
End Sub

Private Sub btnScreenBounds_Click(ByVal sender As Object, _
    ByVal e As System.EventArgs) Handles btnScreenBounds.Click

    RaiseEvent ScreenBoundsChanged(My.Computer.Screen.Bounds)
    MessageBox.Show(My.Computer.Screen.Bounds.ToString, _
        strApplicationName)
End Sub

Private Sub btnScreenWorkingArea_Click(ByVal sender As Object, _
    ByVal e As System.EventArgs) Handles btnScreenWorkingArea.Click

    RaiseEvent ScreenWorkingAreaChanged(My.Computer.Screen.WorkingArea)
    MessageBox.Show(My.Computer.Screen.WorkingArea.ToString, _
        strApplicationName)
End Sub
```

How It Works

In this example you specify the Event statement, the event name, and the parameters that the event will return to define an event. Most events for controls are going to be Click or Changed; thus, you have specified the different button names suffixed with the word Changed.

The Application Copyright button returns the application copyright as a string; thus, the parameter for the ApplicationCopyrightChanged event is specified as a String data type. The Screen Bounds and Screen Working Area buttons return the screen information in a Rectangle structure; thus, you specified the Rectangle structure as the data type for these events:

```vb
'Public Events
Public Event ApplicationCopyrightChanged(ByVal text As String)
Public Event ScreenBoundsChanged(ByVal bounds As Rectangle)
Public Event ScreenWorkingAreaChanged(ByVal bounds As Rectangle)
```

To raise an event, you have to use the RaiseEvent statement. This looks after the tricky aspect of actually telling the control's owner what event has been raised and passes it the appropriate parameters.

You'll have noticed that when you typed the word RaiseEvent, Visual Studio 2010 IntelliSense kicked in and provided a drop-down list of the events that you defined. This is just another example of how the IDE makes your life as a developer much easier.

In each instance of raising the events, you simply pass the event being raised the data that will be displayed in the message box when the appropriate button is clicked:

```vb
Private Sub btnApplicationCopyright_Click(ByVal sender As System.Object, _
    ByVal e As System.EventArgs) Handles btnApplicationCopyright.Click
```

```
        RaiseEvent ApplicationCopyrightChanged( _
            My.Application.Info.Copyright)

        MessageBox.Show(My.Application.Info.Copyright, _
            strApplicationName)
    End Sub

    Private Sub btnScreenBounds_Click(ByVal sender As Object, _
        ByVal e As System.EventArgs) Handles btnScreenBounds.Click

        RaiseEvent ScreenBoundsChanged(My.Computer.Screen.Bounds)

        MessageBox.Show(My.Computer.Screen.Bounds.ToString, _
            strApplicationName)
    End Sub

    Private Sub btnScreenWorkingArea_Click(ByVal sender As Object, _
        ByVal e As System.EventArgs) Handles btnScreenWorkingArea.Click

        RaiseEvent ScreenWorkingAreaChanged(My.Computer.Screen.WorkingArea)

        MessageBox.Show(My.Computer.Screen.WorkingArea.ToString, _
            strApplicationName)
    End Sub
```

All that remains now is to detect when the event has fired and do something. This is known as *consuming* an event. When a control fires an event, you can hook into the event handler. By doing this, you receive notification that the event has fired and can do something with the data that the event exposes. This is one of the core concepts of the control/event methodology that you have been using throughout this book.

TRY IT OUT Consuming Events

Code file MyNamespaceControl.zip available for download at Wrox.com

For this example, you will wire up events you created. This will be similar to what you have seen before when you handled the click event of a button.

1. Switch to the Forms Designer for Form1 and add three TextBox controls as shown in Figure 14-3. Set the Name properties to **txtApplicationCopyright**, **txtScreenBounds**, and **txtScreenWorkingArea**, respectively.

2. Switch to the Code Editor for Form1 and select MyNamespace1 in the Class Name combo box at the top of the Code Editor. Click in the Method Name combo box, and you'll see your ApplicationCopyrightChanged event in the method name combo box as shown in Figure 14-4. Remember, although you specifically defined three events for this control, you still get all of the other events that were defined on the various base classes that your control class inherits from.

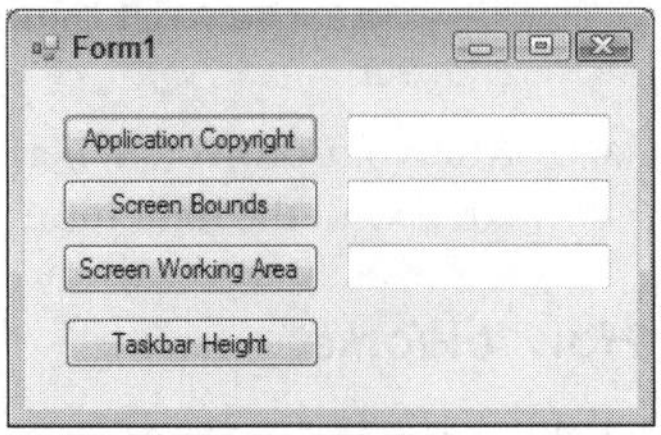

FIGURE 14-3

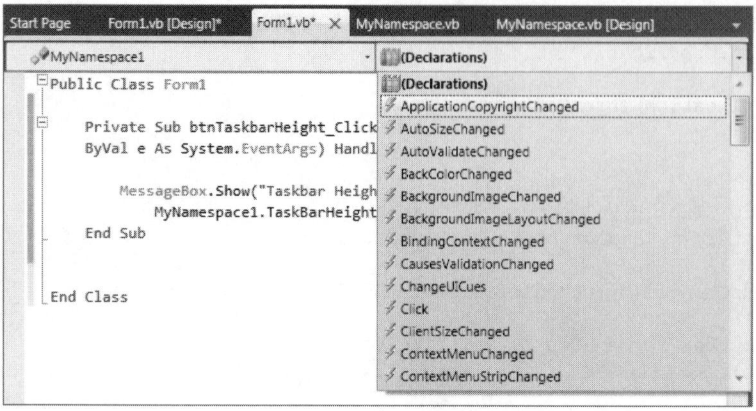

FIGURE 14-4

3. Of course, if you select the control and an event, you are automatically given a handler stub into which you can add your event-handling code, just as you have been doing with the other controls that you've used all along. Select the `ApplicationCopyrightChanged` event in the Method Name combo box. Now add the following bolded code to the `ApplicationCopyrightChanged` event handler:

```
Private Sub MyNamespace1_ApplicationCopyrightChanged(ByVal text As String) _
    Handles MyNamespace1.ApplicationCopyrightChanged

    txtApplicationCopyright.Text = text
End Sub
```

4. Select `MyNamespace1` in the Class Name combo box and the `ScreenBoundsChanged` event in the Method Name combo box. Add the following bolded code:

```
Private Sub MyNamespace1_ScreenBoundsChanged(ByVal bounds As _
    System.Drawing.Rectangle) Handles MyNamespace1.ScreenBoundsChanged

    txtScreenBounds.Text = bounds.ToString
End Sub
```

5. Finally, select `MyNamespace1` in the Class Name combo box and the `ScreenWorkingAreaChanged` event in the Method Name combo box. Add the following bolded code to the `ScreenWorkingAreaChanged` event handler:

```
Private Sub MyNamespace1_ScreenWorkingAreaChanged(ByVal bounds As _
    System.Drawing.Rectangle) Handles MyNamespace1.ScreenWorkingAreaChanged

    txtScreenWorkingArea.Text = bounds.ToString
End Sub
```

6. Run your project. When you click each of the buttons, the corresponding text box will be populated with the data returned by the event, and then the message box will be displayed.

How It Works

In this example, consuming control events in your application is very straightforward and something that you've been doing all along with Button and TextBox controls. You merely select the control name in the Class Name combo box in the Code Editor and the appropriate event in the Method Name combo box and then write the appropriate code to consume, or handle, the event that has been raised by the control. In the case of the MyNamespace control, you are consuming three different events: `ApplicationCopyrightChanged`, `ScreenBoundsChanged`, and `ScreenWorkingAreaChanged`.

For the `ApplicationCopyrightChanged` event, you simply take the text returned from the event and set it in the `Text` property of your text box:

```
Private Sub MyNamespace1_ApplicationCopyrightChanged(ByVal text As String) _
    Handles MyNamespace1.ApplicationCopyrightChanged

    txtApplicationCopyright.Text = text
End Sub
```

The `ScreenBoundsChanged` event is a little different. This event returns data in a `Rectangle` structure, which you must convert to a `String` data type in order to set it in the `Text` property of your text box. This is done using the `ToString` method of the `Rectangle` structure:

```
Private Sub MyNamespace1_ScreenBoundsChanged(ByVal bounds As _
    System.Drawing.Rectangle) Handles MyNamespace1.ScreenBoundsChanged

    txtScreenBounds.Text = bounds.ToString
End Sub
```

The `ScreenWorkingAreaChanged` event is like the `ScreenBoundsChanged` event. This event also returns data in a `Rectangle` structure, which must be converted to a `String` data type before it can be set in the `Text` property of your text box:

```
Private Sub MyNamespace1_ScreenWorkingAreaChanged(ByVal bounds As _
    System.Drawing.Rectangle) Handles MyNamespace1.ScreenWorkingAreaChanged

    txtScreenWorkingArea.Text = bounds.ToString
End Sub
```

DESIGN TIME OR RUNTIME

In certain circumstances, it's useful to know whether your control is in design mode or run mode. The control is in design mode when a form is being designed and the properties of the control are being set; it is in run mode when the form is being run and the control is able to expose methods and events.

As an example, imagine you have a control that establishes a database connection when a certain property is set. It might not be appropriate for that control to establish the connection when the form is being designed, but you will want it to when the application is being run.

Usually, a control itself has a Boolean property called `DesignMode`, which returns `True` if the control is in design mode and `False` if it isn't.

TRY IT OUT   Creating a Control That Understands Design Mode

Code file MyNamespaceControl.zip available for download at Wrox.com

In this Try It Out, you're going to modify the MyNamespace control by adding a Label and Timer control to it. The `Text` property of the label will be updated with the text *Design Mode* when your MyNamespace control is in design mode, and updated with the current time when the control is in run mode.

1. Switch to the Control Designer for the MyNamespace control. Expand the height of the control so that you can place a Label control underneath the last button.

2. Drag a Label control from the Toolbox and center it underneath the last button control. Set the Name property to **lblTime**.

3. Drag and drop a Timer control from the Components tab of the Toolbox onto the Control Designer. The timer will be added to the bottom of the IDE. Accept the default properties for this control and ensure that the Enabled property is set to **False** and that Interval is set to **100**.

4. Switch to the Code Editor for your MyNamespace control. You can detect when your control has been added to a form through the `InitLayout` method, which is defined on `System .Windows.Forms.Control`. This happens both at design time and at runtime. This is the best point to determine which mode you're in and, if appropriate, to start the timer. Add the following bold code:

```
Protected Overrides Sub InitLayout()
    MyBase.InitLayout()

    'Are we in design mode?
    If DesignMode Then
        lblTime.Text = "Design Mode"
    Else
        Timer1.Enabled = True
    End If
End Sub
```

5. The last thing to do is to add code to the `Tick` event of the timer. Select Timer1 in the Class Name combo box at the top of the Code Editor and the `Tick` event in the Method Name combo box. Add the bold code to the `Tick` event handler:

```
Private Sub Timer1_Tick(ByVal sender As Object, _
    ByVal e As System.EventArgs) Handles Timer1.Tick

    'Display the time
    lblTime.Text = Now.ToLongTimeString
End Sub
```

6. You'll need to build the project before the changes to the control can be picked up by your Controls application. Build the project by right-clicking the MyNamespaceControl project in the Solution Explorer and choosing Build from the context menu.

7. Open the Forms Designer for Form1 in the Controls project. Delete the current MyNamespace control from the form and drag a new one from the Toolbox and drop it on your form. You'll see the text `Design Mode`, as shown in Figure 14-5.

8. Run the project. You will see that the `Design Mode` text is replaced by the current time.

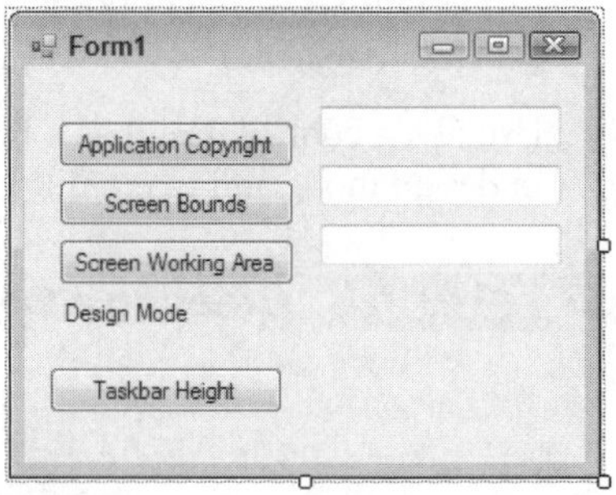

How It Works

In this example, the `InitLayout` method is fired when the control is initialized, both at design time and at runtime. The `DesignMode`

FIGURE 14-5

property of your control returns a `Boolean` value of `True` when the control is in design mode and a value of `False` when the control is in run mode.

If your control is in design mode, you simply want to display the text `Design Mode` on your label control. When the control is in run mode, you want to enable the Timer control, and the Timer control will update the label with the current time:

```
Protected Overrides Sub InitLayout()
    MyBase.InitLayout()

    'Are we in design mode?
    If DesignMode Then
        lblTime.Text = "Design Mode"
    Else
        Timer1.Enabled = True
    End If
End Sub
```

Of course, there are many other occasions when you might want your code to behave differently at runtime than at design time. An example could be that validation rules for a property will be different. In these cases, you would check the control's `DesignMode` property in exactly the same way.

The `Tick` event of the Timer control gets called at the specified interval of the Timer control, which in this case is every 100 milliseconds. When the `Tick` event is fired, you want to update the `Text` property of the Label control with the current time. This is done by retrieving the current long time from the `ToLongTimeString` property of the `Now` object:

```
Private Sub Timer1_Tick(ByVal sender As Object, _
    ByVal e As System.EventArgs) Handles Timer1.Tick

    'Display the time
    lblTime.Text = Now.ToLongTimeString
End Sub
```

Because you made changes to the actual UI of the control, you had to rebuild the control and then delete the current control from Form1 and get a new instance of it from the Toolbox. You don't have to do this when simply making code changes to the control, because those changes are automatically picked up.

CREATING A COMMAND LINK CONTROL

New versions of Windows introduce a lot of new controls in the operating system, such as the Command Link control released with Vista and shown in Figure 14-6. Unfortunately, some of these controls are not available in either the Visual Studio 2010 Toolbox or the .NET Framework. To use those controls in your applications, you need to create a Windows Forms Control that inherits the base control and then sets the appropriate properties and parameters needed to create the control desired.

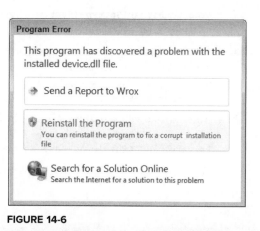

FIGURE 14-6

In this next section, you create a Command Link control that can be used in your own applications. Since this is a new control in the Windows Vista operating system, it is not available in previous Windows operating systems. If you are not running Windows Vista or Windows 7, you can skip this section of the chapter.

Building the Command Link Control

The Command Link control is actually just a Button control with a different style and additional properties. Since your control will inherit from the `Windows.Forms.Button` class, it may be worthwhile to review the section on Inheritance in Chapter 11.

TRY IT OUT Creating the Command Link Control

Code file ButtonExtended.zip available for download at Wrox.com

In this Try It Out, you build the Command Link control. You will use the Win32 API directly in this example. This is considered working with unmanaged code. Unmanaged code is basically code that is not part of the .Net Runtime and includes COM objects, DLLs created in VB 6 and the Win 32 API.

1. Open Visual Studio 2010 and click File ➪ New Project. In the New Project dialog box, select Visual Basic and then Windows under the Installed Templates list and Windows Forms Control Library in the templates list. Enter **ButtonExtended** in the Name field and then click OK.

2. Right-click `UserControl1.vb` in the Solution Explorer and select Delete from the context menu.

3. Right-click the ButtonExtended project in the Solution Explorer and select Add Class from the context menu. In the Add New Item – ButtonExtended dialog box, enter **CommandLink.vb** and click Add.

4. Add the following `Imports` statements at the top of the class:

```
Imports System.Windows.Forms
Imports System.Runtime.InteropServices
Imports System.ComponentModel

Public Class CommandLink
```

5. Since this control inherits from the `Windows.Forms.Button` class, it should have the standard Button icon in the Toolbox. Add the following code above the `Class` statement:

```
<ToolboxBitmap(GetType(System.Windows.Forms.Button))> _
Public Class CommandLink
```

6. Add the following `Inherits` statement so that this control will inherit the base properties and methods in the `Button` class:

```
Public Class CommandLink
    Inherits Button
```

7. Add the following variables, objects, and constants:

```
'Private variables and objects
Private blnUACShield As Boolean = False
```

```
Private strSupplementalExplanation As String = String.Empty
Private objBitmap As Bitmap

'Private constants
Private Const BS_COMMANDLINK As Integer = 14
Private Const BCM_SETNOTE As Integer = 5641
Private Const BCM_SETSHIELD As Integer = 5644
Private Const BM_SETIMAGE As Integer = 247
```

8. You'll need to call some unmanaged code from your Visual Basic 2010 code to so add the following shared functions:

```
'SendMessage API
<DllImport("user32.dll", CharSet:=CharSet.Unicode)> _
Private Shared Function SendMessage(ByVal hWnd As IntPtr, _
    ByVal msg As Integer, ByVal wParam As Integer, _
    ByVal lParam As String) As Integer
End Function

<DllImport("user32.dll")> _
Private Shared Function SendMessage(ByVal hWnd As IntPtr, _
    ByVal msg As Integer, ByVal wParam As Integer, _
    ByVal lParam As Boolean) As Integer
End Function

<DllImport("user32.dll")> _
Public Shared Function SendMessage(ByVal hWnd As IntPtr, _
    ByVal msg As Integer, ByVal wParam As Integer, _
    ByVal lParam As Integer) As Integer
End Function
```

9. You need a constructor for your control to override the default Button style. Add this code to your class:

```
Public Sub New()
    'Set the FlatStyle property
    Me.FlatStyle = FlatStyle.System
End Sub
```

10. A Command Link button is larger than a standard Button control so you need to override the default size of the Button control when a developer adds the control to his or her form. Add this code:

```
Protected Overrides ReadOnly Property DefaultSize() _
    As System.Drawing.Size
    Get
        'Set the new default size of the control
        'when placed on a form
        Return New Size(270, 60)
    End Get
End Property
```

11. The CreateParams property initializes the style of the button so add this code:

```
    Protected Overrides ReadOnly Property CreateParams() _
```

```
            As System.Windows.Forms.CreateParams
            Get
                'Set the style of the Button to CommandLink
                Dim objCreateParams As CreateParams = MyBase.CreateParams
                objCreateParams.Style = objCreateParams.Style Or BS_COMMANDLINK
                Return objCreateParams
            End Get
        End Property
```

12. After initializing the style of the `Button` class to create a Command Link button, the default image on the button is a green arrow. You need to create a property to override the default image and to display the User Access Control (UAC) shield image to indicate that elevated user privileges are needed to perform the actions associated with the Command Link button. Add the following code to create the `UACShield` property:

```
<Category("Appearance"), _
Description("Indicates if the UAC shield icon will be displayed " & _
"on the control."), _
DefaultValue(False)> _
Public Property UACShield() As Boolean
    Get
        Return blnUACShield
    End Get
    Set(ByVal value As Boolean)
        blnUACShield = value
        'Add the shield icon to the control
        SendMessage(Me.Handle, BCM_SETSHIELD, 0, blnUACShield)
    End Set
End Property
```

13. A supplemental explanation is used when a Command Link is not self-explanatory. Add the following code to create the `SupplementalExplanation` property:

```
<Category("Appearance"), _
Description("The optional supplemental explanation for the control."), _
DefaultValue("")> _
Public Property SupplementalExplanation() As String
    Get
        Return strSupplementalExplanation
    End Get
    Set(ByVal value As String)
        strSupplementalExplanation = value
        'Add the supplemental explanation to the control
        SendMessage(Me.Handle, BCM_SETNOTE, 0, value)
    End Set
End Property
```

14. The final bit of code needed will override the default `Image` property of the `Button` class to allow you to display an image other than the default green arrow or UAC shield:

```
<Category("Appearance"), _
Description("The image that will be displayed on the control."), _
DefaultValue(GetType(Nullable))> _
Public Shadows Property Image() As Bitmap
```

```
Get
    Return objBitmap
End Get
Set(ByVal value As Bitmap)
    objBitmap = value
    UACShield = False
    If value IsNot Nothing Then
        'Add the image to the control instead of using the default image
        SendMessage(Me.Handle, BM_SETIMAGE, 1, objBitmap.GetHicon.ToInt32)
    End If
End Set
End Property
```

15. Double-click My Project in the Solution Explorer. The property page for the project will open to the Application tab.

16. Click the Assembly Information button. In the Assembly Information dialog box, enter a description in the Description field, a company name in the Company Name field, and copyright information in the Copyright field. Click OK to save your changes and close the dialog box.

17. Save your project by clicking the Save All button on the toolbar.

18. Right-click the ButtonExtended project in the Solution Explorer and choose Build from the context menu.

19. In the Solution Explorer, double-click the CommandLink.vb file to open the Components Designer. Hover your mouse over the Toolbox to open it and then right-click in the Common Controls tab and select Choose Items from the context menu.

20. In the Choose Toolbox Items dialog box, click the Browse button on the .NET Framework Components tab and browse to the bin\Release folder for this project. In the Open dialog box, select ButtonExtended.dll and then click Open. Then click OK in the Choose Toolbox Items dialog box to close it.

21. Your CommandLink control is now listed in the Toolbox at the bottom of the Common Controls tab. You can move the control up in the list by dragging it to a new location.

22. Close Visual Studio 2010.

In this example, the code starts with three Imports statements. The Button class exists in three different namespaces and you need your control to differentiate which namespace it belongs to, which is why you include the System.Windows.Forms namespace. The System.Runtime.InteropServices namespace is needed to call unmanaged code from your Visual Basic 2010 managed code. The System.ComponentModel namespace is needed to provide the attributes for the control properties that you define:

```
Imports System.Windows.Forms
Imports System.Runtime.InteropServices
Imports System.ComponentModel
```

Each control in the Toolbox has an associated icon. Since this control inherits and extends the Button control, it only makes sense to use the Button controls icon in the Toolbox. The ToolboxBitmapAttribute class is used to specify the icon from the Button control.

> **NOTE** *Although you are using the* `ToolboxBitmapAttribute` *class, you specify only* `ToolboxBitmap` *in the code. This is true for all types of attributes, as you'll discover later when attributes are used on the properties that you defined. The constructor for the* `ToolboxBitmapAttribute` *class in this code uses an object with an embedded image to be used for the icon. You use the* `GetType` *operator to return an object of the* `Button` *class:*
>
> ```
> <ToolboxBitmap(GetType(System.Windows.Forms.Button))> _
> Public Class CommandLink
> ```

Because the `Button` class is the base class for this control, you inherit the `Button` class through the use of the `Inherits` statement:

```
Public Class CommandLink
    Inherits Button
```

Next, you declare the variables, objects, and constants that will be used throughout the code. The `blnUACShield` variable is used to keep track of the `UACShield` property to determine if the UAC Shield icon should be displayed or not. The `strSupplementalExplanation` variable is used to hold the supplemental explanation text when set. The `objBitmap` object is used to hold the image set in the `Image` property.

The following constants are used to set the Button style to Command Link, to set the supplemental explanation text, to set the UAC Shield icon, and to set an image that overrides the default green arrow icon and UAC Shield icon:

```
'Private variables and objects
Private blnUACShield As Boolean = False
Private strSupplementalExplanation As String = String.Empty
Private objBitmap As Bitmap
'Private constants
Private Const BS_COMMANDLINK As Integer = 14
Private Const BCM_SETNOTE As Integer = 5641
Private Const BCM_SETSHIELD As Integer = 5644
Private Const BM_SETIMAGE As Integer = 247
```

The three functions that follow are calls to the `SendMessage` API in unmanaged code in the `user32.dll`. The `SendMessage` API sends a message to a window and in this project, the form hosting the control. Notice that these are overloaded functions differing only in their last parameter. The `DllImportAttribute` class is used to specify that the method defined is exposed through unmanaged code. You pass the DLL name of the unmanaged code to the constructor of the `DllImport` attribute. The first function also specifies the `CharSet` field to indicate to the compiler how to marshal string parameters to the unmanaged code. Here you specify that strings should be sent as Unicode:

```
'SendMessage API
<DllImport("user32.dll", CharSet:=CharSet.Unicode)> _
Private Shared Function SendMessage(ByVal hWnd As IntPtr, _
    ByVal msg As Integer, ByVal wParam As Integer, _
    ByVal lParam As String) As Integer
End Function
```

```
<DllImport("user32.dll")> _
Private Shared Function SendMessage(ByVal hWnd As IntPtr, _
    ByVal msg As Integer, ByVal wParam As Integer, _
    ByVal lParam As Boolean) As Integer
End Function

<DllImport("user32.dll")> _
Public Shared Function SendMessage(ByVal hWnd As IntPtr, _
    ByVal msg As Integer, ByVal wParam As Integer, _
    ByVal lParam As Integer) As Integer
End Function
```

Now you get to the constructor for your class. You have seen the default style for a button in the numerous projects that you have built. You want to override the default style of the button, so you set the `FlatStyle` property to the `System` constant from the `FlatStyle` enumeration. This indicates that the operating system will determine the style to be used:

```
Public Sub New()
    'Set the FlatStyle property
    Me.FlatStyle = FlatStyle.System
End Sub
```

The `DefaultSize` property is used to set the control's initial size when it is created on a form. The `DefaultSize` property is defined as `Overridable`, which allows you to specify the `Overrides` keyword to override the default behavior of this property. Here you define a new default size for the control when it is created on a form:

```
Protected Overrides ReadOnly Property DefaultSize() _
    As System.Drawing.Size
    Get
        'Set the new default size of the control
        'when placed on a form
        Return New Size(270, 60)
    End Get
End Property
```

The `CreateParams` class is used to specify information about the initial state and appearance of a control when it is created. You can also override the `CreateParams` property as shown in the following code. However, it is important that you create a `CreateParams` object and set it to the base class's `CreateParams` object, which is what you have done in the first line of code. This ensures that your control uses the `CreateParams` class defined for the base class that you are inheriting and that your control will work the way it was initially intended in the base class, and then allows you to override the necessary properties to get the look and feel desired.

After you create a `CreateParams` object that is set from the base class's `CreateParams` property, you can then proceed to override the properties of the `CreateParams` class. In the second line of code, you set the `Style` property in the `CreateParams` class using a bitwise combination of the current style plus the style defined in the `BS_COMMANDLINK` constant. This causes your normal button to appear as a Command Link button. Since this is a read-only property, you return the `CreateParams` object that you created here:

```
Protected Overrides ReadOnly Property CreateParams() _
    As System.Windows.Forms.CreateParams
```

```
        Get
            'Set the style of the Button to CommandLink
            Dim objCreateParams As CreateParams = MyBase.CreateParams
            objCreateParams.Style = objCreateParams.Style Or BS_COMMANDLINK
            Return objCreateParams
        End Get
    End Property
```

Next, you want to add some additional properties for the new Command Link control that you are creating. The green arrow shown in the first Command Link in Figure 14-1 is the default icon that is displayed for a Command Link control. To display the User Access Control (UAC) Shield icon (the icon shown in the second Command Link in Figure 14-1) in the Command Link control, you need to create a property to override the default icon. The UACShield property does just that.

This property starts out by defining the CategoryAttribute class that specifies the category in the Properties window that this property will be displayed under when the properties are sorted by category. The DescriptionAttribute class provides the description for this property that gets displayed at the bottom of the Properties window when this property is selected. Finally, the DefaultValueAttribute class provides a default value for this property when the control is created. Since this property gets and sets a Boolean data type, the DefaultValue has been specified as False, indicating that no UAC Shield icon should be displayed by default when the control is created.

The Get portion of this property returns the value contained in the blnUACShield variable. The Set portion of this property first stores the Boolean value set in this property in the blnUACShield variable and then calls the SendMessage API, passing it a number of parameters.

The first parameter is the handle to this control, and the second parameter is the BCM_SETSHIELD constant indicating that the SendMessage API should set or remove a UAC Shield icon from the Command Link control. The third parameter is not used so a value of 0 is passed. The final parameter is a Boolean value indicating whether to set the UAC Shield icon or to remove it. Here you pass the value contained in the blnUACShield variable:

```
    <Category("Appearance"), _
    Description("Indicates if the UAC shield icon will be displayed " & _
    "on the control."), _
    DefaultValue(False)> _
    Public Property UACShield() As Boolean
        Get
            Return blnUACShield
        End Get
        Set(ByVal value As Boolean)
            blnUACShield = value
            'Add the shield icon to the control
            SendMessage(Me.Handle, BCM_SETSHIELD, 0, blnUACShield)
        End Set
    End Property
```

The next property that you create is the SupplementalExplanation property. This property gets or sets the supplemental explanation text that is displayed beneath the main text of the control. A supplemental explanation is optional and thus the DefaultValueAttribute class is specified with an empty string so that this control is initialized with no text set in the SupplementalExplanation property.

The Get portion of this property returns the text contained in the strSupplementalExplanation variable. The Set portion of this property sets the text passed to it in the strSupplementalExplanation variable and then calls the SendMessage API to set the supplemental explanation for this control.

Again, the handle to this control is passed as the first parameter to the `SendMessage` API and then the `BCM_SETNOTE` constant is passed as the second parameter. The third parameter is not used and a value of 0 is passed for that parameter. The final parameter contains the supplemental text in the `value` variable:

```
<Category("Appearance"), _
Description("The optional supplemental explanation for the control."), _
DefaultValue("")> _
Public Property SupplementalExplanation() As String
    Get
        Return strSupplementalExplanation
    End Get
    Set(ByVal value As String)
        strSupplementalExplanation = value
        'Add the supplemental explanation to the control
        SendMessage(Me.Handle, BCM_SETNOTE, 0, value)
    End Set
End Property
```

The final property is the `Image` property, and the code here shadows the `Image` property in the base class. This means that this code redeclares that property, and only this code will be executed. The `CategoryAttribute` and `DescriptionAttribute` classes provide the category and description, respectively, of this property in the Properties window. Notice that the `DefaultValueAttribute` class for this property has been set to the `Nullable` class. The `Nullable` class supports setting a value to nothing. Since this property gets and sets a `Bitmap` object, you must set the `Bitmap` returned from this property to nothing, hence the `Nullable` class. The `GetType` operator returns a `Type` object of the specified type that is passed to it. Since you pass the `Nullable` class to the `GetType` operator, it returns a value of `Nothing`.

The `Get` portion of this property returns the image stored in the `objBitmap` object. The `Set` portion of this property is a little more involved. First, you set the image contained in the value parameter in the `objBitmap` object. Then you call the `UACShield` property, passing it a value of `False` to turn off the UAC Shield icon if it is currently displayed.

Finally, you make sure the value parameter is not `Nothing`, which indicates that the `Image` property is being cleared. If the value parameter is not `Nothing`, then you call the `SendMessage` API, passing it the handle to this control and the `BM_SETIMAGE` constant. You pass a value of 1 for the `wParam` parameter and the integer handle to the image.

You get the handle to the image by calling the `GetHicon` method on the `objBitmap` object, which returns the handle to the image as an `IntPtr` structure. Since the `lParam` parameter of the `SendMessage` API expects an `Integer` data type, you call the `ToInt32` method of the `IntPtr` structure to convert the handle to an `Integer` data type.

After the `SendMessage` API is called, it sets the image in the Command Link control, overriding the default green arrow with the image specified:

```
<Category("Appearance"), _
Description("The image that will be displayed on the control."), _
DefaultValue(GetType(Nullable))> _
Public Shadows Property Image() As Bitmap
    Get
        Return objBitmap
    End Get
    Set(ByVal value As Bitmap)
        objBitmap = value
        UACShield = False
```

```
        If value IsNot Nothing Then
            'Add the image to the control instead of using the default image
            SendMessage(Me.Handle, BM_SETIMAGE, 1, objBitmap.GetHicon.ToInt32)
        End If
    End Set
End Property
```

In Step 20 of the Try It Out, you add the new Command Link control to the Common Components tab of the Toolbox. This ensures that this control is always available in the Toolbox to other applications, as you'll see in the next Try It Out exercise.

Using the Command Link Control

In this Try It Out, you build a simple application that uses the new Command Link control and exercises all of the properties that you added.

TRY IT OUT Using the new CommandLink Control

Code file Command Link Control Demo.zip available for download at Wrox.com

1. In Visual Studio 2010, click File ⇨ New Project. In the New Project dialog box, select Visual Basic and then Windows under the Installed Templates list and Windows Forms Application in the templates list. Enter **Command Link Control Demo** in the Name field and then click OK.

2. Click Form1 in the Forms Designer and then set the form properties as follows:

➤ Set BackColor to White.

➤ Set ControlBox to False.

➤ Set Font to Segoe UI, 8pt.

➤ Set Size to **395, 300**.

➤ Set Text to **Program Error.**

3. Add a Label control to your form and align it to the upper-left corner of your form. Set the following properties of the Label control:

➤ Set AutoSize to False.

➤ Set Font to Segoe UI, 12pt.

➤ Set ForeColor to Navy.

➤ Set Size to **350, 50**.

➤ Set Text to **This program has discovered a problem with the installed device.dll file.**

4. In the Toolbox under the Common Controls tab, drag a CommandLink control and position it beneath the Label control on your form. Set the following properties of this control:

➤ Set Size to **343, 45**.

➤ Set Text to **Send a Report to Wrox.**

5. Drag another CommandLink control from the Toolbox and position it beneath the first one. Set its properties as follows:

➤ Set Size to **343, 65**.

➤ Set SupplementalExplanation to **You can reinstall the program to fix a corrupt installation file.**

➤ Set Text to **Reinstall the Program.**

➤ Set UACShield to True.

6. Drag a third CommandLink control from the Toolbox and position it beneath the last one. Set its properties as follows:

➤ Set Size to **343, 60**.

➤ Set SupplementalExplanation to **Search the Internet for a solution to this problem.**

➤ Set Text to **Search for a Solution Online.**

7. Click the ellipse button in the Image property to invoke the Select Resource dialog box. Click the Import button to invoke the Open dialog box and browse to C:\Program Files\Microsoft Visual Studio 10.0\Common7\VS2010ImageLibrary\1033\VS2010ImageLibrary\Objects\png_format\ WinVista and select the mynet.png file. Click Open in the Open dialog box and then click OK in the Select Resource dialog box.

8. Double-click the CommandLink1 button and add the following bolded code to the event handler:

```
Private Sub CommandLink1_Click(ByVal sender As System.Object, _
    ByVal e As System.EventArgs) Handles CommandLink1.Click

    MessageBox.Show("Sending a report to Wrox.", _
        My.Application.Info.Title, MessageBoxButtons.OK)
End Sub
```

9. In the Class Name combo box, select CommandLink2, and in the Method Name combo box, select the Click event. Add the following code to the event handler:

```
Private Sub CommandLink2_Click(ByVal sender As Object, _
    ByVal e As System.EventArgs) Handles CommandLink2.Click

    MessageBox.Show("Reinstalling the program.", _
        My.Application.Info.Title, MessageBoxButtons.OK)
End Sub
```

10. Select CommandLink3 in the Class Name combo box and select the Click event in the Method Name combo box. Add the bolded code to the event handler:

```
Private Sub CommandLink3_Click(ByVal sender As Object, _
        ByVal e As System.EventArgs) Handles CommandLink3.Click

    MessageBox.Show("Searching the Internet.", _
        My.Application.Info.Title, MessageBoxButtons.OK)
    Me.Close()
End Sub
```

11. Save your project by clicking the Save All button on the toolbar.

12. Run your project. When your form displays it should look similar to the one shown in Figure 14-7. The Command Link with the blue line around it is the default button. Simply pressing the Enter key will invoke the `Click` event handler for it. Also note that as you hover your mouse over each Command Link, the Command Link getting the focus fades in with a gray background and the Command Link losing focus fades out from a gray background back to a white background.

13. Clicking the third Command Link displays the message dialog box and then closes the form.

Program Error

This program has discovered a problem with the installed device.dll file.

➔ Send a Report to Wrox

⊙ Reinstall the Program
You can reinstall the program to fix a corrupt installation file

🔍 Search for a Solution Online
Search the Internet for a solution to this problem

FIGURE 14-7

How It Works

In this example, the CommandLink control works the same way as any other control in the Toolbox. You drag the control onto your form, resize it if necessary, and then set the properties of the control. You then wire up the appropriate event handler for the control to perform the actions needed.

You'll notice that when you drag a CommandLink control from the Toolbox onto your form, the green arrow is the default icon displayed. To change the default green arrow to the UAC Shield icon, you set the `UACShield` property to `True`. To provide your own image, as shown in the third Command Link in Figure 14-7, you set the `Image` property to the image desired.

Changing the `Text` property of the control changes the main label of the control providing a one-line explanation of the controls function. Supplemental explanation text is not displayed since the `SupplementalExplanation` property has an empty string as its default value. If a supplemental explanation is required for the control, you set the `SupplementalExplanation` property to provide more details.

The default event handler for the Command Link is the `Click` event, just as it is for the Button control. That's because this control inherits the `Button` class, so it inherits all of its properties, events, and methods. You merely change the style of the control through your implementation of this class and provide additional properties to enhance the control's appearance.

For design concepts, usage patterns, and guidelines for the Command Link, refer to the MSDN Command Links article at `http://msdn.microsoft.com/en-us/library/aa511455.aspx`.

SUMMARY

This chapter showed two ways of creating Windows Forms controls with some encapsulated functionality. You looked at building a user control that aggregated a number of existing controls usefully. You extended the new control with properties, methods, and events. This control, once compiled, was shown in the Toolbox under its own tab.

You also took a look at how to create a control that inherits the base class of an existing control, changing its appearance and adding additional properties to enhance its appearance. This Command-Link control was added to the Toolbox under the Common Controls tab, making it available to all applications that you create.

To summarize, you should know:

- What a Windows Forms control is and how it works
- How to create a Windows Forms control
- How to add methods and events to your control
- How to code for design time and runtime
- How to create a control that inherits from an existing control

EXERCISES

1. User controls are a good example of which key principle of object-oriented design — encapsulation or polymorphism?

2. There are two properties that you can set to explain to the user what the Command Link control will do. What are they?

3. What are the two main ways to reuse controls between applications?

4. What method should you override to determine when a user control has been added to a form?

5. There is a property that will tell you if the control is in runtime or design time. What is its name and what data type is it?

6. Add a property to the MyNamespace control called `SuppressMsgBox`, which contains a `Boolean` value. Add code to the `Click` event handlers for each of the buttons on this control to show the message box when the `SuppressMsgBox` property is `False`, and to suppress the message box when this property is `True`.

▶ WHAT YOU HAVE LEARNED IN THIS CHAPTER

TOPIC	CONCEPTS
Create a Windows Form control	Create a Windows Forms Control Library and add your controls and code.
Expose properties and methods of a Windows Form control	Add public functions and properties to allow consumers of your control access to this functionality.
Inherit a control to create a new one	Inherit the base control that provides the functionality you wish to extend.
Determine how to code for design time or runtime	Use the property `DesignMode`.

15

Accessing Databases

WHAT YOU WILL LEARN IN THIS CHAPTER:

➤ Learning what a database really is

➤ Examining the SQL SELECT statement

➤ Examining data access components

➤ Examining data binding in Windows Forms

➤ Using the data access wizards in Visual Studio 2010

Most applications manipulate data in some way. Visual Basic 2010 applications often manipulate data that comes from relational databases. To do this, your application needs to interface with relational database software such as Microsoft Access, Microsoft SQL Server, Oracle, or Sybase.

Visual Studio 2010 provides the data access tools and wizards to connect to these databases and retrieve and update their data. In this chapter, you will look at some of these tools and wizards and use them to retrieve data from a database.

The next chapter concentrates on writing code directly, which gives you more flexibility and control than relying on Visual Studio 2010 to create it for you. With practice, writing code will also take less time than working through a wizard.

> **NOTE** *In order to work through the exercises in this chapter, you will need Microsoft Access 2000 or later. The screenshots and example code in this chapter are created using Access 2007.*

WHAT IS A DATABASE?

A database consists of one or more large, complex files that store data in a structured format. The database engine, in your case Microsoft Access, manages the file or files and the data within those files.

Microsoft Access Objects

A Microsoft Access database file, which has the extension *.mdb,* contains tables, queries, forms, reports, pages, macros, and modules, which are referred to as *database objects.* That's a lot of information in one large file, but Microsoft Access manages this data quite nicely. Forms, reports, pages, macros, and modules are generally concerned with letting users work with and display data. You will be writing Visual Basic 2010 applications to do this, so the only database objects you're really concerned about at the moment are tables and queries.

Tables

A table contains a collection of data, which is represented by one or more columns and one or more rows of data. Columns are typically referred to as fields in Microsoft Access, and the rows are referred to as *records.* Each field in a table represents an attribute of the data stored in that table. For example, a field named First Name would represent the first name of an employee or customer. This field is an attribute of an employee or customer. A record in a table contains a collection of fields that form a complete set of attributes of one instance of the data stored in that table. For example, suppose a table contains two fields: First Name and Last Name. These two fields in a single record describe the name of that one person. This is illustrated in Figure 15-1.

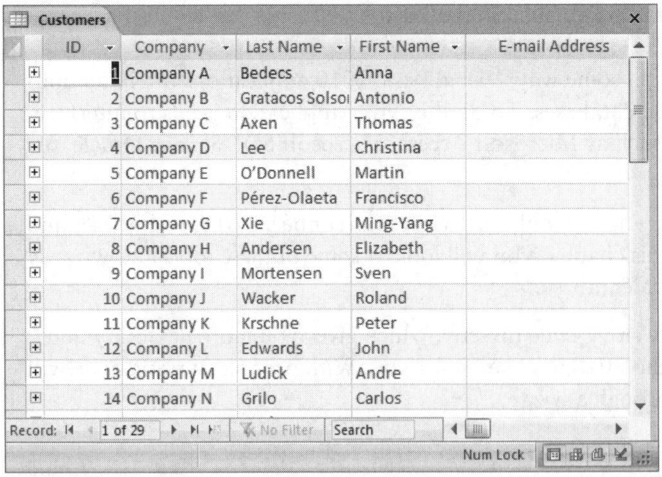

Customers					
ID	Company	Last Name	First Name	E-mail Address	
1	Company A	Bedecs	Anna		
2	Company B	Gratacos Solsoi	Antonio		
3	Company C	Axen	Thomas		
4	Company D	Lee	Christina		
5	Company E	O'Donnell	Martin		
6	Company F	Pérez-Olaeta	Francisco		
7	Company G	Xie	Ming-Yang		
8	Company H	Andersen	Elizabeth		
9	Company I	Mortensen	Sven		
10	Company J	Wacker	Roland		
11	Company K	Krschne	Peter		
12	Company L	Edwards	John		
13	Company M	Ludick	Andre		
14	Company N	Grilo	Carlos		

Record: 1 of 29   No Filter   Search   Num Lock

FIGURE 15-1

Queries

A *query* in a database is a group of Structured Query Language (SQL) statements that allow you to retrieve and update data in your tables. Queries can be used to select, insert, delete, or even update all of the data or specific data in one or more tables.

Query objects in Microsoft Access are a hybrid of two types of objects in SQL Server: views and stored procedures. Using database query objects can make your Visual Basic 2010 code simpler, because you have fewer complex SQL queries included in your code. They can also make your programs faster, because database engines can precompile execution plans for queries when you create them, whereas the SQL code in a Visual Basic 2010 program needs to be reinterpreted every time it's used.

To really understand the implications of queries, you need to learn some SQL. Fortunately, compared to other programming languages, basic SQL is really simple.

THE SQL SELECT STATEMENT

The American National Standards Institute (ANSI) defines the standards for ANSI SQL. Most database engines implement ANSI SQL to some extent and often add some features specific to the given database engine.

The benefit of ANSI SQL is that once you learn the basic syntax for SQL, you have a solid grounding from which you can code the SQL language in almost any database. All you need to learn is a new interface for the database that you are working in. Many database vendors extended SQL to use advanced features or optimizations for their particular database. It is best to stick with ANSI standard SQL in your coding whenever possible, in case you want to change databases at some point.

The SQL SELECT statement selects data from one or more fields in one or more records and from one or more tables in your database. Note that the SELECT statement only selects data — it does not modify the data in any way.

The simplest allowable SELECT statement is like this:

```
SELECT * FROM Employees;
```

The preceding statement means "retrieve every field for every record in the Employees table." The * indicates "every field." Employees indicates the table name. Officially, SQL statements in Microsoft Access should end in a semicolon. It usually doesn't matter if you forget the semicolons, as Access will add them automatically. On other database platforms, you may not need to terminate each statement with a semicolon.

If you wanted to retrieve only first names and last names, you can provide a list of field names instead of an asterisk (*):

```
SELECT [First Name], [Last Name] FROM Employees;
```

You need to enclose these field names in square brackets because they contain spaces. The square brackets indicate to the SQL interpreter that even though there is a space in the name, it should treat First Name as one object name and Last Name as another object name. Otherwise, the interpreter would be unable to follow the syntax.

SQL is a lot like plain English — even a nonprogrammer could probably understand what it means. Now say you wanted to retrieve only the employees whose last names begin with D. To do this, you add a WHERE clause to your SELECT statement:

```
SELECT [First Name], [Last Name]
FROM Employees
WHERE [Last Name] LIKE 'D*';
```

A WHERE clause limits the selection of data to only those records that match the criteria in the WHERE clause. The preceding SELECT statement would cause the database to look at the Last Name column and select only those records where the employee's last name begins with the letter D.

Last, if you want to retrieve these items in a particular order, you can, for example, order the results by first name. You just need to add an ORDER BY clause to the end:

```
SELECT [First Name], [Last Name]
FROM Employees
WHERE [Last Name] LIKE 'D*'
ORDER BY [First Name];
```

This means that if you have employees named Angela Dunn, Zebedee Dean, and David Dunstan, you will get the following result:

```
Angela    Dunn
David     Dunstan
Zebedee   Dean
```

You're specifying a specific command here, but the syntax is pretty simple — and very similar to how you would describe what you want to an English speaker. Usually, when ordering by a name, you want to order in an ascending order so that A comes first and Z comes last. If you were ordering by a number, though, you might want to have the bigger number at the top — for example, so that a product with the highest price appears first. Doing this is really simple — just add DESC (short for descending) to the ORDER BY clause, which causes the results to be ordered in descending order:

```
SELECT [First Name], [Last Name] FROM Employees
                WHERE [Last Name] LIKE 'D*' ORDER BY [First Name] DESC;
```

The D* means "begins with a D followed by anything." If you had said *D* it would mean "anything followed by D followed by anything" — basically, "contains D." The preceding command would return the following:

```
Zebedee   Dean
David     Dunstan
Angela    Dunn
```

You can summarize this syntax in the following way:

```
SELECT select-list
   FROM table-name
   [WHERE search-condition]
   [ORDER BY order-by-expression [ASC | DESC]]
```

This means that you must either provide a list of fields to include or use a * to select them all. You must provide a table name. Optionally, you can choose to provide a search condition. You can also choose to provide an order by expression, and if you do, you can make it either ascending or descending.

SQL gets considerably more complicated when you start working with several tables in the same query. But, for various reasons, you don't need to do this all that much when working with Visual Basic 2010.

QUERIES IN ACCESS

SQL is really a basic programming language, and if you are a programmer who needs to access databases, you will need to use it. However, Microsoft Access provides wizards and visual tools that enable novice programmers to write queries without knowing SQL. Even for SQL programmers, these can sometimes prove useful. These tools, demonstrated in this section, end up producing SQL statements that you can view and modify if you wish, so they can be a good way to learn more about SQL.

TRY IT OUT Creating a Customer Query

In this Try It Out, you use Access to create a simple query that will select customer information from the Customer table in the `Northwind.mdb` database. You'll need to ensure that the sample databases were installed when you installed Microsoft Access or Microsoft Office. You'll create this query and then view the SQL `SELECT` statement that gets generated by Access.

1. For Access 2000: Open Microsoft Access and click the Open icon on the toolbar. In the Open dialog box, navigate to `C:\Program Files\Microsoft Office\Office11\Samples\` and open `Northwind.mdb`. Then click the OK button.

For Access 2003: Open Microsoft Access and click the Help menu. Next, choose Sample Databases and then choose Northwind Sample Database. If the samples are not installed, you will be prompted to install them. They are stored in the same location as the Access 2000 database based on the Office installation directory.

> **NOTE** *The path to Microsoft Office will vary depending on the version you have installed and the installation path chosen at setup.*

For Access 2007: Open Microsoft Access and click the Sample Template Category. From the Sample list, choose Northwind 2007. Next, click the Download button and then follow the onscreen instructions from MS Access. You can close the help window if it opens. After installation, you may see a Login Dialog. If so, close it. If you do not see a Login Dialog, you need to follow the instructions on the Startup Screen to enable content on the Message Bar.

2. When the database opens, you will see the Navigation Pane on the left. Click the arrow at the top of the pane and select Object Type and All Access Objects as shown in Figure 15-2. You can use this to gather related objects of any type, in any way you want.

3. Since you want to take a look at how an SQL SELECT statement is built by Access, click Create in the Ribbon.

4. You are going to build a new query, so click Query Design in the Ribbon (see Figure 15-3).

5. The Show Table dialog box appears and allows you to select one or more tables to be in your query. You only want to select one table: Customers. Click the Customers table and then click the Add button to have this table added to the Query Designer. Then click the Close button to close the Show Table dialog box.

6. The Customers table is displayed with all available fields plus an asterisk. You can select the fields that you want to be added to your query, or you can select the asterisk, which will select all fields from the table. For this exercise you will just select a few fields for your query. Double-click Company in the Customers table to add it to the first column in the grid below the table. The Field and Table cells are automatically filled in. You also want to sort the data by this field, so click in the Sort cell and choose Ascending to have the results of your query sorted by this field.

FIGURE 15-2

Your screen should now look like Figure 15-4. Notice that the primary key for the table has a key beside it: ID. A primary key is a special column that cannot be duplicated, and it guarantees that all rows in the table will be unique.

FIGURE 15-3

7. You now need to add the Last Name field to your grid. Double-click this field in the Customers table and it will be automatically added to the next available column in the grid. Then add Job Title in the same way. Your completed design should now look like the one in Figure 15-5.

8. Click the Save icon on the toolbar, enter the name **CustomerQuery** in the Save As dialog box, and then click OK.

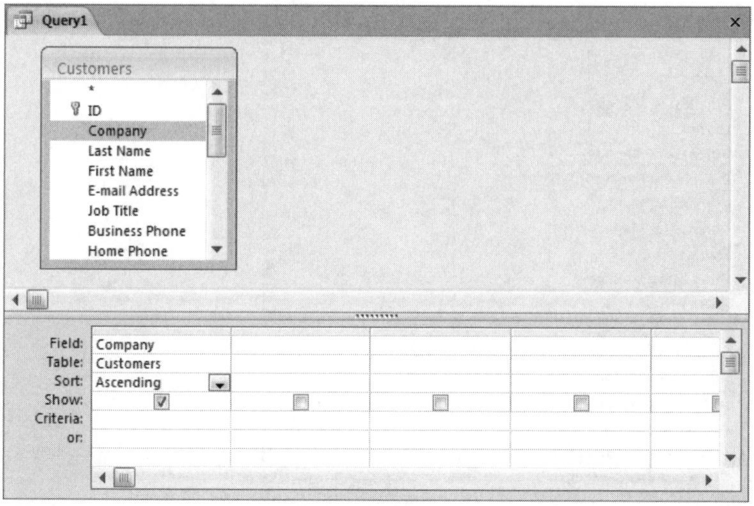

FIGURE 15-4

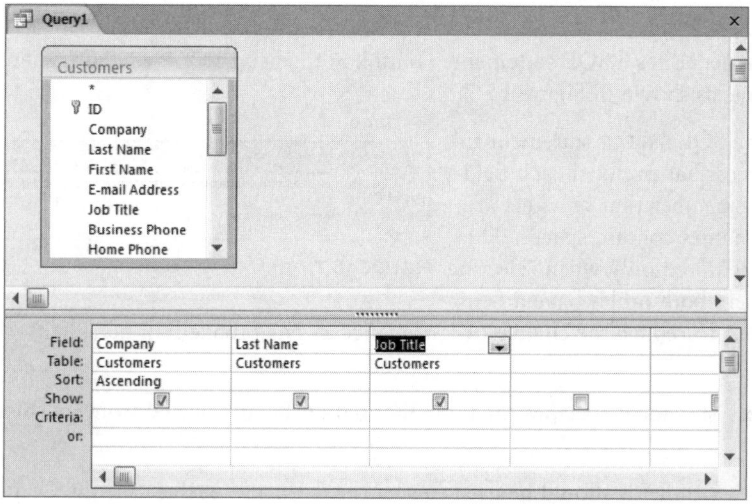

FIGURE 15-5

9. On the toolbar, click the Run icon, indicated by an exclamation point (!), and you will see results similar to the ones shown in Figure 15-6. Notice that the results are sorted on the Company field in ascending order.

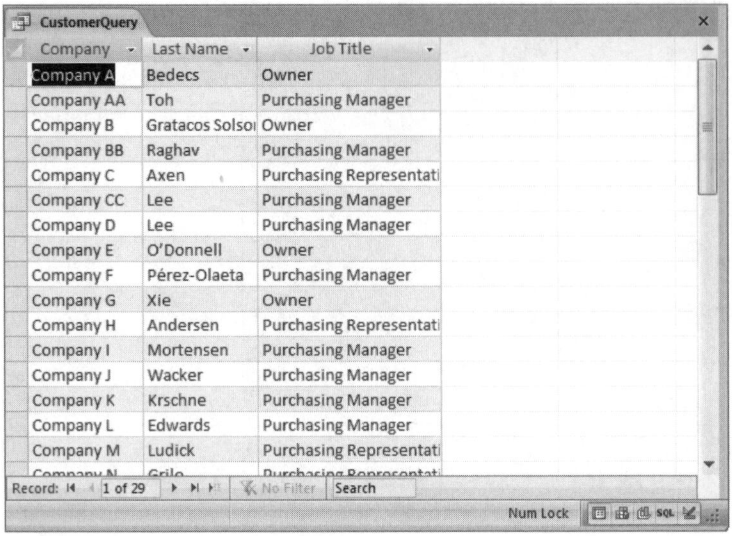

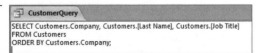

FIGURE 15-6

How It Works

Based on your choices, Access generates a SQL statement. To look at it, click the View ⇨ SQL View. This will display the SQL statements as shown in Figure 15-7.

Notice that you have the basic SQL SELECT statement followed by the field names. Access has prefixed each field name with the table name. Remember that brackets are required only when the field names contain spaces. The table name prefix is actually required only when selecting data from multiple tables where both tables have a field with the same name. However, to reduce the chance of errors, Access has prefixed all fields with the table name.

```
CustomerQuery
SELECT Customers.Company, Customers.[Last Name], Customers.[Job Title]
FROM Customers
ORDER BY Customers.Company;
```

FIGURE 15-7

The FROM clause in your SELECT statement specifies the table that data is being selected from (in this case, the Customers table).

The ORDER BY clause specifies which fields should be used to sort the data, and in this case the Company field has been specified.

How does this SQL statement actually get built? When you first started creating this query you added a table name. Before any fields were added to the grid, Access generated the following SQL statement:

```
SELECT
FROM Customers;
```

Of course, this by itself is not a valid SQL statement. When you added the first field and set the sort order for that field, the following SQL statement was generated — which is valid:

```
SELECT Customer.Company
FROM Customers
ORDER BY Customers.Company;
```

As you continued to add fields, the rest of the field names were added to the SQL statement until the complete SQL statement shown in Figure 15-7 was generated.

The next section discusses the basic data access components that are needed in Windows Forms to display data. Since you have been using Microsoft Access in your examples here, the focus is on the data access components provided in Visual Studio 2010 that assist you in accessing the data in an Access database.

FIGURE 15-8

DATA ACCESS COMPONENTS AND CONTROLS

Start by looking at three of the data access components in Visual Basic 2010 that you can use for retrieving and viewing data from the database: Binding-Source, TableAdapter, and DataSet. The BindingSource and DataSet components are located in the Toolbox under the Data tab, as shown in Figure 15-8. The TableAdapter can be automatically generated depending on the path you take when adding data access components, as you'll soon discover. The following sections take a brief look at all of these and two new controls.

> **NOTE** *These components are known as* data components *and are simply classes, like everything else in the .NET Framework. In this chapter, you will simply see how to use some of them in a Windows application. Data components are discussed as a whole in the next chapter.*

DataSet

The DataSet is a cache of data that is stored in memory. It's a lot like a mini database engine, but its data exists in memory. You can use it to store data in tables, and using the DataView component (covered in Chapter 16), you can query the data in various ways.

The DataSet is very powerful. In addition to storing data in tables, it stores a rich amount of metadata, or "data about the data." This includes things like table and column names, data types, and the information needed to manage and undo changes to the data. All of this data is represented in memory in Extensible Markup Language (XML). A DataSet can be saved to an XML file and then loaded back into memory very easily. It can also be passed in XML format over networks, including the Internet.

Because the DataSet component stores all of the data in memory, you can scroll through the data both forward and backward, and make updates to the data in memory. You'll explore the power of the DataSet component in more detail in the next chapter. In this chapter, you will simply be using it to store data and bind it to a control on your form.

DataGridView

The DataGridView control is a container that allows you to bind data from your data source and have it displayed in a spreadsheet-like format, displaying the columns of data horizontally and the rows of data vertically.

The DataGridView also provides many properties that allow you to customize the appearance of the component itself, as well as properties that allow you to customize the column headers and the display of data.

More important, though, are the quick links at the bottom of the Properties window for the Data-GridView, which allow you to customize the appearance of the DataGridView itself through several predefined format styles.

BindingSource

The BindingSource acts like a bridge between your data source (DataSet) and your data-bound controls (that is, controls that are bound to data components). Any interaction with the data from your controls goes through the BindingSource, which in turn communicates with your data source.

For example, your DataGridView control will be initially filled with data. When you request that a column be sorted, the DataGridView control will communicate that intention to the BindingSource, which in turn communicates that intention to the data source.

The BindingSource is the component that you will bind to the DataSource property of your controls.

BindingNavigator

The BindingNavigator control provides a standard UI that enables you to navigate through the records in your data source. It looks very similar to the record navigator shown at the bottom of Figure 15-6.

The BindingNavigator control is bound to your BindingSource component much like the DataGridView control is. When you click the Next button in the BindingNavigator, it in turn sends a request to the BindingSource for the next record, and the BindingSource in turn sends the request to the data source.

TableAdapter

There's one last component to talk about: the TableAdapter. This component does not reside in the Toolbox but can be automatically generated for you depending on how you add your data access components to your project.

The TableAdapter contains the query that is used to select data from your database, as well as con-nection information for connecting to your database. It also contains methods that will fill the DataSet in your project with data from the database. You can also choose to have the TableAdapter generate INSERT, UPDATE, and DELETE statements based on the query that is used to select data.

The TableAdapter is covered in more detail in Chapter 17.

DATA BINDING

Data binding means taking data referenced by your BindingSource and binding it to a control. In other words, the control will receive its data from your data access components, and the data will be automatically displayed in the control for the user to see and manipulate. In Visual Basic 2010, most controls support some level of data binding. Some are specifically designed for it, such as the DataGridView and TextBox. In your next Try It Out, you will be binding data from a BindingSource to a DataGridView control, so this is where you want to focus your attention. Later in this chapter you'll bind data to a TextBox control.

TRY IT OUT | **Binding Data to a DataGridView Control**

Code file Northwind Customers DataGridView.zip available for download at Wrox.com

In this Try It Out, you will be using the data access wizards in Visual Studio 2010 to create the data objects necessary to bind data to a DataGridView control. You will be using the Northwind sample database again as your data source.

1. Create a new Windows Forms Application project named **Northwind Customers DataGridView**.

2. Click the Data tab in the Toolbox and then drag a DataGridView control from the toolbox and drop it on your form. The DataGridView control will display the DataGridView Tasks dialog box, as shown in Figure 15-9.

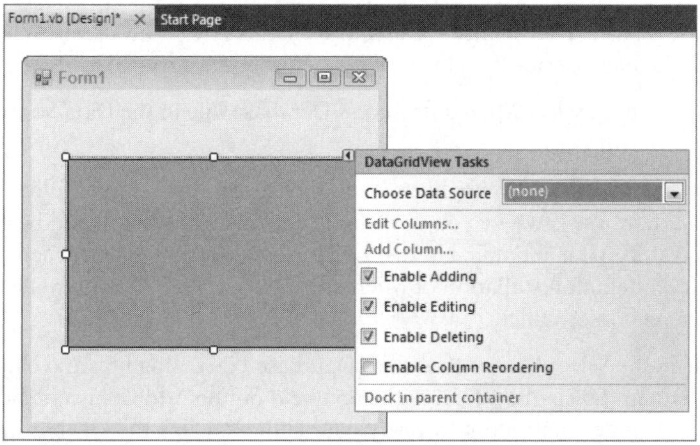

FIGURE 15-9

3. Click the drop-down arrow in the Choose Data Source combo box and then click the Add Project Data Source link at the bottom of the list that is displayed. This displays the Data Source Configuration Wizard.

4. The Choose a Data Source Type screen allows you to choose the data source for your data. As you can see from this screen, shown in Figure 15-10, you have several data source options. You can click the Database icon for connecting to various databases such as SQL Server, Oracle, and

Access; the Web Service icon for connecting to a web service; or the Object icon for connecting to your business logic components. Click the Database icon and then click the Next button.

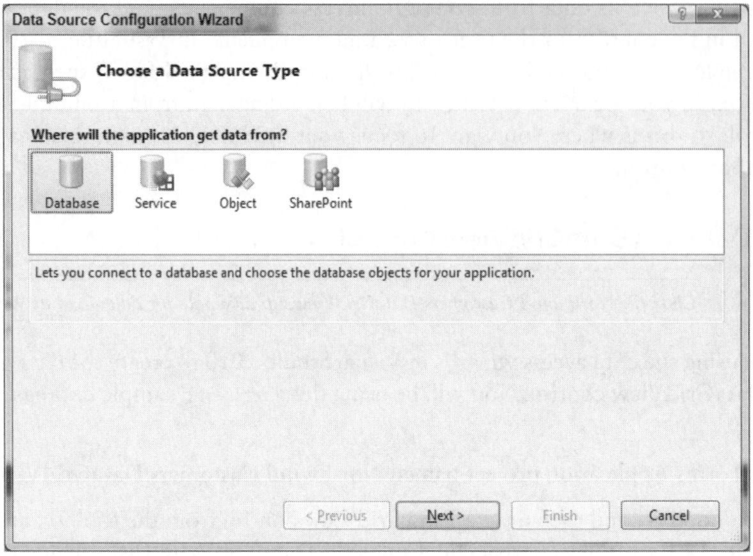

FIGURE 15-10

5. The next screen is for Database Model. The Choose Dataset and click Next. In the Choose Your Data Connection screen, click the New Connection button.

6. In the Choose Data Source dialog box, select Microsoft Access Database File in the Data Source list and then click the Continue button.

7. In the Add Connection dialog box, click the Browse button and navigate to the samples folder for Microsoft office. For 2007, the database is where you downloaded it. By default, it would be in your document library. In Access 2003, it should be in the folder `C:\Program Files\Microsoft Office\Office11\Samples\` for a default installation of Microsoft Office 2003 (11 is the version and will change based on your version of Office).

8. Select the `Northwind` database in the Select Microsoft Access Database File dialog box and click the Open button to have the path and filename added to the text field on the Add Connection dialog box. You can click the Test Connection button to verify your choices. Click the OK button when you are done to close the Add Connection dialog box and then click the Next button on the Choose Your Data Connection screen.

9. The next dialog is for the connection. If you made no changes to your database, accept the default settings. Test your connection with the Test Connection button to ensure it is correct and click OK.

10. Now you are back to the first screen. Click Next to continue. You will be prompted with a dialog box that informs you that the data file is not part of your project and asks if you want to add it. Click the Yes button in this dialog box.

11. Click the Next button on the Save the Connection String to the Application Configuration File screen.

12. The Choose Your Database Objects screen allows you to select the data that your application needs. Here you have the option to select data directly from the tables in your database, data generated from the execution of various views and stored procedures, or data generated from the execution of functions.

13. You'll be using the query that you created in the last Try It Out exercise, so expand the Views node in the Database objects list and then select the check box for CustomerQuery as shown in Figure 15-11. If you expand CustomerQuery, you'll see the columns that are returned from this query. Click the Finish button when you are done.

At this point, the wizard will generate a DataSet named Northwind_2007DataSet, a Binding-Source named CustomerQueryBindingSource, and a TableAdapter named CustomerQuery-TableAdapter.

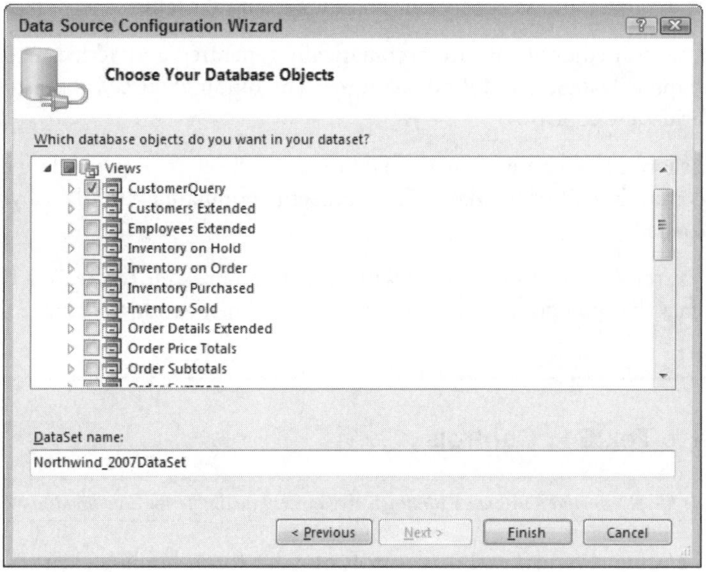

FIGURE 15-11

14. Because you will not be adding, editing, or deleting records from this table, uncheck the check box next to these options in the DataGridView Tasks dialog box. If you don't see this, click on Data-GridView and an arrow will appear at the top right. Click this arrow and you will see the DataGridView Tasks dialog box. You will, however, want to implement sorting in your Data-GridView control, so check the check box next to Enable Column Reordering. When you are done, click the title bar of the form to hide the dialog.

15. Click the DataGridView control and, in the Properties window, set the Dock property to Fill.

16. At this point you can run your project to see the results. Click the Start button on the toolbar. Your form will be displayed with the DataGridView control populated with data.

You can click the column headers to have the data in the DataGridView sorted in ascending order. Clicking the same column header again will sort the data in descending order. Each sort order will be indicated with an arrow pointing up for ascending and down for descending.

How It Works

At this point you have not written a single line of code to achieve these results, which just goes to prove how powerful the data wizards in Visual Basic 2010 are.

The preceding approach for this example is the easiest and most straightforward approach for data access. You start by adding a DataGridView control to your form, which prompts you with the Tasks dialog box for the DataGridView.

This dialog box allows you to create a new Data Source via the Data Source Configuration Wizard, which walks you through a series of steps. First, you identify the type of data source that you wanted to use. Then you specify the type of database object that you want to use to retrieve your data; in this step you merely chose to use a specific table in your database and select specific columns from that table.

When you click the Finish button, several components are automatically generated and added to your project. These include the TableAdapter, DataSet, and BindingSource. The BindingSource is bound to the DataSource property of the DataGridView control.

Remember that the BindingSource's job is to communicate the data needs of the control to the data source, which in this case is the DataSet containing all of the data. The DataSet is populated with data by the TableAdapter when your form is loaded.

The most important point of this exercise is to show the ease with which you are able to create a data-bound application and the simple fact that you do not have to write a single line of code to achieve the end results.

TRY IT OUT   **Binding Data to TextBox Controls**

> *Code file Northwind Customers BindingNavigator.zip available for download at Wrox.com*

In this Try It Out exercise, you'll be using several TextBox controls on your form, binding each text box to a certain field in your BindingSource. You'll then use a BindingNavigator control to navigate through the records in your DataSet.

1.   Create a new Windows Forms Application project named **Northwind Customers BindingNavigator**.

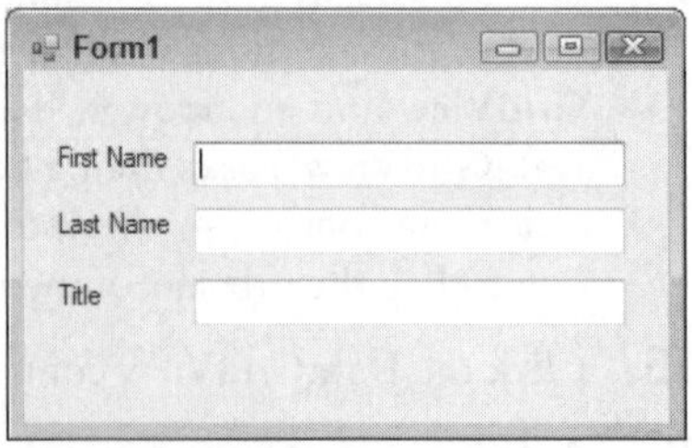

2.   Add three Label controls and three TextBox controls to your form. Arrange the controls so that your form looks similar to Figure 15-12, and set the `Text` properties of the Label controls.

3.   Click the first text box on your form and then expand the `(DataBindings)` property in the Properties window by clicking the plus sign next to it. Then click the `Text` property

FIGURE 15-12

under the DataBindings property. Now click the drop-down arrow for the Text property.

At this point you'll see the Data Source window shown in Figure 15-13. Click the Add Project Data Source link to invoke the Data Source Configuration Wizard, which you saw in the previous Try It Out exercise.

4. Select the Database icon in the Choose a Data Source Type screen and click the Next button. In the Database Model dialog, choose DataSet and click Next.

5. In the Choose Your Data Connection screen, click the New Connection button.

6. In the Add Connection dialog box, click the Browse button and navigate to where the Northwind database is located. This is the same location as the previous example. Select the Northwind database in the Select Microsoft Access Database File dialog box and click the Open button to have the path and filename added to the text field on the Add Connection dialog box. Test the connection and click the OK button when you are done to close the Add Connection dialog box, and then click the Next button on the Choose Your Data Connection screen.

FIGURE 15-13

You will be prompted with a dialog box that informs you that the data file is not part of your project and asks if you want to add it. Click the Yes button in this dialog box.

7. Click the Next button on the Save the Connection String to the Application Configuration File screen.

8. In the Choose Your Database Objects screen, expand the Tables node in the Database objects list and then expand the Customers table. Select the check box for First Name, Last Name, and Job Title. Click Finish.

9. Click the drop-down arrow next to the Text property in the Properties window. At this point, you'll see the Data Source window shown in Figure 15-14. Expand the Other Data Sources node, the Project Data Sources node, the Northwind_2007DataSet node, and finally the Customers node.

Now click the First Name field. The window will close, and the Text field under the DataBindings property will be bound to the First Name field in your DataSet.

If you look at the bottom of the IDE, you'll notice that a Northwind_2007DataSet, CustomersBindingSource, and Customers-TableAdapter have been automatically generated.

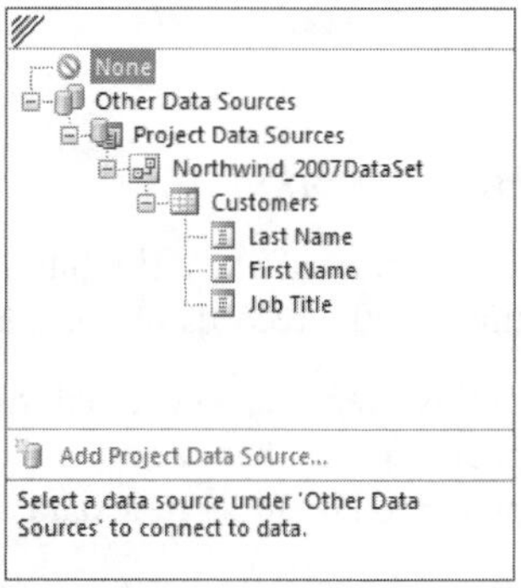

FIGURE 15-14

10. Click the second text box on your form, and then select the Text property under the DataBindings property in the Properties window. Now click the drop-down arrow for the Text property. Expand the CustomersBindingSource node in the Data Source window, and then click the Last Name field.

> **NOTE** *This is not exactly what you did in step 9. Be sure to click CustomersBindingSource or you will have a new Binding Source added to your project and the text boxes will change together.*

11. Click the third text box on your form, and then click the `Text` property under the `DataBindings` property in the Properties window. Click the drop-down arrow for the `Text` property, expand the CustomersBindingSource node in the Data Source window, and then click the Job Title field.

12. Return to the Toolbox, drag a BindingNavigator control from the Data tab, and drop it on your form. The BindingNavigator control will be automatically docked to the top of the form.

13. In the Properties window, locate the `BindingSource` property, and then click that field. Now click the drop-down arrow for the `BindingSource` property and choose CustomersBinding-Source from the list.

14. Finally, click the Start button on the toolbar to run your project. Your form that is displayed should look similar to the one shown in Figure 15-15. You'll be able to navigate through the records in your data source, navigating backward and forward as well as being able to go the first and last record.

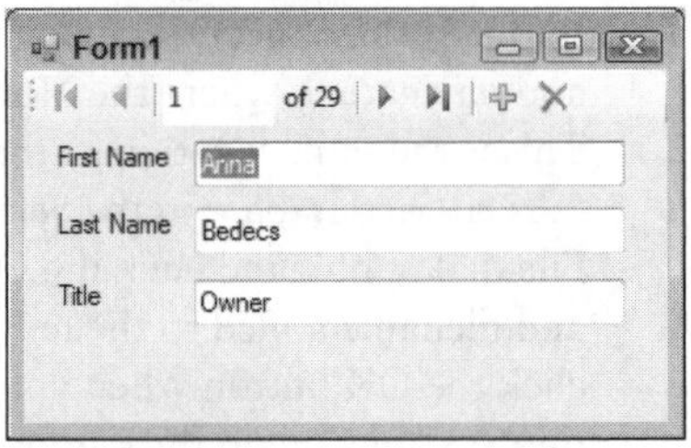

FIGURE 15-15

> **NOTE** *Clicking the Delete button will delete records from your DataSet but will not delete records from the database. Likewise, clicking the Add button will add an empty record to your DataSet but not to the database. You would need to write some code to actually have the database updated with the changes from your DataSet.*

How It Works

The beauty of using the BindingNavigator control is that you've quickly built a form that will navigate through the records of your database without you having to write a single line of code.

In this example, you added three Label and TextBox controls to your form. You then set the `DataBindings` properties of the text boxes. When you set the `Text DataBindings` property of the first text box, you are prompted to add a new data source, which again invokes the Data Source Configuration Wizard.

You use the Data Source Configuration Wizard in this exercise in the same manner as you did in the previous exercise. When you complete the Data Source Configuration Wizard, it automatically generates a TableAdapter, DataSet, and BindingSource. You are then able to choose which field in the DataSet to bind to the `DataBindings Text` property.

When you add the BindingNavigator control to your form, setting it up is a matter of simply choosing the BindingSource that is generated by the Data Source Configuration Wizard in the `BindingSource` property in the Properties window.

Again, this exercise has demonstrated the simplicity with which you can create data-bound applications without the need to write any code.

SUMMARY

You started this chapter by exploring what a database actually is and then looked at the SQL `SELECT` statement. You put this knowledge to use by creating a query in the `Northwind.mdb` database to see the SQL statements that Access generated for you.

You then took a look at the basics of binding data to controls on a form, specifically the DataGridView control and TextBox controls. You have examined the necessary basic data access components required to retrieve data from an Access database and bind that data to your controls. You used the components and controls provided in the Data tab of the Toolbox for your data access, and used the wizards to generate the necessary code to connect to the database and retrieve the data.

After working through this chapter, you should know:

➤ What a database is and the basic objects that make up a database

➤ How to use the SQL `SELECT` statement to select data from a database

➤ How to use the Data Source Configuration Wizard to create the data access components needed to perform data binding

➤ How to bind data to a DataGridView control

➤ How to bind data to TextBox controls and use the BindingNavigator control

You have seen that the wizards provided in Visual Studio 2010 make it simple to bind data quickly to the controls on a form. Sometimes, however, you need more control over how you interact with the data in a database and how you bind the data to the controls on a form. Chapter 16 takes a different approach to data binding by programmatically binding data to controls on a form. You will also be exploring the data access components in more detail and will learn how to set their properties and execute their methods from your code.

EXERCISES

1. How would you write a query to retrieve the `Name`, `Description`, and `Price` fields from a table called `Product`?

2. What would you add to the query to retrieve only items with DVD in their description?

3. How would you order the results so that the most expensive item comes first?

4. What do you put around column names that have spaces in them?

5. In Visual Studio 2010, what control can you use to navigate through data in a Windows Forms Application?

6. What is the terminating character for a SQL command you must use in MS Access?

► **WHAT YOU HAVE LEARNED IN THIS CHAPTER**

TOPIC	CONCEPTS
How to read data from a database	Use the SQL Select statement to read data. Filter data with a Where clause. Sort data using Order By.
Understanding the data controls and components	DataSet: Use this to store data in memory DataGridView: Use this to display data BindingSource: Use this to connect controls with data BindingNavigator: Use this to navigate through your data TableAdapter: Use this to fill your dataset and store information about the queries used for accessing the data
Data binding	Connecting your data to the controls in your application

16

Database Programming with SQL Server and ADO.NET

WHAT YOU WILL LEARN IN THIS CHAPTER:

- ➤ About ADO.NET objects
- ➤ Binding data to controls
- ➤ Searching for and sorting in-memory data using ADO.NET DataView objects
- ➤ Selecting, inserting, updating, and deleting data in a database using ADO.NET

Chapter 15 introduced database programming. You obtained data from a single table in an Access database and displayed it on a grid. You managed to give the user some cool features while writing virtually no code.

You used wizards that wrote most of the code for you — including setting up the connection, configuring the data adapter, and generating a typed dataset. This works great for simple database access using one or two tables, but writing the code yourself can give you a lot more control.

This chapter dives much deeper into the topic of database access. The database access technologies you used in the previous chapter, including components for retrieving data, storing data in memory, and binding data to controls, are collectively called *ADO.NET*. In this chapter, you explore how you can use the built-in capabilities of ADO.NET to retrieve and update data from databases. You will also learn to manipulate, filter, and edit data held in memory by the `DataSet`.

The data you extract will be bound to controls on your form, so you also need to explore binding more thoroughly. You will see how you can use controls to view one record at a time (for example, using text boxes) and how to navigate between records, using the `CurrencyManager` object.

You will also learn how to access SQL Server databases using the `SqlClient` data provider. As mentioned in the previous chapter, `SqlClient` is significantly faster than `OleDb`, but it works only with SQL Server databases. To complete the exercises in this chapter, you need to have access to a version of SQL Server 2008. One is installed with Visual Studio. The chapter is based on SQL Server 2008 but the code should work with SQL Server 2005 with only minor adjustments, if any. As a beginner, it will be easier for you to use SQL Server 2008 without the worry of minor changes. The database can reside in SQL Server 2008 on your local machine or in SQL Server on a network. This chapter has examples of SQL Server 2008 Express running locally. The database the examples use is the `pubs` database from Microsoft.

You can download SQL Server 2008 Express, without cost, from `www.microsoft.com/sql` and choose the link for users who already have SQL Server installed. The Web Platform Installer will not allow you to install another instance and Visual Studio installs one for you. Select the version with tools. You can also enter the following URL directly: `blogs.msdn.com/ sqlexpress/archive/2009/06/15/installing-sql-server-2008-guidance.aspx`.

Here are some notes for installing SQL Server 2008 Express (Runtime with Management Tools):

➤ For Chapter 16, you should install a named instance of `SQLEXPRESS` to avoid having to customize the code.

➤ Chapter 16 uses mixed mode authentication to allow a user name and password to be passed into SQL Server. The chapter uses the `sa` login with a password of `wrox`, which has system administrator rights. This is not normally how you would log in your application to SQL Server. For production, create a login that has a few rights as possible to use or use windows authentication where you can give rights to users or groups.

➤ To run SQL Server 2008 on Windows 7 you have to install SQL Server 2008 Service Patch 1 or later.

➤ Select to install the database engine.

➤ Be sure to select mixed mode authentication. The `sa` account will not be active unless mixed mode authentication is selected.

➤ To use the examples in this chapter, set the `sa` password to `wrox`.

➤ When selecting user accounts for services, use the network service or local service account.

To locate a copy of the `pubs` database, go to the following resources:

➤ SQL Server 2000 scripts and instructions can be downloaded from `www.microsoft.com/ downloads/details.aspx?FamilyID=06616212-0356-46A0-8DA2-EEBC53A68034`. This script will work with 2008 versions. This is the easiest place to get the database.

➤ If the links are a hassle to type, just go to `www.microsoft.com/downloads` and search for SQL Server Sample Databases. The search results will contain the preceding link.

➤ The msi package you download and install will install to `C:\SQL Server 2000 Sample Databases` (the drive may vary based on your configuration). You can then open the file `instpubs.sql` into SQL Management Studio and execute the code, and the `pubs` database will be created and loaded with data.

ADO.NET

ADO.NET is designed to provide a *disconnected architecture*. This means that applications connect to the database to retrieve a load of data and store it in memory. They then disconnect from the database and manipulate the in-memory copy of the data. If the database needs to be updated with changes made to the in-memory copy, a new connection is made and the database is updated. The main in-memory data store is the `DataSet`, which contains other in-memory data stores, such as `DataTable`, `DataColumn`, and `DataRow` objects. You can filter and sort data in a `DataSet` using `DataView` objects, as you will see later in the chapter.

Using a disconnected architecture provides many benefits, of which the most important to you is that it allows your application to *scale up*. This means that your database will perform just as well supporting hundreds of users as it does supporting ten users. This is possible because the application connects to the database only long enough to retrieve or update data, thereby freeing available database connections for other instances of your application or other applications using the same database.

ADO.NET Data Namespaces

The core ADO.NET classes exist in the `System.Data` namespace. This namespace, in turn, contains some child namespaces. The most important of these are `System.Data.SqlClient` and `System.Data.OleDb`, which provide classes for accessing SQL Server databases and OLE (Object Linking and Embedding) DB–compliant databases, respectively. You've already used classes from the `System.Data.OleDb` namespace in the previous chapter, where you used `OleDbConnection` and `OleDbDataAdapter`. In this chapter, you use `System.Data.SqlClient` with its equivalent classes, including `SqlConnection` and `SqlDataAdapter`.

Another child namespace also exists in the `System.Data` namespace: `System.Data.Odbc`. The `System.Data.Odbc` namespace provides access to older Open Database Connectivity (ODBC) data sources that do not support the `OleDb` technology.

The `System.Data.SqlClient`, `System.Data.OleDb`, and `System.Data.Odbc` namespaces are known as *data providers* in ADO.NET. Although other data providers are available, this book concentrates on only the first two.

In this chapter, you access SQL Server databases using the `SqlClient` namespace. However, in ADO.NET, the different data providers work in a very similar way, so the techniques you use here can be easily transferred to the `OleDb` classes. Also, the techniques you learned in the previous chapter using `OleDb` apply to `SqlClient` classes. With ADO.NET, you use the data provider that best fits your data source — you do not need to learn a whole new interface, because all data providers work in a very similar way.

As you start working with ADO.NET, you will soon learn how the pieces fit together, and this chapter helps you in that reaching that goal.

Because the space here is limited, you will focus on the specific classes that are relevant to the example programs in this chapter. The following list contains the ADO.NET classes, from the `System.Data.SqlClient` namespace, that you will be using:

➤   `SqlConnection`

➤   `SqlDataAdapter`

➤   `SqlCommand`

➤   `SqlParameter`

Remember that these are specifically `SqlClient` classes, but that the `OleDb` namespace has very close equivalents.

You can use the `Imports` keyword so you do not have to fully qualify members of the `SqlClient` namespace in your code, as shown in the following fragment:

```
Imports System.Data.SqlClient
```

If you want to use the core ADO.NET classes, such as `DataSet` and `DataView`, without typing the full name, you must import the `System.Data` namespace, as shown here:

```
Imports System.Data
```

You should already be familiar with importing different namespaces in your project. However, to be thorough, you also cover this when you go through the hands-on exercises.

Next, we'll take a look at the main classes in the `System.Data.SqlClient` namespace.

The SqlConnection Class

The `SqlConnection` class is at the heart of the classes discussed in this section because it provides a connection to an SQL Server database. When you construct a `SqlConnection` object, you can choose to specify a *connection string* as a parameter. The connection string contains all the information required to open a connection to your database. If you don't specify one in the constructor, you can set it using the `SqlConnection.ConnectionString` property. In the previous chapter, Visual Studio .NET built a connection string for you from the details you specified in the Data Link Properties dialog box. However, it is often more useful or quicker to write a connection string manually — so let's take a look at how connection strings work.

Working with the Connection String Parameters

The way that the connection string is constructed depends on what data provider you are using. When accessing SQL Server, you usually provide a `Server` and a `Database` parameter, as shown in Table 16-1.

TABLE 16-1: Server and Database Parameters

PARAMETER	DESCRIPTION
Server	The name of the SQL Server that you want to access. This is usually the name of the computer that is running SQL Server. You can use (local) or localhost if SQL Server is on the same machine as the one running the application. If you are using named instances of SQL Server, then this parameter would contain the computer name followed by a backslash followed by the named instance of SQL Server.
Database	The name of the database to which you want to connect.

You also need some form of authentication information, which you can provide in two ways: by using a user name and password in the connection string or by connecting to SQL Server using the NT account under which the application is running. If you want to connect to the server by specifying a user name and password, you need to include additional parameters in your connection string, as shown in Table 16-2.

TABLE 16-2: Additional Parameters When Connecting with a User Name

PARAMETER	DESCRIPTION
User ID	The user name for connecting to the database. An account with this user ID needs to exist in SQL Server and have permission to access the specified database.
Password	The password for the specified user.

However, SQL Server can be set up to use the Windows NT account of the user who is running the program to open the connection. In this case, you don't need to specify a user name and password. You just need to specify that you are using *integrated security*. (The method is called integrated security because SQL Server is integrating with Windows NT's security system, providing the most secure connection because the User ID and Password parameters need not be specified in the code.) You do this using the Integrated Security parameter, which you set to True when you want the application to connect to SQL Server using the current user's NT account.

Of course, for this to work, the user of the application must have permission to use the SQL Server database. This is granted using the SQL Server Management Studio.

To see how these parameters function in a connection string to initialize a connection object, consider the following code fragment. It uses the SqlConnection class to initialize a connection object that uses a specific user ID and password in the connection string:

```
Dim objConnection As SqlConnection = New _
    SqlConnection("Server=localhost\WROX;Database=pubs;" & _
    "User ID=sa;Password=wrox;")
```

This connection string connects to an SQL Server database. The Server parameter specifies that the database resides on the local machine. The Database parameter specifies the database that you want to access — in this case it is the pubs database. Finally, the User ID and Password parameters specify the User ID and password of the user defined in the database. As you can see, each parameter has a value assigned to it using =, and each parameter-value pair is separated by a semicolon.

A great resource for help with just about any kind of connection string is www.connectionstrings.com. You can find just about anything you need to know about any type of data connection.

Opening and Closing the Connection

After you initialize a connection object with a connection string, as shown previously, you can invoke the methods of the SqlConnection object such as Open and Close, which actually open and close a connection to the database specified in the connection string. An example of this is shown in the following code fragment:

```
' Open the database connection..
objConnection.Open()

' .. Use the connection

' Close the database connection..
objConnection.Close()
```

Although many more properties and methods are available in the SqlConnection class, the ones mentioned so far are all you really need to complete the hands-on exercises, and they should be enough to get you started.

The SqlCommand Class

The SqlCommand class represents an SQL command to execute against a data store. The command is usually a select, insert, update, or delete query, and can be an SQL string or a call to a stored procedure. The query being executed may or may not contain parameters.

In the example in Chapter 15, the Data Adapter Configuration Wizard generated a command object for you (although in that case it was an OleDbCommand). In that case, a data adapter used the command to fill a dataset. You look at how to write code to do this later in the chapter. For the moment, you'll look at command objects alone. You learn how they relate to data adapters in the next section.

The constructor for the SqlCommand class has several variations, but the simplest method is to initialize a SqlCommand object with no parameters. Then, after the object has been initialized, you can set the properties you need to perform the task at hand. The following code fragment shows how to initialize a SqlCommand object:

```
Dim objCommand As SqlCommand = New SqlCommand()
```

When using data adapters and datasets, there isn't much call for using command objects on their own. They are mainly used for executing a particular select, delete, insert, or update, so that is what you do in this chapter. You can also use command objects with a data reader. A *data reader* is an alternative to a DataSet that uses fewer system resources but provides far less flexibility. In this book, you concentrate on using the DataSet because it is the more common and useful of the two.

The Connection Property

Certain properties must be set on the SqlCommand object before you can execute the query. The first of these properties is Connection. This property is set to a SqlConnection object, as shown in the next code fragment:

```
objCommand.Connection = objConnection
```

For the command to execute successfully, the connection must be open at the time of execution.

The CommandText Property

The next property that must be set is the CommandText property. This property specifies the SQL string or stored procedure to be executed. Most databases require that you place all *string* values in single quote marks, as shown here in bold:

```
Dim objConnection As SqlConnection = New _
            SqlConnection("server=(local);database=pubs;user id=sa;password=")
Dim objCommand As SqlCommand = New SqlCommand()
objCommand.Connection = objConnection
objCommand.CommandText = "INSERT INTO authors " & _
                "(au_id, au_lname, au_fname, contract) " & _
                "VALUES('123-45-6789', 'Barnes', 'David', 1)"
```

The INSERT statement is a very simple one that means "Insert a new row into the authors table. In the au_id column put '123-45-6789', in the au_lname column put 'Barnes', in the au_fname column put 'David', and in the contract column put '1'."

This is the basic way that INSERT statements work in SQL. You have INSERT INTO followed by a table name. After that is a series of column names, in parentheses. You then have the VALUES keyword followed by a set of values to be inserted into the columns that you've just named and in the same order.

This assumes that you know the values to insert when you are writing the program, which is unlikely in most cases. Fortunately, you can create commands with parameters and then set the values of these parameters separately.

The Parameters Collection

Placeholders are variables prefixed with an at (@) sign in the SQL statement; they get filled in by parameters. For example, if you wanted to update the authors table as discussed in the previous section but didn't know the values at design time, you would do this:

```
Dim objConnection As SqlConnection = New _
            SqlConnection("server=(local);database=pubs;user id=sa;password=")
Dim objCommand As SqlCommand = New SqlCommand()
objCommand.Connection = objConnection
objCommand.CommandText = "INSERT INTO authors " & _
                "(au_id, au_lname, au_fname, contract) " & _
                "VALUES(@au_id,@au_lname,@au_fname,@au_contract)"
```

Here, instead of providing values, you provide placeholders. Placeholders, as mentioned, always start with an @ symbol. They do not need to be named after the database column that they represent, but it is often easier if they are, and it helps to self-document your code.

Next, you need to create parameters that will be used to insert the values into the placeholders when the SQL statement is executed. You create and add parameters to the Parameters collection of the SqlCommand object. The term *parameters* here refers to the parameters required to provide data to your SQL statement or stored procedure, *not* to the parameters that are required to be passed to a Visual Basic 2010 method.

You can access the Parameters collection of the SqlCommand object by specifying the Parameters property. After you access the Parameters collection, you can use its properties and methods to create one or more parameters in the collection. The easiest way to add a parameter to a command is demonstrated in the following example:

```
Dim objConnection As SqlConnection = New _
                SqlConnection("server=(local);database=pubs;user id=sa;password=")
Dim objCommand As SqlCommand = New SqlCommand()
objCommand.Connection = objConnection
objCommand.CommandText = "INSERT INTO authors " & _
                "(au_id, au_lname, au_fname, contract) " & _
                "VALUES(@au_id,@au_lname,@au_fname,@au_contract)"
objCommand.Parameters.AddWithValue ("@au_id", txtAuId.Text)
objCommand.Parameters.AddWithValue ("@au_lname", txtLastName.Text)
objCommand.Parameters.AddWithValue ("@au_fname", txtFirstName.Text)
objCommand.Parameters.AddWithValue ("@au_contract", chkContract.Checked)
```

The AddWithValue method here accepts the name of the parameter and the object that you want to add. In this case, you are using the Text property of various Text box objects on a (fictitious) form for most of the columns. For the Contract column you use the Checked property of a check box on the same form. In previous versions of ADO.NET, you could use the add method to add a parameter with a value. That overload is now obsolete.

The ExecuteNonQuery Method

Finally, you can execute the command. To do this, the connection needs to be opened. You can invoke the ExecuteNonQuery method of the SqlCommand object. This method executes the SQL statement and causes the data to be inserted into the database. It then returns the number of rows that were affected by the query, which can be a useful way to check that the command worked as expected. To complete your code fragment, you need to open the connection, execute the query, and close the connection again:

```
Dim objConnection As SqlConnection = New _
    SqlConnection("server=(local);database=pubs;user id=sa;password=")
Dim objCommand As SqlCommand = New SqlCommand()
objCommand.Connection = objConnection
objCommand.CommandText = "INSERT INTO authors " & _
    "(au_id, au_lname, au_fname, contract) " & _
    "VALUES(@au_id,@au_lname,@au_fname,@au_contract)"
objCommand.Parameters.AddWithValue("@au_id", txtAuId.Text)
objCommand.Parameters.AddWithValue("@au_lname", txtLastName.Text)
objCommand.Parameters.AddWithValue("@au_fname", txtFirstName.Text)
objCommand.Parameters.AddWithValue("@au_contract ", chkContract.Checked)
objConnection.Open()
objCommand.ExecuteNonQuery()
objConnection.Close()
```

The SqlDataAdapter Class

The SqlDataAdapter supports only SQL Server databases. You can configure an SqlDataAdapter using wizards or in code. This chapter explains how to configure and use an SqlDataAdapter in code.

Data adapters act as bridges between your data source and in-memory data objects such as the DataSet. To access the data source, they use the command objects you've just looked at. These command objects are associated with connections, so the data adapter relies on command and connection objects to access and manipulate the data source.

The SqlDataAdapter class's SelectCommand property is used to hold an SqlCommand that retrieves data from the data source. The data adapter then places the result of the query into a DataSet or DataTable. The SqlDataAdapter also has UpdateCommand, DeleteCommand, and InsertCommand properties. These are also SqlCommand objects, used to write changes made to a DataSet or DataTable back to the data source. This may all seem complicated, but in fact the tools are really easy to use. You learned enough SQL in the previous chapter to write a SelectCommand, and there are tools called *command builders* that you can use to automatically create the other commands based on this.

The following section takes a look at the SelectCommand property, and then examines how you can create commands for updating, deleting, and inserting records.

The SelectCommand Property

The SqlDataAdapter class's SelectCommand property is used to fill a DataSet with data from an SQL Server database, as shown in Figure 16-1.

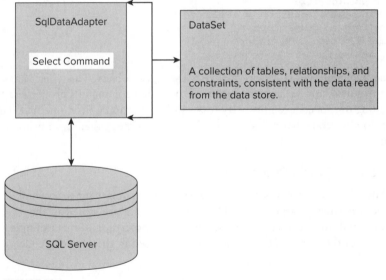

FIGURE 16-1

When you want to read data from the data store, you must set the SelectCommand property of the SqlDataAdapter class first. This property is an SqlCommand object and is used to specify what data to select and how to select that data. Therefore, the SelectCommand property has properties of its own, and you need to set them just as you would set properties on a normal SQLCommand. You've already seen the following properties of the SqlCommand object:

➤ Connection: Sets the SqlConnection object to be used to access the data store.

➤ CommandText: Sets the SQL statements or stored procedure name to be used to select the data.

In the previous examples of `SqlCommand` objects, you used straight SQL statements. If you want to use stored procedures, you need to be aware of an additional property, `CommandType`, which sets a value that determines how the `CommandText` property is interpreted.

In this chapter, you are going to concentrate on SQL statements, but stored procedures are often useful too, particularly if they already exist in the database. If you want to use one, set the `CommandText` property to the name of the stored procedure (remember to enclose it in quote marks because the compiler treats this as a string), and set the `CommandType` property to `CommandType.StoredProcedure`.

Setting SelectCommand to SQL Text

Take a look at how you set these properties in code. The code fragment that follows shows the typical settings for these properties when executing SQL text:

```
' Declare SqlDataAdapter object..
Dim objDataAdapter As New SqlDataAdapter()

' Assign a new SqlCommand to the SelectCommand property
objDataAdapter.SelectCommand = New SqlCommand()

' Set the SelectCommand properties..
objDataAdapter.SelectCommand.Connection = objConnection
objDataAdapter.SelectCommand.CommandText = _
    "SELECT au_lname, au_fname FROM authors " & _
    "ORDER BY au_lname, au_fname"
```

The first thing that this code fragment does is declare the `SqlDataAdapter` object. This object has a `SelectCommand` property set to a new `SqlCommand`; you just need to set that command's properties. You set the properties by first setting the `Connection` property to a valid connection object, one that will already have been created before the code that you see here. Next, you set the `CommandText` property to your SQL `SELECT` statement.

Setting SelectCommand to a Stored Procedure

This next code fragment shows how you could set these properties when you want to execute a *stored procedure*. A stored procedure is a group of SQL statements that are stored in the database under a unique name and are executed as a unit. The stored procedure in this example (`usp_select_author_titles`) uses the same SQL statement that you used in the previous code fragment:

```
' Declare SqlDataAdapter object..
Dim objDataAdapter As New SqlDataAdapter()

' Assign a new SqlCommand to the SelectCommand property
objDataAdapter.SelectCommand = New SqlCommand()

' Set the SelectCommand properties..
objDataAdapter.SelectCommand.Connection = objConnection
objDataAdapter.SelectCommand.CommandText = "usp_select_author_titles"
objDataAdapter.SelectCommand.CommandType = CommandType.StoredProcedure
```

The `CommandText` property now specifies the name of the stored procedure that you want to execute instead of the SQL string that was specified in the previous example. Also notice the `CommandType`

property. In the first example, you did not change this property because its default value is
CommandType.Text, which is what you need to execute SQL statements. In this example, it is set to a
value of CommandType.StoredProcedure, which indicates that the CommandText property contains the
name of a stored procedure to be executed.

Using Command Builders to Create the Other Commands

The SelectCommand is all you need to transfer data from the database into your DataSet. After you
let your users make changes to the DataSet, though, you will want to write the changes back to the
database. You can do this by setting up command objects with the SQL for inserting, deleting, and
updating. Alternatively, you can use stored procedures. Both of these solutions require knowledge of
SQL outside the scope of this book. Fortunately, there is an easier way; you can use *command builders*
to create these commands. It takes only one more line:

```
' Declare SqlDataAdapter object..
Dim objDataAdapter As New SqlDataAdapter()

' Assign a new SqlCommand to the SelectCommand property
objDataAdapter.SelectCommand = New SqlCommand()

' Set the SelectCommand properties..
objDataAdapter.SelectCommand.Connection = objConnection
objDataAdapter.SelectCommand.CommandText = "usp_select_author_titles"
objDataAdapter.SelectCommand.CommandType = CommandType.StoredProcedure
' automatically create update/delete/insert commands
Dim objCommandBuilder As SqlCommandBuilder = New SqlCommandBuilder
(objDataAdapter)
```

Now you can use this SqlDataAdapter to write changes back to a database. You look more at this later
in the chapter. For now, look at the method that gets data from the database to the DataSet in the first
place: the Fill method.

The Fill Method

You use the Fill method to populate a DataSet object with the data that the SqlDataAdapter object
retrieves from the data store using its SelectCommand. However, before you do this you must first
initialize a DataSet object.

```
' Declare SqlDataAdapter object..
Dim objDataAdapter As New SqlDataAdapter()

' Assign a new SqlCommand to the SelectCommand property
objDataAdapter.SelectCommand = New SqlCommand()

' Set the SelectCommand properties..
objDataAdapter.SelectCommand.Connection = objConnection
objDataAdapter.SelectCommand.CommandText = "usp_select_author_titles"
objDataAdapter.SelectCommand.CommandType = CommandType.StoredProcedure

' Create the DataSet
Dim objDataSet as DataSet = New DataSet()
```

Now that you have a `DataSet` and `SqlDataAdapter`, you can fill your `DataSet` with data. The `Fill` method has several overloaded versions, but you will be discussing the one most commonly used. The syntax for the `Fill` method is shown here:

```
SqlDataAdapter.Fill(DataSet, string)
```

The `DataSet` argument specifies a valid `DataSet` object that will be populated with data. The `string` argument gives the name you want the table to have in the `DataSet`. Remember that one `DataSet` can contain many tables. You can use any name you like, but usually it's best to use the name of the table from which the data in the database has come. This helps you self-document your code and makes the code easier to maintain.

The following code fragment shows how you invoke the `Fill` method. The string `"authors"` is specified as the *string* argument. This is the name you want to use when manipulating the in-memory version of the table; it is also the name of the table in the data source.

```
' Declare SqlDataAdapter object..
Dim objDataAdapter As New SqlDataAdapter()

'Create an instance of a new select command object
objDataAdapter.SelectCommand = New SqlCommand

' Set the SelectCommand properties..
objDataAdapter.SelectCommand.Connection = objConnection
objDataAdapter.SelectCommand.CommandText = "usp_select_author_titles"
objDataAdapter.SelectCommand.CommandType = CommandType.StoredProcedure

' Create the DataSet
Dim objDataSet as DataSet = New DataSet()

' Fill the DataSet object with data..
objDataAdapter.Fill(objDataSet, "authors")
```

The `Fill` method uses the `SelectCommand.Connection` property to connect to the database. If the connection is already open, the data adapter will use it to execute the `SelectCommand` and leave it open after it's finished. If the connection is closed, then the data adapter will open it, execute the `SelectCommand`, and then close it again.

You now have data in memory and can start manipulating it independently of the data source. Notice that the `DataSet` class does not have `Sql` at the start of its class name. This is because `DataSet` is not in the `System.Data.SqlClient` namespace; it is in the parent `System.Data` namespace. The classes in this namespace are primarily concerned with manipulating data in memory, rather than obtaining data from any particular data source. Once you have the data loaded into a `DataSet`, it no longer matters what data source it came from (unless you need to write it back). Let's have a look at two of the classes in this namespace: the `DataSet` and the `DataView`.

The DataSet Class

The `DataSet` class is used to store data retrieved from a data store and stores that data in memory on the client. The `DataSet` object contains a collection of tables, relationships, and constraints that are consistent with the data read from the data store. It acts as a lightweight database engine all by itself, enabling you to store tables, edit data, and run queries against it using a `DataView` object.

The data in a `DataSet` is disconnected from the data store, and you can operate on the data independently from the data store. You can manipulate the data in a `DataSet` object by adding, updating, and deleting the records. You can apply these changes back to the original data store afterwards using a data adapter.

The data in a `DataSet` object is maintained in Extensible Markup Language (XML), which is discussed in detail in Chapter 18, meaning that you can save a `DataSet` as a file or easily pass it over a network. The XML is shielded from you as a developer, and you should never need to edit the XML directly. All editing of the XML is done through the properties and methods of the `DataSet` class. Many developers like using XML and will sometimes choose to manipulate the XML representation of a `DataSet` directly, but this is not essential.

Like any XML document, a `DataSet` can have a *schema,* a file that describes the structure of the data in one or more XML files. When you generated a typed `DataSet` in the previous chapter, an XML Schema Definition (XSD) file was added to the Solution Explorer, as shown in Figure 16-2.

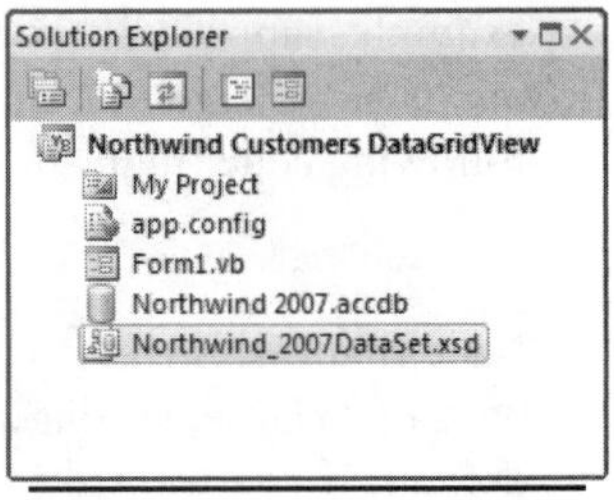

This file is an XML schema for the data that the `CustomerDataSet` would hold. From this, Visual Studio .NET was able to create a class that inherited from the `DataSet` and that used this particular schema. A `DataSet` schema contains information about the tables, relationships, and constraints stored in the `DataSet`. Again, this is shielded from you, and you do not need to know XML to work with a `DataSet`.

FIGURE 16-2

Because the `DataSet` contains the actual data retrieved from a data store, you can bind the `DataSet` to a control or controls to have them display (and allow editing of) the data in the `DataSet`. You did this a bit in Chapter 15, and you will see more later in this chapter.

DataView

The `DataView` class is typically used for sorting, filtering, searching, editing, and navigating the data from a `DataSet`. A `DataView` is *bindable,* meaning it can be bound to controls in the same way that the `DataSet` can be bound to controls. Again, you learn more about data binding in code later in this chapter.

A `DataSet` can contain a number of `DataTable` objects; when you use the `SqlDataAdapter` class's `Fill` method to add data to a `DataSet`, you are actually creating a `DataTable` object inside the `DataSet`. The `DataView` provides a custom view of a `DataTable`; you can sort or filter the rows, for example, as you can in an SQL query.

You can create a `DataView` from the data contained in a `DataTable` that contains only the data that you want to display. For example, if the data in a `DataTable` contains all authors sorted by last name and first name, you can create a `DataView` that contains all authors sorted by first name and then last name. Or, if you wanted, you could create a `DataView` that contained only last names or certain names.

Although you can view the data in a `DataView` in ways different from the underlying `DataTable`, it is still the same data. Changes made to a `DataView` affect the underlying `DataTable` automatically, and changes made to the underlying `DataTable` automatically affect any `DataView` objects that are viewing that `DataTable`.

The constructor for the `DataView` class initializes a new instance of the `DataView` class and accepts the `DataTable` as an argument. The following code fragment declares a `DataView` object and initializes it using the `authors` table from the `DataSet` named `objDataSet`. Notice that the code accesses the `Tables` collection of the `DataSet` object, by specifying the `Tables` property and the table name:

```
' Set the DataView object to the DataSet object..
Dim objDataView = New DataView(objDataSet.Tables("authors"))
```

The Sort Property

Once a `DataView` has been initialized and is displaying data, you can alter the view of that data. For example, suppose you want to sort the data in a different order than in the `DataSet`. To sort the data in a `DataView`, you set the `Sort` property and specify the column or columns that you want sorted. The following code fragment sorts the data in a `DataView` by author's first name and then last name:

```
objDataView.Sort = "au_fname, au_lname"
```

Note that this is the same syntax as the `ORDER BY` clause in an SQL `SELECT` statement. As in the SQL `ORDER BY` clause, sorting operations on a `DataView` are always performed in an ascending order by default. If you wanted to perform the sort in descending order, you would need to specify the `DESC` keyword, as shown here:

```
objDataView.Sort = "au_fname, au_lname DESC"
```

The RowFilter Property

When you have an initialized `DataView`, you can filter the rows of data that it will contain. This is similar to specifying a `WHERE` clause in an SQL `SELECT` statement; only rows that match the criteria will remain in the view. The underlying data is not affected, though. The `RowFilter` property specifies the criteria that should be applied on the `DataView`. The syntax is similar to the SQL `WHERE` clause. It contains at least a column name followed by an operator and the value. If the value is a string, it must be enclosed in single quote marks, as shown in the following code fragment, which retrieves only the authors whose last names are `Green`:

```
' Set the DataView object to the DataSet object..
objDataView = New DataView(objDataSet.Tables("authors"))
objDataView.RowFilter = "au_lname = 'Green'"
```

If you want to retrieve all rows of authors except those with the last name of `Green`, you would specify the not equal to operator (`<>`) as shown in this example:

```
' Set the DataView object to the DataSet object..
objDataView = New DataView(objDataSet.Tables("authors"))
objDataView.RowFilter = "au_lname <> 'Green'"
```

You can also specify more complex filters, as you could in SQL. For example, you can combine several criteria using an `AND` operator:

```
objDataView.RowFilter = "au_lname <> 'Green' AND au_fname LIKE 'D*'"
```

This returns authors whose last names are not `Green` and whose first names begin with `D`.

The Find Method

If you want to search for a specific row of data in a DataView, you invoke the Find method. The Find method searches for data in the sort key column of the DataView. Therefore, before invoking the Find method, you first need to sort the DataView on the column that contains the data that you want to find. The column that the DataView is sorted on becomes the sort key column in a DataView object.

For example, suppose you want to find the author who has a first name of Ann. You would need to sort the DataView by first name to set this column as the sort key column in the DataView, and then invoke the Find method, as shown in the following code fragment:

```
Dim intPosition as Integer
objDataView.Sort = "au_fname"
intPosition = objDataView.Find("Ann")
```

If it finds a match, the Find method returns the position of the record within the DataView. Otherwise, the DataView returns a null value, indicating that no match was found. If the Find method finds a match, it stops looking and returns only the position of the first match. If you know there is more than one match in your data store, you could filter the data in the DataView, a subject that is covered shortly.

The Find method is not case sensitive, meaning that to find the author who has a first name of Ann, you could enter either Ann or ann.

The Find method looks for an exact case-insensitive match, so this means that you must enter the whole word or words of the text that you are looking for. For example, suppose you are looking for the author who has the first name of Ann. You cannot enter An and expect to find a match; you must enter all the characters or words that make up the author's name. Notice that the following example specifies all lowercase letters, which is perfectly fine:

```
Dim intPosition as Integer
objDataView.Sort = "au_fname"
intPosition = objDataView.Find("ann")
```

You have seen that a DataView can be sorted on more than one column at a time. To do so, you need to supply an array of values to the Find method instead of just a single value. For example, you may want to find where Simon Watts appears in the DataView, if at all:

```
Dim intPosition As Integer
Dim arrValues(1) As Object
objDataView.Sort = "au_fname, au_lname"

' Find the author named "Simon Watts".
arrValues(0)= "Simon"
arrValues(1) = "Watts"
intPosition = objDataView.Find(arrValues)
```

THE ADO.NET CLASSES IN ACTION

You've now looked at the basics of the ADO.NET classes and how they enable you to retrieve and insert data into SQL Server. No doubt your head is spinning from information overload at this point, so the best way to ensure that you understand how to use all of the objects, methods, and properties that you have been looking at is to actually use them. In the next two Try It Outs, you'll see how to exploit the power of the `DataSet` object to expose data to your users. You may find that you want to come back and reread the previous section after you've completed the Try It Outs; this will help to clarify ADO.NET in your mind.

The first Try It Out implements the `SqlConnection`, `SqlDataAdapter`, and `DataSet` classes. You will see firsthand how to use these classes in a simple example in which you need to retrieve read-only data and display that data in a data grid. In fact, what you do here is very similar to the example in the previous chapter, but you will be doing it in code instead of using wizards.

> **NOTE** When writing your programs, you can often use a combination of wizards and coding to create powerful programs quickly and easily. The components created in the previous chapter by drag and drop can be manipulated in code in exactly the same way as objects created in code. In the previous chapter, you used wizards almost all the time. In this chapter you concentrate on code.

Examining a DataSet Example

Before you dive into the details of creating the program, take a look at the data and the relationships of the data that you want to display. The data that you want comes from the Pubs database in SQL Server. If you are using SQL Server 2000, SQL Server 2005, or SQL Server 2008, you should be seeing the exact same data. Newer versions SQL Server do not come with the Pubs database. The link to get the database is at the beginning of the chapter.

You want to display a list of authors, their book titles, and the price of their books. Figure 16-3 shows the tables that this data resides in and also the relationship of the tables.

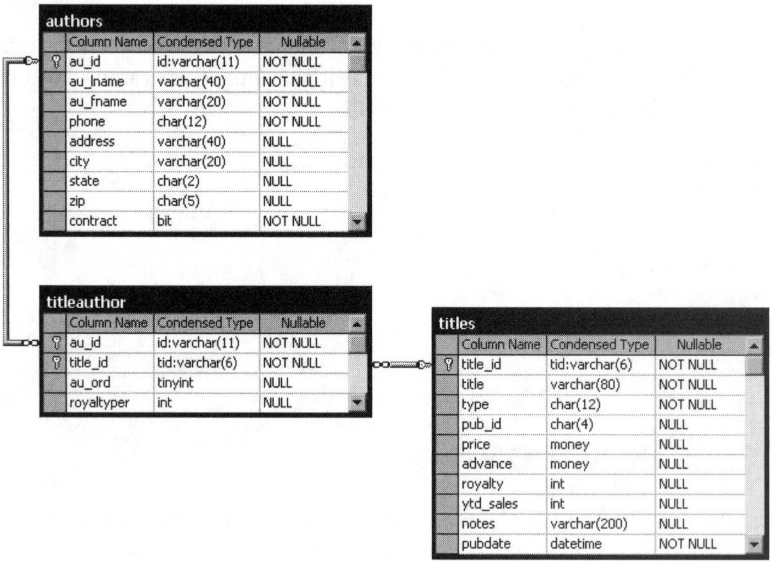

FIGURE 16-3

You want to display the author's first and last names, which reside in the authors table, and the title and price of the book, which reside in the titles table. Because an author can have one or more books and a book can have one or more authors, the titles table is joined to the authors table via a *relationship table* called titleauthor. This table contains the many-to-many relationship of authors to books.

Having looked at the table relationships and knowing what data you want, consider the SQL SELECT statement that you need to create to get this data:

```
SELECT au_lname, au_fname, title, price
FROM authors
JOIN titleauthor ON authors.au_id = titleauthor.au_id
JOIN titles ON titleauthor.title_id = titles.title_id
ORDER BY au_lname, au_fname
```

The first line of the SELECT statement shows the columns that you want to select. The second line shows the main table from which you are selecting data, which is authors.

The third line *joins* the titleauthor table to the authors table using the au_id column. Therefore, when you select a row of data from the authors table, you also get every row in the titleauthor table that matches the au_id in the selected row of the authors table. This join returns only authors who have a record in the titleauthor table.

The fourth line joins the titles table to the titleauthor table using the title_id column. Hence, for every row of data that is selected from the titleauthor table, you select the corresponding row of data (having the same title_id value) from the titles table. The last line of the SELECT statement sorts the data by the author's last name and first name using the ORDER BY clause.

TRY IT OUT DataSet Example

Code file DatasetExample.zip is available for download at Wrox.com

Now, you'll create a project in this Try It Out.

1. Create a new Windows Forms application called **DatasetExample**.

2. Set the following properties of the form:
   - ➤ Set Size to **600, 230**.
   - ➤ Set StartPosition to **CenterScreen**.
   - ➤ Set Text to **Bound DataSet**.

3. From the Toolbox, locate the DataGridView control under the Windows Forms tab and drag it onto your form. Set the properties of the DataGridView as follows:
   - ➤ Set Name to **grdAuthorTitles**.
   - ➤ Set Anchor to **Top, Bottom, Left, Right**.
   - ➤ Set Location to **0, 0**.
   - ➤ Set Size to **592, 203**.

4. Add the `Imports` statements for the namespaces you will use. Open the code window for your form and add the namespaces in bold at the very top of your code:

```
' Import Data and SqlClient namespaces..
Imports System.Data
Imports System.Data.SqlClient

Public Class Form1

End Class
```

5. You need to declare the objects necessary to retrieve the data from the database, so add the following bold code. Ensure that you use a user ID and password that have been defined in your installation of SQL Server:

```
Public Class Form1
    Dim objConnection As New SqlConnection _
        ("server=localhost\WROX;database=pubs;user id=sa;password=wrox")

    Dim objDataAdapter As New SqlDataAdapter()
    Dim objDataSet As New DataSet()
End Class
```

6. To add a handler for the form's `Load` event, select `(Form1 Events)` in first combo box the `(General)` and then select `Load` in the second combo box `(Declarations)`. Insert the following bold code:

```
Private Sub Form1_Load(ByVal sender As Object, ByVal e As System.EventArgs) _
        Handles Me.Load
    ' Set the SelectCommand properties..
    objDataAdapter.SelectCommand = New SqlCommand()
    objDataAdapter.SelectCommand.Connection = objConnection
    objDataAdapter.SelectCommand.CommandText = _
        "SELECT au_lname, au_fname, title, price " & _
        "FROM authors " & _
        "JOIN titleauthor ON authors.au_id = titleauthor.au_id " & _
        "JOIN titles ON titleauthor.title_id = titles.title_id " & _
        "ORDER BY au_lname, au_fname"
    objDataAdapter.SelectCommand.CommandType = CommandType.Text

    ' Open the database connection..
    objConnection.Open()

    ' Fill the DataSet object with data..
    objDataAdapter.Fill(objDataSet, "authors")

    ' Close the database connection..
    objConnection.Close()

    ' Set the DataGridView properties to bind it to our data..
    grdAuthorTitles.AutoGenerateColumns = True
    grdAuthorTitles.DataSource = objDataSet
    grdAuthorTitles.DataMember = "authors"

    ' Clean up
    objDataAdapter = Nothing
    objConnection = Nothing
End Sub
```

7. Run the project. You should see results similar to what is shown in Figure 16-4.

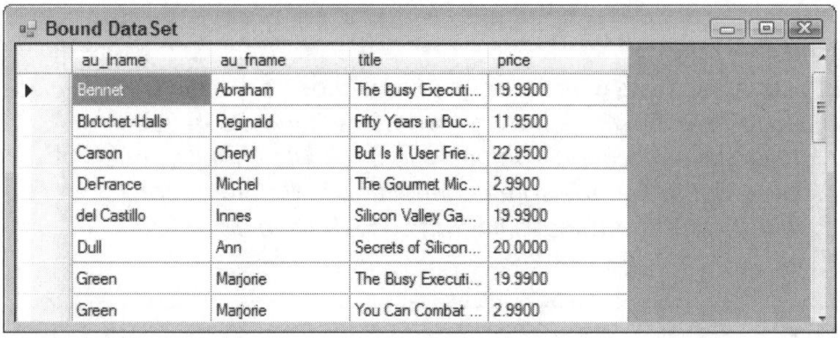

au_lname	au_fname	title	price
Bennet	Abraham	The Busy Executi...	19.9900
Blotchet-Halls	Reginald	Fifty Years in Buc...	11.9500
Carson	Cheryl	But Is It User Frie...	22.9500
DeFrance	Michel	The Gourmet Mic...	2.9900
del Castillo	Innes	Silicon Valley Ga...	19.9900
Dull	Ann	Secrets of Silicon...	20.0000
Green	Marjorie	The Busy Executi...	19.9900
Green	Marjorie	You Can Combat ...	2.9900

FIGURE 16-4

8. Note that the DataGridView control has built-in sorting capabilities. If you click a column header, the data in the grid will be sorted by that column in ascending order. If you click the same column again, the data will be sorted in descending order.

> **NOTE** *Note that error handling has been omitted from the exercise, to preserve space. You should always add the appropriate error handling to your code. Review Chapter 10 for error-handling techniques.*

How It Works

To begin, you first imported the following namespaces:

```
' Import Data and SqlClient namespaces..
Imports System.Data
Imports System.Data.SqlClient
```

Remember that the System.Data namespace is required for the DataSet and DataView classes, and that the System.Data.SqlClient namespace is required for the SqlConnection, SqlDataAdapter, SqlCommand, and SqlParameter classes. You will be using only a subset of the classes just mentioned in this example, but you do require both namespaces.

Then you declared the objects that were necessary to retrieve the data from the database. These objects were declared with class-level scope, so you placed those declarations just inside the class:

```
Public Class Form1
    Inherits System.Windows.Forms.Form

    Dim objConnection As New SqlConnection _
        ("server=localhost\WROX;database=pubs;user id=sa;password=wrox")

    Dim objDataAdapter As New SqlDataAdapter()
    Dim objDataSet As DataSet = New DataSet()
```

The first object that you declared was an SqlConnection object. Remember that this object establishes a connection to your data store, which in this case is SQL Server.

The next object that you declared was an SqlDataAdapter object. This object is used to read data from the database and populate the DataSet object.

The last object in your declarations was the `DataSet` object, which serves as the container for your data. Remember that this object stores all data in memory and is not connected to the data store.

> **NOTE** *In this particular example, there was no need to give these objects class-level scope. You use them in only one method, and they could have been declared there. However, if your application enabled users to write changes back to the database, you would want to use the same connection and data adapter objects for reading and writing to the database. In that case, having class-level scope would be very useful.*

With your objects defined, you placed some code to populate the `DataSet` object in the initialization section of the form. Your `SqlDataAdapter` object is responsible for retrieving the data from the database. Therefore, you set the `SelectCommand` property of this object. This property is an `SqlCommand` object, so the `SelectCommand` has all the properties of an independent `SqlCommand` object:

```
' Set the SelectCommand properties..
objDataAdapter.SelectCommand = New SqlCommand()
objDataAdapter.SelectCommand.Connection = objConnection
objDataAdapter.SelectCommand.CommandText = _
    "SELECT au_lname, au_fname, title, price " & _
    "FROM authors " & _
    "JOIN titleauthor ON authors.au_id = titleauthor.au_id " & _
    "JOIN titles ON titleauthor.title_id = titles.title_id " & _
    "ORDER BY au_lname, au_fname"
```

First, you initialize the `SelectCommand` by initializing an instance of the `SqlCommand` class and assigning it to the `SelectCommand` property.

Then you set the `Connection` property to your connection object. This property sets the connection to be used to communicate with your data store.

The `CommandText` property is then set to the SQL string that you wanted to execute. This property contains the SQL string or stored procedure to be executed to retrieve your data. In this case you used an SQL string, which was explained in detail earlier.

After all of the properties are set, you open your connection, fill the dataset, and then close the connection again. You open the connection by executing the `Open` method of your `SqlConnection` object:

```
' Open the database connection..
objConnection.Open()
```

You then invoke the `Fill` method of the `SqlDataAdapter` object to retrieve the data and fill your `DataSet` object. In the parameters for the `Fill` method, you specify the `DataSet` object to use and the table name. You set the table name to `authors`, even though you are actually retrieving data from several tables in the data store:

```
' Fill the DataSet object with data..
objDataAdapter.Fill(objDataSet, "authors")
```

After you fill your `DataSet` object with data, you need to close the database connection. You do that by invoking the `Close` method of the `SqlConnection` object:

```
' Close the database connection..
objConnection.Close()
```

As you learned earlier, you do not have to open and close the connection explicitly. The `Fill` method of the `SqlDataAdapter` executes the `SelectCommand` and leaves the connection in the same state as when the method was invoked. In this case, the `Fill` method left the connection open. If you did not explicitly write code to open and close the connection, the `SqlDataAdapter.Fill` method would open and close the connection for you.

Then you set some properties of the `DataGridView` to bind your data to it. The first of these properties is the `AutoGenerateColumns` property. Here you let the control create all of the columns you needed by setting the `AutoGenerateColumns` property to `True`. The next property is the `DataSource` property, which tells the `DataGridView` where to get its data:

```
' Set the DataGridView properties to bind it to our data..
grdAuthorTitles.AutoGenerateColumns = True
grdAuthorTitles.DataSource = objDataSet
grdAuthorTitles.DataMember = "authors"
```

The `DataMember` property selects the table in the data source, and here you set it to `authors`, which is the table used in your `DataSet` object.

Then, to free memory, you clean up the objects that are no longer being used:

```
' Clean up
objDataAdapter = Nothing
objConnection = Nothing
```

When you ran the example, the `DataGridView` control read the schema information from the `DataSet` object (which the `DataSet` object created when it was filled) and created the correct number of columns for your data in the DataGridView control. It has also used the column names in the schema as the column names for the grid, and each column had the same default width. The DataGridView also read the entire `DataSet` object and placed the contents into the grid.

TRY IT OUT   Changing the DataGridView Properties

Code file DatasetExample.zip is available for download at Wrox.com

In this Try It Out, you use some of the DataGridView properties to make this a more user-friendly display of data.

1.   Here are some changes you can make to make your **DataGridView** more user-friendly:

➤   Add your own column header names.

➤   Adjust the width of the column that contains the book titles so that you can easily see the full title.

➤   Change the color of every other row so that the data in each one stands out.

➤   Make the last column in the grid (which contains the price of the books) right-aligned.

You can do all this by making the following modifications in bold to your code in the `Form1_Load` method:

```
' Set the DataGridView properties to bind it to our data..
grdAuthorTitles.DataSource = objDataSet
grdAuthorTitles.DataMember = "authors"
```

```
' Declare and set the currency header alignment property..
Dim objAlignRightCellStyle As New DataGridViewCellStyle
objAlignRightCellStyle.Alignment = DataGridViewContentAlignment.MiddleRight

' Declare and set the alternating rows style..
Dim objAlternatingCellStyle As New DataGridViewCellStyle()
objAlternatingCellStyle.BackColor = Color.WhiteSmoke
grdAuthorTitles.AlternatingRowsDefaultCellStyle = objAlternatingCellStyle

' Declare and set the style for currency cells ..
Dim objCurrencyCellStyle As New DataGridViewCellStyle()
objCurrencyCellStyle.Format = "c"
objCurrencyCellStyle.Alignment = DataGridViewContentAlignment.MiddleRight

' Change column names and styles using the column index
grdAuthorTitles.Columns(0).HeaderText = "Last Name"
grdAuthorTitles.Columns(1).HeaderText = "First Name"
grdAuthorTitles.Columns(2).HeaderText = "Book Title"
grdAuthorTitles.Columns(2).Width = 225

' Change column names and styles using the column name
grdAuthorTitles.Columns("price").HeaderCell.Value = "Retail Price"
grdAuthorTitles.Columns("price").HeaderCell.Style =_ objAlignRightCellStyle
grdAuthorTitles.Columns("price").DefaultCellStyle = objCurrencyCellStyle

' Clean up
objDataAdapter = Nothing
objConnection = Nothing
objCurrencyCellStyle = Nothing
objAlternatingCellStyle = Nothing
objAlignRightCellStyle = Nothing

End Sub
```

2. Run your project again. You should now see results similar to what is shown in Figure 16-5. You can compare this figure to Figure 16-4 and see a world of difference. It's amazing what setting a few properties will do to create a more user-friendly display.

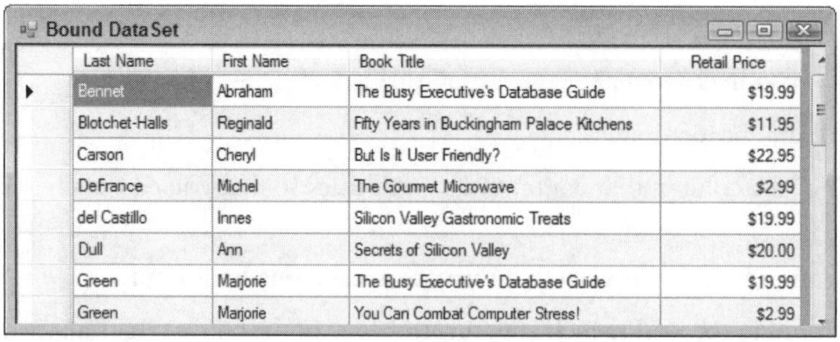

Last Name	First Name	Book Title	Retail Price
Bennet	Abraham	The Busy Executive's Database Guide	$19.99
Blotchet-Halls	Reginald	Fifty Years in Buckingham Palace Kitchens	$11.95
Carson	Cheryl	But Is It User Friendly?	$22.95
DeFrance	Michel	The Gourmet Microwave	$2.99
del Castillo	Innes	Silicon Valley Gastronomic Treats	$19.99
Dull	Ann	Secrets of Silicon Valley	$20.00
Green	Marjorie	The Busy Executive's Database Guide	$19.99
Green	Marjorie	You Can Combat Computer Stress!	$2.99

Bound Data Set

FIGURE 16-5

How It Works

The DataGridView uses inherited styles to format the output table the users see. Style inheritance enables you to apply default styles that cascade to all cells, rows, columns, or headers under the parent style. Then, you can change only individual items that do not match the default styles. The architecture of styles is very powerful. You can set individual style properties or create your own DataGridViewCellStyle objects to set multiple style properties and reuse them.

To start, you declare a DataGridViewCellStyle object. Then you change the alignment to middle right, which enables you to align the price column later:

```
' Declare and set the currency header alignment property..

Dim objAlignRightCellStyle As New DataGridViewCellStyle
    objAlignRightCellStyle.Alignment = DataGridViewContentAlignment.MiddleRight
```

The first thing that you do here is alternate the background color of each row of data. This helps each row of data stand out and makes it easier to see the data in each column for a single row. The Color structure provides a large list of color constants, as well as a few methods that can be called to generate colors:

```
' Declare and set the alternating rows style..
Dim objAlternatingCellStyle As New DataGridViewCellStyle()
objAlternatingCellStyle.BackColor = Color.WhiteSmoke
grdAuthorTitles.AlternatingRowsDefaultCellStyle = objAlternatingCellStyle
```

Next, changes to the currency cells for Retail Price are set up. You change the format to currency and right-align the column:

```
' Declare and set the style for currency cells ..
Dim objCurrencyCellStyle As New DataGridViewCellStyle()
objCurrencyCellStyle.Format = "c"
objCurrencyCellStyle.Alignment = DataGridViewContentAlignment.MiddleRight
```

Some changes to the format of the DataGridView are easy to make at the property level. Column titles can simply be changed by accessing the column and setting HeaderText or HeaderCell.Value properties. You set both properties in the code that follows.

You changed the book Title column width to 225 to display the title in a more readable format.

```
' Change column names and styles using the column index
grdAuthorTitles.Columns(0).HeaderText = "Last Name"
grdAuthorTitles.Columns(1).HeaderText = "First Name"
grdAuthorTitles.Columns(2).HeaderText = "Book Title"
grdAuthorTitles.Columns(2).Width = 225
```

Next, you set the styles on the Price column based on the style objects above. What is great about using style objects is you can apply the same styles to multiple objects. For example, if you have three columns that hold dollar amounts, you can set up one style object and reuse this style on all three columns.

```
' Change column names and styles using the column name
grdAuthorTitles.Columns("price").HeaderCell.Value = "Retail Price"
grdAuthorTitles.Columns("price").HeaderCell.Style = objAlignRightCellStyle
grdAuthorTitles.Columns("price").DefaultCellStyle = objCurrencyCellStyle
```

You have now seen how to bind the DataSet object to a control, in this case a **DataGridView** control. In the next Try It Out, you expand on this knowledge by binding several controls to a DataView object and by using the `CurrencyManager` object to navigate the data in the `DataView` object. However, before you get to that point, the following section describes data binding and how you can bind data to simple controls, such as the TextBox control, and how to navigate the records.

DATA BINDING

The **DataGridView** control is a great tool for displaying all your data at one time. You can also use it for editing, deleting, and inserting rows, provided you have the logic to write changes back to the data source. However, you will often want to use a control to display a single column value from one record at a time. In cases like these, you need to bind individual pieces of data to simple controls, such as a TextBox, and display only a single row of data at a time. This type of data binding gives you more control over the data, but it also increases the complexity of your programs, because you must write the code both to bind the data to the controls and to navigate between records. This section takes a look at what is involved in binding data to simple controls, and how to manage the data bindings.

In this discussion, the term *simple controls* refers to controls that can display only one item of data at a time, such as a TextBox, a Button, a CheckBox, or a RadioButton. Controls such as ComboBox, ListBox, and DataGridView can contain more than one item of data and are not considered simple controls when it comes to data binding. Generally speaking, nonsimple controls have particular properties intended for binding to a data object such as a `DataTable` or `Array`. When binding to simple controls, you are actually binding a particular item of data to a particular property.

BindingContext and CurrencyManager

Each form has a built-in `BindingContext` object that manages the bindings of the controls on the form. Because the `BindingContext` object is already built into each form, you don't need to do anything to set it up.

The `BindingContext` object manages a collection of `CurrencyManager` objects. The `CurrencyManager` is responsible for keeping the data-bound controls in sync with their data source and with other data-bound controls that use the same data source. This ensures that all controls on the form are showing data from the same record. The `CurrencyManager` manages data from a variety of objects, such as `DataSet`, `DataView`, `DataTable`, and `DataSetView`. Whenever you add a data source to a form, a new `CurrencyManager` is automatically created. This makes working with data-bound controls very convenient and simple.

> **NOTE** The `CurrencyManager` gets its name because it keeps the controls current with respect to the data in the data source. The controls do not represent currency (monetary amounts).

If you have multiple data sources in your form, you can declare a `CurrencyManager` variable and set it to refer to the appropriate `CurrencyManager` object for a given data source in the collection managed by the `BindingContext` object. You then have the capability to manage the data in the data-bound controls explicitly.

The following code fragment, using the DataSet object that you have been using in the previous example, defines and sets a reference to the CurrencyManager that manages the data source containing the local authors table. First, the code declares a variable using the CurrencyManager class. Then it sets this CurrencyManager variable to the currency manager for the DataSet object (objDataSet) contained in the BindingContext object. The CType function is used to return an object that is explicitly converted. The CType function accepts two arguments: the expression to be converted and the type to which the expression is to be converted. Because the expression is to evaluate to a CurrencyManager object, CurrencyManager is specified for the type argument:

```
Dim objCurrencyManager As CurrencyManager
objCurrencyManager = _
    CType(Me.BindingContext(objDataSet), CurrencyManager)
```

After you have a reference to the data source object, you can manage the position of the records using the Position property, as shown in the following example. This example advances the current record position in the objDataSet object by one record:

```
objCurrencyManager.Position += 1
```

If you wanted to move backward one record, you would use this code:

```
objCurrencyManager.Position -= 1
```

To move to the first record contained in the DataSet object, you would use the following:

```
objCurrencyManager.Position = 0
```

The Count property of the CurrencyManager contains the number of records in the DataSet object managed by the CurrencyManager. Therefore, to move to the very last record, you would use the following code:

```
objCurrencyManager.Position = objCurrencyManager.Count - 1
```

Note that this code specifies the Count value minus one. Because the Count property contains the actual number of records and the DataSet object has a base index of zero, you must subtract one from the Count value to get the index to the last record.

Binding Controls

When you want to bind a data source to a control, you set the DataBindings property for that control. This property accesses the ControlBindingsCollection class. This class manages the bindings for each control, and it has many properties and methods. The method of interest here is Add.

The Add method creates a binding for the control and adds it to the ControlBindingsCollection. The Add method has three arguments, and its syntax is shown here:

```
object.DataBindings.Add(propertyname, datasource, datamember)
```

In this syntax, note the following:

➤   *object* represents a valid control on your form.

➤   The *propertyname* argument represents the property of the control to be bound.

➤ The *datasource* argument represents the data source to be bound and can be any valid object, such as a `DataSet`, `DataView`, or `DataTable`, that contains data.

➤ The *datamember* argument represents the data field in the data source to be bound to this control.

An example of how the `Add` method works is shown in the following code. This example binds the column name `au_fname` in the `objDataView` object to the `Text` property of a text box named `txtFirstName`:

```
txtFirstName.DataBindings.Add("Text", objDataView, "au_fname")
```

Sometimes, after a control has been bound, you may want to change the bindings for that control. To do this, you can use the `Clear` method of the `ControlBindingsCollection`. The `Clear` method clears the collection of all bindings for this control. Then you can make the change you need. An example of this method is shown in the following code fragment:

```
txtFirstName.DataBindings.Clear()
```

Now that you have had a look at the `BindingContext`, `CurrencyManager`, and `ControlBindings Collection` objects, learn how all of these pieces fit and work together in a practical hands-on exercise.

Binding Example

The following Try It Out demonstrates not only how to use the `BindingContext`, `CurrencyManager`, and `ControlBindingsCollection` objects, but also how to use the `DataView`, `SqlCommand`, and `SqlParameter` classes.

> **NOTE** *You will be using the query from the previous example as the base for your new query, and will again display all authors' first and last names, as well as their book titles and the prices of their books. However, this example differs from the last one in that it displays only one record at a time.*

You use the `CurrencyManager` object to navigate the records in the `DataView` object and provide the functionality to move forward and backward, as well as to the first and last records.

TRY IT OUT **Binding Simple Controls**

Code file BindingExample.zip available for download at Wrox.com

To build this example, follow these steps:

1. Create a new Windows Forms application project called **BindingExample**. Set the various form properties as follows:

➤ Set `FormBorderStyle` to **FixedDialog**.

➤ Set `MaximizeBox` to **False**.

➤ Set `MinimizeBox` to **False**.

➤ Set `Size` to **430, 360.**

➤ Set `StartPosition` to **CenterScreen.**

➤ Set `Text` to **Binding Controls.**

2. Drag a ToolTip control from the Toolbox and drop it on your form to add it to the designer.

3. You are going to add objects to the form such that the form ends up looking like Figure 16-6.

The steps that follow provide the controls you need but do not specify the exact layout. The cosmetic properties are not as important; you can approximate the layout visually based on Figure 16-6.

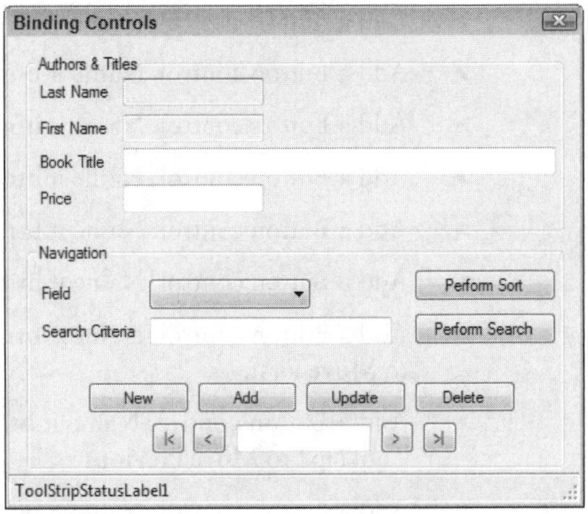

FIGURE 16-6

4. Add a GroupBox control to the form. You can find the GroupBox controls under the Containers node in the Toolbox. Set the GroupBox1 properties according to the following list:

➤ Set `Text` to **Authors && Titles.**

5. Using this list, add the required controls to GroupBox1 and set their properties:

➤ Add a Label control. Set `Text` to **Last Name.**

➤ Add a Label control. Set `Text` to **First Name.**

➤ Add a Label control. Set `Text` to **Book Title.**

➤ Add a Label control. Set `Text` to **Price.**

➤ Add a TextBox control. Name it **txtLastName** and set `ReadOnly` to **True.**

➤ Add a TextBox control. Name it **txtFirstName** and set `ReadOnly` to **True.**

➤ Add a TextBox control. Name it **txtBookTitle.**

➤ Add a TextBox control. Name it **txtPrice.**

6. Now add a second GroupBox and set its properties according to this list:

➤ Set `Text` to **Navigation.**

7. In GroupBox2, add the following controls:

➤ Add a Label control. Set `Text` to **Field.**

➤ Add a Label control. Set `Text` to **Search Criteria.**

➤ Add a ComboBox control. Name it **cboField** and set `DropDownStyle` to **DropDownList.**

➤ Add a TextBox control. Name it **txtSearchCriteria.**

➤ Add a TextBox control. Name it **txtRecordPosition** and set `TabStop` to **False;** `TextAlign` to **Center.**

➤ Add a Button control. Name it **btnPerformSort** and set Text to **Perform Sort**.

➤ Add a Button control. Name it **btnPerformSearch** and set Text to **Perform Search**.

➤ Add a Button control. Name it **btnNew** and set Text to **New**.

➤ Add a Button control. Name it **btnAdd** and set Text to **Add**.

➤ Add a Button control. Name it **btnUpdate** and set Text to **Update**.

➤ Add a Button control. Name it **btnDelete** and set Text to **Delete**.

➤ Add a Button control. Name it **btnMoveFirst** and set Text to |<; ToolTip on ToolTip1 to **Move First**.

➤ Add a Button control. Name it **btnMovePrevious** and set Text to <; ToolTip on ToolTip1 to **Move Previous**.

➤ Add a Button control. Name it **btnMoveNext** and set Text to >; ToolTip on ToolTip1 to **Move Next**.

➤ Add a Button control. Name it **btnMoveLast** and set Text to >|; ToolTip on ToolTip1 to **Move Last**.

8. Finally, add a StatusStrip control. Leave its name as the default StatusStrip1, and its default location and size. Click the new StatusStrip1 control on the form; you have an option to add a StatusLabel control in the menu. Select StatusLabel from the menu and leave the default settings.

9. When you are done, your completed form should look like the one shown in Figure 16-6.

10. Again, you need to add imports to the namespaces needed. To do this, switch to Code Editor view and then insert the following lines of code at the very top:

```
' Import Data and SqlClient namespaces..
Imports System.Data
Imports System.Data.SqlClient
```

11. Next you need to declare the objects that are global in scope to this form, so add the following bold code:

```
Public Class Form1
    ' Declare objects..
    Dim objConnection As New SqlConnection _
        ("server=localhost\WROX;database=pubs;user id=sa;password=wrox;")
    Dim objDataAdapter As New SqlDataAdapter( _
        "SELECT authors.au_id, au_lname, au_fname, " & _
        "titles.title_id, title, price " & _
        "FROM authors " & _
        "JOIN titleauthor ON authors.au_id = titleauthor.au_id " & _
        "JOIN titles ON titleauthor.title_id = titles.title_id " & _
        "ORDER BY au_lname, au_fname", objConnection)
    Dim objDataSet As DataSet
    Dim objDataView As DataView
    Dim objCurrencyManager As CurrencyManager
```

> **NOTE** Be sure to update the connection string to match your settings for the user ID and password, and also set the Server to the machine where SQL Server is running if it is not your local machine.

12. The first procedure you need to create is the `FillDataSetAndView` procedure. This procedure, along with the following procedures, is called in your initialization code. Add the following code to the form's class, just below your object declarations:

```
Private Sub FillDataSetAndView()
    ' Initialize a new instance of the DataSet object..
    objDataSet = New DataSet()

    ' Fill the DataSet object with data..
    objDataAdapter.Fill(objDataSet, "authors")

    ' Set the DataView object to the DataSet object..
    objDataView = New DataView(objDataSet.Tables("authors"))

    ' Set our CurrencyManager object to the DataView object..
    objCurrencyManager = CType(Me.BindingContext(objDataView), CurrencyManager)
End Sub
```

13. The next procedure you need to create actually binds the controls on your form to your `DataView` object:

```
Private Sub BindFields()
    ' Clear any previous bindings..
    txtLastName.DataBindings.Clear()
    txtFirstName.DataBindings.Clear()
    txtBookTitle.DataBindings.Clear()
    txtPrice.DataBindings.Clear()

    ' Add new bindings to the DataView object..
    txtLastName.DataBindings.Add("Text", objDataView, "au_lname")
    txtFirstName.DataBindings.Add("Text", objDataView, "au_fname")
    txtBookTitle.DataBindings.Add("Text", objDataView, "title")
    txtPrice.DataBindings.Add("Text", objDataView, "price")

    ' Display a ready status..
    ToolStripStatusLabel1.Text = "Ready"
End Sub
```

14. Now you need a procedure that displays the current record position on your form:

```
Private Sub ShowPosition()
    'Always format the number in the txtPrice field to include cents
    Try
        txtPrice.Text = Format(CType(txtPrice.Text, Decimal), "##0.00")
        Catch e As System.Exception
            txtPrice.Text = "0"
        txtPrice.Text = Format(CType(txtPrice.Text, Decimal), "##0.00")
    End Try

    ' Display the current position and the number of records
    txtRecordPosition.Text = objCurrencyManager.Position + 1 & _
        " of " & objCurrencyManager.Count()
End Sub
```

15. You've added some powerful procedures to your form, but currently there is no code to call them. You want these procedures, as well as some other code, to execute every time the form loads.

Therefore, return to the Form Designer, double-click the Form Designer, and add the following bold code to the `Form_Load` method (note that you must click an area outside of the `GroupBox` controls):

```
Private Sub Form1_Load(ByVal sender As System.Object, _
                       ByVal e As System.EventArgs) Handles MyBase.Load
    ' Add items to the combo box..
    cboField.Items.Add("Last Name")
    cboField.Items.Add("First Name")
    cboField.Items.Add("Book Title")
    cboField.Items.Add("Price")

    ' Make the first item selected..
    cboField.SelectedIndex = 0

    ' Fill the DataSet and bind the fields..
    FillDataSetAndView()
    BindFields()

    ' Show the current record position..
    ShowPosition()
End Sub
```

16. To add the code for your navigation buttons, you need to switch back and forth between the Design and Code views, double-clicking each button and then adding the code, or you can select the buttons in the `Class Name` combo box and then select the `Click` event in the `Method Name` combo box. Add the following code in bold to the procedure for the `btnMoveFirst` button first:

```
Private Sub btnMoveFirst_Click(ByVal sender As Object, _
            ByVal e As System.EventArgs) Handles btnMoveFirst.Click
    ' Set the record position to the first record..
    objCurrencyManager.Position = 0

    ' Show the current record position..
    ShowPosition()
End Sub
```

17. Add the code in bold to the `btnMovePrevious` button next:

```
Private Sub btnMovePrevious_Click(ByVal sender As Object, _
            ByVal e As System.EventArgs) Handles btnMovePrevious.Click
    ' Move to the previous record..
    objCurrencyManager.Position -= 1

    ' Show the current record position..
    ShowPosition()
End Sub
```

18. The next procedure you want to add code to is the `btnMoveNext` procedure:

```
Private Sub btnMoveNext_Click(ByVal sender As Object, _
            ByVal e As System.EventArgs) Handles btnMoveNext.Click
    ' Move to the next record..
    objCurrencyManager.Position += 1

    ' Show the current record position..
    ShowPosition()
End Sub
```

19. The final navigation procedure that you need to code is the btnMoveLast procedure:

```
Private Sub btnMoveLast_Click(ByVal sender As Object, _
         ByVal e As System.EventArgs) Handles btnMoveLast.Click
    ' Set the record position to the last record..
    objCurrencyManager.Position = objCurrencyManager.Count - 1

    ' Show the current record position..
    ShowPosition()
End Sub
```

20. At this point, you have entered a lot of code and are probably anxious to see the results of your work. Run the project to see how your DataView object gets bound to the controls on the form and to see the CurrencyManager object at work as you navigate through the records.

After your form displays, you should see results similar to Figure 16-7. The only buttons that work are the navigation buttons, which change the current record position. Test your form by navigating to the next and previous records and by moving to the last record and the first record. Each time you move to a new record, the text box between the navigation buttons will be updated to display the current record.

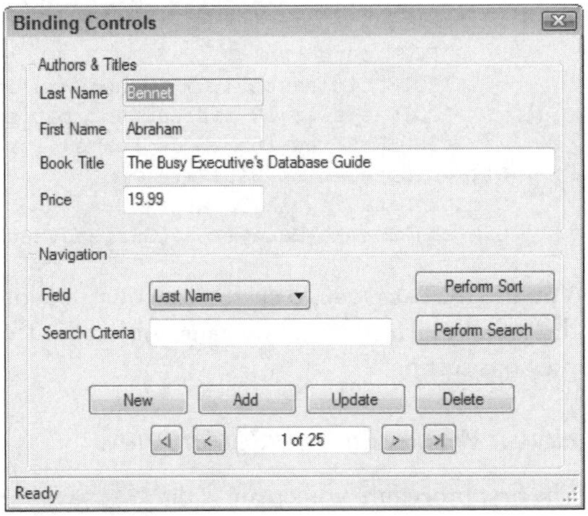

While you are on the first record, you can try to move to the previous record but nothing will happen because you are already on the first record. Likewise, you can move to the last record and try to navigate to the next record and nothing will happen, because you are already on the last record.

FIGURE 16-7

If you hover your mouse pointer over the navigation buttons, you will see a ToolTip indicating what each button is for. This just provides a nicer interface for your users.

> **NOTE** *Error handling has been omitted from the exercise to preserve space. You should always add the appropriate error handling to your code. Please review Chapter 10 for error-handling techniques.*

How It Works: Namespaces and Object Declaration

As usual, you import the System.Data and System.Data.SqlClient namespaces. Next, you declare the objects on your form. The first three objects should be familiar to you, because you used them in your last project.

Take a closer look at the initialization of the SqlDataAdapter object. You use a constructor that initializes this object with a string value for the SelectCommand property and an object that represents a connection to the database. This constructor saves you from writing code to manipulate the SqlDataAdapter properties; it's already set up.

The SELECT statement that you use here is basically the same as in the previous project, except that you add a couple more columns in the *select list* (the list of columns directly following the word SELECT).

The au_id column in the select list is prefixed with the table name authors, because this column also exists in the titleauthor table. Therefore, you must tell the database which table to get the data from for this column. Likewise for the title_id column, except that this column exists in the titles and titleauthor tables:

```
Dim objConnection As New SqlConnection _
    ("server=bnewsome;database=pubs;user id=sa;password=!p@ssw0rd!;")
Dim objDataAdapter As New SqlDataAdapter( _
    "SELECT authors.au_id, au_lname, au_fname, " & _
    "titles.title_id, title, price " & _
    "FROM authors " & _
    "JOIN titleauthor ON authors.au_id = titleauthor.au_id " & _
    "JOIN titles ON titleauthor.title_id = titles.title_id " & _
    "ORDER BY au_lname, au_fname", objConnection)
Dim objDataSet As DataSet
Dim objDataView As DataView
Dim objCurrencyManager As CurrencyManager
```

You use the DataView to customize your view of the records returned from the database, and stored in the DataSet. The CurrencyManager object controls the movement of your bound data, as shown in the previous section.

How It Works: FillDataSetAndView

The first procedure you create is the FillDataSetAndView procedure. This procedure, which will be called in your code, will get the latest data from the database and populate your DataView object.

First, you need to initialize a new instance of the DataSet object. You do this here because this procedure might be called more than once during the lifetime of the form. If it is, you do not want to add new records to the records already in the DataSet; you always want to start afresh:

```
Private Sub FillDataSetAndView()
    ' Initialize a new instance of the DataSet object..
    objDataSet = New DataSet()
```

Next, you invoke the Fill method on objDataAdapter to populate the objDataSet object. Then you specify that your DataView object will be viewing data from the authors table in the DataSet object. Remember that the DataView object allows you to sort, search, and navigate through the records in the DataSet:

```
' Fill the DataSet object with data..
objDataAdapter.Fill(objDataSet, "authors")

' Set the DataView object to the DataSet object..
objDataView = New DataView(objDataSet.Tables("authors"))
```

After you initialize your DataView object, you want to initialize the CurrencyManager object. Remember that the BindingContext object is built into every Windows form and contains a collection of

`CurrencyManager`s. The collection contains the available data sources, and you choose the `DataView` object:

```
' Set our CurrencyManager object to the DataView object..
objCurrencyManager = _
    CType(Me.BindingContext(objDataView), CurrencyManager)
```

How It Works: BindFields

The next procedure that you create (`BindFields`) binds the controls on your form to your `DataView` object. This procedure first clears any previous bindings for the controls and then sets them to your `DataView` object.

> **NOTE** *It is important to clear the bindings first because after you modify the* `DataView` *object by adding, updating, or deleting a row of data, the* `DataView` *object will show only the changed data. Therefore, after you update the database with your changes, you must repopulate your* `DataView` *object and rebind your controls. If you didn't do this, the data that would actually be in the database and the data in the* `DataView` *may not be the same.*

Using the `DataBindings` property of the controls on your form, you execute the `Clear` method of the `ControlBindingsCollection` class to remove the bindings from them. Notice that the controls that you bound are all the text boxes on your form that will contain data from the `DataView` object:

```
Private Sub BindFields()
    ' Clear any previous bindings to the DataView object..
    txtLastName.DataBindings.Clear()
    txtFirstName.DataBindings.Clear()
    txtBookTitle.DataBindings.Clear()
    txtPrice.DataBindings.Clear()
```

After you clear the previous bindings, you can set the new bindings back to the same data source, the `DataView` object. You do this by executing the `Add` method of the `ControlBindingsCollection` object returned by the `DataBindings` property. As described earlier, the `Add` method has three arguments, shown in the code that follows:

➤   The first argument is *propertyname* and specifies the property of the control to be bound. Because you want to bind your data to the `Text` property of the text boxes, you have specified `"Text"` for this argument.

➤   The next argument is the *datasource* argument, which specifies the data source to be bound. Remember that this can be any valid object, such as a `DataSet`, `DataView`, or `DataTable`, that contains data. In this case, you are using a `DataView` object.

➤   The last argument specifies the *datamember*. This is the data field in the data source that contains the data to be bound to this control. Note that you have specified the various column names from the `SELECT` statement that you executed in the previous procedure.

```
' Add new bindings to the DataView object..
txtLastName.DataBindings.Add("Text", objDataView, "au_lname")
```

```
txtFirstName.DataBindings.Add("Text", objDataView, "au_fname")
txtBookTitle.DataBindings.Add("Text", objDataView, "title")
txtPrice.DataBindings.Add("Text", objDataView, "price")
```

The last thing you do in this procedure is set a message in the status bar using the `Text` property of `ToolStripStatusLabel1`:

```
' Display a ready status..
ToolStripStatusLabel1.Text = "Ready"
End Sub
```

How It Works: ShowPosition

The `CurrencyManager` object keeps track of the current record position within the `DataView` object.

The `price` column in the `titles` table in `Pubs` is defined as a `Currency` data type. Therefore, if a book is priced at $40.00, the number that you get is `40`; the decimal portion is dropped. The `ShowPosition` procedure seems like a good place to format the data in the `txtPrice` text box, because this procedure is called whenever you move to a new record:

```
Private Sub ShowPosition()
    'Always format the number in the txtPrice field to include cents
    Try
        txtPrice.Text = Format(CType(txtPrice.Text, Decimal), "##0.00")
    Catch e As System.Exception
        txtPrice.Text = "0"
        txtPrice.Text = Format(CType(txtPrice.Text, Decimal), "##0.00")
    End Try

    ' Display the current position and the number of records
    txtRecordPosition.Text = objCurrencyManager.Position + 1 & _
                             " of " & objCurrencyManager.Count()
End Sub
```

This part of the function is enclosed in a `Try ... Catch` block in case the `txtPrice` is empty. If `txtPrice` is empty, the `Format` function throws a handled exception, and the exception handler defaults the price to `0`. The second line of code in this procedure uses the `Format` function to format the price in the `txtPrice` text box. This function accepts the numeric data to be formatted as the first argument and a format string as the second argument. For the format function to work correctly, you need to convert the string value in the `txtPrice` field to a `decimal` value using the `CType` function.

The last line of code displays the current record position and the total number of records that you have. Using the `Position` property of the `CurrencyManager` object, you can determine which record you are on. The `Position` property uses a zero-based index, so the first record is always `0`. Therefore, you specified the `Position` property plus `1` to display the true number.

The `CurrencyManager` class's `Count` property returns the actual number of items in the list, and you are using this property to display the total number of records in the `DataView` object.

How It Works: Form_Load

Now that you've looked at the code for the main procedures, you need to go back and look at your initialization code.

You have a combo box on your form that will be used when sorting or searching for data. This combo box needs to be populated with data representing the columns in the DataView object. You specify the Add method of the Items property of the combo box to add items to it. Here you are specifying text that represents the columns in the DataView object in the same order that they appear in the DataView object:

```
'Add any initialization after the InitializeComponent() call

' Add items to the combo box..
cboField.Items.Add("Last Name")
cboField.Items.Add("First Name")
cboField.Items.Add("Book Title")
cboField.Items.Add("Price")
```

After you have loaded all of the items into your combo box, you want to select the first item. You do this by setting the SelectedIndex property to 0. The SelectedIndex property is zero-based, so the first item in the list is item 0:

```
' Make the first item selected..
cboField.SelectedIndex = 0
```

Next, you call the FillDataSetAndView procedure to retrieve the data, and then call the BindFields procedure to bind the controls on your form to your DataView object. Finally, you call the ShowPosition procedure to display the current record position and the total number of records contained in your DataView object:

```
' Fill the DataSet and bind the fields..
FillDataSetAndView()
BindFields()

' Show the current record position..
ShowPosition()
```

How It Works: Navigation Buttons

The procedure for the btnMoveFirst button causes the first record in the DataView object to be displayed. This is accomplished using the Position property of the CurrencyManager object. Here you set the Position property to 0, indicating that the CurrencyManager should move to the first record:

```
' Set the record position to the first record..
objCurrencyManager.Position = 0
```

Because your controls are bound to the DataView object, they always stay in sync with the current record in the DataView object and display the appropriate data.

After you reposition the current record, you need to call the ShowPosition procedure to update the display of the current record on your form:

```
' Show the current record position..
ShowPosition()
```

Next, you add the code for the btnMovePrevious button. You move to the prior record by subtracting 1 from the Position property. The CurrencyManager object automatically detects and handles the beginning position of the DataView object. It will not let you move to a position prior to the first record; it just quietly keeps its position at 0:

```
' Move to the previous record..
objCurrencyManager.Position -= 1
```

Again, after you have repositioned the current record being displayed, you need to call the `ShowPosition` procedure to display the current position on the form.

In the `btnMoveNext` procedure, you want to increment the `Position` property by 1. Again, the `CurrencyManager` automatically detects the last record in the `DataView` object and will not let you move past it:

```
' Move to the next record..
   objCurrencyManager.Position += 1
```

You call the `ShowPosition` procedure to display the current record position.

When the `btnMoveLast` procedure is called, you want to move to the last record in the `DataView` object. You accomplish this by setting the `Position` property equal to the `Count` property minus one. Then you call the `ShowPosition` procedure to display the current record:

```
' Set the record position to the last record..
objCurrencyManager.Position = objCurrencyManager.Count—1

' Show the current record position..
ShowPosition()
```

TRY IT OUT   Including Sorting Functionality

Code file BindingExample.zip is available for download at Wrox.com

Now that you have built the navigation, you move on to add sorting functionality to this project in this Try It Out.

1. Double-click the Perform Sort button on the form in design mode to have the empty procedure added to the form class, or select the button in the Class Name combo box and then select the Click event in the Method Name combo box. Insert the following bold code in the `btnPerformSort_Click` event procedure:

```
Private Sub btnPerformSort_Click(ByVal sender As Object, _
        ByVal e As System.EventArgs) Handles btnPerformSort.Click
    ' Determine the appropriate item selected and set the
    ' Sort property of the DataView object..
    Select Case cboField.SelectedIndex
        Case 0 'Last Name
            objDataView.Sort = "au_lname"
        Case 1 'First Name
            objDataView.Sort = "au_fname"
        Case 2 'Book Title
            objDataView.Sort = "title"
        Case 3 'Price
            objDataView.Sort = "price"
    End Select

    ' Call the click event for the MoveFirst button..
    btnMoveFirst_Click(Nothing, Nothing)

    ' Display a message that the records have been sorted..
    ToolStripStatusLabel1.Text = "Records Sorted"
End Sub
```

2. Test the new functionality by running it; click the Start button to compile and run it. Select a column to sort and then click the Perform Sort button. You should see the data sorted by the column that you have chosen. Figure 16-8 shows the data sorted by book price.

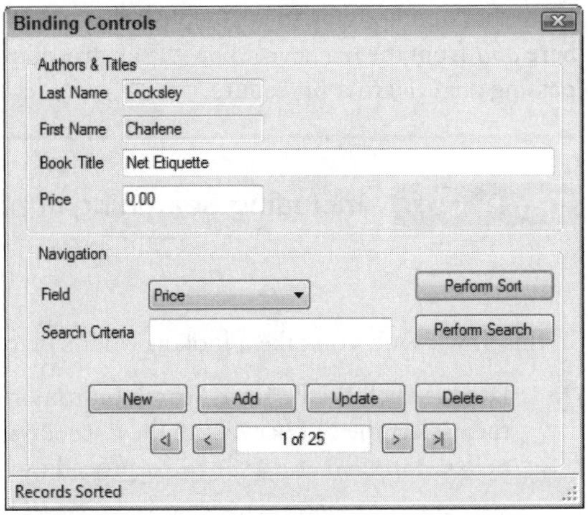

How It Works

First, you determine which field you should sort on. This information is contained in the cboField combo box.

```
' Determine the appropriate item selected
    and set the
' Sort property of the DataView object..
Select Case cboField.SelectedIndex
    Case 0 'Last Name
        objDataView.Sort = "au_lname"
    Case 1 'First Name
        objDataView.Sort = "au_fname"
    Case 2 'Book Title
        objDataView.Sort = "title"
    Case 3 'Price
        objDataView.Sort = "price"
End Select
```

FIGURE 16-8

Using a Select Case statement to examine the SelectedIndex property of the combo box, you can determine which field the user has chosen. After you have determined the correct entry in the combo box, you can set the Sort property of the DataView object using the column name of the column that you want sorted. After the Sort property has been set, the data is sorted.

After the data has been sorted, you want to move to the first record, and there are a couple of ways you can do this. You can set the Position property of the CurrencyManager object and then call the ShowPosition procedure, or you can simply call the btnMoveFirst_Click procedure, passing it Nothing for both arguments. This is the procedure that would be executed had you actually clicked the Move First button on the form.

The btnMoveFirst_Click procedure has two arguments: ByVal sender As Object and ByVal e As System.EventArgs. Because these arguments are required (even though they're not actually used in the procedure), you need to pass something to them, so you pass the Nothing keyword. The Nothing keyword is used to disassociate an object variable from an object. Thus, by using the Nothing keyword, you satisfy the requirement of passing an argument to the procedure but have not passed any actual value:

```
' Call the click event for the MoveFirst button..
btnMoveFirst_Click(Nothing, Nothing)
```

After the first record has been displayed, you want to display a message in the status bar indicating that the records have been sorted. You did this by setting the Text property of the status bar as you have done before.

Note that another way to accomplish this is to have a procedure called `MoveFirst`, and to call that from here *and* from the `btnMoveFirst_Click` procedure. Some developers would opt for this method instead of passing `Nothing` to a procedure.

TRY IT OUT Including Searching Functionality

Code file BindingExample.zip is available for download at Wrox.com

In this Try It Out, you take a look at what's involved in searching for a record.

1. Double-click the Perform Search button or select the button in the `Class Name` combo box and then select the `Click` event in the `Method Name` combo box, and add the following bold code to the `btnPerformSearch_Click` event procedure:

```
Private Sub btnPerformSearch_Click(ByVal sender As Object, _
        ByVal e As System.EventArgs) Handles btnPerformSearch.Click
    ' Declare local variables..
    Dim intPosition As Integer

    ' Determine the appropriate item selected and set the
    ' Sort property of the DataView object..
    Select Case cboField.SelectedIndex
        Case 0 'Last Name
            objDataView.Sort = "au_lname"
        Case 1 'First Name
            objDataView.Sort = "au_fname"
        Case 2 'Book Title
            objDataView.Sort = "title"
        Case 3 'Price
            objDataView.Sort = "price"
    End Select

    ' If the search field is not price then..
    If cboField.SelectedIndex < 3 Then
        ' Find the last name, first name, or title..
        intPosition = objDataView.Find(txtSearchCriteria.Text)
    Else
        ' otherwise find the price..
        intPosition = objDataView.Find(CType(txtSearchCriteria.Text, Decimal))
    End If
    If intPosition = -1 Then
        ' Display a message that the record was not found..
        ToolStripStatusLabel1.Text = "Record Not Found"
    Else
        ' Otherwise display a message that the record was
        ' found and reposition the CurrencyManager to that
        ' record..
        ToolStripStatusLabel1.Text = "Record Found"
        objCurrencyManager.Position = intPosition
    End If

    ' Show the current record position..
    ShowPosition()
End Sub
```

2. Test the searching functionality that you added. Run the project and select a field in the `Field` combo box that you want to search on, and then enter the search criteria in the Search Criteria text box. Finally, click the Perform Search button.

If a match is found, you see the first matched record displayed, along with a message in the status bar indicating that the record was found, as shown at the bottom of Figure 16-9. If no record was found, you see a message in the status bar indicating the record was not found.

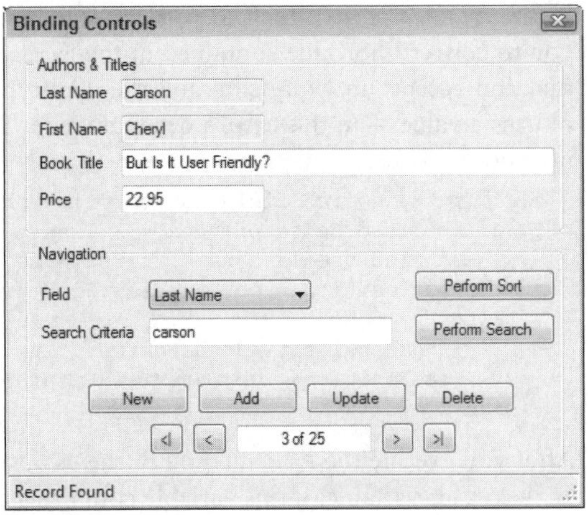

FIGURE 16-9

How It Works

This is a little more involved than previous Try It Outs because there are multiple conditions that you must test for and handle, such as a record that was not found. The first thing that you do in this procedure is declare a variable that will receive the record position of the record that has been found or not found:

```
' Declare local variables..
Dim intPosition As Integer
```

Next, you sort the data based on the column used in the search. The `Find` method searches for data in the sort key. Therefore, by setting the `Sort` property, the column that is sorted on becomes the sort key in the `DataView` object. You use a `Select Case` statement, just as you did in the previous procedure:

```
' Determine the appropriate item selected and set the
' Sort property of the DataView object..
Select Case cboField.SelectedIndex
    Case 0 'Last Name
        objDataView.Sort = "au_lname"
    Case 1 'First Name
        objDataView.Sort = "au_fname"
    Case 2 'Book Title
        objDataView.Sort = "title"
    Case 3 'Price
        objDataView.Sort = "price"
End Select
```

The columns for the authors' first and last names, as well as the column for the book titles, all contain text data. However, the column for the book price contains data that is in a currency format. Therefore, you need to determine which column you are searching on; and if that column is the price column, you need to format the data in the `txtSearchCriteria` text box to a decimal value.

Again, you use the `SelectedIndex` property of the `cboField` combo box to determine which item has been selected. If the `SelectedIndex` property is less than 3, you know that you want to search on a column that contains text data.

You then set the `intPosition` variable to the results returned by the `Find` method of the `DataView` object. The `Find` method accepts the data to search for as the only argument. Here you pass it the data contained in the `Text` property of the `txtSearchCriteria` text box.

If the `SelectedIndex` equals 3, you are searching for a book with a specific price, and this requires you to convert the value contained in the `txtSearchCriteria` text box to a decimal value. The `CType` function accepts an expression and the data type that you want to convert that expression to and returns a value — in this case, a decimal value. This value is then used as the search criterion by the `Find` method:

```
' If the search field is not price then..
If cboField.SelectedIndex < 3 Then
    ' Find the last name, first name or title..
    intPosition = objDataView.Find(txtSearchCriteria.Text)
Else
    ' otherwise find the price..
    intPosition = objDataView.Find(CType(txtSearchCriteria.Text, Decimal))
End If
```

After you execute the `Find` method of the `DataView` object, you need to check the value contained in the `intPosition` variable. If this variable contains a value of -1, no match was found. Any value other than -1 points to the record position of the record that contains the data. Therefore, if the value in this variable is -1, you want to display a message in the status bar indicating that no record was found.

If the value is greater than -1, you want to display a message that the record was found, and position the `DataView` object to that record using the `Position` property of the `CurrencyManager` object:

```
ToolStripStatusLabel1.Text = "Record Found"
objCurrencyManager.Position = intPosition
```

> **NOTE** It is worth noting that the `Find` method of the `DataView` object performs a search looking for an exact match of characters. There is no wildcard search method here, so you must enter the entire text string that you want to search for. The case, however, does not matter, so the name "Ann" is the same as "ann"; you do not need to be concerned with entering proper case when you enter your search criteria.

Last, you want to show the current record position, which you do by calling the `ShowPosition` procedure.

TRY IT OUT Adding Records

Code file BindingExample.zip is available for download at Wrox.com

Now all that is left is to add the functionality to add, update, and delete records. Take a look at what is required to add a record first.

1. Add just two lines of code to the `btnNew_Click` procedure:

```
Private Sub btnNew_Click(ByVal sender As Object, _
            ByVal e As System.EventArgs) Handles btnNew.Click
    ' Clear the book title and price fields..
    txtBookTitle.Text = ""
    txtPrice.Text = ""
End Sub
```

2. Add code to the btnAdd_Click procedure. This procedure, which is responsible for adding a new record, has the largest amount of code by far of any of the procedures you have coded or will code in this project. That's because of the relationship of book titles to authors and the primary key used for book titles:

```
Private Sub btnAdd_Click(ByVal sender As Object, _
        ByVal e As System.EventArgs) Handles btnAdd.Click
    ' Declare local variables and objects..
    Dim intPosition As Integer, intMaxID As Integer
    Dim strID As String
    Dim objCommand As SqlCommand = New SqlCommand()

    ' Save the current record position..
    intPosition = objCurrencyManager.Position

    ' Create a new SqlCommand object..
    Dim maxIdCommand As SqlCommand = New SqlCommand _
        ("SELECT MAX(title_id) AS MaxID " & _
        "FROM titles WHERE title_id LIKE 'DM%'", objConnection)

    ' Open the connection, execute the command
    objConnection.Open()
    Dim maxId As Object = maxIdCommand.ExecuteScalar()

    ' If the MaxID column is null..
    If maxId Is DBNull.Value Then
        ' Set a default value of 1000..
        intMaxID = 1000
    Else
        ' otherwise set the strID variable to the value in MaxID..
        strID = CType(maxId, String)

        ' Get the integer part of the string..
        intMaxID = CType(strID.Remove(0, 2), Integer)

        ' Increment the value..
        intMaxID += 1
    End If

    ' Finally, set the new ID..
    strID = "DM" & intMaxID.ToString

    ' Set the SqlCommand object properties..
    objCommand.Connection = objConnection
    objCommand.CommandText = "INSERT INTO titles " & _
        "(title_id, title, type, price, pubdate) " & _
        "VALUES(@title_id,@title,@type,@price,@pubdate);" & _
        "INSERT INTO titleauthor (au_id, title_id) VALUES(@au_id,@title_id)"

    ' Add parameters for the placeholders in the SQL in the
    ' CommandText property..

    ' Parameter for the title_id column..
    objCommand.Parameters.AddWithValue ("@title_id", strID)

    ' Parameter for the title column..
    objCommand.Parameters.AddWithValue ("@title", txtBookTitle.Text)
```

```
    ' Parameter for the type column
    objCommand.Parameters.AddWithValue ("@type", "Demo")
    ' Parameter for the price column..
    objCommand.Parameters.AddWithValue ("@price", txtPrice.Text).DbType _
                            = DbType.Currency

    ' Parameter for the pubdate column
    objCommand.Parameters.AddWithValue ("@pubdate", Date.Now)

    ' Parameter for the au_id column..
    objCommand.Parameters.AddWithValue _
                ("@au_id", BindingContext(objDataView).Current("au_id"))

    ' Execute the SqlCommand object to insert the new data..
    Try
        objCommand.ExecuteNonQuery()
    Catch SqlExceptionErr As SqlException
        MessageBox.Show(SqlExceptionErr.Message)
    End Try

    ' Close the connection..
    objConnection.Close()

    ' Fill the dataset and bind the fields..
    FillDataSetAndView()
    BindFields()

    ' Set the record position to the one that you saved..
    objCurrencyManager.Position = intPosition

    ' Show the current record position..
    ShowPosition()

    ' Display a message that the record was added..
    ToolStripStatusLabel1.Text = "Record Added"
End Sub
```

3. Run your project. Choose an author for whom you want to add a new title and then click the New button. The Book Title and Price fields will be cleared, and you are ready to enter new data to be added, as shown in Figure 16-10. Take note of the number of records in the DataView (25 in Figure 16-10).

4. Enter a title and price for the new book and click the Add button. You will see a message in the status bar indicating that the record has been added, and you will see that the number of records has changed (to 26), as shown in Figure 16-11.

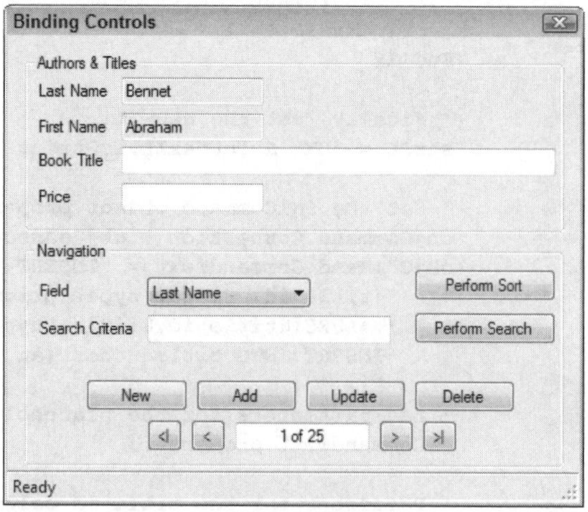

Now that you have added a record, examine what you actually did.

FIGURE 16-10

How It Works

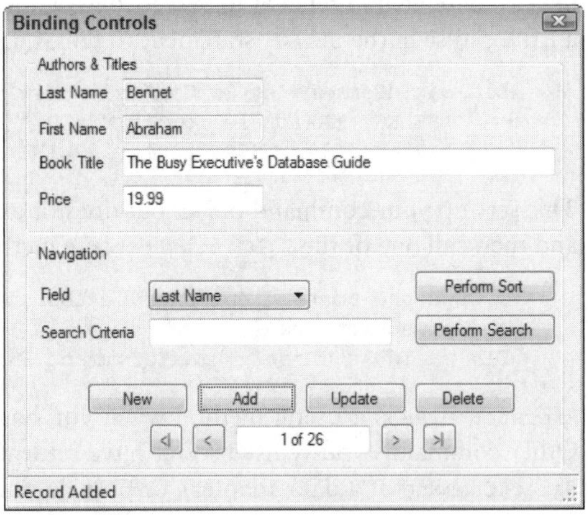

Remember that the only data you can add is a new book title and its price, so instead of selecting the data in each of these fields, deleting it, and then entering the new data, you want to be able to simply click the New button. The job of the New button is to clear the Book Title and Price fields for you. All you need to do is set the Text properties of these text boxes to an empty string as shown here:

```
' Clear the book title and price fields..
txtBookTitle.Text = ""
txtPrice.Text = ""
```

When you click the New button, the fields are cleared. If you are updating or editing a record, those changes are lost. You would normally put logic into your application to prevent that problem, but for this example that type of validation was left out.

FIGURE 16-11

The primary key used in the titles table is not the database's Identity column. Identity columns use a sequential number and automatically increment the number for you when a new row is inserted. Instead of an Identity column, the primary key is made up of a category prefix and a sequential number. This means that you must first determine the maximum number used in a category and then increment that number by 1 and use the new number and category prefix for the new key.

The first thing that you want to do in the btnAdd_Click event procedure is declare your local variables and objects that will be used here. The intPosition variable will be used to save the current record position, and the intMaxID variable will be used to set and increment the maximum sequential number for a category. The strID will be used to store the primary key from the authors table and to set the new key for the authors table. Finally, the objCommand object will be used to build a query to insert a new record into the titleauthor and titles tables.

Before you do anything, you want to save the position of the current record that you are on. This enables you to go back to this record once you reload the DataView object, which will contain the new record that you add in this procedure:

```
intPosition = objCurrencyManager.Position
```

You need to execute a command on the database to determine what ID to give your new title. You use an SqlCommand object to do this, passing in an SQL string and the connection that you use throughout your program. This SQL string selects the maximum value in the title_id column, where the title_id value begins with the prefix of DM.

There is no category for demo, so you add all of the test records under this category and use the category prefix of DM, enabling you to identify quickly the records that you have inserted just in case you want to get rid of them manually later.

Because the MAX function you use is an *aggregate function* (meaning that it is a function that works on groups of data), the data is returned without a column name. Therefore, you use the AS keyword in the

SELECT statement and tell SQL Server to assign a column name to the value — in this case, MaxID. You use a LIKE clause in the SELECT statement to tell SQL Server to search for all values that begin with DM:

```
Dim maxIdCommand As SqlCommand = New SqlCommand( _
    "SELECT MAX(title_id) AS MaxID " & _
    "FROM titles WHERE title_id LIKE 'DM%'", objConnection)
```

This sets up your command object but doesn't execute it. To execute it, you need to open the connection and then call one of the SqlCommand execute methods. In this case you use ExecuteScalar:

```
' Open the connection, execute the command
objConnection.Open()
Dim maxId As Object = maxIdCommand.ExecuteScalar()
```

ExecuteScalar is a useful method when you have a database command that returns a single value. Other commands you've used so far have returned a whole table of values (you have used these as the SelectCommand of a data adapter), or no values at all (you have executed these with ExecuteNonQuery). In this case, you are interested in only one number, so you can use ExecuteScalar. This returns the first column of the first row in the result set. In this case, there is only one column and one row, so that is what you get.

You want to check for a Null value returned from the command, so you compare the resulting Object against the Value property of the DBNull class:

```
' If the MaxID column is null..
If maxId Is DBNull.Value Then
```

If the expression evaluates to True, you have no primary key in the titles table that begins with DM, so you set the initial value of the intMaxID variable to a value of 1000. You choose 1000 because all of the other primary keys contain a numeric value of less than 1000:

```
' Set a default value of 1000..
intMaxID = 1000
```

If the column value evaluates to False, then you have at least one primary key in the titles table that begins with DM. In this case, you need to obtain the integer portion of this ID to work out which integer to use for your ID. To do this, you must convert your maxId object to a String:

```
Else
    ' otherwise set the strID variable to the value in MaxID..
    strID = CType(maxId, String)
```

Then you can extract the integer portion of the key by using the Remove method of the string variable, strID. The Remove method removes the specified number of characters from a string. You specify the offset at which to begin removing characters and the number of characters to be removed. This method returns a new string with the removed characters. In this line of code, you are removing the prefix of DM from the string so that all you end up with is the integer portion of the string. You then use the CType function to convert the string value, which contains a number, to an Integer value, which you place in the intMaxID variable. Finally, you increment it by one to get the integer portion of the ID that you will use:

```
    ' Get the integer part of the string..
    intMaxID = CType(strID.Remove(0, 2), Integer)
    ' Increment the value..
    intMaxID += 1
End If
```

After you get the integer part, you build a new primary key in the `strID` variable by concatenating the numeric value contained in the `intMaxID` variable with the prefix `DM`:

```
' Finally, set the new ID..
strID = "DM" & intMaxID.ToString
```

Next, you build the SQL statements to insert a new row of data into the `titles` and `titleauthor` tables. If you look closely, there are two separate `INSERT` statements in the `CommandText` property of your `objCommand` object. The two `INSERT` statements are separated by a semicolon, which enables you to concatenate multiple SQL statements. The SQL statements that you build use placeholders that are filled in by the `SqlParameter` objects.

> **NOTE** *Because of the relationship between the* `titles` *table and the* `authors` *table, you must first insert a new title for an author into the* `titles` *table and then insert the relationship between the title and the author in the* `titleauthor` *table. Your* `INSERT` *statements are specifying the columns that you want to insert data into and then the values that are to be inserted, some of which are represented by placeholders.*

You have seen the properties of the `SqlCommand` object before. This time, however, you are using properties rather than the constructor. You set the `Connection` property to an `SqlConnection` object and then set the `CommandText` property to the SQL string that you want executed — in this case, the two separate `INSERT` statements:

```
objCommand.Connection = objConnection
objCommand.CommandText = "INSERT INTO titles " & _
    "(title_id, title, type, price, pubdate) " & _
    "VALUES(@title_id,@title,@type,@price,@pubdate);" & _
    "INSERT INTO titleauthor (au_id, title_id) VALUES(@au_id,@title_id)"
```

You then add entries to the `Parameters` collection property for each of your placeholders in the preceding SQL statements. Where the same parameter name is used twice in the `CommandText` property — as `title_id` is here — you need only one `SqlParameter` object:

```
' Add parameters for the placeholders in the SQL in the
' CommandText property..

' Parameter for the title_id column..
objCommand.Parameters.AddWithValue ("@title_id", strID)

' Parameter for the title column..
objCommand.Parameters.AddWithValue ("@title", txtBookTitle.Text)

' Parameter for the type column
objCommand.Parameters.AddWithValue ("@type", "Demo")

' Parameter for the price column..
objCommand.Parameters.AddWithValue _
                    ("@price", txtPrice.Text).DbType = DbType.Currency

' Parameter for the pubdate column
objCommand.Parameters.AddWithValue ("@pubdate", Date.Now)
```

```
' Parameter for the au_id column..
objCommand.Parameters.AddWithValue ("@au_id", BindingContext _
    (objDataView).Current("au_id"))
```

For the @title_id parameter, you use the strID variable that you created and set earlier in this method. For the @title parameter, you use the text in the Book Title text box entered by the user. For the @price parameter, you use the text in the Price text box. However, the Text property is a String. SQL Server cannot automatically convert between a String and a Currency data type, so you specify that the parameter is of the DbType.Currency data type.

For @au_id you need to use the ID of the currently selected author. There are no bound controls for the au_id column, so you need to use some code to obtain the value. Take a close look at that particular statement:

```
BindingContext(objDataView).Current("au_id")
```

Here you are getting the form's BindingContext for the objDataView data source, which is the one you're using for all of your bound controls. When you're accessing a DataView through BindingContext, the Current property returns a DataRowView object. This object represents the view of the particular row that the user is currently looking at. You are then able to select a particular column from that row, thus giving you a specific value. Here, of course, you are obtaining the au_id column.

The remaining parameters indicate that the new record is a Demo record, and timestamp the record with the current date and time:

```
' Parameter for the type column
objCommand.Parameters.AddWithValue ("@type", "Demo")

' Parameter for the pubdate column
objCommand.Parameters.AddWithValue ("@pubdate", Date.Now)
```

After you add all your parameters, you execute the command using the ExecuteNonQuery method. This causes your SQL statements to be executed and the data inserted. After your new data is inserted, you close the database connection.

This is the one spot in your code that is really subject to failure, so very basic error handling is included here. You execute your INSERT statement inside the Try block of your error handler, and if an error is encountered, the code in the Catch block is executed. The code there simply displays a message box that shows the error encountered:

```
' Execute the SqlCommand object to insert the new data..
Try
    objCommand.ExecuteNonQuery()
Catch SqlExceptionErr As SqlException
    MessageBox.Show(SqlExceptionErr.Message)
Finally
    ' Close the connection..
    objConnection.Close()
End Try
```

Then the FillDataSetAndView and BindFields procedures are called to reload the DataView object and to clear and rebind your controls. This ensures that all new data is added, updated, or deleted in the tables in SQL Server.

You then reposition the DataView object back to the record that was being displayed by setting the Position property of the CurrencyManager using the intPosition variable. This variable was set using the current record position at the beginning of this procedure.

> **NOTE** *The position that you set here is only approximate. It does not take into account any records that have been inserted or deleted by someone else or you. It is possible that the title you just inserted for a specific author could be returned prior to the title that was displayed before. If you need more detailed control over the actual record position, you need to add more code to handle finding and displaying the exact record that was displayed; however, this is a topic beyond the scope of this book.*

After you reposition the record that is being displayed, you call the `ShowPosition` procedure to show the current record position.

Finally, you display a message in the status bar indicating that the record has been added.

TRY IT OUT **Updating Records**

Code file BindingExample.zip is available for download at Wrox.com

In this Try It Out, you code the `btnUpdate_Click` procedure. This procedure is a little simpler because all you need to do is update existing records in the `titles` table. You do not have to add any new records, so you do not have to select any data to build a primary key.

1. To the `btnUpdate_Click` event procedure, add the following bold code:

```
Private Sub btnUpdate_Click(ByVal sender As Object, _
        ByVal e As System.EventArgs) Handles btnUpdate.Click
    ' Declare local variables and objects..
    Dim intPosition As Integer
    Dim objCommand As SqlCommand = New SqlCommand()

    ' Save the current record position..
    intPosition = objCurrencyManager.Position

    ' Set the SqlCommand object properties..
    objCommand.Connection = objConnection
    objCommand.CommandText = "UPDATE titles " & _
        "SET title = @title, price = @price WHERE title_id = @title_id"
    objCommand.CommandType = CommandType.Text

    ' Add parameters for the placeholders in the SQL in the
    ' CommandText property..

    ' Parameter for the title field..
    objCommand.Parameters.AddWithValue ("@title", txtBookTitle.Text)

    ' Parameter for the price field..
    objCommand.Parameters.AddWithValue ("@price", txtPrice.Text).DbType _
        = DbType.Currency

    ' Parameter for the title_id field..
    objCommand.Parameters.AddWithValue _
        ("@title_id", BindingContext(objDataView).Current("title_id"))
```

```
' Open the connection..
objConnection.Open()

' Execute the SqlCommand object to update the data..
objCommand.ExecuteNonQuery()

' Close the connection..
objConnection.Close()

' Fill the DataSet and bind the fields..
FillDataSetAndView()
BindFields()

' Set the record position to the one that you saved..
objCurrencyManager.Position = intPosition

' Show the current record position..
ShowPosition()

' Display a message that the record
was updated..
ToolStripStatusLabel1.Text = "Record
Updated"
End Sub
```

2. Run your project. You can update the price of the book that you have just added, or you can update the price of another book. Choose a book, change the price in the Price field, and then click the Update button.

When the record has been updated, you see the appropriate message in the status bar and the record will still be the current record, as shown in Figure 16-12.

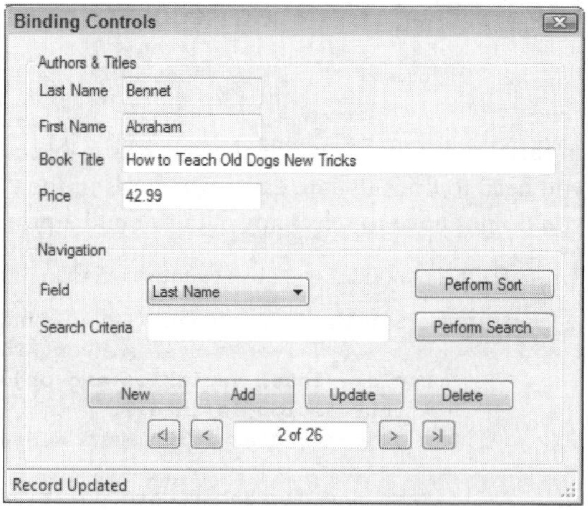

FIGURE 16-12

How It Works

As always, the first thing that you want to do is declare your variables and objects. You need one variable to save the current record position and one object for the SqlCommand object. Next, you save the current record position just as you did in the last procedure.

By adding the following code, you set the Connection property of the SqlCommand object using your objConnection object. Then you set the CommandText property using an SQL string. The SQL string here contains an UPDATE statement to update the Title and Price columns in the titles table. Note that there are three placeholders in this UPDATE statement: Two placeholders are for the title and price, and one is for the title_id in the WHERE clause:

```
' Set the SqlCommand object properties..
objCommand.Connection = objConnection
objCommand.CommandText = "UPDATE titles " & _
    "SET title = @title, price = @price WHERE title_id = @title_id"
objCommand.CommandType = CommandType.Text
```

After you set the `CommandText` property, you set the `CommandType` property to indicate that this is an SQL string.

You need to add the appropriate parameters to the `Parameters` collection. The first parameter that you add is for the `title` column in your UPDATE statement. The title of the book is coming from the `Text` property of the `txtBookTitle` text box on your form.

The second parameter is for the `price` in your UPDATE statement. This parameter is used to update the price of a book, and the data is coming from the `txtPrice` text box on your form. You again need to set the `DbType` explicitly for this parameter.

This last parameter was for your WHERE clause in the UPDATE statement. The data for the `Value` property comes directly from the form's `BindingContext`, as the `au_id` did in the Adding Records example.

The rest of the procedure is similar to the `btnAdd_Click` event procedure.

TRY IT OUT Deleting Records

Code file BindingExample.zip is available for download at Wrox.com

You code the final procedure, `btnDelete_Click`, in this Try It Out.

1. To include delete functionality in your project, add the following bold code to the `btnDelete_Click` event procedure:

```
Private Sub btnDelete_Click(ByVal sender As Object, _
            ByVal e As System.EventArgs) Handles btnDelete.Click
    ' Declare local variables and objects..
    Dim intPosition As Integer
    Dim objCommand As SqlCommand = New SqlCommand()

    ' Save the current record position—1 for the one to be
    ' deleted..
    intPosition = Me.BindingContext(objDataView).Position - 1

    ' If the position is less than 0 set it to 0..
    If intPosition < 0 Then
        intPosition = 0
    End If

    ' Set the Command object properties..
    objCommand.Connection = objConnection
    objCommand.CommandText = "DELETE FROM titleauthor " & _
            "WHERE title_id = @title_id;" & _
            "DELETE FROM titles WHERE title_id = @title_id"

    ' Parameter for the title_id field..
    objCommand.Parameters.AddWithValue _
        ("@title_id", BindingContext(objDataView).Current("title_id"))

    ' Open the database connection..
    objConnection.Open()
```

```
    ' Execute the SqlCommand object to update the data..
    objCommand.ExecuteNonQuery()

    ' Close the connection..
    objConnection.Close()

    ' Fill the DataSet and bind the fields..
    FillDataSetAndView()
    BindFields()

    ' Set the record position to the one that you saved..
    Me.BindingContext(objDataView).Position = intPosition

    ' Show the current record position..
    ShowPosition()

    ' Display a message that the record
    was deleted..
    ToolStripStatusLabel1.Text = "Record
    Deleted"
End Sub
```

2. To test this functionality, run your project, choose any book that you want to delete, and then click the Delete button. Before you delete a book, however, take note of the record count that is displayed on the form (see Figure 16-13). You may see an error because of a constraint in the database. This is because there is sales data for this book. Find the book you added and it will not have sales data associated with it.

    After the delete has been performed, you will see one less record in the record count on the form.

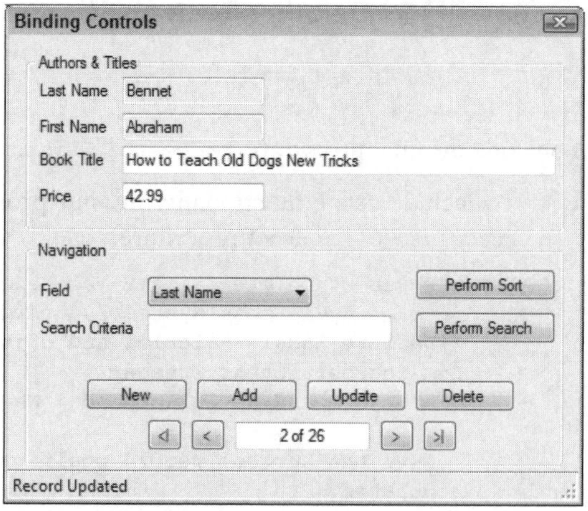

FIGURE 16-13

How It Works

This procedure is a little more involved than the `btnUpdate_Click` procedure because of the relationship of `titles` to `authors`. Remember that there is a relationship table to join `authors` and `titles`. You must delete the row in the `titleauthor` relationship table before you can delete the row of data in the `titles` table. Therefore, you need two DELETE statements in your SQL string.

Note that this time after you declare your variables, you specify the Position property minus 1. This allows the user to be on the last record and delete it. You also allowed the user to be on the first record as you check the value of the `intPosition` variable. If it is less than 0, then you know that the user was on the first record, so you set it to 0; this means that when you restore the record position later, it is again on the first record.

Note also that you did not use the `CurrencyManager` object this time. Instead, you used the `BindingContext` object and specified the `objDataView` object as the object to be manipulated. Remember that the `BindingContext` object is automatically part of the form; there is nothing you need to do to add it. The

BindingContext object is used here to demonstrate how to use it and so that you know that you do not have to use the CurrencyManager object to navigate the records contained in the objDataView:

```
' Declare local variables and objects..
Dim intPosition As Integer
Dim objCommand As SqlCommand = New SqlCommand()

' Save the current record position-1 for the one to be
' deleted..
intPosition = Me.BindingContext(objDataView).Position - 1

' If the position is less than 0 set it to 0..
If intPosition < 0 Then
    intPosition = 0
End If
```

When you set the properties of your SqlCommand object, the SQL string specified in the CommandText property contains two DELETE statements separated by a semicolon. The first DELETE statement deletes the relationship between the titles and authors tables for the book being deleted. The second DELETE statement deletes the book from the titles table:

```
' Set the Command object properties..
objCommand.Connection = objConnection
objCommand.CommandText = "DELETE FROM titleauthor " & _
    "WHERE title_id = @title_id;" & _
    "DELETE FROM titles WHERE title_id = @title_id"
```

Again, you use a placeholder for the primary keys in WHERE clauses of your DELETE statements.

This statement uses only one placeholder. The next line sets it up in the normal way:

```
' Parameter for the title_id field..
objCommand.Parameters.AddWithValue ("@title_id", _
    BindingContext(objDataView).Current("title_id"))
```

The rest of the code is the same as the code for the previous two methods, and should be familiar by now. That wraps up this project. It is hoped that you have gained some valuable knowledge about data binding and how to perform inserts, updates, and deletes using SQL to access a database.

Remember that error handling is a major part of any project. Except for one place in your code, it was omitted to conserve space. You also omitted data validation, so trying to insert a new record with no values could cause unexpected results and errors.

SUMMARY

This chapter covers a few very important ADO.NET classes, particularly the SqlConnection, SqlDataAdapter, SqlCommand, and SqlParameter classes. You saw firsthand how valuable these classes can be when selecting, inserting, updating, and deleting data. These particular classes are specifically for accessing SQL Server.

You also saw the DataSet and DataView classes from the System.Data namespace put to use, and you used both of these classes to create objects that were bound to the controls on your forms. Of particular interest to this discussion is the DataView object, as it provides the functionality to sort and search data. The DataView class provides the most flexibility between the two classes because you can also present a subset of data from the DataSet in the DataView.

You saw how easy it is to bind the controls on your form to the data contained in either the DataSet or the DataView. You also learned how to manage the navigation of the data in these objects with the CurrencyManager class. This class provides quick and easy control over navigation.

This chapter has demonstrated using manual control over the navigation of data on the form and manual control over the insertion, update, and deletion of data in a data store. You should use the techniques that you learned in this chapter when you need finer control of the data, especially when dealing with complex table relationships such as you have dealt with here.

To summarize, after reading this chapter you should:

➤ Feel comfortable using the ADO.NET classes discussed in this chapter

➤ Know when to use the DataSet class and when to use the DataView class

➤ Know how to bind controls on your form manually to either a DataSet or a DataView object

➤ Know how to use the CurrencyManager class to navigate the data in a DataSet or DataView object

➤ Know how to sort and search for data in a DataView object

EXERCISES

1. What properties do you need to set for a SQL Server connection string when passing a user name and password?

2. Which method do you execute when updating data using a SQLCommand object?

3. Why would you use Integrated Security in your connection string?

4. If you do not need to create update/delete/insert commands, how do you have them created automatically?

5. What method do you use to populate a dataset with data?

► **WHAT YOU HAVE LEARNED IN THIS CHAPTER**

TOPIC	CONCEPTS
Installing SQL Server	Where to find a version of SQL Server to download and install.
Using `SQLConnection`, `SQLDataAdapter`, `SQLCommand`, `SQLParameter` classes.	Use these common ADO.Net classes to insert, update, read, and delete data.
Working with `DataSet` and `DataView` classes.	Getting data from the database. Binding to controls and sorting data.
Navigating and updated data on a form.	Using the `CurrencyManager` and `BindingContext` to navigate through bound data on a form. Within the same example, use the controls along with ADO.Net classes to add, update, and delete data.

17

Dynamic Data Web Site

WHAT YOU WILL LEARN IN THIS CHAPTER:

➤ How to create a Dynamic Data Website

➤ How to change the look and feel of pages

➤ How to change the design of individual controls

Now that you have seen how to work with databases in a Windows application, let's learn how to work with data using a web application. Starting with SP1 of Framework 3.5 and Visual Studio 2008, a new site template was shipped. This new template is included in Visual Studio 2010. This template, named Dynamic Data Web Site, allows you to create a data driven site in minutes. The best part about using the new template is that you get a working website with the ability to create, read, update, and delete data in a database without writing any code.

CREATING A DYNAMIC DATA LINQ TO SQL WEB SITE

This section provides an overview of how to create a website to manage data in the Pubs database. You go through a simple wizard, make minor adjustments to the solution and then you have it. You will be amazed in just a few minutes.

TRY IT OUT   Creating a Dynamic Data Web Site

Code file DDA.zip is available for download at Wrox.com

1. Start this project by choosing File ➪ New Web Site. Make sure Visual Basic is the language, and select ASP.NET Dynamic Data Linq to SQL. For the location, change the drop-down box to File System and enter *[The default path for VS 2010]*\DDA. A default path for Windows 7 will look like C:\Users\Bryan\Documents\Visual Studio 2010\WebSites\DDA. Click OK to create a file system site that will use the built-in development web server for testing. The New Web Site dialog box is shown in Figure 17-1.

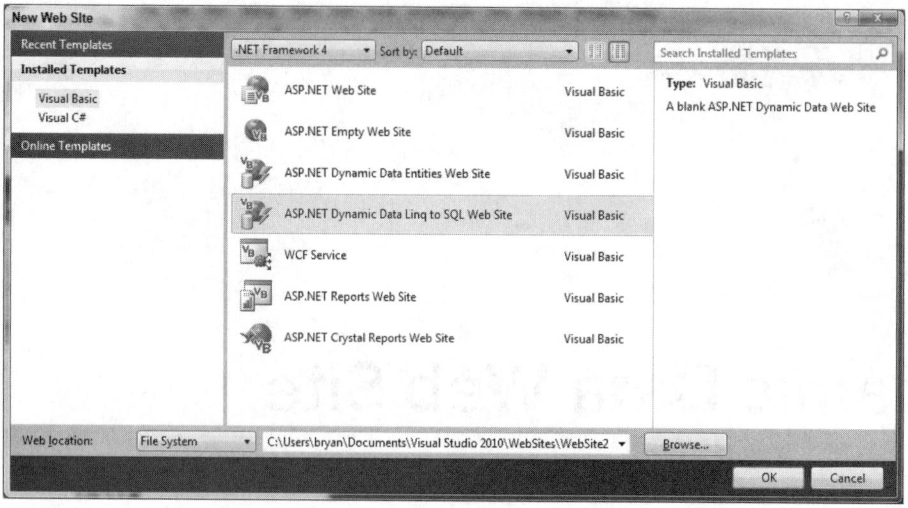

FIGURE 17-1

2. Visual Studio creates many default folders and files for the website. Your Solution Explorer window will look like what is shown in Figure 17-2. You will learn more about these pages later in this chapter.

3. You now have a website set up. Next, you need a database to connect the application to. To add a database, right-click App_Data in Solution Explorer and choose Add Existing Item. The Add Existing Item dialog will display. First, change the file type to Data files in the drop-down menu in the lower-right corner of the window. Now, browse for the pubs database you created in Chapter 16. You need to find Pubs.mdf, which should be in your SQL Server data folder. If you installed your SQL Server and pubs database based on Chapters 15 and 16, you can find the database at C:\Program Files\Microsoft SQL Server\MSSQL10.WROX\MSSQL\DATA. Your Add Existing Item dialog will look similar to Figure 17-3. After finding the database, click Add to continue.

You may see an error if you are not running Visual Studio as an administrator. See Figure 17-4.

If you see this message, you need to close Visual Studio and open it again running as administrator. To do this, right-click the shortcut in your menu and choose Run as Administrator. After reopening and running as administrator, repeat step 3.

FIGURE 17-2

4. Next, you will create the data model. To do this, first create an App_Code folder. Right-click the solution in Solution Explorer and select Add ASP.NET Folder and then select App_Code.

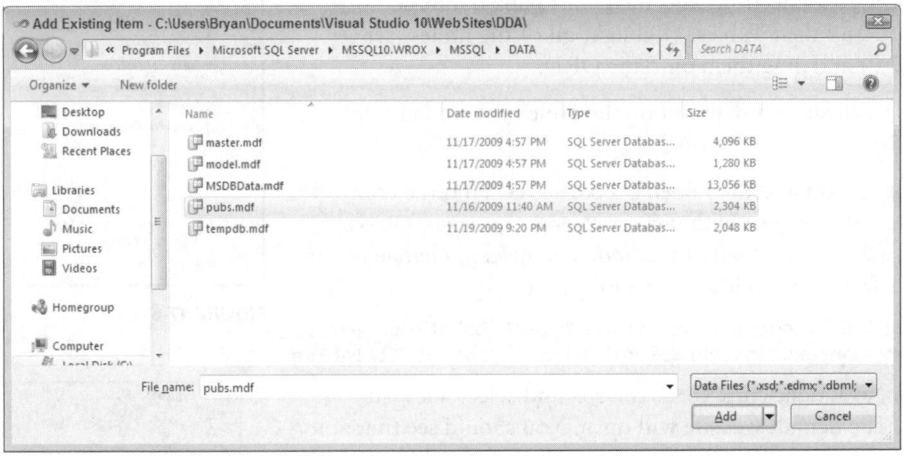

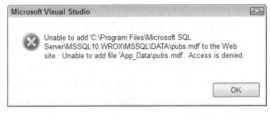

FIGURE 17-3

5. Right-click the new App_Code folder and click Add New Item. Choose the LINQ to SQL Classes template and change the name to **Pubs.dbml** in the Add New Item dialog, as shown in Figure 17-5.

6. Now click Add and you will see the Object Relational Designer (ORD). Click the Server Explorer Link in the ORD. Server Explorer, shown in Figure 17-6, will open.

FIGURE 17-4

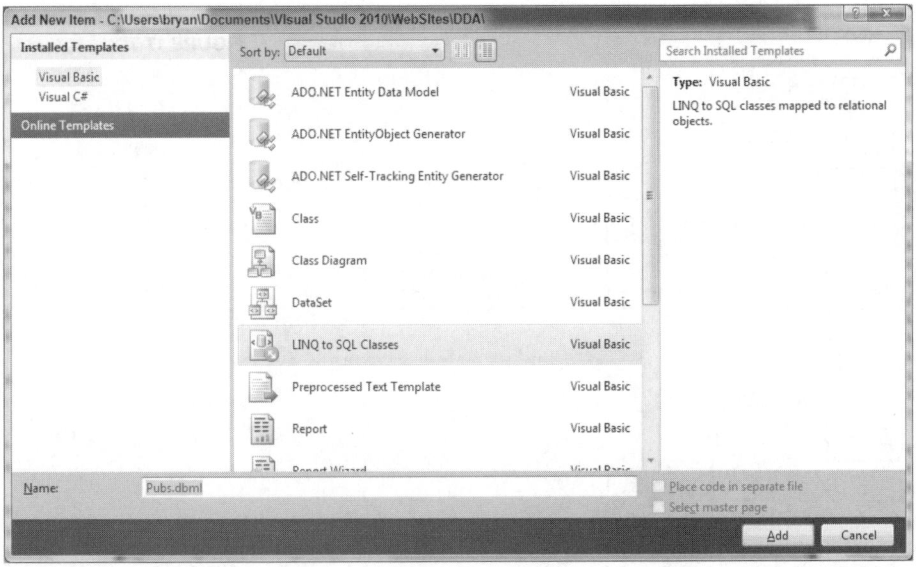

FIGURE 17-5

7. Expand Data Connections and then your `pubs` database (pubs.mdf), and then Tables. Highlight all of the tables (see Figure 17-7) and drag them onto the ORD.

The ORD will show a diagram on the tables you added (see Figure 17-8).

8. Save your project and then open `Global.asax`. Find the commented line that begins with `DefaultModel.RegisterContext` inside of the `RegisterRoutes` method. You need to change this to match the following code and uncomment it:

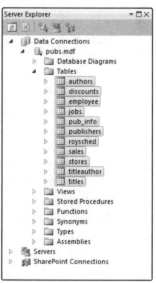

FIGURE 17-6

```
DefaultModel.RegisterContext(GetType(PubsDataContext), _
    New ContextConfiguration() With {.ScaffoldAllTables = True})
```

9. That's it. Now right-click `Default.aspx` and select View in Browser. The default website will open. You should see the same site shown in Figure 17-9. Click some of the links and play a little bit. You will be amazed at what you have created.

How It Works

You have completed your first Dynamic Data website, and Visual Studio did all of the work for you. First, you created a new Dynamic Data LINQ to SQL website. In this step, the core site files were created.

Next you added data. In this step, you found the .mdf file for your `pubs` database. Visual Studio then created a copy of the database for use by the site. There are other methods of data access, such as attaching directly to the database file.

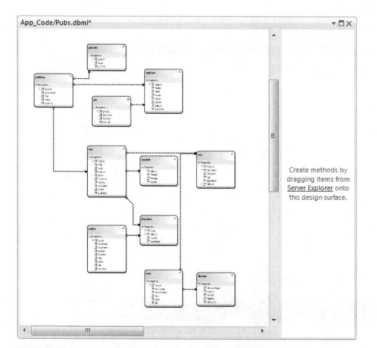

FIGURE 17-8

FIGURE 17-7

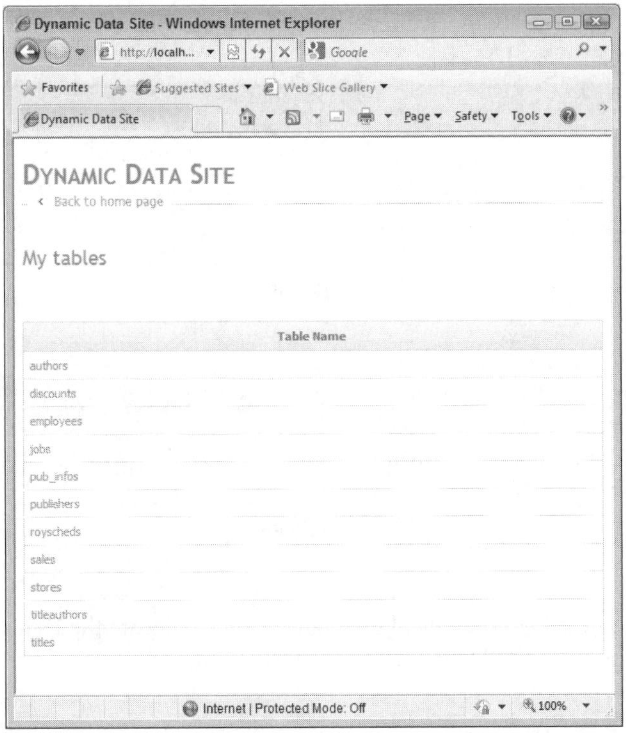

FIGURE 17-9

In the third step, you created the data model. To accomplish this you added a special folder ASP.NET(App_Code) to the site. Inside of the new folder, you created the data model by adding LINQ to SQL Classes and mapping the tables using the Object Relational Designer. This created all of the classes needed to handle the basic CRUD operations.

Finally, you added the context registration to the Pubs Data Context that was created. This basically hooks up the website to the data.

Here, you set `ScaffoldAllTables` to `True`. This tells the site to add CRUD operations for all tables in the database. You can set this to `False` and use table-level scaffolding to remove access to certain tables. Global scaffolding is easy to set up and may create security risks so use it with care.

This exercise demonstrated how easy it is to create the Dynamic Data website. In the next section, you will learn how to change the design of the default site you just created.

Customizing the Design of a Dynamic Data Web Site

When you create dynamic data websites, you get an incredible amount of functionality out of the box. The only drawback is that site has a basic design that will not work for many applications. Don't let this deter you. You can easily change the design of the site to meet just about any requirement using built-in templates.

There are four types of templates discussed next. You can use these to make the site look completely different.

Page Templates

You use Page templates to change the look of tables in the site. These templates can change the look of all tables or specific tables. Page templates are located in DynamicData ➪ PageTemplates (see Figure 17-10).

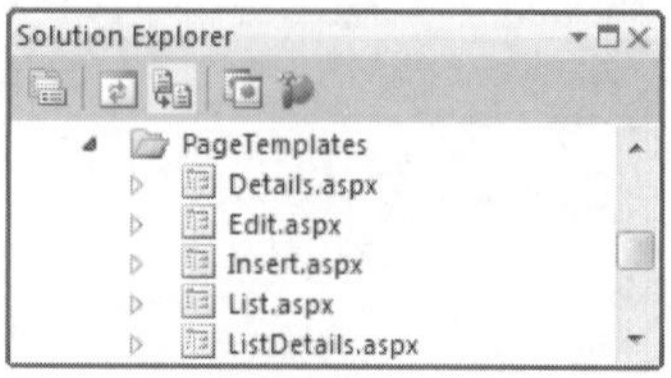

FIGURE 17-10

Entity Templates

Entity templates are user controls to change the layout of tables. This approach gives you more control than using Page templates. For example, you can change the way insert, edit, and view tables are rendered independently. To locate the Entity templates, open Solution Explorer and select DynamicData ➪ EntityTemplates (see Figure 17-11).

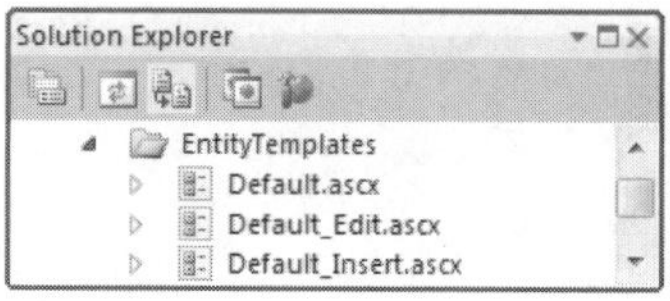

FIGURE 17-11

Field Templates

To change the way a specific data type is rendered, you use Field templates. You can locate the Field templates by opening Solution Explorer and selecting DynamicData ➪ FieldTemplates (see Figure 17-12).

Filter Templates

When you want to change the way the filters are displayed for the tables, change the Filter templates. Filter templates are user controls that allow site users to select data to be displayed in each table. To access the Filter templates, open Solution Explorer and select DynamicData ➪ Filters (see Figure 17-13).

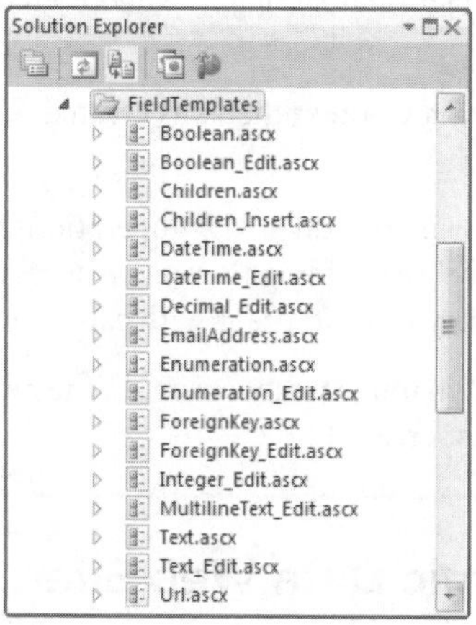

FIGURE 17-12

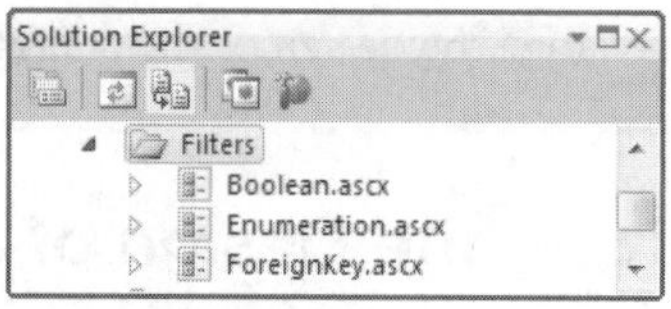

FIGURE 17-13

TRY IT OUT Changing the Look and Feel of a Dynamic Data Web Site

Code file DDA.zip is available for download at Wrox.com

In this Try It Out, you will make updates to the site using Page templates and Field templates.

1. Return to the DDA website. In Solution Explorer, right-click `List.aspx` located at DynamicData ➪ PageTemplates and choose View Markup. Look for the following `H2` element:

   ```
   <h2 class="DDSubHeader"><%= table.DisplayName%></h2>
   ```

   Change it as follows:

   ```
   <h2 class="DDSubHeader">View or update table: <%= table.
   DisplayName.ToUpper%></h2>
   ```

2. View the changes in the site and you will see your change to the page heading, as shown in Figure 17-14.

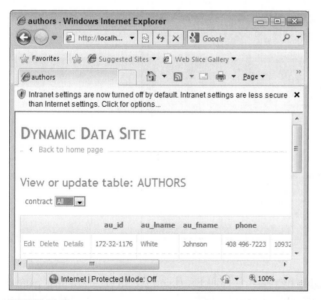

FIGURE 17-14

3. Go back to Visual Studio and switch to Design View on `List.aspx`. To switch between Design View and Markup View press Shift+F7. Right-click GridView1 and select AutoFormat. GridView1 is shown in Figure 17-15.

4. The AutoFormat dialog will open, showing the available formats for the GridView control. Select Brown Sugar as shown in Figure 17-16 and click OK.

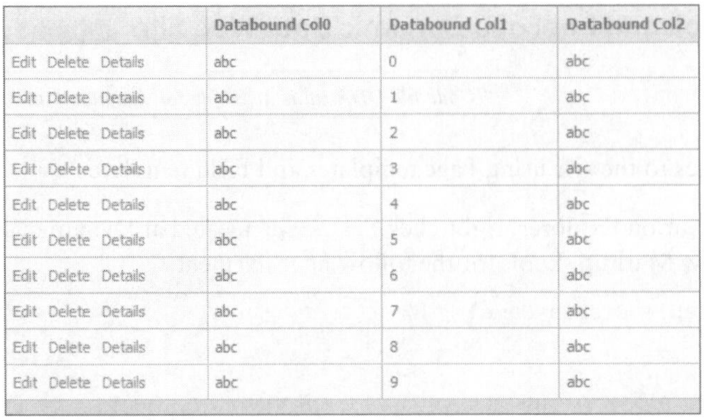

	Databound Col0	Databound Col1	Databound Col2
Edit Delete Details	abc	0	abc
Edit Delete Details	abc	1	abc
Edit Delete Details	abc	2	abc
Edit Delete Details	abc	3	abc
Edit Delete Details	abc	4	abc
Edit Delete Details	abc	5	abc
Edit Delete Details	abc	6	abc
Edit Delete Details	abc	7	abc
Edit Delete Details	abc	8	abc
Edit Delete Details	abc	9	abc

FIGURE 17-15

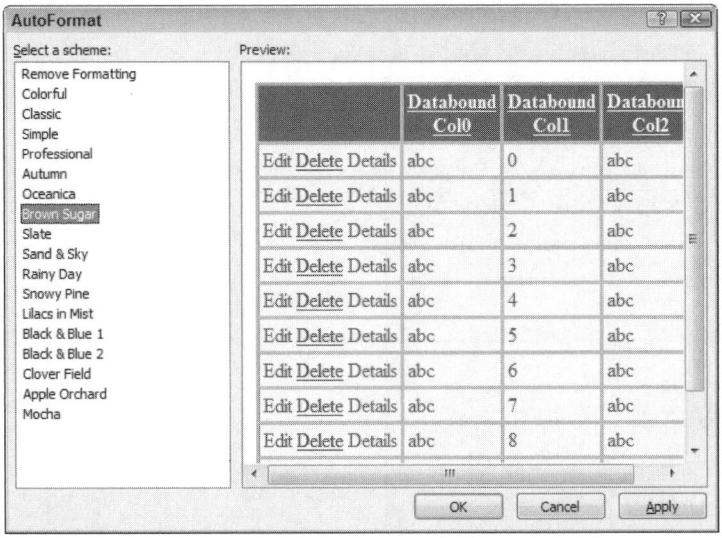

FIGURE 17-16

5. Run the application without debugging by pressing Ctrl+F5. If you see an error that the page cannot be found, you need to set the start page. To do so, right-click Default.aspx in the Solution Explorer and click Set as Start Page. Run again and the default page will open. Click the link to the Sales table and you will see the Brown Sugar theme, as shown in Figure 17-17.

6. To change the way text boxes look in edit mode, locate the Text_Edit.ascx page in the FieldTemplates folder in Solution Explorer. Right-click the file and select View Designer.

7. Select the TextBox1 control. In the Properties Window, set BackColor to Black and ForeColor to White.

8. To test your changes, press Ctrl+F5. When the site opens, click the link to authors and then click one of the Edit links. You will see the new text box design with a white font and a black background. Your site should look like Figure 17-18.

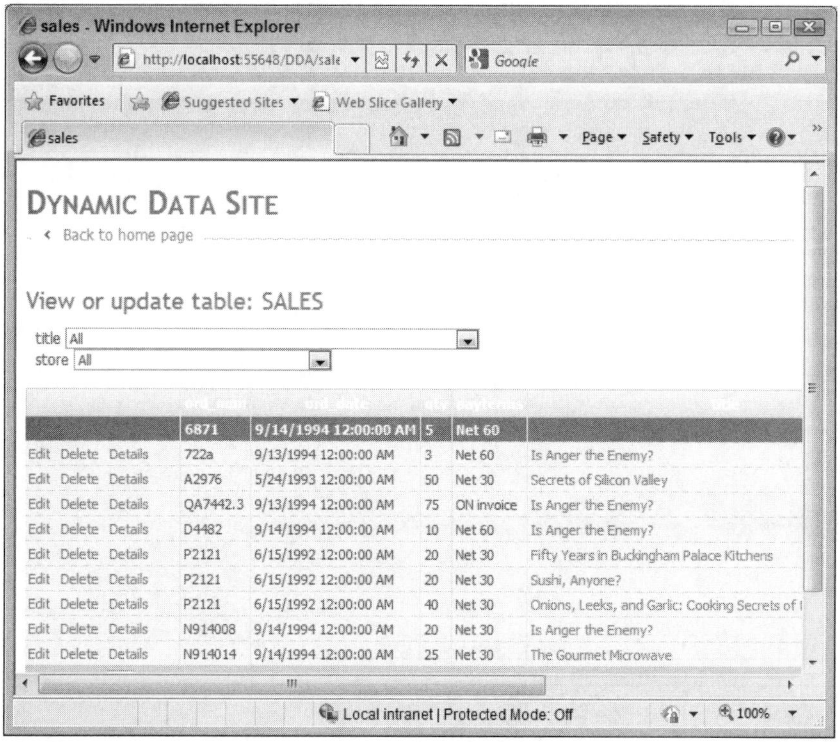

FIGURE 17-17

How It Works

In the previous exercise, you were able to change the way the site looked. Changing Dynamic Data Web Sites is accomplished by using templates.

The first change you made was to the text in the markup of the List template. You added the text **View or update table:** to every page on the site by changing one line of code:

```
<h2 class="DDSubHeader">View or update table: <%=
     table.DisplayName.ToUpper%></h2>
```

The site uses this template when listing table data unless a specific table has a template that overrides this one.

Next, you updated the design on the GridView control. For this change, you used the AutoFormat dialog to select a theme for the data GridView
controls. The change affected all tables in the site.

What happened behind the scenes is the GridView control's markup was updated. Figure 17-19 shows the GridView code before the formatting was applied. Figure 17-20 shows the same GridView after

FIGURE 17-18

FIGURE 17-19

FIGURE 17-20

applying the Brown Sugar theme. If you look closely, you will see all of the styles that were added. You can customize the GridView control just about any way you can imagine using these same styles.

The final change was for Textboxes on the edit and insert pages. This change affected all text fields in the database that display as a textbox. It altered the text boxes that display text, making the font white and the background black. If you want to change the design of integer data, you make the same change to the `Integer_Edit.acsx` page.

SUMMARY

In this chapter, you learned how simple it is to create Dynamic Data websites. Using the built-in wizards, you were able to create a complete data maintenance website for the pubs database. After going through the exercises, you should be able to create a data driven site for any of your databases in just minutes. This tool is extremely powerful and as you saw, based on templates. You have access to open the templates and change them so the site can be customized in just about any way you see fit.

EXERCISES

1. How do you change the way date and time fields are displayed in a Dynamic Data website in edit mode?

2. How do you change the way insert pages are displayed in a Dynamic Data website?

3. What type of template do you use to change the way the site looks for just one table?

► **WHAT YOU HAVE LEARNED IN THIS CHAPTER**

TOPIC	CONCEPTS
Creating Dynamic Data websites	Know how to create the site, add a database, create the data model, and set up the site to connect to the database
Customizing pages in Dynamic Data websites	Understand how to use the Page and Entity templates to change the look and feel of the website
Customizing controls in Dynamic Data websites	Understand how to use the Field template to change the look and feel of the website
Customizing filters in Dynamic Data websites	Understand how to use the Filter template to change the look and feel of the website
Scaffolding	Setting `ScaffoldAllTables` to `True` makes all tables available. You can set scaffolding at the table level or globally.

18

ASP.NET

WHAT YOU WILL LEARN IN THIS CHAPTER:

➤ A basic overview of web applications (thin-client applications)

➤ The advantages of Web Forms versus Windows Forms

➤ Understanding the control toolbox

➤ Exploring client and server processing

➤ Assessing the possible locations for websites in VS 2010 (IIS and ASP.NET Development Server)

➤ Gaining an understanding of tools for data validation, navigation, security, data entry, and look and feel

As we look to the future, the Internet is sure to increase its presence in business, so it follows that developers need to gain knowledge of building robust, dynamic websites. In this chapter, you will learn about building Web Forms applications. You will focus on the basics for website development and moving to database-driven applications. With Visual Studio 2010, you will be building data-driven sites in no time.

Visual Studio 2010 is the best tool for creating ASP.NET sites on the market today. It provides you with the best IntelliSense, debugging, and control library to create websites written in Visual Basic. You can build ASP.NET websites (sometimes referred to as Web Forms applications), web services, and even sites targeted for mobile devices in VS 2010. In addition, you do not need IIS or any web server to host your site with VS 2010; ASP.NET Development Server is a built-in web server you can use to host your sites while developing them.

> **NOTE** *Before you get your first look at the code, you will have a short lesson on the building blocks developers use to create web applications.*

THIN-CLIENT ARCHITECTURE

In previous chapters, you have seen thick-client applications in the form of Windows Forms applications. Most of the processing is completed by the client application you built earlier, and many of the applications stood on their own and needed no other applications or servers. In web development, conversely, most of the processing is completed on the server and then the result is sent to the browser.

When you develop Web Forms applications, you do not have to distribute anything to the user. Any user who can access your web server and has a web browser can be a user. You must be careful with the amount of processing you place on the client. When you design a thin-client system, you must be aware that your users or customers will use different clients to access your application. If you try to use too much processing on the client, it may cause problems for some users. This is one of the major differences between Windows and Web Forms applications. You will learn about the major difference between these two types of Visual Studio 2010 applications later in this chapter.

When dealing with a Windows Forms application, you have a compiled program that must be distributed to the user's desktop before they can use it. Depending upon the application, there may also be one or more supporting DLLs or other executables that also need to be distributed along with the application.

In thin-client architecture, there is typically no program or DLL to be distributed. Users merely need to start their browsers and enter the URL of the application website. The server hosting the website is responsible for allocating all resources the web application requires. The client is a navigation tool that displays the results the server returns.

All code required in a thin-client application stays in one central location: the server hosting the website. Any updates to the code are immediately available the next time a user requests a web page.

Thin-client architecture provides several key benefits. First and foremost is the cost of initial distribution of the application — there is none. In traditional client/server architecture, the program would have to be distributed to every client who wanted to use it, which could be quite a time-consuming task if the application is used in offices throughout the world.

Another major benefit is the cost of distributing updates to the application — again, there is none. All updates to the website and its components are distributed to the web server. Once an update is made, it is immediately available to all users the next time they access the updated web page. In traditional client/server architecture, the updated program would have to be distributed to every client, and the updates could take days or weeks to roll out. Thin-client architecture allows a new version of an application to be distributed instantly to all the users without having to touch a single desktop.

Another major benefit is that you can make changes to the back-end architecture and not have to worry about the client. Suppose, for example, that you want to change the location of the database from a low-end server to a new high-end server. The new server would typically have a new machine name. In a traditional client/server application, the machine name of the database server is stored in the code or Registry setting. You would need to modify either the code or the Registry setting for every person who uses the application. In thin-client architecture, you simply need to update the setting of the web server to point to the new database server and you are in business, and so are all of the clients.

You can see that in a thin-client architecture model, any client with a browser can access your website and immediately have access to updates. In fact, if your changes were transparent to the user, the client wouldn't even know that changes had been made.

Now that you have a basic understanding of thin-client architecture, let's look at how Web Forms work.

WEB FORMS VERSUS WINDOWS FORMS

In this section, you will get an overview of the advantages of both Windows Forms and Web Forms. This will give you an idea of when you build each type of application to solve a customer's problem. You will almost always have to choose between these two types of architecture when building solutions, so it is important to understand some of the advantages of both.

Windows Forms Advantages

Windows Forms applications have advantages in some types of systems. Typically, applications that require a responsive interface, such as a point-of-sale system at a retail store, are Windows Forms applications. Also, in most cases, processor-intensive applications such as games or graphics programs are better suited to a Windows Forms program.

A major advantage of Windows Forms is trust. When a user installs the application, it is given trust in the current zone. With this high-enough level of trust, you can store data and state about the current session on the local computer. The user can run the application and it can interact with the local file system or Registry seamlessly. Trust is very limited, however, for an Internet application.

Another advantage is having control over the client application. This allows you to build a very powerful, rich user interface. As you will see, numerous controls are not available to a Web Form (although this is becoming less of a difference) to permit the developer to create user-friendly applications. Windows Forms allow for a more ample user interface.

Also, application responsiveness is an advantage with Windows Forms. With most or all of the processing being done on the client, the need to send data over the wire can be reduced. Any amount of data sent to servers can cause latency. For an application running locally on a computer, the normal events are handled more quickly. In addition, the speed of data transmission over a local network is much faster than the typical Internet connection. This speed enables data to move across the wire faster and create less of a bottleneck for the user.

Web Forms Advantages

Although the advantages of Web Forms may seem to be greater than the advantages of Windows Forms, don't permit this to transform you into a full-time web developer for every project. There will always be times when Windows Forms are a better solution.

The greatest advantage of a web application is distribution. To distribute a Web Forms application, just install it on the web server. That's it. There's no need to create an installation for every version of Windows, or ship CDs. When you make a change, just publish the change to the web server; and the next time customers access the site, they will use the latest application.

Version control, or change control, is another advantage. With all of your application code at the same location, making changes is a breeze. You never have to worry about one user on version 8 and another on version 10; all users access the same application. As soon as you publish a change, all users see the update — with no user intervention necessary.

You may be familiar with the term *platform independence*. Web applications have it. It doesn't matter what type of computer the user has — as long as there is a browser and a connection to your web server, the user can access your application. There is no need to build application versions for different operating systems.

These advantages can add up to many thousands of dollars of savings compared to a Windows application. Being able to make quick changes and maintain one code base are great advantages. Still, there are times when a web application will not provide an adequate user experience. Make sure you evaluate both options for every project. Now, let's look more closely at Web Forms development.

WEB APPLICATIONS: THE BASIC PIECES

In its simplest form, a web application is just a number of web pages. In order for the user to access the web pages, there must be a web server and browser. A request is made by the browser for the page on the server. The server then processes the web page and returns the output to the browser. The user sees the page inside the browser window. The pages that the users see may contain HyperText Markup Language (HTML), cascading style sheets (CSS), and client-side script. Finally, the page displays in the browser for the user. This section presents a basic overview of each piece of the system.

Web Servers

There are many web servers on the market today. The most well-known web servers in use today are Microsoft Internet Information Services (IIS) and Apache. For this book, you will focus exclusively on IIS.

Browsers

Every user of a Web Forms application must have a browser. The five most popular browsers are Microsoft Internet Explorer (IE), Firefox, Chrome, Safari, and Opera. When you develop public websites, you must be aware that the site may render differently in each browser. You will find that IE is the most lenient when it comes to valid HTML; and we will focus on IE8 for this book. The controls you use in Visual Studio will render browser-specific code to make your applications appear correctly in all browsers. You still need to test each version your users will use to access your application.

HyperText Markup Language

Also known as HTML, this is the presentation, or design layout, of the web page. HTML is a tag-based language that allows you to change the presentation of information. For example, to make text bold in HTML, just place the <b> tag around the text. The following text is an example of HTML:

```
<p>This is <b>bold</b> in HTML.</p>
```

If the previous text is then rendered by a browser, it would be displayed like this:

This is **bold** in HTML.

Browsers will interpret HTML and should conform to the standards from the World Wide Web Consortium (W3C). The W3C was created to develop common protocols for the Web in the 1990s. You can read more about the W3C at their website, at www.w3.org.

Although VS 2010 allows you to design ASP.NET websites without firsthand knowledge of HTML, you gain experience with hands-on exercises creating web pages with HTML later in the chapter.

JavaScript

A major part of web development is client-side script. If you are creating an application for the public that uses client-side script, you need to use JavaScript for support in all browsers. VBScript is a Microsoft-centric language that is more like Visual Basic syntax and slowly going away. You may see it in old code. Just know that is only supported by Internet Explorer. You will probably never create new code using VBScript for client-side scripting..

Client-side scripting is typically used for data validation and dynamic HTML (DHTML). Validation scripts enforce rules that may require the user to complete a field on the screen before continuing. DHTML scripts allow the page to change programmatically after it is in memory on the browser. Expanding menus is an example of DHTML. Currently, IE supports more DHTML than is required by the W3C, so you may have to create DHTML for each target browser.

One of the great features of Visual Studio 2010 is the validation and navigation controls. You can drag these controls onto your web page without writing any client-side script. In most instances, you can manage with these controls, but for others you will need to be self-sufficient in the creation of client-side script. For this reason, you will write some of your own scripts later in this chapter.

Cascading Style Sheets

Cascading style sheets (CSS) allows for the separation of layout and style from the content of a web page. You can use CSS to change fonts, colors, alignment, and many other aspects of web page presentation. The best thing about CSS is that it can be applied to an entire site. By using a master CSS page, you can easily maintain and quickly change the look and feel of the entire website by changing one page. You will learn more about CSS in this chapter.

ACTIVE SERVER PAGES

With Visual Studio 2010, you create websites using Active Server Pages or ASP.NET. This makes it easy to create dynamic, data-driven websites. This section explains the features and benefits of ASPX or Web Forms.

Benefits of ASP.NET Web Pages

When you create web applications, you could use many solutions. The most common types of pages are Active Server Pages (.asp and .aspx), JavaServer Pages (.jsp), Cold Fusion Pages (.cfm) and basic HTML (.htm or .html). In this book, you mainly focus on ASPX, but you will see some HTML also.

Execution time is one benefit for which ASP.NET stands out above the rest. When an ASP.NET page is requested the first time, a compiled copy is placed into memory on the server for the next request. This offers great performance gains over interpreted languages.

Using Visual Studio 2010 to design your applications also makes a big difference in productivity. The .NET Framework supplies thousands of namespaces, objects, and controls for use in developing Web Forms applications. In addition, ASP.NET also supports all .NET-compatible languages. By default, Visual Basic and C# are available in Visual Studio 2010.

Special Website Files

When you work with ASP.NET, you will see many special files. These files are very important, and each could have an entire chapter written about it. The two files discussed here, global.asax and web.config, enable you to make sitewide changes from one location. There is much more to learn about these than we can present in a single chapter, and you can do research at http://www.msdn.com.

Global.asax

The global.asax file allows you to add code to certain application-level events. The most common events are Application_Start, Application_End, Session_Start, Session_End, and Application_Error. The application start and end events fire when the actual web application inside of IIS changes state. The application start event will fire with the first request to a website after the server or IIS is restarted. The session events fire on a per user/browser session on the web server. When you save data to the user's session, you must be careful. This data will be saved for every user/browser that is browsing the application, which can create an extra load on the server. You can use the final event, Application_Error, to log all unhandled exceptions in one common place. Make sure to redirect users to a friendly error page after logging the error.

Web.config

Web.config is exactly what it appears to be — a configuration file for the web application; it is an XML document. You can update many application settings for security, errors, and much, much more. In most production apps, you store your connection string to the database here.

Development

As you build Web Forms applications in Visual Studio 2010, you will work in the IDE you are familiar with from Windows Forms applications. As you work with web pages, you have the option to use what is known as a *code-behind page*. This enables you to keep your application logic separate from the presentation code. You have three views to work from: Design, Source, and Code view, the common ways to build applications. Design and Source view are for the .aspx page that contains the user interface and data validation. Code view is the .vb file that is the code-behind page. Visual Studio 2010 makes creating web sites an easy task.

Controls: The Toolbox

The default controls you will use to build web applications are all in the Toolbox. If you do not see the Toolbox, press Ctrl+Alt+X to view it. The controls are organized by category. The standard category, along with its controls, is shown in Figure 18-1.

BUILDING WEB SITES

In this section, you will create a small web application demonstrating different aspects of web development. In accomplishing this, you will see how the basics of Web Forms applications work.

Creating a Web Form for Client- and Server-Side Processing

The Web Form in this Try It Out contains HTML and server controls. The HTML controls have client-side processing, and the server controls process the code on the server.

FIGURE 18-1

| TRY IT OUT | Server and Client-Side Processing |

Code file Client_ServerProcessing.zip is available for download at Wrox.com

This example will introduce you to your first custom web site.

1. Start this project by choosing File ➪ New Web Site. Make sure Visual Basic is the language, and select ASP.NET web site. For the Location, change the drop-down box to File System and enter **[The default path for VS 2010]\Client_ServerProcessing**. A default path for Windows 7 will look like `C:\Users\Bryan\Documents\Visual Studio 2010\WebSites\Client_ServerProcessing`. Click OK to create a file system site that will use the built-in development web server for testing. The New Web Site dialog box will look like Figure 18-2.

2. Visual Studio will create the default folders and files for the website. Take a look at the `Default.aspx`, shown in Figure 18-3. The `Default.aspx` page will be open in the IDE. The page already has a master page and default design created. You will learn more about master pages later in this chapter.

3. Remove the content inside the ContentPlaceHolder control. This is the control named MainContent. Click inside of the ContentPlaceHolder, press Ctrl+A and then delete. Now you want to add the following standard controls to `to MainContent` while in Design mode. (To get to Design mode, while viewing the `.aspx` page, click the Design option on the lower-left corner of the pane, or simply press Shift+F7.) You are only allowed to add controls inside of the ContentPlaceHolder because the page has a master page. Do not worry about the position of the controls for now, but make sure you use controls from the Standard and HTML tabs on the toolbox.

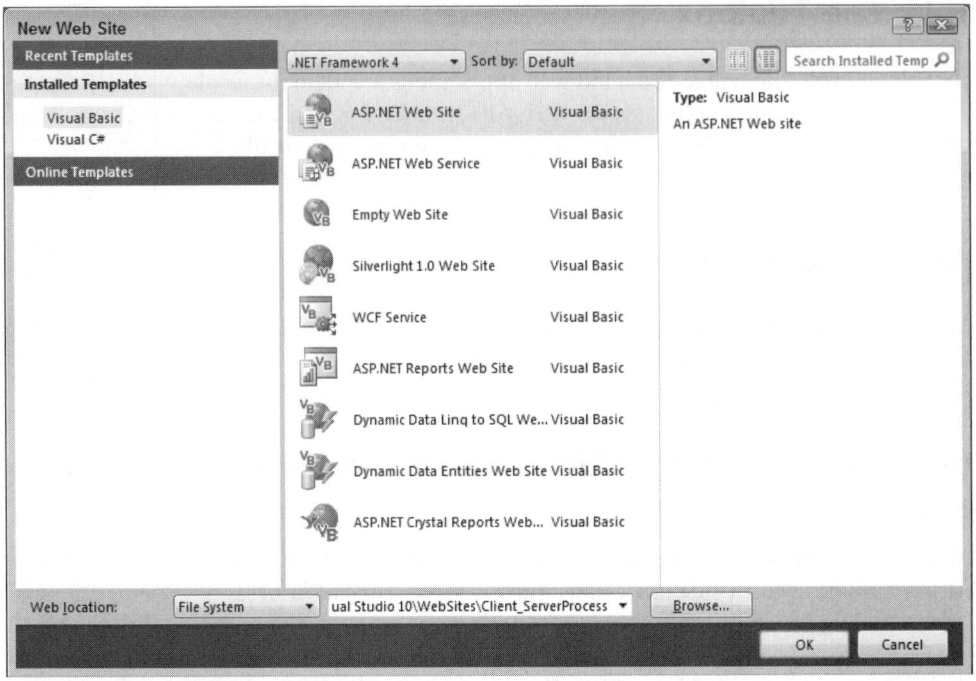

FIGURE 18-2

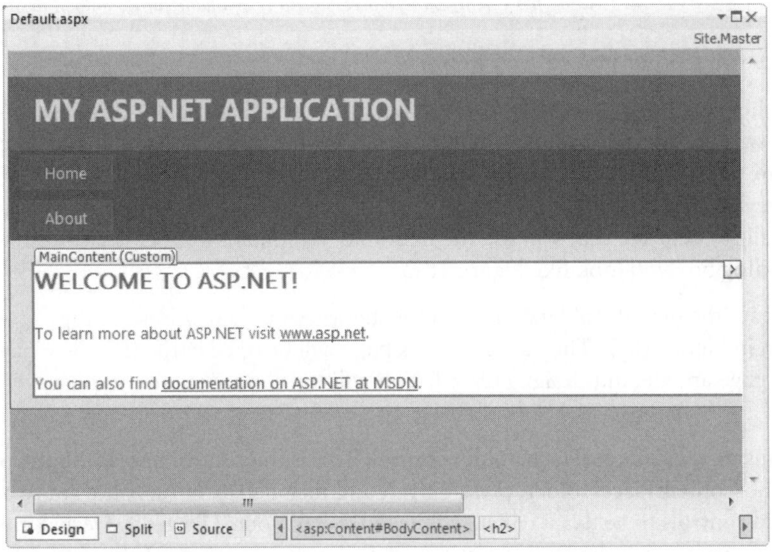

FIGURE 18-3

> *NOTE* The area at the bottom of the Default.aspx page that has Design, Split, Source, and other HTML tags on the right is known as the tag navigator.

When adding the following controls to the form, you can arrange them in any order you want for now. To make designing the layout easier, put your cursor inside MainContent and press your Enter key five or six times. This will add space to your work area. This is a basic way to lay out your pages, and normally you would use either CSS layout or table layout for your websites. You will learn more about layout later in this chapter.

➤ From the Standard controls tab, add one Button and two Label controls.

➤ From the HTML controls tab, add one Input (Button) control.

4. Change the properties of the controls as follows (refer to Figure 18-4 as a guide):

➤ Set the ID of the Standard:Button to **btnServer** and the Text to **Server**.

➤ Set the ID of the HTML:Input (Button) to **btnClient** and the Text to **Client**.

➤ Set the ID of the upper Standard:Label to **lblServer**; set ClientIDMode to **Static** and the Text to **Server**.

➤ Set the ID of the lower Standard:Label to **lblClient**; set ClientIDMode to **Static** and the Text to **Client**.

5. You have to enter line breaks and spaces on the page to move the controls around. This is called *relative positioning*; each control is placed relative to the previous control. Arrange the controls so they resemble Figure 18-4. When you finish, press Ctrl+F5 to run the project without debugging and see the page in the browser. You will be asked to modify the web.config page to enable debugging. Choose the option to enable debugging and click OK.

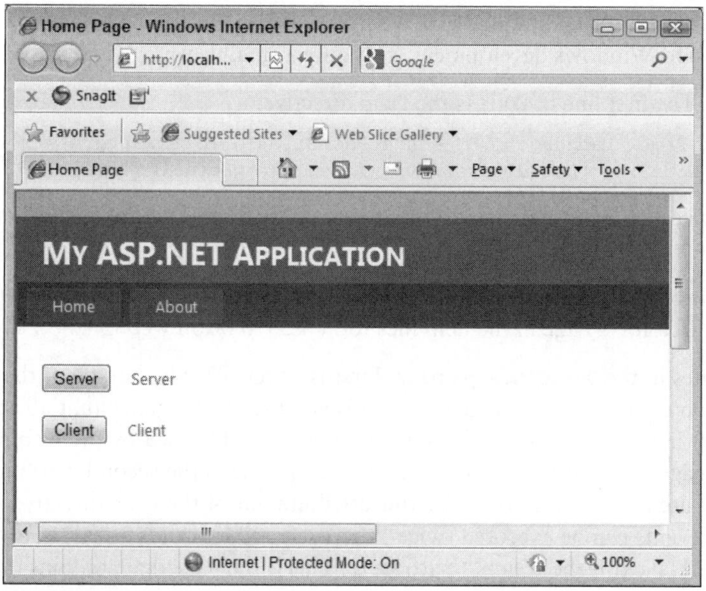

FIGURE 18-4

6. Close the browser and go back to Visual Studio 2010. Double-click the btnServer to jump to the `btnServer_Click` event handler. Depending on your settings, you will be either on the code-behind page or working in the source of the `.aspx` page. Add the following bolded code to the event:

```
Protected Sub btnServer_Click(ByVal sender As Object, _
    ByVal e As System.EventArgs) Handles btnServer.Click
    lblServer.Text = `Changed"
End Sub
```

Run the program again and test the button's `Click` event. The label will display `Changed` after you click the Server button.

7. Close the browser and go back to Visual Studio 2010. Create an event handler for the HTML Input (Button) and add a title to the page. (Make sure you have the `Default.aspx` page open in the IDE and that the Properties window has DOCUMENT selected.) To add a title, find the `Title` property and set it to **My First Page**. On the tag navigator, click Source to change to HTML view. In the Client Object & Events combo box, choose `btnClient`. Next, select `onclick` in the event combo box and add the following bolded code to the event that VS 2010 creates (note that JavaScript is case sensitive):

```
function btnClient_onclick() {
  document.getElementById(`lblClient").innerText = `Changed";
  document.getElementById(`lblServer").innerText = `Server";
}
```

8. Run the project again by pressing Ctrl+F5. Test both buttons.

How It Works

Now you can see that Web Forms development is very similar to Windows Forms development. This is one of the benefits of .NET development and Visual Studio 2010. Microsoft has made it easy for any developer to switch from client server to web to Windows development with only a small learning curve.

First, consider the HTML source. The first line of code is the `Page` directive:

```
<%@ Page Title="My First Page" Language="VB" MasterPageFile="~/Site.Master"
AutoEventWireup="false" CodeFile="Default.aspx.vb" Inherits="_Default" %>
```

Depending on the mode you develop in, you may see different default attributes set by Visual Studio 2010.

The `Page` directive has over 30 attributes that can be set. Only the default attributes are discussed here, but if you want to explore the rest, search for **@Page** in the help files for VS 2010 or on web.

Take a look at the default attributes in the `Default.aspx` page. First is TITLE. This is the title of the page displayed in the browser. Then you see the `Language` attribute. This is set to the language that all server code will compile into. Then there is `MasterPageFile`. This is the mater page file used by the web page (you'll learn more about master pages later in the chapter). `AutoEventWireup` is the second attribute. Visual Studio 2010 sets this attribute to `false`. If you leave this attribute out of the `Page` directive, the default value is `true`, and certain events can be executed twice. Microsoft recommends always setting the `AutoEventWireup` attribute to `false`. Next is the `CodeFile` attribute. This is the page that contains the code when using a separate code file or the code-behind page. Finally, there is the Inherits attribute. This is simply the class name from which the page will inherit.

The JavaScript for client button click is next. The only event is the OnClick event of the btnClient control. Client side code is added to the HeadContent based on the master page. When you click the client button, this procedure executes. The first line of the subroutine uses the getElementById function to find the object in the document that has an ID of lblClient. Once it is found, the innerText is set to Changed. The same function is used to find the lblServer object on the next line. The innerText is then changed to Server. This is added to reset the Server button's label.

```
<asp:Content ID="HeaderContent" runat="server" ContentPlaceHolderID="HeadContent">
    <script language="javascript" type="text/javascript">
// <![CDATA[

        function btnClient_onclick() {
          document.getElementById("lblClient").innerText = "Changed";
          document.getElementById("lblServer").innerText = "Server";
        }

// ]]>
    </script>
</asp:Content>
```

What you may not notice is the difference in the way each button performs event handling. It is hard to notice when running locally, but go back to the web page and watch the status bar of the browser while you click each button. When you click the Server button, the page actually calls the web server to process the event.

The Client button did not call back to the server; the browser handled the event itself. ClientIDMode is where you can set the behavior of the ID you will use in your script. Using Static will force the control's ID to be the client ID. This is by far the easiest option. You should be careful not to duplicate names in controls when using Static.

Now you are at the next Content tag. This is where you added the controls:

```
<asp:Content ID="BodyContent" runat="server" ContentPlaceHolderID="MainContent">
```

When you click the Server button, the contents of the form are actually submitted to the server.

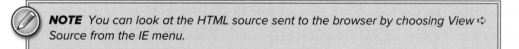

> **NOTE** You can look at the HTML source sent to the browser by choosing View ⇨ Source from the IE menu.

The browser knows that btnServer is a submit button. The function of a submit button is to pass form data back to a web server.

The final portion of the code on the Default.aspx page is the markup for the controls. These are the controls you placed onto the design area of the form:

```
<br />
<asp:Button ID="btnServer" runat="server" Text="Server" />
  
```

```
        <asp:Label ID="lblServer" runat="server" Text="Server"
            ClientIDMode="Static">
        </asp:Label>
        <br />
        <br />
        <input id="btnClient" type="button" value="Client"
            onclick="return btnClient_onclick()" />   
        <asp:Label ID="lblClient"
            runat="server" Text="Client" ClientIDMode="Static">
            </asp:Label>
        <br />
        <br />
</asp:Content>
```

Finally, look at the `Default.aspx.vb` page. In the code for the `OnClick` event of the btnServer control, you set the text of the label to `Changed`:

```
Partial Class _Default
    Inherits System.Web.UI.Page

    Protected Sub btnServer_Click(ByVal sender As Object, _
        ByVal e As System.EventArgs) Handles btnServer.Click
        lblServer.Text = "Changed"
    End Sub

End Class
```

You have completed your first ASP.NET page. In this exercise, you saw a few basic controls and learned that client and server code are handled differently. In the next section, you will learn where you can host websites with Visual Studio 2010.

Website Locations with VS 2010

When you create a new site, you have a choice of locations for the site. The example in this chapter uses the File System location for the website, as shown in Figure 18-5. One advantage of this location is that the web server is not accessible to external users.

There are three other ways to work with website projects, as you can see in the left panel of the Choose Location window. The first is using local IIS (see Figure 18-6).

If you have a local web server, you can host your application there. This allows others to see the site and test it. The second option is to use an FTP site. In this case, you are most likely using a hosting company. All you have to do is add the location and authentication information, and you can code your application on the production server. You can see the setup screen for an FTP site in Figure 18-7.

The final option is a Remote Site. Again, this also may be used when you use a hosting company. If your hosting company supports FrontPage Extensions, you can use this option, as shown in Figure 18-8.

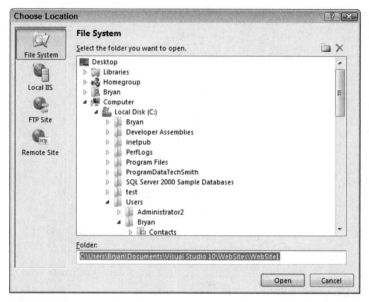

FIGURE 18-5

FIGURE 18-6

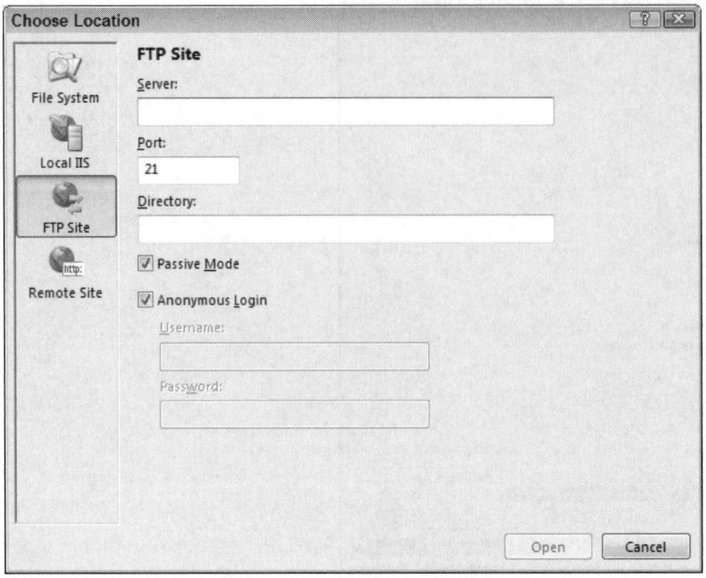

FIGURE 18-7

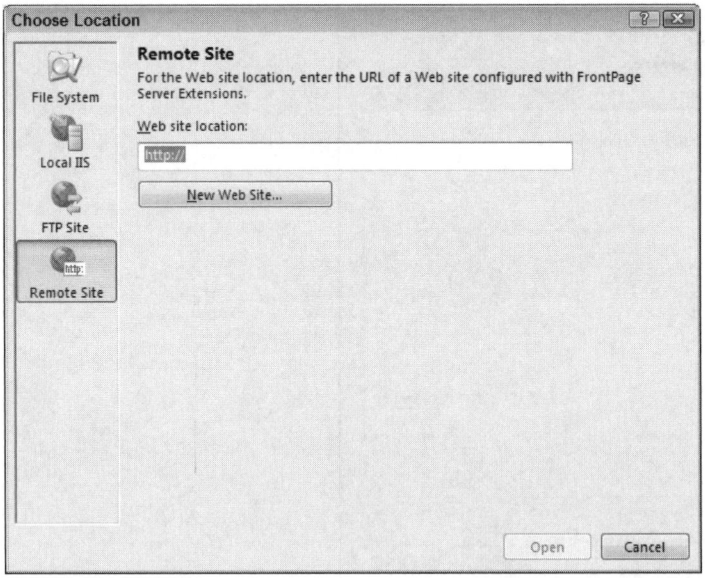

FIGURE 18-8

Performing Data Entry and Validation

One of the basic functions of almost every website is to gather some kind of information from the user. You have undoubtedly seen screens that have links such as Contact Us or Create an Account. Anywhere you see a text box on a web page, data entry and validation are probably taking place.

TRY IT OUT Data Entry and Validation

Code file DataEntry.zip is available for download at Wrox.com

In this Try It Out, you learn the basics of using built-in validation controls and accessing the data the user enters into the web page.

1. Create a new website located on the file system and name it **DataEntry** by choosing File ⇨ New Web Site from the menu.

2. Add four labels, three text boxes, and one button to the `Default.aspx` page. Make sure you use server controls from the Standard tab of the Toolbox. You need to remove the default content as you did in the previous example. Select each control you added and use the Format menu to set each control's positioning to Absolute (under Format, select Set Position ⇨ Absolute). Finally, align the controls to resemble Figure 18-9.

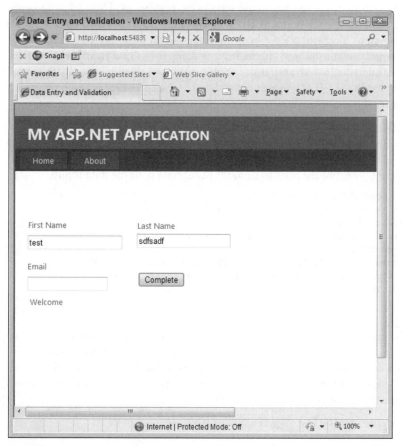

FIGURE 18-9

3. Set the properties of the eight controls and the document. You may want to use the Source view to make the changes to the control properties, as it is easier to make changes in this mode.

> ➤ Set the `Title` of the `Document` to **Data Entry and Validation**.

> ➤ Set the `ID` of the `Button` to **btnComplete** and the `Text` to **Complete**.

> ➤ Set the `ID` of the upper-left `TextBox` to **txtFirstName**.

> ➤ Set the `ID` of the upper-right `TextBox` to **txtLastName**.

> ➤ Set the `ID` of the lower `TextBox` to **txtEmail**.

> ➤ Set the `Text` of the upper-left `Label` to **First Name**.

> ➤ Set the `Text` of the upper- right `Label` to **Last Name**.

> ➤ Set the `Text` of the middle `Label` to **Email**.

> ➤ Set the `Text` of the lower `Label` to **Welcome** and the `ID` to **lblWelcome**.

4. Test the page by pressing Ctrl+F5. When the page opens, you will test three items. First, enter your name and e-mail address and then click the Complete button. The page will post back to the server, and the HTML returned will still have your data in the text boxes. This is default behavior known as *view state*. Second, type the text **<SCRIPT>alert "Hi"</SCRIPT>** into the First Name text box and click Complete. You will see the error message shown in Figure 18-10. ASP.NET has a feature called *request validation* that checks for any dangerous input from the user unless you explicitly turn it off. Finally, test the tab order. You can control the tab order by the order in which the controls appear in the HTML source or by the `TabIndex` property on each control. You can change the tab order if it is not correct.

5. It is time to do something with the data the user enters. First, you need to open the code-behind page. The easiest way to do this is to press F7. Next, add an event handler for page load. To do this, select (Page Events) from the Objects combo box on the left and `Load` from the Events combo box. Add the following bolded code to update `lblWelcome` with the data input:

```
Protected Sub Page_Load(ByVal sender As Object, _
        ByVal e As System.EventArgs) Handles Me.Load
    If Page.IsPostBack Then
        `If this is a postback and not the initial page load
        `Display the data to the user
        Me.lblWelcome.Text = `Hello" + Me.txtFirstName.Text + ` " + _
        Me.txtLastName.Text + `<BR>" + `Your email address is" + _
        Me.txtEmail.Text
    End If
End Sub
```

6. Add validation to the input. Visual Studio has built-in controls just for this. To see the controls, switch to `Default.aspx`. From the Toolbox, select the Validation tab, which includes prebuilt controls to assist with data validation. Add two RequiredFieldValidator controls and one ValidationSummary control to the form. Use the Format ➪ Set Postion menu to set each control's positioning to absolute. Align the controls similar to Figure 18-12.

Set the following properties for the first `RequiredFieldValidator`:

> ➤ Set `ID` to **rfvFirstName**.

> ➤ Set `Display` to **None**.

➤ Set `ControlToValidate` to **txtFirstName**.

➤ Set `ErrorMessage` to **First name is required.**

Set the following properties for the second `RequiredFieldValidator`:

➤ Set `ID` to **rfvEmail**.

➤ Set `Display` to **None**.

➤ Set `ControlToValidate` to **txtEmail**.

➤ Set `ErrorMessage` to **Email is required.**

➤ Set ValidationSummary's ID to **ValidationSummary.**

Your page should look like Figure 18-11 when you finish.

FIGURE 18-10

7. Run your project and try to submit blank entries for first name and e-mail. You will see two error messages similar to those displayed in Figure 18-12.

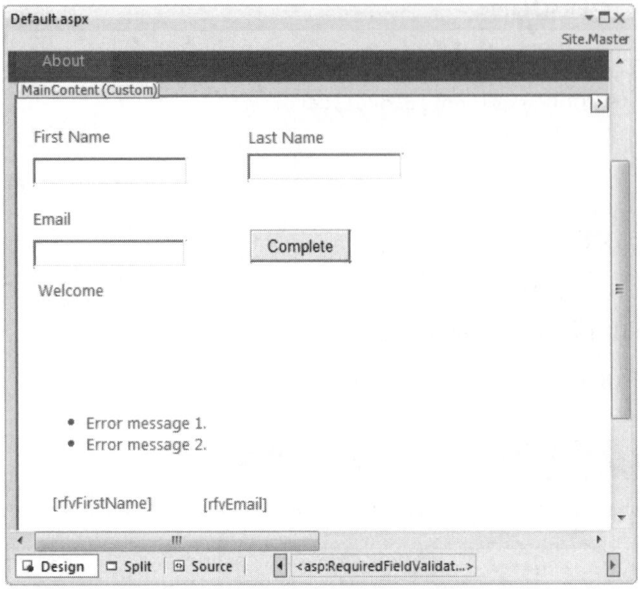

FIGURE 18-11

> **NOTE** *This quick example explains how easy data validation is in ASP 4.0. Other controls are available for enforcing data validation. The CompareValidator control tests a control to ensure that it matches a value. This value can be a constant, another control, or even a value from a data store. RangeValidator tests whether a value is within a specified range. For example, you can test to ensure that a person is between 18 and 35 years old.*

How It Works

Without writing any code, you are able to require that data entry fields are completed on a web page. You take advantage of controls already created for quick and hearty data validation.

You use the RequiredFieldValidator control to make sure the user entered data. You set a couple of properties on the control. You set the ErrorMessage to a string that displays in the ValidationSummary control. Setting Display="None" causes the error message not to be shown inside of the RequiredField-Validator control. The required property, ControlToValidate, is set to the ID of the control that was required.

```
<asp:RequiredFieldValidator ID="rfvFirstName" display="None"
    ControlToValidate="txtFirstName" runat="server"
    ErrorMessage="First name is required."
    style="z-index: 1; left: 37px; top: 478px;
    position: absolute"></asp:RequiredFieldValidator>
```

NOTE *The style attribute is added by Visual Studio when using absolute positioning. With absolute positioning, you can drag and drop controls where you want them.*

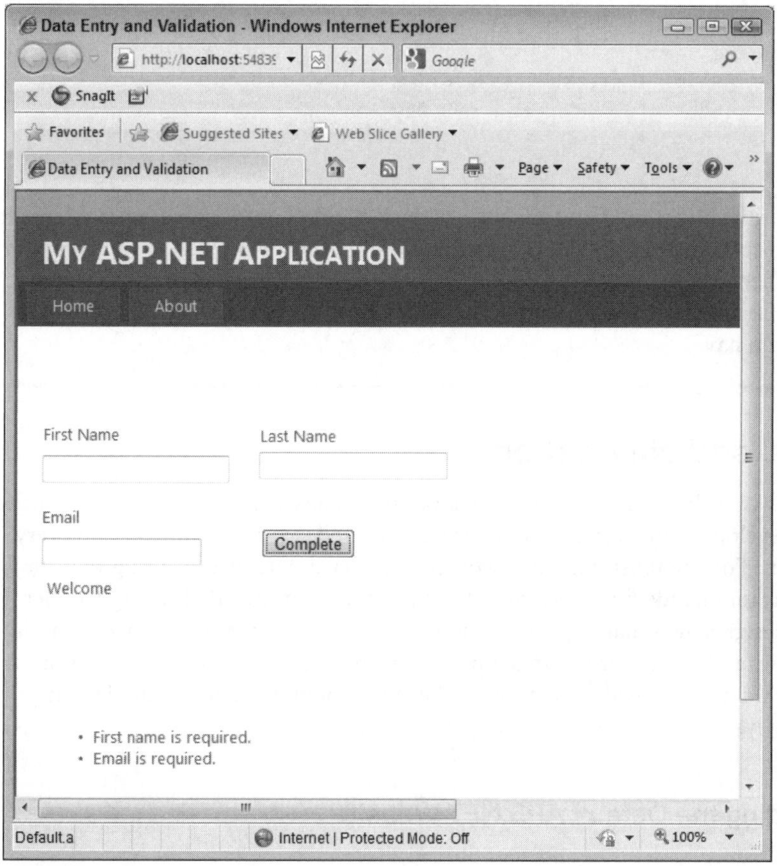

FIGURE 18-12

You use the ValidationSummary control as a central location for displaying all error messages. If you decide not to use a summary object, you could set the Display property of the individual validation controls to Static or Dynamic. That way, the error messages are displayed within the validation control. No property changes are needed to use the ValidationSummary control. You just add it to the form at the location you want to display validation messages.

```
<asp:ValidationSummary ID="ValidationSummary" runat="server"
    style="z-index: 1; left: 25px; top: 414px;
    position: absolute;
    height: 34px;     width: 920px" />
```

The only code you write is added to the Page_Load event. Here, you tested for a postback using the IsPostBack property of the Page object. If it was a postback, you display the name and e-mail entered by the user. You can still use the Page_Load event in VS 2010. To insert the event automatically, go into design view on the aspx page and double-click on the page (not on any controls). The event will be generated and you will be brought to the new event in the code-behind.

```
If Page.IsPostBack Then
    `If this is a post back and not the initial page load
    `Display the data to the user
    Me.lblWelcome.Text = `Hello" + Me.txtFirstName.Text + ` " + _
    Me.txtLastName.Text + `<BR>" + `Your email address is" + _
    Me.txtEmail.Text
End If
```

There are more controls to help with validation. Controls such as the RangeValidator can be used to ensure that the value entered is within a specified range. The CompareValidator control enables you to compare the value of one control to another or to a constant. For more complex validation there are two other controls: CustomValidator and RegularExpressionValidator. With these, you can basically handle any type of validation requirement you have.

Site Layout, Themes, and Navigation

In the past, a major drawback of web development was maintaining a consistent design across an entire site in a manageable way. Developers created user controls and inserted server-side includes in every page to try to accomplish this. For the most part, this worked. The hard part was ensuring that the opening tags that were in certain include files were closed in the pages that included them. Another cause of frustration for the designer was making sure all user controls or include files displayed in the same location. This took time, and with every changed page, someone had to make sure the entire site looked OK. Today, Visual Studio provides the tools you need to maintain a consistent layout for design, navigation, and security.

TRY IT OUT   **Understanding the Default APS.NET Website**

Code file DefaultSite.zip is available for download at Wrox.com

Login controls, navigation controls, and master pages are the tools to accomplish a consistent website. You will learn about all three in this Try It Out.

1.   Create a new site and name the project **DefaultSite**. When the site is created, it is set up with most if not all of your basic needs. If you take a look at the site features, you will see login capability, a common design theme, and a menu system. This basic site is all you need to have your own site ready in no time.

2.   Run the site and click on the links, register and login. That's a lot of functionality; let's go through the highlights.

How It Works

As you have seen in other parts of Visual Studio, you can do a lot with built-in tools. When you create a new ASP.NET site, the site includes the most common functionality, such as a menu, a login module, and master pages. All you have to do is go in and modify these to work the way you want them to. First, let's look at the master page and what it contains.

Master pages are the key to a consistent look and feel for your websites. By defining a common look and feel, developers of other pages will not be able to change their appearance when creating the new pages (they will inherit your specified look and feel). When creating a new page, you have access to update the ContentPlaceHolders. This makes it easy to add pages and just focus on their content, and not worry about other areas of the website being affected.

Take a look at the `Site.master` page created by default. This example focuses on a couple of important items in the source. At the top you will see some required HTML. As a developer, you will be able to leave most of this alone. Let's go through each part of the basic HTML briefly.

The next line in the source code is the `!DOCTYPE` element. This tells IE6 and later that the document conforms to the XHTML 1.0 Document Type Definition (DTD) specified by the W3C for English:

```
<!DOCTYPE html PUBLIC "-//W3C//DTD XHTML 1.0 Strict//EN"
    "http://www.w3.org/TR/xhtml1/DTD/xhtml1-strict.dtd">
```

The actual HTML root element is next. You will see this element with no attributes set in many instances. Here VS has specified that the namespace for custom tags will be `http://www.w3.org/1999/xhtml`. If you browse to this site, you will see that this is the XHTML namespace defined by the W3C. `xml:lang="en"` tells the browser the content is in English:

```
<html xmlns="http://www.w3.org/1999/xhtml" xml:lang="en">
```

After the root HTML element is the HEAD element. Children of this element are items that are not rendered, but they may affect how the page is displayed. You will place SCRIPT, META, TITLE, LINK, STYLE, and other elements here to define the page's look and feel.

The first element is TITLE. This is the title the browser displays for the page. Next, a LINK tag tells the browser that there is a cascading style sheet related to this document, and its location. Finally, a Content-PlaceHolder in the HEAD element allows you to add to what you need to each page of the site:

```
Also, Please break the following pink code as it will be broken in production.<!DOCTYPE
    html PUBLIC "-//W3C//DTD XHTML 1.0 Strict//EN"
    "http://www.w3.org/TR/xhtml1/DTD/xhtml1-strict.dtd">
<html xmlns="http://www.w3.org/1999/xhtml" xml:lang="en">
<head runat="server">
    <title></title>
    <link href="~/Styles/Site.css" rel="stylesheet"
        type="text/css" />
    <asp:ContentPlaceHolder ID="HeadContent" runat="server">
    </asp:ContentPlaceHolder>
</head>
```

Next you will see BODY, FORM, DIV and H1 elements or tags. Both tags BODY and FORM are required. The BODY tag contains all HTML content; and all your ASPX controls need to be inside of the FORM tag. These tags are typically not changed except for applying styles. The DIV and H1 are HTML elements for content. These are used for layout along with many other HTML elements. This example does not go into detail about the HTML elements because it's more than we can cover in a chapter. As a developer, you just need to focus on learning the code for this chapter; you can work on the layout as you learn more.

There are three more controls of interest on the master page.

➤ **asp:Menu:** This control has many needed options. You can nest menus that will drop down or appear horizontally when needed. You can also dynamically bind the menu to an XML site map file. Of course, the menu control can be skinned using themes and styles.

➤ **asp:LoginView:** This control is used with other login controls that implement .NET membership for authentication. When a page is rendered, you can display different views to authenticated users versus anonymous users using templates (AnonymousTemplate and LoggedInTemplate). As shown in the default site, a login link or welcome message with logout is a typical use of this control.

➤ **asp:ContentPlaceHolder:** This is for developers to add content to new pages.

TRY IT OUT **The Menu Control**

Code file DefaultSite.zip is available for download at Wrox.com

In this Try It Out, you will see the menu control in more detail.

1. Open the `Site.Master` file in Visual Studio and locate the asp:Menu control. Before making any changes, be sure to run the site and see how the menu functions. By default there are two menu items: Home and About. Add a nested menu after About as shown:

```
<Items>
    <asp:MenuItem NavigateUrl="~/Default.aspx" Text="Home"/>
    <asp:MenuItem NavigateUrl="~/About.aspx" Text="About"/>
    <asp:MenuItem NavigateUrl="~/About.aspx" Text="Test">
        <asp:MenuItem NavigateUrl="~/About.aspx" Text="Submenu" />
    </asp:MenuItem>
</Items>
```

2. Change the menu to be aligned vertically. To do this, change the `Orientation="Horizontal"` to `Orientation="Vertical"` for the asp:Menu control. Refresh the website, and now you will see a vertical menu as shown in Figure 18-13.

How It Works

The built-in menu control is easy to work within your websites. You can go in and manually change the menu items to adjust the varying levels of a simple or complex menu. To add new menus and submenus, you added new menu items with nesting. This added a new test menu that dropped down with a submenu:

```
<asp:MenuItem NavigateUrl="~/About.aspx" Text="Test">
    <asp:MenuItem NavigateUrl="~/About.aspx" Text="Submenu" />
</asp:MenuItem>
```

Next, you converted the menu from a horizontal orientation to a vertical one by changing one property:

```
Orientation="Vertical"
```

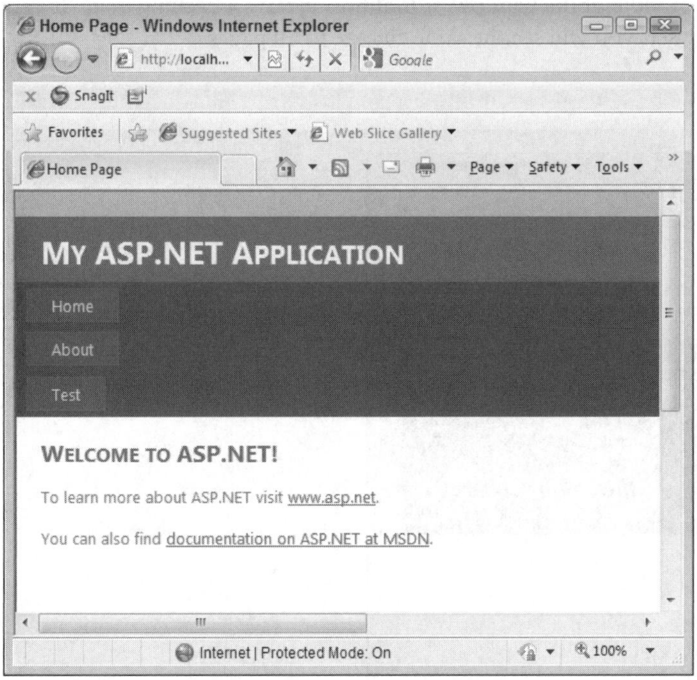

FIGURE 18-13

TRY IT OUT   Master Pages

Code file DefaultSite.zip is available for download at Wrox.com

In this exercise, you will see how quickly you can change the look and feel of a site with CSS (cascading style sheets), master pages, and themes.

1. In the default site, open the `Default.aspx` page in a browser and in Visual Studio. The easy way to view a web page in your solution is to right-click it in Solution Explorer and choose View in Browser.

2. Change the H1 contents from My ASP.NET Application to **Master Pages are easy**. Refresh your web page and you will see what is shown in Figure 18-14. Browse other pages of the site and you will see your new message on all of them.

3. That was a simple demonstration of the power of master pages. Now you will change the location of the login view for the entire site. To accomplish this, go back to the master page in Visual Studio. You will notice that the `DIV` containing the LoginView control has a class of `loginDisplay`. Open `Site.css` under the Styles menu and locate the block for loginDisplay. Once you find it, change the `text-align` attribute from `center` to `middle` and set `color` to `red`. Go back to your browser and press Ctrl+F5 to force a refresh in IE, because the browser will cache the CSS pages and it may be hard to get the latest changes to show in your browser. If you don't see the braces turn red and the login move to the middle of the window, it is almost always a caching issue. If you check other pages in your browser, you will see the same change to all pages.

```
text-align: center;
color: red
```

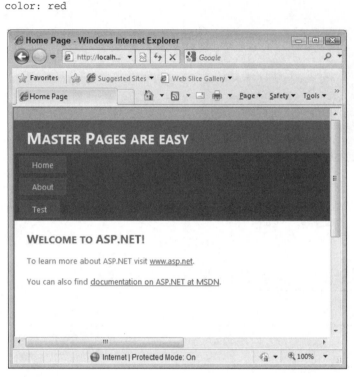

FIGURE 18-14

4. Next, you will add a new content page and apply the same look and feel as the entire site. Right-click the website name in Solution Explorer and choose Add New Item. Select Web Form and give it a name of **News.aspx**. Make sure to check the "Place code in separate file" and "Select master page" check boxes as shown in Figure 18-15. When prompted to select a master page, choose Site.master. You should see that the site design is on the new page already.

5. Add a Button to the ContentPlaceHolder and set its text to **Click Here**. Take a look at your new page in the browser and you will see your changes.

6. The new Button looks fine with the default, but for this site you will add a theme for buttons so all buttons will look the same. In Solution Explorer, right-click the website and choose Add ASP.NET Folder and then click Theme. Visual Studio adds two folders: App_Themes and Theme1. Right-click the Theme1 folder in Solution Explorer and choose Add New Item. In the Add New Item dialog, select Skin File, name it **Button.skin,** and click OK.

7. Your new Skin file will open in the IDE. Add the following code to it:

```
<asp:Button runat="server" BackColor="Black" ForeColor="White" />
```

8. On the `News.aspx` page, add the attribute `Theme` to the `Page` directive at the top and set it to Theme1. After refreshing the browser, you will see a black button with white text. The updated code is as follows:

```
<%@ Page Title="" Language="VB" MasterPageFile="~/Site.master"
    AutoEventWireup="false" CodeFile="News.aspx.vb" Inherits="News"
    Theme="Theme1" %>
```

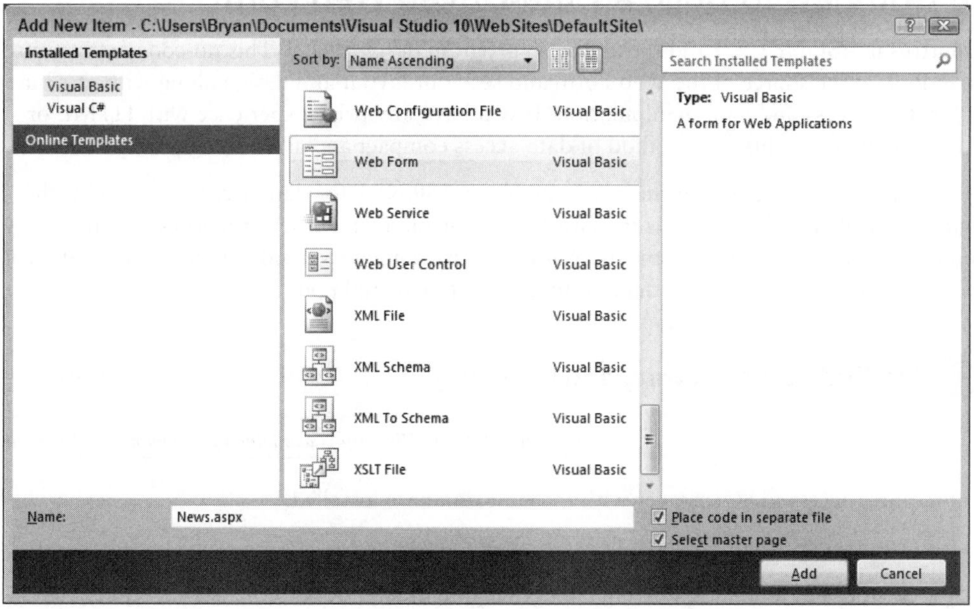

FIGURE 18-15

How It Works

To see how quick it is to change a master page and have it affect the entire site, you updated the page heading to `Master Pages are easy`. Every page on the site that uses that master page will immediately display the change to the end users. This can be a very powerful tool when you set up applications this way for long-term success. Maintaining applications over a few years can be very difficult. Without the use of features like this, a simple change might require a change to every page on the site, which could take days or even weeks. Be sure to take advantage of master pages in your websites.

Next, you used CSS to alter the display properties of the login link. Because it was on the master page, it was changed on every other page also. CSS is very powerful and you can do much more than this with it. Almost any property that affects how an object looks in a browser can be changed via CSS. Even a global change such as changing all the text in every `DIV` tag can be done using a simple block of CSS. Here, you used a class that defined the scope of the CSS. Instead of a class, you could have used `DIV`, and all `DIV` tags would have been affected.

You can apply the master page to any new page to give it the look and feel of the site instantly. In this case, you applied the `Site.master` to the `News.aspx` page you added.

Themes are similar to CSS. You can apply skins to server controls and package them together as a theme. Then you apply the theme at the page level as shown in this example or you can apply it globally. You can make up new themes and just by changing that one property give the entire site a fresh new look.

Using the GridView to Build a Data-Driven Web Form

The data controls in ASP.NET 2.0 add the ability to program *declaratively*. This no-code architecture allows you to look at the source of the Web Form and see your layout and design along with attributes that allow for data access and data manipulation. If you have any prior experience with HTML or ASP.NET 1.1, you will find this new method of data access compact and astoundingly simple.

In this Try It Out, you will see two of the best controls in ASP.NET for data access. The first is the SqlDataSource control, and the second is the GridView control. You will set properties and attributes of these controls and also their child elements. Without writing any server-side or client-side code, you will create a web application to display data in the pubs database and update it.

TRY IT OUT   No-Code Data Viewing and Updating

Code file DataGridView.zip is available for download at Wrox.com

This Try It Out requires access to SQL Server with the pubs database installed.

1. Create a new empty website and name it **DataGridView**. Add a `Default.aspx` web form.

2. Use the Source view and add the following changes highlighted in bold to the `Default.aspx` page. Be sure to change the values of the ConnectionString to match your development environment.

```
<%@ Page Language="VB" AutoEventWireup="false"
CodeFile="Default.aspx.vb" Inherits="_Default" %>
<!DOCTYPE html PUBLIC "-//W3C//DTD XHTML 1.0 Transitional//EN"
"http://www.w3.org/TR/xhtml1/DTD/xhtml1-transitional.dtd">
<html xmlns="http://www.w3.org/1999/xhtml"> <head runat="server">
<head runat="server">
    <title>Grid View</title>
</head>
<body>
<form id="form1" runat="server">
<div>
    <asp:SqlDataSource ID="sdsAuthors" Runat="server"
                    ProviderName = "System.Data.SqlClient"
                    ConnectionString = "Server=localhost\wrox; User ID=sa;
                    Password=wrox;Database=pubs;"
                    SelectCommand = "SELECT au_id, au_lname,
                    au_fname, phone,
                    address, city, state, zip FROM authors"
                    UpdateCommand = "UPDATE authors
                    SET au_lname = @au_lname,
                    au_fname = @au_fname, phone = @phone,
```

```
                        address = @address,
                        city = @city, state = @state, zip = @zip
                        WHERE au_id = @au_id" >
    </asp:SqlDataSource>

    <asp:GridView ID="gdvAuthors" Runat="server"
     DataSourceID="sdsAuthors" AllowPaging="True" AllowSorting="True"
     AutoGenerateColumns="false" DataKeyNames="au_id" >
        <PagerStyle BackColor="Gray" ForeColor="White"
          HorizontalAlign="Center" />
        <HeaderStyle BackColor="Black" ForeColor="White" />
        <AlternatingRowStyle BackColor="LightGray" />
        <Columns>
          <asp:CommandField ButtonType="Button" ShowEditButton="true" />
          <asp:BoundField Visible="false" HeaderText="au_id"
                          DataField="au_id" SortExpression="au_id">
                          </asp:BoundField>
          <asp:BoundField HeaderText="Last Name" DataField="au_lname"
                          SortExpression="au_lname"></asp:BoundField>
           <asp:BoundField HeaderText="First Name" DataField="au_fname"
                          SortExpression="au_fname"></asp:BoundField>
          <asp:BoundField HeaderText="Phone" DataField="phone"
                          SortExpression="phone"></asp:BoundField>
          <asp:BoundField HeaderText="Address" DataField="address"
                          SortExpression="address"></asp:BoundField>
          <asp:BoundField HeaderText="City" DataField="city"
                          SortExpression="city"></asp:BoundField>
          <asp:BoundField HeaderText="State" DataField="state"
                          SortExpression="state"></asp:BoundField>
          <asp:BoundField HeaderText="Zip Code" DataField="zip"
                          SortExpression="zip"></asp:BoundField>
        </Columns>
      </asp:GridView>
  </div>
  </form>
  </body>
  </html>
```

3. Run the application without debugging by pressing Ctrl+F5. You will see a data grid display similar to the one shown in Figure 18-16.

4. Test the functions of the grid. At the bottom, you can move to any page of the data. In addition, sorting is available by clicking any of the column headers. After trying both of these, update a row. To edit an author's data, click the Edit button on the left of the author's row. The screen refreshes, and you will see a new grid that looks like the one in Figure 18-17.

Change any field and click the Update button to make the change permanent. You can cancel a change by clicking any link or button other than the Update button.

How It Works

Now that was easy. By adding two controls, you created a fairly robust data access page. We'll explain how this happened.

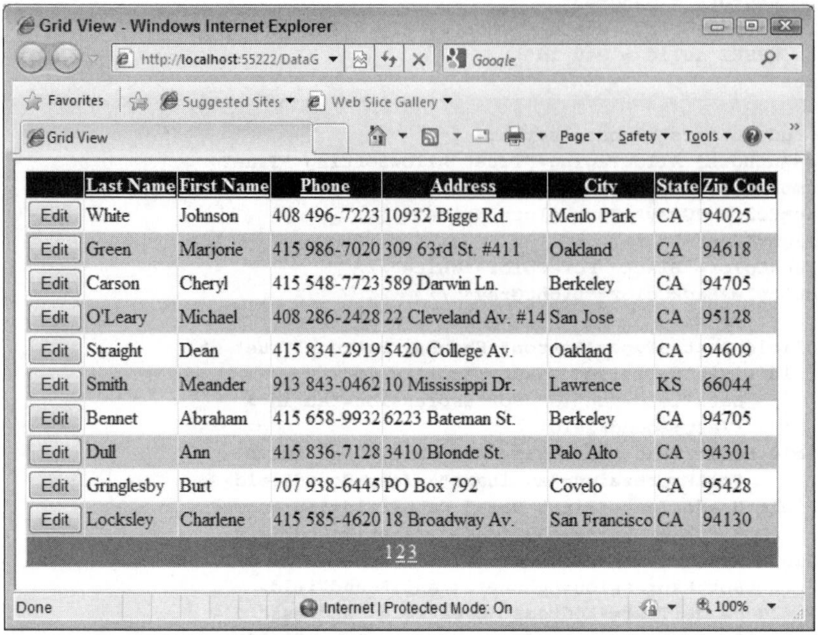

FIGURE 18-16

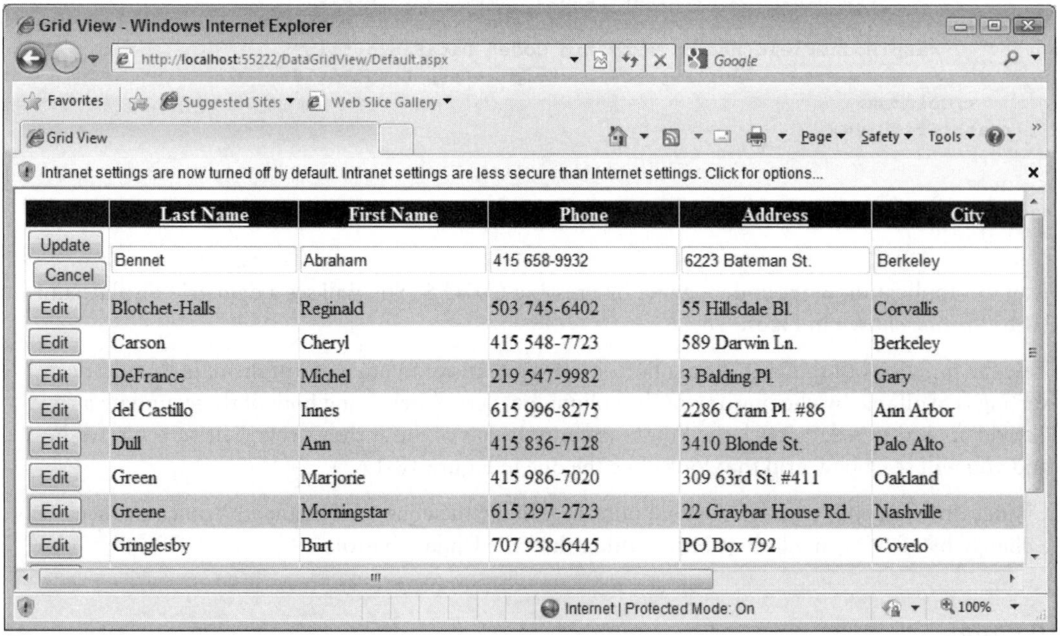

FIGURE 18-17

First, you create the SqlDataSource control. Table 18-1 explains each attribute you add or change for the SqlDataSource control.

TABLE 18-1: SqlDataSource Controls

ATTRIBUTE OR ELEMENT	DESCRIPTION
ID	The control's identifier
Runat	Specifies that the code for the control is run at the server before the page is sent to the browser
ProviderName	Used to set the provider to access the data store. In this case, it is `System.Data.SqlClient`, the managed provider for SQL Server.
ConnectionString	This string value is used to gain access to the database resource, pubs.
SelectCommand	The SQL statement passed to the database to retrieve the data that is displayed in the grid. This could be a stored procedure name.
UpdateCommand	The SQL statement that is used to update the data. You could use a stored procedure name in place of the SQL statement in this case.

The code follows:

```
<asp:SqlDataSource ID="sdsAuthors" Runat="server"
                   ProviderName = "System.Data.SqlClient"
                   ConnectionString = "Server=localhost\wrox;
                   User ID=sa;
                   Password=wrox;Database=pubs;"
                   SelectCommand = "SELECT au_id, au_lname,
                   au_fname, phone,
                   address, city, state, zip FROM authors"
                   UpdateCommand = "UPDATE authors
                   SET au_lname = @au_lname,
                   au_fname = @au_fname, phone = @phone,
                   address = @address,
                   city = @city, state = @state, zip = @zip
                   WHERE au_id = @au_id" >
</asp:SqlDataSource>
```

The second control you add to the form is the GridView. Its attributes are described in Table 18-2.

The GridView control code is as follows:

```
<asp:GridView ID="gdvAuthors" Runat="server"
 DataSourceID="sdsAuthors" AllowPaging="True"
 AllowSorting="True"
 AutoGenerateColumns="false" DataKeyNames="au_id" >
   <PagerStyle BackColor="Gray" ForeColor="White"
     HorizontalAlign="Center" />
```

```
      <HeaderStyle BackColor="Black" ForeColor="White" />
      <AlternatingRowStyle BackColor="LightGray" />
      <Columns>
        <asp:CommandField ButtonType="Button"
            ShowEditButton="true" />
        <asp:BoundField Visible="false" HeaderText="au_id"
            DataField="au_id" SortExpression="au_id">
            </asp:BoundField>
        <asp:BoundField HeaderText="Last Name"
            DataField="au_lname"
            SortExpression="au_lname"></asp:BoundField>
         <asp:BoundField HeaderText="First Name"
            DataField="au_fname"
            SortExpression="au_fname"></asp:BoundField>
         <asp:BoundField HeaderText="Phone" DataField="phone"
            SortExpression="phone"></asp:BoundField>
         <asp:BoundField HeaderText="Address" DataField="address"
            SortExpression="address"></asp:BoundField>
         <asp:BoundField HeaderText="City" DataField="city"
            SortExpression="city"></asp:BoundField>
         <asp:BoundField HeaderText="State" DataField="state"
            SortExpression="state"></asp:BoundField>
         <asp:BoundField HeaderText="Zip Code" DataField="zip"
            SortExpression="zip"></asp:BoundField>
      </Columns>
    </asp:GridView>
```

TABLE 18-2: GridView Attributes

ATTRIBUTE OR ELEMENT	DESCRIPTION
ID	The control's identifier.
Runat	Defines that the code for the control is run at the server before the page is sent to the browser.
DataSourceID	The ID of the SqlDataSource object is used here.
AllowPaging	Can be set to True or False. Turns on paging features of the grid.
AllowSorting	Can be set to True or False. Turns on sorting features of the grid.
AutoGenerateColumns	Can be set to True or False. Determines how the GridView creates the columns automatically.
DataKeyNames	The primary key used by the database table.
PagerStyle	This element defines the style of the paging area of the grid.
HeaderStyle	This element defines the style of the header row area of the grid.
AlternatingRowStyle	This element defines the style of the every other row of the grid.

TABLE 18-2 (*continued*)

ATTRIBUTE OR ELEMENT	DESCRIPTION
`Columns`	A collection of column objects.
`asp:CommandField`	Two properties of this object are used. The first is `ButtonType`. This is set to a type of button. You can insert a button, image, or link as a value. If left blank, the default is link.
`BoundField`	This element allows for the binding of the data to the grid. For a better user interface, you use the `Visible` property to hide the primary key column. Also, you set the `SortExpression` of each column. This converts every column header to a link. When clicked, the data is sorted by that column. Next, you change the column headers with the `HeaderText` property. If this is blank, the column names are used as headers. Finally, the field to bind to is set using the `DataField` property.

SUMMARY

In this chapter, you learned what thin-client development is. You saw the advantages of Web Forms and Windows Forms and why you would choose one type of application over the other. Maybe the low distribution cost of web applications is a major factor in your decision to create a web application over a Windows application.

You also learned about the basic pieces that constitute a typical web application. From layout and formatting to database integration, you gained knowledge of the best features of ASP.NET and how they are implemented. Finally, you designed a code-free page that updated data in a database.

If you like web development, there is much more to learn than can be explained in one chapter. To continue learning, we recommend navigating to Wrox.com and clicking the ASP.NET link to find more resources to take you to the next level of web development.

You should know how to:

➤   Choose between Web Forms and Windows Forms applications to suit your purpose

➤   Use the toolbox for ASP.NET

➤   Create a Web Site project in Visual Studio 2010

➤   Handle client and server web form events

➤   Use built-in controls for data validation

➤   Choose between the possible locations for websites in Visual Studio 2010

➤   Decide when to use themes, master pages, CSS, and the Menu control

➤   Use a GridView and a SqlDataSource to read and update data in a SQL database

EXERCISES

1. If you wanted to build a design and layout that can be inherited by Web Form pages, how would you do it?

2. To change the way elements of the page appear, you have two good options when designing web pages. What are they?

3. What type of data source do you bind the menu control to?

4. What property do you set to have static client IDs for server controls?

5. Name one control you can use to help validate form data.

▶ **WHAT YOU HAVE LEARNED IN THIS CHAPTER**

TOPIC	CONCEPTS
Client and server events	Some events (client) are handled by the browser while others (server) are handled by the web server.
Data Validation	In ASP.NET, you can use built in validation controls to ensure your user input is valid.
Website layout and design.	Use master pages, themes, CSS and the Menu control to design your site.
Accessing data on the web	You can use the GridView control to bring your data to the web.

19

Visual Basic 2010 and XML

WHAT YOU WILL LEARN IN THIS CHAPTER:

➤ Gain a deeper understanding of XML and what it looks like

➤ Learn how to read and write XML files

➤ Learn how to serialize and deserialize XML data

➤ Learn how to navigate through an XML document

➤ Learn how to change existing XML data and add new data to an XML document

Put simply, Extensible Markup Language (XML) is used for exchanging data between applications. Although it has been around for some time, XML has established itself as the de facto data exchange standard for Internet applications. Today, XML is used not only on the Internet, but also to exchange data between many different platforms and applications.

In this chapter, you are not going to get bogged down in the details regarding XML, such as its validation and well-formedness. Instead, you get a general introduction to XML, and then you look at its role with Visual Basic 2010. After that, you focus on using XML inside an application.

UNDERSTANDING XML

The need for XML is simple: In commercial environments, applications need to exchange information in order to integrate. This integration is more applicable to the line-of-business software that a company may have, rather than to desktop productivity applications such as Microsoft Office. For example, a company may have invested in a piece of software that enables it to track the stock in its warehouse — that piece of software would be an example of line-of-business software.

In the past, integration has been very difficult to achieve, and XML, together with web services, represents technologies designed to reduce the difficulty and cost involved in software integration. In reducing the difficulty of software integration, there is an add-on benefit in terms of the ease with which more general data/information exchange can occur.

For example, imagine you are a coffee retailer who wants to place an order with a supplier. The old-school technique of doing this is to phone or fax your order. However, this introduces a human element into the equation. It is likely that your own line-of-business applications (telling you what products you have sold) are suggesting that you buy more of a certain machine or certain blend of coffee. From that suggestion, you formulate an order and transmit it to your supplier. In the case of phone or fax orders, a human being at the supplier then has to transcribe the order into his or her own line-of-business system for processing.

An alternative way of carrying out this order would be to get the suggestion that has been raised by your line-of-business system to create an order automatically in the remote system of your supplier. This makes life easier and more efficient for both you and the management of your chosen supplier. However, getting to a point where the two systems are integrated in this way requires a lot of negotiation, coordination, and cost. Thus, it is more relevant for people who do a lot of business with each other.

Before the Internet, for two companies to integrate in this way, specific negotiations had to be undertaken to set up some sort of proprietary connection between the two companies. With the connection in place, data is exchanged not only in order to place the order with the supplier, but also for the supplier to report the status of the order back to the customer. With the Internet, this proprietary connection is no longer required. As long as both parties are on the Internet, data exchange can take place.

However, without a common language on which this data exchange can be based, the problem is only half solved. XML is this common language. As the customer, you can create an XML document that contains the details of the order. You can use the Internet to transmit that order written in XML to the supplier, either over the Web, through e-mail, or by using web services. The supplier receives the XML document, decodes it, and raises the order in their system. Likewise, if the supplier needs to report anything back to the customer, they can construct a different document (again using XML), and use the Internet to transmit it back again.

The actual structure of the data contained within the XML document is up to the customer and supplier to decide. (Usually it's for the supplier to decide upon and the customer to adhere to.) This is where the *extensible* in XML comes in. Any two parties who wish to exchange data using XML are completely free to decide exactly what the documents should look like.

This does not sound amazing, because companies in the past and even today still use comma-separated files. These files had a format and worked similarly, so what does XML have that the previous formats did not?

XML is a lot more descriptive, and it can be validated against a schema. A *schema* defines what the XML document or fragment should look like. Even without a schema, XML can potentially describe itself well enough for others to ascertain what the data is. In line with the benefits of previous file formats, XML is also a text-based format. This means that XML can be moved between platforms using Internet technologies such as e-mail, the Web, FTP, and other file copy techniques. Traditional software integration was difficult when binary data had to be moved between platforms such as Windows, Unix, Macintosh, AS/400, or OS/390, so the fact that XML is text-based makes it easier to send data across platforms.

What Does XML Look Like?

If you have any experience with HTML, XML is going to look familiar to you. In fact, both have a common ancestor in Standard Generalized Markup Language (SGML). In many ways, XML is not a language, as the name suggests, but rather a set of rules for *defining your own* markup languages that enable the exchange of data. XML is not a stand-alone technology either; in fact, a great many different related specifications dictate what you can and cannot do with XML. Such specifications include the following (not the best late-night reading, at least if you want to be an alert and attentive reader):

- ➤ URIs (Uniform Resource Identifiers): `www.ietf.org/rfc/rfc2396.txt`
- ➤ UTF-8 (Unicode Transformation Format): `www.utf-8.com/`
- ➤ XML (Extensible Markup Language): `www.w3.org/TR/REC-xml`
- ➤ XML Schema: `www.w3.org/XML/Schema`
- ➤ XML Information Set: `www.w3.org/TR/xml-infoset/`

Although the specifications may not beat a book such as this in terms of format, layout, and ease of understanding, they have a lot to offer the XML fan. If you feel up to it, you can read more about XML after this introduction.

XML is tag-based, meaning the document is made up of *tags* that contain data. Here is how you might choose to describe this book in XML:

```
<Book>
    <Title>Beginning VB 2010</Title>
    <ISBN>xxxx502228</ISBN>
    <Publisher>Wrox</Publisher>
</Book>
```

In XML, you delimit tags using the < and > symbols. There are two sorts of tags: start tags such as `<Title>`, and end tags such as `</Title>`. Together, the tags and the content between them are known as an *element*. In the previous example, the `Title` element is written like this:

```
<Title>Beginning VB 2010</Title>
```

The `ISBN` element looks like this:

```
<ISBN>xxxx502228</ISBN>
```

And the `Publisher` element looks like this:

```
<Publisher>Wrox</Publisher>
```

Note that elements can contain other elements. In this case, for example, the `Book` element contains three sub-elements:

```
<Book>
    <Title>Beginning VB 2010</Title>
```

```
    <ISBN>xxxx502228</ISBN>
    <Publisher>Wrox</Publisher>
</Book>
```

> **NOTE** The structure formed by elements nested inside other elements can also be represented as a tree with, for example, Title, ISBN, and Publisher as branches from the root Book. Therefore, terms such as node, parent, and child are often used instead of element.

If you were given this XML document, you would need to have an understanding of its structure. Usually, the company that designed the structure of the document will tell you what it looks like. In this case, someone might tell you that if you first look for the Book element and then the Title element, you will determine the title of the book. The value between the <Title> start tag and the </Title> end tag is the title (in this case, Beginning VB 2010.)

As in HTML, XML can also use what are known as attributes. An *attribute* is a named piece of information descriptive to the node (element) wherein it is located. When you use attributes, you must enclose them in quotes. Here is the same XML fragment as the previous one, but this time using attributes:

```
<Book>
        <Title ISBN="xxxx502228">Beginning VB 2010</Title>
    <Publisher>Wrox</Publisher>
    </Book>
```

XML is largely common sense, which is one of the things that make it so simple. For example, you can probably guess what the following document represents, even though you may have only just started thinking about XML:

```
<Books>
   <Book>
      <Title>Beginning VB 2010</Title>
      <ISBN>xxxx502228</ISBN>
      <Publisher>Wrox</Publisher>
   </Book>
   <Book>
      <Title>Professional Visual Basic.Net</Title>
      <ISBN>1861005555</ISBN>
      <Publisher>Wrox</Publisher>
   </Book>
</Books>
```

XML for Visual Basic Newcomers

As a newcomer to programming and Visual Basic, it is unlikely that you will be undertaking projects that involve complex integration work. If XML is so popular because it makes systems integration so much easier, how is it relevant to a newcomer?

The answer to this question is that, in addition to being a great tool for integration, XML is also a great tool for storage and general data organization. Before XML, the two ways that an application could store its data were by using a separate database or by having its own proprietary file format with code that could save into and read from it.

In many cases, a database is absolutely the right tool for the job, because you need the fast access, shared storage, and advanced searching facilities that a database such as Access or SQL Server gives you. In other cases, such as with a graphics package or word processor, building your own proprietary format is the right way to go. The reasons for this will vary — for example, you may want the application to be light and you don't want the hassle of showing users how to set up and maintain a database, or you simply don't want to deal with the licensing implications of needing a separate application to support yours.

XML gives you a new way of storing application data, although it is still based on the concept of defining your own proprietary application storage format. The key difference, in contrast to formats such as .doc files for Word documents, however, is that the XML storage format is a universal standard.

The Rules

There are some simple rules to learn when using XML. Master these and you will be ready to go:

➤ All XML elements must have a closing tag.

➤ XML tags are case sensitive.

➤ XML elements must be properly nested.

➤ XML documents must have a root element

➤ XML attribute values must be quoted.

➤ Special characters must be encoded

    ➤ < should be <

    ➤ > should be >

    ➤ ' should be '

    ➤ " should be "

    ➤ & should be &

THE ADDRESS BOOK PROJECT

You're going to build a demonstration application that enables you to create an XML file format for an address book. You'll be able to create a list of new addresses and save the whole lot as an XML file on your local disk. You'll also be able to load the XML file and walk through the addresses one by one.

Creating the Project

As always, the first thing you have to do is create a new project.

TRY IT OUT   Creating the Project

Code file address book.zip is available for download at Wrox.com

In this Try It Out, you will create the project and lay out the form.

1.   Open Visual Studio 2010 and select File ⇨ New Project from the menu. Create a new Visual Basic .NET Windows Forms Application project and name it **Address Book**.

2.   The Forms Designer for Form1 will open. Change its Text property to **Address Book**. Then add 10 text boxes, 12 labels, and a button to the form so that it looks like Figure 19-1.

For a quick way to create the form, add one label and one text box aligned properly at the top of the form. Select both of these controls by holding down the left mouse button and then dragging the mouse over both the label and text box. Make sure the mouse pointer is not on a control or you will just move the control. When you release the left mouse button, both controls will be selected. Also, you can right-click on each of the controls while pressing the Ctrl or Shift key to select them.

Once you have them both selected, you can copy and paste them by pressing Ctrl+C and then Ctrl+V. You will now have a copy of the controls aligned toward the center of the form. If you press Ctrl+Up Arrow while the controls are selected, they will move up and align to the other controls. You can use Ctrl+Down Arrow at the end of the controls to move the controls down.

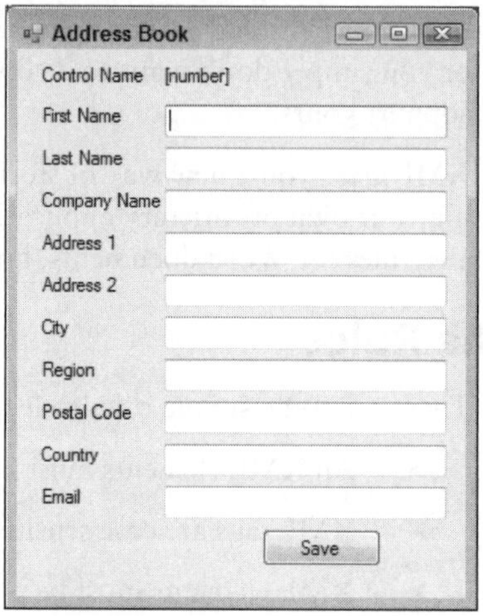

FIGURE 19-1

3.   The text boxes should be named as follows:

   1.   txtFirstName

   2.   txtLastName

   3.   txtCompanyName

   4.   txtAddress1

   5.   txtAddress2

   6.   txtCity

   7.   txtRegion

   8.   txtPostalCode

   9.   txtCountry

 10.   txtEmail

4.   Set the text properties of the labels and button to match Figure 19-1.

5. The button should be named **btnSave**. Finally, the Label control marked (number) should be called **lblAddressNumber**.

That's all you need to do with respect to form design. Let's move on and write some code to save the data as an XML file.

The SerializableData Class

Your application is going to have two classes: `Address` and `AddressBook`. `Address` will be used to store a single instance of a contact in the address book. `AddressBook` will store your entire list of addresses and provide ways for you to navigate through the book.

Both of these classes will be inherited from another class called `SerializableData`. This base class will contain the logic needed for saving the addresses to disk and loading them back again. In XML parlance, the saving process is known as *serialization,* and the loading process is known as *deserialization.*

TRY IT OUT   Building SerializableData

Code file address book.zip is available for download at Wrox.com

In this Try It Out, you're going to build the `SerializableData` and `Address` classes so that you can demonstrate saving a new address record to disk.

1. The first class you need to build is the base `SerializableData` class. Using the Solution Explorer, right-click the Address Book project and select Add ➪ Class. Call the new class **SerializableData** and click Add.

2. Right-click the project in Solution Explorer and choose Add Reference. Click the .NET tab and then select `System.XML`. Next, add these namespace import directives at the top of the class definition:

```
Imports System.IO
Imports System.Xml.Serialization

Public Class SerializableData
End Class
```

3. Next, add these two methods to the class:

```
' Save—serialize the object to disk..
Public Sub Save(ByVal filename As String)
    ' make a temporary filename..
    Dim tempFilename As String
    tempFilename = filename & ".tmp"
    ' does the file exist?
    Dim tempFileInfo As New FileInfo(tempFilename)
    If tempFileInfo.Exists = True Then tempFileInfo.Delete()
    ' open the file..
    Dim stream As New FileStream(tempFilename, FileMode.Create)
    ' save the object..
    Save(stream)
```

```
    ' close the file..
    stream.Close()
    ' remove the existing data file and
    ' rename the temp file..
    tempFileInfo.CopyTo(filename, True)
    tempFileInfo.Delete()
End Sub


' Save—actually perform the serialization..
Public Sub Save(ByVal stream As Stream)
    ' create a serializer..
    Dim serializer As New XmlSerializer(Me.GetType)
    ' save the file..
    serializer.Serialize(stream, Me)
End Sub
```

4. Add a new class called **Address**. Set the class to derive from SerializableData, like this:

```
Public Class Address
    Inherits SerializableData
End Class
```

5. Next, add the fields to the class that will be used to store the address details:

```
Public Class Address
    Inherits SerializableData

    ' fields..
    Public FirstName As String
    Public LastName As String
    Public CompanyName As String
    Public Address1 As String
    Public Address2 As String
    Public City As String
    Public Region As String
    Public PostalCode As String
    Public Country As String
    Public Email As String
End Class
```

6. Go back to the Forms Designer for Form1 and double-click the Save button to have the Click event handler created. Add this bolded code to it:

```
Private Sub btnSave_Click(ByVal sender As System.Object, _
    ByVal e As System.EventArgs) Handles btnSave.Click
    ' create a new address object..
    Dim address As New Address()
    ' copy the values from the form into the address..
    PopulateAddressFromForm(address)
    ' save the address..
    Dim filename As String = DataFilename
    address.Save(filename)
    ' tell the user..
    MsgBox("The address was saved to " & filename)
End Sub
```

7. Visual Studio highlights the fact that you haven't defined the `DataFilename` property or the `PopulateAddressFromForm` method by underlining these respective names. To remove these underlines, first add the `DataFileName` property to the Form1 code:

```
' DataFilename—where should we store our data?
Public ReadOnly Property DataFilename() As String
    Get
        ' get our working folder..
        Dim folder As String
        folder = Environment.CurrentDirectory
        ' return the folder with the name "Addressbook.xml"..
        Return folder & "\AddressBook.xml"
    End Get
End Property
```

8. Now you need to add the `PopulateAddressFromForm` method to your Form1 code:

```
' PopulateAddressFromForm—populates Address from the form fields..
Public Sub PopulateAddressFromForm(ByVal address As Address)
    ' copy the values..
    address.FirstName = txtFirstName.Text
    address.LastName = txtLastName.Text
    address.CompanyName = txtCompanyName.Text
    address.Address1 = txtAddress1.Text
    address.Address2 = txtAddress2.Text
    address.City = txtCity.Text
    address.Region = txtRegion.Text
    address.PostalCode = txtPostalCode.Text
    address.Country = txtCountry.Text
    address.Email = txtEmail.Text
End Sub
```

9. Run the project and fill in an address.

10. Click the Save button. A message box lets you know where the file has been saved.

11. Use Windows Explorer to navigate to the folder that this XML file has been saved into. Double-click it, and Internet Explorer should open and list the contents. What you see should be similar to the contents listed here:

```
    <?xml version="1.0" ?>
<Address xmlns:xsi="http://www.w3.org/2001/XMLSchema-instance"
    xmlns:xsd="http://www.w3.org/2001/XMLSchema">
<FirstName>Bryan</FirstName>
<LastName>Newsome</LastName>
<CompanyName>Wiley Publishing</CompanyName>
<Address1>11 First Avenue</Address1>
<Address2 />
<City>No where</City>
<Region>South East</Region>
<PostalCode>28222</PostalCode>
<Country>USA</Country>
<Email>Bryan@email.com</Email>
</Address>
```

How It Works

Look at the XML that's been returned. For this discussion, you can ignore the first line, starting `<?xml`, because all that's doing is saying, "Here is an XML version 1.0 document." You can also ignore the `xmlns` attributes on the first and second lines, because they merely provide some extra information about the file, which at this level is something you can let .NET worry about and don't need to get involved with. With those two parts removed, this is what you get:

```
<Address>
  <FirstName>Bryan</FirstName>
  <LastName>Newsome</LastName>
  <CompanyName>Wiley Publishing</CompanyName>
  <Address1>11 First Avenue</Address1>
  <Address2 />
  <City>No where</City>
  <Region>South East</Region>
  <PostalCode>28222</PostalCode>
  <Country>USA</Country>
  <Email>Bryan@email.com</Email>
</Address>
```

You can see how this is pretty similar to the code described previously in this chapter — you have start tags and end tags, and when taken together these tags form an element. Each element contains data, and it's pretty obvious that, for example, the `CompanyName` element contains Bryan's company name.

You'll notice as well that there are `Address` start and end tags at both the top and the bottom of the document. All of the other elements are enclosed by these tags, which means that each of the elements in the middle belongs to the `Address` element. The `Address` element is the first element in the document and is therefore known as the *top-level element* or *root element*.

It's worth noting that an XML document can only have one root element; all other elements in the document are child elements of this root.

Look at the `<Address2 />` line. By placing the slash at the end of the tag, you're saying that the element is empty. You could have written this as `<Address2></Address2>`, but that would consume more storage space in the file. The `XmlSerializer` class itself chooses the naming of the tags, which is discussed later in this chapter.

So now you know what was created; but how did you get there? Follow the path of the application from the clicking of the Save button.

The first thing this method did was create a new `Address` object and call the `PopulateAddressFromForm` method, which just reads the `Text` property for every text box on the form and populates the matching property on the `Address` object:

```
Private Sub btnSave_Click(ByVal sender As System.Object, _
    ByVal e As System.EventArgs) Handles btnSave.Click
    ' create a new address object..
    Dim address As New Address()
    ' copy the values from the form into the address..
    PopulateAddressFromForm(address)
```

Then, you ask the `DataFilename` property (which you wrote in step 7 of this Try It Out) to give you the name of a file to which you can save the data. You do this by using the `Environment.CurrentDirectory` property to return the folder that the address book is executing in and then tacking `"\AddressBook.xml"` to the end of this directory pathway. This is going to be the convention you use when saving and loading files with your application — you won't bother with giving the user the opportunity to save a specific file. Rather, you'll just assume that the file you want always has the same name and is always in the same place:

```
' save the address..
Dim filename As String = DataFilename
```

You then call the `Save` method on the `Address` object. This method is inherited from `SerializableData`, and in a moment you'll take a look at what this method actually does. After you've saved the file, you tell the user where it is:

```
        address.Save(filename)
        ' tell the user..
        MsgBox ("The address was saved to " & filename)
End Sub
```

It's the two `Save` methods on `SerializableData` that are the really interesting part of this project. The first version of the method takes a filename and opens the file. The second version of the method actually saves the data using the `System.Xml.Serialization.XmlSerializer` class, as you'll soon see.

When you save the file, you want to be careful. You have to save over the top of an existing file, but you also want to make sure that if the file save fails for any reason, you don't end up trashing the only good copy of the data the user has. This is a fairly common problem with a fairly common solution: You save the file to a different file, wait until you know that everything has been saved properly, and then replace the existing file with the new one.

To get the name of the new file, you just tack `.tmp` onto the end. For example, if the given filename were `C:\MyPrograms\AddressBook\AddressBook.xml`, you'd actually try and save to `C:\MyPrograms\AddressBook\AddressBook.xml.tmp`. If this file exists, you delete it by calling the `Delete` method:

```
' Save—serialize the object to disk..
Public Sub Save(ByVal filename As String)
        ' make a temporary filename..
        Dim tempFilename As String
        tempFilename = filename & ".tmp"
        ' does the file exist?
        Dim tempFileInfo As New FileInfo(tempFilename)
        If tempFileInfo.Exists = True Then tempFileInfo.Delete()
```

When the existing `.tmp` file is gone, you can create a new file. This returns a `System.IO.FileStream` object:

```
' open the file..
Dim stream As New FileStream(tempFilename, FileMode.Create)
```

You then pass this stream to another overloaded `Save` method. You'll go through this method in a moment, but for now all you need to know is that this method does the actual serialization of the data.

Then, you close the file:

```
' close the file..
stream.Close()
```

Finally, you replace the existing file with the new file. You do this with `CopyTo` (the `True` parameter you pass to this method means "overwrite any existing file") and then delete the temporary file:

```
        ' remove the existing data file and
```

```
        ' rename the temp file..
        tempFileInfo.CopyTo(filename, True)
        tempFileInfo.Delete()
    End Sub
```

The other version of `Save` takes a `Stream` argument instead of a `String` and looks like this:

```
' Save—actually perform the serialization..
Public Sub Save(ByVal stream As Stream)
    ' create a serializer..
    Dim serializer As New XmlSerializer(Me.GetType)
    ' save the file..
    serializer.Serialize(stream, Me)
End Sub
```

The `System.Xml.Serialization.XmlSerializer` class is what you use to actually serialize the object to the stream that you specify. In this case, you're using a stream that points to a file, but later in this chapter you'll use a different kind of file.

`XmlSerializer` needs to know ahead of time what type of object it's saving. You use the `GetType` method to return a `System.Type` object that references the class you actually are saving, which in this case is `Address`. The reason `XmlSerializer` needs to know the type is because it works by iterating through all of the properties on the object, looking for ones that are both readable and writable (in other words, ones that are not flagged as read-only or write-only). Every time it finds such a property, `XmlSerializer` writes the property to the stream, which in this case means that the property subsequently gets written to the `AddressBook.xml` file.

`XmlSerializer` bases the name of the element in the XML document on the name of the matching property. For example, the `FirstName` element in the document matches the `FirstName` property on `Address`. In addition, the top-level element of `Address` matches the name of the `Address` class; in other words, the root element name matches the class name. `XmlSerializer` is a great way of using XML in your programs because you don't need to mess around with creating and manually reading XML documents — it does all the work for you.

Loading the XML File

In the next Try It Out, you'll be adding the methods necessary to deserialize the XML back into data that you can work with in your application.

TRY IT OUT Loading the XML File

Code file is address book.zip available for download at Wrox.com

Now, you will add code to load the address back from the XML file on the disk.

1. Using the Solution Explorer, open the code editor for `SerializableData`. Add these two methods:

```
' Load—deserialize from disk..
Public Shared Function Load(ByVal filename As String, _
            ByVal newType As Type) As Object
    ' does the file exist?
```

```
            Dim fileInfo As New FileInfo(filename)
            If fileInfo.Exists = False Then
                ' create a blank version of the object and return that..
                Return System.Activator.CreateInstance(newType)
            End If
            ' open the file..
            Dim stream As New FileStream(filename, FileMode.Open)
            ' load the object from the stream..
            Dim newObject As Object = Load(stream, newType)
            ' close the stream..
            stream.Close()
            ' return the object..
            Return newObject
        End Function

        ' Load-actually perform the deserialization
        Public Shared Function Load(ByVal stream As Stream, _
                        ByVal newType As Type) As Object
            ' create a serializer and load the object..
            Dim serializer As New XmlSerializer(newType)
            Dim newObject As Object = serializer.Deserialize(stream)
            ' return the new object..
            Return newobject
        End Function
```

2. Go back to the Forms Designer for Form1. Add a new button. Set the `Text` property of the new button to **&Load** and the `Name` to **btnLoad**.

3. Double-click the Load button and add the following bolded code to the event handler:

```
Private Sub btnLoad_Click(ByVal sender As System.Object, _
        ByVal e As System.EventArgs) Handles btnLoad.Click
    ' load the address using a shared method on SerializableData..
    Dim newAddress As Address = _
     SerializableData.Load(DataFilename, GetType(Address))
    ' update the display..
    PopulateFormFromAddress(newAddress)
End Sub
```

4. You'll also need to add this method to Form1:

```
' PopulateFormFromAddress-populates the form from an
' address object..
Public Sub PopulateFormFromAddress(ByVal address As Address)
    ' copy the values..
    txtFirstName.Text = address.FirstName
    txtLastName.Text = address.LastName
    txtCompanyName.Text = address.CompanyName
    txtAddress1.Text = address.Address1
    txtAddress2.Text = address.Address2
    txtCity.Text = address.City
    txtRegion.Text = address.Region
    txtPostalCode.Text = address.PostalCode
    txtCountry.Text = address.Country
    txtEmail.Text = address.Email
End Sub
```

5. Run the project and click the Load button or press Alt+L. The address should be loaded from the XML file and displayed on the screen. After clicking the Load button, you should see what you typed and saved previously, as shown in Figure 19-2.

How It Works

Deserialization is the opposite of serialization. It can be used to load the XML data from the file, whereas before you saved the XML data to the file. (Note that the word "file" is used here for simplification. In fact, you can serialize to and deserialize from any kind of stream.)

Whenever you ask XmlSerializer to deserialize an object for you, it creates a new object. You can use this functionality to get XmlSerializer to create a new object for you, rather than having to create one yourself. This is a good candidate for an overloaded method on the SerializableData object. You create an overloaded method called Load, the first version of which takes a filename and a System.Type object. This Type object represents the type of object you ultimately want to end up with. Specifically, you'll need to pass in a Type object that tells XmlSerializer where to find a list of properties that exist on your Address object.

FIGURE 19-2

Because XmlSerializer doesn't save .NET class namespaces or assembly information into the XML file, it relies on an explicit statement saying which class the file contains; otherwise things get ambiguous. (Imagine you had 100 assemblies on your machine, each containing a class called Address. How could XmlSerializer know which one you mean?)

Obviously, when the method is called, the first thing you do is check to see whether the file exists. If it doesn't, you return a blank version of the object you asked for:

```
' Load—deserialize from disk..
Public Shared Function Load(ByVal filename As String, _
                ByVal newType As Type) As Object
    ' does the file exist?
    Dim fileInfo As New FileInfo(filename)
    If fileInfo.Exists = False Then
        ' create a blank version of the object and return that..
        Return System.Activator.CreateInstance(newType)
    End If
```

If the file does exist, you open it and pass it to the other version of Load, which you'll see in a moment. You then close the file and return the new object to the caller:

```
    ' open the file..
    Dim stream As New FileStream(filename, FileMode.Open)
    ' load the object from the stream..
    Dim newObject As Object = Load(stream, newType)
    ' close the stream..
    stream.Close()
    ' return the object..
    Return newObject
End Function
```

The other version of Load uses the XmlSerializer again, and as you can see, it's no more complicated than when you used it last time — except, of course, that the Deserialize method returns a new object:

```
Public Shared Function Load(ByVal stream As Stream, _
                ByVal newType As Type) As Object
    ' create a serializer and load the object..
    Dim serializer As New XmlSerializer(newType)
    Dim newObject As Object = serializer.Deserialize(stream)
    ' return the new object..
    Return newobject
End Function
```

When it's deserializing, XmlSerializer goes through each of the properties on the new object that it has created, again looking for ones that are both readable and writable. When it finds one, it takes the value stored against it in the XML document and sets the property. The result: You are returned a new object, fully populated with the data from the XML document.

Once you've called Load and have received a new Address object back, you pass the new object to PopulateFormFromAddress:

```
Private Sub btnLoad_Click(ByVal sender As System.Object, _
        ByVal e As System.EventArgs) Handles btnLoad.Click
    ' load the address using a shared method on SerializableData..
    Dim newAddress As Address = _
     SerializableData.Load(DataFilename, GetType(Address))
    ' update the display..
    PopulateFormFromAddress(newAddress)
End Sub
```

Changing the Data

To prove that nothing funny is going on, in the next Try It Out you'll change the XML file using Notepad and try clicking the Load button again.

TRY IT OUT   Changing the Data

Code file address book.zip is available for download at Wrox.com

This example will prove this code works. Follow the next 2 steps, to be sure your code is working.

1. Open Windows Notepad and load the XML file into it. Inside the FirstName element, change the name that you entered to something else. Then save the file and exit Notepad.

2. Go back to the Address Book program. Click the Load button again. The new name that you entered will be loaded.

How It Works

What you've done here is proven that XmlSerializer does indeed use the AddressBook.xml file as the source of its data. You changed the data, and when you loaded the Address object again, the FirstName property was indeed changed to the new name that you entered.

Sending E-mail

For the following Try It Out, you'll see how you can integrate this application with an e-mail client such as Outlook or Outlook Express using the e-mail data from your addresses. You'll be using the `Process` class to start the e-mail client associated with the `mailto` protocol, as shown shortly.

TRY IT OUT   Sending E-mail from the Client

Code file address book.zip is available for download at Wrox.com

1.   Go back to the Form1 designer and, using the Toolbox, draw a LinkLabel control underneath the Email label. Set its `Text` property to **Send Email** and change its `Name` property to **lnkSendEmail** as shown in Figure 19-3.

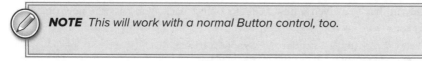

> **NOTE** *This will work with a normal Button control, too.*

2.   Double-click the LinkLabel control. This creates an event handler for the `LinkClicked` event. Add this code:

```
Private Sub lnkSendEmail_LinkClicked(ByVal sender
As System.Object, _
   ByVal e As System.Windows.Forms.LinkLabelLink
ClickedEventArgs) _
   Handles lnkSendEmail.LinkClicked
      ' start the e-mail client..
      System.Diagnostics.Process.Start("mailto:" &
txtEmail.Text)
End Sub
```

3.   Run the project and click the Load button. Ensure you have an e-mail address entered in the Email field and then click the Send Email link. Your e-mail client should display a new mail message with the To: field filled in with your e-mail address.

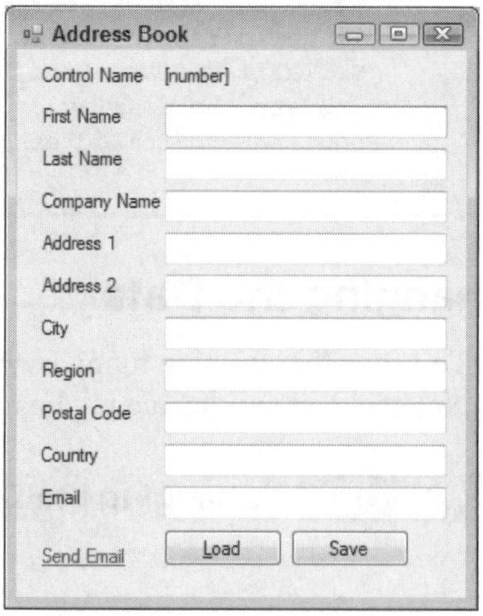

FIGURE 19-3

How It Works

Windows has a built-in capability to decode Internet addresses and fire up the programs that are associated with them.

When an e-mail client such as Outlook or Outlook Express is installed, it registers a protocol called `mailto` with Windows, just as when a web browser such as Internet Explorer is installed it registers the protocol `HTTP`, familiar to anyone who browses the Web.

If you were to close the mail message, click the Start button from the Windows taskbar, select Run, enter **mailto:** followed by the e-mail address from your program, and then click OK, the same mail message would appear.

In your code, you take the current value of the txtEmail field and put `mailto:` at the beginning. This turns the e-mail address into a URL. You then call the shared `Start` method on the `System.Diagnostics.Process` class, passing it this URL:

```
Private Sub lnkSendEmail_LinkClicked(ByVal sender As System.Object, _
  ByVal e As System.Windows.Forms.LinkLabelLinkClickedEventArgs) _
  Handles lnkSendEmail.LinkClicked
    ' start the e-mail client..
    System.Diagnostics.Process.Start("mailto:" & txtEmail.Text)
End Sub
```

The `Start` method behaves in exactly the same way as the Run dialog. Both tap into Windows' built-in URL-decoding functionality. In this case, you've used this functionality to integrate your application with Outlook. However, if you had specified a protocol of `http:` rather than `mailto:`, your application could have opened a web page. Likewise, if you had supplied a path to a Word document or an Excel spreadsheet, the application could open those too. Note that when you're working with a file, you don't need to supply a protocol — for example, you only need to do this:

```
c:\My Files\My Budget.xls
```

Creating a List of Addresses

The purpose of this Try It Out is to build an application that enables you to store a list of addresses in XML. At the moment you can successfully load just one address, so now you have to turn your attention to managing a list of addresses.

TRY IT OUT   **Creating AddressBook**

Code file address book.zip is available for download at Wrox.com

The class you're going to build to store this is called `AddressBook`. This class will inherit from `SerializableData` because ultimately you want to get to a point where you can tell the `AddressBook` object to load and save itself to the XML file without you having to do anything.

1. Using Solution Explorer, create a new class called `AddressBook`.

2. Add this namespace declaration:

```
Imports System.Xml.Serialization

Public Class AddressBook
End Class
```

3. Set the class to inherit from `SerializableData` as shown in the bolded code:

```
Imports System.Xml.Serialization

Public Class AddressBook
    Inherits SerializableData
End Class
```

4. To store the addresses, you're going to use a `System.Collections.ArrayList` object. You also need a method that you can use to create new addresses in the list. Add the following bolded member and method to the class:

```
Imports System.Xml.Serialization
Public Class AddressBook
    Inherits SerializableData

    ' members..
    Public Items As New ArrayList()

    ' AddAddress—add a new address to the book..
    Public Function AddAddress() As Address
        ' create one..
        Dim newAddress As New Address()
        ' add it to the list..
        Items.Add(newAddress)
        ' return the address..
        Return newAddress
    End Function
End Class
```

5. Open the Code Editor for Form1. Add these members to the top of the class:

```
Public Class Form1
    ' members..
    Public AddressBook As AddressBook
    Private _currentAddressIndex As Integer
```

6. Next, add this property to Form1:

```
' CurrentAddress—property for the current address..
ReadOnly Property CurrentAddress() As Address
    Get
        Return AddressBook.Items(CurrentAddressIndex—1)
    End Get
End Property
```

7. Then add this property to Form1:

```
' CurrentAddressIndex—property for the current address..
Property CurrentAddressIndex() As Integer
    Get
        Return _currentAddressIndex
    End Get
    Set(ByVal Value As Integer)
        ' set the address..
        _currentAddressIndex = Value
        ' update the display..
        PopulateFormFromAddress(CurrentAddress)
        ' set the label..
        lblAddressNumber.Text = _
        _currentAddressIndex & " of " & AddressBook.Items.Count
    End Set
End Property
```

8. Double-click the form to create the `Load` event for `Form1` and add the following bolded code to the handler:

```
Private Sub Form1_Load(ByVal sender As System.Object, _
      ByVal e As System.EventArgs) Handles MyBase.Load
  ' load the address book..
  AddressBook = _
    SerializableData.Load(DataFilename, GetType(AddressBook))
  ' if the address book only contains one item, add a new one..
  If AddressBook.Items.Count = 0 Then AddressBook.AddAddress()
  ' select the first item in the list..
  CurrentAddressIndex = 1
End Sub
```

9. Now that you can load the address book, you need to be able to save the changes. From the left drop-down list, select (Form1 Events). From the right list, select FormClosed. Add the bolded code to the event handler, and also add the `SaveChanges` and `UpdateCurrentAddress` methods:

```
Private Sub Form1_FormClosed(ByVal sender As Object, ByVal e As _
      System.Windows.Forms.FormClosedEventArgs) Handles Me.FormClosed
  ' save the changes..
  UpdateCurrentAddress()
  SaveChanges()
End Sub

' SaveChanges—save the address book to an XML file..
Public Sub SaveChanges()
    ' tell the address book to save itself..
    AddressBook.Save(DataFilename)
End Sub
' UpdateCurrentAddress—make sure the book has the current
' values currently entered into the form..
Private Sub UpdateCurrentAddress()
    PopulateAddressFromForm(CurrentAddress)
End Sub
```

Before you run the project, it's very important that you delete the existing `AddressBook.xml` file. If you don't, `XmlSerializer` will try to load an `AddressBook` object from a file containing an `Address` object, and an exception will be thrown.

10. Run the project. Don't bother entering any information into the form, because the save routine won't work — we've deliberately introduced a bug to illustrate an issue with `XmlSerializer`. Close the form, and you should see the exception thrown, as shown in Figure 19-4.

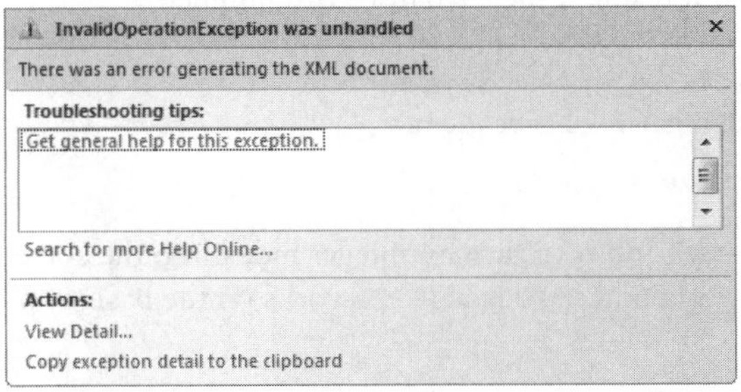

FIGURE 19-4

How It Works (or Why It Doesn't!)

When the form is loaded, the first thing you do is ask `SerializableData` to create a new `AddressBook` object from the `AddressBook.xml` file. Because you deleted this before you ran the project, this file won't exist; and, if you recall, you rigged the `Load` method so that if the file didn't exist it would just create an instance of whatever class you asked for. In this case, you get an `AddressBook`:

```
Private Sub Form1_Load(ByVal sender As System.Object, _
        ByVal e As System.EventArgs) Handles MyBase.Load
    ' load the address book..
    AddressBook = _
        SerializableData.Load(DataFilename, GetType(AddressBook))
```

However, the new address book won't have any addresses in it. You ask `AddressBook` to create a new address if the list is empty:

```
    ' if the address book only contains one item, add a new one..
    If AddressBook.Items.Count = 0 Then AddressBook.AddAddress()
```

At this point, either you'll have an `AddressBook` object that's been loaded from the file and therefore contains a set of `Address` objects, or you'll have a new `AddressBook` object that contains one blank address. You set the `CurrentAddressIndex` property to 1, meaning the first item in the list:

```
    ' select the first item in the list..
    CurrentAddressIndex = 1
End Sub
```

The setter for the `CurrentAddressIndex` property does a number of things. First, it updates the private `_currentAddressIndex` member:

```
' CurrentAddressIndex—property for the current address..
Property CurrentAddressIndex() As Integer
    Get
        Return _currentAddressIndex
    End Get
    Set(ByVal Value As Integer)
        ' set the address..
        _currentAddressIndex = Value
```

Then the setter uses the `CurrentAddress` property to get the `Address` object that corresponds to whatever `_currentAddressIndex` is set to. This `Address` object is passed to `PopulateFormFromAddress`, whose job it is to update the display:

```
        ' update the display..
        PopulateFormFromAddress(CurrentAddress)
```

Finally, it changes the `lblAddressNumber` control so that it displays the current record number:

```
        ' set the label..
        lblAddressNumber.Text = _
            _currentAddressIndex & " of " & AddressBook.Items.Count
    End Set
End Property
```

You'll just quickly look at `CurrentAddress`. This property's job is to turn an integer index into the corresponding `Address` object stored in `AddressBook`. However, because `AddressBook` works on the basis of an

`ArrayList` object that numbers items from `0`, and your application starts numbering items at `1`, you have to decrement your index value by `1` to get the matching value from `AddressBook`:

```
' CurrentAddress—property for the current address..
ReadOnly Property CurrentAddress() As Address
    Get
        Return AddressBook.Items(CurrentAddressIndex—1)
    End Get
End Property
```

All good so far, but why is `XmlSerializer` throwing an exception? Well, the problems occur when you close the application. This fires the `FormClosed` method, which ultimately calls the `Save` method of `AddressBook`.

As you know, to save an object to disk, `XmlSerializer` walks through each of the properties looking for those that are readable and writable. So far, you've used `XmlSerializer` only with `System.String`, but when the object comes across a property that uses a complex type, such as `Address`, it uses the same principle — in other words, it looks through all of the properties of the complex type. If properties on that that object return complex types, it will drill down again. What it's doing is looking for simple types that it knows how to turn into text and write to the XML document.

However, some types cannot be turned into text, and at this point `XmlSerializer` chokes. The `ArrayList` object that you're using to store a list of addresses had some properties that cannot be converted to text, which is why the exception is being thrown. What you need to do is provide an alternative property that `XmlSerializer` can hook into in order to get a list of addresses and tell it not to bother trying to serialize the `ArrayList`.

Ignoring Members

Although `XmlSerializer` cannot cope with certain data types, it has no problems with arrays. You've also seen that `XmlSerializer` has no problems with your `Address` class, simply because this object doesn't have any properties of a type that `XmlSerializer` cannot support.

TRY IT OUT   **Ignoring Members**

Code file address book.zip is available for download at Wrox.com

In the next Try It Out, you'll provide an alternative property that returns an array of `Address` objects and tells `XmlSerializer` to keep away from the `Items` property because `XmlSerializer` cannot deal with `ArrayList` objects.

1.   Open the Code Editor for `AddressBook`. Find the `Items` property and prefix it with the `System.Xml.Serialization.XmlIgnore` attribute:

```
Public Class AddressBook
    Inherits SerializableData

    <XmlIgnore()>Public Items As New ArrayList
```

2. Now, add this new property to the `AddressBook` class:

```
' Addresses–property that works with the items
' collection as an array..
Public Property Addresses() As Address()
    Get
        ' create a new array..
        Dim addressArray(Items.Count-1) As Address
        Items.CopyTo(addressArray)
        Return addressArray
    End Get
    Set(ByVal Value As Address())
        ' reset the arraylist..
        Items.Clear()
        ' did you get anything?
        If Not Value Is Nothing Then
            ' go through the array and populate items..
            Dim address As Address
            For Each address In Value
                Items.Add(address)
            Next
        End If
    End Set
End Property
```

3. Run the project and then close the application; this time everything functions correctly. Run the project again, and then enter some data into the address fields. Close the application and you should find that `AddressBook.xml` does contain data. (We've removed the `xmlns` and `?xml` values for clarity here.)

```
<AddressBook>
  <Addresses>
    <Address>
      <FirstName>Bryan</FirstName>
      <LastName>Newsome</LastName>
      <CompanyName>Company</CompanyName>
      <Address1 />
      <Address2 />
      <City />
      <Region />
      <PostalCode />
      <Country />
      <Email />
    </Address>
  </Addresses>
</AddressBook>
```

How It Works

The XML that got saved into your file proves that your approach works, but why?

At this point, your `AddressBook` object has two properties: `Items` and `Addresses`. Both are read/write properties, so both are going to be examined as candidates for serialization by `XmlSerializer`. As you know, `Items` returns an `ArrayList` object, and `Addresses` returns an array of `Address` objects.

However, you have now marked Items with the XmlIgnore attribute. This means, not surprisingly, that XmlSerializer ignores the property, despite the fact that it is readable and writable. Instead, the serializer moves on to the Addresses property.

The Get portion of the Addresses property is what interests you. All you do is create a new array of Address objects and use the CopyTo method on the ArrayList to populate it:

```
' Addresses—property that works with the items
' collection as an array..
Public Property Addresses() As Address()
    Get
        ' create a new array..
        Dim addressArray(Items.Count—1) As Address
        Items.CopyTo(addressArray)
        Return addressArray
    End Get
    Set(ByVal Value As Address())
        ..
    End Set
End Property
```

When XmlSerializer gets an array of objects that it can deal with, all it does is iterate through the array, serializing each of these contained objects in turn. You can see this in the XML that you received: The structure of the XML contained within the Addresses element exactly matches the structure of the XML you saw when you tested the process and wrote a single Address object to the file:

```
<AddressBook>
  <Addresses>
    <Address>
      <FirstName>Bryan</FirstName>
      <LastName>Newsome</LastName>
      <CompanyName>Company</CompanyName>
      <Address1 />
      <Address2 />
      <City />
      <Region />
      <PostalCode />
      <Country />
      <Email />
    </Address>
  </Addresses>
</AddressBook>
```

Loading Addresses

If you're lucky, loading addresses should just work! Close the program and run the project again. You will see a record like the one shown in Figure 19-5. The Load button doesn't work at this point, but don't worry; you don't need it anymore.

You already set up the project to load the address book the first time you ran the project after creating the AddressBook class itself. This time, however, AddressBook.Load can find a file on the disk, so rather than create a blank object, it's getting XmlSerializer to deserialize the lot. As XmlSerializer has no problems writing arrays, you can assume that it has no problem reading them.

It's the Set portion of the Addresses property that does the magic this time. When working with this property, be careful if you are passed a blank array (in other words, Nothing); you want to prevent exceptions being thrown:

```
' Addresses—property that works with the items
' collection as an array..
Public Property Addresses() As Address()
    Get
        ..
    End Get
    Set(ByVal Value As Address())
        ' reset the arraylist..
        Items.Clear()
        ' did you get anything?
        If Not Value Is Nothing Then
            ' go through the array and populate items..
            Dim address As Address
            For Each address In Value
                Items.Add(address)
            Next
        End If
    End Set
End Property
```

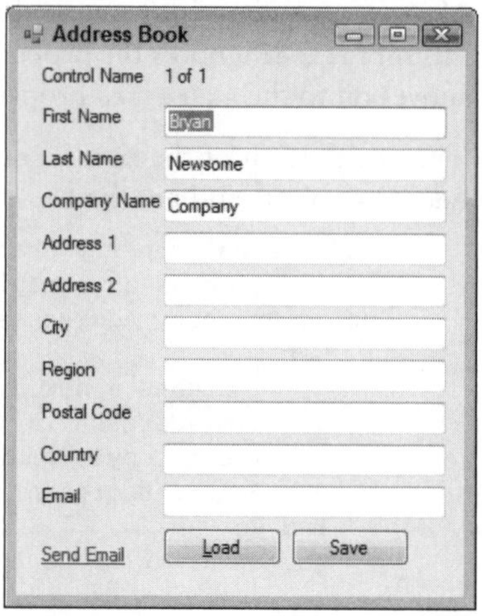

FIGURE 19-5

For each of the values in the array, all you have to do is take each one in turn and add it to the list.

Adding New Addresses

Now you'll look at how you can add new addresses to the list.

TRY IT OUT **Adding New Addresses**

Code file address book.zip is available for download at Wrox.com

In this Try It Out, you'll be adding four new buttons to your form. Two of the buttons enable you to navigate through the list of addresses, and two buttons enable you to add and delete addresses.

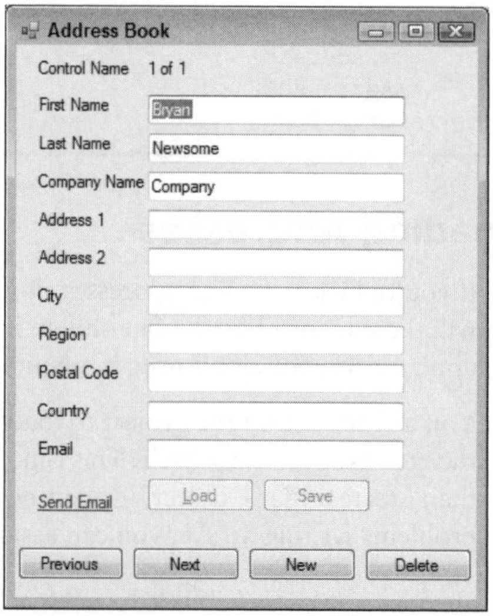

1. Open the Forms Designer for Form1 and disable the Load and Save buttons before adding the four new buttons shown at the bottom of Figure 19-6.

2. Name the buttons in turn **btnPrevious, btnNext, btnNew,** and **btnDelete** and set their Text properties to **Previous, Next, New,** and **Delete,** respectively.

3. Double-click the New button to create a Click handler. Add the bolded line to the event handler, and add the AddNewAddress method:

FIGURE 19-6

```
Private Sub btnNew_Click(ByVal sender As System.Object, _
        ByVal e As System.EventArgs) Handles btnNew.Click
    AddNewAddress()
End Sub

Public Function AddNewAddress() As Address
    ' save the current address..
    UpdateCurrentAddress()

    ' create a new address..
    Dim newAddress As Address = AddressBook.AddAddress
    ' update the display..
    CurrentAddressIndex = AddressBook.Items.Count
    ' return the new address..
    Return newAddress
End Function
```

4. Run the project. Click New and a new address record is created. Enter a new address.

5. Close the program and the changes will be saved. Open AddressBook.xml and you should see the new address.

How It Works

This time you have a new Address object added to the XML document. It is contained within the Addresses element, so you know that it is part of the same array.

The implementation was very simple — all you had to do was ask AddressBook to create a new address, and then you updated the CurrentAddressIndex property so that it equaled the number of items in the AddressBook. This had the effect of changing the display so that it went to record 2 of 2, ready for editing.

However, before you actually do this, it is important that you save any changes the user might have made. With this application, you are ensuring that any changes the user makes will always be persisted into the XML file. Whenever the user closes the application, creates a new record, or moves backward or forward in the list, you want to call UpdateCurrentAddress so that any changes are saved:

```
Public Function AddNewAddress() As Address
    ' save the current address..
    UpdateCurrentAddress()
```

After you've saved any changes, it is safe to create the new record and show it to the user:

```
    ' create a new address..
    Dim newAddress As Address = AddressBook.AddAddress
    ' update the display..
    CurrentAddressIndex = AddressBook.Items.Count
    ' return the new address..
    Return newAddress
End Function
```

Navigating Addresses

Now that you can add new addresses to the address book, you need to wire up the Next and Previous buttons so that you can move through the list. In this Try It Out, you'll be adding the code that reads the next or previous address from the array of addresses maintained by the AddressBook class.

To make the navigation work, you will need to read from the array. Before reading the next or previous address, however, you'll also want to ensure that any changes made to the current address are updated, and you'll be calling the appropriate procedures to update the current address before navigating to a new address.

1.   Open the Forms Designer for Form1. Double-click the Next button to create a new `Click` handler. Add this code and the associated `MoveNext` method:

```
Private Sub btnNext_Click(ByVal sender As System.Object, _
    ByVal e As System.EventArgs) Handles btnNext.Click
    MoveNext()
End Sub

Public Sub MoveNext()
    ' get the next index..
    Dim newIndex As Integer = CurrentAddressIndex + 1
    If newIndex > AddressBook.Items.Count Then
        newIndex = 1
    End If
    ' save any changes..
    UpdateCurrentAddress()
    ' move the record..
    CurrentAddressIndex = newIndex
End Sub
```

2.   Next, flip back to the Forms Designer and double-click the Previous button. Add the bolded code:

```
Private Sub btnPrevious_Click(ByVal sender As System.Object, _
    ByVal e As System.EventArgs) Handles btnPrevious.Click
    MovePrevious()
End Sub

Public Sub MovePrevious()
    ' get the previous index..
    Dim newIndex As Integer = CurrentAddressIndex-1
    If newIndex = 0 Then
        newIndex = AddressBook.Items.Count
    End If
    ' save changes..
    UpdateCurrentAddress()
    ' move the record..
    CurrentAddressIndex = newIndex
End Sub
```

3.   Run the project. You should now be able to move between addresses.

How It Works

All you've done here is wire up the buttons so that each one changes the current index. By incrementing the current index, you move forward in the list. By decrementing it, you move backward.

However, it's very important that you don't move outside the bounds of the list (in other words, try to move to a position before the first record or after the last record), which is why you check the value and adjust it as appropriate. When you move forward (MoveNext), you flip to the beginning of the list if you go off the end. When you move backward (MovePrevious), you flip to the end if you go past the start.

In both cases, you ensure that before you actually change the CurrentAddressIndex property, you call UpdateCurrentAddress to save any changes:

```
Public Sub MoveNext()
    ' get the next index..
    Dim newIndex As Integer = CurrentAddressIndex + 1
    If newIndex > AddressBook.Items.Count Then
        newIndex = 1
    End If
    ' save any changes..
    UpdateCurrentAddress()
    ' move the record..
    CurrentAddressIndex = newIndex
End Sub
```

Deleting Addresses

To finish the functionality of your address book, you'll deal with deleting items. When deleting items, you must take into account that the item you are deleting is the last remaining item. In this case, you have to provide the appropriate code to add a new blank address.

TRY IT OUT Deleting Addresses

Code file address book.zip is available for download at Wrox.com

This Try It Out provides this and all necessary functionality to delete an address properly.

1. Go back to the Forms Designer for Form1 and double-click the Delete button. Add the following code to the event handler, and add the DeleteAddress method:

```
Private Sub btnDelete_Click(ByVal sender As System.Object, _
        ByVal e As System.EventArgs) Handles btnDelete.Click
    ' ask the user if they are ok with this?
    If MsgBox("Are you sure you want to delete this address?", _
        MsgBoxStyle.Question Or MsgBoxStyle.YesNo) = _
        MsgBoxResult.Yes Then
        DeleteAddress(CurrentAddressIndex)
    End If
End Sub

' DeleteAddress—delete an address from the list..
Public Sub DeleteAddress(ByVal index As Integer)
    ' delete the item from the list..
    AddressBook.Items.RemoveAt(index—1)
    ' was that the last address?
    If AddressBook.Items.Count = 0 Then
```

```
                ' add a new address?
                AddressBook.AddAddress()
        Else
                ' make sure you have something to show..
                If index > AddressBook.Items.Count Then
                        index = AddressBook.Items.Count
                End If
        End If
        ' display the record..
        CurrentAddressIndex = index
    End Sub
```

2.   Run the project. You should be able to delete records from the address book. Note that if you delete the last record, a new record is automatically created.

How It Works

The algorithm you've used here to delete the records is an example of how to solve another classic programming problem.

Your application is set up so that it always has to display a record. That's why, when the program is first run and there is no AddressBook.xml, you automatically create a new record. Likewise, when an item is deleted from the address book, you have to find something to present to the user.

To physically delete an address from the disk, you use the RemoveAt method on the ArrayList that holds the Address objects:

```
    ' DeleteAddress—delete an address from the list..
    Public Sub DeleteAddress(ByVal index As Integer)
        ' delete the item from the list..
        AddressBook.Items.RemoveAt(index–1)
```

Again, notice here that because you're working with a zero-based array, when you ask to delete the address with an index of 3, you actually have to delete the address at position 2 in the array.

The problems start after you've done that. It could be that you've deleted the one remaining address in the book. In this case, because you always have to display an address, you create a new one:

```
    ' was that the last address?
    If AddressBook.Items.Count = 0 Then
        ' add a new address?
        AddressBook.AddAddress()
```

Alternatively, if there are items in the address book, you have to change the display. In some cases, the value that's currently stored in CurrentAddressIndex will be valid. For example, if you had five records and are looking at the third one, _currentAddressIndex will be 3. If you delete that record, you have four records, but the third one as reported by _currentAddressIndex is still 3 and is still valid. However, as 4 has now shuffled into 3's place, you need to update the display.

It could be the case that you've deleted the last item in the list. When this happens, the index isn't valid, because the index would be positioned over the end of the list. (Suppose you have four items in the list; delete the fourth one, and you only have three, but _currentAddressIndex would be 4,which isn't valid.) Therefore, when the last item is deleted, the index will be over the end of the list, so you set it to be the last item in the list:

```
Else
    ' make sure you have something to show..
    If index > AddressBook.Items.Count Then
        index = AddressBook.Items.Count
    End If
End If
```

Whatever actually happens, you still need to update the display. As you know, the `CurrentAddressIndex` property can do this for you:

```
    ' display the record..
    CurrentAddressIndex = index
End Sub
```

Testing at the Edges

This brings us to a programming technique that can greatly help you test your applications. When writing software, things usually go wrong at the edge. For example, suppose you have a function that takes an integer value, but in order for the method to work properly, the value supplied must lie between 0 and 99.

When your algorithm works properly when you give it a valid value, test some values at the boundaries of the valid data. For example: −1, 0, 99, and 100. In most cases, if your method works properly for one or two of the possible valid values, it works properly for the entire set of valid values. Testing a few values at the edge shows you where potential problems with the method lie.

A classic example of this is with your `MoveNext` and `MovePrevious` methods. If you had 100 addresses in your address book and tested only that `MoveNext` and `MovePrevious` worked between numbers 10 and 20, it most likely would have worked between 1 and 100. However, the moment you move past 100 (in other words, "go over the edge"), problems can occur. If you hadn't handled this case properly by flipping back to 1, for example, your program would have crashed.

INTEGRATING WITH THE ADDRESS BOOK APPLICATION

So far, you've built an application that is able to save and load its data as an XML document. You've also taken a look at the document as it's been changing over the course of the chapter, so by now you should have a pretty good idea of what an XML document looks like and how it works.

The beginning of this chapter pitched XML as a technology for integrating software applications. It then went on to say that for newcomers to Visual Basic, using XML for integration is unlikely to be something that you would do on a daily basis, so you've been using XML to store data. In the rest of this chapter, we're going to demonstrate why XML is such a good technology for integration. What you'll do is build a separate application that, with very little work, is able to read in and understand the proprietary data format that you've used in `AddressBook.xml`.

Using XML is an advanced topic, so if you would like to learn more about the technology and its application, try the following books:

➤ *Beginning XML, 2nd Edition* (Wrox, 2001)

➤ *Visual Basic .NET and XML: Harness the Power of XML in VB.NET Applications* (Wiley, 2002)

Demonstrating the Principle of Integration

Before you build the application that can integrate with your address book application, you should try to understand the principles involved. Basically, XML documents are good for integration because they can be easily read, understood, and changed by other people. Old-school file formats require detailed documentation to understand and often don't evolve well — that is, when new versions of the format are released, software that worked with the old formats often breaks.

XML documents are typically easily understood. Imagine you'd never seen or heard of your address book before, and look at this XML document:

```
<Addresses>
    <Address>
        <FirstName>Bryan</FirstName>
        <LastName>Newsome</LastName>
        <CompanyName>Wiley</CompanyName>
        <Address1>123 Main St</Address1>
        <Address2 />
        <City>Big City</City>
        <Region>SE</Region>
        <PostalCode>28222</PostalCode>
        <Country>USA</Country>
        <Email>Bryan@email.com</Email>
    </Address>
</Addresses>
```

Common sense tells you what this document represents. You can also perceive how the program that generated it uses it. In addition, you can use the various tools in .NET to load, manipulate, and work with this document. To an extent, you still need to work with the people who designed the structure of the document, especially when more esoteric elements come into play, but you can use this document to some meaningful effect without too much stress.

Provided that you know what structure the document takes, you can build your own document or add new things to it. For example, if you know that the Addresses element contains a list of Address elements, and that each Address element contains a bunch of elements that describe the address, you can add your own Address element using your own application.

To see this happening, you can open the AddressBook.xml file in Notepad. You need to copy the last Address element (complete with the contents) to the bottom of the document, but make sure it remains inside the Addresses element. Change the address data to something else.

XML tags are case sensitive so be sure that your start and end tags have matching names. In XML, <Root><Tag></tag></root> is not valid.

Here's mine:

```xml
<?xml version="1.0" encoding="utf-8"?>
<AddressBook xmlns:xsi="http://www.w3.org/2001/XMLSchema-instance"
xmlns:xsd="http://www.w3.org/2001/XMLSchema">
  <Addresses>
    <Address>
      <FirstName>Bryan</FirstName>
      <LastName>Newsome</LastName>
      <CompanyName>Company</CompanyName>
      <Address1 />
      <Address2 />
      <City />
      <Region />
      <PostalCode />
      <Country />
      <Email />
    </Address>
    <Address>
      <FirstName>Bryan</FirstName>
      <LastName>Newsome</LastName>
      <CompanyName>Wiley</CompanyName>
      <Address1>123 Main St</Address1>
      <Address2 />
      <City>Big City</City>
      <Region>SE</Region>
      <PostalCode>28222</PostalCode>
      <Country>USA</Country>
      <Email>Bryan@email.com</Email>
    </Address>
  </Addresses>
</AddressBook>
```

Finally, if you save the file and run the address book application, you should find that you have two addresses and that the last one is the new one that you added. This shows that you can manipulate the document and gain some level of integration.

Reading the Address Book from Another Application

To further the illustration, what you do in the next Try It Out is build a completely separate application from Address Book that's able to load in the XML file that Address Book uses and do something useful with it.

TRY IT OUT   Reading Address Book Data

Code file address list.zip is available for download at Wrox.com

For this example, you'll extract all of the addresses in the file and display a list of names with their matching e-mail addresses.

1. Create a new Windows Forms Application project. Call it **Address List**.

2. On Form1, draw a ListBox control. Change its `IntegralHeight` property to **False,** its `Dock` property to **Fill,** and its `Name` to **lstEmails,** as shown in Figure 19-7.

3. Double-click the form's title bar. Add this code to the `Load` event handler. Remember to add a reference to `System.Xml.dll` and add this namespace declaration:

FIGURE 19-7

```vb
Public Class Form1

Private Sub Form1_Load(ByVal sender As System.
    Object, _
        ByVal e As System.EventArgs) Handles
    MyBase.Load
    ' where do we want to get the XML from..
    Dim filename As String = _
        "C:\Users\Bryan\Documents\Visual Studio 10\Projects\Address " & _
        "Book\bin\Debug\ AddressBook.xml"
    ' open the document..
    Dim reader As New XmlTextReader(filename)
    ' move to the start of the document..
    reader.MoveToContent()
    ' start working through the document..

    Dim addressData As Collection = Nothing
    Dim elementName As String = Nothing
    Do While reader.Read
        ' what kind of node to we have?
        Select Case reader.NodeType
            ' is it the start of an element?
            Case XmlNodeType.Element
                ' if it's an element start, is it "Address"?
                If reader.Name = "Address" Then
                    ' if so, create a new collection..
                    addressData = New Collection()
                Else
                    ' if not, record the name of the element..
                    elementName = reader.Name
                End If
            ' if we have some text, try storing it in the
            ' collection..
            Case XmlNodeType.Text
                ' do we have an address?
                If Not addressData Is Nothing Then
                    addressData.Add(reader.Value, elementName)
                End If
            ' is it the end of an element?
            Case XmlNodeType.EndElement
                ' if it is, we should have an entire address stored..
                If reader.Name = "Address" Then
                    ' try to create a new listview item..
                    Dim item As String = Nothing
                    Try
```

```
                item = addressData("firstname") & _
                        " " & addressData("lastname")
                item &= " (" & addressData("email") & ")"
            Catch
            End Try
            ' add the item to the list..
            lstEmails.Items.Add(item)
            ' reset..
            addressData = Nothing
        End If
    End Select
Loop
End Sub

End Class
```

The preceding code assumes that your `AddressBook.xml` will be in `C:\Users\Bryan\Documents\Visual Studio 10\Projects\Address Book\bin\Debug`. If yours isn't, change the filename value specified at the top of the code.

4. Run the project; you should see something like what is shown in Figure 19-8. Notice that addresses without an e-mail address display without problems, as the `Email` element in your XML file contains an empty string value instead of a null value, as is typically found in databases.

FIGURE 19-8

How It Works

To fully appreciate the benefit of this exercise (and therefore the benefit of XML), imagine that before writing the application you'd never seen the XML format used by the Address Book application. Because XML is a text-based format, you're able to open it in a normal text editor, read it, and make assumptions about how it works. You know that you want to get a list of names and e-mail addresses, and you understand that you have an array of `Address` elements, each one containing the three elements you need: `FirstName`, `LastName`, and `Email`. All that remains is to extract and present the information.

Since announcing .NET, Microsoft has a made a big deal about how it is built on XML. This shows in the .NET Framework support for XML, which offers a dazzling array of classes for reading and writing XML documents. The `XmlSerializer` object that you've been using up until now is by far the easiest one to use, but it relies on your having classes that match the document structure exactly. Therefore, if you are given a document from a business partner, you won't have a set of classes that matches the document. As a result, you need some other way to read the document and fit it into whatever classes you do have.

In your Address List project, you don't have applicable `AddressBook` or `Address` classes, so you had to use some classes to step through a file. The one you're using is `System.Xml.XmlTextReader`. This class provides a pointer that starts at the top of the document and, on command, moves to the next part of the document. (Each of these parts is called a *node*.) The pointer will stop at anything, and this includes start tags, end tags, data values, and whitespace.

So, when you start, the first thing `XmlTextReader` tells you about is this node:

```
<?xml version="1.0" encoding="utf-8"?>
```

When you ask it to move on, it tells you about this node:

```
<AddressBook xmlns:xsi="http://www.w3.org/2001/XMLSchema-instance"
     xmlns:xsd="http://www.w3.org/2001/XMLSchema">
```

Then, when you ask it to move on again, it tells you about this node:

```
<Addresses>
```

Then it tells you about `<Address>`, `<FirstName>Bryan</FirstName>`, and `<LastName>`, and so on until it gets to the end of the document. In between each one of these, you may or may not get told about whitespace nodes. By and large, you can ignore these.

What your algorithm has to do, then, is get hold of an `XmlTextReader` and start moving through the document one piece at a time. When you first start, the pointer is set ahead of the first node in the document. Each call to `Read` moves the pointer along one node, so the first call to `Read` that you see at the start of the `Do ... While` loop actually sets the pointer to the first node:

```
Private Sub Form1_Load(ByVal sender As System.Object, _
          ByVal e As System.EventArgs) Handles MyBase.Load
    ' where do you want to get the XML from..
    Dim filename As String = _
"C:\Users\Bryan\Documents\Visual Studio 10\Projects\Address " & _
  "Book\bin\Debug\AddressBook.xml\AddressBook.xml"

    ' open the document..
    Dim reader As New XmlTextReader(filename)
    ' move to the start of the document..
    reader.MoveToContent()
    ' start working through the document..
    Dim addressData As Collection, elementName As String
    Do While reader.Read
```

You can use the `NodeType` property of `XmlTextReader` to find out what kind of node you're looking at. If you have an `Element` node, then this maps directly onto a start tag in the document. You can use the `Name` property to get the name of the tag. When you find the `<Address>` start tag, you create a new collection called `addressData`. If the start tag that you're looking at isn't the `<Address>` tag, then you store the name in `elementName` for later use:

```
    ' what kind of node to we have?
    Select Case reader.NodeType
        ' is it the start of an element?
        Case XmlNodeType.Element
            ' if it's an element start, is it "Address"?
            If reader.Name = "Address" Then
                ' if so, create a new collection..
                addressData = New Collection()
            Else
                ' if not, record the name of the element..
                elementName = reader.Name
            End If
```

Alternatively, the node you get might be a lump of text. If this is the case, then you check to see whether `addressData` points to a `Collection` object. If it does, you know that you are inside an `Address` element.

Remember, you've also stored the name of the element that you are looking at inside `elementName`. This means that if `elementName` is set to `FirstName`, you know you're in the `FirstName` element, and therefore the text element you're looking at must be the first name in the address. You then add this element name and the value into the collection for later use:

```
' if we have some text, try storing it in the
' collection..
Case XmlNodeType.Text
    ' do we have an address?
    If Not addressData Is Nothing Then
        addressData.Add(reader.Value, elementName)
    End If
```

As you work through the file, you'll get to this point for each of the elements stored in the `Address` element. Effectively, by the time you reach `</Address>`, `addressData` will contain entries for each value stored against the address in the document.

To detect when you get to the `</Address>` tag, you need to look for `EndElement` nodes:

```
' is it the end of an element?
Case XmlNodeType.EndElement
```

When you get one of these, if `Name` is equal to `Address`, then you know that you have reached `</Address>`, and this means that `addressData` should be fully populated. You form a string and add it to the list:

```
' if it is, you should have an entire address stored..
If reader.Name = "Address" Then
    ' try to create a new listview item..
    Dim item As String
    Try
        item = addressData("firstname") & _
                " " & addressData("lastname")
        item &= " (" & addressData("email") & ")"
    Catch
    End Try
    ' add the item to the list..
    lstEmails.Items.Add(item)
    ' reset..
    addressData = Nothing
End If
```

You'll notice that in your `Try ... Catch` you won't do anything if an exception does occur. To keep this example simple, you're going to ignore any problems that do occur. Specifically, you'll run into problems if the `Address` element you're looking through has sub-elements missing — for example, you might not always have an e-mail address for each address, as shown earlier in Figure 19-8.

You then continue the loop. For each iteration of the loop, `XmlTextReader.Read` is called, which advances the pointer to the next node. If there are no more nodes in the document, `Read` returns `False`, and the loop stops:

```
        End Select
    Loop
End Sub
```

It is hoped that this example has illustrated the power of XML from a software integration perspective. With very little work, you've managed to integrate the Address Book and Address List applications together.

If you want to experiment with this a little, try adding and deleting addresses from the Address Book. You'll need to close the program to save the changes to `AddressBook.xml`, but each time you start Address List, you should see the changes you made.

SUMMARY

This chapter introduced the concept of XML. XML is a language based on open standards and can be used as a tool for software integration. Within a single organization, XML can be used to transport data across platforms easily. It also enables two organizations to define a common format for data exchange; and because XML is text-based, it can easily be moved around using Internet technologies such as e-mail, the Web, and FTP. XML is based on building a document constructed of tags and data.

XML is primarily used for integration work to make the tasks of data transportation and exchange easier; and you, as a newcomer to Visual Basic and programming in general, are unlikely to do integration work (as it's typically done by developers with a lot of experience). Nevertheless, this chapter helped you get an idea of what this is all about by focusing on using the `System.Xml.Serialization.XmlSerializer` class to save entire objects to disk (known as *serialization*). This same object was used to load objects from disk (known as *deserialization*). You built a fully functional address book application that was able to use an XML file stored on the local computer as its primary source of data.

To round off the chapter and to demonstrate that XML is great for software integration work, you wrote a separate application that was able to load and make sense of the XML document used by the Address Book application.

At this point, you should:

➤   Have a better understanding of XML and know what it looks like

➤   Know the basic rules for using XML

➤   Be able to serialize and deserialize XML data into objects

➤   Be able to manipulate XML data in your applications

➤   Be able to use the `XMLTextReader` class to walk through an XML document

EXERCISES

1.   Name two reasons to use XML to integrate systems or store data.

2.   In what two items do you store data in XML?

3.   Is this valid XML? `<Root><one att="red" /></root>`

4.   Is this valid XML? `<Root><one att="red" >Me & you</one></Root>`

5.   Is this valid XML? `<Root><one><att>Me</one></att></Root>`

▶ **WHAT YOU HAVE LEARNED IN THIS CHAPTER**

TOPIC	CONCEPTS
XML	XML files must contain a root element, are tag-based, case sensitive, self describing, and based on a widely used standard.
Working with XML Files	You can easily serialize and deserialize XML data to and from files to work with it as a data source.
Exchanging data with applications.	You can open XML in many applications, including text editors, and share the data between these applications.

20

Deploying Your Application

WHAT YOU WILL LEARN IN THIS CHAPTER:

- ➤ Deployment concepts and terminology
- ➤ How to deploy a ClickOnce Application with Visual Studio 2010
- ➤ How to create a setup program with Visual Studio 2010
- ➤ How to edit the installer user interface

Deploying an application can be a complicated process, especially when dealing with large, complex applications. A wealth of knowledge is required about nearly every aspect of a deployment. A large software installation for Windows requires knowledge ranging from Registry settings, MIME types, and configuration files to database creation and manipulation. Companies tend to rely on dedicated deployment software for these large installations, together with key people who understand the processes involved. However, Visual Studio 2010 does provide some basic deployment functionality, which is tremendously helpful for the standard developer and smaller installations.

Under the Visual Studio 2010 banner, you can create many different types of applications, from desktop to web applications and services. All of these have varying degrees of complexity or peculiarities when it comes installation time.

Since this is a beginner's guide, this chapter provides an overview of deployment.

WHAT IS DEPLOYMENT?

Deployment is the activity of delivering copies of an application to other machines so that the application runs in the new environment. It is the larger, architectural view for what you may know as installation or setup. There is a subtle difference between deployment and installation.

Deployment is the art of distribution. In other words, deployment is the way in which software is delivered. Installation or setup is a process, whereby you load, configure, and install the software. In other words, an *installation* is what you do to configure the software, and *deployment* is how you get it where you want it.

With this terminology, a CD is a deployment mechanism, as is the Internet. The two deployment mechanisms may have different installation requirements. For example, if an installation is on a CD, you may have all the additional dependent software on that CD. Delivery of the same application via the Internet might require users to visit additional sites to gather all the dependent software. Another example that may affect the installation option is one in which you may have written an installation in JavaScript. This may work fine when executed on a machine by a user who has the correct Windows user rights, but would not work through Internet Explorer. These kinds of considerations are important when deciding upon your best deployment option. The type of installations you require could also vary per application.

Now that you have an understanding of the terminology, it's time to learn how to deploy applications using Visual Studio 2010.

ClickOnce Deployment

ClickOnce deployment is the concept of sending an application or its referenced assemblies to the client in a way that allows self-updating applications. You have three distribution options for a ClickOnce application: file share, web page, or external media (CD, DVD, and so on). ClickOnce deployment has both benefits and limitations. It is a useful deployment option for small- to medium-size applications.

The benefits of ClickOnce deployment include three major factors. First, using this deployment option allows for self-updating Windows applications. You can post the latest version of the application at the original location, and the next time the user runs the application, it will install the latest version and run it. Next, any user can install most ClickOnce applications with only basic user security. With other technologies, administrator privileges are required. Finally, the installation has little impact on the user's computer. The application can run from a secure per-user cache and add entries only to the Start menu and the Add/Remove Programs list. For programs that can run in the Internet or intranet zones that do not need to access the Global Assembly Cache (GAC), this is a terrific deployment solution for distribution via the web or a file share. If you distribute the ClickOnce application through external media, the installation will be run with higher trust and have access to the GAC.

TRY IT OUT   **Deploying a ClickOnce Application from the Web**

Code file ClickOnce.zip and Publish.zip is available for download at Wrox.com

In this Try It Out, you learn how to deploy a ClickOnce application from the Web.

1. Create a new Windows Forms Application named **ClickOnce**.

2. On Form1, add a button and label. Change the button's Name property to **btnVersion** and the Text property to **Version**. Change the label Name to **lblVersion** and clear the Text property.

3. Add the following bolded code to the Click event for btnVersion:

```
Private Sub btnVersion_Click(ByVal sender As System.
  Object, ByVal e As _
    System.EventArgs) Handles btnVersion.Click
      lblVersion.Text = "Version 1.0"
End sub
```

FIGURE 20-1

4. Test the form. When the user clicks the button, the label should display Version 1.0. Your form should look like Figure 20-1.

5. Prepare to publish the assembly to the Web.

> *✎* **NOTE** *If you do not have IIS installed, you can publish the file to a local or network drive. Just remember how you chose to publish the assembly. You will need to be running Visual Studio with elevated privileges to complete this. You may need to close Visual Studio: right-click the shortcut, and choose Run as Administrator to launch the software.*

6. Right-click the ClickOnce project in the Solution Explorer and choose Publish from the context menu. The Publish Wizard opens (see Figure 20-2). Choose a location to publish the file. In this example, choose a directory on the local computer like C:\Bryan\Publish.

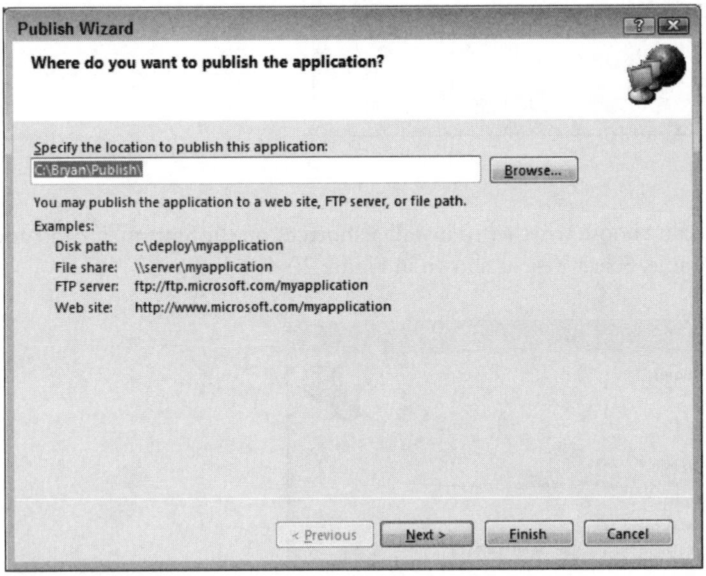

FIGURE 20-2

> *✎* **NOTE** *You will need to share this folder. Here the folder is shared as Publish. To share a folder in Windows 7 with other users on the network or this computer, navigate to the folder in Windows Explorer and right click the folder to bring up the context menu. Choose Share With and then Specific People. At your work, you would choose a group of users that could access the shared folder or network share. For this example, just select or enter Everyone and then click Add. Next, click Share and then click Done to share the folder.*

After setting the location, click Next.

7. Specify how users will install the application. Select the radio button for "From a UNC Path or file share." Enter the UNC path as `\\localhost\Publish` or however you named your file share in step 6 (see Figure 20-3).

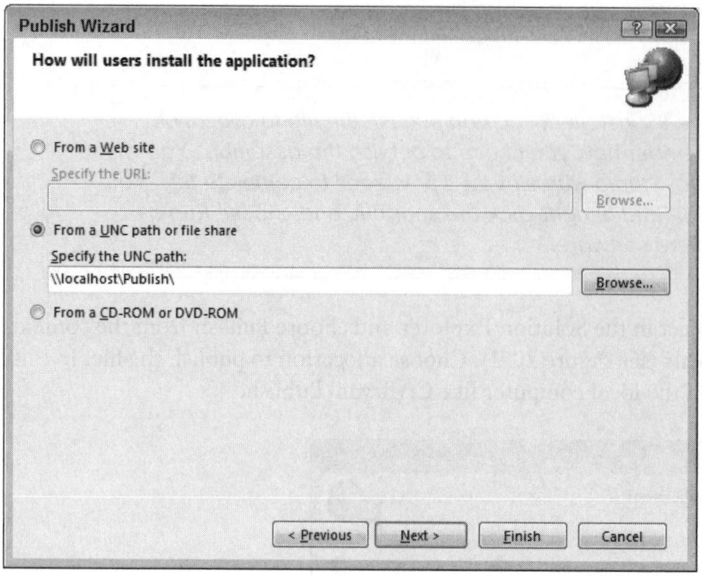

FIGURE 20-3

8. Click Next. In this step you can choose whether to install a shortcut on the Start menu and add a listing in Add/Remove Programs. Select Yes, as shown in Figure 20-4.

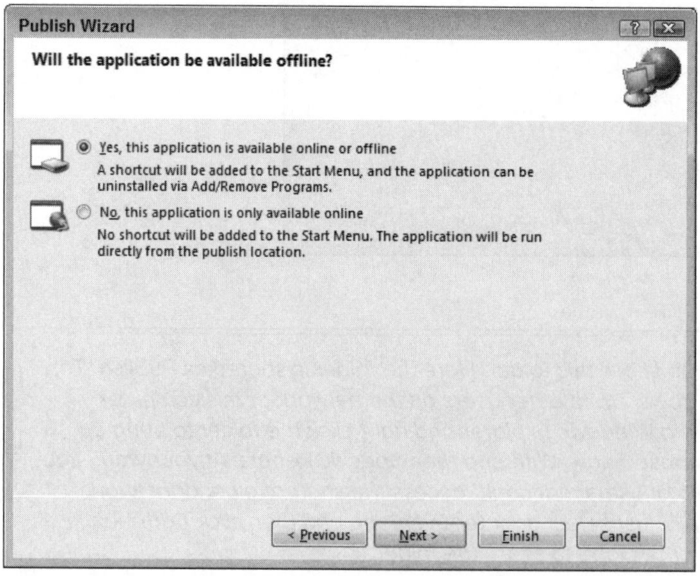

FIGURE 20-4

9. You will see the summary of your choices. Click Finish to complete the wizard. The setup files will be copied to the file share.

10. When you run the install from the share, you may see a few security warnings, such as the one shown in Figure 20-5. If you see this, just click Install to continue. The form you created will open. Click the Version button and you will see Version 1.0. You can close the form. Check the Program Files directory; you will see firsthand that no files were added for the ClickOnce application, and a new shortcut has been added to the Start menu.

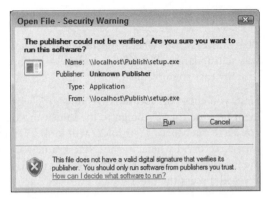

FIGURE 20-5

11. To update the application and see the self-updating capabilities in action, go back to the ClickOnce Windows application in Visual Studio and change the button Click event to update the label to **Version 1.1**. Your Click event handler should look like this:

```
Private Sub btnVersion_Click(ByVal sender As System.Object, ByVal e As _
    System.EventArgs) Handles btnVersion.Click
    lblVersion.Text = "Version 1.1"
End Sub
```

12. Test the application to make sure the label now displays Version 1.1.

13. Right-click the project in Solution Explorer and choose Properties from the context menu. This time you will not use the wizard to publish the assembly. Click the Publish tab on the left side of the main window.

14. Take a look at the options. You can see all the choices you made using the wizard. Be sure to set the action for updates. To do this, click the Updates button and select the check box for "The application should check for updates." Click the radio button to check before the application starts. All you have to do is scroll down to the bottom right of the Publish window and click Publish Now.

15. Notice at the bottom of Visual Studio that it notes that Publish succeeded.

16. Run the application using the shortcut on the Start menu. You will be prompted to update the application. Click OK (see Figure 20-6). After the form opens, click the Version button; the text of the label indicates that the application is updated to Version 1.1.

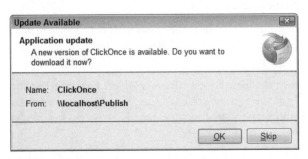

FIGURE 20-6

How It Works

That was easy, but what happened? After a few clicks, you deployed a Windows Forms application that was self-updating. Behind the scenes, Visual Studio completed many tasks that make this deployment strategy easy to implement.

First, you chose the location to publish the assembly: `C:\Bryan\Publish` was created to host the deployment files for you. If you go to the folder and open the Application Files folder, you will see each version you have published. Your folder will look like Figure 20-7. Note that each version of the assembly has its own directory. By default, the .NET Framework is installed if the user does not have the correct version of the Framework. The installer would download it from Microsoft. Feel free to browse around the directory. We will discuss the other files later.

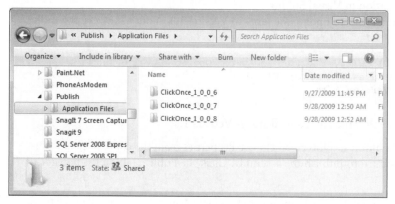

FIGURE 20-7

Next, you choose how the users will install the application. Here you tell the wizard how to deliver the application to the users' computers.

The next step of the wizard enables you to specify whether offline access is allowed. If you decide to allow offline access, a shortcut is added to Add/Remove Program files and the Start menu. The application is also installed to a secure cache on your computer. If you decide not to allow offline access, the user must return to the publishing location to launch the application on each use. In this case, the user would be required to have access to the share to launch the application for each use.

That's it. When you click Finish, Visual Studio 2010 goes to work. What happens behind the scenes is not magic. Actually, you could manually complete everything without Visual Studio if you ever needed to do so.

Referring back to Figure 20-7, take another look at the files. Here's what happened: First, the application was deployed. Then a subdirectory was created for the current version's files. Also, required manifest files were generated and placed under the root and version subdirectory. Finally, a `setup.exe` file for deployment was created.

To install the application, you navigated to the Share and ran Setup. Each time you launch the installed application, a check is made to see whether a newer version is available. When a new version is available, you are notified and presented with the option to install the update. ClickOnce deployment has a large number of deployment options. This exercise only scratched the surface.

XCOPY Deployment

XCOPY deployment gets its name from the MS DOS xcopy command. XCOPY is a copy procedure that simply copies a directory and all files, including subfolders. This is commonly associated with web applications, but with Visual Studio 2010 it can also apply to a desktop application. Since a standard .NET assembly does not need any form of registration, it fully supports this option. XCOPY does not work with shared assemblies because they require installation (if they are used from the Global Assembly Cache). You learn more about shared assemblies later in this chapter. When you use XCOPY for desktop applications, you have to create any shortcuts or menu items via a script or manually. You would typically use XCOPY for web site deployment and for testing and prototypes of Windows Forms applications.

CREATING A VISUAL STUDIO 2010 SETUP APPLICATION

Visual Studio 2010 supports the Windows Installer. But what is it? Windows Installer, which gets installed with Visual Studio 2010, is a general platform for installing applications in Windows. It provides a lot of functionality, such as uninstall capabilities and transactional installation options (the ability to roll back if something fails) as well as other general features. Many of these features are either built in (so that you do not have to do anything) or are configurable, extensible, or both.

The Visual Studio 2010 Windows Installer support has made it easier to create a simple installation. Visual Studio has provided templates in the New Project dialog for this purpose.

Visual Studio 2010 exposes four main templates for creating Windows Installer projects:

➤ **Setup Project** for desktop or general setup

➤ **Web Setup Project** for web applications or web services

➤ **Merge Module,** a package that can only be merged into another setup

➤ **Cab Project,** which creates a package that can be used as a type of install

Finally, Visual Studio 2010 also has a Setup Wizard Project, which aids you in creating one of the Windows Installer templates listed here.

When you are creating setup applications, always be aware of the user. By default, all of the applications you will create with Visual Studio 2010 require version 4 of the .NET Framework on the installation system. For internal applications, you will know what prerequisites are installed on each computer, but in many cases you will deliver your application to users with no idea of the target system configuration. When you are not sure of the user's configuration, it is up to you to make all required components available.

Visual Studio 2010 makes the process of including prerequisites easy. Most common requirements can be included (bootstrapped) by selecting a check box. By default, the .NET Framework is automatically bootstrapped. Any setup application that is created with the default settings will prompt the end user to install version 4 of the Framework if it is not installed prior to setup.

TRY IT OUT Creating a Setup Application

Code file Prerequisite.zip is available for download at Wrox.com

In this Try It Out, you create a setup application.

1. Open Visual Studio and create a New Windows Forms application named **Prerequisite**. You will not make any changes to the form design or code.

2. Save All and then build the project.

3. Add a setup project named **Installer** to the solution, as shown in Figure 20-8. To add a new project, choose File ⇨ Add ⇨ New Project from the main menu bar.

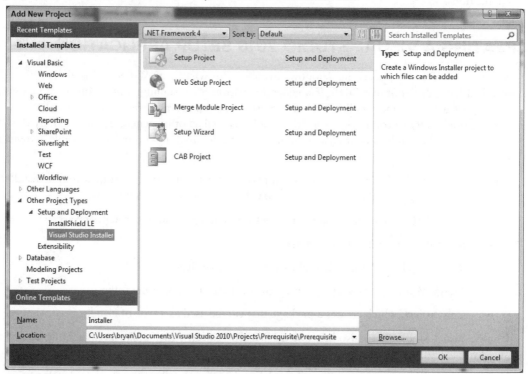

FIGURE 20-8

When Visual Studio creates the project, it adds a Designer. There are three main folders in the left pane of the designer: Application Folder, User's Desktop, and User's Programs Menu (see Figure 20-9).

4. In the Solution Explorer, right-click the Installer project and choose Properties.

5. Find the Prerequisite button to the right and click it. You will see the Prerequisites form, as shown in Figure 20-10. Notice that by default, the .NET Framework 4 Client Profile is selected, along with Windows Installer 3.1.

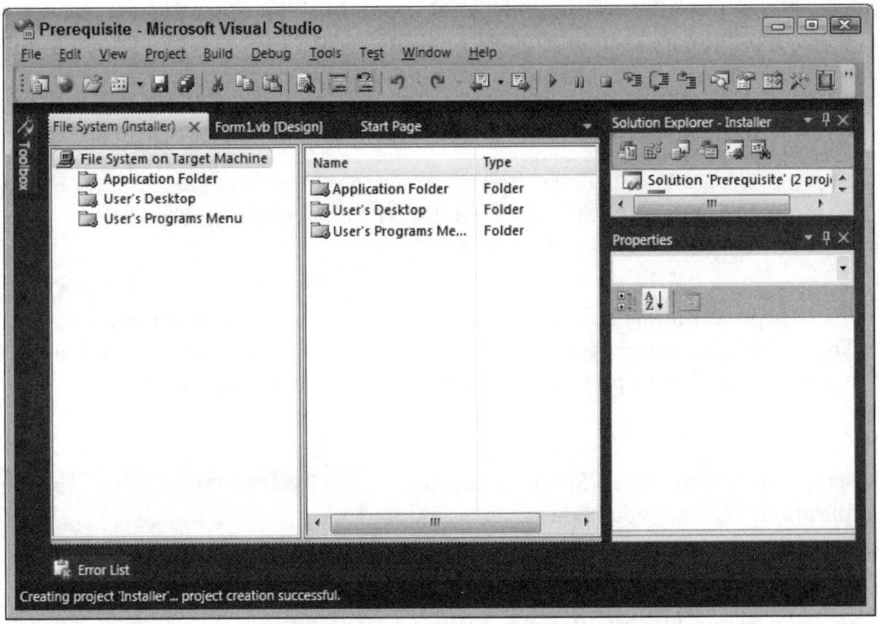

FIGURE 20-9

6. Select the check box beside Microsoft Visual Basic PowerPacks 10.0 and click OK twice to both dialogs. Note that by default, the components are set to download from the vendor's website.

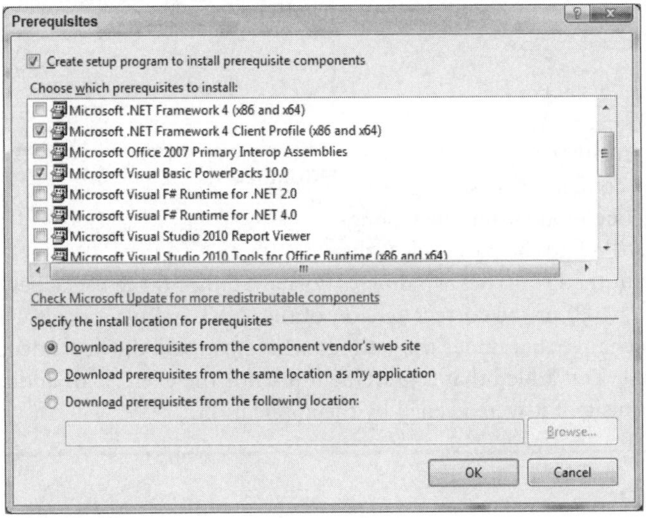

FIGURE 20-10

7. Right-click the Application Folder node in the designer (left pane) and select Add Project Output. The form will look like Figure 20-11.

8. Select Primary output from the Add Project Output Group form and click OK.

9. Right-click Primary output from Prerequisite, which you just added. From the context menu, select Create a Shortcut to Primary Output from Prerequisite. Rename the shortcut **Prerequisite**. Right-click the newly created shortcut and select Cut from the context menu. On the left pane, right-click User's Programs Menu and click Paste.

10. Save and build the Installer project.

> **NOTE** *You may see some warnings about a public key error when building these next few Try It Outs. You can ignore these.*

11. Right-click the Installer project in the Solution Explorer and select Install. A Windows Installer will be loaded. This is the Setup project you have just created. Remember the shortcut you added to the User's Programs menu. Take a peek at your menu and you will see the shortcut.

How It Works

When you create the setup application, Visual Studio creates a Windows Installer application. Changes you make, such as adding the ClickOnce program to the project, are included in the Installer database file.

In this example, you add one executable. It is also possible to add many other types of files, including text files, help files, and other assemblies.

When you build the project, two files are created:

➤ The msi file

➤ An installation loader named setup.exe

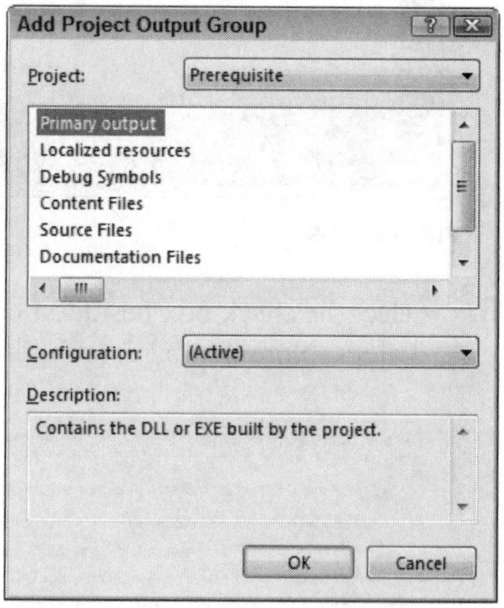

You can see these files in your <solution directory>\Installer\Release or <solution directory>\Installer\Debug folder. Your files will be stored in either the Release folder or the Debug folder, depending on your configuration settings.

FIGURE 20-11

You can change between release and debug mode using the Configuration Manager under the build menu. To find the path, select the solution and look at the Path property in the Properties window of Visual Studio. If the user does not have Microsoft Visual Basic PowerPacks 10.0 or the correct version of the .NET Framework, it will be downloaded from the vendor. You can change that under the settings where you add the dependency for Microsoft Visual Basic PowerPacks 10.0. You added that requirement just for the exercise of adding it. Normally, you would only add a prerequisite if it were needed by the application.

USER INTERFACE EDITOR

Installations can be configured to meet almost any need, with Visual Studio 2010. One of the easiest ways to make your installation look professional is to customize the user interface during installation. A tool, User Interface Editor, is available to do just this.

With the User Interface Editor, you can configure the installation to do just about anything you want. You can add prebuilt dialogs such as a license agreement. A number of customizable dialogs are also available. You can even add a custom dialog to ensure that a valid serial number is entered during installation.

TRY IT OUT Customizing the User Interface

Code file UserInterface.zip is available for download at Wrox.com

In this Try It Out, you will customize the installation of a setup application. This exercise demonstrates only some of the options, of course — almost every aspect of the installation is customizable.

1. Open Visual Studio and create a New Setup Project. Name the project **UserInterface**.

2. Select View ⇨ Editor ⇨ User Interface from the menu. The editor will open, as shown in Figure 20-12. You will see two main items, Install and Administrative Install, both of which have customizable interfaces. The administrative install is for a special type of installation that we will not explain in detail; it is used when an administrator installs an application image to a network share.

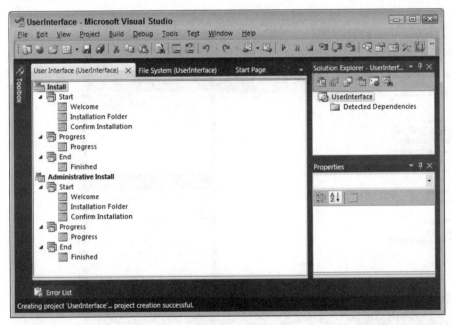

FIGURE 20-12

3. Under the Install node at the top, right-click Start and choose Add Dialog from the context menu. The Add Dialog window will appear (see Figure 20-13).

4. Select the License Agreement dialog and click OK. By default, the dialog box will be added as the last dialog under the Start node. You will make the dialog box the second window the user sees by moving it up the tree node. Right-click the License Agreement dialog box and choose Move Up until it is the second dialog box. Your project will look similar to Figure 20-14.

5. This is where you would normally add a license agreement file using the `LicenseFile` property. The only requirement is that is it must be in Rich Text Format (RTF). For this example, leave this property blank.

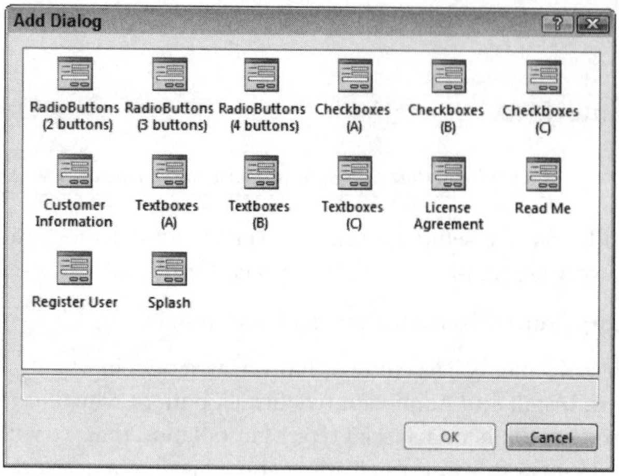

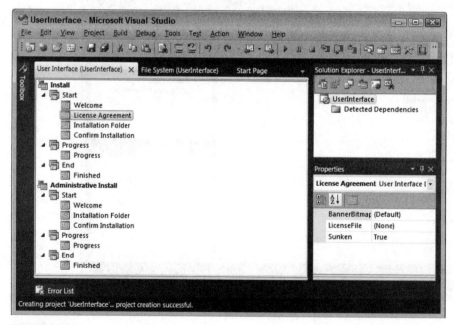

FIGURE 20-13

FIGURE 20-14

6. Add a Customer Information dialog box and make it the third step under the Start process. Change the `SerialNumberTemplate` property to **%%-###-%%%** and the `ShowSerialNumber` to **True**.

7. That is all it takes. Just build the application and install. To install, you can right-click the project in Solution Explorer and choose Install. You will see the License Agreement dialog box as the second screen of the installation. The third step is the Customer Information screen.

10. In the Customer Information screen, enter 77-000-777 for the serial number (see Figure 20-15).

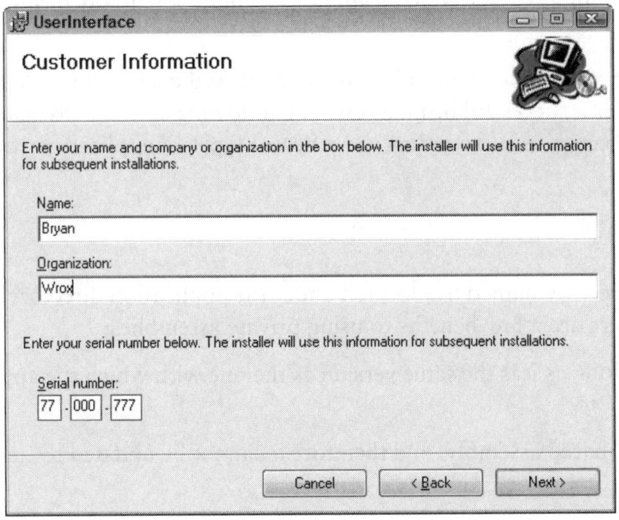

FIGURE 20-15

11. Complete the installation by clicking Next through the rest of the steps.

How It Works

Wow. How easy is that? You customize the installation package with just a few clicks of the mouse. Visual Studio makes it easy for you to have complete control over the installation interface.

The second step of the installation is the license agreement you add. After agreeing to install the application, Visual Studio adds the dialog boxes in the order you choose.

The third dialog is the Customer Information screen. Without a valid serial number, the installation would abort. You create a valid serial number based on the `SerialNumberTemplate` property you changed to `%%-###-%%%`. The `%` character signifies that a required digit is included in the algorithm, and the `#` character is entered for digits that are not included. The serial number algorithm sums up all required digits and then divides the sum by 7. If the remainder is 0, the serial number entered passed validation. So, the first two and the last three digits are added together for a total of 35. Then 35 is divided by 7 for a remainder of 0, and you are allowed to install the application.

DEPLOYING DIFFERENT SOLUTIONS

Deploying applications is actually a large and complex task, made easier by various tools. However, if you consider a large suite of applications such as Microsoft Office, you will notice that there can be a vast number of files. All these files require explicit locations or Registry entries. They all tie together to make the application work. In addition to size, there can also be many other complexities, such as database creation: What happens if the database already exists? What happens with the data that is already there? This kind of activity, commonly referred to as *migration*, could potentially mean a lot of work for an installation expert.

Having multiple application types can also make an installation complex, and detailed knowledge of the different applications is required for a successful installation. The following sections discuss some items related to different deployment scenarios surrounding the different types of applications that can be created with Visual Studio 2010.

Private Assemblies

Private assemblies are installed in a directory named `bin` located under the application directory. These files are private to the application. There are a few benefits to using private assemblies:

➤ No versioning is required, as long as it is the same version as the one with which the application was built.

➤ The private assembly is not a shared assembly, and therefore it cannot be updated by another application (at least it is not meant to be).

➤ You can manually replace the assembly as long as it is the same version.

➤ It enables XCOPY deployment (the ability simply to copy and paste files to a location and have it work).

➤ You can make changes to the assembly, and if two different applications use it, you can update one independently from the other.

➤ No configuration or signing (see the following section) is necessary. It just works.

➤ It is great for small utility assemblies or application-specific code.

Private assemblies have the following negatives:

➤ When you have multiple applications using one assembly, you have to deploy the assembly to the `bin` directory of each application.

➤ You would normally have to include the assembly in each setup project where it is used.

➤ Versioning is not enforced, as it is in a shared assembly.

➤ It is not strongly named, which means someone could spoof your assembly.

> **NOTE** *Spoofing an assembly is when someone creates an assembly that looks identical to yours and replaces yours with the spoofed copy. This spoofed copy could behave in malicious ways.*

Shared Assemblies

Shared assemblies are actually more stable than private assemblies, and they have a thorough approach to assembly deployment. A shared assembly can also behave like a private assembly, so all the benefits of that approach apply here too. The traditional shared assembly is different because of the extra work you need to do and the extra capabilities it then gains.

A shared assembly is like going back in time. In Windows 3.1, the main deployment location for these kinds of DLLs was the `Windows\System` directory. Then you were advised to have these files in the local application path, which enabled easier installation and uninstallation. Today, the `System` directory concept returns in a new guise named the Global Assembly Cache (GAC). However, the strong naming of assemblies is a definite step up.

To install a shared assembly, you have to add the file to a new folder named `Global Assembly Cache`. By default, this folder is not visible in the three default folders that are listed. To add the GAC folder you must right-click the node named File System on Target Machine and select Add Special Folder Global Assembly Cache.

> **NOTE** *Note that any project type can use a shared assembly, including a web application.*

A shared assembly offers the following main benefits:

➤ It is signed and cannot be spoofed.

➤ It has strong versioning support and configuration options.

➤ It is stored in one central location and does not need to be copied to the `bin` directory of every application that uses it.

➤ Many different versions can be running side by side.

Shared assemblies have the following negatives:

➤ You have to sign the assembly.

➤ You have to be careful not to break compatibility with existing applications; otherwise, you have to configure the different versions.

➤ Configuration can be a nightmare, depending on the requirements.

Deploying Desktop Applications

In the second project, you created a setup for a desktop application. For that you installed only one executable. It had no dependencies other than the .NET Framework, which is always required. In a more complete application, you may have various assemblies, WinForm controls, or other files that you created for the application. Installing a private assembly with the Setup project means that you include the file by adding it to the setup application.

Deploying Web Applications

A web application, when using private assemblies, can be simple to deploy. You can use the Visual Studio 2010 Web Application setup project to create a simple web setup. The setup creates a virtual directory and copies the files you specify to the physical directory location.

Deploying XML Web Services

A web service is deployed in much the same way as a web application. It also has a virtual directory. The files that it requires are somewhat different, though. You need to deploy the `asmx` and `discovery` files together with the assembly.

Useful Tools

This section describes a few tools that either come with .NET or are in Windows already for you to use. When creating an installation, you need to test it by installing it on various machines. Sometimes, when things do not go according to plan, you may need to do some or all of the tasks manually to see which one was the cause of the problem.

For example, perhaps you suspect that the `ASPNET_WP.dll` process has become unstable or broken in some fashion and has affected the installation. In this scenario, you may want to restart IIS before you run the install. In a similar vein, perhaps an assembly that was supposed to be registered in the GAC as a shared assembly cannot be found by the client; you may want to register it manually to check whether there was a problem with the registration. The following list briefly describes the tools you may need to use:

➤ **ASPNET_RegIIS:** The `aspnet_regiis.exe` command line tool can be found in the `<sysdir>\Microsoft.NET\Framework\<version>` directory. This tool makes it an easy task to reinstall various aspects of the ASP.NET runtime and change settings for ASP.NET in IIS.

➤ **IISReset:** IISReset simply restarts IIS without requiring you to open the IIS management console. Simply open a DOS prompt and type **IISReset**, and it will immediately restart IIS.

➤ **ILDasm:** If you want to inspect the metadata of an assembly, MSIL Disassembler is the tool for the job. With this tool, you can inspect everything from the namespaces to the version. Start MSIL Disassembler by typing **ildasm** at a Visual Studio command prompt.

➤ **GACUtil:** This is a Visual Studio command-line tool for registering/unregistering assemblies from the Global Assembly Cache. The `/I` option is for registering the assembly, and the `/u` option is for unregistering.

➤ **RegAsm:** This Visual Studio command-line utility is used for creating the necessary Component Object Model (COM) information from an assembly. This is used when you need to expose an assembly for COM Interop. The `regasm` tool includes switches for registering/unregistering type libraries.

➤ **InstallUtil:** This is a Visual Studio command-line tool for executing the Installer classes within an assembly. This can execute the InstallerHelper sample you did earlier in this chapter.

➤ **MageUI (Manifest Generation and Editing Tool):** This is a graphical tool for generating, editing, and signing the application and deployment manifest for ClickOnce applications. Run MageUI from a Visual Studio command prompt to start the tool. A command-line version of this tool, `Mage.exe`, is available if you prefer to not have the user interface.

SUMMARY

We hope you enjoyed looking at some general aspects of deployment. In the first section of this chapter, you were introduced to some terminology, and then you learned how to create a ClickOnce application and a simple Setup application inside Visual Studio. You also learned the positives and negatives of private versus shared assemblies. Ultimately, we hope you learned that there is potentially a lot to learn in this area, from getting to know more about the features of the Windows Installer templates to learning how to do more with ClickOnce deployment.

To summarize, you should know how to:

➤ Create a ClickOnce deployment application

➤ Create a Visual Studio 2010 setup application

➤ Use general deployment terms such as XCOPY, and understand the differences between shared versus private assemblies

➤ Edit the installer user interface

EXERCISES

1. Where are shared assemblies stored?

2. How are updates handled when using ClickOnce deployment?

3. Name two dialog boxes you can add to a setup project in Visual Studio 2010.

4. How do you arrange the order of dialog boxes in the user interface of installations?

► **WHAT YOU HAVE LEARNED IN THIS CHAPTER**

TOPIC	CONCEPTS
ClickOnce Deployment	Applications will update when a new version is released. Windows applications can be released from a remote location like a website or file share. You can choose whether to allow the user to run the application when not connected to the network or website. This is a very easy way to manage application installs to users in remote locations and keep them updated.
XCOPY Deployment	A simple copy process. No shortcuts are created.
Setup Application	You can add a setup project to your solution to build an `msi/setup` file installation. This is the standard deployment method most of us are used to. You have complete control of the setup process.
User Interface Editor	Use the editor to add, remove, or reorder the dialogs the the user will see during installation.You can add many prebuilt dialogs like: License, Register User, Read Me, Splash, Customer Information, and others.

A

Exercise Solutions

CHAPTER 1

Code file Chapter 1\ Exercise 1.zip.

1. Create a Windows application with a Textbox control and a Button control that will display whatever is typed in the text box when the user clicks the button.

A. To display the text from a text box on a form when the user clicks the button, you add the following bolded code to the button's Click event handler:

```
Private Sub btnDisplay_Click(ByVal sender As System.Object, _
ByVal e As System.EventArgs) Handles btnDisplay.Click

  'Display the contents of the text box
  MessageBox.Show(txtInput.Text, "Exercise 1")
End Sub
```

CHAPTER 3

1. Create a Windows application with two button controls. In the Click event for the first button, declare two Integer variables and set their values to any number that you like. Perform any math operation on these variables and display the results in a message box.

In the Click event for the second button, declare two String variables and set their values to anything that you like. Perform a string concatenation on these variables and display the results in a message box.

A.   The first part of this exercise requires you to declare two `Integer` variables and set their values, and then to perform a math operation of these variables and display the results in a message box. The variables can be declared and set as:

```
'Declare variables and set their values
Dim intX As Integer = 5
Dim intY As Integer = 10
```

➤   To perform a math operation and display the results can be performed as:

```
'Multiply the numbers and display the results
MessageBox.Show("The sum of " & intX.ToString & " * " & _
intY.ToString & " = " & intX * intY, "Exercise 1")
```

➤   The second part of this exercise requires you to declare two `String` variables and set their values, and then to concatenate the variables and display the results in a message box. The `String` variables can be declared and set as:

```
'Declare variables and set their values
Dim strOne As String = "Visual Basic "
Dim strTwo As String = "2010"
```

➤   To concatenate the variables and display the results, you could write code such as:

```
'Concatenate the strings and display the results
MessageBox.Show(strOne & strTwo, "Exercise 1")
```

2.   Create a Windows application with a text box and a button control. In the button's `Click` event, display three message boxes. The first message box should display the length of the string that was entered into the text box. The second message box should display the first half of the string, and the third message box should display the last half of the string.

A.   This exercise requires you to display the length of the string entered into a text box, and then display the first half of the string and the last half of the string. To display the length of the string, you can use the `Length` property of the `Text` property of the text box, as shown here:

```
'Display the length of the string from the TextBox
MessageBox.Show("The length of the string in the TextBox is " & _
txtInput.Text.Length, "Exercise 2")
```

➤   To display the first half of the string, you need to use the `Substring` method with a starting index of `0`, and for the length you use the length of the string divided by `2`, as shown here. Don't forget that with the Option Strict option turned on, you must convert the results of a division operation to an `Integer` data type for use in the `SubString` method:

```
'Display the first half of the string from the TextBox
MessageBox.Show(txtInput.Text.Substring(0, _
CType(txtInput.Text.Length / 2, Integer)), "Exercise 2")
```

➤   To display the last half of the string you again use the `Substring` method but this time you simply give it a starting index of the length of the string divided by `2`, as shown here:

```
'Display the last half of the string from the TextBox
MessageBox.Show(txtInput.Text.Substring( _
CType(txtInput.Text.Length / 2, Integer)), "Exercise 2")
```

CHAPTER 4

1. When using a `Select Case` statement, how do you allow for multiple items in the `Case` statement?

A. Separate the items with commas.

2. What is the difference between a `Do Until` and a `Loop Until Do` loop?

A. With a `Loop Until` statement it will always run the code one time.

3. Is "Bryan" and "BRYAN" the same string as Visual Basic sees it?

A. No. These strings are different. You can have your code run case-insensitive comparisons so they look the same when you want your code to see them as equal.

4. When you use the `string.compare` method, what is the last parameter (a Boolean parameter) used for?

A. It indicates whether or not to use a case-sensitive comparison.

5. In a `Select Case` statement, how do you put in a catch all case for items that do not have a match?

A. `Case Else`

6. When writing a `For Each` Loop, how do you have the loop iterate backwards?

A. Use the `Step` keyword and give it a negative value.

7. What keyword do you use to exit a loop early?

A. `Exit`

CHAPTER 5

1. What keyword do you use to keep the values in an array that you `ReDim`? Where do you insert it?

A. `Preserve`. In the statement to redimension (after `ReDim`) the array.

2. How do you order an array?

A. By using the `sort` method.

3. Are arrays zero-based or one-based?

A. Arrays are zero-based.

4. Why would you use an enumeration in code?

A. To provide clarity and prevent invalid values from being submitted.

5. When initializing an array with values, what characters do you use to enclose the values?

A. Brackets `{}`.

6. How does a constant differ from a normal variable?

A. It cannot be changed during runtime.

7. Structures are simpler and similar to what object?

A. A class.

8. Hashtables provide a fast mechanism for what?

A. Lookups. Hashtables are very fast at looking up key-value pairs.

CHAPTER 6

1. WPF makes it easy for organizations to separate which parts of software development?

A. WPF makes it easy to separate business logic from presentation logic or user interface design.

2. XAML is based on another type of language. What is it?

A. XAML is based on XML.

3. What property do you set to position a WPF control in a Grid control?

A. To position WPF controls, you need to set the margin property of the control.

4. In WPF design, you cannot place controls onto a window class, as the window does not have a design surface. To place controls onto a form, Visual Studio adds what container by default?

A. The grid container is the default container for designing a form.

CHAPTER 7

1. Name two controls you can use when adding a toolbar to your form.

A. You can use the following controls when adding a toolbar to your form: ToolStrip, ToolStripButton, ToolStripSeparator, ToolStripProgressBar, ToolStripTextBox, ToolStripDropDownButton, and ToolStripComboBox.

2. What property do you set to display text to users when they hover over a button on a toolbar?

A. You set ToolTipText to display text to users when they hover over a button on the toolbar.

3. When you create a WPF and Windows application you design different objects that are very similar. In a Windows application, you design a form. What do you design in a WPF application?

A. When creating WPF applications you design a window, not a form.

4. To work with a textbox so a user can add many lines of text, what property must be set to `true` in a Windows Forms application?

A. `Multiline` must be set to `True`.

5. Why would you want to show a form using the `ShowDialog` method?

A. To show a form modally, you would open it using `ShowDialog`. This forces the user to act on the form.

CHAPTER 8

1. To display a dialog box to the user, what method do you use?

A. Use the `ShowDialog` method to display a dialog box to the user.

2. What method do you call to display a message box?

A. Use the `Show` method to display a message box to the user.

3. Name the five different ways to display an icon to the user on a message box.

A. The five different ways to show an icon are as follows:

    a. No icon

    b. Information icon

    c. Error icon

    d. Exclamation icon

    e. Question mark icon

4. How do you determine which button was pressed on a message box?

A. Use the `DialogResult` enumeration to determine which button was pressed.

5. If you need to write basic code, where should you look for a simple example inside of Visual Studio?

A. Simple code examples can be found by inserting snippets inside of Visual Studio.

CHAPTER 9

1. How do you add the commonly used menus and toolbars to either a MenuStrip or ToolStrip control?

A. To add commonly used items, you can choose Insert Standard Items from the control's context menu.

2. How do you add a custom context menu to a TextBox control?

A. First you create a ContextMenuStrip control and then you set the control's `ContextMenuStrip` property to the new menu you added.

3. How do you add a shortcut to a menu item, such as Alt+F?

A. To provide an access key such as Alt+F for the File menu, you add & before the shortcut character.

4.   How do you add a shortcut to a menu item, such as Ctrl+C?

A.   To add a shortcut to a menu, use the `ShortcutKeys` property.

CHAPTER 10

1.   What window do you use to track a specific variable while debugging?

A.   To track specific variables, use the Watch window.

2.   How do you look at all of the variables in scope while debugging?

A.   You can see variables in scope by using the Locals windows.

3.   How do you best add error handling to your code?

A.   The best way to add error handling is by using the `Try ... Catch` block. You can also use `Finally` to always run code whether an error occurs or not.

4.   Sometimes you need to cause errors to happen in your code. What keyword do you use to cause errors?

A.   To cause an error, use the `Throw` keyword.

5.   While debugging, how do you move to the very next statement?

A.   `Step Into` enables you to move the next statement.

CHAPTER 11

1.   Modify your `Car` class to implement the `IDisposable` interface. In the `Main` procedure in `Module1`, add code to dispose of the `objCar` object after calling the `DisplaySportsCarDetails` procedure.

A.   The code should now look like this for the `Main` procedure in `Module1`.

```
Sub Main()
'Create a new sports car object
Dim objCar As New SportsCar

'Set the horsepower and weight(kg)
objCar.HorsePower = 240
objCar.Weight = 1085

'Display the details of the car
DisplayCarDetails(objCar)
DisplaySportsCarDetails(objCar)

'Dispose of the object
objCar.Dispose()
objCar = Nothing
```

```
'Wait for input from the user
Console.ReadLine()
End Sub
```

The `Car` class should look like this.

```
Namespace CarPerformance
  Public Class Car
      Implements IDisposable

      Public Color As String
      Public HorsePower As Integer

      Private intSpeed As Integer
      Private intNumberOfDoors As Integer

      'Speed - read-only property to return the speed
      Public ReadOnly Property Speed() As Integer
          Get
              Return intSpeed
          End Get
      End Property

      'Accelerate - add mph to the speed
      Public Sub Accelerate(ByVal accelerateBy As Integer)
          'Adjust the speed
          intSpeed += accelerateBy
      End Sub

      'NumberOfDoors - get/set the number of doors
      Public Property NumberOfDoors() As Integer
          'Called when the property is read
          Get
              Return intNumberOfDoors
          End Get
          'Called when the property is set
          Set(ByVal value As Integer)
              'Is the new value between two and five
              If value >= 2 And value <= 5 Then
                  intNumberOfDoors = value
              End If
          End Set
      End Property

      'IsMoving - is the car moving?
      Public Function IsMoving() As Boolean
          'Is the car's speed zero?
          If Speed = 0 Then
              Return False
          Else
              Return True
          End If
      End Function
```

```
        'Constructor
        Public Sub New()
            'Set the default values
            Color = "White"
            intSpeed = 0
            intNumberOfDoors = 5
        End Sub

        'CalculateAccelerationRate - assume a constant for a normal car
        Public Overridable Function CalculateAccelerationRate() As Double
            'If we assume a normal car goes from 0-60 in 14 seconds,
            'that's an average rate of 4.2 mph/s
            Return 4.2
        End Function

        Private disposedValue As Boolean = False        ' To detect redundant calls

        ' IDisposable
        Protected Overridable Sub Dispose(ByVal disposing As Boolean)
            If Not Me.disposedValue Then
                If disposing Then
                    ' TODO: free other state (managed objects).
                End If

                ' TODO: free your own state (unmanaged objects).
                ' TODO: set large fields to null.
            End If
            Me.disposedValue = True
        End Sub

#Region " IDisposable Support "
    ' This code added by Visual Basic to correctly implement the disposable
pattern.
        Public Sub Dispose() Implements IDisposable.Dispose
            ' Do not change this code.  Put cleanup code in Dispose(ByVal
disposing As Boolean) above.
            Dispose(True)
            GC.SuppressFinalize(Me)
        End Sub

#End Region

    End Class
End Namespace
```

2.   Modify the code in the Main procedure in Module1 to encapsulate the declaration and usage of the SportsCar class in a Using ... End Using statement. Remember that the Using ... End Using statement automatically handles disposal of objects that implement the IDisposable interface.

A.   The code should now look like this for the Main procedure in Module1.

```
Sub Main()
'Create a new sports car object
Using objCar As New SportsCar
'Set the horsepower and weight(kg)
objCar.HorsePower = 240
objCar.Weight = 1085

'Display the details of the car
DisplayCarDetails(objCar)
DisplaySportsCarDetails(objCar)
End Using

'Wait for input from the user
Console.ReadLine()
End Sub
```

CHAPTER 12

1. Modify the Favorites Viewer project to select the first favorite in the ListView control automatically after it has been loaded so that the LinkLabel control displays the first item when the form is displayed.

You also need to modify the Load event in Form1, and ensure that the ListView control contains one or more items before proceeding. You do this by querying the Count property of the Items property of the ListView control. Then you select the first item in the ListView control using the lstFavorites.Items(0).Selected property and call the Click event for the ListBox control to update the LinkLabel control.

A.
```
Private Sub Viewer_Load(ByVal sender As Object, _
    ByVal e As System.EventArgs) Handles Me.Load

    Try
        'Create and use a new instance of the Favorites class
        Using objFavorites As New Favorites

            'Scan the Favorites folder
            objFavorites.ScanFavorites()

            'Process each objWebFavorite object in the
            'favorites collection
            For Each objWebFavorite As WebFavorite In _
                objFavorites.FavoritesCollection

                'Declare a ListViewItem object
                Dim objListViewItem As New ListViewItem

                'Set the properties of the ListViewItem object
                objListViewItem.Text = objWebFavorite.Name
```

```
                    objListViewItem.SubItems.Add(objWebFavorite.Url)

                    'Add the ListViewItem object to the ListView
                    lvwFavorites.Items.Add(objListViewItem)
                Next

            End Using
        Catch ExceptionErr As Exception
            'Display the error
            MessageBox.Show(ExceptionErr.Message, "Favorites Viewer", _
                MessageBoxButtons.OK, MessageBoxIcon.Warning)
        End Try

        'If one or more items exist...
        If lvwFavorites.Items.Count > 1 Then
            'Select the first item
            lvwFavorites.Items(0).Selected = True
            lvwFavorites_Click(Nothing, Nothing)
        End If

    End Sub
```

CHAPTER 13

1. When you compile a Class Library project, what type of file is created?

A. A .dll (Dynamic Link Library) file.

2. Where are signed assemblies stored to be shared on a computer?

A. In the GAC (Global Assembly Cache)

3. How do you install assemblies into the GAC?

A. By dragging the dll into the C:\windows\assembly folder or by running Gacutil.exe.

4. What command would you use to create a key pair file named MyKeyPair.snk?

A. sn -k MyKeyPair.snk

5. When does the task bar redraw?

A. When you mouse over it.

6. If you use a third-party dll and do not have the documentation, how would you investigate the properties and methods available to you?

A. Use the Object Browser. Press F2 as a shortcut to view the Object Browser.

CHAPTER 14

1. User controls are a good example of which key principle of object-oriented design — encapsulation or polymorphism?

A. Encapsulation.

2. There are 2 properties that you can set to explain to the user what the Command Link control will do. What are they?

A. `SupplementalExplanation` and `Text`

3. What are the two main ways to reuse controls between applications?

A. The first is to add the control's source file to every project in which you need the control. The second way is to build a control library.

4. What method should you override to determine when a user control has been added to a form?

A. `InitLayout`

5. There is a property that will tell you if the control is in runtime or design time. What is its name and what data type is it?

A. `DesignMode`, Boolean

6. Add a property to the MyNamespace control called `SuppressMsgBox`, which contains a `Boolean` value. Add code to the `Click` event handlers for each of the buttons on this control to show the message box when the `SuppressMsgBox` property is `False`, and to suppress the message box when this property is `True`.

A. The following shows the code for this exercise:

```
Public Property SuppressMsgBox() As Boolean
    Get
        Return blnSuppressMsgBox
    End Get
    Set(ByVal value As Boolean)
        blnSuppressMsgBox = value
    End Set
End Property

Private Sub btnApplicationCopyright_Click(ByVal sender As System.Object, _
    ByVal e As System.EventArgs) Handles btnApplicationCopyright.Click

    RaiseEvent ApplicationCopyrightChanged( _
        My.Application.Info.Copyright)

    If Not blnSuppressMsgBox Then
        MessageBox.Show(My.Application.Info.Copyright, _
            strApplicationName)
    End If
End Sub

Private Sub btnScreenBounds_Click(ByVal sender As Object, _
    ByVal e As System.EventArgs) Handles btnScreenBounds.Click

    RaiseEvent ScreenBoundsChanged(My.Computer.Screen.Bounds)

    If Not blnSuppressMsgBox Then
```

```
                    MessageBox.Show(My.Computer.Screen.Bounds.ToString, _
                        strApplicationName)
                End If
            End Sub


            Private Sub btnScreenWorkingArea_Click(ByVal sender As Object, _
                ByVal e As System.EventArgs) Handles btnScreenWorkingArea.Click

                RaiseEvent ScreenWorkingAreaChanged(My.Computer.Screen.WorkingArea)

                If Not blnSuppressMsgBox Then
                    MessageBox.Show(My.Computer.Screen.WorkingArea.ToString, _
                        strApplicationName)
                End If
            End Sub
```

CHAPTER 15

1. How would you write a query to retrieve the Name, Description, and Price fields from a table called Product?

A. SELECT Name, Description, Price FROM Product;.

2. What would you add to the query to retrieve only items with DVD in their description?

A. WHERE Description LIKE "*DVD*

3. How would you order the results so that the most expensive item comes first?

A. ORDER BY Price DESC

4. What do you put around column names that have spaces in them?

A. Square brackets are used for column names with spaces, such as [First Name].

5. In Visual Studio 2010, what control can you use to navigate through data in a Windows Forms Application?

A. You can use a BindingNavigator to move through data in a Windows application.

6. What is the terminating character for a SQL command you must use in MS Access?

A. You must terminate your SQL commands with a semicolon in MS Access.

CHAPTER 16

1. What properties do you need to set for a SQL Server connection string when passing a user name and password?

A. You need to set Server, User ID, Password and Database.

2. Which method do you execute when updating data using a `SQLCommand` object?

A. `ExecuteNonQuery` is the method to use to run update queries.

3. Why would you use Integrated Security in your connection string?

A. You would use Integrated Security when you want to access the database and have the security of the current application user.

4. If you do not need to create update/delete/insert commands, how do you have them created automatically?

A. Use a `SqlCommandBuilder` to create update/delete/insert commands.

5. What method do you use to populate a dataset with data?

A. Use the `Fill` method to populate a `DataSet`.

CHAPTER 17

1. How do you change the way date and time fields are displayed in a Dynamic Data website in edit mode?

A. Changing the `DateTime_Edit.ascx` Field Template will change the way date and time fields appear.

2. How do you change the way insert pages are displayed in a Dynamic Data website?

A. Changing the `Insert.aspx` Page template will change the way insert pages are shown.

3. What type of template do you use to change the way the site looks for just one table?

A. Use an Entity Template to change the design for just one table.

CHAPTER 18

1. If you wanted to build a design and layout that can be inherited by Web Form pages, how would you do it?

A. To create a design other Web Forms can inherit you should implement master pages.

2. To change the way elements of the page appear, you have two good options when designing web pages. What are they?

A. When creating Web Forms, you can use themes and skins or cascading style sheets to update the appearance of elements.

3. What type of data source do you bind the menu control to?

A. You can bind the menu control to a site map (XML file).

4. What property do you set to have static client IDs for server controls?

A. Set the `ClientIDMode` property to `Static` to force a static client ID.

5. Name one control you can use to help validate form data.

A. You can use a `RequiredFieldValidator` to force users to enter data when submitting a form. Other controls are `CompareValidator`, `CustomValidator`, `RangeValidator`, and `RegularExpressionValidator`.

CHAPTER 19

1. Name two reasons to use XML to integrate systems or store data.

A. You should use XML because it is human readable, it is a common standard, cross-platform integration is possible, and it can be validated against a schema.

2. In what two items do you store data in XML?

A. Elements and attributes.

3. Is this valid XML? `<Root><one att="red" /></root>`

A. No, it is not. The closing tag for `Root` is not cased properly and does not match.

4. Is this valid XML? `<Root><one att="red" >Me & you</one></Root>`

A. No, it is not. The text for element `one` cannot contain `&`. To make it valid, replace `Me & you` with `Me &amp; you`

5. Is this valid XML? `<Root><one><att>Me</one></att></Root>`

A. No, it is not. The tags are not nested properly. `<att>` must close before `<one>` because it is nested inside of `<one>`. The correct XML would look like this:

```
<Root><one><att>Me</att></one></Root>.
```

CHAPTER 20

1. Where are shared assemblies stored?

A. Shared assemblies are stored in the Global Assembly Cache.

2. How are updates handled when using ClickOnce deployment?

A. Updates are handled automatically when using ClickOnce.

3. Name two dialog boxes you can add to a setup project in Visual Studio 2010.

A. Two dialogs that can be added to setup projects are Customer Information and License Agreement. A few others are Read Me, Register User, and Splash.

4. How do you arrange the order of dialog boxes in the user interface of installations?

A. To change the order of dialogs, right-click the dialog and select move up or move down.

```vb
Public Property SuppressMsgBox() As Boolean
    Get
        Return blnSuppressMsgBox
    End Get
    Set(ByVal value As Boolean)
        blnSuppressMsgBox = value
    End Set
End Property
Private Sub btnApplicationCopyright_Click(ByVal sender As System.Object, _
    ByVal e As System.EventArgs) Handles btnApplicationCopyright.Click

    RaiseEvent ApplicationCopyrightChanged( _
        My.Application.Info.Copyright)

    If Not blnSuppressMsgBox Then
        MessageBox.Show(My.Application.Info.Copyright, _
            strApplicationName)
    End If
End Sub

Private Sub btnScreenBounds_Click(ByVal sender As Object, _
    ByVal e As System.EventArgs) Handles btnScreenBounds.Click

    RaiseEvent ScreenBoundsChanged(My.Computer.Screen.Bounds)

    If Not blnSuppressMsgBox Then
        MessageBox.Show(My.Computer.Screen.Bounds.ToString, _
            strApplicationName)
    End If
End Sub

Private Sub btnScreenWorkingArea_Click(ByVal sender As Object, _
    ByVal e As System.EventArgs) Handles btnScreenWorkingArea.Click

    RaiseEvent ScreenWorkingAreaChanged(My.Computer.Screen.WorkingArea)

    If Not blnSuppressMsgBox Then
        MessageBox.Show(My.Computer.Screen.WorkingArea.ToString, _
            strApplicationName)
    End If
End Sub
```

B

Where to Now?

Now that you have come to the end of this book, you should have a relatively good idea of how to write code using Visual Basic 2010. The topics and example code covered in this book have been designed to provide you with a firm foundation, but that foundation is just the beginning of your journey. In fact, this book is just one of the many steps you are going to take on your road to becoming a full-fledged Visual Basic 2010 programmer. Although you have come a long way, there is still a lot farther to go, and you will certainly have many more questions on the way.

Where will you get these questions answered? And then, what next?

This appendix offers you some advice about what your possible next steps could be. As you can imagine, a number of different routes are open to any one person. The path you choose will probably depend on your goals and what you are being asked to do by your employer. Some readers will want to continue at a more general level with some knowledge about all aspects of Visual Basic 2010, while others may want to drill down into more specific areas.

It is extremely important not to take a long break before carrying on with Visual Basic 2010. If you do so, you will find that you quickly forget what you have learned. The trick is to practice. You can do this in a number of ways:

> Continue with the examples from this book. Try to add more features and more code to extend the examples. Try to merge and blend different samples together.

> You may have an idea for a new program. Go on and write it.

> Try to get a firm understanding of the terminology.

> Read as many articles as you can. Even if you do not understand them at first, bits and pieces will come together.

> Make sure you communicate your knowledge. If you know other programmers, get talking and ask questions.

> Consult our online and offline resources for more information.

The rest of this appendix lists available resources, both online and offline, to help you decide where to go next.

ONLINE RESOURCES

Basically, there are thousands of places you can go online for help with any problems you may have. The good news is that many of them are free. Whenever you come across a problem — and, unfortunately, you will — there are always loads of people out there willing to help. These unknown souls include others who were at the same stage as you and may have had a similar problem, or experts with a great deal of knowledge. The key is not to be intimidated and to use these resources as much as you like. Remember, everyone was a complete beginner at some point and has had many of the same experiences as you.

This section begins by examining the P2P site provided by Wrox, followed by some of the more general sites available. If you can't find what you want through any of the sites listed here or if you have some time and want to explore, just search for **Visual Basic 2010** and you will be on your way!

P2P.Wrox.com

P2P provides programmer-to-programmer support on mailing lists, forums, and newsgroups, in addition to a one-to-one e-mail system. You can join any of the mailing lists for author and peer support in Visual Basic 2010 (plus any others you may be interested in).

You can choose to join the mailing lists, and you can receive a weekly digest of the list. If you don't have the time or facilities to receive mailing lists, you can search the online archives using subject areas or keywords.

Should you wish to use P2P for online support, go to `http://p2p.wrox.com`. On P2P, you can view the groups without becoming a member. These lists are moderated, so you can be confident about the information presented. Also, junk mail and spam are deleted, and your e-mail address is protected.

Microsoft Resources

Probably one of the first sites you'll intuitively turn to is the Microsoft site (`http://www.microsoft.com`). That makes sense, because it is full of information, including support, tips, hints, downloads, and newsgroups. To see more newsgroups, navigate to `http://www.microsoft.com/communities/`.

There are also a number of sites on MSDN that you may find to be very helpful, including the following:

- ➤ **Visual Studio:** `http://msdn.microsoft.com/en-us/vstudio/`
- ➤ **MSDN Library:** `http://msdn.microsoft.com/library/`
- ➤ **Microsoft Developer Network:** `http://msdn.microsoft.com/`
- ➤ **Microsoft Visual Basic:** `http://msdn.microsoft.com/en-us/vbasic/`
- ➤ **.NET Framework download site:** `http://msdn.microsoft.com/netframework/downloads/`
- ➤ **CodePlex:** `http://www.codeplex.com/` (hosted by Microsoft)

➤ **ASP .NET Resources:** `http://www.asp.net/`

➤ **Channel 9:** `http://channel9.msdn.com/`

Other Resources

As mentioned earlier, hundreds of online sites discuss Visual Basic 2010. These sites give everything from news on moving from Visual Basic 2008 to Visual Basic 2010, to listings of up and coming conferences worldwide. Although you can do a search for Visual Basic 2010, the number of sites returned can be extremely overwhelming. Let's look at three of these possible sites.

A place to find sample code and examples is at `http://www.freevbcode.com/` or `http://www.4guysfromrolla.com/` At these sites, you can find great articles and tips to take your skills to the next level. Both sites have forums or message boards for your questions and answers.

You can get a journal, *The Visual Studio Magazine,* from a similar user group. Again, this journal is backed by meetings and four yearly conferences, along with a website, `http://www.devx.com/vb/`, which can give e-mail updates. On the website, you have access to a number of different areas both in Visual Basic and other related and nonrelated Visual Studio areas.

Of course, these are just three among the many out there, to help you get started. Remember, however, that the Internet is not the only place to find information, so the next section looks at some resources not found on the Web.

OFFLINE RESOURCES (BOOKS)

Wrox Press is committed to providing books that will help you develop your programming skills in the direction that you want. We have a selection of tutorial-style books that build on the Visual Basic 2010 knowledge gained here. These will help you to specialize in particular areas. Here are the details of a couple of key titles.

➤ *Professional Visual Basic 2010 and .NET 4*, Wiley Publishing 2010

- ➤ Visual Studio 2010
- ➤ Objects and Visual Basic
- ➤ Custom Objects
- ➤ Common Language Runtime
- ➤ Declarative Programming with Visual Basic
- ➤ Exception Handling and Debugging
- ➤ TDD with Visual Basic
- ➤ Arrays, Collections, Generics
- ➤ Transactions
- ➤ Using XML
- ➤ ADO.NET and LINQ

- ➤ Entity Framework
- ➤ Working with SQL Server
- ➤ Services (XML/WCF)
- ➤ Windows Forms
- ➤ Advanced Windows Forms
- ➤ User Controls
- ➤ WPF Desktop Applications
- ➤ Blend
- ➤ Silverlight
- ➤ Silverlight and Services
- ➤ Working with ASP.NET
- ➤ ASP.NET Advanced Features
- ➤ ASP.NET MVC
- ➤ Live/Mesh/Azure
- ➤ SharePoint
- ➤ VSTO
- ➤ Windows Workflow (WF)
- ➤ Localization
- ➤ Com-Interop
- ➤ Network Programming
- ➤ Application Services
- ➤ Assemblies and Reflection
- ➤ Security
- ➤ Threading
- ➤ Deployment
- ➤ Visual Basic Compiler
- ➤ Visual Basic Power Pack Tools
- ➤ Workflow 2008 Specifics
- ➤ Enterprise Services
- ➤ *Visual Basic 2010 Programmer's Reference*, Wiley Publishing 2010
  - ➤ Introduction to the IDE
  - ➤ Menus, Toolbars, and Windows

- Customization
- Windows Form Designer
- WPF Designer
- Visual Basic Code Editor
- Debugging
- Selecting Windows Forms Controls
- Using Windows Forms Controls
- Windows Forms
- Selecting WPF Controls
- Using WPF Controls
- WPF Windows
- Program and Module Structure
- Data Types, Variables, and Constants
- Operators
- Subroutines and Functions
- Program Control Statements
- Error Handling
- Database Controls and Objects
- LINQ
- Custom Controls
- Drag and Drop, and the Clipboard
- UAC Security
- OOP Concepts
- Classes and Structures
- Collection Classes
- Generics
- Drawing Basics
- Brushes, Pens, and Paths
- Text
- Image Processing
- Printing
- Reporting

➤   Configuration and Resources

➤   Streams

➤   File System Objects

➤   WCF

➤   Useful Namespaces

➤   Useful Control Properties, Methods, and Events

➤   Variable Declarations and Data Types

➤   Windows Forms Controls and Components

➤   Visual Basic Power Packs

➤   Form Objects

➤   Graphics

➤   Useful Exception Classes

➤   Date and Time Format Specifiers

➤   Other Format Specifiers

➤   The Application Class

➤   The My Namespace

➤   Streams

➤   File System Classes

INDEX

Z